COLLINS & BROWN

This page contains letters extricated from the front covers of 14 different albums. We ruined these perfectly good album sleeves so that you may join in the competition to name their source.
We invite you to identify and name as many as you can by artist and title. This can be done by clicking on to the Competitions page at www.thisdayinmusic.com, and then the words 'Cover Competition'. Fill in your suggestions as to the 14, get as many as you can, and you will be contacted with your results and prizes.

The competition closes on December 25th 2006, at which point all entrants will be e-mailed the results.

The Editorial Board,
This Day In Music

THIS DAY

First published in Great Britain in 2005 by
Collins & Brown
The Chrysalis Building
Bramley Road
London W10 6SP

An imprint of Chrysalis Books Group plc

Volume © Chrysalis Books Group plc 2005
Text © Neil Cossar 2005

1 3 5 7 9 8 6 4 2

British Library Cataloguing-in-Publication Data:
A catalogue record for this book is available from
the British Library.

ISBN 1-84340-298-X

Commissioning Editor: Chris Stone
Designer: Anthony Cohen
Thanks to Antar Archive

Reproduction by
Anorax Imaging Ltd, UK
Printed and bound by
Kyodo Printing Co (S'Pore) Pte Ltd

YOU REALLY SHOT ME!

Kinks star Ray is hit as he chases pair after mugging

BRITNEY'S HITS MAKE BOSS £2bn

By IAN KING and NICOLE LAMPERT

THE tycoon behind the hits of Britney Spears was last night celebrating a £2billion payday.

Clive Calder sold his record company Zomba — which also boasts 'NSYNC and the Backstreet Boys — to German-owned giant BMG Music.

Mr Calder, who is credited with discovering Britney after she auditioned at his studios, started Zomba in 1975 and his first big British act was Billy Ocean.

He also released hits for Tight Fit, ex-Page Three girl Sam Fox and the first album by cult band The Stone Roses.

Talent

The reclusive South African, 56, was dubbed the Howard Hughes of pop after it emerged that he has a separate air supply to his New York offices because of an allergy.

An ex-workmate said: "Clive is very quiet and unassuming and hates publicity. Unlike most showbiz people, he's not at all flamboyant, but he has a talent for picking big stars.

"He's very quietly spoken and works very hard. He's always the first in the office and the last one out."

Discovery . . . Britney

JOHN LENNON SHOT DEAD

THE NEW STANDARD

PCL PRESENTS

THE WHITE STRIPES
PLUS GUESTS

Under 14s must be accompanied by an adult
www.glasgow-academy.co.uk

GLASGOW ACADEMY
121 Eglinton Street, Glasgow

THU 10 APR 2003 7:00 PM

PRICE: 15.00

IN MUSIC

CIVIC COLISEUM | **FRI. FEB. 3**

KNOXVILLE — AT 8:30 P. M.
ADMISSION $2.50 - $3.00 - $3.50
Tickets on Sale at COLISEUM BOX OFFICE - TUCKER'S RECORD SHOP on The Mall

APO SHOWS PRESENT

★ OTIS REDDING ★
"TRY A LITTLE TENDERNESS"

★ THE MARVELETTES
"THE HUNTER GETS CAPTURED BY THE GAME"

AARON NEVILLE
"TELL IT LIKE IT IS"

JAMES AND BOBBY PURIFY
"I'M YOUR PUPPET" · "WISH YOU DIDN'T HAVE TO GO"

THE ORIGINAL **DRIFTERS**

LORRAINE ELLISON
"STAY WITH ME"

SAD SAM
M.C.

IRWIN C. WATSON
THE TV COMEDIAN

TOUR DIRECTION: UNIVERSAL ATTRACTIONS, 200 W. 57th ST. - NEW YORK CITY

THE SUN, Monday, May 27, 1998   7

I AM SO GUTTED

Clapton agony as blaze wrecks his £1.5m home

By BRIAN FLYNN

ROCK legend Eric Clapton told last night how he plunged into his blazing home to rescue his priceless guitar collection.

Don't fret, Eric ... a haggard Clapton yesterday   Picture: MATT DICKENS

Wrecked ... fireman go into house

Houston drug inquiry

Los Angeles: The singer, Whitney Houston, left, is under investigation for allegedly trying to smuggle 15.2 grams of marijuana out of Hawaii (Grace Bradberry writes). A local newspaper said that a security officer at Keahold-Kona Airport, who has limited powers of arrest, found the drug when he asked Houston to open her handbag. She walked away when he tried to detain her.

ROCK SUPERSTAR'S SKELETON FOUND

THE skeleton of Manic Street Preachers' star Richey Edwards was found last night – eight years after his mystery disappearance.
Full story: Page 7

1st January

BORN ON THIS DAY

1950 Morgan Fisher – keyboardist with Mott The Hoople, who had the 1972 UK No.3 & US No.37 single 'All The Young Dudes' – a song David Bowie gave to the band on hearing that they were about to split up.

1956 Diane Warren, US songwriter, who has written over 80 US Top 20 hits including: Aerosmith, 'I Don't Want To Miss A Thing'; LeAnn Rimes, 'How Do I Live' and Toni Braxton, 'Un-Break My Heart'. She has also written hits for Cher, Celine Dion, Eric Clapton, TLC, Michael Bolton, Rod Stewart and Ace Of Base.

1958 Joseph Saddler (Grandmaster Flash), who had a 1982 UK No.8 single 'The Message'. A major force in early rap music, he was given his nickname due to his rapid hand movements on the record decks.

ON THIS DAY

1953 country singer Hank Williams died of a heart attack aged 29. He made his first record in 1946 and went on to score 36 Top 10 US country hits – his best-known being 'You're Cheatin Heart'. Over 20,000 mourners attended his funeral.

1957 BBC Television aired its new rock 'n' roll show *Cool For Cats* for the first time in the UK.

1960 Johnny Cash played his first free concert for the inmates of San Quentin Prison, California. Future country star Merle Haggard was in the audience.

Eric Clapton wed Melia McEnery on this day in 2003.

1962 The Beatles auditioned for Decca Records in West Hampstead, London. They were told two months later that they had failed the audition.

1964 the first edition of the BBC TV show *Top Of The Pops* was transmitted from an old church hall in Manchester. Introduced by DJ Jimmy Saville, acts miming to their latest releases included The Rolling Stones, The Dave Clark Five, The Hollies and The Swinging Blue Jeans.

1964 UK blues artist Alexis Korner died. He had been a major force behind the UK R&B scene, formed Blues Incorporated with Charlie Watts, enjoyed hits with CCS and been a writer and radio presenter.

1965 The Yardbirds (with Eric Clapton) played two shows at The Odeon Cinema, Hammersmith, London.

1968 *Billboard* magazine reported that for the first time ever albums had outsold singles in the US – album sales had reached over 192 million units.

1971 Radio Luxembourg aired over seven hours of continuous Beatles music to celebrate the group's tenth year in the music business. Every track played was a single or LP track by The Beatles, or a song from their solo albums.

Marc Bolan started to release records through his own label in 1972.

1972 Marc Bolan signed with EMI to release records in the UK on his own T. Rex Wax Co. label.

1977 The Clash played the opening night at punk's first real venue, The Roxy Club in London.

1977 Wings were at No.1 on the UK singles chart with 'Mull Of Kintyre'. It became the first single to sell over two million copies in the UK.

1984 UK blues artist Alexis Korner died. He had been a major force behind UK R&B, formed Blues Incorporated with Charlie Watts, enjoyed hits with CCS and was a writer and radio presenter.

2002 Welsh singer Shakin' Stevens spent several hours in police custody after being arrested for drink driving.

BORN ON THIS DAY

1936 Roger Miller, singer, guitarist and TV star. In 1965 he had a UK No.1 & US No.4 single with 'King Of The Road'. He won four Grammy Awards in 1965 including Best Country & Western Album. Roger died of lung cancer on October 25th 1991, aged 56.

1942 Chick Churchill – keyboardist for Ten Years After, who had a 1970 UK No.10 single with 'Love Like A Man'.

1957 Ricky Van Shelton, US country singer, scored 10 country No.1s, including duets with Dolly Parton and Brenda Lee.

1963 Keith Gregory, who was the bass guitarist for The Wedding Present. During 1992 the UK band released one single every month, which gave them 12 Top 30 hits. This resulted in their being the only group ever to score more than 10 new UK hits in one year.

1967 Robert Gregory – drummer for Babybird, who had a 1996 UK No.3 single with 'You're Gorgeous' and a 1996 UK No. 9 album with *Ugly Beautiful*.

ON THIS DAY

1926 the first issue of *The Melody Maker* went on sale in the UK, priced at 3d. The monthly magazine was for "all who are interested in the production of popular music". The first issue provided dance band news, a feature on ukuleles and information on how to read music by sight.

1968 the entire shipment of John and Yoko's album *Two Virgins* was seized by authorities in New Jersey due to the full frontal nude photograph of the couple on the cover.

1969 Led Zeppelin played the first of four nights at the Whisky A Go Go, Los Angeles during their first US tour, supported by the Alice Cooper band.

1969 filming began at Twickenham Studios of The Beatles rehearsing for the *Let It Be* album. The project ran into several problems, including George Harrison walking out on the group on January 10th.

1971 George Harrison's *All Things Must Pass* started a seven week run at No.1 on the US album chart, making Harrison the first solo Beatle to score a US No.1 album.

1971 BBC TV aired the first of a 13 week series, *It's Cliff Richard*, featuring resident guests singer and actress Una Stubbs and Shadows guitarist Hank Marvin.

1976 appearing at the second day of the Great British Music Festival at London's Olympia were Bad Company, Nazareth, Ronnie Lanes Slim Chance, Pretty Things and Be Bop Deluxe. Tickets were £3.50 ($5.95).

1979 Sex Pistol's bass player Sid Vicious went on trial in New York accused of murdering his girlfriend, Nancy Spungen.

1980 US singer Larry Williams *(top)* died from gunshot wounds aged 45. The Beatles and The Jam covered his songs, while Williams himself had a 1957 US No.5 single with 'Short Fat Mannie'.

1981 David Lynch of The Platters died of cancer. The band had had a 1959 UK & US No.1 single with 'Smoke Gets In Your Eyes'.

1985 Rolling Stone Ron Wood married his girlfriend Jo in Gerrards Cross, Buckinghamshire. Guests included Keith Richard, Bill Wyman, Charlie Watts, Ringo Starr, Rod Stewart and Jeff Beck.

1994 singer Dannii Minogue married Julian McMahon (the son of Billy McMahon, Australia's Prime Minister during the 1970s), in Melbourne, Australia. Dannii's new mother-in-law, Lady Sonia McMahon, was unhappy with the wedding and was quoted as saying, "I hope I break a leg so I don't have to go".

1996 Arrested Development announced they had split up. The US group released two albums and had the US No.1 single 'Tennessee'.

2002 Backstreet Boy Nick Carter was arrested in a Tampa, Florida nightclub after being involved in a fight. Police said that Carter was arguing with a woman and when they asked him to leave, he continued arguing. He was arrested on a misdemeanour count of resisting a law enforcement officer without violence.

2004 Daniel Bedingfield suffered two fractured vertebrae in his neck after the jeep he was driving rolled over and crashed when on holiday in New Zealand. Emergency workers had to cut the singer free before he could be taken to hospital.

> "I basically became a musician because of Elvis Presley."
> **John Lennon**

BORN ON THIS DAY

1926 Sir George Martin, 1960s EMI in-house record producer and so-called "fifth Beatle". He produced all but one of The Beatles' albums, as well as working with comedy acts The Goons and Beyond The Fringe. Martin received a knighthood in 1996.

1941 Van Dyke Parks, US songwriter and producer. He worked with Brian Wilson on the *Smile* album, played keyboards on The Byrds' song 'Eight Miles High' and produced Ry Cooder, Randy Newman and Judy Collins.

1945 Stephen Stills, guitarist and vocalist in Buffalo Springfield, Crosby, Stills & Nash and Manassas. Crosby, Stills, Nash & Young had a 1969 UK No.17 single with 'Marrakesh Express' and a 1970 US No.1 album with *Déjà vu*. Stills had a 1971 solo UK No.37 single with 'Love The One Your With'.

ON THIS DAY

1957 Guy Mitchell was at No.1 on the UK singles chart with 'Singing The Blues'. The song was also a US No.1.

1963 Cliff Richard was at No.1 on the UK singles chart with 'The Next Time / Bachelor Boy'. This was his sixth UK No.1.

1964 appearing at The Glenlyn Ballroom, London, The Rolling Stones supported by The Detours (The Who).

1964 The Beatles were seen for the first time ever on US TV when a clip from the BBC's *The Mersey Sound* showing the group playing 'She Loves You' was shown on *The Jack Parr Show*.

1967 having received a US army draft notice, Beach Boy Carl Wilson refused to be sworn in, on the grounds of a conscientious objector.

1967 The Bee Gees were at No.1 on the Australian singles chart with the single 'Spickes and Speckes'.

1969 to the horror of the producer, when appearing live on *The Lulu TV Show* Jimi Hendrix stopped performing his new single after a few bars and instead launched into a version of Cream's 'Sunshine Of Your Love' as a tribute to the band – who had split a few days earlier.

1970 B. J. Thomas started a four week run at No.1 on the US singles chart with 'Raindrops Keep Falling On My Head'. The song was featured in the film *Butch Cassidy and the Sundance Kid*.

1970 The Beatles recorded what would be their last song together, 'I Me Mine'. A decade later it was the title of George Harrison's autobiography.

1974 Bob Dylan and The Band started a 39 date US tour, Dylan's first live appearance for over seven years. There were more than five million applications for the 660,000 tickets.

1976 The Bay City Rollers went to No.1 on the US singles chart with 'Saturday Night'. At the height of their US success, the Scottish group signed a deal to promote breakfast cereal.

1979 The Hype appeared at McGonagils, Dublin. The band was later to be known as U2.

1981 David Bowie made his final appearance as the Elephant Man in the Broadway show.

1992 Simple Minds singer Jim Kerr married actress Patsy Kensit at the Chelsea register office.

1999 Steps scored their first UK No.1 single with their version of The Bee Gees song 'Tragedy'.

2000 Luciano Pavarotti agreed to pay the Italian authorities £1.6 million ($2.72 million) after losing an appeal against tax evasion charges. It was reported that the singer was worth £300 million ($510 million) at the time.

2002 Liam and Noel Gallagher topped a poll of celebrities you would least like to live next to, getting 40 percent of the vote. The brothers from Oasis were voted as "Neighbours From Hell" by readers of *Your Home* magazine.

2002 Zak Foley, bass guitarist with EMF, died. He was aged 31.

STEREO-SPECTRUM

BEATS!!!!
THE MERSEYSIDE SOUND!

THE NEW BEAT FROM BRITAIN !!!!!

I Want To Hold Your Hand · This Is What I Mean · Tell Me I'm The One · Joshua · Maybe I Will
I Saw Her Standing There · Seems To Me · Got To Get Another Girl · Your Kind Of Love · There I Go

DESIGN UCP-170

Not really the Beatles at all actually. Beware of imitations.

BORN ON THIS DAY

1956 Bernard Sumner – guitarist and vocalist with Warsaw, Joy Division (who had a 1980 UK No.13 single with 'Love Will Tear Us Apart'), New Order (who had a 1983 UK No.9 single with 'Blue Monday') and Electronic (who had a 1991 UK No.8 single with 'Get The Message').

1960 Michael Stipe – vocalist with R.E.M., who had a 1991 UK No.6 & US No.10 single with 'Shiny Happy People' plus over 20 Top 40 UK singles. They also had a 1992 UK No.1 & US No.2 album with *Automatic For The People*.

ON THIS DAY

1936 *Billboard* magazine introduced the first-ever pop music chart that ranked records on national sales. Big band violinist Joe Venuti was the first No.1.

1954 Elvis Presley made his second visit to the Memphis recording service and cut two songs onto a 10in acetate, 'Casual Love Affair' and 'I'll Never Stand In Your Way'. Studio boss Sam Phillips asked Presley to leave his phone number.

1962 Liverpool's *Mersey Beat* published its first popularity poll, with The Beatles in first place and Gerry And The Pacemakers voted second.

1967 The Jimi Hendrix Experience played the first of what would be over 240 gigs in this year when they appeared at the Bromel Club, Bromley. (Many of the concerts consisted of two shows per night.)

1970 Chauffeur Neil Boland was accidentally killed when The Who's drummer Keith Moon ran over him. Moon was trying to escape from a gang of skinheads after a fight broke out at a pub in Hatfield, England. Moon had never passed his driving test.

1975 Elton John started a two week run at No.1 on the US singles chart with his version of The Beatles' 'Lucy In The Sky With Diamonds'. His third US No.1, the song featured John Lennon on guitar.

1976 former Beatles roadie Mal Evans was shot dead by police at his Los Angeles apartment. His girlfriend had called the police when she found Evans upset with a rifle in his hand. When they arrived, he pointed the gun at the police – who opened fire.

Our Skinhead hero eyes up Keith Moon's Roller.

1977 The Sex Pistols shocked passengers and airline staff at Heathrow Airport when they spat and vomited boarding a plane to Amsterdam.

1986 Phil Lynott of Thin Lizzy died of heart failure and pneumonia after being in a coma for eight days following a drug overdose.

1992 Simply Red went back to No.1 on the UK album chart for a five week run with *Stars*. This was the third time the album had been at the top of the charts.

2001 Courtney Love filed a lawsuit against her alleged stalker claiming that Lesley Barber, the ex-wife of her current boyfriend Jim Barber, drove over her foot. This had forced her to forfeit her role in a forthcoming film and lost her the £200,000 ($340,000) fee that went with it.

2001 US rapper Vanilla Ice spent the night in jail after allegedly ripping out some of his wife's hair during a row while driving on Interstate 595. Ice (born Robert Van Winkle) told police he pulled out some of his wife's hair to prevent her from jumping out of their truck's window. He was released the following morning from Broward County Jail in Fort Lauderdale on $3,500 bail.

2004 Britney Spears had her surprise marriage annulled less than 55 hours after tying the knot in Las Vegas with childhood friend Jason Alexander *(below)*. Her lawyers filed for an annulment, saying Spears, "lacked understanding of her actions to the extent that she was incapable of agreeing to the marriage".

2005 the owner of a recording studio where Eminem had recorded his *Slim Shady* LP was found shot dead. A.J. Abdallah was discovered by a business colleague at the Detroit studio. Police suggested that a robbery may also have taken place. Mr Abdallah had lived in an apartment above the studio on Eight Mile Road, the Detroit street that inspired the title of Eminem's 2002 film *8 Mile*.

Spears rapidly unties knot
By Philip Pank

BRITNEY SPEARS's marriage to a childhood friend has been proclaimed annulled by a judge after two short days.

The singer herself admitted that marriage to the pop star had been a mistake. "We made a mistake," she realised what we did was not the right thing to do", Jason Alexander, 22, said. "It wasn't the right way to go about it and we wanted to fix the mistake. We sat down and said 'That wasn't a very cool thing we did'."

The star's lawyers secured an annulment at Clark County Family Court on the ground that she had not fully understood what she was doing.

Mr Alexander told an interviewer from the Access Hollywood website how, after two days of drinking and partying, the proposal had been made in a Las Vegas hotel suite. "We'd had a really good time and it was Saturday night and Saturday morning actually. It was crazy. We were looking at the lights in the city, thinking, this is a really beautiful night. We were just looking at each other and said 'Let's do something wild, crazy. Let's go get married, just for the hell of it'."

Spears donned a white baseball cap, pulled a white garter over the knee of her ripped jeans and left to immortalise her charade with a rare-time sweetheart from her home town of Kentwood, Louisiana.

They married at the Little White Wedding Chapel in the Strip after a stop at a club at 3.30am. Judge Lisa M. Brown signed the annulment order at 12.50pm yesterday.

David Chesnoff, the lawyer called in to clear things up, said of the annulment: "Jason agreed to this completely. They've made a wise decision. They are friends."

He complained for annulment filed in the Family Court, claimed that "Plaintiff Spears lacked understanding of her actions to the extent that she was incapable of agreeing to the marriage. Before entering into the marriage the plaintiff and defendant did not know each other's likes and dislikes, each other's desires to have or not have children and each other's desires as to state of residence. Upon learning of each other's desires, they are incompatible that there was a want of understanding of each other's actions in entering into this marriage."

Mr Alexander has not ruled out seeing Miss Spears. "As far as anything else goes, I don't know what's going to happen," he said.

Wedding belle: Britney Spears's marriage is over

BORN ON THIS DAY

1923 Sam Phillips, the founder of Sun Records – which was the first label to record Elvis Presley. Phillips also recorded Carl Perkins, Ike Turner, B.B. King and Jerry Lee Lewis. He died on August 30th 2003.

1940 Athol Guy – singer with The Seekers, who had a 1965 UK No.1 single with 'I'll Never Find Another You'.

1949 George Brown – singer with Kool & The Gang, who had a 1981 US No.1 & UK No.7 single with 'Celebration' as well as over 15 other UK Top 40 hits.

1950 Chris Stein – guitarist with Blondie, who had five UK No.1 singles including the 1979 UK & US No.1 single 'Heart Of Glass'. Blondie also had a 1978 worldwide No.1 album with *Parallel Lines*.

1964 Phil Thornalley, songwriter, and bass guitarist who worked with Johnny Hates Jazz and The Cure. He also co-wrote Natalie Imbruglia's worldwide hit 'Torn'.

1969 Brian Warner (a.k.a. Marilyn Manson) has had a 1998 US No.1 album with *Mechanical Animals* and a UK No. 12 single with 'The Dope Show'. He named himself after Marilyn Monroe and Charles Manson.

ON THIS DAY

1966 The Who appeared on a new BBC TV programme, *The Whole Scene Going*.

1967 appearing at The Marquee Club, London were Pink Floyd.

1968 Jimi Hendrix was jailed for one day in Stockholm, Sweden on drink charges after going berserk and destroying everything in his room at the Goteberg Hotel.

1972 David Bowie played two shows at Green's Playhouse, Glasgow, Scotland.

1974 Yes scored their first UK No.1 album with the double set *Tales From The Topographic Oceans*.

1978 The Sex Pistols started a US tour in Atlanta, Georgia before an audience of 500 people.

1979 jazz musician and bandleader Charles Mingus died aged 56. His final project was *Mingus*, a collaboration with Joni Mitchell.

1979 Prince made his live debut at the Capri Theater, Minneapolis.

1983 Everything But The Girl made their live debut at the ICA in London. They took their name from a second-hand furniture store in Hull.

1987 young Welsh chorister Aled Jones announced his retirement from pop music at the age of 16, in order to study for his O'level exams. (Jones had scored the 1985 UK Top 5 hit 'Walking On Air'.)

1989 in *Melody Maker*'s Readers Poll results: The Mission won best band, best live act, best single and album; Morrissey won male singer; Julianne Regan, female singer; worst LP was Bros with *Push* and the best new band was House Of Love.

1991 Iron Maiden went to No.1 on the UK singles chart with 'Bring Your Daughter To The Slaughter'. It became the lowest-selling No.1 since 1960, with just over 42,000 copies sold in its first week.

1991 Madonna went to No.1 on the US singles chart with 'Justify My Love', which was co-written with Lenny Kravitz.

1997 Sonny Bono was killed in a skiing accident at

Congressman Bono (Californian variety as opposed to Dublin) in suitable man-of-the-woods pose.

YOU REALLY SHOT ME!
Kinks star Ray is hit as he chases pair after mugging

a resort near Lake Tahoe, aged 62. Bono who was one half of Sonny and Cher, which scored the 1965 UK & US No.1 single 'I Got You Babe'. He had also since become a US Congressman.

1998 Ken Forssi, bass guitarist with Love, died of brain cancer aged 55. Love scored the 1966 US No.33 single '7 And 7 Is' and had a 1968 UK No.24 album with *Forever Changes*.

2001 Kirsty MacColl was laid to rest at a private ceremony, ahead of a public memorial to pay tribute to her life. The singer/songwriter was killed in a boating accident on December 18th 2000.

2004 Kinks singer Ray Davies was shot in the leg while on holiday in New Orleans *(above)*. He was shot when running after two men who stole his girlfriend's purse at gunpoint. Davies was admitted to the Medical Center of Louisiana but his injuries were not considered serious.

2002 in UK pop magazine Smash Hits the "Best Singles Of 2001" had Kylie Minogue at No.3 with 'Can't Get You Out Of My Head', No.2 was Shaggy's 'It Wasn't Me' and at No.1 was S Club 7 with 'Don't Stop Movin'.

BORN ON THIS DAY

1929 Wilbert Harrison, singer, who had a 1959 US No.1 single with 'Kansas City'. He also wrote 'Let's Work Together', which was a hit for Canned Heat and Bryan Ferry.

1944 Van McCoy, singer and producer, who had a 1975 US No.1 & UK No.3 single with 'The Hustle'. He also produced Gladys Knight and Aretha Franklin. McCoy died on July 6th 1979 aged 38.

1946 Syd Barrett – original guitarist and vocalist with Pink Floyd, he left in 1968. Barrett released one solo album, *Barrett*, in 1970.

1947 Sandy Denny – UK folk singer and member of Fairport Convention. She died on April 21st 1978 after falling down the stairs at a friend's house. She sung on the Fairport Convention 1969 UK No.21 single 'Si Tu Dois Partir' and also worked as a solo artist. She featured on the Led Zeppelin track 'Battle Of Evermore'.

1953 Malcolm Young – guitarist with AC/DC, who had a 1980 UK No.36 single with 'Whole Lotta Rosie' and a 1980 UK No.1 & US No.14 album *Back In Black* – the latter sold over ten million copies.

1959 Kathy Sledge – singer with Sister Sledge, who had a 1979 US No.2 single with 'We Are Family' and a 1985 UK No.1 with 'Frankie'.

1964 Mark O'Toole – bass guitarist with Frankie Goes To Hollywood, who had a 1984 UK No.1 & US No.10 single with 'Relax' and six other UK Top 40 singles.

ON THIS DAY

1956 Elvis Presley performed in the gym at Randolph High School in Mississippi; this was the last time he ever appeared in a small auditorium.

1958 Gibson guitars launched its "Flying V" electric guitar.

1964 the first night of a 14-date tour, "Group Scene 1964", featuring The Rolling Stones, The Ronettes, Marty Wilde, The Swinging Blue Jeans and Dave Berry And The Cruisers at the Granada Theatre, Harrow on The Hill, Middlesex.

1968 Irish singer Val Doonican was at No.1 on the UK album chart with *Val Doonican Rocks, But Gently.*

1968 The Beatles *Magical Mystery Tour* started an eight week run at No.1 on the US album chart, the group's 11th US chart topper.

1970 Crosby, Stills, Nash & Young made their UK live debut at the Royal Albert Hall, London.

1973 Carly Simon's 'You're So Vain' (with Mick Jagger on backing vocals), started a three week run at No.1 on the US singles chart.

1977 EMI Records dropped The Sex Pistols, giving the band £40,000 ($68,000) to release them from their contract.

1979 The Village People scored their only UK No.1 single with 'Y.M.C.A.'. At its peak the single was selling over 150,000 copies a day.

1987 Eric Clapton started what became an annual event by playing six shows at the Royal Albert Hall, London.

1990 Phil Collins started a three week run at No.1 on the US album chart with *...But Seriously.*

1993 it was reported that David Bowie had lost over £2.5 million ($4.25 million) in unpaid royalties to an Italian Mafia-linked bootleg fraud.

1996 James Brown's wife Adrienne died in a Los Angeles hospital, aged 47, after suffering a heart attack during a major plastic surgery operation.

1997 two bronze busts worth £50,000 ($85,000) were stolen from a garden at George Harrison's estate in Henley-on-Thames, Oxfordshire. Thieves had climbed a 3m (10ft) wall and cut the figures of two monks from their stone plinths.

"Cheer up guys". The Sex Pistols, dropped by EMI in 1977.

2001 Pink Floyd guitarist David Gilmour won the right to his dot com name. Dave took legal action in his battle to reclaim davidgilmour.com from Andrew Herman, who had registered the URL and was selling Pink Floyd merchandise through the site.

2004 US CD sales rose for the first time in four years, despite the growing popularity of legal digital music downloads.

BORN ON THIS DAY

1937 Paul Revere – keyboardist and leader of Paul Revere And The Raiders, who had a 1971 US No.1 single with 'Indian Reservation' as well as 14 other US Top 30 hit singles.

1942 Danny Williams, singer, who had a 1961 UK No. 1 with 'Moon River'.

1944 Mike McGear – singer with The Scaffold, who had a 1968 Christmas UK No.1 single with 'Lily The Pink'. McGear is the brother of Paul McCartney.

1948 Kenny Loggins – singer/songwriter and one half of Loggins & Messina 1971–76. He had a 1984 US No.1 & UK No. 6 single with 'Footlose', from the film of the same name.

1959 Kathy Valentine – bass guitarist with The Go-Go's, who had a 1982 US No.2 single with 'We Got The Beat' and a 1982 UK No.47 single with 'Our Lips Are Sealed'.

1974 John Rich – bass guitarist and vocalist for Lonestar, who had a 2000 US No.1 & UK No. 21 single with 'Amazed'.

ON THIS DAY

1955 'Rock Around The Clock' by Bill Haley And His Comets entered the UK chart for the first time, peaking at No.17.

1961 Johnny Tillotson was at No.1 on the UK singles chart with 'Poetry In Motion'.

1964 Harmonica player Cyril Davies died of leukaemia aged 32. Davies was a driving force in the early 60s blues movement and formed Blues Incorporated with Alexis Korner.

1970 Led Zeppelin kicked off an eight-date UK tour at Birmingham Town Hall.

1973 appearing live at Newcastle City Hall, England, was David Bowie.

1980 Hugh Cornwell of The Stranglers was found guilty of possession of heroin, cocaine and cannabis. He was fined £300 ($510) and sentenced to three months in Pentonville prison.

Hugh gets some 'inside information'... from Pentonville Prison.

1982 singles reviewed in this week's *Smash Hits* included: Haircut 100's 'Love Plus One', XTC's 'Senses Working Overtime' and Robert Palmer's 'Some Guys Have All The Luck'. OMD had the front cover and there were interviews with Adam Ant, Squeeze and Dollar.

1984 Madonna was at No.1 on the US singles chart with 'Like A Virgin'.

1989 Kylie Minogue and Jason Donovan started a three week run at No.1 on the UK singles chart with 'Especially For You'.

1990 appearing at Wembley Arena, London was Chris Rea on his "Road To Hell" tour.

1993 R.E.M. played a Greenpeace benefit show at the 40 Watt Club, Athens, Georgia, for 500 people. The show was recorded on a solar-powered mobile recording studio.

1994 Oasis started recording their debut album *Definitely Maybe* at Monrow studios, South Wales.

2003 *The Beatles Book Monthly* closed down after 40 years. Author Sean O'Mahony, who set up the magazine in 1963, said there was nothing more to say as the number of things the former Beatles are doing gets less as the years go on.

2004 drummer John Guerin died of pneumonia aged 64. He had worked with Joni Mitchell, Frank Zappa, Linda Rondstadt, Gram Parsons and Todd Rundgren.

Several dusty *Beatles Book Monthly* magazines, destined for ebay no doubt.

BORN ON THIS DAY

1935 Elvis Aaron Presley, the King of rock 'n' roll. He had his first No.1 in 1956 – the US No.1 & UK No.2 single 'Heartbreak Hotel'. His first UK No.1 single was in 1957, with 'All Shook Up', and he went on to have over 100 US & UK Top 40 singles from 1956–2004. He died on August 16th 1977.

1937 Shirley Bassey, singer. She first charted in the UK in 1957, scored the 1970 UK No.4 single with a cover of the George Harrison song 'Something' and also had hits with the James Bond themes 'Goldfinger' and 'Diamonds are Forever'.

Singing: "Goldfingaaaah".

1946 Robert Krieger – guitarist with The Doors, who had a 1967 US No.1 & UK No.49 single with 'Light My Fire' and a 1971 US No.14 & UK No.22 single 'Riders On The Storm'.

1947 David Bowie, singer/songwriter. He had his first UK Top 40 single in 1969 with 'Space Oddity', which also went No.1 in the UK in 1975. He has had over 50 UK Top 40 hits including five No.1s and two US No.1s – such as 1975's 'Fame' and 1983's 'Lets Dance'. He also made two albums with Tin Machine, in 1991 and 1992.

1948 Paul King – guitarist and vocalist with Mungo Jerry, who had a 1970 UK No.1 & US No.3 single with 'In The Summertime'.

1969 R. Kelly, singer, writer and producer, who has had a 1994 US No.1 single with 'Bump N' Grind' and a 1997 UK No.1 single with 'I Believe I Can Fly'.

1973 Sean Paul, singer, who had a 2003 US No.1 & UK No.4 single with 'Get Busy'.

ON THIS DAY

1957 Bill Haley And His Comets started the first ever "rock & roll tour" of Australia, playing two sold out nights in Sydney.

1966 The Beatles started a six week run at No.1 on the US album chart with *Rubber Soul*, the group's seventh US chart topper. The group also started a three week run at No.1 on the US singles chart with 'We Can Work It Out', their 11th US No.1 single.

1979 Canadian rock band Rush were named the country's official Ambassadors Of Music by the Canadian government.

1982 Olivia Newton-John was at No.1 on the US singles chart with 'Physical'.

1991 Steve Clark, guitarist with Def Leppard, was found dead at his Chelsea flat by his girlfriend after a night of heavy alcohol consumption combined with prescription drugs.

1993 Elvis Presley became the first rock 'n' roll artist to be honoured by the US Postal Service when they issued a commemorative stamp featuring him.

1996 a Los Angeles court found Robert Hoskins guilty of five counts of stalking, assault and making terrorist threats to Madonna. Hoskins had twice scaled the walls of the singer's estate and had threatened to slash her throat from ear to ear.

2000 Christina Aguilera started a two week run at No.1 on the US singles chart with 'What A Girl Wants'. She ended Santana's 12 week run at No.1 with 'Smooth'.

The many faces of David Bowie, born on this day in 1947.

2001 a woman who believed that Axl Rose communicated with her via telepathy was arrested for stalking the Guns N' Roses singer for a second time. Police detained Karen Jane McNeil after she was spotted loitering outside his house.

2004 the estate of George Harrison started a $10 million (£5.8 million) legal action against Dr Gilbert Lederman of Staten Island University Hospital, claiming the doctor coerced Harrison to sign souvenirs. The main allegations of the legal action was that Dr Lederman got an extremely sick Harrison to sign his son's guitar and autographs for his two daughters.

BORN ON THIS DAY

1941 Joan Baez, US singer/songwriter who had a 1971 UK No.6 single with 'The Night They Drove Old Dixie Down'.

1944 Jimmy Page – guitarist and producer with The Yardbirds then Led Zeppelin, who had a 1969 US No.4 single with 'Whole Lotta Love'. The band's fourth album, released in 1971 and featuring the rock classic 'Stairway To Heaven', has sold over 11 million copies. Page was also in The Honeydrippers (with Robert Plant, Jeff Beck and Nile Rodgers), who had a 1984 US No.3 single with 'Sea Of Love'. As a session guitarist in the 60s Page played on 'Here Comes The Night' by Them, 'Shout' by Lulu and The Who's 'Can't Explain'.

Scott Engel stares at pop career in horror.

1944 Scott Engel – vocalist for The Walker Brothers, who had a 1966 UK No.1 & US No.13 single with 'The Sun Ain't Gonna Shine Anymore'.

1950 David Johansen – vocalist with The New York Dolls, who released a 1973 album *New York Dolls*. He was Buster Poindexteras as part of the Saturday Night Live house band in the late 1980's.

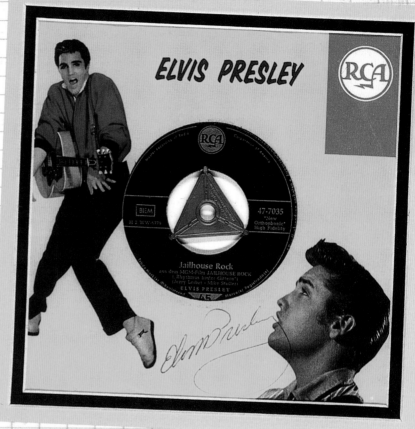

Elvis, back in jail after 48 years.

1967 Dave Matthews – guitarist and vocalist, The Dave Matthews Band, who had a 1998 US No.1 album with *Before These Crowded Streets*, a 2001 US No.1 album with *Everyday* and a 2001 UK No.35 single with 'The Space Between'.

1978 A.J. McLean – vocalist with The Backstreet Boys, who had a 1997 US No.2 single with 'Quit Playing Games With My Heart' and a 1999 UK No.1 single with 'I Want It That Way'.

ON THIS DAY

1963 drummer Charlie Watts joined The Rolling Stones after leaving Blues Incorporated.

1973 Mick Jagger was refused a Japanese visa on an account of a 1969 drug conviction, which caused The Rolling Stones to cancel a forthcoming tour.

1976 Queen were at No.1 on the UK singles chart with 'Bohemian Rhapsody'.

1979 the music for the UNICEF concert taking place in New York featured Rod Stewart, The Bee Gees, Earth, Wind and Fire, Abba and Donna Summer.

1982 The Human League went back to No.1 on the UK album chart for three weeks with *Dare*.

1988 Whitney Houston scored her sixth consecutive No.1 in the US with 'So Emotional'.

2000 the chauffeur who drove Puff Daddy and his girlfriend Jennifer Lopez from a nightclub after a shooting was reported to be co-operating with prosecutors. Puff Daddy faced up to 15 years in jail for allegedly pulling a gun in a New York club.

2005 Elvis Presley went to No.1 on the UK singles chart with 'Jailhouse Rock'. The single sold just 21,262 copies to reach No.1, the lowest sales ever for a UK chart topper since data began in 1969.

BORN ON THIS DAY

1917 Jerry Wexler, producer and record company executive. He was the co-owner of Atlantic Records, vice president at Warner Brothers and worked with Ray Charles, Phil Spector, Dr John, Dusty Springfield, Dire Straits and Bob Dylan.

1927 US teen idol singer Johnnie Ray, who had a 1956 UK No.1 & US No.2 single with 'Just Walking In The Rain', plus over 20 Top 40 singles between 1952 and 1960. He died of liver failure on February 21st 1990.

1943 Jim Croce, US singer/songwriter who had a 1973 US No.1 single with 'Time In A Bottle'. He was killed in a plane crash on the way to a concert on September 20th 1973.

1945 Rod Stewart, singer/songwriter. He was a member of The Hoochie Coochie Men, Steampacket, Shotgun Express, Jeff Beck Group and The Faces (who had a UK No.6 & US No.17 single with 'Stay With Me'). As a solo artist he had a 1971 UK & US No.1 single with 'Maggie May', plus five other UK No.1s and over 35 Top 40 hits. His 1971 debut album *Every Picture Tells A Story* was the first album ever to simultaneously be No.1 in the UK & US.

1948 Donald Fagen – vocalist and keyboardist with Steely Dan, who had a 1973 US No.11 single with 'Reeling In The Years' and nine other US Top 30 hits.

1953 Pat Benatar, singer who had a 1985 UK No.17 single with 'Love Is A Battlefield'.

1955 Luci Martin – vocalist with Chic, who had a 1978 US No.1 & UK No.7 single with 'Le Freak'.

1964 Brad Roberts – vocalist and guitarist with Crash Test Dummies, who had a 1994 UK No.2 & US No.4 single with 'Mmm Mmm Mmm Mmm'.

1973 Aerlee Taree – vocalist with Arrested Development, who had a 1992 UK No.2 single with 'People Everyday'.

1979 Chris Smith – rapper/singer with Kris Kross, who had a 1992 US No.1 & UK No.2 single with 'Jump'. The duo of Chris Smith and Chris Kelly were 12 and 13 respectively when they recorded the song.

ON THIS DAY

1956 Elvis Presley made his first recordings for RCA Records at The Methodist television, radio and TV Studios in Nashville. 'Heartbreak Hotel' was one of the songs recorded during this session.

1957 Tommy Steele And The Steelmen were at No.1 on the UK singles chart with 'Singing The Blues'. Guy Mitchell had been at No.1 the previous week with his version of the song and then returned to No.1 the following week.

1965 John Lennon appeared on UK TV's Peter Cook and Dudley Moore show, *Not Only But Also.*

1976 C.W. McCall went to No.1 on the US singles chart with 'Convoy', while it made No.2 in the UK. C.W. McCall was in fact an advertising agent whose real name was Bill Fries.

1976 Deep Purple split up at the end of a UK tour. David Coverdale went on to form Whitesnake, while Jon Lord and Ian Paice formed a band with Tony Ashton. The classic line up of Blackmore, Gillan, Glover, Lord and Paice reformed in 1984.

1977 Keith Richards was fined £750 ($1,275) with £250 ($425) costs after being found guilty of possessing cocaine.

1978 The Sex Pistols make their US TV debut on the show *Variety.*

Pictured here for the first time: the Crash Test Dummies' two missing Ms.

Page 2 — New Musical Express 10th January, 1981

"When everyone likes you, you've had it." Adam Ant.
So farewell then, Adam Ant, all things must pass. Our hearts go out to you at this season of goodwill. After more than three balmy years of being abused and reviled, all this adulation must be kind of hard to take.
Pic: Peter Anderson

UK SINGLES

This Week	Last Week			Weeks in	Highest
1	(17)	Imagine.............John Lennon (Apple)		2	1
2	(1)	**Starting Over** John Lennon/Yoko Ono (WEA/Geffen)		8	1
3	(8)	Antmusic.............Adam & The Ants (CBS)		3	3
4	(3)	There's No One Quite Like Grandma St Winifred's School Choir (MFP)		4	3

1981 John Lennon's 'Imagine' started a four week run at No.1 on the UK singles chart, ten years after it was recorded *(above)*. Lennon had two other songs in the Top 5 this week, 'Happy Christmas, (War Is Over)' and '(Just Like) Starting Over'. 'Imagine' was voted by the viewers of BBC TV as having the best lyrics of all time in a poll broadcast in October 1999.

1999 Norman Cook scored his third UK No.1 single under the name of Fatboy Slim with 'Praise You'. Cook's other No.1s were with The Housemartins and Beats International.

2005 Spencer Dryden, drummer with Jefferson Airplane, died of cancer at his home in California aged 66. Dryden was the nephew of Charlie Chaplin.

BORN ON THIS DAY

1958 Vicki Peterson – guitarist and vocalist with The Bangles, who had a 1986 UK No.2 single with the Prince song 'Manic Monday' and a 1986 US No.1 single with 'Walk Like An Egyptian'.

1968 Tom Dumont – keyboardist for No Doubt, who had a 1997 UK No.1 single with 'Don't Speak'.

1971 Mary J. Blige, US singer who had a 1997 US No.1 album with *Share My World*, a 1999 UK No.4 single with 'As' and a 2001 US No.1 single 'Family Affair'.

1971 Tom Rowlands of The Chemical Brothers, who had a 1996 UK No.1 single with 'Setting Sun'.

ON THIS DAY

1958 the release date for the Elvis Presley single 'Jailhouse Rock' was put back a week because the Decca Records pressing plant in the UK were unable to meet the 250,000 advance orders.

1963 The Beatles recorded their first national TV show, *Thank Your Lucky Stars*. They mimed to 'Please Please Me'.

1964 *Ring Of Fire* by Johnny Cash became the first country album to go to No.1 on the US chart.

1965 The Righteous Brothers arrived in Britain for a promotional visit, appearing on *Ready Steady Go!*, *Scene At 6.30* and *Discs A Go-Go*.

1967 The Jimi Hendrix Experience recorded 'Purple Haze'. Jimi also signed to the new record label Track Records on this day.

1978 appearing at Newcastle City Hall, England was Elvis Costello And The Attractions.

1981 appearing at the Hope & Anchor, London were Blancmange and support Depeche Mode. Tickets cost £1 ($1.7).

1986 The Pet Shop Boys scored their first UK No.1 single with 'West End Girls'.

1992 Nirvana appeared on NBC-TV's *Saturday Night Live*. Also on this day the band went to No.1 on the US album chart with *Nevermind*.

2000 Gary Glitter was released from prison after serving half of a four month sentence for possessing child pornography downloaded from the Internet. Glitter was told he would have to go on the sex offenders' register for seven years.

2000 Whitney Houston was under investigation after allegedly trying to smuggle 15.2 grams of Marijuana out of Hawaii. A security officer found the drug in the singer's handbag, who then walked away when he tried to detain her.

2002 Mickey Finn from T. Rex died of kidney and liver problems aged 55.

2003 Britain's oldest rockers came out winners in The Pollstar listing of the Top 10 grossing US tours of 2002: Paul McCartney $68m (£40m), The Rolling Stones $58m (£34m), Elton John $47m (£27.6m), The Who $20m (£11.8m), Ozzy Osbourne $18m (£10.6m), Peter Gabriel $10m (£5.88m), Yes $6m (£3.5m), Elvis Costello $5m (£2.94m), The Moody Blues $4m (£2.35m) and Jethro Tull $3m (£1.76m).

2003 Girls Aloud singer Cheryl Tweedy was arrested after an alleged attack in a nightclub in Guildford, England. The *Popstars – The Rivals* winner was accused of punching a lavatory attendant.

2003 a haul of 500 Beatles tapes known as the "Get Back sessions" stolen in the 1970s were found after UK police cracked a major bootleg operation in London and Amsterdam. Five men were arrested *(above)*.

2005 Former Bread guitarist and Academy Award-winning songwriter Jimmy Griffin died at his home in Nashville at the age of 61 after suffering from cancer.

FAB FOUR: In 1969

5 held in Beatles tape theft

By PATRICK MULCHRONE

FIVE hundred original Beatles tapes stolen 30 years ago were found by police investigating a bootleg scam.

Five people were arrested yesterday – two in West London and three, including a Briton, near Amsterdam.

Officers said a "substantial amount of tapes" were recovered with other items from the Beatles' record company Apple.

It followed a year long investigation by the International Federation of the Phonographic Industry and City of London Police.

The reel-to-reel tapes contain the Get Back sessions, recorded in 1969 for an album of that name which was shelved.

They vanished shortly after recording sessions. Pirate copies have turned up in the UK, Europe and the US over the years.

Stephen Bailey, boss of the Beatle Shop in Liverpool, which sells music and memorabilia, said: "These tapes would be worth millions if published."

A spokesman for Paul McCartney would not comment yesterday.

THE BANGS — GETTING OUT OF HAND

The Bangles before the band's name change.

CARLING LIVE .COM

BORN ON THIS DAY

1941 Long John Baldry – vocalist in Bluesology. As a soloist he had a 1967 UK No.1 single with 'Let The Heartaches Begin'.

1946 Cynthia Robinson – vocalist with Sly And The Family Stone, who had a 1971 US No.1 & 1972 UK No.15 single with 'Family Affair'.

1960 Charlie Gillingham – keyboardist for Counting Crows, who had a 1994 UK No.28 single with 'Mr Jones' and a 1996 US No.1 album with *Recovering The Satellites*.

1965 Greg Kriesel – bass guitarist with The Offspring, who had a 1999 UK No.1 & US No. 59 single with 'Pretty Fly, (For A White Guy' and a 1999 US No.6 & UK No.10 album with *Americana*.

1968 Raekwon of Wu-Tang Clan, who had a 1997 US & UK No.1 album with *Wu-Tang Forever*.

1974 Melanie Chisholm a.k.a. Mel C or Sporty Spice of The Spice Girls, who had a 1996 UK No.1 & 1997 US No.1 single with 'Wannabe'. As a solo artist Melanie had a 2000 UK No.1 single with 'Never Be The Same Again'.

ON THIS DAY

1974 Jim Croce started a five week run at No.1 on the US album chart with *You Don't Mess Around With Jim*.

1974 The Rolling Stones released the single 'Brown Sugar', the first on the band's own label. The track was from the *Sticky Fingers* album.

1974 The Steve Miller Band were at No.1 on the US singles chart with 'The Joker', the first of three No.1s. It reached No.1 in the UK chart in 1990.

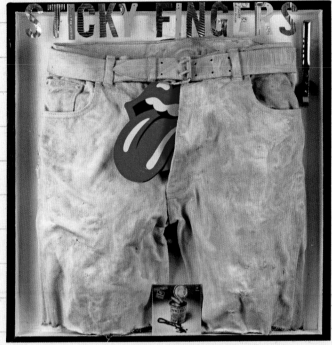

Super-rare Canadian artwork for the withdrawn release of the Rolling Stones album.

1975 the first night of a UK tour kicked off under the banner of The Warner Brothers Music Show *(left)*. It featured Little Feat, Montrose, Tower Of Power, and The Doobie Brothers.

1977 EMI Records issued a statement saying it felt unable to promote The Sex Pistols records in view of the adverse publicity generated over the last two months.

1977 The Police had their first rehearsal, held at drummer Stewart Copeland's London flat, with Henri Padovani on guitar, Sting on bass and Andy Summers on guitar.

1981 it was reported that the White House had expanded its record library by including albums by Bob Dylan, Kiss and The Sex Pistols.

1992 Bob Geldof was arrested after a disturbance on a Boeing 727 that had been grounded for five hours at Stansted Airport.

1993 Van Morrison failed to turn up at the Rock And Roll Hall Of Fame induction dinner, making him the first living inductee not to attend.

1995 Snoop Doggy Dogg was charged in Los Angeles for possession of marijuana and drug paraphernalia.

2000 teenage diva Charlotte Church sacked her manager Jonathan Shalit. Shalit had won her a five album deal with Sony Records and helped the singer with her career – which had earn her £6 million ($10.2 million) to date.

2001 British Airways staff complained about Oasis singer Liam Gallagher after he had grabbed a stewardess' bottom, refused to stop smoking and had thrown objects around the cabin during a flight from London to Rio De Janeiro.

2003 Bee Gee Maurice Gibb died in Miami following a heart attack during abdominal surgery, aged 53.

2004 singer/songwriter Randy Van Warmer died from leukaemia. He had had a 1979 US No.4 & UK No.8 single with 'Just When I Needed You Most'.

2005 it was announced that the Strawberry Field children's home immortalized by The Beatles was to close. The home in Woolton, Liverpool was made famous when John Lennon wrote 'Strawberry Fields Forever' after playing there as a child.

13th January

BORN ON THIS DAY

1955 Fred White – drummer with Earth, Wind and Fire, who had a 1975 US No.1 single with 'Shining Star' and a 1981 UK No.3 single with 'Let's Groove'.

1961 Graham McPherson (a.k.a. Suggs) – vocalist with Madness, who had a 1982 UK No.1 single 'House Of Fun' plus over 20 other UK Top 40 singles. As a solo artist Suggs had a 1995 UK No.7 single with a cover of The Beatles' song 'I'm Only Sleeping'.

1964 David McClusky – drummer with The Bluebells, who had a 1993 UK No.1 single with the reissued 'Young At Heart'.

1970 Zach de la Rocha – vocalist with Rage Against The Machine, who had a 1996 US No.1 album with *Evil Empire* and a 1993 UK No.16 single with 'Bullet In The Head'.

ON THIS DAY

1962 Chubby Checker went back to No.1 on the US singles chart with 'The Twist'. The song first went to No.1 in September 1960 and became the only record in American chart history to top the charts on two separate occasions.

1973 Eric Clapton made his stage comeback at the Rainbow Theatre, London, with Pete Townshend and friends.

1973 Slade scored their first UK No.1 album with *Slayed*.

1978 The Police started recording their first album at Surrey Sound studios, Surrey, England with producer Nigel Gray.

1979 Soul singer Donny Hathaway committed suicide when he fell from a 15th floor New York hotel window. Hathaway had scored the 1972 UK No.29 single with Roberta Flack 'Where Is The Love' and had a 1978 US No.2 single with 'The Closer I Get'.

1981 appearing at The Venue, London was Bow Wow Wow. Tickets cost £3 ($5.10).

1984 BBC Radio 1 announced a ban on 'Relax' by Frankie Goes To Hollywood, after DJ Mike Read called it obscene. A BBC TV ban also followed, but the song still went on to become a UK No.1 – spending a total of 48 weeks on the UK chart.

1986 Sex Pistol members John Lydon, Steve Jones and Paul Cook, as well as the mother of Sid Vicious, sued former manager Malcom McClaren for £1 million ($1.7 million). They settled out of court.

1990 New Kids On The Block had their second UK No. 1 single with 'Hangin' Tough'.

1999 Steps had a UK No.1 single with 'Heartbeat/Tragedy'.

2003 Diana Ross appeared in a US court charged with driving while twice over the drink driving limit. Police in Tucson reported that Miss Ross could not walk in a straight line, touch her nose or count to 30 after she had been stopped for swerving across the road.

2003 Pete Townshend was arrested on suspicion of child porn offences. Police officers impounded seven computers from his £15 million ($25.5 million) home in Richmond, Surrey.

What is a straight road to some was a long and winding one to poor Diana in 2003.

BORN ON THIS DAY

1936 Clarence Carter, blind US singer and guitarist who had a 1970 US No.4 & UK No.2 single with 'Patches'.

1938 Allen Toussaint, US singer, songwriter and producer, who has worked with Paul Simon, Joe Cocker, The Band, Lee Dorsey and The Neville Brothers.

1948 Tim Harris – drummer with The Foundations, who had a 1967 UK No.1 single with 'Baby Now That I've Found You' and a 1969 US No.3 single with 'Build Me Up A Buttercup'.

1959 Chas Smash – horn player with Madness, who had a 1982 UK No.1 single with 'House Of Fun' plus over 20 other UK Top 40 hits.

1967 Zakk Wylde – guitarist in the Ozzy Osbourne Band, who had a 1986 UK No.20 single with 'Shot In The Dark'.

1968 James Todd Smith, (a.k.a. LL Cool J), who had a 1987 UK No.8 single with 'I Need Love'.

1969 Dave Grohl – drummer for Nirvana, who had a 1991 UK No.7 & 1992 US No.6 single with 'Smells Like Teen Spirit'. This was taken from the 1991 album *Nevermind*, which spent over two years on the UK chart and made US No.1 in 1992. Since then he has formed the Foo Fighters, who had a 1995 UK No.5 single with 'This Is A Call'.

1974 Denise Van Outen, actress and singer who had a 2002 UK No. 23 single with Andy Williams 'Can't Take My Eyes Off You'. The song set a new record for the biggest age gap of a duo to have a hit: 45 years.

ON THIS DAY

1963 Drummer Charlie Watts made his live debut with The Rolling Stones at The Flamingo Jazz Club, Soho, London.

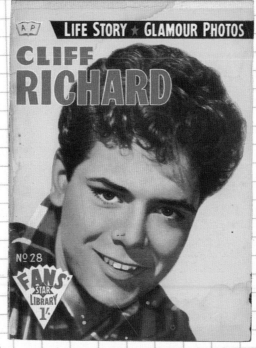

1967 Cliff Richard *(above)* told music weekly *NME* that he was retiring from show business to teach religious education in schools.

1970 Diana Ross made her last appearance with The Supremes at The Frontier Hotel, Las Vegas.

1972 Stevie Wonder kicked off a 15 date UK tour at London's Hammersmith Odeon.

1978 The Sex Pistols played their last live gig at Winterland, San Francisco, (they reformed in 96).

1984 Paul McCartney made history by becoming the first artist to have a No.1 in a group, (The Beatles), in a duo, (with Stevie Wonder), in a trio, (with Wings) and as a solo artist when he went to No.1 on the UK singles chart with 'Pipes Of Peace'.

1989 Bobby Brown went to No.1 on the US singles chart with 'My Prerogative'.

1989 compilation albums were excluded from the UK chart and were listed in the new Top 20 Compilation Albums listing.

1992 Jerry Nolan, drummer with The New York Dolls, died from a fatal stroke.

1993 US alternative group The Pixies announced that they had split. They reformed in 2004.

1996 Oasis went to No.1 on the UK album chart with *(What's the story) Morning Glory?*

2003 the sister of Jerry Lee Lewis, keyboardist Linda Gail Lewis, dropped a claim of sex discrimination against Van Morrison. Lewis had claimed that Morrison had publicly humiliated her on stage and had tried to ruin her life by asking her for sex. She withdrew her claim after discussions with her lawyer. Morrison denied all the allegations.

2005 a $100,000 (£58,823) statue honouring the late punk guitarist Johnny Ramone was unveiled by his widow Linda at the Hollywood Forever Cemetery. Johnny died from prostate cancer in September 2004 at the age of 55. Hundreds turned out for the ceremony, including Tommy Ramone – the only surviving band member. Dee Dee Ramone died of a drugs overdose in 2002 and Joey died in 2001 of lymphatic cancer.

One good reason to exclude compilation albums from the charts (1989).

BORN ON THIS DAY

1893 Ivor Novello, songwriter and actor. There is an annual British award named after him. Novello died on March 6th 1951.

1941 Don Van Vliet, (a.k.a. Captain Beefheart). His albums included *Safe As Milk*, *Trout Mask Replica* and *Strictly Personal*.

1942 Edward Bivens – vocalist with The Manhattans, who had a 1976 US No.1 & UK No.4 single with 'Kiss And Say Goodbye'.

1947 Pete Waterman, producer, TV presenter and part of the Stock Aitken Waterman team. He booked the first-ever tour for The Bay City Rollers, signed Musical Youth and Nik Kershaw and during the 70s was promotion consultant for John Travolta. He had a 1987 UK No.13 hit with 'Roadblock'. He dominated UK pop in the mid- to late 1980s as part of Stock Aitken Waterman, the most successful pop writers and producers of all time. They produced Bananarama, Kylie Minogue, Rick Astley and Jason Donovan. He became a judge on UK TV's *Popstars*.

1948 Ronnie Van Zant – vocalist with Lynyrd Skynyrd, who had a 1974 US No.8 single with 'Sweet Home Alabama' and a 1982 UK No.21 single with 'Freebird'. He died in a plane crash on October 20th 1977.

1952 Melvyn Gale – celloist in the Electric Light Orchestra, who had a 1979 UK No.3 & US No.4 single with 'Don't Bring Me Down', plus 26 other Top 40 hits.

1953 Boris Blank of Yello, who had a 1988 UK No.7 single with 'The Race'.

1965 Adam Jones – guitarist with Tool, who had a 2001 US No.1 album with *Lateralus*.

1967 Lisa Velez – vocalist for Lisa Lisa & Cult Jam, who had a 1987 US No.1 single with 'Head To Toe'.

1969 Ice Cube, rapper who had a 1994 UK No.22 single with 'Bop Gun' and a 1992 US No.1 US album with The Predator. He was also a member of N.W.A. who had a 1990 UK No.26 single with 'Express Yourself'

ON THIS DAY

1958 The Everly Brothers made their debut on British TV appearing on *The Perry Como Show*.

1961 The Supremes signed a worldwide recording contract with Motown Records.

1965 The Who released their first single 'I Can't Explain'. Jimmy Page played guitar on the track, which went on to reach No.8 in the UK chart.

1967 The Rolling Stones were forced to change the lyrics of 'Let's Spend The Night Together' to 'Let's Spend Some Time Together' when appearing on the US TV's *The Ed Sullivan Show*.

1972 Don McLean's 'American Pie' started a four week run at No.1 in the US singles chart.

1977 Abba scored their second UK No.1 album when *Arrival* went to the top of the charts.

1977 The Eagles went to No.1 on the US album chart with *Hotel California*, the group's third US No.1 album.

1977 UK singer Leo Sayer went to No.1 on the US singles chart with 'You Make Me Feel Like

Dancing'. It was the first of two US No.1s for the singer.

1980 The Ramones appeared live on UK BBC TV's *The Old Grey Whistle Test*.

1983 Men At Work started a four week run at No.1 in the US singles chart with 'Down Under', the group's second US No.1. It was also a No.1 in the UK.

1994 singer/songwriter Harry Nilsson died in his sleep. He had recorded 'Everybody's Talkin' from the film *Midnight Cowboy*. He also wrote hits for Three Dog Night and The Monkees, and had a UK & US No.1 single with his version of the Badfinger Evans/Ham song 'Without You'.

1998 harmonica player Junior Wells died. He had worked with Muddy Waters, Van Morrison and Carlos Santana.

2002 the 80s pop legend Adam Ant was admitted to a mental ward 24 hours after being charged by police for pulling a gun on staff in a London pub.

2004 it was announced that album sales in the UK rose by 7.6 percent in 2003 to a record high. Almost 121 million artist albums were sold.

Ivor Novello, not looking too well, these days.

A young Don McLean receives some sound advice on home baking!

BORN ON THIS DAY

1937 Bob Bogle – guitarist with The Ventures, who had a 1960 UK No.4 single with 'Perfidia' and a 1960 US No.2 with 'Walk Don't Run'.

1942 Raymond Philips – keyboardist for The Nashville Teens, who had a 1964 UK No.6 & US No.16 single with 'Tobacco Road'.

1942 William Francis – keyboardist and vocalist with Dr. Hook, who had a 1972 UK No.2 & US No.5 single with 'Sylvia's Mother'.

1959 Helen Folasade Adu (a.k.a. Sade), singer, who had a 1984 UK No.6 single with 'Your Love Is King' and a 1985 US No.5 single with 'Smooth Operator'.

1965 Maxine Jones – singer with En Vogue, who had a 1992 US No.2 & UK No.4 single with 'My Lovin'.

1979 Aaliyah, US singer and actress who had a 2000, US No.1 single with 'Try Again' and a posthumous 2002 UK No.1 single with 'More Than A Woman'. She was killed in a plane crash in the Bahamas on August 25th 2001.

1981 Nick Valensi – guitarist with The Strokes, who had a 2001 UK No.14 single with 'Last Nite'.

ON THIS DAY

1957 The Cavern Club *(top)* opened in Liverpool. It became the home of many Liverpool bands, including The Beatles.

1964 The Dave Clark Five were at No.1 on the UK singles chart with 'Glad All Over'. This was the group's only UK No.1.

1970 John Lennon's London art gallery exhibit of erotic lithographs, "Bag One", was raided by detectives from Scotland Yard who confiscated eight exhibits that were deemed to be indecent.

1973 Bruce Springsteen appeared at Villanova University in front of an audience of 25 people.

THE Cavern CLUB

MEMBERSHIP CARD
1962 SEASON

Ending 31st December, 1962

1977 *Starsky And Hutch* TV actor David Soul was at No.1 on the UK singles chart with 'Don't Give Up On Us', his first of two No.1 UK singles.

1978 Sex Pistol Sid Vicious fell through a glass door at a San Francisco hotel, took a drug overdose and was rushed to hospital.

1980 Paul McCartney was jailed for nine days in Tokyo for marijuana possession after being found with 219g (7.7oz) on his arrival at Narita Airport.

1987 Presenter Jools Holland was suspended from Channel 4's UK music show *The Tube* for six weeks after using the phrase "groovy fuckers" during a live trailer broadcast in children's hour.

1988 24 years after The Beatles first topped the chart, George Harrison went to No.1 in the US with 'Got My Mind Set On You'.

1988 Tina Turner gave herself a place in the record books when she performed in front of 182,000 people in Rio De Janerio. This was the largest audience ever for a single artist.

1992 Eric Clapton recorded his unplugged session for MTV.

1999 Brandy started a two week run at No.1 on the US singles chart with the Diane Warren song 'Have You Ever', which was a No.13 hit in the UK.

2000 it was reported that Mick Jagger had lost the chance of a knighthood because of his errant ways. British Prime Minister Tony Blair had second thoughts about the message it would give about family values.

2003 Steve Strange, of 80s band Visage, told a London court he was robbed of a bracelet given to him by Kylie Minogue after being beaten over the head in central London.

2004 Michael Jackson appeared in court and pleaded not guilty to seven charges of child molestation. The singer, who arrived 21 minutes late, was told off by the Santa Barbara judge – who said, "Mr Jackson, you have started out on the wrong foot here."

2005 Elvis Presley's single 'One Night' made chart history by becoming the 1,000th UK No.1 single. Elvis, who had led the previous week's chart with 'Jailhouse Rock', had now scored more No.1 UK hits than any other artist. He had 20 No.1s, so beating The Beatles' 17 chart toppers.

Do not arise Sir Mick Jagger

Eben Black
Chief Political Correspondent

Mick Jagger: too naughty for knighthood.

BORN ON THIS DAY

1927 Eartha Kitt *(below)*, US female singer who had a 1955 UK No.7 single with 'Under The Bridges Of Paris' and a 1989 UK No.32 single with Bronski Beat, 'Cha Cha Heels'.

1943 Chris Montez, UK singer who had a 1962 UK No.2 & US No.4 single with 'Let's Dance'.

1948 Mick Taylor – guitarist in John Mayall's Bluesbreakers who then joined The Rolling Stones in 1969. While he was with them they had a 1971 US No.1 & UK No.2 single with 'Brown Sugar'.

1955 Steve Earle, US singer/songwriter who had a 1988 UK No.45 single with 'Copperhead Road' and a country and independent No.1 album with *Trancendental Blues*. Johnny Cash, Emmylou Harris, Gretchen Peters, Shawn Colvin and Eddi Reader have all covered his songs.

1956 Paul Young, singer who had a 1983 UK No.1 single with 'Wherever I Lay My Hat, That's My Home' and a 1985 US No.1 single with 'Everytime You Go Away'. He had been part of The Streetband, who had had a 1978 UK No.18 single with 'Toast' then singer for Q-Tips, a soul covers band.

1959 Susanna Hoffs – guitarist and vocalist with The Bangles, who had a 1986 UK No.2 single with the Prince song 'Manic Monday' and a 1986 US No.1 single with 'Walk Like An Egyptian'.

1960 John Crawford – bass guitarist and keyboardist for Berlin, who had a 1986 UK & US No.1 single with 'Take My Breath Away'.

1963 Andy Rourke – bass guitarist from The Smiths, who had a 1984 UK No.10 single with 'Heaven Knows I'm Miserable Now', plus 15 other UK Top 40 singles.

1966 Shabba Ranks, singer who had a 1993 UK No.3 single with 'Mr Loverman'.

1971 Kid Rock (a.k.a. Robert James Ritchie), US singer who had a 2000 US No.2 album with *History Of Rock*.

ON THIS DAY

1963 appearing at The Marquee Club, London were the Cyril Davis All Stars, The Velvets and, bottom of the bill, The Rolling Stones.

1966 NBC-TV bought *The Monkees* series, placing it on their 1966 autumn schedule.

1967 the *Daily Mail* ran the story about a local council survey finding 4,000 holes in the road in Lancashire, inspiring John Lennon's contribution to The Beatles' song 'A Day In The Life'.

1967 The Jimi Hendrix Experience recorded a session for Radio Luxembourg's "Ready Steady Radio". The band ran up a bar bill of £2, 5 shillings ($6.21), which they were unable to pay.

1970 The Doors appeared at New York's Felt Forum.

1974 Dean Martin's son Dino Martin was arrested after attempting to sell two AK-47 machine guns to an undercover agent.

1982 Tommy Tucker died, aged 48, after being overcome by poisonous fumes while renovating the floors of his New York home. He had written the 1964 US No.11 hit 'Hi Heel Sneakers'.

1987 Kate Bush started a two week run at No.1 on the UK album chart with *The Whole Story*.

1994 Donny Osmond took part in a charity boxing match held in Chicago against former Partridge Family member Danny Bonaduce. Donny lost 2–1.

1998 Savage Garden started a two week run at No.1 on the US singles chart with 'Truly Madly Deeply.'

The Monkees ponder their hectic 1966 schedule.

2003 a long-lost recording featuring John Lennon and Mick Jagger was set to spark a bidding war at a London auction. The acetate record was recorded in 1974 with Jagger singing the blues song 'Too Many Cooks' and Lennon playing guitar. The track had never been released because the two artists were both singed to different record companies.

BORN ON THIS DAY

1941 Bobby Goldsboro, US singer who had a 1968 US No.1 & UK No.2 single with 'Honey'.

1941 David Ruffin of The Temptations, who had a 1971 US No.1 & UK No. 8 single with 'Just My Imagination' and reissued 'My Girl' to have UK No.2 in 1992. As a solo artist he had a 1975 US No.9 & UK No.10 single with 'Walk Away From Love'. He died of a drug overdose on June 1st 1991.

1944 Legs Larry Smith – drummer with the Bonzo Dog Doo Dah Band *(right)*, who had a 1968 UK No.5 single with 'I'm The Urban Spaceman'.

1959 Bob Rosenberg, who formed Will To Power. The group had a 1988 US No.1 & 1989 UK No.6 single with 'Baby I Love Your Way/Freebird'.

1971 Jonathan Davis – vocalist with Korn, who had a 1998 UK No.23 single with 'Got The Life' and a 1998 US No.1 album with *Follow The Leader*.

1983 Samantha Mumba, singer and actress who had a 2000 UK No.2 & US No.4 single with 'Gotta Tell You' and a 2001 UK No.3 single with 'Always Come Back To'.

ON THIS DAY

1960 Johnny Preston started a three week run at No.1 on the US singles chart with 'Running Bear', which was also No.1 in the UK.

1964 The Beatles made their US chart debut when 'I Want To Hold Your Hand' entered the chart at No.45. It went on to spend seven weeks at the No.1 position.

1969 Led Zeppelin played the second of three sold out nights at The Grande Ballroom, Detroit in Michigan during the band's debut North American tour.

1970 appearing at The Fairfield Hall, Croydon, England was Pink Floyd.

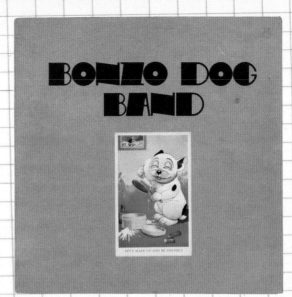

1974 ex-members from Free (Paul Rodgers and Simon Kirke), Mott The Hoople (Mick Ralphs) and King Crimson (Boz Burrell) formed Bad Company.

1975 Barry Manilow scored his first US No.1 single when 'Mandy', (originally titled 'Brandy') went to the top of the charts.

1975 Status Quo were at No.1 on the UK singles chart with 'Down Down', the group's only UK No.1 from 50 Top 40 hits.

1981 Wendy O'Williams of The Plasmatics was arrested on stage at Milwaukee and was charged with the offence of simulating sex with a sledgehammer.

1986 Guns N' Roses appeared at The Roxy Club in Hollywood, California.

Houston drug inquiry

Los Angeles: The singer, Whitney Houston, left, is under investigation for allegedly trying to smuggle 15.2 grams of marijuana out of Hawaii (Grace Bradberry writes). A local newspaper said that a security officer at Keahold-Kona Airport, who has limited powers of arrest, found the drug when he asked Houston to open her handbag. She walked away when he tried to detain her.

Inflexible friend

Nairobi: A Kenyan businessman who was carried into a bank on a stretcher to get money to pay for emergency hospital treatment was turned away because he did not have his cash card with him. *The East African Standard*

1991 three fans were killed during a crush in a crowd during an AC/DC gig in Salt Lake City.

1991 the first of three nights at Wembley Arena for The Brits 91, which featured the Happy Mondays, James, 808 state, The Cure, Jesus Jones, The Quire Boys, Thunder and The Little Angels. Tickets £12.50 ($21.25) for each day.

1996 Lisa Marie Presley divorced Michael Jackson after less then two years of being married.

1995 Grateful Dead guitarist Jerry Garcia escaped without injury after crashing his BMW into a guard rail near Mill Valley, California.

2000 Whitney Houston was under investigation after allegedly trying to smuggle 15.2 grams of Marijuana out of Hawaii.

2001 Oasis guitarist Noel Gallagher was granted a quickie divorce from Meg Matthews at the High Court in London. The couple split up in the previous September, eight months after Meg had given birth to their daughter Anais.

2004 Jennifer Lopez's divorce from her second husband Cris Judd became final. Lopez and Judd married in 2001, after meeting when filming the video to 'Love Don't Cost A Thing' but split the next year. He was expected to get a $15 million (£8.8 million) settlement from the divorce.

BORN ON THIS DAY

1935 Johnny O'Keefe, singer known as "Australia's King of rock 'n' roll". He co-wrote and had the 1958 Australian hit with, 'Real Wild Child', which was covered by Iggy Pop in 1986. O'Keefe died on October 6th 1978.

1939 Phil Everly *(below)*, singer/songwriter of The Everly Brothers, who had a 1958 UK & US No.1 single with 'All I Have To Do Is Dream', plus over 25 other Top 40 hits.

1943 Janis Joplin, US singer who had a 1971 US No.1 single with 'Me And Bobby McGee' and a 1971 US No.1 album with *Pearl*. She died on October 4th 1970 after an accidental heroin overdose.

1946 Dolly Parton, US singer/songwriter and actress who had a 1976 UK No.7 single with 'Jolene' and a 1981 US No.1 single with '9 To 5'. She also wrote 'I Will Always Love You', a UK & US No.1 for Whitney Houston.

1949 Robert Palmer, singer/songwriter who was part of Vinegar Joe . As a solo artist he had a 1986 US No.1 & UK No.5 single with 'Addicted To Love'. He died on September 25th 2003, aged 54.

1951 Dewey Bunnell – vocalist and guitarist with America, who had a 1972 US No.1 & UK No.3 'Horse With No Name'.

1957 Mickey Virtue – keyboardist with UB40, who had a 1983 UK No.1 & 1988 US No.1 single with 'Red Red Wine' and over 30 other UK Top 40 hits.

ON THIS DAY

1959 The Platters' 'Smoke Gets In Your Eyes' started a three week run at No.1 on the US singles chart.

1967 Pink Floyd and Marmalade played at The Marquee Club, London.

1967 The Monkees were at No.1 on the UK singles chart with 'I'm A Believer', the group's only UK No.1.

1971 The Beatles *White Album* was played in the courtroom at the Sharon Tate murder trial to find out if any songs could have influenced Charles Manson and his followers to commit murder.

1980 'Brass In Pocket' gave The Pretenders their first UK No.1 single. The band's self-titled debut album started a four week run at No.1 on the UK chart on this day too.

1980 Pink Floyd's *The Wall* started a 15 week run at No.1 on the US album chart. The group's third US No.1, it went on to sell over eight million copies.

1988 Bon Jovi and Motley Crue manager Doc

Norah has a choice of three keys to sing in.

McGheep pleaded guilty to importing more than 18,140kg (40,000lb) of marijuana into the US.

1990 singer Mel Appleby died of pneumonia aged 23. She had been one half of the duo Mel & Kim.

1993 Fleetwood Mac reformed to perform at Bill Clinton's inauguration. The band's 'Don't Stop' was used as the theme for his campaign.

1997 Madonna won the Best Actress award for *Evita* at the Golden Globe Awards.

1998 Carl Perkins died aged 65, after suffering two strokes. He had written the classic rock 'n' roll song 'Blue Suede Shoes'.

2003 Norah Jones started a three week run at No.1 on the US album chart with *Come Away With Me*, which was also a UK No.1.

BORN ON THIS DAY

1924 Slim Whitman, American country singer who had a 1955 UK No.1 single with 'Rose Marie' – while his US hits included 'Cattle Call' and 'Keep It A Secret'.

1933 Ron Townson – singer in The 5th Dimension, who had a 1969 US No.1 & UK No.11 single with 'Aquarius'. He died on August 3rd 2001.

1942 Billy Powell of The O'Jays, who had a 1973 US No.1 & UK No.9 single with 'Love Train'. Powell died on May 26th 1982.

1943 Rick Evans – singer with Zager & Evans, who had a 1969 US & UK No.1 single with 'In The Year 2525'.

1945 Eric Stewart – guitarist, keyboardist and vocalist. He was a member of Mindbenders, who had a 1966 UK No.2 single with 'Groovy Kind Of Love', Hotlegs, who had a 1970 UK No.2 single with 'Neanderthal Man' and 10CC, who had a 1975 UK No.1 & US No. 2 single with 'I'm Not In Love' – plus ten other Top 30 hits.

1946 Jimmy Chambers – singer with Londonbeat, who had a 1990 UK No.2 & 1991 US No.1 single with 'I've Been Thinking About You'.

1950 Paul Stanley – guitarist and vocalist with Kiss, who had a 1974 US No.5 single with 'On And On', a 1976 US No 11 album *Rock and Roll Over* (that spent 26 weeks on the chart) and a 1987 UK No.4 single with 'Crazy Crazy Nights'.

1969 Nicholas Jones (a.k.a. Nicky Wire) – bass guitarist with the Manic Street Preachers, who had a 1996 UK No.2 single with 'A Design For Life' plus 2 UK No.1 singles.

1971 Gary Barlow – vocalist, pianist and songwriter for Take That, who had a 1995 UK No.1 single with 'Back For Good' plus seven other UK No.1 singles. As a solo artist he had a 1996 UK No.1 single with 'Forever Love'. He has also written songs for Donny Osmond, Charlotte Church, Bryan McFadden and Atomic Kitten.

1979 Rob Bourdon – drummer for Linkin Park, who had a 2002 US No.2 & UK No.4 single with 'In The End' and a 2002 US No.2 & 2001 UK No.4 album *Hybrid Theory*.

1979 Will Young, singer and UK TV's *Pop Idol* winner, who had a 2002 UK No.1 single with 'Anything Is Possible/Evergreen'.

ON THIS DAY

1966 The Spencer Davis Group were at No.1 on the UK singles chart with 'Keep On Running'.

1967 *The Monkees* TV show was shown for the first time in the UK.

1968 one hit wonders John Fred And The Playboy Band started a two week run at No.1 on the US singles chart with 'Judy In Disguise, (With Glasses)', it made No.3 in the UK. The song was inspired by The Beatles' 'Lucy In The Sky With Diamonds'.

1975 the US Top 5 singles of the year were: No.5, Stevie Wonder, 'Boogie On Reggae Woman'; No.4, Ohio Players, 'Fire'; No.3, Barry Manilow, 'Mandy'; No.2, Neil Sedaka, 'Laughter In The Rain' and No.1, The Carpenters, 'Please Mr. Postman'.

1979 appearing at London's Hammersmith Odeon were Chic. The group's latest single 'Le Freak' had reached No.7 on the UK chart.

1982 during an Ozzy Osbourne concert in Des Moines, Iowa a member of the audience threw an unconscious bat onto the stage. Thinking it was one of his rubber fakes, Ozzy picked it up and bit off its head. The singer was later taken to hospital to be given a rabies injection.

1986 Stevie Wonder and Bob Dylan appeared at a concert to celebrate the first Martin Luther King Day in the US.

1990 Michael Bolton started a three week run at No.1 on the US singles chart with 'How Am I Supposed To Live Without You', the singer's first No.1 as well as the first No.1 single of the 90s in the US.

1996 Bobby Brown was fined $1,000 (£560), sentenced to two years probation and ordered to attend anger management classes after assaulting a security guard.

1999 Bill Albaugh of the Lemon Pipers died. They had had the 1967 US No.1 single 'Green Tambourine'.

2001 a memorial service was held for Kirsty MacColl, who was killed in a boating accident off the coast of Mexico in December 2000. Bono and Billy Bragg were among the friends and fans that attended St Martin-in-the-Fields Church, London.

2002 George Harrison had the posthumous UK No.1 single with the re-release of the 1971 former No.1 'My Sweet Lord'. Harrison's single replaced Aaliyah's 'More Than A Woman', making it the only time in chart history that one deceased artist had taken over from another at No.1.

POP IDOL EXCLUSIVE

WILL: I'M GAY

- It's totally no big deal, just part of who I am
- Family and friends know ..it's never been a secret
- Everyone is supportive and I'm very happy

The Pop Idol winner breaks his news to the world!

BORN ON THIS DAY

1939 DJ Wolfman Jack, who had been master of ceremonies for the rock 'n' roll generation of the 60s on radio and later on television during the 70s. He died of a heart attack on July 1st 1995.

1941 Richie Havens, *(below)* folk singer who had a 1971 US No.16 single with his version of George Harrisons' 'Here Comes The Sun' and appeared at Woodstock, Newport and Isle Of Wight festivals.

1942 Edwin Starr, singer who had a 1970 US No.1 and UK No.3 single with 'War'. He died on April 2nd 2003 at 61.

1942 Mac Davis, singer/songwriter who had a 1972 US No.1 single with 'Baby Don't Get Hooked On Me' – which reached No.29 in the UK. He also wrote 'In The Ghetto' and 'Don't Cry Daddy' for Elvis Presley.

1950 Billy Ocean, singer who had a 1988 US No.1 & UK No.3 single with 'Get Out Of My Dreams Get Into My Car'.

1958 Anita Baker, US soul singer who had a 1986 UK No.13 single with 'Sweet Love' and a 1998 US No.1 album with *Giving You The Best That I Got*.

1965 Jam Master Jay (a.k.a. Jason Mizell), former member of Run DMC. He was killed by an assassin's single bullet on October 30th 2002. The group had a 1986 UK No.8 single with Aerosmith 'Walk This Way' and a 1998 UK No.1 single with 'It's Like That'.

1976 Emma Bunton – Baby Spice of The Spice Girls, who had a 1996 UK No.1 & 1997 US No.1 single with 'Wannabe'. She later had a 2001 UK No.1 solo single with 'What Took You So Long'.

ON THIS DAY

1965 The Rolling Stones and Roy Orbison were met by 3,000 screaming fans at Sydney Airport when they arrived for a tour in Australia.

1966 George Harrison married Patti Boyd at Leatherhead Register Office in Surrey with Paul McCartney as best man. George had first met Patti on the set of The Beatles movie *A Hard Day's Night*.

1970 Elvis Presley's last film *Change Of Habit* was released.

1974 appearing at Newcastle City Hall, England were T. Rex. Tickets cost £1.50 ($2.55).

1978 the soundtrack album *Saturday Night Fever* started a 24 week run at No.1 on the US album charts. It went on to sell over 30 million copies worldwide, making it the bestselling film soundtrack album of all time.

1984 soul singer Jackie Wilson died. Wilson had been in care after suffering a heart attack during a stage performance in 1975. Van Morrison wrote the song 'Jackie Wilson Said' as a tribute to the singer, which was later covered by Dexy's Midnight Runners.

1989 Six weeks after his death Roy Orbison started a three week run at No.1 on the UK album chart with *The Legendary Roy Orbison* collection.

1992 Billy Idol pleaded guilty to assault and battery charges after an incident outside a West Hollywood restaurant. He was fined $2,700 (£1,588) and ordered to appear in a series of anti-drug commercials.

1997 'Colonel' Tom Parker, Elvis Presley's manager and agent, died aged 87. Born Andreas van Kuijk, a Dutch immigrant who changed his name as soon as he arrived in the US, Parker never applied for a green card and feared deportation his entire life. He also briefly managed country singers Eddy Arnold and Hank Snow.

2001 Limp Bizkit started a two week run at No.1 on the UK singles chart with 'Rollin'.

2002 singer and actress Peggy Lee died. She had scored the 1958 US No. 8 & UK No.5 single 'Fever' and also worked with Benny Goodman, Randy Newman and Quincy Jones.

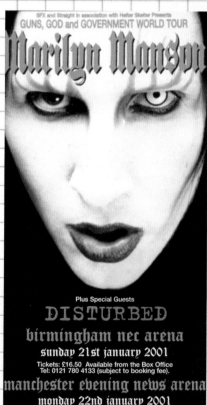

Marilyn Manson appearing at the Birmingham NEC in 2001.

BORN ON THIS DAY

1931 Sam Cooke, US soul singer who had a 1957 US No.1 & UK No.29 single with 'You Send Me' and a 1986 UK No.2 single with 'Wonderful World' (it was first released in 1960). He died on December 11th 1964.

1940 Addie Harris of vocal group The Shirelles, who had a 1961 US No.1 & UK No. 4 single with 'Will You Love Me Tomorrow'. She died on June 10th 1982.

1947 Malcolm McLaren, Sex Pistols manager and solo artist who had a 1983 UK No.3 single with 'Double Dutch'.

1953 Steve Perry – vocalist with Journey, who had a 1982 US No.2 single with 'Open Arms'. As a solo artist he had a 1984 US No.3 single with 'Oh, Sherrie'.

1962 Michael Hutchence – vocalist with INXS, who had a 1988 UK No.2 & US No.1 single with 'Need You Tonight'. He was found dead on November 22nd 1997 in a hotel suite in Sydney, Australia, aged 37. Hutchence's body was found naked behind the door to his room; he had apparently hanged himself with his own belt.

Michael Hutchence and friends in the studio.

1965 Steven Adler – drummer with Guns N' Roses, who had a 1988 US No.1 & 1989 UK No.6 single with 'Sweet Child O' Mine'.

1980 Benjamin Moody – guitarist for Evanescence, who had a 2003 UK No.1 & US No.5 single with 'Bring Me To Life' and a 2003 UK No.1 & US No.3 album with Fallen.

ON THIS DAY

1966 The Beach Boys went into the studio to record 'Wouldn't It Be Nice'.

1967 The Monkees performed live for the very first time at The Cow Palace, San Francisco to a sell-out crowd.

1972 David Bowie 'came out' as bisexual during a Melody Maker interview with reporter Michael Watts.

1972 Don Mclean's album American Pie, started a seven week run at No.1 in the US album chart.

1977 Wings went to No.1 on the US album chart with Wings Over America, Paul McCartney's sixth US No.1 album after leaving The Beatles.

1980 This week's US Top 5 singles were: No.5, Rupert Holmes, 'Escape, (The Pina Colada Song)'; No.4, Smokey Robinson, 'Cruisin'; No.3, Kenny Rogers, 'Coward Of The County'; No.2, Captain And Tennille, 'Do That To Me One More Time' and No.1, Michael Jackson, 'Rock With You'.

1983 the new 24-hour music video network MTV started broadcasting to the West Coast of America after being picked up by Group W Cable, Los Angeles.

1986 appearing at Glasgow Exhibition Centre, Scotland were Frankie Goes To Hollywood. Tickets cost £8 ($13.60).

1987 one hit wonder Steve 'Silk' Hurley was at No.1 on the UK singles chart with 'Jack Your Body', the first "house" record to top the charts.

1988 Faith No More made their live UK debut at Dingwalls, London at the start of a 13 date tour.

1992 Mariah Carey's stepfather went to court seeking damages, claiming that he had paid for her Manhattan apartment, a car and dental work in her early years on the understanding that she would repay him when she became successful.

1994 D:Ream had their first UK No.1 single with 'Things Can Only Get Better'. It stayed at No.1 for four weeks.

2000 Savage Garden went to No.1 on the US singles chart with 'I Knew I Loved You'.

2001 The Strokes released their first record, 'The Modern Age' EP, on Rough Trade Records in the UK.

2004 Ryan Adams broke a wrist after falling during a sell-out show at the Royal Court Theatre in Liverpool. Adams fell from the stage and suffered a fractured wrist. A fan said, "One minute he was on the stage and the next he had disappeared. He went down with a thud and we couldn't believe he was trying to continue singing."

OZZY: I WANT BABY!

Let's hope it's not quads, Oz

Brace yourself – Ozzy and Sharon are back in action

OZZY Osbourne's wife Sharon has revealed the rocker longs for another baby after cheating death in a quad bike accident.

Ozzy Osbourne announces he wants another baby with wife Sharon.

EM GIRL'S RAP

RAPPER Eminem's ex-wife moved last yesterday after admitting possessing cocaine. Kim Mathers, who admitted 31 marijuana in 2001 after being arrested...

BORN ON THIS DAY

1910 Django Reinhardt, jazz guitarist. He badly burned the third and fourth fingers of his left hand in a house fire when aged 18. Doctors suggested he play the guitar to keep his fingers flexible, and it was this that gave him his two-fingered guitar style. He worked with Stephane Grappelli and Duke Ellington. Reinhardt died of a stroke on May 15th 1953.

1948 Anita Pointer – singer with The Pointer Sisters, who had a 1981 US No.2 single with 'Slow Hand' and a 1984 UK No.2 single with 'Automatic'.

1950 Bill Cunningham – bass guitarist and pianist for The Box Tops, who had a 1967 US No.1 & UK No.5 single with 'The Letter'.

1950 Pat Simmons – guitarist and vocalist for The Doobie Brothers, who had a 1979, US No.1 single with 'What A Fool Believes' and a 1993 UK No.7 single with 'Long Train Runnin'.

1953 Robin Zander – vocalist with Cheap Trick, who had a 1979 UK No.29 & US No.17 single with 'I Want You To Want Me' and a 1988 US No.1 single with 'The Flame'.

ON THIS DAY

1956 rock 'n' roll fans in Cleveland that were aged under 18 were banned from dancing in public (unless accompanied by an adult), after Ohio Police introduced a law dating back to 1931.

1965 'Downtown' made Petula Clark the first UK female singer to have a No.1 on the US singles chart since Vera Lynn in 1952. It was a No.2 hit in the UK.

> "If there's not drama and negativity in my life, all my songs will be boring."
> **Eminem**

1971 Steel Mill played their final show when they appeared at the Upstage Club, Ashbury Park, New Jersey. The band's singer, Bruce Springsteen, formed new bands during the rest of the year; Bruce Springsteen Jam, Dr. Zoom And The Sonic Boom and The Bruce Springsteen Band.

1971 George Harrison became the first solo Beatle to have a No.1 when 'My Sweet Lord' went to the top of the UK singles charts.

1971 Dawn started a three week run at No.1 on the US singles chart with 'Knock Three Times', the group's first No.1, which was also a UK No.1.

1977 Patti Smith broke her spine when she fell off the stage at a gig in Tampa, Florida.

1978 Adam And The Ants made their radio debut on Radio 1's "John Peel Show".

1978 Terry Kath of Chicago accidentally shot himself dead while cleaning what he believed was an unloaded gun. Kath's last words were "Don't worry it's not loaded" as he put the gun to his head and pulled the trigger. The guitarist and singer was killed instantly.

1980 appearing at the Liverpool Philharmonic was Marvin Gaye, with Edwin Starr as support.

1988 Michael Jackson went to No.1 on the US singles chart with 'The Way You Make Me Feel', which was a No.3 hit in the UK.

1990 Allen Collins from Lynyrd Skynyrd died of pneumonia after being ill for several months. Collins had survived a plane crash in 1977 that killed two other band members.

1990 David Bowie announced his forthcoming and final world tour, "Sound And Vision", during which he would invite each local audience to decide on a "greatest hits" running order – this was organized through local radio stations.

2001 an English coroner criticized the rap singer Eminem's lyrics as depressing at an inquest into the death of a school boy who threw himself in front of a train.

2001 former rubbish collector Mark Oliver was found guilty by a London court of stealing luggage belonging to Victoria Beckham from Heathrow Airport. Police issued a list of the £23,000 ($39,100) worth of clothes.

2003 R. Kelly was arrested on new child pornography charges. The singer was detained in Miami after police said digital sex pictures were discovered at his home in Florida last June.

2005 One of the biggest charity concerts since Live Aid raised £1.25 million ($2 million) for victims of the tsunami disaster in Asia. The concert held at The Millennium Stadium, Cardiff featured Eric Clapton, Manic Street Preachers, Keane, Charlotte Church, Snow Patrol, Embrace, Feeder, Craig David and Liberty X.

BORN ON THIS DAY

1933 Zeke Carey of The Flamingos, who had a 1959 US No.11 single with 'I Only Have Eyes For You' – this was a 1975 UK No.1 hit for Art Garfunkel. Carey died on December 24th 1999.

1941 Aaron Neville – vocalist for The Neville Brothers, who had a 1966 US No.2 single with 'Tell It Like It Is' and 1989 UK No.2 single with Linda Ronstadt 'Don't Know Much'.

1941 Neil Diamond, singer/songwriter who had a 1970 US No.1 & UK No.3 single with 'Cracklin' Rose' plus over 30 US & 10 UK Top 40 singles. He also wrote 'I'm A Believer', which was a No.1 for The Monkees. Many acts – including Elvis Presley, Lulu and Deep Purple – have covered his songs.

1941 Ray Stevens, singer/songwriter who had a 1970 US No.1 & UK No.6 single with 'Everything Is Beautiful' and a 1974 US & UK No.1 single with 'The Streak'.

1945 Tammi Terrell, singer, who died of a brain tumour on March 16th 1970 after collapsing into Marvin Gaye's arms on stage during a duet of 'That's All You Need To Get By'. Terrell had undergone eight brain operations in 18 months. She had had hits with Marvin Gaye, including the 1967 US No.5 'Your Precious Love'.

1947 Warren Zevon, singer/songwriter. He had played piano with The Everly Brothers, recorded over 15 solo albums and the 1978 solo US No.21 single 'Werewolves Of London'. He died on September 7th 2003.

1949 John Belushi, actor and singer, who was Joliet 'Jake' Blues in The Blues Brothers and recorded the 1990 UK No.12 single 'Everybody Needs Somebody To Love'. He died of a drug overdose on March 5th 1982.

1955 Jools Holland, keyboardist with Squeeze then Jools Holland's Big Band and TV presenter on *The Tube, Juke Box Dury* and *Later...* He had a 1979 UK No.2 single with Squeeze, 'Up The Junction'.

ON THIS DAY

1958 Elvis Presley was at No.1 on the UK singles chart with 'Jailhouse Rock'. It became the first-ever single to enter the chart at No.1 and was Presley's second UK No.1.

1962 Brian Epstein signed a management deal with The Beatles.

1968 Georgie Fame was at No.1 on the UK singles chart with 'The Ballad Of Bonnie and Clyde'.

1970 Black Sabbath kicked off a 24 date UK tour at Birmingham Town Hall with support band Wild Turkey. Also on this day Led Zeppelin appeared at Leeds Town Hall, England.

1976 Bob Dylan started a five week run at No.1 on the US album chart with *Desire*.

"Woodstock wasn't about anything. It was just a whole new market for tie-dye tee-shirts."

Bob Dylan

1976 Diana Ross went to No.1 on the US singles chart with 'Theme From Mahogany', the singer's third US No.1 – it was a No.5 hit in the UK.

1977 appearing at the Roxy, London, were the Buzzcocks supported by Chelsea. Also appearing at the venue over the last week had been The Damned, The Boys, The Adverts, Slaughter And The Dogs and Squeeze.

1978 workers at EMI's record-pressing plant refused to press copies of the Buzzcocks forthcoming release 'What Do I Get' because of the title on the B-side 'Oh Shit'.

1979 The Clash released their first single in the US, 'I Fought The Law' (written by Sonny Curtis of Buddy Holly's Crickets).

1980 appearing at The Blitz Club, London were Spandau Ballet.

1981 Adam And The Ants started a 10 week run at No.1 on the UK chart with their debut album *Kings Of The Wild Frontier*.

1981 Steve Tyler of Aerosmith was hospitalized after being involved in a crash on his motorbike.

1995 David Cole, producer and keyboardist of C&C Music Factory, died of meningitis aged 32. He had had a 1991 UK No.4 single with 'Things That Make You Go Hmmm...' and a 1991 US No.1 single with 'Gonna Make You Sweat'. He had produced Mariah Carey, Whitney Houston and Aretha Franklin.

1998 Oasis went to No.1 on the UK singles chart with 'All Around The World'. It had the longest running time for a No.1 with a total duration of 9 minutes 38 seconds.

1999 The Offspring went to No.1 on the UK singles chart with 'Pretty Fly, For A White Guy'.

2003 David Palmer, former keyboard player for Jethro Tull, changed his name to Dee Palmer after a successful sex change operation. Palmer was the keyboard player for Jethro Tull between 1969 and 1980.

BORN ON THIS DAY

1915 folk singer/songwriter Ewan MacColl, composer of 'The First Time Ever I Saw Your Face', which was a hit for Roberta Flack in 1971. MacColl died on October 22nd 1989.

1931 Stig Anderson, producer, who worked with Abba. He died of a heart attack on September 12th 1997.

1938 Etta James, singer who scored nine US Top 40 hits during the 60s, and also had a 1996 UK No.5 single with 'I Just Want To Make Love To You'.

1954 Robert Finch – vocalist with KC & The Sunshine Band, who had a 1975 US No.1 single with 'That's The Way I Like It' and a 1983 UK No.1 single with 'Give It Up'.

1956 Andy Cox, guitarist. With The Beat he had a 1983 UK No.3 single with 'Can't Get Used To Losing You'. He then joined the Fine Young Cannibals, who had a 1989 US No.1 & UK No.5 single with 'She Drives Me Crazy'.

1958 Gary Tibbs – bass guitarist for Roxy Music then Adam And The Ants. The latter band had a 1981 UK No.1 single with 'Stand And Deliver' plus 15 other Top 40 UK singles.

1981 Alica Keys, US singer/songwriter who had a 2001 US No.1 & UK No.3 single with 'Fallin' and 2001 US No.1 & UK No.7 album with *Songs In A Minor*.

ON THIS DAY

1960 the original cast recording of *The Sound Of Music* started a 16 week run at No.1 on the US album chart.

1964 Phil Spector appeared as a guest on this week's UK TV show *Juke Box Jury*.

1975 The Carpenters went to No.1 on the US singles chart with their version of The Marvelettes' 1961 hit 'Please Mr. Postman'.

1978 Joy Division made their live debut when they played Pips in Manchester.

1980 The Specials made their US live debut when they appeared at New York's Hurrah club.

1983 The Allman Brothers' bass guitarist Lamar Williams died of cancer, aged 36.

1984 Yoko Ono donated £250,000 ($425,000) to Liverpool old people's home Strawberry Fields.

1986 Norwegian group A-Ha were at No.1 in the UK with 'The Sun Always Shines On TV'. They became the first-ever Norwegian act to score a UK No.1.

1989 Bobby Brown was arrested for an overtly sexually suggestive performance after a show in Columbus. He was fined $652 (£384) under the anti-lewdness ordinance law.

1989 Madonna started divorce proceedings for the second time from Sean Penn at Los Angeles County Court and moved into a new three bedroom house in Hollywood Hills.

1992 Guns N' Roses played at The Thomas & Mack Center in Las Vegas during a 14 date US tour.

2001 millionaire pop impresario Jonathan King was charged with a further ten offences of sexually abusing children. The charges dated back to the 1970s. King was granted bail. He was later jailed.

2004 Katie Melua started a three week run at No.1 on the UK album chart with her debut release *Call Off The Search*.

Jonathan King to face new charges

By Lewis Smith

JONATHAN KING, 55, the millionaire pop impresario, was charged yesterday with a further ten offences of sexually abusing children. He has already appeared in court on three charges of sexually abusing boys under the age of 16.

The new charges involved allegations dating back to the 1970s.

Earlier this week he was rearrested and questioned for nine hours by Surrey police before being released on bail.

Shortly after his court appearance in November last year, under his real name of Kenneth George King, he said: "I categorically deny these absurd allegations about events from 28 years ago."

A spokesman for the pop tycoon, who first rose to fame at the age of 21 with the hit single *Everyone's Gone To The Moon*, said last year that Mr King regarded such claims as an occupational hazard.

After his chart success he moved into record management and later founded his own recording company. He helped to launch the popular group Genesis and promoted the Bay City Rollers.

He is widely known for his work as a television presenter and radio disc jockey. In 1990 he was asked to revise the Brit Awards show and in 1997 he was named Man of the Year by the British Phonographic Industry. Mr King was granted bail to appear next month.

The gates at the entrance to Strawberry Fields. Currently for sale on ebay, buyer sends articulated lorry to collect!

marquee

90 Wardour St., W.1.   **01-437 6603**

OPEN EVERY NIGHT FROM 7.00 p.m. to 11.00 p.m.
REDUCED ADMISSION FOR STUDENTS AND MEMBERS

Wed. 25th Jan. (Adm 75p)	Sun. 29th Jan. (Adm 75p)
SALT Plus friends & Jerry Floyd	**ROOGGALATOR** Plus support & Nick Leigh
Thurs. 26th Jan. (Adm 65p) **ADAM & THE ANTS** Plus support & Ian Fleming	Mon. 30th Jan. (Adm 65p) **THE KILL JOYS** Plus friends & Jerry Floyd
Fri. 27th Jan. (Adm £1) Welcome Return of . . . **THE SAINTS**	Tues. 31st Jan. (Adm 70p) **BETHNAL —** **SPEEDOMETERS** & Joe Lung
Sat. 28th Jan. (Adm 75p) **THE DEPRESSIONS** **THE PIRHANAS** & Ian Fleming	Wed. 1st Feb. (Adm 75p) **SALT** Plus support & Jerry Floyd

Hamburgers and other hot & cold snacks are available

BORN ON THIS DAY

1934 Huey "Piano" Smith, US R&B pianist who had a 1958 US No.9 single with 'Don't You Just Know It' and also played on Frankie Ford's hit 'Sea Cruise'.

1949 Derek Holt – multi-instrumentalist and vocalist with the Climax Blues Band, who had a 1976 UK No.10 & 1977 US No.3 single with 'Couldn't Get It Right'.

1957 Norman Hassan – percussionist with UB40, who had a 1983 UK No.1 & 1988 US No.1 single with 'Red Red Wine' and over 30 other Top 40 hit singles.

1963 Andrew Ridgeley – vocalist with Wham!, who had a 1984 UK & US No.1 single 'Wake Me Up Before You Go Go' plus 10 other UK Top 20 hit singles.

1963 Jazzie B, Soul II Soul member and producer. Soul II Soul had a 1989 UK No.1 single with 'Back To Life'.

ON THIS DAY

1961 Elvis Presley was at No.1 on the UK singles chart with 'Are You Lonesome Tonight?'. This was the singer's sixth UK No.1.

1965 Keith Richards had his shirt torn off and Mick Jagger was forced to leave the stage after 50 fans invaded it during a gig at The Town Hall, Brisbane, Australia.

1970 John Lennon wrote, recorded and mixed his new single 'Instant Karma' all in one day.

1973 Sweet were at No.1 on the UK singles chart with 'Blockbuster'. This was the group's only UK No.1 of 15 Top 40 hits.

1974 Ringo Starr went to No.1 on the US singles chart with his version of the Johnny Burnette 1960 hit 'You're Sixteen' — it was a No.3 hit in the UK.

1977 Former Fleetwood Mac guitarist Peter Green was committed to a mental hospital following an incident when he threatened his accountant Clifford Adams with an air rifle when he was trying to deliver a £30,000 ($51,000) royalty cheque to him.

1980 Prince made his TV debut on the US show *American Bandstand*.

1986 Allen Collins from Lynyrd Skynyrd crashed his car, which paralyzed him from the waist down and killed his girlfriend Debra Jean Watts.

1989 US soul singer Donnie Elbert died of a stroke aged 53. He had had a 1972 US No. 22 & UK No.11 single with 'I Can't Help Myself, (Sugar Pie Huney Bunch)'.

1991 Cher made a special video for the troops involved in Desert Storm during the Gulf War. Cher's video, *Canteen*, featured Janet Jackson, Paul Simon, Van Halen and Bonnie Raitt.

1991 Queen had their second UK No.1 with 'Innuendo'. It was the third-longest No.1 song of all time, behind The Beatles' 'Hey Jude' and Simple Minds' 'Belfast Child'.

2003 Billy Joel was airlifted to hospital after his car smashed into a tree. The singer lost control of his Mercedes S500 and skidded for 91m (100 yds) before crashing. The accident happened in The Hamptons near New York.

2003 B2K and Puff Daddy went to No.1 on the US singles chart with 'Bump Bump Bump.'

2003 Justin Timberlake went to No.1 on the UK album chart with his debut solo album *Justified*, which spent over a year on the UK chart.

2004 John Lydon was one of ten contestants to take part in the latest *I'm A Celebrity... Get Me Out Of Here* UK TV show set in the Australian outback. The former Sex Pistols singer was seen by 11 million viewers on the first night covered in bird seed being pecked by giant ostriches. Lydon, who was paid £25,000 ($42,500) to appear in the show, walked off the jungle set after four days.

Billy . . hit tree in Merc

Billy Joel's car horror

SINGER Billy Joel was airlifted to hospital early yesterday after his car smashed into a tree.

The star, 54, lost control of the Mercedes S500 and skidded for 100 yards before crashing.

He was alone when the accident happened in the millionaire's playground of The Hamptons, near New York, where he has a mansion.

The singer — whose hits include Uptown Girl, about ex-wife Christie Brinkley — alerted emergency services on his mobile phone.

Police said alcohol was not a reason for the crash.

Joel, who survived a motorbike accident in 1983, was released from Stony Brook University Hospital after treatment.

Police said: "It was a bad accident. It was bordering on freezing but it was dry."

TON-UP BIKERS

Five thousand Harley-Davidson bike fans are expected at a 100th birthday party for the firm at Butlins in Minehead.

BORN ON THIS DAY

1918 Elmore James, US blues guitarist and singer who wrote 'Shake Your Money Maker', which was covered by Fleetwood Mac in 1968. He influenced Jimi Hendrix, BB King and Keith Richards. James died on May 24th 1963.

1945 Nick Mason – drummer with Pink Floyd, who had a 1973 US No.1 & UK No.2 album with *Dark Side Of The Moon*.

1946 Nedra Talley – vocalist with The Ronettes, who had a 1963 US No.2 & UK No.4 single with 'Be My Baby'.

1951 Seth Justman – keyboardist and vocalist with The J. Geils Band, who had a 1982 US No.1 & UK No.3 single with 'Centerfold'.

1968 Mike Patton – vocalist for Faith No More, who had 1993 UK No.3 and US No.4 single with 'I'm Easy'.

1974 Mark Owen – vocalist with Take That, who had a 1995 UK No.1 single with 'Back For Good' plus seven other UK No.1 singles. As a solo artist he had a 1996 UK No.3 single with 'Child'. He was also the winner of UK TV show *Celebrity Big Brother* in 2002.

ON THIS DAY

1958 Little Richard entered The Oakwood Theological College in Huntsville, where he was ordained as a Seventh Day Adventist minister.

1962 Joey And The Starlighters were at No.1 on the US singles chart with 'Peppermint Twist, Part 1'.

1966 The Overlanders were at No.1 on the UK singles chart with their version of The Beatles' song 'Michelle'. This was the group's only UK hit.

1968 The Bee Gees made their live debut in the US when they played at the Anaheim Center, California.

1971 David Bowie arrived in the US for the first time. He couldn't play live because of work permit restrictions, but attracted publicity when he wore a dress at a promotion event.

1973 Roxy Music won "the most promising new name" section in the *NME* readers' poll.

1973 'Superstition' gave Stevie Wonder his second No.1 single in the US, ten years after his first No.1.

1977 The Clash signed to CBS Records UK.

1979 Ian Dury And The Blockheads were at No.1 on the UK singles chart with 'Hit Me With Your Rhythm Stick'.

1980 Def Leppard played the first of two nights at The Marquee, London. Tickets cost £2 ($3.40).

1980 Dexy's Midnight Runners kicked off a 26 date UK tour at London's Music Machine.

1984 Madonna made her first appearance in the UK, on TV music programme *The Tube*, performing 'Holiday'. The show was broadcast live from the Hacienda Club in Manchester.

1990 Kylie Minogue *(above)* had her third UK No.1 single with 'Tears On My Pillow', originally a US hit for Little Anthony And The Imperials in 1958.

1996 Babylon Zoo started a five week run at No.1 on the UK singles chart with 'Spaceman', the fastest-selling non-charity single ever (it sold 420,000 copies in six days).

1998 James Brown was charged with possession of marijuana and unlawful use of a firearm after police were called to his South Carolina home.

2004 R&B singer Faith Evans and her husband were charged with possession of cocaine and marijuana in Atlanta, Georgia.

FOXES at the NEW REGENT — WEST STREET BRIGHTON — opposite Top Rank Suite

Fri. 27th Jan (tickets at the door)

WIRE
plus Adam + the Ants
+ D. J. Peter Fox

Fri. Feb 3rd — Slaughter + The Dogs + Psycho

BORN ON THIS DAY

1927 Ronnie Scott, jazz musician. Formed his own nine-piece group in 1953, opened the first Ronnie Scott's night club in London in 1959. He played with

his own groups at the club, in between presenting the cream of the world's jazz musicians. He died on December 23rd 1996.

1946 Rick Allen – bass guitarist with The Box Tops, who had a 1967 US No.1 & UK No.5 single with 'The Letter'.

1968 Sarah McLachlan, singer/songwriter who also put the Lilith Fair US tour together. She had a 1997 US No.2 album with *Surfacing*.

1977 Joseph Fatone – member of *NSYNC, who had a 2000 US No.1 single with 'It's Gonna Be Me' and a 1999 UK No.5 single with 'I Want You Back'.

1980 Nicolas Carter – singer with the Backstreet Boys, who had a 1997 US No.2 single with 'Quit Playing Games With My Heart' and a 1999 UK No.1 single with 'I Want It That Way'.

ON THIS DAY

1956 Elvis Presley made the first of four weekly appearances on the TV programme *Stage Show*, performing 'Shake Rattle And Roll/Flip, Flop And Fly' and 'I Got A Woman'. One of the hosts from the show was overheard saying "he can't last".

1965 The Moody Blues were at No.1 on the UK singles chart with 'Go Now!', the group's only UK No.1.

1965 The Who made their first appearance on UK TV show *Ready Steady Go!*

1978 The Fleetwood Mac album *Rumours* went to No.1 on the UK album chart – it was also a No.1 in the US. The album went on to sell over 15 million copies worldwide and spent over 440 weeks on the UK chart.

1983 British rock 'n' roll singer Billy Fury died of heart failure. He had had a 1961 UK No.3 single with 'Halfway To Paradise', plus 25 other Top 40 UK singles.

1984 Frankie Goes To Hollywood started a five week run at No.1 on the UK singles chart with 'Relax'. *Top Of The Pops* were unable to feature the song due to a BBC ban.

1985 the recording took place for 'We Are The World' the US equivalent of Band Aid. Written by Michael Jackson and Lionel Richie, the all-star cast included Stevie Wonder, Tina Turner, Bruce Springsteen, Diana Ross, Bob Dylan, Ray Charles, Daryl Hall, John Oates and Cyndi Lauper.

1988 eleven years after it was released, The Sex Pistols album *Never Mind The Bollocks, Here's The Sex Pistols* went Gold in the US with sales of over 500,000.

1994 Paul and Linda McCartney attended the premiere of *Wayne's World II* in London. The couple then went on to Hard Rock Café, where the film star Mike Myers presented them with a cheque for LIPA (the Liverpool Institute for Performing Arts) for £25,000 ($42,500).

1995 TLC started a four week run at No.1 on the US singles chart with 'Creep', the group's first US No.1. It made No.6 in the UK the following year.

1998 Oasis guitarist Noel Gallagher played a 20 minute solo gig at the King's Head, an English pub in Santa Monica.

2000 Sax player Thomas "Beans" Bowles died of prostate cancer. He had played on many Motown sessions, including Marvin Gaye's 'What's Going On' and The Supremes' 'Baby Love'.

2001 Jennifer Lopez started a two week run at No.1 on the US album chart with *J.Lo*.

2001 Limp Bizkit started a two week run at No.1 on the UK album chart with *Chocolate Starfish*.

2001 Shaggy, featuring Ricardo Rikrot, started a two week run at No.1 on the US singles chart with 'It Wasn't Me'. It was also a No.1 in the UK.

2003 H-Town singer Keven Conner was killed in a car crash in Houston, aged 28. Conner died when an S.U.V. ran a red light and crashed into the car he was a passenger in, which had just picked him up from the recording studio.

2004 Elvis Presley fans expressed their anger at plans to cut up a rare tape of the singer's early songs and sell the snippets at auction. US firm Master Tape Collection said the tape would be cut into two-inch snippets and sold for £270 ($460) each.

2005 Drummer and singer Jim Capaldi died of stomach cancer aged 60. He had been a member of Traffic, who had a 1967 UK No.2 single with 'Hole In My Shoe' and also had success as a solo artist with the 1975 UK No.4 single 'Love Hurts'.

The original unofficial release of Sex Pistols debut.

BORN ON THIS DAY

1889 Leadbelly (Hurrdi William Ledbetter), blues musician. He wrote 'Goodnight Irene', 'The Rock Island Line' and 'The Midnight Special.' He was once jailed for shooting a man dead during an argument over a woman. Leadbelly died on December 6th 1949.

1933 French singer and guitarist Sacha Distel, who had a 1970 UK No.10 single with 'Raindrops Keep Falling On My Head'. He died on July 22nd 2004.

1938 James Jamerson, bass guitarist with The Funk Brothers. They played on many Motown hits by The Temptations, Marvin Gaye, The Four Tops and Martha And The Vandellas. He died of a heart attack on August 22nd 1983 aged 45.

1943 Tony Blackburn, DJ on Radio Caroline and the first DJ on BBC Radio 1. (The first song played was 'Flowers In The Rain' by The Move). Blackburn was crowned "King of the jungle" in 2003 after winning the UK TV show *I'm A Celebrity... Get Me Out Of Here* set in the Australian outback.

1952 Thomas Erdelyi, (a.k.a. Tommy Ramone) – drummer with The Ramones, who had a 1977 UK No.22 single with 'Sheena Is A Punk Rocker'.

1953 Louie Perez – member of Los Lobos, who had a 1987 UK & US No.1 single with 'La Bamba'.

1954 Rob Manzoli – guitarist with Right Said Fred, who had a 1991 US No.1 & UK No.2 single with 'I'm Too Sexy' and a 1993 UK No.1 album with *Up*.

ON THIS DAY

1964 the first date on a twice nightly UK package tour with Dusty Springfield, Bobby Vee and The Swinging Blue Jeans, kicked off at The Adelphi Theatre, Slough.

1969 Fleetwood Mac scored their only UK No.1 single with the instrumental 'Albatross'.

1972 the triple album *The Concert For Bangladesh* went to No.1 on the UK album chart. It was organized by George Harrison to raise funds for the people caught up in the war and famine from the area.

British DJ Tony Blackburn presents his own board game, *Chartbuster*.

1977 former backing band for The Temptations, Rose Royce went to No.1 on the US singles chart with 'Car Wash', a No.9 hit in the UK.

1979 16-year-old Brenda Spencer killed two people and wounded nine others when she fired from her house onto the entrance of San Diego's Grover Cleveland Elementary School with a .22-calibre rifle her father gave her for Christmas. When asked why she did it, she answered "I don't like Mondays". The Boomtown Rats *(right)* went on to write and record a song based on the event.

1982 flying back from Cannes, France Gary Numan made a forced landing after running low on fuel at an RAF base outside Southampton. The press ran stories that he had in fact crash landed on the A3057.

1983 Australian group Men At Work went to No.1 on the British and American singles and album charts simultaneously with 'Down Under' and *Business As Usual*. The last artist to achieve this was Rod Stewart in 1971.

1986 Stevie Nicks from Fleetwood Mac married Kim Anderson, a Warner Brothers Records promotion man.

1989 Marc Almond started a four week run at No.1 on the UK singles chart with 'Something's Gotten Hold Of My Heart', which had guest vocals from Gene Pitney.

1992 Willie Dixon, blues singer and guitarist, died. He had written classic songs including, 'You Shook Me', 'I Can't Quit You Baby' and 'Little Red Rooster'. He was a major influence on The Rolling Stones and Led Zeppelin.

2001 a New York based data company issued a chart listing sales of posthumous albums. The idea came about after radio stations wanted to distinguish between proper recordings when the artists were alive and CDs released after they died. Mike Shalett, founder of SoundScan, said there was only one problem — what to call the chart? The Top 5 chart had The Doors at No.5, Eva Cassidy at 4, Jimi Hendrix at 3, Bob Marley at 2 and 2Pac at No.1.

BORN ON THIS DAY

1941 Joe Terranova – singer with Danny & The Juniors, who had a 1958 US No.1 & UK No.3 single with 'At The Hop'.

1942 Martyn Balin – vocalist with Jefferson Airplane, who had a 1967 US No.18 single with 'White Rabbit'.

1943 Sandy Deane – member of vocal group Jay & the Americans, who had a 1969 US No.6 single with 'This Magic Moment' plus nine other US Top 30 hits.

1947 Steve Marriott, *(right)* guitarist and singer/songwriter. He was a major influence on many UK bands. Marriott was a member of Small Faces, who had a 1967 UK No.3 & US No.16 single with 'Itchycoo Park' plus the 1968 No.1 UK album *Ogden's Nut Gone Flake* and Humble Pie, who had a 1969 UK No.4 single with 'Natural Born Bugie'. He died in a house fire on April 20th 1991.

1961 Jody Watley – vocalist for Shalamar, who had a 1980 US No.8 single with 'The Second Time Around' and a 1982 UK No.5 single with 'A Night To Remember'. As a solo artist she had a 1987 UK No.13 single, with 'Looking For A New Love' and a 1989 US No.2 single with 'Real Love'. Destiny's Child covered the Watley penned song 'Sweet Sixteen'.

ON THIS DAY

1956 Elvis Presley started recording what would be his first album at RCA's New York Studios. Songs recorded included his version of Carl Perkin's 'Blue Suede Shoes'.

1961 The Shirelles started a two week run at No.1 on the US singles chart with 'Will You Love Me Tomorrow' – it reached No.4 in the UK.

1964 The Searchers were at No.1 on the UK singles chart with 'Needles And Pins'. This was the group's second UK No.1.

1969 the rooftop gig took place with The Beatles appearing live on top of the Apple building. It lasted for just over 40 minutes and it was the last time The Beatles performed live.

1970 Marc Bolan married June Child at the Kensington registry office. They divorced in 1975.

1970 Edison Lighthouse were at No.1 on the UK singles chart with 'Love Grows (Where My Rosemary Goes)'.

1972 Paul McCartney wrote and recorded his protest song 'Give Ireland Back To The Irish' within 24 hours of Bloody Sunday, when 13 Catholics were killed by British paratroopers.

1973 Kiss made their live stage debut at The Coventry Club, Queens, New York.

1978 appearing at the Vortex, Wardour Street, London were The Police.

1982 Paul McCartney appeared on BBC radio's "Desert Island Discs". His selections included: Elvis

Music agent Dennis Farriss (father of INXS band members Tim, John and Andrew) ran the INXS fan club too!

Presley's 'Heartbreak Hotel'; Chuck Berry's 'Sweet Little Sixteen'; John Lennon's 'Beautiful Boy' and Little Richards' 'Tutti Frutti'.

1988 during a court case involving Holly Johnson and ZTT Records it was revealed that Frankie Goes To Hollywood had not played on their hits 'Relax' and 'Two Tribes'. The court was told that top session musicians were used to make the records.

1988 INXS had their first US No.1 hit single with 'Need You Tonight'.

1988 Tiffany was at No.1 on the UK singles chart with 'I Think We're Alone Now', the singer's only UK No.1 single.

1990 unhappy with the reissue of the band's early single 'Sally Cinnaman' The Stone Roses trashed their former record company Revolver FM's offices and threw paint over cars. The band were arrested and charged with criminal damage.

1990 Bob Dylan was honoured in France and became a commander in the Order of Arts and Letters.

1999 after spending 11 weeks on the US singles chart Britney Spears started a two week run at No.1 with '...Baby One More Time'. Britney's debut album also went to No.1 on the US chart on the same day.

1999 in the *NME* readers' poll results the winner of "The pop personality that you would like as your doctor" was won by Australian singer Natalie Imbruglia *(left)*.

(Card reads:) TELEPHONE 381 2177 RUG SPECIALISTS — Dowland Farriss Pty. Ltd. *Agents & Distributors* — 511 HAY STREET, JOLIMONT WESTERN AUSTRALIA 6014 — DENNIS FARRISS Director

BORN ON THIS DAY

1946 Terry Kath – guitarist with Chicago, who had a 1976 UK & US No.1 single with 'If You Leave Me Now'. Kath accidentally shot himself dead on January 23rd 1978.

1951 Harry Wayne Casey – lead vocalist with KC & The Sunshine Band, who had a 1975 US No.1 single with 'That's The Way, I Like It' and a 1983 UK No.1 single with 'Give It Up'.

1951 Phil Collins, drummer, pianist, vocalist and actor. He was a member of Genesis, who had a 1986 US No.1 single 'Invisible Touch' and a 1992 UK No.7 single with 'I Can't Dance' plus six UK No.1 albums. As a solo artist he had a 1988 UK & US No.1 single with 'A Groovy Kind Of Love' plus six other US No.1s and four UK No.1 albums. His acting roles include *Oliver*, *Buster* and *Miami Vice*.

1951 Phil Manzanera – guitarist with Roxy Music, who had a 1972 UK No.4 single 'Virginia Plain' plus 15 other UK Top 40 singles.

1956 John Lydon (a.k.a. Johnny Rotten) – singer with the Sex Pistols, who had a 1977 UK No.2 single with 'God Save The Queen' and a 1977 UK No.1 album *Never Mind The Bollocks Here's The Sex Pistols*. He went on to be part of Public Image Ltd, who had a 1983 UK No.5 single with 'This Is Not A Love Song'.

1961 Lloyd Cole – singer, songwriter and guitarist for Lloyd Cole And The Commotions, who had a 1985 UK No.19 single with 'Brand New Friend'. As

a solo artist he had a 1995 UK No.24 with 'Like Lovers Do'.

1981 Justin Timberlake, singer. He was formerly part of *NSYNC, who had a 2000 US No.1 single 'Its Gonna Be Me' and a 1999 UK No.5 single with 'I Want You Back'. As a solo artist he had a 2003 UK No.2 & US No.3 single with 'Cry Me A River'.

ON THIS DAY

1957 Decca Records announced that Bill Haley And His Comets' 'Rock Around The Clock' had sold over a million copies in the UK.

Former *NSYNC hunk Justin Timberlake.

Even the waxwork Robbie Williams attracts legions of adoring female fans.

1967 taking time out from filming the promo for 'Strawberry Fields Forever' John Lennon bought a 1843 poster from an antiques shop in Surrey. This provided him with most of the lyrics for the song 'Being For The Benefit Of Mr Kite', recorded on *Sgt Pepper's*.

1970 The Jackson Five went to No.1 on the US singles chart with 'I Want You Back'. The song was originally written for Gladys Knight & The Pips and was the first of four No.1s for the group. It made No.2 in the UK.

1976 Abba's single 'Mamma Mia' knocked Queen's 'Bohemian Rhapsody' off the UK No.1 spot after it had had a nine week run at the top of the charts.

1976 *Sounds* readers' poll winners included: Queen who won best album for *A Night At The Opera*, best single single for 'Bohemian Rhapsody', and best band. Best musician went to Mike Oldfield; best female singer Maddy Prior; from Steeleye, Span, best new band went to Rainbow and The Bay City Rollers won bore of the year.

1978 Talking Heads made their UK TV debut on *The Old Grey Whistle Test*.

1988 appearing at The Mean Fiddler, London were the Red Hot Chili Peppers.

2003 Robbie Williams topped a chart based on UK album sales from the past five years. The ex-Take That singer had sold 9.7 million albums in Britain, an average of over 5,000 every day. The Corrs were in second place with 5.8 million sales, Westlife third with 5.1 million, Madonna in fourth with 5 million and The Beatles in fifth with 4.7 million.

a tribute to the BEATLES

NOT THE BEATLES

BORN ON THIS DAY

1937 Don Everly of The Everly Brothers, who had a 1958 UK & US No.1 single with 'All I Have To Do Is Dream' plus over 25 other UK hit singles.

1937 Ray Sawyer – vocalist with Dr. Hook, who had a 1972 US No.5 & UK No.2 single with 'Sylvia's Mother' plus nine other US Top 40 hits.

1938 Jimmy Carl Black – drummer with Frank Zappa, who had a 1970 UK No.9 album Hot Rats.

Jimmy Black by Schenkel.

1939 Joe Sample – keyboardist with The Crusaders, who had a 1979 UK No.5 single with 'Street Life'.

1948 Rick James, US singer who had a 1980 UK No.41 single with 'Big Time', a 1981 US No.3 album with Street Songs and a 1981 US No.16 single with 'Super Freak Part 1'. Jame was found dead at his home on August 6th 2004.

1954 Mike Campbell – guitarist with Tom Petty & The Heartbreakers, (1989 UK No.28 single 'I Won't Back Down'.

1957 Dennis Brown, reggae singer, who had a 1979 UK No.14 single with 'Money In My Pocket'. He died on July 1st 1999.

1968 Lisa Marie Presley, daughter of Elvis. She married Michael Jackson in 1994, but separated from him on December 10th 1995.

1969 Patrick Wilson – drummer with Weezer, who had a 1995 UK No.12 single with 'Buddy Holly'.

1971 Ron Welty – drummer with The Offspring, who had a 1999 UK No.1 & US No. 59 single with 'Pretty Fly, (For A White Guy)' and a 1999 US No.6 & UK No.10 album with *Americana*.

ON THIS DAY

1949 RCA Records issued the first ever 45rpm single. This invention made jukeboxes possible.

1964 The Beatles started a seven week run at No.1 on the US singles chart with 'I Want To Hold Your Hand', the first US No.1 by a UK act since The Tornados' 'Telstar' in 1962 It was the first of three consecutive No.1s for the group.

1969 Tommy James & The Shondells started a two week run at No.1 on the US singles chart with 'Crimson And Clover', the group's second and last No.1. Billy Idol had a 1987 US No.1 with 'Mony Mony', which had been a No.3 hit for Tommy James in 1968.

1972 Chuck Berry had his first UK No.1 single with a live recording of a song he'd been playing live for over 20 years – 'My Ding A Ling'. UK public morality campaigner Mary Whitehouse attempted to have the song banned.

1975 Neil Sedaka had his second US No.1 single with 'Laughter In The Rain', over 12 years after his last chart topper 'Breaking Up Is Hard To Do'.

1986 Diana Ross married Norwegian shipping magnate Arne Naess in Geneva. Stevie Wonder performed at the reception. The couple divorced in 2000.

1986 music publisher Dick James died of a heart attack aged 65. He had worked with many UK 60s acts, including The Beatles.

1988 The Cars announced they were breaking up after 12 years of working together.

1995 Richey James, guitarist with the Manic Street Preachers, vanished leaving no clues to his whereabouts. He left The Embassy Hotel in London at 7am, leaving behind his packed suitcase. His car was found on the Severn Bridge outside Bristol 16 days later.

2001 a collection of Sir Elton John's private photos on display at a museum in Atlanta were withdrawn. The exhibition, which included snaps of nude men, was said to be too explicit – some school trips to the museum had been cancelled.

RCA launch their first single and the entire 'Rock And Roll' movement. Remy Ray was a master of the "Hula Twist" as you can see.

BORN ON THIS DAY

1934 Skip Battin – bass guitarist with The Byrds, who had a 1965 US & UK No.1 single with 'Mr Tambourine Man'. He was also a member of New Riders Of The Purple Sage and The Flying Burrito Brothers. Battin died on July 6th 2003.

1940 Alan Caddy – guitarist with The Tornados, who had a 1962 UK & US No.1 single with 'Telstar'. This was the first major hit from a UK act on the US chart. Caddy died on August 16th 2000.

1942 Graham Nash – guitarist and vocalist with The Hollies, then Crosby, Stills, Nash & Young, who had a 1969 UK No.17 single with 'Marrakesh Express' and a 1970 album with *Deja Vu*.

1946 Howard Bellamy of the Bellamy Brothers, who had a 1976 US No.1 single with 'Let Your Love Flow' and a 1979 UK No.3 single 'If I Said You Had A Beautiful Body Would You Hold It Against Me?'.

1947 Peter Lucia –drummer with Tommy James & The Shondells, who had a 1966 US No.1 single with 'Hanky Panky' and a 1968 UK No.1 single with 'Mony Mony'.

1948 Alan McKay – guitarist with Earth, Wind and Fire, who had a 1975 US No.1 single with 'Shining Star' and a 1981 UK No.3 single 'Let's Groove'.

1963 Eva Cassidy, US singer. She is the only artist to score three posthumous UK No.1 albums: 2001's *Songbird*; 2002's *Imagine* and 2003's *American Tune*. In 2001 she also had a UK No. 42 single with 'Over The Rainbow'. Eva died of cancer on November 1st 1996, aged 33.

1969 John Spence, singer and original member of No Doubt in the late 80s. He committed suicide on December 21st 1987 by shooting himself.

1971 Ben Mize – drummer for Counting Crows, who had a 1994 UK No.28 single with 'Mr Jones' and a 1996 US No.1 album with *Recovering The Satellites*.

ON THIS DAY

1959 appearing at Surf Ballroom, Clear Lake, Iowa were Buddy Holly, Richard Valens and The Big Bopper. This was their last-ever gig before they were killed in a plane crash the following day.

1966 The Rolling Stones released '19th Nervous Breakdown'. It went on to be a No.2 hit on the US & UK singles chart.

1973 Keith Emerson of ELP injured his hands when his piano, which was rigged to explode as a stunt, detonated prematurely during a concert in San Francisco.

1974 Barbra Streisand started a four week run at No.1 on the US singles chart with the theme from the film *The Way We Were*. The single won an Oscar and a Grammy as "song of the year".

1974 The Carpenters started a four week run at No.1 on the UK album chart with *The Singles 1969–73*, which featured 12 hits and the US No.1 'Top Of The World'. The album went back to the top of the charts on three other occasions.

1979 Sex Pistols bass player Sid Vicious died of a heroin overdose in New York. There had been a party in his flat to celebrate Vicious' release on $50,000 (£29,412) bail pending his trial for the murder of his former girlfriend, Nancy Spungen, the previous October. Party guests, said that Vicious had taken heroin at midnight.

2001 Bad Manners singer Buster Bloodvessel was told he was "too fat" to survive an urgently needed operation. Buster collapsed on stage during a show in Italy but doctors felt that his huge 190kg (30 stone) frame might not make it through surgery. The following year he had his stomach stapled. His weight dropped from 31 stone to 13 in just 10 months.

Bad Manners singer 'too fat for operation'

By Adam Sherwin

BUSTER BLOODVESSEL, the 30-stone performer, was told last night that he was "too fat" to survive an urgently needed operation.

The rotund Bad Manners singer, famed for performing a high-kicking cancan in women's clothing, collapsed on stage during a concert in Italy.

The bald frontman, who boasts of drinking ten pints a day and admits to an "obsession with kebabs", has had a strangulated hernia diagnosed.

Doctors in Perugia realised they faced a challenge when the 40-year-old, whose real

Buster Bloodvessel: "an obsession with kebabs"

make a television series in which he eats his way across

2002 performersmoney.com was launched by The P.P.L. (Phonographic Performance Ltd), for artists to check if they were owed any of the £10 million ($17 million) in unclaimed money. It showed that Michael Jackson was owed over £100,000 ($170,000) for 'Say, Say, Say', Stevie Wonder had money owing for 'Ebony And Ivory' and Ray Davies of The Kinks was owed a six-figure fee for 'You Really Got Me'. Director Dominic McGonigal said "If anyone has seen Rick Astley please let him know he is still earning money from his hits."

2003 Russian girl duo Tatu started a four week run at No.1 on the UK singles chart with 'All The Things She Said'.

2003 Jennifer Lopez started a three week run at No.1 on the US singles chart with 'All I Have'.

2005 Former Libertines frontman Pete Doherty was arrested on suspicion of theft and assault and was held in custody at a north London police station after an alleged incident at a hotel in Clerkenwell, central London.

Explosive performance-enhancer for any ELP concert, and what gave Prog fan George Michael an idea…

BORN ON THIS DAY

1940 Angelo D'Aleo – vocalist with Dion And The Belmonts, who had a 1961 US No.1 & UK No.11 single with 'Runaround Sue'.

1943 Dennis Edwards – vocalist with The Temptations, who had a 1971 US No.1 & UK No.8 single with 'Just My Imagination' and reissued 'My Girl', a UK No.2 in 1992.

1943 Eric Haydock – bass guitarist with The Hollies, who have had over 25 Top 40 singles since 1963, including: the 1972 US No.2 single 'Long Cool Woman In A Black Dress' and the 1988 UK No.1 single 'He Ain't Heavy, He's My Brother' – which was first released in 1969.

1947 Dave Davies – guitarist with The Kinks, who had a 1964 UK No.1 & US No.7 with 'You Really Got Me', a 1967 UK No.2 single with 'Waterloo Sunset' plus 19 other UK Top 40 singles.

1947 Melanie Safka *(right)*, singer/songwriter who had a 1971 US No.1 & 1972 UK No.4 single with 'Brand New Key'.

1949 Arthur "Killer" Kane, bass guitarist of The New York Dolls, who had a 1973 album *New York Dolls*. Kane died in Los Angeles on July 13th 2004, due to complications from leukaemia, aged 55.

1959 Lol Tolhurst – keyboardist with The Cure, who had a 1989 US No.2 single with 'Love Song', a 1992 UK No.6 single with 'Friday I'm In Love' and over 20 other UK Top 40 singles).

ON THIS DAY

1959 Buddy Holly, The Big Bopper and Ritchie Valens hired a light aircraft to take them on to the next date of a US tour. In bad weather the plane crashed in the Iowa countryside, killing all on board.

1967 producer Joe Meek shot his landlady Violet Shenton and then shot himself at his flat in London. Meek produced The Tornados' 'Telstar', the first No.1 in the US by a British group.

1967 appearing at The Civic Coliseum, Knoxville, Tennessee *(right)* were Otis Redding, The Marvelettes, Aaron Neville, James and Bobby Purify and The Drifters. Tickets cost $2.50–3.50 (£1.47–2.06).

1968 The Lemon Pipers went to No.1 on the US singles chart with 'Green Tambourine', which was a No.7 UK hit.

1973 Elton John started a three week run at No.1 on the US with the single 'Crocodile Rock'. This was his first of five US No.1 singles.

1979 Blondie had the first of five UK No.1 singles with 'Heart Of Glass'.

1979 The Blues Brothers went to No.1 on the US album chart with *Briefcase Full Of Blues*.

1990 Bob Dylan started a six night residency at London's Hammersmith Odeon.

1990 for the first time ever, the UK Top 3 singles featured non-British and non-American acts – Ireland's Sinead O'Connor, Australia's Kylie Minogue and Belgium's Technotronic. Sinead O'Connor had her first No.1 single with 'Nothing Compares To U'.

1993 appearing at The Wheatsheaf, Stoke On Trent, England were Radiohead.

2003 the exclusive documentary *Living With Michael Jackson* was shown on UK television. Reporter Martin Bashir had spent eight months with the star. The show's editor said, "viewers will not believe what they're seeing".

2004 Sean "P. Diddy" Combs settled a $3 million (£1.76 million) court case filed by his former driver after an incident in 1999. Wardell Fenderson had driven Mr Combs and his then-girlfriend Jennifer Lopez away from a New York nightclub where three people had been wounded in a shooting. Mr Fenderson said he was traumatized by having guns in the car and being ordered to ignore police orders to stop, for which he was arrested.

BORN ON THIS DAY

1941 John Steel – drummer with The Animals, who had a 1964 UK & US No.1 single with 'House Of The Rising Sun'.

1944 Florence LaRue – singer with The 5th Dimension, who had a 1969 US No.1 & UK No.11 single with 'Aquarius'.

1947 Margie and Mary Ann Ganser – vocalists for The Shangri-Las, who had a 1964 US No.1 & UK No.11 single with 'Leader Of The Pack'. Margie died on July 28th 1996.

1948 Alice Cooper (a.k.a. Vincent Furnier) – singer with Earwigs then the Alice Cooper Band, who had a 1972 UK No.1 & US No.7 single with 'School's Out'.

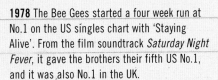

Alice Cooper tools up before School's Out.

1950 James Dunn – vocalist for The Stylistics, who had a 1975 US No.1 single with 'You Make Me Feel Brand New', a 1975 UK No.1 single with 'Can't Give You Anything But My Love' and 15 other UK Top 40 singles.

1963 Wasserman – guitarist with The Offspring, who had a 1999 UK No.1 & US No. 59 single with 'Pretty Fly, (For A White Guy)' and a 1999 US No.6 & UK No.10 album with *Americana*.

1975 Natalie Imbruglia, actress and singer who had a 1997 UK No.2 single with 'Torn' and a 1997 UK No.5 album with *Left Of The Middle*.

ON THIS DAY

1965 The Righteous Brothers were at No.1 on the UK singles chart with 'You've Lost That Lovin' Feeling'. It was also a US No.1 at the same time.

1967 The Monkees' self-titled debut album *(right)* started a seven week run at No.1 on the UK chart.

1970 John Lennon and Yoko Ono donated their hair for an auction in aid of the Black Power movement.

1978 Abba started a seven week run at No.1 on the UK chart with *The Album*, their third No.1 LP.

1978 appearing at the Oasis, Swindon, England were Talking Heads plus special guests Dire Straits.

1978 The Bee Gees started a four week run at No.1 on the US singles chart with 'Staying Alive'. From the film soundtrack *Saturday Night Fever*, it gave the brothers their fifth US No.1, and it was also No.1 in the UK.

1983 singer Karen Carpenter died aged 32 of a cardiac arrest at her parent's house. The coroner's report gave the cause of death as imbalances associated with anorexia nervosa.

1983 The Smiths appeared at The Hacienda, Manchester.

1984 Culture Club started a three week run at No.1 on the US singles chart with 'Karma Chameleon', the group's fifth US Top 10 hit – it was also a No.1 in the UK.

1984 Eurythmics scored their first UK No.1 album with their second release *Touch*, which featured the singles 'Here Comes The Rain Again', 'Who's That Girl' and 'Right By Your Side'.

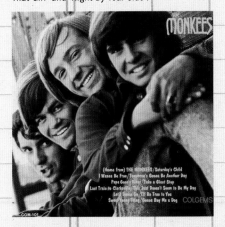

1992 appearing at The Borderline in London were Pearl Jam. Tickets cost £5 ($8.50).

1999 soul singer Gwen Guthrie died of cancer. She had worked with Aretha Franklin and Stevie Wonder and written songs for Sister Sledge and Roberta Flack.

2000 Bjorn Ulvaeus confirmed that the members of Abba had turned down a $1 billion (£0.58 billion) offer by American and British consortium to reform the group. "It is a hell of a lot of money to say no to, but we decided it wasn't for us," band member Benny Andersson told the Swedish newspaper *Aftonbladet*.

2003 Courtney Love was arrested at Heathrow airport for "endangering an aircraft" on a transatlantic flight. The singer was said to have hurled abuse at the cabin crew on the flight from Los Angeles to London after her nurse, who was in an economy seat, was barred access to Love in the upper-class cabin.

BORN ON THIS DAY

1935 Alex Harvey – vocalist and guitarist with the Sensational Alex Harvey Band, who had a 1975 UK No.7 single with 'Delilah'. Harvey died on February 4th 1982.

1941 Barrett Strong, US songwriter who wrote many Motown hits with Norman Whitfield including, 'Money', 'War', 'Ball Of Confusion' and 'Papa Was A Rolling Stone'.

1942 Corey Wells – vocalist for Three Dog Night, who had a 1970 UK No.3 & US No.1 single with 'Mamma Told Me Not To Come'.

1943 Chuck Winfield – trumpet player with Blood, Sweat & Tears, who had a 1969 US No.2 & UK No.35 single with 'You've Made Me So Very Happy'.

1944 Al Kooper, guitarist, keyboardist and producer. He was part of The Royal Teens, who had a 1958 US No.3 single with 'Shorts Shorts' then Blood, Sweat & Tears, who had a 1969 US No.12 & UK No.35 single with 'You've Made Me So Very Happy'. He also played organ on Dylan's 'Like A Rolling Stone'.

1948 David Denny – guitarist with the Steve Miller Band, who had a 1974 US No.1 & 1990 UK No.1 single with 'The Joker'.

1964 Duff McKagan – bass player for Guns N' Roses, who had a 1998 US No.1 & 1989 UK No.6 single with 'Sweet Child O' Mine'.

1968 Chris Barron – vocalist with The Spin Doctors, who had a 1993 UK No.3 & US No.7 single with 'Two Princes'.

1969 Bobby Brown, singer. He was in New Edition, who had a 1983 UK No.1 & US No.46 single with 'Candy Girl'. As a solo artist he had a 1988 UK No.6 & 1989 US No.1 single with 'My Prerogative'. Brown married Whitney Houston on July 18th 1992.

ON THIS DAY

1957 Bill Haley arrived from New York on the liner Queen Elizabeth at Southampton for his UK concert debut and was greeted by 5,000 fans. He was also the first American rock artist to tour the UK.

1966 Petula Clark had her second No.1 in the US singles chart with 'My Love' (it made No. 4 in the UK).

1969 The Move was at No.1 on the UK singles chart with 'Blackberry Way', the group's only UK No.1.

1972 T. Rex was at No.1 on the UK singles chart with 'Telegram Sam', the group's third UK No.1.

1983 Def Leppard's album *Pyromania* started a 92 week run on the US charts. It never reached No.1 but sold over six million copies in the US.

1983 Toto went to No.1 on the US singles with 'Africa'. The song made No.3 in the UK.

1991 Bill Drummond and Jimmy Cauty of KLF were arrested in Battersea, London after painting a logo on a *Sunday Times* billboard ad.

1999 *NSYNC made a guest appearance on *Sabrina The Teenage Witch* on US TV.

2000 Shirelles singer Doris Coley died of breast cancer aged 58. The Shirelles had had a 1961 US No.1 & UK No.4 single with 'Will You Love Me Tomorrow?'.

2004 prosecutors in the murder case of producer Phil Spector demanded that a fingernail overlooked by police investigating Lana Clarkson's shooting should be put forward as evidence. They claimed the fingernail, blackened with gunpowder, could indicate that the 40-year-old actress killed herself at Spector's Los Angeles mansion. Spector, had denied murdering Clarkson.

After '66 Petula Clark allegedly embarked on an ill-fated prog-rock-duo project. Best now forgotten!

BORN ON THIS DAY

1942 John London, session bass player. He worked with The Monkees, Linda Ronstadt, James Taylor and The Nitty Gritty Dirt Band. London died on February 12th 2000.

1945 Bob Marley, singer/songwriter and guitarist who had a 1981 UK No.8 single with 'No Woman No Cry', plus over ten other UK Top 40 singles and the 1976 US No.8 & UK No. 15 album 'Rastaman Vibration'. Marley died of cancer on May 11th 1981. The 1984 *Best Of* album spent 330 weeks on the UK chart. In 1990, February 6th was proclaimed a national holiday in Jamaica to commemorate his birth. Inducted into the Rock and Roll Hall of Fame in 1994.

1950 Mike Batt, songwriter and Womble. He had a 1974 UK No.3 single with 'Remember You're A Womble'. He also composed 'Bright Eyes', a 1979 UK No.1 single for Art Garfunkel.

1950 Natalie Cole, singer who had a 1989 UK No.2 single with 'Miss You Like Crazy'. Natalie is the daughter of Nat "King" Cole.

Genuine Womble skin.

1962 Axl Rose – vocalist for Guns N' Roses, who had a 1988 US No.1 & 1989 UK No.6 single with 'Sweet Child O' Mine'.

1966 Rick Astley, singer who had a 1987 UK & US No.1 single with 'Never Gonna Give You Up'.

ON THIS DAY

1958 George Harrison joined Liverpool group The Quarrymen.

1965 The Righteous Brothers started a two week run at No.1 on the US singles chart with the Phil Spector produced 'You've Lost That Lovin' Feelin'. The song was also No.1 in the UK for the duo, who were not related in any way.

1965 The Rolling Stones' second album *Rolling Stones No.2* started a three week run at No.1 on the UK charts.

1970 Eric Clapton played the first of two nights at The Filmore East, New York.

1981 composer Hugo Montenegro died in California. He had written the 1968 UK No.1 & US No.2 single 'The Good, The Bad And The Ugly' from the soundtrack to the Clint Eastwood spaghetti western film of the same name.

1982 Kraftwerk were at No.1 on the UK singles chart with 'The Model/Computer Love', the first German act to have an UK No.1.

1982 the J. Geils Band started a six week run at No.1 on the US singles chart with 'Centrefold', the band's only US No.1. It was a No.3 hit in the UK. The band's album *Freeze-Frame* started a four week run at No.1 on the US album chart on the same day.

1989 reggae producer King Tubby *(above right)* died after being shot in the street outside his home. He had worked with Robbie Shakespeare, Sly Dunbar and Carlton Barrett.

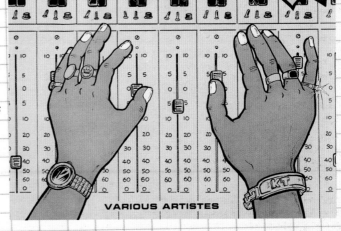

1990 Billy Idol suffered serious injuries when he failed to pull up at a stop sign and crashed from his Harley-Davidson motorbike into a car.

1990 over 200 women filed court actions against Chuck Berry after it was alleged that he had been secretly filming them in the toilets of the restaurant he owned.

1998 Beach Boy Carl Wilson died, aged 51, after a long battle with lung cancer.

1998 Austrian singer Falco was killed in a car accident. He had previously scored the 1986 UK & US No.1 single 'Rock Me Amadeus'.

2004 US singer Faith Evans and her husband Todd Russaw agreed to enrol in a rehabilitation programme. Prosecutors said charges for alleged possession of cocaine and marijuana would be dropped if they successfully completed the 13-week rehab scheme.

BORN ON THIS DAY

1934 US sax player King Curtis who worked with John Lennon and played on The Coasters' 'Yakety Yak'. He was stabbed to death by a vagrant on the front steps of his New York home on August 13th 1971.

1948 Jimmy Greenspoon – organist with Three Dog Night, who had a 1970 UK No.3 & US No.1 single with 'Mamma Told Me Not To Come'.

1949 Alan Lancaster – bass guitarist with Status Quo, who had a 1977 UK No.3 single with 'Rockin' All Over The World' plus 50 other UK Top 75 singles since 1968. Lancaster left the band in 1984.

1962 David Bryan – keyboardist with Bon Jovi, who had a 1987 US No.1 & UK No.4 single with 'Livin' On A Prayer'.

1962 Garth Brooks, country singer who had a 1991 US No.1 album with *Ropin' The Wind* (which spent 70 weeks on the US chart) and a 1994 UK No.13 single with 'The Red Strokes'. Brooks was the biggest-selling artist of the 90s, enjoying over 60 million sales.

1975 Wes Borland – guitarist with Limp Bizkit, who had a 2001 UK No.1 single with 'Rollin' and a US & UK No.1 album in 2000 with *Chocolate Starfish and the Hotdog Flavoured Water*.

The actual 4 shillings used to see The Rolling Stones.

ON THIS DAY

1959 the funeral of Buddy Holly took place at The Tabernacle Baptist Church in Lubbock, Texas.

1963 appearing at The Manor House, London were The Blues By Six plus The Rolling Stones. Tickets cost 4 shillings ($0.56).

1964 Pan-Am flight PA 101 arrived at New York's Kennedy Airport bringing The Beatles to the US for the first time and causing riotous scenes as they touched down.

1967 Robin, Maurice and Barry Gibb of The Bee Gees returned to the UK after living in Australia for nine years.

1967 Mike Nesmith and Mickey Dolenz from The Monkees appeared on UK TV's *Top Of The Pops*.

1970 Led Zeppelin scored their first UK No.1 album with *Led Zeppelin II*. Featuring the US single 'Whole Lotta Love', it went on to stay in the chart for 138 weeks and sold over six million copies in the US.

1970 one hit wonders Shocking Blue went to No.1 on the US singles chart with 'Venus', making them the first Dutch act to top the US charts. It made No.8 in the UK; Bananarama took the song to No.8 on the UK chart in 1986.

1976 Bob Dylan started a five week run at No.1 on the US album chart with *Desire*, his second US No.1.

1976 Paul Simon started a three week run at No.1 on the US singles chart with '50 Ways To Leave Your Lover', the singer's first solo US No.1.

1981 John Lennon was at No.1 on the UK singles chart with 'Woman', his third No.1 in seven weeks.

1987 George Michael and Aretha Franklin were at No.1 on the UK singles chart with 'I Knew You Were Waiting (For Me)'. The song, written by Simon Climie, gave Aretha her first UK No.1

almost 20 years after her first hit.

1989 Georgia state representative Billy Randall introduced a bill to make Little Richards' 'Tutti Frutti' the state's official rock song.

1999 Blondie went to No.1 on the UK singles chart with 'Maria', giving the group their sixth UK No.1 single, 20 years after their first.

2000 Big Punisher died of a heart attack, aged 28. The rapper had weighed 318kg (50 stone) when he had the attack.

2004 Queen's single 'We Will Rock You' topped a poll of music fans to find the greatest rock

The withdrawn UK Led Zeppelin single, 'Whole Lotta Love'.

anthem of all time. The 1977 song beat the band's classic 'Bohemian Rhapsody' into second place in a survey of 1,000 people carried out for the UCI cinema chain. The poll was done to mark the release of new Jack Black film comedy *School of Rock*.

BORN ON THIS DAY

1943 Creed Bratton – guitarist with Grass Roots, who had a 1968 US No.5 single with 'Midnight Confessions', plus 13 other US Top 40 singles.

1946 Adolpho De La Para – drummer for Canned Heat, who had a 1970 UK No.2 & US No.26 single with 'Let's Work Together'.

1946 Paul Wheatbread – drummer with Gary Puckett And The Union Gap, who had a 1968 UK No.1 & UK No.2 single with 'Young Girl'.

1948 Dan Seals – singer, songwriter, England Dan & John Ford Coley, who had a 1976 US No.2 & UK No.26 single with 'I'd Really Love To See You Tonight'.

1961 Vince Neil – vocalist with Motley Crue, who had a 1988 UK No.23 single with 'You're All I Need' and a 1989 US No.1 album with *Dr Feelgood*.

1977 Dave "Phoenix" Ferrel – bass guitarist with Linkin Park, who had a 2002 US No.2 & UK No.4 single with 'In The End' and a 2002 US No.2 & 2001 UK No.4 album with *Hybrid Theory*.

ON THIS DAY

1960 Mark Dinning went to No.1 on the US singles chart with 'Teen Angel', which was a No.37 hit in the UK.

1964 The Ronettes greeted The Beatles on their first visit to the US, interviewing them for radio.

1969 *TBC* by The Supremes with Temptations went to No.1 on the US album chart.

1973 Max Yasgur died of a heart attack, aged 53. Yasgur was the owner of the Woodstock farm where the 1969 festival was held.

1975 Bob Dylan went to No.1 on the US album chart with *Blood On The Tracks*.

1975 The Ohio Players went to No.1 on the US singles chart with 'Fire', the group's first of two US No.1s.

1980 the divorce became final between David and Angie Bowie. He won custody of their son Zowie, now known as Joe. Angie received a £30,000 ($51,000) settlement.

Away from prying cameras, a couple of Beautiful People betray the smelly-hippy stigma on Max Yasgur's farm.

1981 R.E.M. made their first-ever recording sessions at Bombay Studios Smyrna, Georgia. Tracks included 'Gardening At Night', 'Radio Free Europe' and '(Don't Go Back To) Rockville'.

1986 Billy Ocean started a four week run at No.1 on the UK singles chart with 'When The Going Gets Tough, The Tough Get Going', as featured in the film *The Jewel Of The Nile*. The video was banned in the UK because it featured non-musician union members.

1990 US singer Del Shannon died of self-inflicted gunshot wounds. Shannon had had a 1961 UK and US No.1 single with 'Runaway', plus 9 US & 12 other UK Top 40 singles.

1992 UK act Right Said Fred started a three week run at No.1 on the US singles chart with 'I'm Too Sexy', which was a No.2 hit in the UK.

1994 Oasis were forced to cancel their first foreign tour after they were deported from Holland. The band were involved in a drunken brawl on a cross-channel ferry, resulting in members of the band being arrested and locked in the brig.

2001 Eminem made his live UK concert debut when he appeared at The Manchester Arena.

2002 Bob Wooler died, aged 76. He was the resident DJ and booker at Liverpool's Cavern Club during the early 60s.

2005 Pete Doherty was released from jail on bail after four nights when his manager paid the remaining £100,000 ($170,000) bail to Highbury Corner Magistrates Court, London. The ex-Libertines star had been charged with robbery and blackmail after a fracas at a London hotel. His bail arrangements stated he would not be able to leave his house between 22:00pm and 07:00am every night and must be accompanied by a security guard or his manager.

THE CAVERN   Membership Number M № 05038

(The following information to be entered in block capitals)

Member's First Names KENNETH
Member's Surname ALLCROFT
Member's Full Address 1 SYCAMORE TERRACE HAYFIELD VIA STOCKPORT
Date of Joining JAN 28/64   Fee paid 10/-
Member's Signature Kenneth Allcroft

The Cavern, 8-12 Mathew Street, Liverpool.   Tel: 236 7881 (STD. 051)

A genuine membership pass from Liverpool's Cavern Club.

BORN ON THIS DAY

1939 Barry Mann, US singer/songwriter. He wrote many early 60s pop hits, including 'Saturday Night At The Movies', 'You've Lost That Loving Feeling' and 'Walking In The Rain' and also had the 1961 US No.7 solo single 'Who Put The Bomp, In The Bomp, Bomp, Bomp'.

1940 Brian Bennett – drummer with The Shadows, who had a 1963 UK No.1 single with 'Foot Tapper' plus 28 other UK Top 40 singles. The group also had hits with Cliff Richard.

1942 Carole King, US singer/songwriter (who wrote many songs with Gerry Goffin), who had a 1962 UK No.3 & US No.22 single with 'It Might As Well Rain Until September' and a 1970 US No.1 album *Tapestry* (which has sold over 15 million copies). She was a Grammy award winner in 1971.

1947 Joe Ely, country singer who toured with The Clash in the late 70s and was also a one-time member of Linda Ronstadt's band.

1947 Major Harris – vocalist with The Delfonics, who had a 1968 US No.4 & 1971 UK No.19 single with 'La-La Means I Love You'.

1951 Dennis Thomas – saxophonist with Kool & The Gang, who had a 1981 US No.1 & UK No.7 single with 'Celebration' and a 1984 UK No.2 single 'Joanna' plus over 15 other Top 40 hits.

1960 Holly Johnson – vocalist. He was a member of Big In Japan before joining Frankie Goes To Hollywood, who had a 1984 UK No.1 & US No.10 single with 'Relax'. As a solo artist he had a 1989 UK No.4 with 'Love Train' and a 1989 UK No.1 album with *Blast*.

1964 Rachel Bolan – bass player with Skid Row, who had a 1989 US No.4 & 1990 UK No.12 single with '18 and Life'.

ON THIS DAY

1963 Paul And Paula started a three week run at No.1 on the US singles charts with 'Hey Paula'. The song made No.8 in the UK.

1964 The Beatles made their US live debut on CBS-TV's *The Ed Sullivan Show*. They performed five songs, including their current No.1 'I Want To Hold Your Hand', and were watched by an estimated 73 million people.

1967 Canadian conductor Percy Faith died, aged 67. He scored the 1960 US No.1 'Theme From A Summer Palace', which had nine weeks at the top.

1967 the film for 'Penny Lane/Strawberry Fields Forever' was shown on BBC TV's *Top Of The Pops*. It was the first Beatles single not to make No.1 since 1963, being held off the top by Engelbert Humperdinck's 'Release Me'.

1972 Paul McCartney's Wings played the first night of a UK College tour in Nottingham. The group arrived unannounced, asking social secretaries if they would like them to perform that evening.

1981 Bill Haley was found dead, fully clothed on his bed at his home in Harlington, from a heart attack. Haley had sold over 60 million records during his career.

1982 George Harrison presented UNICEF with a cheque for $9 million (£5.3 million), ten years after the fundraising concert for Bangladesh.

1985 Madonna started a three week run at No.1 on the US album chart with *Like A Virgin*.

1986 Pete Townshend, Chrissie Hynde and The Communards played a charity show at London's Albert Hall for the victims of a volcanic eruption in Colombia.

2001 Eminem beefed up security for his UK shows following the threat of gay rights protests. Campaigners said the rapper was a homophobe who fuelled prejudice with hate-filled lyrics.

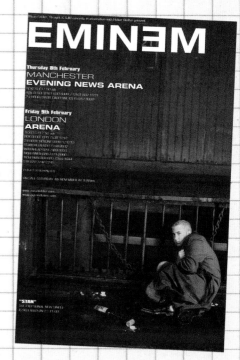

2002 Billboard published the Top 5 selling albums in the world from 2001: Britney Spears' *Britney*, $7m (£4.1m); Shaggy's *Hotshot*, $7.2m (£4.24m); Destiny's Child's *Survivor*, $7.8m (£4.6m); Linkin Park's *Hybrid*, $8.5m (£5m) and Dido's *No Angel*, $8.6m (£5.06m) sales.

BORN ON THIS DAY

1914 Larry Adler, mouth organist, worked as a soloist with many of the world's major symphony orchestras. He played with countless artists from Fred Astaire to George Gershwin and later with Elton John and Sting. Recorded the 1994 tribute album *Glory Of Gershwin*. He died on August 7th 2001, aged 87.

1929 composer Jerry Goldsmith who created the music for classic movies and television shows such as *Star Trek*, *Planet Of The Apes*, *The Man From U.N.C.L.E.* and *Dr. Kildare*. He died from cancer on July 21st 2004, aged 75.

1937 Roberta Flack, singer who had a 1972 US No.1 single with 'The First Time Ever I Saw Your Face' and a 1973 US No.1 & UK No.6 single with 'Killing Me Softly With His Song'.

1940 Jimmy Merchant — member of R&B vocal group Frankie Lymon And The Teenagers, who had a 1956 UK No.1 & US No.6 single with 'Why Do Fools Fall In Love?'.

1962 Cliff Burton — bass player with Metallica. Burton was killed on September 27th 1987, when the band's tour bus crashed as it was travelling between Stockholm and Copenhagen.

1977 Rosanna Tavarez — member of vocal group Eden's Crush, who had a 2001 US No.1 single with 'Get Over Yourself', (the first female group to debut at number one with their first single). Formed after its members auditioned for the reality series *Popstars*

ON THIS DAY

1942 Glen Miller became the first person to be awarded a Gold disc, for his 'Chattanooga Choo Choo' single.

1958 Frank Sinatra started a five week run at No.1 on the US album chart with *Come Fly With Me*.

The work of Jerry Goldsmith. Just to be fair we present the spin-off *The Girl From Uncle* as well.

1962 Henry Mancini went to No.1 on the US album chart with the soundtrack to *Breakfast At Tiffany's*.

1968 The Four Tops' *Greatest Hits* was at No.1 on the UK album chart, the first No.1 album for the Tamla Motown label.

1972 David Bowie appeared at the Tolworth Toby Jug, London. This was the opening date of his Ziggy Stardust tour.

1973 Elton John had his first UK No.1 album when *Don't Shoot Me I'm Only The Piano Player* started a six week run at the top of the charts.

1974 producer Phil Spector was injured in a car crash. He needed extensive plastic surgery, which dramatically altered his looks.

1975 Dave Alexander, bass player with Iggy Pop And The Stooges, died from pneumonia, aged 28.

1976 Elvis Presley was made a police reserve for the Memphis police.

1977 The Clash started recording their debut album at the CBS studios in London.

1979 Rod Stewart started a four week run at No.1 on the US singles chart with 'Da Ya Think I'm Sexy?', his third US No.1. It was also a No.1 in the UK. Also on this day Rod started a three week run at No.1 on the US album chart with *Blondes Have More Fun*.

1990 Paula Abdul started a three week run at No.1 on the US singles chart with 'Opposites Attract', her fourth US No.1 and a No.2 hit in the UK.

1998 Axl Rose was charged with disorderly conduct following a row with a baggage handler at Arizona Airport. He was released on bail.

2004 Diana Ross was sentenced to two days in jail after pleading "no contest" to a drink driving charge. She was allowed to enter her plea over the telephone from New York, and her lawyer said the singer would serve her term at a prison near her Los Angeles home. Ross was arrested in December 2002 after tests indicated she was twice over the drink-drive limit.

2005 Prince topped *Rolling Stone* magazine's annual list of the year's biggest money earners after his 2004 tour grossed over $90 million (£53 million). Madonna came in second place after earning $54.9 million (£34.3 million) and Metallica came third with $43 million (£25.3 million).

BORN ON THIS DAY

1935 Gene Vincent, US rock 'n' roll singer who had a 1956 US No.7 & UK No.16 single with 'Be Bop A Lula'. He died on October 12th 1971.

1939 Gerry Goffin, songwriter of over 20 US hits with Carol King, including: The Shirelles' ''Will You Still Love Me Tomorrow'; The Drifters' 'Up On The Roof'; The Chiffons' 'One Fine Day' and Herman's Hermits' 'I'm Into Something Good'.

1940 Bobby "Boris" Pickett, singer who had a 1962 US No.1 & 1973 UK No.3 single with 'The Monster Mash'.

1963 Sheryl Crow, singer/songwriter who had a 1994 US No.2 & UK No.4 single with 'All I Wanna Do' and a 1993 UK No.8 album *Tuesday Night Music Club*. She had previously worked as a backing singer on the Michael Jackson "Bad" tour.

1977 Mike Shinoda – guitarist and vocalist with Linkin Park, who had a 2002 US No.2 & UK No.4 single with 'In The End' and a 2002 US No.2 & 2001 UK No.4 album with *Hybrid Theory*.

1979 Brandy, singer who had a 1998 US No.1 and UK No.2 single with Monica, 'The Boy Is Mine'.

1981 Kelly Rowland – singer with Destiny's Child, who had a 2000 US No.1 & UK No.3 single with 'Say My Name' and a 2001 US & UK No.1 single & album with 'Survivor'. As a solo artist she had a 2003 UK No.2 single with 'Stole' and a 2002 US No.1 single with Nelly, 'Dilemma'.

ON THIS DAY

1958 Michael Holliday was at No.1 on the UK singles chart with 'The Story Of My Life'. The song gave the writers Bacharach and David their first UK No.1 hit.

1963 in less then ten hours, The Beatles recorded ten new songs for their first album plus four others, which would be the next singles. Lennon's vocal on The Isley Brothers' 'Twist And Shout' was recorded in one take to complete the album.

ORIGINAL MOTION PICTURE SOUNDTRACK ALBUM

GROUPIE GIRL

Polydor STANDARD

A SALON PRODUCTION
FOR WORLD RELEASE BY EAGLE FILMS LTD

1967 saw the release of the Hollywood blockbuster 'Groupie Girl' epic, shown only in dimly lit cinemas and in back-rooms of bars after hours.

1969 The Monkees set a new record when their second album, *More Of The Monkees*, jumped from No.122 to the top of the US chart. It stayed in pole position for 18 weeks.

1973 a local charity raised over £500 ($850) selling bedsheets and pillowcases used by the Rolling Stones after a show in Auckland, New Zealand.

1982 U2 kicked off a 32 date US tour in New Orleans.

1985 The Police won the outstanding contribution to British music at the fourth annual Brit Awards held in London. Prince won Best solo artist.

1987 The Smiths were at No.1 in the UK indie charts with 'Shoplifters Of The World Unite'.

1989 Paula Abdul started a three week run at No.1 on the US singles chart with 'Straight Up', the first of three No.1s for her in 1989. It was a No.3 hit in the UK.

1992 Motley Crue fired their singer Vince Neil when he turned up for rehearsals, claiming that his passion for the band had been overtaken by his involvement with racing cars. (He rejoined the band in 1997).

2000 Spice Girl Geri Halliwell appeared in court to give evidence over the dispute with Aprilla Motorcycles. The company was suing the Spice Girls for £1.6 million ($2.72 million) over lost advertising as sponsors for the 1998 Spiceworld world tour.

2003 The British Phonographic Industry reported its biggest sales decline in decades, with the biggest slump in a single year since the birth of the CD market in the early 1980s. Piracy, illegal duplication and distribution of CDs, by international criminals was blamed for the decrease.

BORN ON THIS DAY

1915 Lorne Greene, star of the NBC TV show *Bonanza*. He had a US No.1 single 'Ringo', which made him the second Canadian to have a US No.1 single – it was a No.22 hit in the UK. Greene died on September 11th 1987.

1935 Ray Manzarek – keyboardist with The Doors, who had a 1967 US No.1 & UK No.9 single with 'Light My Fire' and a 1971 US No.14 & UK No.22 single 'Riders On The Storm'.

1945 Joe Schermie – bass guitarist with Three Dog Night, who had a 1970 UK No.3 & US No.1 single with 'Mamma Told Me Not To Come'.

1950 Steve Hackett *(right)*, guitarist with Genesis, who had a 1974 UK No.21 single 'I Know What I Like (In Your Wardrobe)'. Hackett went solo in 1977.

1952 Michael McDonald, keyboardist and vocalist with The Doobie Brothers, who had a 1979 US No.1 single with 'What A Fool Believes' plus 1993 UK No.7 single with 'Long Train Runnin'.

1959 Per Gessle – songwriter and singer with Roxette, who had a 1990 US No.1 & UK No.3 single with 'It Must Have Been Love'.

1968 Chynna Phillips of vocal group Wilson Phillips, who had a 1990 US No.1 & UK No.6 single with 'Hold On'. Phillips is the daughter of Michelle Gilliam from the Mamas And The Papas.

1970 Jim Creeggan, bassist for Barenaked Ladies, who had a 1998 US No.1 & UK No.5 single with 'One Week'.

ON THIS DAY

1956 Dean Martin was at No.1 on the UK singles chart with 'Memories Are Made Of This'.

1965 Pye Records announced that they had signed "the British Bob Dylan", when they added Donovan to their label.

1967 15 police officers raided "Redlands", the home of Keith Richards, and took away various substances for forensic tests.

1969 'If Paradise Is Half As Nice' by Amen Corner was at No.1 on the UK singles chart.

1970 John Lennon performed 'Instant Karma', on BBC TV's *Top Of The Pops*, becoming the first Beatle to have appeared on the show since 1966.

1972 Al Green went to No.1 on the US singles chart with 'Let's Stay Together', his only US chart topper. Tina Turner took the song to No.26 in 1984.

1977 The Police recorded their first single, 'Fall Out' for £150 ($255) at Pathway Studios, London.

1980 appearing at London's Hammersmith Palais were Iggy Pop and The Psychedelic Furs. Tickets cost £3 ($5.10).

1989 Aretha Franklin lost a court case against Broadway producer Ashton Springer, who sued for $1 million (£0.58 million) when Aretha failed to turn up for rehearsals for the stage show "Sing Mahalia Sing" – blaming her fear of flying on the non appearance.

1994 Alice In Chains entered the US album chart at No.1 with *Jar Of Flies*.

1994 Celine Dion started a four week run at No.1

on the US singles chart with 'The Power Of Love', the singer's first US No.1. It was also a No.4 hit in the UK.

1997 U2 launched their "Popmart" world tour at the Manhattan KMart discount store. The tour started in Las Vegas on April 25th.

2000 Mariah Carey started a two week run at No.1 on the US singles chart with 'Thank God I Found You'.

2000 blues singer Screamin' Jay Hawkins died, aged 70. A Golden Gloves boxing champion at 16, he had been married nine times, spent two years in jail and was temporarily blinded by one of his flaming props on stage in 1976. He recorded 'I Put A Spell On You' in 1956, which was covered by The Animals and Nina Simone.

2003 Former Doors drummer John Densmore took out legal action against The Doors' keyboard player Ray Manzarek and guitarist Robby Krieger for breach of contract, trademark infringement and unfair competition. The band had reformed with ex-Cult singer Ian Astbury and former Police drummer Stewart Copeland. Densmore said "It shouldn't be called The Doors if it's someone other than Jim Morrison singing."

The Police: recording on a shoestring.

2005 a train was named after Clash frontman Joe Strummer at a ceremony in Bristol. The diesel train, owned by Cotswold Rail, was named after the singer who had died aged 50 in 2002.

BORN ON THIS DAY

1919 Tennessee Ernie Ford, singer and TV presenter, who had a 1955 US No.1 & 1956 UK No.1 single with 'Sixteen Tons'. It was Capitol Records' first No.1 of the rock era. Ford died on October 17th 1991.

1920 Boudleaux Bryant, songwriter with his wife Felice. They wrote The Everly Brothers' hits, 'Bye Bye Love', 'All I Have To Do Is Dream' and 'Wake Up Little Susie' as well as 'Raining In My Heart', which was a hit for Buddy Holly. Bryant died on June 25th 1987.

1944 Peter Tork – vocalist, keyboardist and bass guitarist for The Monkees, who had a 1967 UK & US No.1 single 'I'm A Believer' plus 10 US & 8 UK Top 40 singles.

1950 Peter Gabriel – vocalist for Genesis and solo artist. Genesis had a 1974 UK No.21 single with 'I Know What I Like (In Your Wardrobe)'. Gabriel left Genesis in 1975 to pursue a solo career, during which he has had a 1986 US No.1 & UK No.4 single with 'Sledgehammer', which was taken from the 1986 UK No.1 & US No.2 album *So*.

1956 Peter Hook – bass guitarist for Joy Division, who had a 1980 UK No.13 single with 'Love Will Tear Us Apart', then New Order, who had a 1983 UK No.9 single with 'Blue Monday', Revenge and Monaco, who had a 1997 UK No.11 single 'What Do You Want From Me?'

1974 Robbie Williams – vocalist with Take That, who had a 1995 UK No.1 single with 'Back For Good' and seven other UK No.1 singles. He left to pursue a solo career and since then has had a 1998 UK No.1 single with 'Millennium' and four other UK No.1 singles). 1997 UK No.1 album *Life Thru A Lens* spent 123 weeks on the UK chart.

Peter Gabriel examines his art collection for insurance purposes.

ON THIS DAY

1961 Frank Sinatra launched his own record label, Reprise Records, which was to become the home of Neil Young, Jimi Hendrix, Joni Mitchell, Randy Newman and The Beach Boys.

1967 The Monkees announced that from now on they would be playing on their own recordings instead of using session musicians.

1971 The Osmonds started a five week run at No.1 on the US singles chart with 'One Bad Apple'. The group had been appearing on the *Andy Williams Show* and then the *Jerry Lewis Show* from 1962.

1974 David Bowie turned down an offer from the Gay Liberation group to compose "the world's first Gay National Anthem".

1980 police raided the home of John Lydon, who greeted them waving a ceremonial sword. The only illegal item found was tear gas, claimed to be for defence against intruders.

1981 "One Plus One" cassettes were launched by Island Records. One side had one of their artists' albums and the other was blank so that people could record on it!

1982 The Jam became the first band since The Beatles to play two numbers on the same edition of *Top Of The Pops* when they performed ' Town Called Malice' and 'Precious', their double A-sided No.1.

1982 the marble slab was stolen from the grave of Lynyrd Skynyrd's singer Ronnie Van Zant. Police found it two weeks later in a dried-up river bed.

1989 Michael Jackson fired his manager, Dileo, who reportedly sought a $60 million (£35.3 million) settlement to prevent him revealing Jackson's lifestyle to the press.

1996 Take That split up. The biggest band of the 90s announced their demise in front of the press at The Hilton in Manchester. They had had seven No.1 singles and two No.1 albums. They released one more single and a *Greatest Hits* album.

1998 former Stones Roses singer Ian Brown was arrested by police at Manchester Airport after an incident during a flight from Paris. He was found guilty in August the same year and jailed for four months. British Airways also banned him from flying with the airline.

2002 Country singer/songwriter Waylon Jennings died after a lengthy fight with diabetes. He had had a 1980 US No.21 single with 'Theme From The Dukes Of Hazard' plus country No.1 hits. He also played bass with Buddy Holly in 1959.

2004 Eminem's ex-wife Kimberly Mathers was jailed for a month after being found using cocaine while on probation. Mathers was also put on a 90 day drug abuse programme.

EMINEM'S EX-WIFE IS JAILED

RAP star Eminem's ex-wife was caged for a month yesterday – after using cocaine while on probation.

Kimberly Mathers, 28, will be put on a 90-day drug abuse programme after serving her term in Michigan.

She was sentenced to two years' probation last month for cocaine possession and driving offences.

She has a seven-year-old daughter, Hailie Jade, with Eminem, 31.

The couple had a stormy relationship and Eminem, whose real name is Marshall Mathers III, has rapped about killing her in his songs.

Rap . . . Kimberly in court yesterday

BORN ON THIS DAY

1945 Vic Briggs – guitarist with The Animals, who had a 1964 UK & US No.1 single with 'House Of The Rising Sun'.

1947 Tim Buckley, singer/songwriter who recorded the 1972 album *Greetings From LA*. His singer/ songwriter son Jeff Buckley drowned while swimming in 1997. Tim himself died on June 29th 1975 of a heroin and morphine overdose.

1951 Kenny Hyslop – drummer. He was a member of Slik, who had a 1976 UK No.1 single with 'Forever And Ever', then Skids, who had a 1979 UK No.10 single with 'Into The Valley', and Simple Minds, who had a 1985 US No.1 single with 'Don't You, Forget About Me' and a 1989 UK No.1 single with 'Belfast Child'.

1972 Rob Thomas – vocalist for Matchbox 20, who had a 1998 UK No.38 single with 'Push' and a 2000 US No.1 single with 'Bent'. Thomas also sang on the 1999 US No.1 single by Santana, 'Smooth'.

Lou Reed, John Farriss, Elton and Prince used this special ancient advisory kit for their Valentine's Day weddings.

ON THIS DAY

1968 Manfred Mann were at No.1 on the UK singles chart with their version of the Bob Dylan song 'Mighty Quinn'. It was a No.10 hit in the US.

1970 the compilation album *Motown Chartbusters Vol 3* went to No.1 on the UK chart, featuring Diana Ross And The Supremes, Stevie Wonder, The Temptations and The Four Tops.

1970 The Who appeared at Leeds University, England. The show was recorded for the band's forthcoming *Live At Leeds* album.

1972 John Lennon and Yoko Ono started a week long run as co-hosts on the *Mike Douglas* US TV show.

1973 David Bowie collapsed on stage during a concert at Radio City Music Hall, New York.

Buckley's greeting card from L.A.

1974 Daryl Dragon and Toni Tennille (of Captain And Tennille) married in Virginia City, while on a promotional tour of the States.

1977 US singer/songwriter Janis Ian received 461 Valentine's Day cards after indicating in the lyrics of her song 'At Seventeen' that she had never received any.

1978 Dire Straits began recording their first album at Basing Street Studios, London. The whole project cost £12,500 ($21,250) to produce.

1980 Lou Reed married Sylvia Morales at a ceremony in his New York apartment.

1984 Elton John married Renate Blauer in Sydney, Australia.

1987 Bon Jovi started a four week run at No.1 on the US singles chart with 'Livin' On A Prayer', the group's second US No.1, and a No.4 hit in the UK.

1990 The Rolling Stones played the first of ten nights at the Korakuen Dome, Tokyo, Japan. The shows were seen by over 500,000 fans, making the band $20 million (£11.76 million).

1992 Jon Farriss from INXS married actress Leslie Bega.

1992 the film *Wayne's World*, which had a brief cameo appearance from Meat Loaf, premiered in the US.

1996 T.A.F.K.A.P. married Mayte Garcia in a Minneapolis church. He composed a special song for his wife, 'Friend, Lover, Sister, Mother/Wife', which she heard for the first time when they had their first wedding dance.

1998 Usher started a two week run at No.1 on the US singles chart with 'Nice & Slow'.

1998 Celine Dion's 'My Heart Will Go On' set a new record for the most radio plays in the US, with 116 million plays in one week.

1999 Lenny Kravitz scored his first UK No.1 single with 'Fly Away'. The single had been used on a TV ad for cars.

2003 Stolen reel-to-reel studio recordings by The Beatles were found in Australia. Police recovered the tapes of the band's 1968 *White* album and the *Abbey Road* album after they were advertised for sale in a Sydney newspaper. Australian police had been tipped off by British detectives from Operation Acetone, an investigation into thefts of original Beatles music from Abbey Road studios in London in the 1960s .

2004 Dave Holland, former drummer with Judas Priest, was jailed for eight years for indecent assault and the attempted rape of a 17-year-old boy. The youth, who had learning difficulties, had been taking drum lessons from Holland.

BORN ON THIS DAY

1941 Brian Holland, part of the Holland/Dozier/Holland songwriting production team. They wrote for Motown, The Supremes, Marvin Gaye, The Four Tops, Martha Reeves & The Vandellas, Freda Payne and Chairmen Of The Board.

1944 Denny Zager – singer with Zager & Evans, who had a 1969 US & UK No.1 single with 'In The Year 2525'.

1944 Mick Avory – drummer with The Kinks, who had a 1964 UK No.1 & US No.7 with 'You Really Got Me', a 1967 UK No.2 single with 'Waterloo Sunset' plus 19 other UK Top 40 singles.

1945 John Helliwell – sax player with Supertramp, who had a 1979 UK No.7 & US No.6 single with 'The Logical Song'.

1959 Ali Campbell – vocalist with UB40, who had a 1983 UK No.1 & 1988 US No.1 single with 'Red Wine' and over 30 other Top 40 hit singles. As a solo artist he had a 1995 UK No.5 single with 'That Look In Your Eye'.

1960 Mikey Craig – bass player with Culture Club, who had a 1983 UK No.1 & 1984 US No.12 single with 'Karma Chameleon' plus seven other UK Top 10 singles.

ON THIS DAY

1961 Jackie Wilson was shot by Juanita Jones, a female fan who had gone to his New York apartment demanding to see him. The gun went off as he tried to disarm her, and it left him with a stomach wound.

1964 The Beatles scored their first US No.1 album with *Meet The Beatles!* It stayed in pole position for eleven weeks.

1964 The Dave Clark Five appeared on the UK TV show *Thank Your Lucky Stars*.

1965 singer Nat King Cole died of lung cancer. He had had a 1955 US No.2 single with 'A Blossom Fell', a 1957 UK No.2 single with 'When I Fall In Love' plus over 20 other US & UK Top 40 singles. He was also the father of singer Natalie Cole.

1968 US blues harmonica player Little Walter died from injuries incurred in a street fight. He had been the first harmonica player to amplify his harp, giving it a distorted echoing sound.

1968 the Lennons and Harrisons arrived in India to study meditation with the Maharishi. McCartney and Starr arrived four days later. Ringo returned before the others, comparing the experience to being like a Butlins holiday camp.

1969 singer Vickie Jones was arrested on fraud charges for impersonating Aretha Franklin in concert at Fort Myers, Florida. No one in the audience had asked for their money back.

1969 Sly & The Family Stone started a four week run at No.1 on the US singles chart with 'Everyday People', their first No.1.

1977 Glen Matlock was fired from The Sex Pistols and replaced by Sid Vicious.

1981 Mike Bloomfield, guitarist, died of a drug overdose. He had been a member of the Paul Butterfield band and Electric Flag. He also played on Dylan's album *Highway 61 Revisited*.

1988 Def Leppard were forced to cancel a concert in El Paso, Texas when they received threats that the gig would be disrupted. This was after singer Jo Elliot had referred to El Paso as "the place with all those greasy Mexicans".

1991 Kelly Emberg, ex-girlfriend of Rod Stewart, filed a $25 million (£14.7 million) palimony suit in Los Angeles.

2002 *Kerrang!* magazine overtook the *New Musical Express* for the first time to become the bestselling UK weekly music publication. It claimed new bands such as Limp Bizkit and Linkin Park had given them a new teenage audience.

Dave Clark and his bunch of fives.

Not quite what it seems: everyone was cashing in on The Beatles fame in the 1960s.

BORN ON THIS DAY

1935 Sonny Bono, singer who had a 1965 UK & US No.1 single, 'I Got You Babe', with Cher. He became a US Congressman in 1994. Bono was killed in a skiing accident on January 5th 1997, aged 62.

1939 Harold and Herbie Kalin, members of The Kalin Twins who had a 1958 UK No.1 & US No.5 single with 'When'. The brothers were the first twins to score a No.1 record.

1956 James Ingram, US singer who had a 1987 UK No.8 single with Linda Ronstadt, 'Somewhere Out There', and a 1990 US No.1 single with 'I Don't Have The Heart'.

1961 Andy Taylor – guitarist with Duran Duran, who had a 1983 UK No.1 single with 'Is There Something I Should Know' plus 25 other UK Top 40 singles and a 1984 US No.1 single 'The Reflex'. Taylor was also part of The Power Station, who had a 1985 UK No.14 single with 'Some Like It Hot'.

1972 Taylor Hawkins – drummer who has worked with Alanis Morrisette and the Foo Fighters. The latter had a 1995 UK No.5 single with 'This Is A Call'.

ON THIS DAY

1967 Petula Clark was at No.1 on the UK singles chart with 'This Is My Song', the singer's second UK No.1.

1972 Charlie Watts' wife Shirley was arrested at Nice Airport for swearing and hitting custom's officials.

1974 Bob Dylan started a four week run at No.1 on the US album chart with *Planet Waves*, his first US No.1.

---

30 Disc—February 16, 1974

LIVE DATES

Queen

Blackpool Winter Gardens (March 1). Plymouth Guildhall (3). Cambridge Corn Exchange (9). Croydon Greyhound (10). Dagenham Roundhouse (12). Cheltenham Town Hall (14). Glasgow University (15). Stirling University (16). Birmingham Barbarella's (17). Cleethorpes Winter Garden (19). Manchester University (20). Sunderland Locarno (22). Colchester Woods (24). Aberystwyth University (28). Penzance Winter Gardens (29). Taunton County Ballroom (30). London Rainbow (31).

Cockney Rebel

Dunstable Civic Hall (February 28). Salford University (March 1). Dagenham Roundhouse (5). Hereford Flamengo (8). Bristol Boobs (18). Plymouth Guildhall (19). Swindon Brunel Rooms (20). Liverpool University (21). Scarborough Penthouse (22). Croydon Greyhound (24). Sheffield Poly (27). Colchester Woods (31).

1974 during a tour of America the members of Emerson, Lake & Palmer were arrested in Salt Lake City after swimming naked in the hotel pool. They were each fined $75 (£44).

1975 Cher started her own weekly hour of music and comedy show on CBS-TV.

1985 Bruce Springsteen went to No.1 on the UK album chart with *Born In The USA*, his first UK No.1 album.

1985 Wham's 'Careless Whisper' started a three week run at No.1 in the US charts. It was the duo's second US No.1.

1991 Queen scored their seventh UK No.1 album with *Innuendo*.

1991 The Simpsons *(right)* were at No.1 on the UK singles chart with 'Do The Bartman'.

1999 winners at The Brit Awards included Robbie Williams for Best British solo artist, Best single 'Angels' and Best video 'Millennium'. The Manic Street Preachers won Best British group and Natalie Imbruglia won Best female artist and newcomer.

2002 thieves broke into George Michael's London home and stole over £100,000 ($170,000) worth of paintings, jewellery and designer clothes and drove off in his £80,000 ($136,000) Aston Martin DB7. They also caused £200,000 ($340,000) worth of damage to his home.

2003 Massive Attack went to No.1 on the UK album chart with *100th Window*.

2003 50 Cent was at No.1 on the US album chart with his debut album *Get Rich Or Die Tryin*, which was a No.2 hit in the UK.

2004 US singer Doris Troy died. She had been a session singer with Dionne Warwick, sang on Pink Floyd's *Dark Side Of The Moon* and released an album on The Beatles' Apple label. She had also had a 1964 UK No.37 single with 'Whatcha Gonna Do About It' and a 1963 US No. 10 hit 'Just One Look'.

BORN ON THIS DAY

1905 Orville "Hoppy" Jones — bass singer and cello player with the Ink Spots, who had a 1955 UK No.10 single with 'Melody Of Love'. Died October 18th 1944.

1922 Tommy Edwards, singer who had a 1958 US & UK No.1 single with 'It's All In The Game' (written by US Vice President Charles Dawes). Edwards died on October 22nd 1968, aged 47.

1941 Gene Pitney, singer who had a 1962 US No.4 single with 'Only Love Can Break A Heart', a 1967 solo UK No.5 & 1989 UK No.1 single with Marc Almond, 'Something's Gotten Hold Of My Heart', plus over 15 other US & UK Top 40 hits.

1972 Billie Joe Armstrong — guitarist and vocalist with Green Day, who had a 1995 UK No.7 single with 'Basket Case'.1994 album *Dookie* has sold over 10 million copies. Top Modern Rock Act in US in 1985.

ON THIS DAY

1960 Elvis Presley won his first Gold record for the album *Elvis*.

1960 The Everly Brothers signed a $1 million (£0.7 million) contract with Warner Brothers Records.

1962 Gene Chandler started a three week run at No.1 on the US singles chart with 'Duke Of Earl'.

1966 Nancy Sinatra was at No.1 on the UK singles chart with 'These Boots Are Made For Walking'.

1968 Diana Ross And The Supremes' *Greatest Hits* started a three week run at No.1 on the UK album chart.

1969 Bob Dylan and Johnny Cash recorded together in Nashville at CBS Studios. The track 'Girl From The North Country' appeared on Bob's *Nashville Skyline* album.

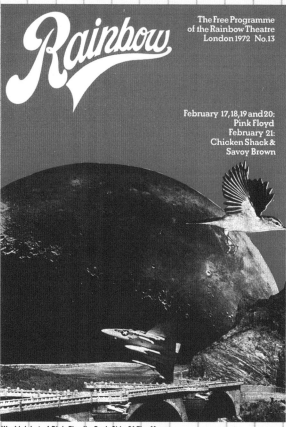

The Free Programme of the Rainbow Theatre London 1972 No.13

February 17,18,19 and 20: Pink Floyd February 21: Chicken Shack & Savoy Brown

World debut of Pink Floyd's *Dark Side Of The Moon*.

1970 Joni Mitchell announced she was retiring from live performances during a concert at London's Royal Albert Hall. She was on stage again by the end of the year.

1971 James Taylor made his TV debut on *The Johnny Cash Show*. Other guests included Neil Young, Linda Ronstadt and Tony Joe White.

1972 Pink Floyd started a three night run at London's Rainbow Theatre. Tickets were £1 ($1.7).

1979 Blondie scored their first UK No.1 album when *Parallel Lines* started a four week run at the top, featuring the singles 'Heart Of Glass', 'Hanging On The Telephone' and 'Sunday Girl'.

1979 The Clash opened the US leg of their "Pearl Harbour 79" North American tour at New York's Palladium.

1980 US country singer Kenny Rogers was at No.1 on the UK singles chart with 'Coward Of The County'.

1989 appearing at the Hordern Pavilion, Sydney, Australia were R.E.M., Hoodoo Gurus and The Go-Betweens.

1996 a Platinum American Express card once belonging to Bruce Springsteen was sold for $4,500 (£2,650) at a New York memorabilia sale. The singer had given the expired card to a waiter in a LA restaurant by mistake and he let him keep it as a souvenir.

1998 songwriter Bob Merrill committed suicide, aged 77. He had written 'How Much Is That Doggie In The Window?' and Barbra Streisand's 'People'.

2000 John Lennon's Steinway piano, on which he composed 'Imagine', went on display at the Beatles Story Museum in Liverpool. The piano was set to be auctioned on the Internet later in the year and was expected to fetch more than £1 million ($1.7 million).

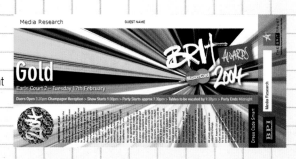

Media Research   GUEST NAME

Gold
Earls Court 2 – Tuesday 17th February
Doors Open 3.30pm Champagne Reception > Show Starts 5.00pm > Party Starts approx 7.30pm > Tables to be vacated by 9.30pm > Party Ends Midnight

BRIT AWARDS 2004
MasterCard

BORN ON THIS DAY

1933 Yoko Ono, artist, singer and wife of John Lennon.

1939 Bobby Hart, singer/songwriter who had a 1968 US No.8 single with Tommy Boyce, 'I Wonder What She's Doing Tonite'. They also wrote 'Last Train To Clarksville', 'I'm Not Your Stepping Stone' and 'Scooby-Doo Where Are You', selling over 40 million records together.

1941 Herman Santigo – singer with Frankie Lymon And The Teenagers, who had a 1956 UK No.1 single with 'Why Do Fools Fall In Love'.

1947 Dennis Deyoung – vocalist and keyboardist with Styx, who had a 1979 US No.1 & 1980 UK No.6 single with 'Babe'.

1953 Robbie Bachman – drummer with Bachman Turner Overdrive, who had a 1974 US No.1 & UK No.2 single with 'You Ain't Seen Nothing Yet'.

1954 John Travolta, actor and singer who had a 1978 UK & US No.1 single with Olivia Newton John, 'You're The One That I Want'.

1965 Dr. Dre – rapper with N.W.A. and record producer, who had a 1990 UK No.26 single with 'Express Yourself'. Dre signed Eminem to his label, producing his *Slim Shady LP* in 1999.

ON THIS DAY

1956 The Platters' 'The Great Pretender', started a two week run at No.1 on the US singles chart. It went to No.5 in the UK.

1962 on weekend leave from marine training, The Everly Brothers appeared on the US *Ed Sullivan Show*. In full uniform and with regulation cropped hair, they sang their new single 'Crying In The Rain'.

1965 The Kinks were at No.1 on the UK singles chart with 'Tired Of Waiting For You', the group's second UK No.1.

1966 Beach Boy Brian Wilson recorded 'Good Vibrations'.

1966 The Rolling Stones kicked off an 11 date tour of Australia at the Commemorative Auditorium, Sydney. They were supported by The Searchers.

1967 The Buckinghams started a two week run at No.1 on the US singles chart with 'Kind Of A Drag', the group's only US No.1. It didn't make the UK chart.

1969 this week's UK Top 5 singles: No.5, 'Dancing In The Street', Martha Reeves And The Vandellas; No.4, 'I'm Gonna Make You Love Me', Diana Ross And The Supremes And The Temptations; No.3, 'Where Do You Go To', Peter Sarstedt; No.2, 'Blackberry Way', The Move and No.1, 'Half As Nice', Amen Corner.

1971 Captain Beefheart And His Magic Band made their New York debut at Unganos.

1972 Los Angeles Radio station KDAY played two new Rolling Stones tracks non-stop for a day after obtaining stolen tapes from a producer's home.

1978 winners at this year's Grammy Awards included: Fleetwood Mac, Album of the year for *Rumours*, The Eagles, Record of the year for 'Hotel California' and The Bee Gees, Best pop vocal performance for 'How Deep Is Your Love'.

Bill Wyman's solo album *Stone Alone*. His professed intention to strike out on his own for good was a little premature, however.

1980 Rolling Stone Bill Wyman said that he intended to leave the band in 1982 on the group's 20th anniversary. He left in 1993.

1984 Simple Minds scored their first UK No.1 album with *Sparkle In The Rain*, the band's sixth release.

1987 Bon Jovi were at No.1 on the US singles chart with 'Livin' On A Prayer'. The song made No.4 in the UK.

1989 Debbie Gibson started a five week run at No.1 on the US album chart with *Electric Youth*.

1989 Fine Young Cannibals scored their only UK No.1 album with *The Raw And The Cooked*.

1998 Oasis' Noel Gallagher's Epiphone Supernova guitar raised £4,600 ($7,820) in aid of Children In Need at a Bonhams auction.

2000 an American court ordered the release of FBI files relating to John Lennon's interests and activities, including his support for the Irish Republican cause and the Workers' Revolutionary Party. The British Government told the US that it wanted the files to remain secret. MI5 also had files on Lennon.

2004 Dido entered a Top 10 of the music world's biggest earners after making £15.8 million ($26.9 million) in 2003. The singer's second album *Life For Rent* was the previous year's biggest selling UK album. The Rolling Stones topped the *Heat* magazine rich list having earned £55.3 million ($94 million) in 2003.

BORN ON THIS DAY

1924 Lee Marvin, actor and singer who had a UK 1970 UK No.1 single with 'Wand'rin Star', taken from the film *Paint Your Wagon*. Marvin died on August 29th 1987.

1940 Smokey Robinson – singer/songwriter, producer and member of The Miracles, who had a 1970 UK & US No.1 single with 'The Tears Of A Clown'. As a solo artist he had a 1981 UK No.1 & US No.2 single with 'Being With You'. He had also become Vice President of Motown Records in 1972.

1943 Lou Christie, US singer who had a 1966 US No.1 single with 'Lightnin' Strikes' and a 1969 UK No.2 single with 'I'm Gonna Make You Mine'.

1946 Pierre Van Den Linden – drummer with Focus, who had a 1973 UK No.4 single with 'Sylvia' and a 1973 US No.9 single with 'Hocus Pocus'.

1948 Toni Iommi – guitarist with Black Sabbath, who had a 1970 UK No.4 single with 'Paranoid'.

1949 Eddie Hardin, keyboards, replaced Steve Winwood, The Spencer Davis Group, (1966 UK No.1 single 'Keep On Running').

1957 Falco, (a.k.a. Hans Holzl), who had a 1986 UK & US No.1 single with 'Rock Me Amadeus'. He was killed in a car accident on February 6th 1998.

1963 Seal, singer/songwriter who had a 1991 UK No.2 single with 'Crazy' and a 1995 US No.1 & UK No.4 single 'Kiss From A Rose'.

ON THIS DAY

1972 Harry Nilsson started a four week run at No.1 on the US singles chart with his version of Badfingers' 'Without You'.

1976 former lead singer with Tower Of Power, Rich

Eddie Hardin in 'irresponsible solo album sleeve shocker'.

Stevens was arrested in connection with the drug-related murders of three men in San Jose, California. Stevens was found guilty of the charges in November 1976.

1977 Leo Sayer had his only UK No.1 single with 'When I Need You'.

1977 Manfred Mann's Earth Band scored a No.1 single in the US with their version of the Bruce Springsteen song 'Blinded By The Light'.

1981 accountant Glenn Kannry pleaded guilty to taking cash from Diana Ross's bank account.

1983 Patti Austin and James Ingram started a two week run at No.1 on the US singles chart with 'Baby Come To Me', which was a No.11 hit in the UK.

1989 billed as "The 1989 World Tour Starts Here", Simply Red played the Edinburgh Playhouse. Tickets cost £10 ($17).

1994 Mariah Carey had her first UK No.1 with her

version of the Peter Ham/Tom Evans song 'Without You'. Nilsson also took the song to No.1 in 1972. Both Ham and Evans committed suicide after an ongoing battle to receive royalties from the song.

1995 Motley Crue drummer Tommy Lee married *Baywatch*'s Pamela Anderson on a Cancun beach. The bride wore a white bikini.

1995 Roxette became the first Western group to perform in Beijing since George Michael in 1984, when they played a concert celebrating the Chinese New Year.

1996 Pulp's Jarvis Cocker was arrested after a stage invasion during Michael Jackson's appearance at the Brit Awards. Cocker was accused of attacking children who were performing with Jackson. All charges were dropped on March 11th.

1996 Bjork was shown on UK breakfast TV attacking a news reporter as she arrived at Thailand Airport. The footage showed the singer pulling the female reporter to the floor and banging her head on the ground. Bjork later apologized.

2000 Savage Garden went back to No.1 on the US singles chart for the second time with 'I Knew I Loved You'.

2004 Johnny Cash's family blocked an attempt by advertisers to use his hit song 'Ring of Fire' to promote haemorrhoid-relief products. The idea is said to have been backed by Merle Kilgore, who co-wrote the song with Cash's wife, June Carter Cash. Cash's daughter Rosanne said the family "would never allow the song to be demeaned like that".

BORN ON THIS DAY

1941 Buffy Sainte-Marie, Canadian singer/songwriter who had a 1971 UK No.7 single with 'Soldier Blue' and a 1972 US No.38 single with 'Mister Can't You See'. She also wrote 'Up Where We Belong', a 1982 US No.1 & UK No.7 for Joe Cocker and Jennifer Warnes.

1946 J. Geils – guitarist for The J. Geils Band, who had a 1982 US No.1 & UK No.3 single with 'Centerfold'.

1950 Walter Becker – bass player, guitarist and vocalist with Steely Dan, who had a 1973 US No.11 single with 'Reeling In The Years' plus nine other US Top 30 hits.

1951 Randy California – guitarist of Spirit, who had a 1969 US No.25 single with 'I Got A Line On You' and a 1981 UK No.40 album *Potato Land*. Randy drowned on January 2nd 1997 when rescuing his 12-year-old son after he was sucked into a riptide in surf off Hawaii.

1967 Kurt Cobain – guitarist and vocalist with Nirvana, who had a 1991 UK No.7 & 1992 US No.6 single with 'Smells Like Teen Spirit'. The song was taken from the 1991 album *Nevermind*, which spent over two years on the UK chart and made US No.1 in 1992. Cobain committed suicide on April 5th 1994.

1975 Brian Littrell of the Backstreet Boys, who had a 1997 US No.2 single with 'Quit Playing Games With My Heart' and a 1999 UK No.1 single with 'I Want It That Way'.

1977 Edwin Graham – drummer with The Darkness, who had a 2003 UK No.2 single with 'I Believe In A Thing Called Love' and a 2003 UK No.1 album with *Permission To Land*.

1985 Volkova Olegovna – singer with Tatu, who had a 2003 UK No.1 single with 'All The Things She Said'.

ON THIS DAY

1960 Jimi Hendrix made his stage debut when he played a show at a high school in Seattle.

1971 appearing at Kingston Poly, London were Yes, supported by Queen. Tickets cost 50p (85c).

1976 all four members of Kiss had their footprints implanted on the pavement outside Grauman's Chinese Theatre in Hollywood.

1980 Bon Scott from AC/DC was pronounced dead on arrival at a London hospital after a heavy night's drinking. The coroner's verdict said that Scott drank himself to death.

1988 Kylie Minogue was at No.1 on the UK singles chart with 'I Should Be So Lucky'. Minogue had become a household name playing Charlene Ramsey in the Australian soap Neighbours. After the track had been turned down by every major UK record company, producer Pete Waterman released the single on his PWL label. Kylie has gone on to score another 30 other Top 30 hit singles.

1991 Bob Dylan was awarded a lifetime achievement award at the third annual Grammy Awards.

1994 Tori Amos went to No.1 on the UK album chart with *Under The Pink*.

2000 All Saints started a two week run at No.1 on the UK singles chart with 'Pure Shores', the group's fourth UK No. 1.

"Among my family, I'm the square one."
Bjork

2003 winners at this year's Brit Awards included: Robbie Williams for British solo artist; Ms Dynamite won British female artist; Best British album went to Coldplay for *A Rush Of Blood*; Best British group also went to Coldplay; Red Hot Chili Peppers won International group; Blue won Best pop act and Liberty X won Best single for 'Just A Little'.

Brian Wilson PERFORMS SMILE

Coming soon... to a face near you!

TOUR 2004
FEBRUARY
LAST FEW TICKETS
20 - 22 **LONDON ROYAL FESTIVAL HALL**
EXTRA PERFORMANCES DUE TO EXCEPTIONAL DEMAND
26 / 27 **LONDON ROYAL FESTIVAL HALL**
020 7960 4242   www.rfh.org.uk
Presented by the South Bank centre

MARCH
MON 1 **BOURNEMOUTH PAVILIONS**
01202 456456
TUE 2 **BRISTOL COLSTON HALL**
0117 922 3686
THU 4 **GLASGOW CLYDE AUDITORIUM**
0870 040 4000
SAT 6 **NEWCASTLE CITY HALL**
0191 261 2606
SUN 7 **LIVERPOOL EMPIRE**
0870 606 3536
MON 8 **BIRMINGHAM SYMPHONY HALL**
0121 780 3333
Presented in association with The Agency Group Ltd

2003 100 people died after pyrotechnics ignited a club during a gig by Great White in West Warwick, Rhode Island. Singer Ty Longley was also killed.

2004 Brian Wilson kicked off an 11 date UK tour at London's Royal Festival Hall. The shows saw Wilson performing the full suite of songs from his unreleased masterpiece 'Smile' - Wilson's "teenage symphony to God."

BORN ON THIS DAY

1933 Nina Simone, US singer who had a 1959 US No.18 single with 'I Love You, Porgy' and a 1968 UK No.2 single with 'Ain't Got No/I Got Life'.

1943 David Geffen, Geffen Records label boss. He first formed Asylum Records and signed The Eagles, Crosby, Stills, Nash & Young, Jackson Browne and Joni Mitchell. He formed Dreamworks in 1995 with Steven Spielberg.

1949 Jerry Harrison – keyboardist and guitarist with Jonathan Richman And The Modern Lovers then Talking Heads (who had a 1983 US No.9 single with 'Burning Down The House' and a 1985 UK No.6 single with 'Road To Nowhere') and Casual Gods.

1951 Vince Welnick – keyboardist with The Tubes, who had a 1977 UK No.28 single with 'White Punks On Dope' and a 1983 US No.10 single with 'She's A Beauty'.

1952 Jean-Jacques Burnel *(right)* – bass player and vocalist with The Stranglers, who had a 1982 UK No.2 single with 'Golden Brown' plus over 20 other UK Top 40 hits.

1961 Ranking Roger – singer with The Beat, who had a 1983 UK No.3 single with 'Can't Get Used To Losing You' and Fine Young Cannibals, who had a 1989 US No.1 & UK No.5 single with 'She Drives Me Crazy'.

1967 Michael Ward – guitarist with The Wallflowers, who had a 1997 US No.3 album with *Bringing Down The Horse*.

1969 James Dean Bradfield – guitarist and singer for the Manic Street Preachers, who had a 1996 UK No.2 single with 'A Design For Life' plus two UK No.1 singles.

1986 Charlotte Church, UK singer who had a 1999 UK No.34 single with 'Just Wave Hello' and a 1998 UK No.4 album with *Voice Of An Angel*.

ON THIS DAY

1961 The Beatles appeared for the very first time at The Cavern Club, Liverpool. They went on to make a total of 292 other appearances at the Club.

1964 The New York band The Echoes recruited a new young unknown piano player, named Billy Joel.

1964 three classic British singles were released: The Rolling Stones' 'Not Fade Away', UK No.3; The Hollies' 'Just One Look', UK No.2 and Billy J. Kramer's 'Little Children', UK No.1.

1970 The Simon & Garfunkel album *Bridge Over Troubled Water* went to No.1 on the UK chart. It went on to stay in the chart for over 300 weeks, returning to the top on eight separate occasions. It spent a total of 41 weeks at No.1.

1976 Florence Ballard of The Supremes died of cardiac arrest, aged 32. She had left The Supremes in 1967, lost an $8 million (£4.7 million) lawsuit against Motown and was living on welfare when she died.

1976 The Four Seasons were at No.1 on the UK singles chart with 'December '63 (Oh What A Night)', the group's only UK No.1.

1977 Fleetwood Mac released their album *Rumours*. It went on to sell more than 15 million

copies worldwide and spent 31 weeks at No.1 on the US chart.

1981 Dolly Parton started a two week run at No.1 on the US charts with '9 To 5', the singer's first No.1. It made No.47 in the UK.

1981 REO Speedwagon went to No.1 on the US album chart with *Hi Infidelity*. The album spent a total of 15 weeks at No.1.

1982 US DJ Murry K. died. He was thought to be the first person to play a Beatles record on radio in the States.

1987 Ben E. King was at No.1 in the UK singles chart with 'Stand By Me'. It had first been released in 1961 and had been featured in the film *Stand By Me*.

2001 Robbie Williams was attacked and thrown from the stage during a concert in Stuttgart, Germany after a man got onto the stage and pushed him into the security pit. The attacker was arrested and taken to a secure psychiatric clinic.

2002 Elton John accused the music industry of exploiting young singers and dumping talented artists for manufactured groups. He said "There are too many average and mediocre acts, it damages real talent getting airplay. It's just fodder."

2004 Mud singer Les Gray died from throat cancer aged 57. The group had a 1974 UK No.1 single with 'Tiger Feet' plus 14 other UK Top 40 singles.

2004 appearing at the Carling Live New Kings of Rock n' Roll (until February 26th) Keane, Snow Patrol, Jet, Longview, Elbow and The Ordinary Boys.

NEW UK TOUR FEBRUARY-MARCH 2004

LIBERTY X

plus special guests

FEBRUARY
Sat 21 MANCHESTER MEN ARENA
0870 190 8000
Sun 22 NOTTINGHAM ARENA
0870 121 0123

BORN ON THIS DAY

1938 Bobby Hendricks – singer with The Drifters, who had a 1960 US No.1 & UK No.2 single with 'Save The Last Dance For Me'.

1943 Mick Green – guitarist with Johnny Kidd & The Pirates (1963 UK No.4 single 'I'll Never Get Over You'). Joined Billy J. Kramer in 1964.

1973 Scott Phillips – drummer with Creed, who had a 2001 US No.1 & UK No.13 single 'With Arms Wide Open' and a 2002 US No.1 album *Weathered*.

1977 James Blunt, singer, songwriter and former Army captain. Had the 2005 UK No.1 album 'Back To Bedlam.'

ON THIS DAY

1960 Percy Faith started a nine week run at No.1 on the US chart with 'Theme From A Summer Place', which was a No.2 hit in the UK.

1962 Elvis Presley was at No.1 in the UK singles chart with 'Rock-A-Hula Baby/Can't Help Falling In Love'. The tracks were from his latest film *Blue Hawaii* and became the singer's tenth UK No.1

1968 Genesis released their first single, 'The Silent Sun'.

1969 appearing at Manchester's Free Trade Hall were Tyrannosaurus Rex. Support act David Bowie performed a one-man mime act.

1975 Scottish group The Average White Band went to No.1 on the US singles chart with 'Pick Up The Pieces', while the band's album *AWB* went to No.1 on the US chart.

1975 Steve Harley And Cockney Rebel had their only UK No.1 single with 'Make Me Smile (Come Up And See Me)'.

1977 The Sex Pistols won "Turkey Of The Year" in this year's *NME* readers' poll.

1978 The Police appeared in a Wrigleys Chewing Gum commercial for US TV. The band dyed their hair blonde for the appearance.

1981 one-hit wonder Joe Dolce had a No.1 UK single with 'Shaddap You Face'.

1986 MTV dedicated a full 22 hours broadcast to The Monkees, showing all 45 episodes of the original Monkees TV series.

1987 Andy Warhol, pop artist and producer, died after a gall bladder operation. Warhol produced and managed The Velvet Underground, designed the 1967 *Velvet Underground And Nico* 'peeled banana' album cover and The Rolling Stones' *Sticky Fingers* album cover.

Sid and Nancy: the courting couple.

1992 Shakespears Sister started an eight week run as the UK No.1 with the single 'Stay'. The duo was made up of ex-Bananarama member Siobhan Fahey and singer Marcella Detroit, who co-wrote 'Lay Down Sally' with Eric Clapton.

1997 Jennifer Lopez married waiter Ojani Noa; they separated a year later.

1997 No Doubt went to No.1 on the UK singles chart with 'Don't Speak'.

1997 The Spice Girls started a four week run at No.1 on the US singles chart with 'Wannabe'. They were the first UK act to score a No.1 in the US for over 18 months.

2000 the engagement ring Sex Pistol Sid Vicious gave to his girlfriend Nancy Spungen went on sale for auction at £1,500 ($2,550). Sid bought the ring from Camden market in 1977.

2001 winners at the 43rd Grammy Awards included: U2, who won Record of the year and Song of the year (songwriters award) with 'Beautiful Day'; Steely Dan won album of the year for *Two Against Nature*; Macy Gray won Female pop vocal for 'I Try'; Sting won Male pop vocal for 'She Walks This Earth'; Eminem won Best Rap album from *The Marshall Mathers LP*; Johnny Cash won Best male country performance for 'Solitary Man' and Shelby Lynne won Best new artist award.

2002 drummer Ronnie Verrell died, aged 77. He had worked with Tom Jones, The Strawbs and Phil Everly and provided the drum licks for Animal in *The Muppet Show*.

2002 two middle-aged women spent the first of eight nights sleeping in a car outside Bournemouth International Centre to make sure they were first in the queue for tickets to Cliff Richard's forthcoming concert.

The original source of U2's 2001 hit.

BORN ON THIS DAY

1944 Johnny Winter – guitarist and vocalist who worked with Rick Derringer and brother Edger Winter – the latter had a 1969 US Top 30 album with *Johnny Winter*.

1944 Mike Maxfield – guitarist with Billy J. Kramer & The Dakotas, who had a 1964 UK No.1 & US No.7 single with 'Little Children'.

1950 Steve Priest – guitarist with Sweet, who had a 1973 UK No.1 single with 'Blockbuster' plus 14 other UK Top 40 singles.

1952 Brad Whitford – guitarist with Aerosmith, who had a 1989 UK No.13 single with 'Love In An Elevator' and a 1998 US No.1 single 'I Don't Want To Miss A Thing'.

1955 Howard Jones – keyboardist and singer/songwriter who had a 1983 UK No.2 single 'What Is Love' plus nine other UK Top 40 singles and a 1986 US No.4 single with 'No One Is To Blame'.

1963 Rob Collins – keyboardist with The Charlatans, who had a 1990 UK No.9 single with 'The Only One I Know'. He was killed in a car crash on July 23rd 1996.

Howard Jones in his 80s heyday.

ON THIS DAY

1961 Petula Clark had her first UK No.1 single with 'Sailor'. During her career she achieved a total of 20 UK Top 40 hits and two US No.1 singles.

1965 filming began on The Beatles' follow up to *A Hard Day's Night* on location in the Bahamas. It had the working title of *Eight Arms To Hold You*.

1974 Suzi Quatro was at No.1 on the UK singles chart with 'Devil Gate Drive', her second UK No.1.

1978 David Coverdale's Whitesnake made their debut at the Sky Bird Club, Nottingham, England.

1978 Sid Vicious and Nancy Spungen were arrested in New York for possession of drugs.

1979 Dire Straits played their first American show when they appeared in Boston.

1985 it was reported that Stevie Wonder had been arrested during an anti-apartheid demonstration outside the South African Embassy in Washington. He was released after being questioned by police.

1991 Whitney Houston achieved her ninth US No.1 single in just over five years with her version of the Sister Sledge song 'All The Man I Need'.

1995 Mevin Franklin of The Temptations died. They had a 1971 US No.1 & UK No.8 single with 'Just My Imagination' and reissued 'My Girl', which became a UK No.2 in 1992.

1998 Oasis were banned for life from flying Cathay Pacific Airlines after "abusive and disgusting behaviour" during a flight from Hong Kong to Perth, Australia.

2003 the *News Of The World* reported that Michael Jackson had undergone scores of painful operations to strip his body of black skin until he appeared white. They also reported that surgeons at a Santa Monica clinic eventually refused him any more treatment. An insider told the paper that Jackson had been anaesthetized on a weekly basis to have his skin peeled and bleached.

2003 Howie Epstein, bass player with Tom Petty And The Heartbreakers, died of a suspected drug overdose in New Mexico.

2003 Norah Jones cleaned up at the 45th Grammy Awards, which was held at Madison Square Garden, New York. The singer/songwriter won: Album of the year for *Come Away With Me*, Record of the year with 'Don't Know Why', Song of the year, Best new artist and Best female pop vocal. Other winners included: Best male pop vocal, John Mayer for 'Our Body Is A Wonderland'; Best male rock vocal, Bruce Springsteen for 'The Rising'; Best female rock vocal, Sheryl Crow for 'Steve McQueen'; Best rock performance by group, Coldplay for 'In My Place' and Best rap album, Eminem for *The Eminem Show*.

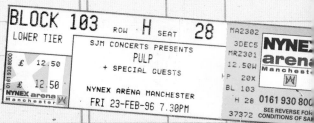

BLOCK 103
LOWER TIER
£ 12.50
£ 12.50
NYNEX arena
Manchester

SJM CONCERTS PRESENTS
PULP
+ SPECIAL GUESTS
NYNEX ARENA MANCHESTER
FRI 23-FEB-96 7.30PM

ROW H SEAT 28

MA2302
3DEC5
MRZ301
12.50W
HP 20X
BL 103
H 28
37372

NYNEX
arena
Manchester

0161 930 800
SEE REVERSE FOR
CONDITIONS OF SA

BORN ON THIS DAY

1942 Paul Jones, singer, harmonica player, actor and radio presenter. He was part of Manfred Mann, who had a 1964 UK & US No.1 single with 'Do Wah Diddy Diddy', and The Blues Band.

1944 Nicky Hopkins *(right)*, session piano player who worked with The Rolling Stones, Jeff Beck, The Beatles, John Lennon, The Who and Small Faces. Hopkins died on September 6th 1994.

1947 Rupert Holmes, writer, producer and singer who had a 1980 US No.1 & UK No.23 single with 'Escape (The Pina Colada Song)'.

1959 Colin Farley – bass player for Cutting Crew, who had a 1987 US No.1 & 1986 UK No.4 single with 'I Just Died In Your Arms Tonight'.

1962 Michelle Shocked, singer/songwriter who had a 1988 airplay hit with 'Anchorage'.

ON THIS DAY

1957 Buddy Holly recorded a new version of 'That'll Be The Day', the title being taken from a phrase used by John Wayne in the film *The Searchers*.

1963 The Rolling Stones started a Sunday night residency at The Station Hotel, Richmond, Surrey; being paid £24 ($41) and appearing on the first night to 66 people.

1969 The Jimi Hendrix Experience played their last-ever British performance when they appeared at the Royal Albert Hall.

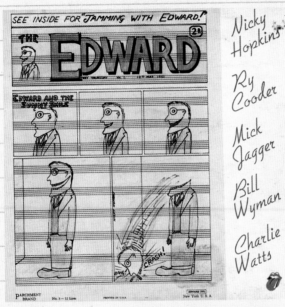

1973 Roberta Flack had her second US No.1 when 'Killing Me Softly With His Song', started a five week run at the top. The song was written about Don McLean.

1973 The Byrds made their final live appearance when they played at The Capitol Theatre in Passaic, New Jersey.

1976 The Eagles' *Greatest Hits* became the first album to be certified platinum by the R.I.A.A. (Recording Industry Association of America). New certifications represented sales of one million copies for albums and two million for singles.

1982 The Police won best British group at the first annual Brit Awards. Adam And The Ants won Best album for *Kings Of The Wild Frontier*.

1982 winners at the Grammy Awards included: John & Yoko, Album of the year for Double Fantasy, Kim Carnes, Song of the year for 'Bette Davis Eyes'; Quincy Jones won Producer of the year and Sheena Easton won Best new act.

1990 50s teen idol Johnnie Ray died of liver failure. Ray scored over 20 Top 40 singles between 1952 and 1960.

1992 Kurt Cobain married Courtney Love in Waikiki, Hawaii. The press reported that the couple was expecting a baby on September 10th.

1997 The Spice Girls won best single with 'Wannabe' at the Brit Awards. Other winners included: Best group Manic Street Preachers; Best dance act, The Prodigy; Best male, George Michael; Best female, Gabrielle and Best newcomer, Kula Shaker.

2000 Carlos Santana won eight awards at this year Grammy Awards. Before the *Supernatural* album, the guitarist had not had a Top 10 album since 1981. Sting won two awards, one for Best pop album and another for Best male pop vocalist. Sir Elton John won the legend award and Phil Collins the Best soundtrack award for Tarzan.

2002 Sting started a two week run at No.1 on the UK album chart with Sting, *The Very Best Of*.

2003 Sir Paul McCartney played a private show in San Diego for the 50th birthday of Wendy Whitworth, the executive producer of CNN's Larry King Show. Sir Paul donated his $1 million (£0.6 million) fee to the Adopt-a-Minefield charity.

2004 Estelle Axton, who helped create the legendary US soul music label Stax, died aged 85. Stax was home to Otis Redding, Rufus Thomas, Isaac Hayes and Booker T & the MGs and the Stax studio, "Soulsville USA", was second only to Motown in its production of soul hits during its 1960s heyday.

BORN ON THIS DAY

1943 George Harrison — guitarist and vocalist with The Beatles. The all-time bestselling album in the UK is The Beatles' *Sgt Pepper's Lonely Hearts Club Band*, with over 4.5 million copies sold. Harrison wrote the 1969 US No.1 & UK No.4 Beatles single 'Something'. As a solo artist he had a 1971 US No.1 album with *All Things Must Pass* and a 1970 worldwide No.1 single with 'My Sweet Lord'. He was also a member of the Travelling Wilburys. Harrison died of cancer on November 29th 2001.

1957 Stuart Wood — guitarist with the Bay City Rollers, who had a 1975 UK No.1 single with 'Bye Bye Baby' plus 11 other UK Top 20 singles and a 1976 US No.1 single 'Saturday Night'.

1959 Mike Peters — guitarist and vocalist with The Alarm, who had a 1983 UK No.17 single with '68 Guns'. Member of Dead Men Walking with Kirk Brandon, (ex Spear Of Destiny), Slim Jim Phantom, (Stray Cats), Glen Matlock (Sex Pistols) and Bruce Watson (Big Country).

ON THIS DAY

1956 Elvis Presley had his first national hit when 'I Forgot To Remember To Forget' went to No.1 on the Billboard Country & Western chart.

1963 the first Beatles single 'Please Please Me' was released in the US on the Vee Jay label, which misspelt the group's name as "The Beatles".

1965 The Seekers were at No.1 on the UK singles chart with 'I'll Never Find Another You'.

GEORGE HARRISON WHEN WE WAS FAB

WHEN WE WAS FAB

GEORGE HARRISON

THE NEW SINGLE PRODUCED BY JEFF LYNNE AND GEORGE HARRISON ON 7" AND 4-TRACK 12"

distributed by **wea** *records ltd.*
a *warner communications company.*

1971 BBC TV aired Led Zeppelin in concert from the Paris Theatre, France.

1977 The Jam signed to Polydor Records UK for £6,000 ($10,200).

1981 winners at this year's Grammy Awards were: Bob Seger, Best rock performance for 'Against The Wind'; Pat Benatar won Best female performance for 'Crimes Of Passion' and Christopher Cross, Best new artist and Best song for 'Sailing'.

1984 The Thompson Twins scored their first UK No.1 album with their third release *Into The Gap*.

1984 Van Halen's 'Jump', started a five week run at No.1 on the US singles chart. The song was a No.7 hit in the UK.

1985 U2 began their first full US arena tour starting at the Dallas Reunion Arena.

FREE SINGLE   NOT FOR SALE

THOMPSON TWINS

Thompson Twins: at No.1 in the album charts in 1984.

1989 Simple Minds were at No.1 on the UK singles chart with 'Belfast Child'. At 6 minutes 39 seconds it became the second longest-running No.1 after The Beatles' 'Hey Jude'.

1995 Madonna started a seven week run at No.1 on the US singles chart with 'Take A Bow'. Co-written with Babyface it made No.16 in the UK.

2000 The Spice Girls were facing a bill of up to £1 million ($1.7 million) after losing a legal battle against the sponsors of their 1988 world tour. The Aprilia Scooter Company had claimed the girls knew of Geri's impending departure.

2001 a feud between two rap music rivals resulted in a shootout in New York's Greenwich Village *(below)*. More than 20 shots were fired outside Hot 97 radio studio as rapper Lil' Kim left after an interview. One man was wounded.

2004 The Rolling Stones topped a US Rich List of music's biggest money makers. The list was based on earnings during 2003 when the band played their "Forty Licks" tour, which made them $212 million, (£124.7m) in ticket, CD, DVD and merchandise sales. The three million fans who went to the shows spent an average of $11 (£6.47) each on merchandise. Bruce Springsteen was listed in second place and The Eagles in third.

Dispute between rap rivals leads to daylight shootout

By James Bone

A FEUD between two rap music rivals appears to have resulted in a shooting in New York's Greenwich Village.

One man was wounded in the back when more than 20 shots were fired in front of the Hot 97 radio studio on Sunday afternoon as the rapper Lil' Kim — known for her blonde hair, bright blue contact lenses and breast implants — left after an interview.

Police said the trouble started when Lil' Kim, whose real name is Kimberly James, ran into another rapper, Kiam Holley, who was arriving to appear on the same hip-hop show. Mr Holley is half of the hardcore rap duo Capone-N-

respective "posses". Moments later a bullet shattered a car window and another hit Effroin Ocasio, a member of Mr Holley's entourage, in the back. Detectives found at least 22 bullets from a 9mm gun and a .38 pistol. Miss James is said to have been at odds with Mr Holley over his support for her rival, Foxy Brown.

Police plan to interview Miss James and Mr Holley. It will not be the first time that Miss James has been questioned about a shooting. In 1999 she was interviewed about an incident outside a studio owned by the rapper Sean "Puff Daddy" Combs, who is now on trial on charges running from a shooting at a Manhattan nightclub.

Lil' Kim she exchanged words with Kiam Holley

Norega. When he and Miss Jones exchanged words, tempers flared among their

BORN ON THIS DAY

1928 Fats Domino, R&B and rock 'n' roll pianist and singer who had a 1957 US No.6 & UK No.6 single with 'Blueberry Hill' and 35 other US Top 40 singles.

1932 Johnny Cash, US country singer/songwriter who had a 1969 US No.2 & UK No.4 single with 'A Boy Named Sue' plus 11 other US Top 40 singles. He had a US TV show in the late 60s–early 70s. Cash died of respiratory failure on September 12th 2003, aged 71.

1945 Bob The Bear Hite – vocalist and harmonica player with Canned Heat, who had a 1968 US No.11 single with 'Going Up The Country' and a 1970 UK No.2 single with 'Let's Work Together'. He died on April 5th 1981.

1947 Sandie Shaw, singer who had a 1964 UK No.1 single with 'There's Always Something There To Remind Me', plus 15 other UK Top 40 singles. She was the first UK act to win the Eurovision Song Contest with 1967's 'Puppet On A String'.

1950 Jonathan Cain – keyboardist with Journey, who had a 1982 US No.2 single with 'Open Arms'.

1953 Michael Bolton, singer who had a 1990 US No.1 & UK No.3 single with 'How Am I Supposed To Live Without You'.

1971 Erykah Badu, US female singer who had a 1997 UK No.12 single with 'On & On' and a 2001 UK No. 23 single with Macy Gray, 'Sweet Baby'.

ON THIS DAY

1955 Billboard reported that for the first time since their introduction in 1949, 45rpm singles were outselling the old 78s.

1958 Perry Como was at No.1 on the UK singles chart with 'Magic Moments', a song written by Burt Bacharach and Hal David. It stayed at No.1 for eight weeks.

1965 guitarist Jimmy Page released a solo single called 'She Just Satisfies'. It didn't chart.

1966 The Beatles' *Rubber Soul* was at No.1 on the US album chart.

1969 Peter Sarstedt was at No.1 on the UK singles chart with 'Where Do You Go To My Lovely?'.

1977 The Eagles went to No.1 on the US singles chart with 'New Kid On Town', the group's third US No.1. It made No.20 in the UK.

1977 Sherman Garnes from Frankie Lymon And The Teenagers died during open heart surgery. The group had had a 1956 UK No.1 and US No.6 single with 'Why Do Fools Fall In Love?'

1979 during a court case between The Sex Pistols and their manager Malcolm McLaren it was revealed that only £30,000 ($51,000) was left of the £800,000 ($1,360,000) the band had earned.

1980 after seeing U2 play at Dublin's National Boxing Stadium in front of 2,400 people Rob Partridge and Bill Stewart from Island Records offered the band a recording contract.

1990 Sinead O'Connor was at No.1 on the UK singles chart with 'Nothing Compares 2 U'.

1991 US songwriter Doc Pomus died. He had written many early 60s hits including, 'Sweets For My Sweet', 'Teenager In Love' and 'Save The Last Dance For Me.'

1994 Toni Braxton went to No.1 on the US album chart with *Toni Braxton*.

1997 Songwriter Ben Raleigh died after setting fire to his bathrobe while cooking. He co-wrote 'Scooby -Doo Where Are You' and 'Tell Laura I Love Her'.

2000 Lonestar started a two week run at No.1 on the US singles chart with 'Amazed'.

2001 winners at the Brit Awards included: Coldplay, who won Best British group and Best British album for *Parachutes*; Robbie Williams, who won Best British male artist and Best single for 'Rock DJ'; Sonique, Best British female artist; Fat Boy Slim, Best dance act ; A1 won Best British newcomer; Westlife won Best pop act; Eminem won Best international male solo artist and U2 won Outstanding contribution to music.

U2: A license to print money from 1980.

BORN ON THIS DAY

1927 Guy Mitchell, US singer who had a 1957 UK & US No.1 single 'Singing The Blues' plus over ten other UK Top 40 singles. Mitchell died on July 1st 1999.

1948 Eddie Gray – guitarist and vocalist with Tommy James & The Shondells, who had a 1966 US No.1 single with 'Hanky Panky' and 1968 UK No.1 single with 'Mony Mony'.

1950 Robert Balderrama – guitarist with ? & The Mysterians, who had a 1966 US No.1 & UK No.37 single with '96 Tears'. The song was also a UK No.17 hit for The Stranglers in 1990.

1957 Adrian Smith – guitarist for Iron Maiden, who had a 1982 UK No.1 album with *The Number Of The Beast* and a 1991 UK No.1 single with 'Bring Your Daughter To The Slaughter'.

1960 Paul Humphreys – keyboardist with Orchestral Manoeuvres In The Dark, who had a 1984 UK No.5 single with 'Locomotion'.

1971 Rozonda "Chilli" Thomas – vocalist with TLC, who had a 1995 US No.1 & UK No.4 single with 'Waterfalls'.

1981 Josh Groban, US singer who had a 2002 US No.7 & UK No.28 album with *Josh Groban*.

ON THIS DAY

1961 Chubby Checker started a three week run at No.1 on the US singles chart with 'Pony Time', his second No.1 of the 60s. It reached No.27 in the UK.

1964 21-year-old former hairdresser and cloakroom attendant at The Cavern club, Cilla Black, was at No.1 on the UK singles chart with 'Anyone Who Had A Heart'. Written by Bacharach and David it was Cilla's first UK No.1. This week's UK Top 10 was the first ever to feature only UK acts.

Arnold Layne himself, as pictured by Joe Boyd.

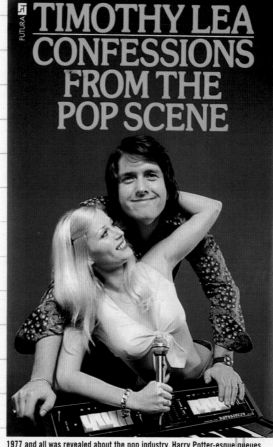

1977 and all was revealed about the pop industry. Harry Potter-esque queues form outside the nation's bookshops.

1965 the first date of a 21-date twice-nightly UK package tour with Del Shannon, Wayne Fontana & the Mindbenders and Herman's Hermits, at Sheffield's City Hall, England.

1967 Pink Floyd recorded their first single, 'Arnold Layne', with producer Joe Boyd.

1971 five months after her death, Janis Joplin started a nine week run at No.1 on the US album chart with *Pearl*.

1972 T. Rex appeared at New York's Carnegie Hall.

1974 Cher filed for divorce from Sonny Bono. She married Gregg Allman on June 27th 1975.

1977 Keith Richards was arrested by the Royal Canadian Mounted Police at Toronto's Harbour Castle Hotel, for possession of heroin and cocaine. Bail was set at $25,000 (£14,705).

1980 winners at the Grammy Awards included: Song of the year, The Doobie Brothers' 'What A Fool Believes'; Album of the year, Billy Joel's *52nd St*; Best new artist, Rickie Lee Jones and Best disco record, 'I Will Survive' by Gloria Gaynor.

1991 James Brown was paroled after two years of a six year prison sentence, imposed for resisting arrest after a car chase across two states.

1993 after 14 weeks at No.1 on the US singles chart, 'I Will Always Love You' gave Whitney Houston the longest-ever US chart topper, taking over from Boyz II Men's hit 'End Of The Road', and becoming the second biggest-selling single in the US.

1999 Britney Spears started a two week run at No.1 on the UK singles chart with 'Baby One More Time'. It went on to be the biggest-selling single of the year. It was also No.1 in the US.

2004 a worker in a supermarket in Aspen, Colorado alerted the police after seeing a man shopping with his face covered by a mask. Police arrived on the scene and identified the man as Michael Jackson, who was in town on holiday with his children.

BORN ON THIS DAY

1942 Brian Jones – guitarist with The Rolling Stones, who had a 1966 UK & US No.1 single with 'Paint It Black'. Jones died on July 3rd 1969 after drowning in his swimming pool under the influence of alcohol and drugs.

1942 Joe South, US singer/songwriter who had a 1969 US No.12 & UK No.6 single with 'Games People Play'. He worked with Bob Dylan, Simon & Garfunkel and Aretha Franklin.

1945 Ronnie Rosman – keyboardist for Tommy James & The Shondells, who had a 1966 US No.1 single 'Hanky Panky' and a 1968 UK No.1 single with 'Mony Mony'.

1957 Cindy Wilson – vocalist with The B-52's, who had a 1990 UK No.2 & US No.3 single with 'Love Shack'.

1957 Ian Stanley – keyboardist for Tears For Fears, who had a 1985 US No.1 & UK No.2 single with 'Everybody Wants To Rule The World'.

1957 Phil Gould – drummer with Level 42,who had a 1986 UK No.3 single with 'Lessons In Love', plus 19 other UK Top 40 singles).

1966 Ian Brown – vocalist with The Stone Roses, who had a 1989 UK No.8 single with 'Fool's Gold' and a 1989 album with *The Stone Roses*. As a solo artist he had a 1998 UK No.5 single with 'My Star'.

ON THIS DAY

1964 The Yardbirds played at the "Rhythm and Blues Festival" at The Town Hall, Birmingham, England.

1968 Frankie Lymon was found dead of a suspected drug overdose at his mother's house in New York . He was 25.

1968 Husband and wife team Esther and Abi Ofarim *(top)* were at No.1 on the UK chart with the single 'Cinderella Rockefella'.

1970 in an interview in *NME*, Fleetwood Mac's Peter Green talked about his plans to give all his money away. He was sent to a mental hospital in 1973. He relaunched his career in the 90s.

1970 Led Zeppelin played a gig in Copenhagen as The Nobs after Eva Von Zeppelin, a relative of the airship designer, threatened to sue if the family name was used in Denmark.

1970 Simon & Garfunkel started a six week run at the top of the US singles chart with 'Bridge Over Troubled Water'. It was also No.1 in the UK in March the same year.

1972 George and Patti Harrison were injured in a car crash. Patti was unconscious for several days.

1974 singer-songwriter Bobby Bloom shot himself in the head at his Hollywood apartment, aged

Cornershop, when all they had was pocket-money.

28. He had had a 1970 US No.8 & UK No.3 single with 'Montego Bay'.

1977 while appearing live on stage Ray Charles was attacked by a member of his audience, who tried to strangle him with a rope.

1984 Michael Jackson won a record seven Grammy Awards including: Album of the year for *Thriller*; Record of the year and Best rock vocal performance for 'Beat It'; Best pop vocal performance, Best R&B performance and Best R&B song for 'Billie Jean', and Best recording for children for *E.T The Extra Terrestrial*.

1985 David Byron, singer with Uriah Heep, died from a heart attack.

1986 George Michael announced that Wham! would officially split during the summer.

1988 k.d. Lang performed at the closing ceremony of the 1988 Winter Olympics in Calgary.

1994 Eric Clapton played his 100th performance at London's Royal Albert Hall, in aid of the "Children In Crisis" charity.

1996 Grammy award winners included: Alanis Morissette, Album of the year for *Jagged Little Pill* and Best female rock vocal and Best song for 'You Oughta Know'; Nirvana's *Unplugged* won Best alternative album and Coolio won Best rap performance with 'Gangsta's Paradise'.

1997 Death Row Records boss Marion "Suge" Knight was sentenced to nine years in prison for violating his probation for a 1995 assault conviction. Under US law, Knight would not be allowed to run Death Row Records while in prison.

1998 Celine Dion started a two week run at No.1 on the US singles chart with 'My Heart Will Go On'.

1998 Cornershop went to No.1 on the UK singles chart with 'Brimful Of Asher'.

BORN ON THIS DAY

1940 Gretchen Christopher – singer with The Fleetwoods, who had a 1959 US No.1 & UK No.6 single with 'Come Softly To Me'.

1976 Ja Rule (a.k.a. Jeffrey Atkins), US rapper who had a 2001 UK No.4 with Jennifer Lopez, 'I'm Real', a 2002 US No.1 & UK No.6 single with 'Always On Time' and a 2001 US No.1 album with *Pain Is Love*.

ON THIS DAY

1964 the first night of a 29 date twice-nightly tour featuring The Searchers, Booby Vee and Dusty Springfield at The Adelphi Cinema, Slough, England.

1968 ex-Supremes singer Florence Ballard married Thomas Chapman in Detroit.

1968 The Beatles' *Sgt Pepper* won Album of the year, Best cover and Best engineered and recorded album at this year's Grammy Awards.

1972 Led Zeppelin played at the Festival Hall, Brisbane, Australia.

1976 10CC kicked off a 30 date UK tour at the Fairfield Hall, Croydon promoting their new album *How Dare You*. Also this week Eric Stewart had been nominated for a Grammy award in America for his work on the Original Soundtrack album.

1977 two members of Lynyrd Skynyrd were knocked unconscious after a scuffle broke out between the band and members of the Metropolitan Police boxing team, who were holding a dinner at the Royal Lancaster Hotel in London.

1980 the glasses that Buddy Holly had been wearing when he died were discovered in a police file in Mason, Iowa after being there for over 21 years.

1992 Mr Big started a three week run at No.1 on the US singles chart with 'To Be With You', a No.3 hit in the UK.

1992 U2's "Zoo TV" tour opened at The Lakeland Civic Centre Arena, Florida.

1996 Status Quo sued Radio 1 for £250,000 ($425,000) on the grounds that the BBC station was breaking the law by not including their new record on their playlist.

1996 Wes Farrell died, aged 56. He was one of the writers behind 'The Partridge Family'. He also wrote 'Hang On Sloopy', which was a 1965 hit for The McCoys.

2000 Eric Clapton was banned from driving for six months after speeding at 45mph in a 30mph zone near his home in Surrey.

2000 Sir Elton John stormed out of the opening of his new Broadway musical show, "Aida", after 15 minutes, complaining that his songs had been ruined.

A Sgt. Pepper's badge from 1968.

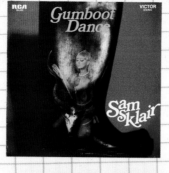

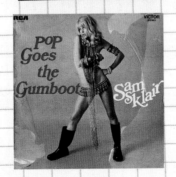

WHAT WERE THEY THINKING OF?

BORN ON THIS DAY

1927 Harry Belafonte, US singer who had a 1957 UK No.1 & US No.12 single with 'Mary's Boy Child' and a 1957 UK No.2 & US No.5 with 'Banana Boat Song'. He also scored over 15 US Top 40 albums, including the 1956 *Calypso*.

1944 Mike D'Abo *(right)*, singer/songwriter with Manfred Mann, who had a 1968 UK No.1 & US No.10 single with 'Mighty Quinn'. He wrote 'Handbags & Gladrags', which was covered by Rod Stewart and the Stereophonics, and 'Build Me Up Buttercup' – a hit for The Foundations.

1944 Roger Daltry – vocalist for The Who, who had a 1965 UK No.2 single with 'My Generation', over 20 other UK hit singles and 16 US Top 40 singles. They also recorded the rock opera albums *Tommy* and *Quadrophenia*.

1958 Nik Kershaw, singer and producer who had a 1984 UK No.2 single with 'I Won't Let The Sun Go Down On Me'.

1973 Ryan Peake – guitarist with Nickelback, who had a 2002 US No.1 & UK No. 4 single with 'How To Remind You' and a 2001 US No.2 & 2002 UK No.2 album with *Silver Side Up*.

ON THIS DAY

1958 Buddy Holly & The Crickets began their only UK tour, a 25 date, twice-nightly package with Des O'Connor, Gary Miller, The Tanner Sisters and Ronnie Keene & His Orchestra.

1961 Elvis Presley signed a five year movie deal with producer Hal Wallis.

1966 Gene Clark of The Byrds announced he was leaving the group due to his fear of flying.

1966 Police were called in after over 100 music fans barricaded themselves inside Liverpool's Cavern Club to protest at the club closing down.

1968 Elton John's first single 'I've Been Loving You Too Long' was released. It didn't chart.

1969 Jim Morrison of The Doors was charged with lewd and lascivious behaviour after showing his penis to the audience during a show in Miami. He was found guilty and sentenced to eight months hard labour. Morrison died in Paris while the sentence was on appeal.

1970 appearing at The Northcote Arms, Middlesex, England was Mott The Hoople, supported by Genesis.

1974 Chris Difford placed an advert in a shop window: "lyricist seeks musician for co-writing". Glen Tillbrook answered the ad. The pair went on to form Squeeze.

1974 Queen began their first headlining UK tour at The Winter Gardens, Blackpool.

1975 Bob Dylan started a two week run at No.1 on the US album chart with *Blood On The Tracks*, his first US No.1.

1975 The Eagles went to No.1 on the US singles chart with 'Best Of My Love', the first of five US No.1s for the band. The highest chart position in the UK for the group was No.8, with the 1977 single 'Hotel California'.

1977 appearing at Friars, Aylesbury, England were Iggy Pop and David Bowie plus The Vibrators.

1979 appearing live at The Hope & Anchor, Islington, London, was Joy Division. Admission was 75p ($1.28).

1980 Blondie were at No.1 on the UK singles chart with 'Atomic', the group's third UK No.1 single.

1989 R.E.M. kicked off the US leg of the "Green World Tour" in Louisville, Kentucky.

1994 Nirvana played their last-ever concert when they appeared at The Terminal Einz in Munich, Germany.

1997 a Motley Crue fan who claimed his hearing had been irreparably damaged after a show in New Jersey had his lawsuit thrown out of court. The judge told Clifford Goldberg, who had sat near the front of the stage, that he knew the risk he was taking.

2001 Sean "Puffy" Combs became the star witness of his own defence in a New York court, claiming he didn't have a gun during a shooting in a New York club. The singer claimed he thought he was being shot at.

Oliver Reed provides a helping hand at Tommy's Holiday camp in the film by The Who.

BORN ON THIS DAY

1943 Lou Reed – singer / songwriter with Velvet Underground, who released the 1967 classic album *The Velvet Underground and Nico*. As a solo artist Reed had a 1973 UK No.10 & US No.16 single with 'Walk On The Wildside' plus a 1997 UK No.1 single with 'Perfect Day'.

1948 Rory Gallagher, Irish blues guitarist, who had a 1970 UK No.18 album with *On The Boards/Taste*. Gallagher died on June 14th 1995.

Lou Reed was not always old and sage-like.

1950 Karen Carpenter – vocalist and drummer with The Carpenters, who had a 1973 UK No.2 single with 'Yesterday Once More' and three US No.1s including the 1975 single 'Please Mr Postman'. She died on February 4th 1983 of anorexia nervosa.

1962 Jon Bon Jovi – vocalist with Bon Jovi, who had a 1987 US No.1 & UK No.4 single 'Livin' On A Prayer'. As a solo artist he had a 1990 UK No.13 single with 'Blaze Of Glory'.

1977 Chris Martin – pianist, guitarist and vocalist with Coldplay, who had a 2000 UK No.4 single with 'Yellow' and the 2005 worldwide No.1 album *X&Y*.

ON THIS DAY

1960 after completing his national service and flying back to America, Elvis Presley stepped on British soil for the first and only time in his life when the plane carrying him stopped for refuelling at Prestwick Airport, Scotland.

1963 The Four Seasons became the first group to have three consecutive No.1s in the US when 'Walk Like A Man' started a three week run at the top. It made No.12 in the UK.

1967 Engelbert Humperdinck was at No.1 on the UK singles chart with 'Release Me'. The singer's first of two No.1s, the song spent six weeks at the top of the chart.

1974 at this year's Grammys Stevie Wonder won four awards: Album of the year for *Innervisions*, Best R&B song and Best vocal for 'Superstition' and Pop vocal performance for 'You Are The Sunshine Of My Life'.

1974 Terry Jacks started a three week run at No.1 on the US singles chart with 'Seasons In The Sun', which was also No.1 in the UK.

1975 an LA policeman who stopped a Lincoln Continental for running a red light was surprised to find Paul McCartney at the wheel, with his wife Linda. The cop detected a smell of marijuana and on searching the car found eight ounces of the drug. Linda was arrested.

1977 The Jam, who had just signed a four year recording contract with Polydor Records, played the first of a five week Wednesday night run at The Red Cow, Hammersmith, London.

1983 a new digital audio system, a 5in (12.7cm) compact disc containing up to one hour of music, was launched by Sony, Philips and Polygram.

Coldplay practice their menacing look.

1985 Wham! started a three week run at No.1 on the US album chart with *Make It Big*, which eventually went on to sell over five million copies in the US.

1989 Madonna started a $5 million (£2.9 million) sponsorship deal with Pepsi Cola.

1991 French singer Serge Gainsbourg died. He was famous for his 1969 UK No.1 duet with Jane Birkin on 'Je T'aime…Moi Non Plus'.

1991 Madonna's 'Rescue Me' entered the US Hot 100 at No.15, making her the highest-debuting female artist in rock history. The record had previously been held by Joy Llayne, whose 1957 single 'Your Wild Heart' entered the chart at No.30.

1991 Mariah Carey started an 11 week run at No.1 on the US album chart with her debut *Mariah Carey*.

1999 UK singer Dusty Springfield died after a long battle against cancer, aged 59.

2002 The *NME* published the winners from this year's Carling Awards: Band of the year, The Strokes; Album of the year, The Strokes, *Is This It*; Best live act, U2; Single of the year, Ash, 'Burn Baby Burn' and Best solo artist, Ian Brown.

2003 singer/songwriter Hank Ballard died from throat cancer. He had written and recorded 'The Twist', but it was only released on the B-side of a record. One year later, Chubby Checker debuted his own version of 'The Twist' on Dick Clark's Philadelphia television show. It topped the charts and launched a dance craze that prompted the creation of other Twist songs, including 'Twist and Shout' by the Isley Brothers and 'Twistin' the Night Away' by Sam Cooke.

Much underrated Ryan brothers appear in Romford in 1967.

BORN ON THIS DAY

1927 Junior Parker, US blues singer/songwriter who wrote 'Mystery Train', which was covered by Elvis Presley. He also worked with BB King and Howlin' Wolf. Parker died on November 18th 1971.

1942 Mike Pender – guitarist and vocalist with The Searchers, who had a 1964 UK No.1 & US No.13 single with 'Needles And Pins'.

1944 Jance Garfat – bass player with Dr. Hook, who had a 1972 US No.5 & UK No.2 single with 'Sylvia's Mother' plus nine other US Top 40 hits.

1947 Jennifer Warnes, singer who had a 1982 US No.1 single 'Up Where We Belong' with Joe Cocker.

1949 Derek "Blue" Weaver – keyboardist with Amen Corner, who had a 1969 UK No.1 single with 'If Paradise Is Half As Nice', then the Strawbs, who had a 1973 UK No.2 single with 'Part Of The Union', and The Bee Gees, who had a 1975 US No.1 with 'Jive Talking'.

1977 Ronan Keating, vocalist with Boyzone, who had a 1996 UK No.1 single with 'Words' plus over 15 other UK Top 10 singles. As a solo artist he had a 1999 UK No.1 single with 'When You Say Nothing At All'.

ON THIS DAY

1966 Neil Young, Stephen Stills and Richie Furay formed Buffalo Springfield in Los Angeles.

1967 a twice-nightly tour kicked off at The ABC in Romford, Essex, UK featuring The Small Faces, Jeff Beck, Roy Orbison and Paul and Barry Ryan.

1969 Led Zeppelin recorded their first BBC Radio 1 session, which was later aired on *Top Gear*.

1973 Slade's 'Cum On Feel The Noize' entered the UK chart at No.1, making Slade the first act to achieve this since The Beatles.

1973 winners at this year's Grammy Awards included: Roberta Flack, who won Song of the year and Record of the year with 'The First Time Ever I Saw Your Face' and Harry Nilsson, who won Best pop vocal performance for 'Without You'.

3/3/99 EXHIBIT Ⓐ

1977 the first night of a UK tour with Johnny Thunders & The Heartbreakers, Cherry Vanilla and The Police kicked off at the Roxy Club, London.

1979 The Bee Gees scored their fourth UK No.1 single with 'Tragedy' and went to No.1 on the US album chat with *Spirits Having Flown*, the brothers' second US No.1 album.

1983 The Eurythmics kicked off a ten date UK tour at The Hacienda, Manchester.

1984 German group Nena were at No.1 on the UK singles chart with '99 Red Balloons'.

1985 Michael Jackson visited Madame Tussauds in London to unveil his waxwork lookalike.

1990 Janet Jackson started a three week run at No.1 on the US singles chart with 'Escapade', her third US No.1. It was a No.17 hit in the UK.

1996 Take That's final single, 'How Deep Is Your Love', started a three week run at UK No.1.

1999 Oasis agreed to pay their former drummer Tony McCarroll a one-off sum of £550,000 ($935,000) after he sued the Manchester band for millions in unpaid royalties. McCarroll had been sacked from the band in 1995.

1999 the first date on a 14 date tour with *NSYNC and B*Witched kicked off in Jacksonville, Florida.

1999 US music professor Peter Jeffrey went to court to sue The Smashing Pumpkins, their promoters and a company who make ear plugs after claiming his hearing was damaged at a concert in Connecticut.

2000 former Bay City Roller, Derek Longmuir was released on bail on charges of downloading child pornographic images from the Internet and keeping indecent videos in his home.

2000 Tom Jones won the Best male artist at this year's Brit Awards. Other winners included Travis for Best band and Best album with *The Man Who*. Best single went to Robbie Williams for 'She's The One', Five won Best pop act, TLC won Best international group, Beck won Best international male and Macy Gray won Best newcomer. Outstanding contribution went to The Spice Girls.

2001 The Stereophonics were forced to change the title of their new album after car manufacturer Daimler Chrysler objected to their use of the copyrighted word "Jeep". The UK title subsequently became *Just Enough Education To Perform*.

BORN ON THIS DAY

1944 Bobby Womack, soul singer and session guitarist who had a 1974 US No.10 single with 'Lookin' For A Love' and a 1993 UK No.27 single with Lulu 'I'm Back For More'.

1948 Chris Squire – bass player with Yes and solo artist. Yes had a 1983 UK No.28 & 1984 US No.1 single with 'Owner Of A Lonely Heart'.

1948 Shakin' Stevens, singer who had a 1981 UK No.1 single with 'This Old House' plus 30 other UK Top 40 singles.

1950 Emilio Estefan – keyboardist with Miami Sound Machine, which had a 1984 UK No.6 single with 'Dr Beat' and a 1989 US No.1 single with 'Don't Wanna Lose You'.

1951 Chris Rea, singer/songwriter and guitarist, who had a 1989 UK No.10 single with 'The Road To Hell'.

1963 Jason Newsted – bassist with Metallica, who had a 1991 UK No.5 single with 'Enter Sandman' and a 1991 US & UK No.1 album with *Metallica*.

1967 Evan Dando – guitarist and vocalist with The Lemonheads, who had a 1993 UK No.14 single with 'Into Your Arms'.

1968 Patsy Kensit – actress, star of the 1986 film *Absolute Beginners* and singer with Eighth Wonder, who had a 1988 UK No.7 single with 'I'm Not Scared'. She was once married to Simple Minds singer Jim Kerr then married Oasis singer Liam Gallagher in 1997 (they divorced in 2000).

ON THIS DAY

1966 John Lennon's statement that The Beatles were "more popular than Jesus Christ" appeared in the *London Evening Standard*, resulting in some US states burning Beatles records. Lennon said; "Christianity will go. It will vanish and shrink. We're more popular then Jesus now; I don't know which will go first, rock 'n' roll or Christianity. Jesus was alright, but his disciples were thick and ordinary."

Chris Squire: a sticker shows his post-mod period after The Syn.

1971 The Rolling Stones announced that they were to become Britain's first rock 'n' roll tax exiles, residing in France.

1977 CBS released The Clash's self-titled first album, but CBS in the US refused to release it until 1979. Americans would go on to buy 100,000 imported copies of *The Clash*, making it one of the biggest-selling import records of all time.

1978 Andy Gibb started a two week run at No.1 on the US singles chart with '(Love Is) Thicker Than Water', giving The Bee Gee's younger brother his second US No.1.

1978 The US Internal Revenue Service carried out a dawn raid at the home of Jerry Lee Lewis and removed cars worth over £100,000 ($170,000) to pay off his tax debts.

Mick Taylor and Keith Richards become accustomed to the occasional Pastis and Pernod in France.

1979 Randy Jackson of The Jackson Five was seriously injured in a car crash, breaking both legs and almost dying in the emergency room when a nurse inadvertently injected him with methadone.

1994 Kurt Cobain was rushed to hospital after overdosing on alcohol and drugs in a Rome hotel during a Nirvana European tour. Cobain had taken 50–60 pills of Rohypnol mixed with champagne. Rumours on the Internet claimed that Kurt was dead.

2001 Village People singer Glenn Hughes died of lung cancer, aged 50.

2003 a noisy neighbour had her stereo system impounded after playing Cliff Richard music too loudly. 23-year-old Sian Davies was fined £1,000 ($1,700) plus court costs after environmental protection officers raided her flat in Porth, Rhondda, Wales and seized 15 amplifiers and speakers, plus 135 CDs and tapes. The disc found in her CD player was the Cliff Richard single, 'Peace in Our Time'. A spokesman for the Cliff Richard Organization said he was delighted to hear of somebody in their early 20s owning one of his many recordings. He added that Cliff would not want anyone to play his music so that it caused a nuisance.

BORN ON THIS DAY

1948 Eddy Grant – singer with The Equals, who had a 1968 UK No.1 single with 'Baby Come Back'. As a solo artist he had a 1982 UK No.1 single with 'I Don't Wanna Dance'.

1952 Alan Clark – keyboardist with Dire Straits, who had a 1985 US No.1 single with 'Money For Nothing' and a 1986 UK No.2 single with 'Walk Of Life'.

1957 Mark E Smith – singer with The Fall, who had a 1987 UK No.30 single with 'There's A Ghost In My House'.

1958 Andy Gibb, younger brother of The Bee Gees. He had a 1978 UK No.10 single with 'An Everlasting Love' and a 1978 US No.1 single with 'Shadow Dancing', which spent seven weeks at the top, plus two other US No.1 singles. Gibb died on March 10th 1988.

1962 Craig and Charlie Reid, singers/songwriters who formed The Proclaimers and had a 1987 UK No.3 single with 'Letter From America'.

1970 John Frusciante – guitarist with Red Hot Chili Peppers, who had a 1992 UK No.26 single with 'Under The Bridge', 1991 US No.3 album *Blood Sugar Sex Magik* and a 2002 UK No.1 album *By The Way*.

ON THIS DAY

1955 Elvis Presley made his TV debut when he appeared on the weekend show *Louisiana Hayride* on KWKH-TV.

Possibly two photos of the same Proclaimer. Possibly not. You decide.

1963 country singer Patsy Cline was killed in a plane crash at Dyersburg, Virginia, along with The Cowboy Copas and Hawkshaw Hawkins. They were travelling to Nashville to appear at a benefit concert for DJ "Cactus" Jack Call, who'd died in a car crash. Cline had been the first country singer to cross over as a pop artist. Two days later country singer Jack Anglin was killed in a car crash on his way to Cline's funeral.

1965 The Mannish Boys (featuring a young David Bowie), released their debut single 'I Pity The Fool'.

1965 The Rolling Stones kicked off their fifth UK tour at The Regal Theatre, Edmonton, London. It was a 14 date package tour with The Hollies, The Konrads and Dave Berry And The Cruisers.

1971 Led Zeppelin started a 12 date "thank you" tour for British fans, appearing at the clubs from their early days and charging the admission price from 1968. The first show was at The Ulster Hall, Belfast.

1973 the former US manager of Jimi Hendrix, Michael Jeffrey, was one of 68 people killed in a plane crash in France. Jeffery was en route to a court appearance in London related to Hendrix.

1975 Rod Stewart met Swedish actress Britt Ekland at a party in Los Angeles. They went on to have a high-profile love affair.

1983 Michael Jackson started a seven week run at No.1 on the US singles chart with 'Billie Jean', his fourth solo US No.1 – it was also No.1 in the UK. And on this day Jackson's album *Thriller* went to No.1 for the first time on the UK album chart; it went on to become the biggest-selling album of all time, with sales of over 40 million.

1992 R.E.M. cleaned up in the *Rolling Stone* Music Awards winning: Album of the year, for *Out Of Time*; Artist of the year; Best single, for 'Losing My Religion'; Best video for 'Losing My Religion'; Best band; Best guitarist and Best songwriter.

2000 former rap artist MC Hammer became a preacher at the Jubilee Christian Center in San Jose. Hammer had been declared bankrupt in 1996 after squandering his $50 million (£29.4 million) fortune.

2000 Madonna went to No.1 on the UK singles chart with her version of the Don McLean hit 'American Pie.' It was her 50th UK hit and the singer's ninth UK No.1.

The very pot used by home-loving Madonna to cook up her version of American Pie.

2002 the first episode of *The Osbournes* TV show was aired on MTV in the US. It focuses on the madman and his family (his wife Sharon and two of their three children). Oblivious to the camera, they bicker, squabble, curse and hang out backstage at Ozzy shows.

BORN ON THIS DAY

1893 Memphis blues artist Walter "Furry" Lewis. He was the first guitarist to play with a bottleneck. He lost a leg in a railroad accident and once supported The Rolling Stones. Joni Mitchell wrote the song 'Furry Sings The Blues' after him. Lewis died on September 14th 1981, aged 88.

1944 Dave Gilmour – guitarist with Pink Floyd, who had a 1973 US No.1 & UK No.2 album *Dark Side Of The Moon*, which spent a record-breaking 741 weeks on the US chart.

1944 Mary Wilson – vocalist with The Supremes, who had a 1964 UK & US No.1 single with 'Baby Love' plus 11 other US No.1 singles.

1945 Hugh Grundy – drummer for The Zombies, who had a 1964 US No.2 & UK No.12 single with 'She's Not There'.

1946 Murray Head, singer who had a 1984 UK No.1 & 1985 US No.3 single with 'One Night In Bangkok'.

1947 Kiki Dee, singer and actress who had a 1976 UK & US No.1 single with Elton John, 'Don't Go Breaking My Heart'.

ON THIS DAY

1961 George Formby, UK singing comedian and ukulele player, died, aged 57. He had made over 20 films and his best-known song is 'Leaning On A Lamp Post'. Formby was made an OBE in 1946.

1965 The Temptations went to No.1 in the US with the Smokey Robinson-penned song 'My Girl', making the group the first male act to have a No.1 for Motown. The single only reached No.43 in the UK but made No.2 when reissued in 1992.

1970 Awareness Records released the Charles Manson album *Lie*. Manson was unable to promote the LP due to the fact he was serving a life sentence for the Sharon Tate murders.

1973 an attempt to bring Elvis Presley to the UK for shows at London's Earl's Court failed.

Dave Gilmour (back-row, third from right) plays the vital midfield-general role.

Promoters had hoped that Elvis would be available during the summer but were told that Elvis had a US tour and filming commitments.

1976 The Eagles started a five week run at No.1 on the US album chart with their *Greatest Hits 1971–1975*. It stayed on the chart for 57 weeks.

1982 The Go-Go's started a six week run at No.1 on the US album chart with *Beauty And The Beast*.

1982 Tight Fit were at No.1 on the UK singles chart with their version of The Tokens' hit 'The Lion Sleeps Tonight'.

1986 Richard Manuel of The Band hung himself from a shower curtain rod in a hotel room in Florida.

1998 Oasis singer Liam Gallagher appeared handcuffed in a Brisbane court and was released on bail on charges of headbutting a fan during a gig in Australia.

2001 a man who hid for a period of 24 hours in the rafters of a cathedral and secretly filmed the christening of Madonna's baby appeared in court. Security staff discovered the man after the ceremony when he made a noise as he climbed down from the rafters.

2004 Diane Richie, the estranged wife of singer Lionel Richie, went to court seeking $300,000 (£176,500) a month in maintenance support. Diane's monthly costs included: $20,000 (£11,800) a year on plastic surgery; $15,000 (£8,824) a month for clothing, shoes and accessories; $5,000 (£2,940) on jewellery and $600 (£353) on massages.

Famous English alternative to plastic surgery and hair-loss.

2004 David Crosby was arrested and charged with criminal possession of a weapon and marijuana after leaving his bag in a New York hotel. The luggage was found by a hotel employee looking for identification – finding instead a handgun and marijuana.

BORN ON THIS DAY

1945 Arthur Lee – guitarist and vocalist with Love, who had a 1966 US No.33 single with '7 And 7 Is' and a 1968 UK No.24 album with *Forever Changes*.

1945 Chris White – bassist with The Zombies, who had a 1964 US No.2 & UK No.12 single with 'She's Not There'.

1946 Matthew Fisher – keyboardist with Procol Harum, who had a 1967 UK No.1 & US No.5 single with 'A Whiter Shade Of Pale'.

1946 Peter Wolf – vocalist for The J. Geils Band, who had a 1982 US No.1 & UK No.3 single with 'Centerfold'. Wolf was once married to actress Faye Dunaway.

1952 Ernie Isley of The Isley Brothers, who had a 1968 UK No.3 single with 'This Old Heart Of Mine' and a 1969 US No.2 single with 'Its Your Thing'.

1977 Paul Cattermole – vocalist with S Club 7, who had a 1999 UK No.1 single with 'Bring It All Back'.

ON THIS DAY

1965 During a Rolling Stones gig at The Palace Theatre in Manchester a teenage fan fell from the circle while the group were on stage. The crowd below broke her fall and she escaped serious injury.

1966 Tina Turner recorded her vocal on the Phil Spector produced 'River Deep Mountain High'. It went on to make No.3 in the UK but only No.88 in the US.

1970 Simon & Garfunkel's album *Bridge Over Troubled Water* started a ten week stay at No.1 on the US chart. The duo had split by the time of release.

1973 During a "Showcase" gig at Max's Kansas City, New York, CBS Records boss John Hammond suffered a heart attack. The event was to mark the signing of his new act Bruce Springsteen.

'The Boss', Bruce Springsteen, surrounded by his heavies.

1976 Elton John was immortalized in wax at Madame Tussauds in London. He was the first rock star to be so since The Beatles.

1987 The Beastie Boys became the first rap act to have a No.1 album in the US with their debut album *Licensed To Ill*.

1991 George Michael was voted the best male singer and sexiest male artist by the readers of *Rolling Stone*.

1999 Boyzone scored their fifth UK No. 1 single with 'When The Going Gets Tough'. It was recorded for the Comic Relief charity and had been a 1986 No.1 single for Billy Ocean.

2000 Oasis singer Liam Gallagher won the Best Dressed Man Award from fashion magazine *GQ*.

2001 the man who discovered Blur, David Balfe, won a high court battle to earn £250,000 ($425,000) in back royalties. Balfe had waged a legal battle for over two years to regain the royalties after selling his Food Records label to EMI in 1994.

2002 former Visage singer Steve Strange was attacked and robbed when on his way to a party in West London. He was robbed of a bracelet given to him by Kylie Minogue and hit over the head, resulting in his needing 18 stitches.

2004 The Smiths' song 'I Know It's Over' topped a poll of tunes that people turn to when they are miserable. This was "The Songs That Saved Your Life" poll run by BBC radio station 6 Music. R.E.M.'s 'Everybody Hurts' and Radiohead's 'Fake Plastic Trees' also made the Top 10.

BORN ON THIS DAY

1942 Ralph Ellis – guitarist and vocalist with The Swinging Blue Jeans, who had a 1964 UK No.2 & US No.24 single with 'Hippy Hippy Shake'.

1943 Andrew Semple – guitarist and vocalist with The Fortunes, who had a 1965 UK No.2 & US No.7 single with 'You've Got Your Troubles'.

1945 Michael Dolenz – vocalist and drummer with The Monkees, who had a 1967 UK & US No.1 single with 'I'm A Believer' plus ten US and eight UK Top 40 singles.

1946 Carole Bayer Sager, singer/songwriter who wrote 'Groovy Kind Of Love', which was a hit for The Mindbenders and Phil Collins. Frank Sinatra, Gene Pitney and Dolly Parton have all recorded her songs. Sager married Burt Bacharach in 1982.

1947 Mike Allsup – guitarist with Three Dog Night, who had a 1970 UK No.3 & US No.1 single with 'Mamma Told Me Not To Come'.

1948 Mel Galley – guitarist with Whitesnake, who had a 1987 US No.1 & UK No.9 single with 'Here I Go Again'.

1954 Cheryl Baker – singer with Bucks Fizz, who had a 1981 UK No.1 single 'Making Your Mind Up', plus 12 other UK Top 40 singles.

1957 Clive Burr – drummer with Iron Maiden, who had a 1982 UK No.1 album with *The Number Of The Beast*.

1958 Gary Numan – singer with the Tubeway Army, who had a 1979 UK No.1 single with 'Are Friends Electric?' As a solo artist he had a 1979 UK No.1 & 1980 US No.9 single with 'Cars' plus 18 other UK Top 40 singles.

1979 Tom Chaplin – vocalist with Keane, who had a 2004 UK No.1 album with *Hopes And Fears*.

ON THIS DAY

1954 The Stargazers were at No.1 on the UK singles chart with 'I See The Moon', the group's second No.1.

1962 The Beatles made their radio debut on the BBC's "Teenagers Turn, (Here We Go)", singing Roy Orbison's 'Dream Baby'.

1965 David Bowie made his TV debut with The Manish Boys on a UK programme called *Gadzooks! It's All Happening* when they performed their current single 'I Pity The Fool'.

1966 Lulu became the first British female singer to appear behind the Iron Curtain when she toured Poland with The Hollies.

1968 appearing at New York's Filmore East, were Albert King, Janis Joplin and Tim Buckley.

1970 Diana Ross made her first performance as a solo act when she appeared in Framingham, Massachusetts.

1973 Paul McCartney was fined £100 ($170) for growing cannabis at his farm in Campbeltown, Scotland. McCartney claimed some fans gave the seeds to him and that he didn't know what they would grow.

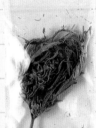

Macca's golden Scottish harvest.

1973 Ron Mckernan, keyboard player with The Grateful Dead, died aged 27 from liver failure brought on by alcohol poisoning.

1975 Olivia Newton John went to No.1 on the US singles chart with 'Have You Ever Been Mellow', the singer's second US No.1.

1986 Diana Ross was at No.1 on the UK singles chart with the Gibb Brothers' written and produced song 'Chain Reaction'.

1986 Whitney Houston went to No.1 on the US album chart with her self-titled album. It spent a total of 14 weeks at the No.1 position.

1990 Cher won the worst dressed female and worst video for 'If I Could Turn Back Time', in the *Rolling Stone* magazine's awards. Donny Osmond won the most unwelcome comeback award.

2001 Winners in *Rock Sound* readers' poll included: Pitchshifter, Best British band; Slipknot, 'Wait & Bleed', Best single; Foo Fighters, 'Breakout', Best video; Marilyn Manson, *Holy Wood*, Best album and Limp Bizkit won Worst band.

2003 singer and actor Adam Faith *(above)* died. He had had a 1959 UK No.1 single with 'What Do You Want', plus over 20 other UK Top 40 singles. His acting roles included the TV series 'Love Hurts'.

BORN ON THIS DAY

1942 Mark Linday - singer, guitarist with Paul Revere & The Raiders, who had a 1971 US No.1 single with 'Indian Reservation' plus 14 other US Top 30 hit singles.

1944 Trevor Burton – guitarist and bass guitarist with The Move, who had a 1969 UK No.1 single with 'Blackberry Way'.

1945 Ron Wilson – drummer with The Surfaris, who had a 1963 US No.2 & UK No.3 single with 'Wipe Out'. Wilson died on May 19th 1989.

1945 Robin Trower – guitarist with Procol Harum, who had a 1967 UK No.1 single & US No.5 with 'A Whiter Shade Of Pale'. Trower also had three Top 20 solo albums.

1946 Jim Cregan – guitarist with Family then Cockney Rebel, who had a 1975 UK No.1 single 'Make Me Smile (Come Up And See Me)'. Cregan also works with Rod Stewart.

1948 Chris Thompson – vocalist with Manfred Mann's Earth Band, who had a 1976 UK No.6 single with 'Blinded By The Light'; this was a US No.1 in 1977.

1951 Frank Rodriguez – keyboardist with ? & The Mysterians, who had a 1966 US No. 1 & UK No.37 single with '96 Tears'. The song was a UK No.17 hit for The Stranglers in 1990.

1958 Martin Fry – vocalist with ABC, who had a 1982 UK No.4 & 1983 US No.18 with 'The Look Of Love' plus nine other UK Top 40 singles.

Radiohead started touring with their highly acclaimed second album *The Bends* in 1995.

ON THIS DAY

1963 appearing at the East Ham Granada, London were Tommy Roe, Chris Montez and, bottom of the bill, The Beatles.

1966 The Beach Boys started recording 'God Only Knows'. It went on to be a UK No.2 single in 1966 and the B-side of 'Wouldn't It Be Nice' in the US.

1967 appearing at the Skyline Ballroom, Hull, Yorkshire were The Small Faces, Family and The Strollers.

1968 Bob Dylan started a ten week run at No.1 on the UK chart with his ninth album *John Wesley Harding*. It was a US No.2 in the same year.

1975 actor Telly Savalas was at No.1 on the UK singles chart with 'If'. Savalas was currently high in the TV ratings playing the policeman Kojak.

1977 *The Jacksons* CBS show was aired for the last time on US TV, finishing at the bottom of the ratings.

1981 Robert Plant played a secret gig at Keele University, England with his new band The Honey Drippers.

1985 Dead Or Alive were at No.1 on the UK singles chart with 'You Spin Me Round (Like A Record)'. It was the first No.1 for the production team of Stock, Aitken and Waterman, who went on to produce over 100 UK Top 40 hits.

1985 Mick Jagger released his solo single 'Just Another Night', which made No.12 in the US and No.32 on the UK charts.

1991 Chris Rea scored his second UK No.1 album with *Auberge*, the follow up to *The Road To Hell*.

1991 Mariah Carey started a two week run at No.1 on the US singles chart with 'Someday', her third US No.1. It went to No.38 in the UK.

1991 'Should I Stay Or Should I Go' gave The Clash their only UK No.1 single after the track was used for a Levi's TV advertisement. The track was first released in 1982.

1995 Radiohead kicked off a 13 date UK tour to promote their new album *The Bends*.

1996 Oasis guitarist Noel Gallagher walked off stage during a gig at the Vernon Valley Gorge ski resort in New Jersey because his hands were too cold to play.

1996 Take That scored their eighth and last UK No.1 single with their version of The Bee Gees' song 'How Deep Is Your Love'. It stayed at the top for three weeks.

1997 Notorious B.I.G. was gunned down and killed as he left a party at the Petersen Automotive Museum in Los Angeles. Born Christopher Wallace, the rapper was pronounced dead on arrival at Cedars Sinai Hospital. He was 24 years old.

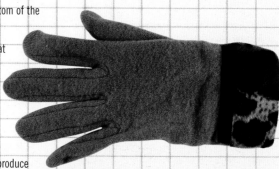

Roadcrew sackings followed the loss of essential equipment for Noel Gallagher.

BORN ON THIS DAY

1940 Dean Torrence – singer with duo Jan & Dean, who had a 1963 US No.1 & UK No.26 single with 'Surf City', which was co-written by Beach Boy Brian Wilson.

1945 Pete Nelson – vocalist with The Flower Pot Men, who had a 1967 UK No.1 single with 'Let's Go To San Francisco'.

1947 Tom Scholz – guitarist and keyboard player with Boston, who had a 1977 UK No.23 single with 'More Than A Feeling' and a 1986 US No.1 single with 'Amanda'.

1963 Jeff Ament – bass player for Pearl Jam, who had a 1992 UK No.15 single with 'Jeremy' and a 1993 US No.1 album with *Vs.*

1964 Neneh Cherry, singer who had a 1988 UK & US No.3 single with 'Buffalo Stance' and a 1994 UK No.3 single with '7 Seconds' with Youssou N'dour.

1965 Edie Brickell, US singer who had a 1989 UK No.31 single with the New Bohemians, 'What I Am'. The song also a 1999 hit for Spice Girl Emma Bunton. Edie married Paul Simon in 1992.

ON THIS DAY

1956 RCA Records placed a half-page ad in *Billboard* magazine claiming that Elvis Presley was "the new singing rage".

1960 UK trade paper *Record Retailer* published the UK's first-ever EP (extended player) chart and LP chart. No.1 EP was 'Expresso Bongo' by Cliff Richard & The Shadows and No.1 LP was *The Explosive Freddy Cannon*.

1962 Bruce Channel started a three week run at No.1 on the US singles chart with 'Hey! Baby'. The song made No.2 on the UK chart.

1967 The Monkees held the No.1 position on the US album chart with *More Of The Monkees*.

1973 Pink Floyd's *Dark Side Of The Moon* was released in the US. Over a 14 year period the album spent over 740 weeks on the chart.

1977 on a trestle-table set up outside Buckingham Palace, London, at 7am in the morning, The Sex Pistols signed to A&M Records. The contract lasted for six days.

1979 Gloria Gaynor started a three-week run at No.1 on the US singles chart with 'I Will Survive'. The song, which was also a No.1 in the UK, was originally a B-side.

1984 Van Halen held the No.1 position on the US singles chart with 'Jump'.

1988 singer and brother of The Bee Gees Andy Gibb died in hospital five days after his 30th birthday. His death followed a long battle with cocaine addiction, which had weakened his heart.

1995 former Stone Roses' manager Gareth Evans' £10 million ($17 million) lawsuit with the band was settled out of court over alleged wrongful dismissal – for an undisclosed sum.

1996 Alanis Morissette won Best album for *Jagged Little Pill*, Best female singer, Best rock album, Best songwriter and Best single at the 25th Juno Awards held in Hamilton, Canada.

2000 Pretenders' Chrissie Hynde was arrested for leading an animal rights protest against the clothing firm Gap, who were accused of using leather from cows slaughtered "illegally and cruelly". The protest took place in a store in Manhattan.

2001 it was reported that US manufacturers Art Asylum planned to send over 100,000 Eminem dolls to shops in the UK. The life-like figure had the rapper's tattoos recreated in detail, including the words "Cut Here" on his neck.

2000 the *Daily Mail* published pictures of Paul McCartney dancing with a cowgirl on the bar of a New York club. McCartney sang along to 'Whole Lotta Shakin' through a megaphone and mimicked a striptease in front of 100 onlookers.

2002 UK TV's *Pop Idol* winner Will Young revealed in an exclusive *News Of The World* interview that he was gay, saying "It's no big deal, it's just part of who I am".

2004 Corey Taylor from Slipknot married his long-time girlfriend, Scarlett.

> "I decided I'd like to enter art college if we flopped in show business."
> **Paul McCartney**

ON THIS DAY

1944 Ric Rothwell – drummer with The Mindbenders, who had a 1965 US No.1 single with 'Game Of Love' and a 1966 UK No.2 single with 'Groovy Kind Of Love'.

1947 Mark Stein – keyboardist with Vanilla Fudge, who had a 1968 US No.6 single with 'You Keep Me Hangin' On'.

1950 Bobby McFerrin, US singer/songwriter, who had a 1988 US No.1 & UK No.2 single with 'Don't Worry Be Happy'.

1968 Lisa Loeb, US singer who had a 1994 US No.1 & UK No.6 single with 'Stay, I Missed You', from the film *Reality Bites*.

1979 Joel Madden (vocalist) and Benji Madden (guitarist and vocalist) with Good Charlotte, who had a 2002 US No.7 album with *The Young And The Hopeless* and a 2003 UK No.6 single with 'Girls and Boys'.

1981 LaToya – singer with Destiny's Child, who had a 2000 US No.1 and worldwide hit single with 'Independent Woman Part 1'.

ON THIS DAY

1963 The Mann Hugg Blues Brothers (later to become Manfred Mann) played at London's Marquee Club.

1965 Tom Jones *(right)* was at No.1 on the UK singles chart with 'It's Not Unusual'. It was the Welsh singer's first of 16 UK Top 40 hits during the 60s.

1967 The Supremes had their ninth US No.1 single with 'Love Is Here And Now You're Gone'. It made No.17 in the UK.

1967 music publisher Dick James announced that 446 different versions of the Paul McCartney song 'Yesterday' had been recorded so far.

1968 the Otis Redding single 'Dock Of The Bay' went Gold three months after the singer was killed in a plane crash.

1970 winners at this year's Grammy Awards included: Joe South for Song of the year with 'Games People Play'; Crosby, Stills & Nash won Best new artist and The Fifth Dimension won Record of the year with 'Aquarius/Let The Sun Shine In'.

1971 Jim Morrison of The Doors arrived in Paris, booking into The Hotel George's. The following week he moved into an apartment at 17 Rue Beautreillis in Paris. Morrison lived in Paris until his death on July 3rd 1971.

1972 Neil Young went to No.1 on the US & UK album chart with *Harvest*, which featured the hit single 'Heart Of Gold'.

1977 The Clash appeared at The Roxy Club, London supported by The Slits, the first all-female punk group who were making their live debut.

1978 French singer Claude Francois was electrocuted changing a light bulb while standing in his bathtub. He had had the 1976 UK hit 'Tears On The Telephone'.

1978 Meat Loaf's *Bat Out Of Hell* album began a 416 week run on the UK chart, going on to sell over two million copies.

1978 the debut single from Kate Bush, 'Wuthering Heights', a song inspired by the Emily Bronte novel, started a four week run at No.1 on the UK singles chart.

1989 Debbie Gibson started a five week run at No.1 on the US album chart with *Electric Youth*.

1989 'Too Many Broken Hearts' gave Australian actor turned singer Jason Donovan his first solo UK No.1 single.

1993 Oasis recorded their first demos at The Real People's Studio in Liverpool. The set included 'Rock 'n' Roll Star', 'Columbia' and 'Fade Away'.

1996 Pulp singer Jarvis Cocker walked free from Kensington police station after police failed to charge him with any criminal offence following his "stage invasion" during Michael Jackson's performance at the Brit Awards in London on February 19th 1996.

2000 Destiny's Child went to No.1 on the US singles chart with 'Say My Name'.

2001 Dave Matthews Band started a two week run at No.1 on the US album chart with *Everyday*.

BORN ON THIS DAY

1917 Leonard Chess, the founder of the Chess record label, which was home to John Lee Hooker, Chuck Berry, Bo Diddley and Jimmy Reed. Chess died of a heart attack on October 16th 1969, aged 52.

1942 Paul Kantner – guitarist with Jefferson Airplane, who had a 1967 US No.18 single with 'White Rabbit'.

1946 Liza Minnelli, singer, actress, dancer and daughter of Judy Garland and film director Vincente Minnelli. She was in the 1970 film *Cabaret* and had a 1989 UK No.6 single with 'Losing My Mind'.

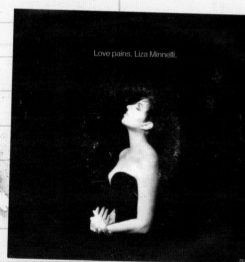

Love pains. Liza Minnelli.

Lisa Minelli in 'great record shocker'.

1948 James Taylor, singer/songwriter, who had a 1971 US No.1 & UK No.4 single with 'You've Got A Friend'. His first album was released on The Beatles' Apple label. Taylor married Carly Simon in 1972.

1949 Mike Gibbins – drummer and vocalist with Badfinger, who had a 1970 UK No.4 & US No.7 single with 'Come And Get It'.

1957 Marlon Jackson – singer with The Jackson Five, who had a 1970 US No.1 & UK No.2 single with 'I Want You Back'. As The Jacksons they had a 1977 UK No.1 single with 'Show You The Way To Go'.

1969 Graham Coxon – guitarist with Blur, who had a 1994 UK No.1 album with *Park Life*, which spent over two years on the UK chart, a 1995 UK No.1 single with 'Country House' plus over 12 other UK Top 40 singles.

1979 Peter Doherty – guitarist and vocalist of The Libertines, who had a 2004 UK No.1 album with *The Libertines*. He now fronts Babyshambles.

ON THIS DAY

1955 Jazz saxophonist Charlie Parker died of a heart attack in New York while watching Tommy Dorsey's Orchestra on television. He was 34.

1958 Jazz singer Billie Holiday was sentenced to a year's probation by a Philadelphia court after being found guilty of narcotics possession.

1969 Paul McCartney married Linda Eastman at Marylebone registry office, London. George Harrison and his wife Patti were late for the wedding after being arrested in the morning and charged with possession of 120 joints of marijuana.

1974 John Lennon made the headlines after an incident at the Troubadour Club in West Hollywood when out on a drinking binge with Harry Nilsson. Lennon hurled insults at the Smothers Brothers, who were playing in the club, and punched their manager before being forcibly removed from the venue.

1977 The Sex Pistols were involved in a fight at London's Speakeasy Club with Bob Harris, presenter of BBC 2's *The Old Grey Whistle Test*. It resulted in one of the show's engineers needing 14 stitches in his head.

1981 Bow Wow Wow were forced to cancel the first dates of a UK tour after Greater London Council stated that singer Annabella Lwin, aged 15, would be guilty of truancy.

1983 Welsh singer Bonnie Tyler had her only UK No.1 single with 'Total Eclipse Of The Heart'.

1983 U2 scored their first UK No.1 album with

War, which went on to spend a total of 147 weeks on the chart and featured the singles 'New Year's Day' and 'Two Hearts Beat As One'.

1988 Rick Astley started a two week run at No.1 on the US singles chart with 'Never Gonna Give You Up'. The song was also a No.1 in the UK.

1994 Swedish group Ace Of Base started a six week run at No.1 on the US singles chart with 'The Sign', which was a No.2 hit in the UK.

1995 The Spin Doctors played a gig at singer Chris Barron's old school in Princeton and raised $10,000 (£5,882) towards a trip to France and the UK for the school choir.

2001 Judy Garland's 'Over The Rainbow' was voted the Song Of The Century in a poll published in *America*. Musicians, critics and fans compiled the list, which was published by the R.I.A.A. The highest-placed UK act was The Rolling Stones' 'Satisfaction', in 16th place. The Beatles had 'I Want To Hold Your Hand' at No.28.

BORN ON THIS DAY

1939 Neil Sedaka, singer/songwriter who had a 1959 UK No.3 single with 'Oh Carol' plus over 30 US and 14 UK other Top 40 singles, including the 1962 US No.1 & UK No.7 single 'Breaking Up Is Hard To Do'.

1959 Ronnie Rogers – guitarist with T'Pau, who had a 1987 UK No. 1 with 'China In Your Hand' and a 1987 US No.4 single with 'Heart And Soul'.

1960 Adam Clayton – bass player with U2, who had a 1984 UK No.3 single with 'Pride, In The Name Of Love' plus over 25 other UK Top 40 singles and the 1987 UK and worldwide No.1 album *The Joshua Tree*.

1979 Toni Lundow – vocalist with Liberty X, who had a 2002 UK No.1 single with 'Just A Little'.

ON THIS DAY

1956 RCA Records issued the first album and extended play releases by Elvis Presley.

1958 The Recording Industry Association of America (R.I.A.A.) introduced its awards for record sales. The Beatles hold the record for being awarded the most, with 76 platinum certifications.

1960 Johnny Preston was at No.1 on the UK singles chart with 'Running Bear', which was also No.1 in the US.

1965 Eric Clapton left The Yardbirds, apparently dissatisfied with the group's direction.

1965 The Beatles started a two week run at No.1 on the US singles chart with 'Eight Days A Week', the group's seventh US No.1.

1965 Tom Jones made his first major TV appearance on BBC TV's *Billy Cotton Band Show*.

1966 Rod Stewart left Steampacket to start work as a solo artist.

1972 Harry Nilsson was at No.1 on the UK singles chart with his version of The Peter Ham and Tom Evans song 'Without You'. The song was also a No.1 for Mariah Carey in 1994.

1975 Tammy Wynette and George Jones were divorced after six years of marriage.

1976 The Four Seasons started a three week run at No.1 on the US singles chart with 'December

1963 (Oh What A Night)', the group's fifth US No.1 and their only UK No.1.

1977 Manhattan Transfer were at No.1 on the UK singles chart with 'Chanson D'amour', the group's only UK No.1.

1985 Bob Geldof and Midge Ure received the bestselling A-side award at the 30th Ivor Novello Awards for 'Do They Know It's Christmas?'

1993 Canadian rapper Snow (a.k.a. Darrin O'Brien) started a seven week run at No.1 on the US singles chart with 'Informer', which was a No.2 hit in the UK. The rapper had been serving time in prison for G.B.H. when the single was released.

1993 Eric Clapton started a three week run at No.1 on the US album chart with *Unplugged*.

1993 Lenny Kravitz started a two week run at No.1 on the UK album chart with *Are You Gonna Go My Way?*

1993 this week's Radio 1's UK Top 40 Chart Show was in chaos after Gallup, who compiled the chart, got 20 of the 40 positions wrong.

1994 Mariah Carey started a three week run at No.1 on the UK album chart with *Music Box*.

1998 Judge Dread (Alex Hughes) died after collapsing on stage during a performance in Canterbury. He achieved ten UK hit singles during the 70s.

1999 Cher started a four week run at No.1 on the US singles chart with 'Believe', which was also a No.1 in the UK.

1999 TLC went to No.1 on the US album chart with *Fanmail*.

Not earning a packet yet: Rod Stewart on the left.

BORN ON THIS DAY

1933 Quincy Jones, producer, bandleader and musician who had a 1978 US No.1 single with 'Stuff Like That' and a 1981 UK No.11 single with 'Razzamatazz'. He also had great success as a producer, working on, for example, Michael Jackson's *Thriller* and *Off The Wall*.

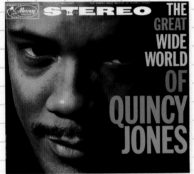

1945 Walter Parazaider – sax player with Chicago, who had a 1976 UK & US No.1 single with 'If You Leave Me Now'.

1946 Jim Pons – bass guitarist with The Turtles, who had a 1967 US No.1 single 'Happy Together', and UK No. 4 with 'She'd Rather Be With Me'.

1983 Jordan Taylor Hanson – keyboardist and vocalist with Hanson, who had a 1997 UK & US No.1 single with 'MMMbop'.

ON THIS DAY

1973 Elton John was at No.1 on the US singles chart with 'Crocodile Rock'.

1981 Eric Clapton was hospitalized with bleeding ulcers, which caused a US tour to be cancelled. He was back in hospital five weeks later after being involved in a car crash.

1981 Roxy Music were at No.1 on the UK singles chart with their version of the John Lennon song 'Jealous Guy'.

1983 Jon Bon Jovi, Richie Sambora and Alec John Such formed Bon Jovi.

1985 appearing live at Sheffield City Hall, England was Frankie Goes To Hollywood.

1985 Dead Or Alive were kicked off UK TV music show *The Tube* after admitting they were incapable of appearing "live".

1987 Boy George scored his first UK No.1 single as a solo artist with the David Gates' song 'Everything I Own'. The song was also a UK No.1 for Ken Boothe in 1974.

1987 Huey Lewis & The News went to No.1 on the US singles chart with 'Jacob's Ladder'. The song was not a hit in the UK.

London's Borderline Club under the name of "Bingo Hand Job".

1998 Will Smith started a three week run at No.1 on the US singles chart with 'Getting' Jiggy Wit It'.

1999 Stereophonics went to No.1 on the UK album chart with *Performance And Cocktails*, making them only the third Welsh band to score a No.1. It was also the first No.1 album for Richard Branson's V2 label.

2001 former Spice Girl Geri Halliwell was banned from driving for six weeks and fined £400 ($680) for speeding in her Aston Martin DB7. Geri had been snapped on a speed camera doing 60mph in a 30mph zone.

Frankie Goes to Hollywood, backstage in Sheffield 1985.

1990 Flea and Chad Smith from The Red Hot Chili Peppers were arrested for sexually harassing a woman on Daytona Beach, Florida. They were each fined $1,000 (£588).

1990 Michael Jackson was voted artist of the decade at the annual Soul Train Awards.

1991 R.E.M. played the first of two nights at

2001 Peter Blake, who designed The Beatles' classic *Sgt. Pepper* album cover, sued the group's record company for more money.

2002 Alicia Keys played a show in a suite at the House of Commons after young Labour MP David Lammy had booked the American singer. Lammy said he'd arranged the show in an attempt to make Parliament more accessible to young people.

BORN ON THIS DAY

1931 James Mitchell – baritone saxophonist with The Memphis Horns, who worked with Al Green, Aretha Franklin, Sam And Dave, Elvis Presley, The Doobie Brothers and Otis Redding. Mitchell died on December 18th 2000.

1932 Arif Mardin, producer and arranger who has worked with Aretha Franklin, Bette Midler, Roberta Flack, Wilson Pickett, Average White Band, The Bee Gees and Norah Jones.

1941 Mike Love – singer with The Beach Boys, who had a 1966 UK & US No.1 single with 'Good Vibrations' plus over 25 other US & UK Top 40 singles and a 1966 US No.10 & UK No.2 album *Pet Sounds*.

1944 Sly Stone – vocalist, guitarist and keyboardist with Sly And The Family Stone, who had a 1968 UK No.7 & US No.8 single with 'Dance To The Music' and a 1969 US No.1 single with 'Everyday People'.

1947 Ry Cooder – guitarist who was a member of Captain Beefheart's Magic Band. As a solo artist he had a 1979 album with *Bop Till You Drop* as well as writing the 1985 film soundtrack album *Paris, Texas*.

1962 Terence Trent D'arby, singer who had a 1988 UK No.2 single with 'Sign Your Name' plus eight other UK Top 40 hits. In the US he had the 1988 No.1 single 'Wishing Well'.

1964 Rockwell (a.k.a. Kennedy Gordy), singer who had a 1984 US No 2 & UK No.6 single with 'Somebody's Watching Me'. Rockwell is the son of Motown boss Berry Gordy.

1972 Mark Hoppus – bass player and vocalist with Blink 182, who had a 2000 UK No.2 single with 'All The Small Things' and a 2001 US No.1 album with *Take Off Your....*

1975 Will.i.am – rapper and producer with the Black Eyed Peas, who had a 2003 UK No.1 single with 'Where Is The Love'.

ON THIS DAY

1955 Elvis Presley signed a management contract with Colonel Tom Parker. Parker had previously managed the Great Parker Pony Circus – one of the acts was a troupe of dancing chickens!

1969 Cream started a two week run at No.1 on the UK chart with their album *Goodbye*. It was a No.2 hit in the US.

1969 Tommy Roe started a four week run at No.1 on the US singles chart with 'Dizzy', which was also No.1 in the UK for Vic Reeves and the Wonder Stuff in 1991.

1975 Led Zeppelin went to No.1 on the UK chart with their double album *Physical Graffiti*, the first on their own Swan Song label. The album also spent six weeks at No.1 in the US.

1975 Olivia Newton-John went to No.1 on the US album chart with *Have You Ever Been Mellow*, the singer's second US No.1.

1986 The Bangles were at No.2 on the UK singles chart with 'Manic Monday', a song written by Prince under the pseudonym Christopher.

Colonel Tom Parker holds circus auditions before discovering one Elvis Presley!

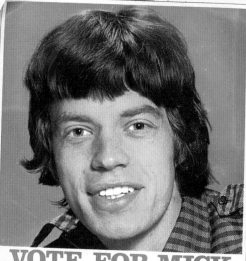

VOTE FOR MICK

It also made No.2 in the US, but was held off No.1 by Prince with 'Kiss'.

1989 The Rolling Stones signed a $70 million (£40 million) contract to play 50 North American dates. It was the largest contract in rock history.

1992 The Beastie Boys appeared live at The Marquee Club in London.

1998 Madonna scored her sixth UK No.1 album with *Ray Of Light*. No other female artist has had more than three UK No.1 albums.

2000 Mick Jagger *(above)* was ordered to increase his child support payments to Brazilian model Luciana Morad from $5,500 (£3,235) a month to $10,000 (£5,888). Mick was asked to confirm that he was the father of her child by the court, while Ms Morad was seeking a $10 million (£3.8 million) settlement.

2002 Yoko Ono unveiled a 2m (7ft) bronze statue of John Lennon overlooking the check-in hall of Liverpool's John Lennon airport. The rebranding of the airport featured a sketch of Lennon's face with the words "Above Us Only Skies".

BORN ON THIS DAY

1942 Jerry Jeff Walker, US singer/songwriter *(right)*. He wrote 'Mr Bojangles', which was a hit for The Nitty Gritty Dirt Band.

1948 Michael Bruce – guitarist for the Alice Cooper Band, who had a 1972 UK No.1 & US No.7 single with 'School's Out'.

1954 Nancy Wilson – vocalist with Heart, who had a 1987 US No.1 & UK No.3 single with 'Alone'.

1972 Andrew Dunlop – guitarist with Travis, who had a 1999 UK No.1 album with *The Man Who* and a 1999 UK No.10 single with 'Why Does It Always Rain On Me?'.

ON THIS DAY

1959 The Platters had the UK No.1 single with 'Smoke Gets In Your Eyes'.

1964 The Beatles set a new record for advance sales in the US with 2,100,000 copies of their forthcoming single 'Can't Buy Me Love'.

1965 The Rolling Stones were at No.1 on the UK singles chart with 'The Last Time', the band's third UK No.1.

1968 the posthumously released Otis Redding single 'Sittin' On The Dock Of The Bay' started a five week run at No.1 on the US chart. It made No.3 in the UK. Otis was killed in a plane crash on December 10th 1967, three days after recording the song.

1969 appearing at "Pop World 69" at London's Wembley Empire Pool were Fleetwood Mac, The Move, Amen Corner, Peter Sarstedt, The Tymes, Harmony Grass and Geno Washington.

1970 Motown singer Tammi Terrell died of a brain tumour after collapsing into Marvin Gaye's arms on stage during a duet of 'That's All You Need To Get By'. Terrell had undergone eight brain operations in 18 months. She had had hits with Marvin Gaye, including the 1967 US No.5 'Your Precious Love'.

1971 winners at this year's Grammy Awards included: Simon & Garfunkel who won Record of the year, Song of the year and Album of the year for 'Bridge Over Troubled Water', while The Carpenters won Best new act and Best vocal performance.

1972 Neil Diamond appeared at The Royal Albert Hall, London.

1972 John Lennon lodged an appeal with the US immigration office in New York after he was served with deportation orders arising from his 1968 cannabis possession conviction.

1973 David Cassidy played the first of six sold-out shows at the Empire Pool, Wembley, London.

1974 Barbra Streisand started a two week run at No.1 on the US album chart with *The Way We Were*, the singer's second US No.1.

1977 after being with the label for just six days The Sex Pistols were fired from A&M due to pressure from other label artists and its Los Angeles head office. 25,000 copies of 'God Save The Queen' were pressed and the band made £75,000 ($127,500) from the deal.

1989 MTV launched a contest to give away Jon Bon Jovi's childhood home.

1989 Bez from the Happy Mondays was arrested at Manchester Airport moments before boarding a flight to Belfast for a gig. He was charged with trying to leave the country, hence breaking bail conditions set after a previous arrest.

1991 all seven members of country star Reba McEntire's band were killed when their plane crashed near San Diego.

1992 during a Metallica gig at Orlando Arena fans dangled an usher by his ankles from the balcony as trouble broke out at the concert. The band was charged $38,000 (£22,353) for repairs and cleaning after the audience trashed the building.

1996 The Ramones performed what they claimed would be their last-ever date in Buenos Aires, Argentina.

2003 Gareth Gates featuring The Kumars started a two week run at No.1 on the UK singles chart with 'Spirit In The Sky'. The song had been a UK No.1 for Norman Greenbaum in 1970 and for Doctor And The Medics in 1986.

2005 Billy Joel checked into a rehabilitation centre for alcohol abuse. A statement from the 55-year-old singer's spokesperson put his latest problems down to "a recent bout of severe gastrointestinal distress.".

BORN ON THIS DAY

1919 Nat King Cole, singer, who had a 1955 US No.2 single with 'A Blossom Fell', a 1957 UK No.2 single with 'When I Fall In Love' and over 20 other US & UK Top 40 singles. He was the father of singer Natalie Cole. Nat died of lung cancer on February 15th 1965.

1941 Clarence Collins – singer with Little Anthony And The Imperials, who had a 1958 US No.4 single with 'Tears On My Pillow'. The song gave Kylie Minogue a UK No.1 in 1990.

1944 John Sebastian – singer/songwriter, guitarist and harmonica player. He was part of The Lovin' Spoonful, who had a 1966 UK No.2 single with 'Daydream' and a 1966 US No.1 single with 'Summer in The City'. As a solo artist he had a 1976 US No.1 single with 'Welcome Back'.

1951 Scott Gorham – guitarist with Thin Lizzy, who had a 1973 UK No.6 single with 'Whisky In The Jar' and a 1976 US No.12 single with 'The Boys Are Back In Town'.

1967 Billy Corgan – vocalist and guitarist for The Smashing Pumpkins, who had a 1995 US No.1 album with *Mellon Collie And The Infinite Sadness* and a 1996 UK No.7 & US No.36 single with 'Tonight Tonight'.

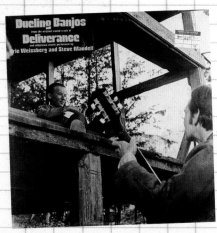

1973 Caroline Corr – drummer, pianist and vocalist with The Corrs, who had a 1998 UK No.3 single with 'What Can I Do?' and their *Talk On Corners* was the bestselling UK album of 1998.

1975 Justin Hawkins *(right)* – vocalist with The Darkness, who had a 2003 UK No.2 single with 'I Believe In A Thing Called Love' and a 2003 UK No.1 album with *Permission To Land*.

1976 Stephen Gately – vocalist with Boyzone, who had a 1996 UK No.1 single with 'Words' plus five other UK No.1 singles. As a solo artist he had a 2000 UK No.3 single with 'New Beginning/Bright Eyes'.

ON THIS DAY

1958 The Champs started a five week run at No.1 on the US singles chart with 'Tequila', which was a No.5 hit in the UK.

1966 The Walker Brothers had their second UK No.1 with the single 'The Sun Ain't Gonna Shine Anymore'. The song was originally recorded by Frankie Valli.

1967 appearing at London's Finsbury Park Astoria, on the first night of a 17 date UK tour were Otis Redding, Eddie Floyd, Carla Thomas, Sam & Dave and Booker T And The MG's.

1968 The Bee Gees made their US television debut when they appeared on *The Ed Sullivan Show*.

1973 Eric Weissberg started a three week run at No.1 on the US album chart with *Dueling Banjos*, which featured the theme from the film *Deliverance (left)*.

1976 appearing at CBGB'S, New York were Johnny Thunders And The Heartbreakers.

1979 Gloria Gaynor started a four week run at No.1 in the UK with 'I Will Survive'.

1997 Elvis Presley Enterprises, of Memphis, Tennessee, lost its court battle to stop London

trader Sid Shaw using the name of "The King" on his souvenirs. The legal tussle with Mr Shaw, who runs a memorabilia shop called Elvisly Yours, had been going on for over 17 years. Speaking after the ruling, Mr Shaw said: "I'm delighted. I've proved that Elvis belongs to all of us – Elvis is part of our history, part of our culture."

1997 US singer Jermaine Stewart died of cancer. In 1986 he had the UK No.2 single 'We Don't Have To...Take Our Clothes Off' and he also worked with Shalamar, The Temptations and Boy George.

2004 The Kinks singer Ray Davies received his CBE medal from the Queen at Buckingham Palace for services to the music industry.

A drumming Corr on her birthday.

2005 Justin Hawkins from The Darkness became the centre of the latest hands-on activity at Madame Tussauds in London. His wax double would judge the air guitar skills of visitors, who were invited to play an imaginary guitar with smoke and music pumping out. Hawkins said: "I find the process of air guitaring rather silly. What makes a good air guitarist? Alcohol."

BORN ON THIS DAY

1938 Charlie Pride, US singer who has scored over 50 country Top 10 hits, including 29 No.1s. He is the most successful black country artist of all time.

1941 Wilson Pickett, US soul singer who had a 1965 UK No.12 & US No. 21 single with 'In The Midnight Hour' plus 15 other US Top 40 singles.

1947 Barry J. Wilson – drummer with Procol Harum, who had a 1967 UK No.1 & US No.5 single with 'Whiter Shade Of Pale'. Wilson died on October 8th 1990.

Brick wall photographed in 1965 as evidence.

1959 Irene Cara, US singer and actress, who had a 1982 UK No.1 & US No.4 single with 'Fame' and a 1983 US No.1 & UK No.2 single with 'Flashdance...What A Feeling'. Cara played Coco Hernandez in Fame.

1963 Vanessa Williams, US singer, former model and beauty queen who had a 1992 US No.1 & UK No.3 single with 'Save The Best To Last'.

1974 Stuart Zender – bass guitarist with Jamiroquai, who had a 1996 UK No.3 single with 'Virtual Insanity' and a 1998 UK No.1 & US No.2 album with Godzilla.

1979 Adam Levine – guitarist and vocalist with Maroon 5, who had a 2004 UK No.1 album with Songs About Jane and a 2004 UK No.4 single 'She Will Be Loved'.

ON THIS DAY

1965 The Rolling Stones were each fined £5 ($8.50) for urinating in a public place. The incident took place at a petrol station after a gig in Romford, Essex, England.

1967 Pink Floyd signed to EMI Records in the UK.

1967 The Beatles scored their 13th US No.1 single with 'Penny Lane'.

1972 Neil Young started a three week run at No.1 on the US singles chart with 'Heart Of Gold'. His only Top 20 hit as a solo artist, it peaked at No.10 on the UK chart.

1972 T. Rex played the first of two sold-out nights at Wembley's Empire Pool. The shows were filmed by Ringo Starr for the Born To Boogie Apple documentary.

1976 The Man Who Fell To Earth film featuring David Bowie premiered in London.

1977 The Clash released their debut single 'White Riot'. It peaked at No.38 in the UK.

1978 The Bee Gees held all Top 3 spots in the US singles charts: 'Night Fever' was at No.1; '(Love is) Thicker Than Water' by brother Andy was at No.2, which had been co-written by Barry Gibb; and 'Emotion' by Samantha Song, written and produced by the Bee Gees, was at No.3.

1978 appearing at the California "Jam II" festival in Ontario, California were Aerosmith, Santana, Heart, Dave Mason, Ted Nugent and Mahogany Rush.

1989 a radio station in California arranged to have all of its Cat Stevens' records destroyed by having a steamroller run over them. This was in protest at the singer's support of The Ayatollah Khomeni.

1991 U2 were fined £500 ($850) after being found guilty of selling condoms illegally at the Virgin Megastore, Dublin.

2004 Courtney Love exposed her breasts during an appearance on David Letterman's TV talk show. The singer, who had her back to the audience, flashed at the presenter while singing the song 'Danny Boy'. After the show, she went on to perform a surprise gig at the Plaid nightclub in Manhattan, where she was alleged to have injured a man by throwing a microphone stand into the crowd. Ms Love was charged with assault and reckless endangerment.

Cat Stevens (centre) who angered a Californian radio station in 1989.

BORN ON THIS DAY

1946 Paul Atkinson – guitarist with The Zombies, who had a 1964 US No.2 & UK No.12 single with 'She's Not There'.

1946 Ruth Pointer – singer with The Pointer Sisters, who had a 1981 US No.2 single with 'Slow Hand' and a 1984 UK No.2 single with 'Automatic'.

1952 Derek Longmuir – drummer with the Bay City Rollers, who had a 1975 UK No.1 single with 'Bye Bye Baby' plus 11 other UK Top 20 singles and a 1976 US No.1 single with 'Saturday Night'.

1953 Ricky Wilson – guitarist with The B-52's, who had a 1990 UK No.2 & US No.3 single with 'Love Shack'. Wilson died on October 12th 1985 of AIDS.

1955 actor and singer Bruce Willis, who had a 1987 UK No.2 single with 'Under The Boardwalk'.

1959 Terry Hall – vocalist with: The Specials, who had a 1981 UK No.1 single with 'Ghost Town'; Fun Boy Three, who had a 1982 UK No.4 single with 'It Ain't What You Do It's The Way That You Do It' with Bananarama; and Colour Field, who had a 1985 UK No.12 single with 'Thinking Of You'. He was also a member of Vegas.

1971 Jack Bessant – bass player with Reef, who had a 1996 UK No.6 single with 'Place Your Hands' and a 1997 UK No.1 album with Glow.

ON THIS DAY

1957 Elvis Presley purchased the stately mansion "Graceland" in Whitehaven, Memphis. He paid $102,500 (£60,295) for the property, which had previously been used by the Graceland Christian Church.

1958 Big Records released 'Our Song' by a teenage duo from Queens, New York called Tom And Jerry. The duo went on to become famous in the 60s under their real names, Paul Simon and Art Garfunkel.

1964 Billy J. Kramer And The Dakotas were at No.1 on the UK singles chart with 'Little Children'. It was the group's second No.1.

1964 UK Prime Minister Harold Wilson presented The Beatles with their awards for Show business personalities of the year for 1963 at London's Dorchester Hotel.

1965 The *Tailor And Cutter* magazine ran an article asking The Rolling Stones to wear ties to save tie makers from financial disaster.

1968 The Jimi Hendrix Experience played two shows at The Capitol Theatre, Ottawa, Canada.

1971 T. Rex were at No.1 on the UK singles chart with 'Hot Love'. This was the group's first of four UK No.1s.

1976 former Free and Back Street Crawler guitarist Paul Kossoff died of heart failure on a flight from Los Angeles to New York, after a long history of drug abuse.

1978 Billy Joel made his UK live debut at London's Drury Lane Theatre.

1981 The J. Geils Band were at No.1 on the US singles chart with 'Centerfold'. Roxy Music had the UK No.1 spot with 'Jealous Guy'.

1982 Randy Rhoads of The Ozzy Osbourne Band, hairdresser Rachel Youngblood and pilot Andrew Aycock were all killed near Orlando, Florida while buzzing the band's tour bus in a light aircraft. The aircraft clipped the bus and crashed.

1996 The second Beatles' *Anthology* series was released. It featured 'Real Love', a track the remaining members of The Beatles recorded using an old demo track of John Lennon's voice.

2001 Geri Halliwell's London home was broken into. The intruder left obscene notes on the walls, stole the singer's computer, hi-fi, threw milk and ribena on the walls and stole a necklace that used to belong to Liz Taylor.

2005 50 Cent became the first solo artist to have three singles in the US Top 5. 'Candy Shop' was at No.1 with 'How We Do' by The Game, (a member of his G-Unit group) was at No.4 and 'Disco Inferno' was at No.5.

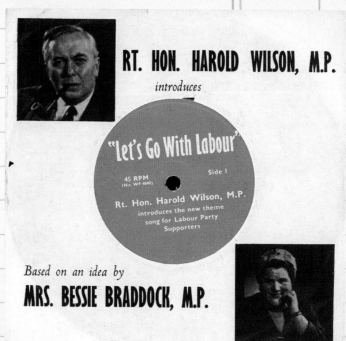

RT. HON. HAROLD WILSON, M.P.
introduces
"Let's Go With Labour"
45 RPM (No. WF 4040) Side 1
Rt. Hon. Harold Wilson, M.P. introduces the new theme song for Labour Party Supporters

Based on an idea by
MRS. BESSIE BRADDOCK, M.P.

Harold Wilson decides that if The Beatles can do it, then so can Bessie Braddock.

BORN ON THIS DAY

1951 Carl Palmer – drummer for: Atomic Rooster, who had a 1971 UK No.4 single with 'The Devil's Answer'; Emerson, Lake and Palmer, who had a 1977 UK No.2 single with 'Fanfare For The Common Man'; and Asia, who had a 1982 US No.4 single with 'Heat Of The Moment'.

1959 Richard Drummie – guitarist with Go West, who had a 1985 UK No.5 single with 'We Close Our Eyes'.

1959 Ian Rossiter – drummer for the Stereo MC's, who had a 1992 UK No.12 single with 'Step It Up'.

1961 Slim Jim Phantom – drummer with The Stray Cats, who had a 1980 UK No.9 single with 'Runaway Boys' and a 1983 US No.3 single with 'Stray Cat Strut'.

1972 Shellie Poole – singer/songwriter with Alisha's Attic, who had a 1996 UK No.14 with 'I Am I Feel'. Poole is the daughter of 60s musician Brian Poole.

1976 Chester Bennington – vocalist with Linkin Park, who had a 2002 US No.2 & UK No.4 single with 'In The End' and a 2002 US No.2 & 2001 UK No.4 album with *Hybrid Theory*.

ON THIS DAY

1961 Elvis Presley started a two week run at No.1 on the US singles chart with 'Surrender', his fifth No.1 of the 60s. It was also a No.1 hit in the UK.

1965 the first of a twice-nightly UK package tour kicked off at London's Finsbury Park Astoria featuring Stevie Wonder, The Miracles, Martha & The Vandellas, The Supremes and The Temptations.

1968 Dave Dee, Dozy, Beaky, Mick And Tich were at No.1 on the UK singles chart with 'The Legend Of Xanadu', the group's only UK No.1.

1968 Eric Clapton, Neil Young, Richie Furay and Jim Mesina were arrested in Los Angeles for "being at a place where it was suspected marijuana was being used". Clapton was later found innocent, while the others paid small fines.

1969 John Lennon married Yoko Ono at the British Consulate Office in Gibraltar.

1970 David and Angela Bowie were married at Beckenham Registry Office. The couple divorced in 1980.

1971 at their own expense the Stones placed full-page advertisements in all the UK's music papers disclaiming any connection with the release of the Decca album *Stone Age*, saying "in our opinion the content is below the standard we try to keep".

1971 Janis Joplin started a two week run at No.1 on the US singles chart with Kris Kristofferson's 'Me And Bobby McGee'. Janis had died the year before on April 10th, aged 27.

1973 Slade were at No.1 on the UK singles chart with 'Cum On Feel The Noize', the group's fourth UK No.1.

1977 Lou Reed was banned from appearing at The London Palladium because of his punk image.

> ## "I was a buffoon and an idiot until the age of 40."
> ## Madonna

1977 T. Rex played their last-ever gig when they appeared at The Locarno in Portsmouth, England.

1980 28-year-old Joseph Riviera held up the Asylum Records office in New York and demanded to see either Jackson Browne or The Eagles, wanting them to finance his trucking operation. He gave himself up when told that neither act was in the office.

1982 Joan Jett And The Blackhearts started a seven week run at No.1 on the US singles chart with 'I Love Rock 'n' Roll', which was a No.4 hit in the UK. The song had been a B-side for 60s band The Arrows.

1990 Gloria Estefan's tour bus was rammed by a tractor trailer on the way to a concert. Emilio Estefan and their son Nayib were injured and Gloria suffered a serious back injury, which required an operation two days later.

1991 Eric Clapton's four-year-son Coner was killed after he fell from a 53rd floor window where he was staying with his mother in New York.

Joseph Riviera, all to win at 28 years old.

2001 Jon, Paul and Bradley from pop group S Club 7 were apprehended by police as they walked through Covent Garden openly smoking a marijuana joint. They were taken to Charing Cross police station, where they were held for four hours.

2002 the *Sun* newspaper reported that Robbie Williams had become a priest. He was ordained via the Internet by the non-denominational Universal Ministries and officiated the wedding of Billy Morrison from rock band The Cult and Jennifer Holliday.

BORN ON THIS DAY

1940 Solomon Burke, US singer known as "The King of rock 'n' soul" who had a 1961 US No.24 single with 'Just Out Of Reach Of My Open Arms' and a 1963 US No.1 R&B hit 'Got To Get You Off My Mind'.

1943 Viv Stanshall – vocalist and ukulele player with Bonzo Dog Doo Dah Band, who had a 1968 UK No.5 single with 'I'm The Urban Spaceman'. Stanshall died on March 5th 1995 in a house fire.

1945 Rosemary Stone – keyboardist with Sly And The Family Stone, who had a 1971 US No.1 & 1972 UK No.15 single with 'Family Affair'.

1946 Ray Dorset – singer/songwriter and guitarist with Mungo Jerry, who had a 1970 UK No.1 & US No.3 single with 'In The Summertime'.

1950 Roger Hodgson – guitarist for Supertramp, who had a 1979 US No.6 & UK No.7 single with 'The Logical Song'.

1951 Russell Thompkins Jr – vocalist for The Stylistics, who had a 1975 US No.1 single with 'You Make Me Feel Brand New', a 1975 UK No.1 single with 'Can't Give You Anything But My Love', plus 15 other UK Top 40 singles.

1967 Keith Palmer – vocalist with The Prodigy, who had a 1996 UK No.1 & US No.30 single with 'Firestarter' and a 1997 UK & US No.1 album with *The Fat Of The Land*.

1980 Deryck "Bizzy D" Whibley – vocalist and guitarist with Sum 41, who had a 2001 UK No.13 single with 'In Too Deep'.

ON THIS DAY

1973 the BBC banned all teenybopper acts *(right)* appearing on UK TV show *Top Of The Pops* after a riot followed a David Cassidy performance.

1976 Iggy Pop and David Bowie were involved in a drug bust at their hotel room in Rochester, New York.

1980 Hugh Cornwell of The Stranglers was sent to Pentonville Prison after losing his appeal against a drugs conviction.

1987 U2 scored their third UK No.1 album with *The Joshua Tree*, which featured the singles 'Where The Streets Have No Name' and 'I Still Haven't Found What I'm Looking For'. *The Joshua Tree* became the fastest-selling album in UK history. It was also a US No.1.

1991 the inventor of The Telecaster and Stratocaster guitars, Leo Fender, died from Parkinson's disease.

1994 Bruce Springsteen won an Oscar for *Streets of Philadelphia*.

1997 Snoop Doggy Dog was sentenced to three years probation and fined $1,000 (£588) for a firearms violation after a handgun was found in his car when he was stopped for a traffic violation.

1999 Blur went to No.1 on the UK album chart with *13*, the band's fourth consecutive No.1. This made them the third act to have had four No.1s in the 90s – Simply Red and R.E.M. being the other two.

2001 Eminem was ordered to pay $476,000 (£280,000) as part of his divorce agreement with his ex-wife Kym. Also as part of the agreement Eminem would keep the "US mansion" and they would share custody of their five-year-old daughter, Hailie Jade.

2001 Michael Jackson's interior decorator told *The Times* newspaper that the singer kept 17 life-size dolls, of both adult and child sizes, all fully dressed in his bedroom for "company".

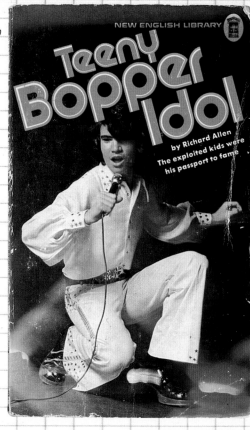

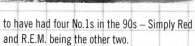

Jimi Hendrix 'sets it alight' on stage with his Fender. Leo would have been horrified.

BORN ON THIS DAY

1936 Roger Whittaker, singer/songwriter who had a 1969 UK No.12 single with 'Durham Town' and a 1975 UK No.2 & US No.19 single with 'The Last Farewell'.

1943 George Benson, US jazz and pop singer and guitarist, who had a 1980 US No.4 & UK No.7 single with 'Give Me The Night'.

1943 Keith Relf – vocalist with The Yardbirds, who had a 1965 UK No.3 & US No.6 single with 'For Your Love'. Relf died on November 14th 1976.

1947 Harry Vanda – guitarist with The Easybeats, who had a 1966 UK No.6 & US No.16 single with 'Friday On My Mind'.

1947 Patrick Olive – percussionist and bass player with Hot Chocolate, who had a 1975 US No.3 single with 'You Sexy Thing', a 1977 UK No.1 single with 'So You Win Again' plus over 25 other Top 40 hits.

1948 Andrew Lloyd Webber, songwriter and producer. With lyricist Tim Rice he wrote "Joseph and the Amazing Technicolor Dreamcoat" for a high school. They later produced "Jesus Christ Superstar" and "Evita", which gave a 1977 UK No.1 single by Julie Covington, 'Don't Cry For Me Argentina'.

1948 Randy Hobbs – bass guitarist with Johnny Winter Group, which became the McCoys. They had a 1965 US No.1 & UK No.5 single with 'Hang On Sloopy'. Hobbs died on August 5th 1993 from a drug overdose, aged 45.

1963 Susanne Sulley – singer with The Human League, who had a 1981 UK No.1 & 1982 US No.1 single with 'Don't You Want Me' plus over 15 other UK Top 40 singles.

1972 Beverly Knight, UK singer who had a 2002 UK No.10 single with 'Shoulda Woulda Coulda'.

Former Yardbirds singer Keith Relf and his new bandmates.

ON THIS DAY

1964 for the first time ever in British recording history, the entire Top 10 singles in this week's chart were by UK acts.

1971 US police arrested all the members from The Allman Brothers Band in Jackson, Alabama for heroin and marijuana possession.

1973 appearing at Manchester's Hard Rock were Traffic, supported by Spooky Tooth.

1975 Frankie Valli went to No.1 on the US singles chart with 'My Eyes Adored You', which was his first solo No.1.

1975 Led Zeppelin started a six week run at No.1 on the US album chart with Physical *Graffiti*, the group's fourth US No.1.

1975 the tartan teen sensations Bay City Rollers were at No.1 on the UK singles chart with 'Bye Bye Baby', the group's first of two UK No.1s.

1978 The Police signed to A&M Records. The band scored over 15 UK Top 40 hits with the label, including the worldwide No.1 'Every Breath You Take'.

1980 Pink Floyd's 'Another Brick In The Wall', started a four week run at No.1 on the US singles chart. It was also No.1 in the UK.

1980 The Jam had their first UK No.1 with their tenth release, 'Going Underground/Dreams Of Children'. It was the first single of the 80s to debut at No.1.

1992 Polygram Records officially announced that Tears For Fears had split up. Roland Orzabal continued using the name Tears For Fears. During their career they scored 15 UK Top 40 singles and two US No.1s.

1994 singer and producer Dan Hartman died. He had worked with Edgar Winter and had a 1978 UK No.8 & US No.29 solo single with 'Instant Replay'.

1997 Puff Daddy featuring Mase started a six week run at No.1 on the US singles chart with 'Can't Nobody Hold Me Down', his first US No.1. It made No.19 in the UK.

2000 Yusuf Islam, the former singer Cat Stevens, joined the campaign to save the Section 28 ban on the promotion of homosexuality in UK schools. He praised peers for fighting the government's plans to scrap Section 28.

Bob Geldof puts World poverty to one side for a moment as he counts the bricks in *The Wall*.

BORN ON THIS DAY

1949 Ric Ocasek – singer/songwriter and guitarist for The Cars, who had a 1978 UK No.3 single with 'My Best Friend's Girl'. The 1984 US No.3 & 1985 UK No.4 'Drive' was used as part of the soundtrack for the "Live Aid" concert.

1953 Chaka Khan (a.k.a. Yvette Marie Stevens), US singer who had a 1984 UK No.1 & US No.3 single with 'I Feel For You' and, with Rufus, a 1974 US No.3 single 'Tell Me Something Good'.

1966 Mark McLoughlin, (a.k.a. Marti Pellow) – vocalist with Wet Wet Wet, who had a 1994 UK No.1 single 'Love Is All Around' – this spent 15 weeks at the top of the charts – plus over 20 other UK Top 40 singles. Pellow left the band in 1999 and then re-joined in 2004.

1968 Damon Albarn – vocalist for Blur, who had a 1994 UK No.1 album with *Park Life* (it spent over two years on the UK chart), a 1995 UK No.1 single with 'Country House' plus over 12 other UK Top 40 singles. Also a member of Gorillaz, who had a 2001 UK No.4 single with 'Clint Eastwood'.

Cheer up Damon, it's your birthday!

1973 John Lennon was ordered to leave the US within 60 days by the immigration authorities. He began a long fight to win his Green Card, which he was given on July 27th 1976.

1974 Cher went to No.1 on the US singles chart with 'Dark Lady', the singer's third solo No.1. It made No.36 in the UK.

1980 The Psychedelic Furs and The Teardrop Explodes appeared at The Lyceum Ballroom, London.

1981 Adam And The Ants kicked off a UK tour at The City Hall, Newcastle Upon Tyne.

1983 The Smiths played at The Rock Garden, London.

1985 Billy Joel married model Christie Brinkley on a boat moored alongside the Statue Of Liberty. The couple divorced in 1993.

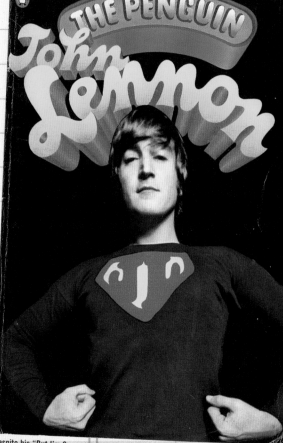

Despite his "But I'm Superman" claims, John Lennon is ordered to leave the USA in 1973.

ON THIS DAY

1961 Elvis Presley had his seventh UK No.1 single with 'Wooden Heart'.

1964 John Lennon's book of verse and rhyme *In His Own Write* was published in the UK.

1972 The film of *The Concert For Bangladesh* featuring George Harrison, Bob Dylan and Eric Clapton, premiered in New York.

1985 Former Creedence Clearwater Revival frontman John Fogerty went to No.1 on the US album chart with *Centerfield*.

1991 R.E.M. scored their first UK No.1 album with their seventh LP *Out Of Time*, which featured the singles 'Losing My Religion' and 'Shiny Happy People'.

1992 Janet Jackson signed with Virgin Records for $16,000,000 (£9,412,000).

1994 Oasis played at The Angel in Bedford, England. They were paid £100 ($170) for the gig.

1996 Celine Dion went to No.1 on the US singles chart with 'Because You Loved Me', her second US No.1. The song was a No.5 hit in UK. On the same day her album *Falling Into You* went to No.1 in the UK album chart.

2005 'Yeah' by Usher featuring Lil Jon and Ludacris was at No.1 on both the US and UK singles chart.

BORN ON THIS DAY

1951 Dougie Thompson – bassist with Supertramp, who had a 1979 US No.6 & UK No.7 single with 'The Logical Song'.

1960 Nena (a.k.a. Gabriele Susanne Kerner), singer who had a 1984 UK No.1 & US No.2 single with '99 Red Balloons'.

1970 Pasemaster Mace – rapper with De La Soul, who had a 1990 UK No.7 single 'The Magic Number'.

1970 Sharon Corr – violinist and vocalist with The Corrs, who had a 1998 UK No.3 single with 'What Can I Do' while *Talk On Corners* was the bestselling UK album of 1998.

ON THIS DAY

1945 Billboard published its first US LP chart. Nat King Cole was at No.1 with 'A Collection Of Favorites'.

1962 at The Barnston Women's Institute were The *Mersey Beat* poll winners, The Beatles. Admission was seven shillings and six pence ($1.05c).

1966 Simon & Garfunkel made their UK singles chart debut with 'Homeward Bound'.

1973 Alice Cooper went to No.1 on the UK album chart with *Billion Dollar Babies*.

1973 at a concert by Lou Reed in Buffalo, New York a fan jumped on stage and bit Lou on the bottom. The man was thrown out of the theatre and Reed completed the show.

1976 transvestite singer Wayne County appeared in court charged with assault after an incident at New York club CBGB's. County had attacked Dictators singer Handsome Dick Manitobe with a mike stand, fracturing his collarbone.

1979 The Bee Gees started a two week run at No.1 on the US singles chart with 'Tragedy', the group's eighth US No.1. It was also No.1 in the UK.

1984 Former Commodores singer Lionel Richie was at No.1 on the UK singles chart with 'Hello'.

1985 'Easy Lover' by former Earth, Wind and Fire singer Philip Bailey and Phil Collins was at No.1 on the UK singles chart.

1990 Canadian singer Alannah Myles started a two week run at No.1 on the US singles chart with 'Black Velvet', which was a No.2 hit in the UK.

1990 Sinead O'Connor went to No.1 on the UK album chart with *I Do Not Want What I Haven't Got*, which featured the single 'Nothing Compares To You'. The album made No.1 in 13 countries and was six weeks at No.1 in the US.

1991 The Black Crowes were dropped as the support act on ZZ Top's tour after repeatedly criticizing the tour sponsor, Miller Beer.

1992 a Chicago court settled the Milli Vanilli class action suit by approving cash rebates of up to $3 (£1.76) to anyone proving they bought the group's music before November 27th 1990, the date the lip synching scandal broke. Milli Vanilli won the 1989 Best new artist Grammy after hits like 'Blame it on the Rain' and 'Girl, You Know It's

Handsome Dick: under attack in 1976.

True', selling 30 million singles and 14 million albums. But in late 1990, the performers were stripped of the award after it was revealed that neither actually sang on the *Milli Vanilli* album.

1997 US soul singer Harold Melvin died, aged 57. He had had a 1972 US No.3 & 1974 UK No.9 single with 'If You Don't Know Me By Know'.

1997 U2 were at No.1 on the US album chart with *Pop*, the band's fifth US No.1 album.

1998 Mark Morrison was jailed for a year after trying to con his way out of doing community service. He sent his minder Gabriel Mafereka instead, who wore sunglasses and hid his hair under a hat so he looked like the star.

2000 a film company paid £635,000, ($1,079,500) for over nine hours of film shot during the 70s by Yoko Ono. The film contained shots of Lennon smoking hash and talking about his political beliefs.

2000 Sir Elton John's "Aida" opened on Broadway. It took Elton 21 days to write the music and five years to make the production.

2002 Gareth Gates became the youngest male solo artist to score a UK No.1 with his debut release 'Unchained Melody'. Gates was 17 years and 255 days old. He had won second place on UK TV's *Pop Idol* show.

BORN ON THIS DAY

1934 US singer Johnny Burnette, who had a 1961 UK No.3 & US No.8 single with 'You're Sixteen'. Killed in a boating accident on Clear Lake, California on August 1st 1964, aged 30.

1938 Hoyt Axton, US singer/songwriter and actor who wrote songs for Elvis Presley, Three Dog Night, John Denver, Ringo Starr and Glen Campbell. Had his own hits with 'When The Morning Comes' and 'Flash Of Fire'. Axton died of a heart attack on October 10th 1999, aged 61.

1942 Aretha Franklin, "The Queen of Soul", who had a 1967 US No.1 & UK No.10 single with 'Respect', a 1968 UK No.4 single 'I Say A Little Prayer', a 1987 UK No.1 single with George Michael 'I Knew You Were Waiting' plus over 15 other UK Top 40 hits.

1947 Elton John, (a.k.a. Reginald Dwight) – singer/songwriter who had a 1971 UK No.7 single with 'Your Song', a 1973 US No.1 single with 'Crocodile Rock' and seven other US No.1s to date. He has also had the biggest-selling single of all time with 1997's 'Candle In The Wind 97', plus over 50 UK Top 40 hit singles.

1949 Nick Lowe *(below)*, musician, songwriter and producer who was also part of bands Brinsley Schwarz and Rockpile. He had a 1978 UK No.7 single with 'I Love The Sound Of Breaking Glass'.

GI Elvis Presley reporting for duty in 1958.

1966 Canadian guitarist and singer Jeff Healey, who has been blind from the age of one..

1975 Melanie Blatt – vocalist with the All Saints, who had a 1998 UK No.1 & US No.4 single with 'Never Ever'.

ON THIS DAY

1958 having been sworn in as Private 53310761 the previous day, Elvis Presley received the regulation short back and sides haircut from army barber James Peterson.

1964 The Beatles made their debut on UK TV show *Top Of The Pops* singing 'Can't Buy Me Love'.

1967 The Turtles started a three week run at No.1 on the US singles chart with 'Happy Together', which made No.12 in the UK.

1967 The Who made their US concert debut in New York as part of a rock 'n' roll extravaganza promoted by DJ Murray the K.

1968 the 58th and final episode of *The Monkees* TV series was broadcast in the US.

1969 John and Yoko started their "bed-in" at The Amsterdam Hilton hotel.

1972 America started a three week run at No.1 on the US singles chart with their debut hit 'Horse With No Name'.

1989 Mike And The Mechanics went to No.1 on the US singles chart with 'The Living Years', which was a No.2 hit in the UK.

1990 Motley Crue's Tommy Lee was arrested for mooning at the audience during a gig in Augusta. Lee was later charged with indecent exposure.

1995 Pearl Jam singer Eddie Vedder was rescued after a riptide carried him 76m (250ft) offshore in New Zealand.

2000 *NSYNC set a new world record after selling a million tickets in one day for a forthcoming tour, netting them over £25 million ($42.5 million).

BORN ON THIS DAY

1917 Rufus Thomas, singer who had a 1963 US No.10 single with 'Walking The Dog' and a 1970 UK No.18 & US No.28 single with 'Do The Funky Chicken'. Thomas died on December 15th 2001.

1944 Diana Ross – singer with The Supremes, who had a 1964 UK & US No.1 single with 'Baby Love' plus over 20 other US & UK Top 40 hits. As a solo artist she had a 1980 US No.1 single with 'Upside Down' and a 1986 UK No.1 single with 'Chain Reaction'.

1948 Richard Tandy – keyboardist and vocalist for the Electric Light Orchestra, who had a 1979 UK No.3 & US No.4 single with 'Don't Bring Me Down' plus 26 other Top 40 UK hits.

1948 Steven Tyler *(below)* – vocalist with Aerosmith, who had a 1989 UK No.13 single with 'Love In An Elevator' and a 1998 US No.1 single with 'I Don't Want

To Miss A Thing'. Their 1989 album *Pump* spent 53 weeks on the US charts.

1968 James Jonas Iha – guitarist with The Smashing Pumpkins, who had a 1995 US No.1 album with *Mellon Collie And The Infinite Sadness* and a 1996 UK No.7 single with 'Tonight Tonight'.

1968 Kenny Chesney, US country singer who had a 2002 US No.1 album with *No Shoes, No Shirt*.

ON THIS DAY

1965 Mick Jagger, Brian Jones and Bill Wyman all received electric shocks from a faulty microphone on stage in Denmark. Wyman was knocked unconscious for several minutes.

1965 The Walker Brothers *(above)* made their UK TV debut on *Ready Steady Go!*

1968 US blues artist Little Willie John died in prison after being convicted of manslaughter. He co-wrote, and was the first to record, 'Fever' and 'Need Your Love So Bad', which was covered by Fleetwood Mac.

1969 Marvin Gaye was at No.1 on the UK singles chart with 'I Heard It Through The Grapevine'. The song had also been a million seller in 1967 for Gladys Knight & The Pips.

1970 Peter Yarrow of Peter, Paul & Mary pleaded guilty to "taking immoral liberties" with a 14-year-old girl in Washington D.C.

1977 Hall and Oates started a three week run at No.1 on the US singles chart with 'Rich Girl', the duo's first US No.1. It was not a hit in the UK.

1980 The Police became the first Western pop group to play in Bombay, India for over ten years when they played a one-off gig in the city.

1983 Duran Duran had their first UK No.1 with their eighth single release 'Is There Something I Should Know?' The group were on a US promotional trip, where they were greeted by 5,000 screaming fans at an instore appearance in New York.

2001 the toy figure of Eminem was facing a ban from UK shops. Woolworths and Hamleys were refusing to stock the dolls. Psychologists warned parents that if they bought the dolls for children they would inadvertently be giving their approval to bad language.

2002 drummer with the Ozzy Osbourne Band Randy Castillon died of cancer.

2003 Kelly Rowland postponed her European tour because of the war in Iraq. The dates were due to start in the UK on April 13th.

2004 Jan Berry of Jan & Dean died after being in poor health from the lingering effects of brain damage from a 1966 car crash.

BORN ON THIS DAY

1950 Tony Banks – keyboardist with Genesis, who had a 1986 US No.1 single with 'Invisible Touch', a 1992 UK No.7 single with 'I Can't Dance' plus over 15 other UK Top 40 hit singles and six UK No.1 albums.

1959 Andrew Farriss – keyboardist with INXS, who had a 1988 UK No.2 & US No.1 single with 'Need You Tonight' and a 1988 US No.3 and worldwide hit album with *Kick*.

1965 Johnny April – bass player with Staind, who had a 2001 US No.1 album with Break The Cycle and a 2001 US No.7 & UK No.15 single with 'It's Been A While'.

1970 Mariah Carey, US singer who was named after 'They Call The Wind Mariah' from the musical "Paint Your Wagon". She had a 1994 UK No.1 single with 'Without You'. To date she has enjoyed over 20 UK Top 40 hits and 12 US No.1 singles.

ON THIS DAY

1953 Walter Stocker – guitarist with Air Supply, who had a 1980 UK No.11 single with 'All Out Of Love' and a 1981 US No.1 single with 'The One That You Love'.

1962 Derrick McKenzie – drummer for Jamiroquai, who had a 1996 UK No.3 single with 'Virtual Insanity' and a 1998 UK No.1 single with 'Deeper Underground'.

1964 The British Invasion continued to make its way around the world, The Beatles having the top six positions on the Australian singles pop chart.

1967 Fats Domino played his first-ever UK date at London's Saville Theatre, supported by The Bee Gees and Gerry And The Pacemakers.

1968 The Beatles were at No.1 on the UK singles chart with 'Lady Madonna', the group's 14th UK No.1 and final No.1 on the Parlophone label.

1971 New York radio station WNBC banned the song 'One Toke Over The Line' by Brewer & Shipley because of its alleged drug references. Other stations around the US followed.

1972 Elvis Presley recorded his last major hit, 'Burning Love'. It made No.2 on the US chart and No.7 in the UK.

1973 Jerry Garcia was arrested after being busted for speeding in New Jersey. Police found cocaine and LSD in his car.

1973 *Rolling Stone* magazine reported that after becoming a disciple of Sri Chinmoy, Carlos Santana had changed his name to "Devadip", which means "the lamp of the light of the Supreme".

1978 The Beatles' parody *All You Need Is Cash* featuring The Rutles was shown in the UK on BBC TV.

1984 Metallica made their UK live debut at the Marquee, London.

1987 U2 performed from the roof of a store in downtown LA to make the video for 'Where The Streets Have No Name', attracting thousands of spectators and bringing traffic to a standstill. The police eventually stopped the shoot.

1991 New Kids On The Block's Donnie Wahlberg was arrested after setting fire to carpets (using a bottle of vodka) at The Seelbach Hotel, Louisville. Wahlberg plea bargained the charge down to criminal mischief and he was ordered to perform fire safety and anti-drug abuse promos.

2000 singer, songwriter, poet and actor Ian Dury *(left)* died after a long battle with cancer, aged 57. Dury had been disabled by polio as a child. He formed Kilburn And The High Roads during the 70s. His first album *New Boots And Panties* became a punk classic, and featured the 1979 UK No.1 single 'Hit Me With Your Rhythm Stick'.

2004 local council officials planned to have a street named after The Darkness in their hometown Lowestoft, Norfolk, England in honour of Justin Hawkins and his band for their recent worldwide success. Hawkins Close or Hawkins Way had been put forward by council officials.

MERSEYSIDE'S OWN ENTERTAINMENTS PAPER

MERSEY BEAT

WHAT'S HAPPENING?
MARCH 1978
WEA NO 11

Vol. 1 No. 13   JANUARY 4-18, 1982   Price THREEPENCE

Rutles   Top Poll!

FULL RESULTS INSIDE

RON NASTY   STIG O'HARA   DIRK McUICKLY   BARRY WOM

DIRK   STIG   NASTY   BARRY

THE RUTLES

The Rutles, notorious Beatles parody act.

BORN ON THIS DAY

1941 Charlie McCoy – multi-instrumentalist who was part of Area Code 615. He wrote the 1970 theme for UK BBC TV music show *The Old Grey Whistle Test* and 'Stone Fox Chase'.

1945 Chuck Portz – bass player for The Turtles, who had a 1967 US No.1 single with 'Happy Together' and a 1967 UK No.4 single with 'She'd Rather Be With Me'.

1948 John Evans – keyboardist with Jethro Tull, who had a 1969 UK No.3 & US No.11 single with 'Living In The Past'.

1948 Milan Williams – keyboard brass and guitar player in The Commodores, who had a 1978 UK & US No.1 single with 'Three Times A Lady'.

1954 Reba McEntire, country singer who sold over 30 million albums during her career.

1969 Cheryl James, "Salt" in Salt-N-Pepa, who had a 1991 UK No.2 single with 'Let's Talk About Sex'.

1969 James Atkin – vocalist with EMF, who had a 1990 UK No.3 & 1991 US No.1 single with 'Unbelievable'.

ON THIS DAY

1957 Elvis Presley appeared live at The Chicago International Theater.

1964 Madame Tussauds, London unveiled the waxwork images of The Beatles, making them the first pop stars to be honoured.

1964 Radio Caroline started broadcasting from the former Danish ferry *Fredericia* in the North Sea.

1968 The Bee Gees kicked off a 24 date UK tour at London's Royal Albert Hall.

1970 Simon & Garfunkel were at No.1 on the UK singles chart with 'Bridge Over Troubled Water', which was the duo's only UK No.1.

1974 blues artist Arthur "Big Boy" Crudup died of a stroke at the age of 69. Crudup wrote 'That's All Right (Mama)', which was a hit for Elvis Presley.

1976 Francis Rossi, Rick Parfitt and Alan Lancaster from Status Quo were arrested after an incident at Vienna Airport. All three were released on bail.

1976 Genesis began their first North American tour since Peter Gabriel left the band, appearing in Buffalo, New York. Phil Collins took over as lead singer.

1981 Blondie started a two week run at No.1 on the US singles chart with 'Rapture', the group's fourth US No.1 and a No.5 hit in the UK.

1981 Elton John's version of The Beatles' 'I Saw Her Standing There' was released as a tribute to John Lennon.

1982 David Crosby was arrested after crashing his car on the San Diego Highway. Police also found cocaine and a pistol in his car.

1987 Mel And Kim were at No.1 on the UK singles chart with 'Respectable', which gave the production team of Stock, Aitken and Waterman their first UK No.1.

Ozzy Osbourne during his Cher period.

1992 over $100,000 (£58,800) worth of damage was caused at The Irvine Meadows Amphitheater, California, when Ozzy Osbourne invited the first two rows of the audience on stage. Several others took up the offer and the band was forced to exit the stage.

1995 country singer Lyle Lovett and actress Julia Roberts announced they were separating after 21 months of marriage.

2001 The artist formerly known as both Puffy and Puff Daddy told MTV he now wanted to be known as P. Diddy.

2001 it was reported that singer/songwriter James Taylor and his wife Caroline Smedvig were expecting twin boys, carried by a surrogate mother who was a family friend.

2004 Usher was at No.1 on the UK album chart with *Confessions*, his second UK No.1 album.

The waxworks Beatles at their 1964 unveiling.

BORN ON THIS DAY

1943 Evangelos Papathanassiou (a.k.a. Vangelis), composer who had a 1981 UK No.12 & 1982 US No.1 single with 'Chariots Of Fire' and released the 1971 album *666 (below)*.

1946 Terry Jacks, singer/songwriter who had a 1974 UK & US No.1 single with 'Seasons In The Sun'. The song was also a UK No.1 hit for Westlife in 1999.

1947 Bobby Kimball – vocalist with Toto, who had a 1983 US No.1 & UK No.3 single with 'Africa'.

1949 Dave Greenfield – keyboardist with The Stranglers, who had a 1986 UK No.2 single with 'Golden Brown' and over 20 other UK Top 40 singles.

1959 Perry Farrell – singer/songwriter who formed Jane's Addiction, who had a 1991 UK No.34 single with 'Been Caught Stealing' and a 1990 US No. 19 album with *Ritual De Lo Habitual*, then Porno For Pyros, who had a 1993 US No.3 & UK No.3 with their self-titled album. He also conceived the US "Lollapalooza" tours.

ON THIS DAY

1943 Chad Allan – vocalist and guitarist with Guess Who, who had a 1970 US No.1 & UK No.19 single with 'American Woman'.

1964 the first night of a tour kicked of at The Coventry Theatre with The Hollies, The Dave Clark Five, The Kinks and The Mojos.

1966 Mick Jagger was injured during a gig in Marseilles after a fan threw a chair at the stage. Mick required eight stitches for the resulting cut.

1966 The Walker Brothers were mobbed by fans as they entered a hotel in Cheshire, resulting in two of the group being concussed.

1969 appearing at the London Free Easter Festival, Bethnal Green were John Lennon and Yoko Ono, Black Sabbath, The Crazy World Of Arthur Brown, Curved Air, J.J. Jackson's Dilemma, Shy Limbs, Spontaneous Music Ensemble, Sunflower Brass Band and Toe Fat.

1975 Labelle went to No.1 on the US singles chart with 'Lady Marmalade', the group's only No.1. British act All Saints had an UK No.1 with the song in 1998 and it was also a hit for Christina Aguilera in 2001.

1975 Led Zeppelin had all of their six albums in the US Top 100 chart in the same week.

1976 Neil Young started a three night run at London's Hammersmith. Tickets cost £1–4 ($1.70–6.80).

1978 David Bowie kicked off his first tour in two years in San Diego, California.

1980 Pink Floyd's *Dark Side Of The Moon* spent its 303rd week on the US album chart, beating the record set by Carole King's album *Tapestry*.

1980 Mantovani, orchestra leader, died aged 74. Scored the 1953 UK No.1 single 'The Song From Moulin Rouge' and the 1957 US No.12 single 'Around The World In Eighty Days'.

1986 Austrian singer Falco started a three week run at No.1 on the US singles chart with 'Rock Me Amadeus, also a No.1 in the UK.

1986 Cliff Richard and The Young Ones were at No.1 on the UK singles chart with a charity version of Cliff Richard's hit from 1959, 'Living Doll'.

1999 The David Bowie Internet Radio Network broadcast its first show for Rolling Stone Radio. The show consisted of Bowie's favourite songs, with him introducing each track.

2000 Phil Collins took out a high court action against two former members of Earth, Wind And Fire. Collins claimed his company had overpaid the musicians by £50,000 ($85,000) in royalties on tracks including 'Sussudio' and 'Easy Lover'.

2001 the man who hid in a cathedral organ to try to video the baptism of Madonna and Guy Ritchie's son Rocco was fined £1,000 ($1,700). He admitted disorderly conduct at Dornoch court in Sutherland.

2005 Neil Young was treated for a brain aneurysm at a New York hospital. Doctors expected the 59-year-old to make a full recovery. The aneurysm was discovered when Young's vision became blurred after the induction ceremony for the Rock and Roll Hall of Fame the previous month.

Perry Farrell – founder of Jane's Addiction, born on this day in 1959.

BORN ON THIS DAY

1942 Graeme Edge – drummer with Moody Blues, who had a 1965 UK No.1 single with 'Go Now' and a 1968 UK No.19 & 1972 US No.2 single with 'Nights In White Satin'.

1945 Eric Clapton, guitarist and singer/songwriter who was part of The Roosters, Casey Jones And The Engineers, John Mayall's Bluesbreakers, Cream (who had a 1967 UK No.11 single with 'I Feel Free') and Derek & The Dominoes (who had a 1972 UK No.7 single with 'Layla'). As a solo artist he had a 1974 US No.1 single with 'I Shot The Sheriff' and a 1992 UK No.5 & US No.25 single with 'Tears in Heaven.

1950 Re Styles – guitarist and vocalist with The Tubes, who had a 1977 UK No.28 single with 'White Punks On Dope' and a 1983 US No.10 single with 'She's A Beauty'.

1955 Randy VanWarmer, singer/songwriter who had a 1979 US No.4 & UK No.8 single with 'Just When I Needed You Most'. He died of leukaemia on January 12th 2004.

1962 MC Hammer, (a.k.a. Stanley Kirk Burrell), rapper who had a 1990 US No.1 album with *Please Hammer Don't Hurt Em* that spent a record-breaking 21 weeks at the top of the chart. He also had a 1990 UK No.3 single with 'U Can't Touch This'.

1964 Tracy Chapman, singer/songwriter who had a 1988 UK No.5 & US No.6 single with 'Fast Car' and a 1988 US & UK No.1 self-titled debut album.

1968 Celine Dion, French-Canadian singer who had a 1994 US No.1 single with 'The Power Of Love', and a 1998 UK No.1 single 'My Heart Will Go On'. She also won the Eurovision Song Contest for Switzerland in 1988.

1979 Norah Jones, singer/songwriter who had a 2002 US & UK No.1 album with *Come Away With Me*. She won eight Grammy Awards in 2003.

Pop pin-ups The Clash in 'lovely boy' bid for acceptance by the nation's teens.

ON THIS DAY

1963 The Chiffons started a four week run at No.1 on the US singles chart with 'He's So Fine', which was a No.16 UK hit. In 1971 George Harrison was taken to court accused of copying the song on his 1970 'My Sweet Lord' and ordered to pay $587,000 (£345,000) to the writers.

1967 the photo session took place at Chelsea Manor studios with Michael Cooper for the cover of The Beatles' *Sgt Pepper* album.

1974 John Denver went to No.1 on the US singles chart with 'Sunshine On My Shoulders', the singer's first of four US No.1s. Denver was killed in a plane crash on October 12th 1997.

1976 The Sex Pistols played their first show at The 100 Club, London. They began a weekly residency at the club in June 1976.

1978 Paul Simonon and Nicky Headon of The Clash were arrested in Camden Town, London after shooting down racing pigeons with air guns from the roof of Chalk Farm Studios. Four police cars and a helicopter were required to make the arrest. Their fines totalled £800 ($1,360).

1978 U2 won £500 ($850) and a chance to audition for CBS Ireland in a talent contest held in Dublin that was sponsored by Guinness.

1991 Gloria Estefan started a two week run at No.1 on the US singles chart with 'Coming Out Of The Dark', which was a No.25 hit in the UK.

2000 Mick Jagger made a nostalgic visit to his old school. He opened the new arts centre named after him at Dartford Grammar. The singer said he had spent the worst years of his life at the school.

BORN ON THIS DAY

1934 Shirley Jones, singer and actress in The Partridge Family, who had a 1970 US No.1 single with 'I Think I Love You' and a 1972 UK No.3 single with 'Breaking Up Is Hard To Do'.

1937 Herb Alpert, trumpeter and vocalist who had a 1968 US No.1 & UK No.3 single with 'This Guy's In Love With You'. He formed A&M Records with Jerry Moss, which at first operated from his garage at home.

1946 Al Nichol – guitarist with The Turtles, who had a 1967 US No.1 single with 'Happy Together' and a 1967 UK No.4 single with 'She'd Rather Be With Me'.

1947 Al Goodman – singer with The Moments, who had a 1970 US No.3 single with 'Love On A Two-Way Street' and a 1975 UK No.3 single with 'Girls'.

1947 Jon-Jon Poulos – drummer with The Buckinghams, who had a 1967 US No.1 single with 'Kind Of A Drag'.

1948 Mick Ralphs – guitarist with Mott The Hoople, who had a 1972 UK No.3 & US No.37 single with 'All The Young Dudes' then Bad Company, who had a 1974 UK No.15 & US No.5 single with 'Can't Get Enough'.

1953 Sean Hooper, keyboardist and vocalist with Huey Lewis & The News, who had a 1985 US No.1 & UK No.11 single with 'The Power Of Love'.

Mick Ralphs, Mott The Hoople guitarist, born on this day in 1948.

1958 Pat McGlynn – guitarist for the Bay City Rollers, who had a 1975 UK No.1 single with 'Bye Bye Baby', 11 other UK Top 20 singles and a 1976 US No.1 single with 'Saturday Night'.

1959 Angus Young – guitarist for AC/DC, who had a 1980 UK No.36 single with 'Whole Lotta Rosie' and a 1980 UK No.1 & US No.14 album *Back in Black* – this sold over 10 million copies.

ON THIS DAY

1958 Chuck Berry's rock 'n' roll classic 'Johnny B. Goode' was released.

1960 Lonnie Donegan was at No.1 on the UK singles chart with 'My Old Man's A Dustman'.

1962 The Beatles played their first gig in the south of England when they appeared at The Subscription Rooms, Stroud on the same bill as The Rebel Rousers.

1962 Connie Francis went to No.1 on the US singles chart with 'Don't Break The Heart That Loves You'. It made No.33 in the UK.

1967 Jimi Hendrix set fire to his guitar live on stage for the first time when he was appearing at The Astoria, London. It was the first night of a 24 date tour with The Walker Brothers, Cat Stevens and Engelbert Humperdink.

1972 The Beatles' Official Fan Club closed. The Beatles' monthly magazine had ceased three years previously.

1973 Donny Osmond was at No.1 on the UK singles chart with his version of 'The Twelfth Of Never', which was a hit single for Johnny Mathis in 1957.

1974 Television appeared at CBGB's in New York.

1976 The Brotherhood Of Man was at No.1 on the UK singles chart with 'Save Your Kisses For Me'. It was the first of three UK No.1s for the group.

1979 *Greatest Hits Vol 2* by Barbra Streisand started a four week run at No.1 on the UK album chart, the singer's first UK No.1 LP.

1984 Kenny Loggins started a three week run at No.1 on the US singles chart with 'Footloose', the theme from the film with the same name. It was a No.6 hit in the UK.

1985 Jeanine Deckers, The Singing Nun, died after taking a overdose of sleeping pills in a suicide pact with a friend. She had had a 1963 US No.1 & UK No.7 single with 'Dominique'.

1986 O'Kelly Isley Of The Isley Brothers died of a heart attack, aged 48.

1995 Jimmy Page escaped being knifed when a fan rushed on stage at a Page and Plant gig at Auburn Hills, Michigan. The fan was stopped by two security guards. After his arrest, he told police he wanted to kill Jimmy Page because of the satanic music he was playing.

2002 Bee Gee Barry Gibb bought his childhood home in Keppel Road, Chorlton, Manchester. Gibb said he was going to clean the house up, rent it out and put a plaque on the wall.

2002 Celine Dion started a four-week run at No.1 on the UK album chart with *A New Day Has Come*, the singer's fifth No.1 album.

2005 Rap record company boss Marion "Suge" Knight was ordered to pay $107m (£57m) to a woman who claimed she helped found the Death Row Records label in 1989. Lydia Harris said she invested in Death Row but was pushed out by Mr Knight.

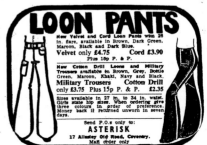

BORN ON THIS DAY

1939 Rudolph Isley – singer with The Isley Brothers, who had a 1973 US No 6 & UK No.14 single with 'That Lady'.

1946 Arthur Conley, soul singer who had a 1967 US No.2 & UK No.7 single with 'Sweet Soul Music'. Conley died of cancer on November 17th 2003.

1946 Ronnie Lane – bass player and vocalist with the Small Faces, who had a 1967 UK No.3 & US No.16 single with 'Itchycoo Park' and a 1968 UK No.1 album with *Ogden's Nut Gone Flake*. The Faces had a 1972 UK No.6 & US No.17 single with 'Stay With Me'. Ronnie then formed Slim Chance, who had a 1974 UK No.5 single with 'How Come'. He died on June 4th 1997, aged 51, after a 20 year battle with multiple sclerosis.

1947 M, (Robin Scott), singer and multi-instrumentalist who had a 1979 US No.1 & UK No.2 single with 'Pop Muzik'.

1948 Jimmy Cliff, Jamaican singer/songwriter who had a 1969 UK No.6 & US No.25 single with 'Wonderful World Beautiful People' and a 1970 UK No.8 version of Cat Stevens' 'Wild World'.

1961 Mark White – guitarist with ABC, who had a 1982 UK No.4 & US No.18 single with 'The Look Of Love' plus nine other UK Top 40 singles.

ON THIS DAY

1955 George Martin became the head of A&R for EMI's Parlophone label.

1961 The Beatles began a three-month residency at The Top Ten Club, Hamburg. The band played for seven hours a night on weekdays and eight hours at weekends, with a 15 minute break every hour.

1966 Pye Records released David Bowie's first solo single, 'Do Anything You Say'. Bowie had previously recorded as David Jones And The Lower Third.

1969 Ambrose Slade (Slade) made their live debut at Walsall Town Hall, Walsall, England.

1969 The Beach Boys announced they were suing their record label Capitol for $2,041,446.64 (£1,200,851) in unpaid royalties.

1970 Earl's Court, London received over one million postal ticket applications for The Rolling Stones' forthcoming six concerts.

Much missed Ronnie Lane of the Small Faces in his travelling show.

1970 50 musicians recorded the orchestral scores for The Beatles tracks 'The Long And Winding Road' and 'Across The Universe' for the Phil Spector produced sessions. The bill for the 50 musicians was £1,126 and 5 shillings, ($1,914).

1972 the three day Mar Y Sol festival in Puerto Rico took place, featuring Rod Stewart, Dr. John, The Allman Brothers, Osibisa, ELP, Alice Cooper and The Mahavishnu Orchestra. Security was simple as the event took place on an island accessible by ticket only.

1975 The Bay City Rollers' TV series *Shang-A-Lang* premiered on ITV in the UK.

1976 the Buzzcocks played their debut live gig when they appeared at Bolton Institute Of Technology.

1976 AC/DC played at The Red Cow, Hammersmith, London making their live debut in the UK.

1984 Marvin Gaye was shot dead by his father during a violent argument at his parent's home in Los Angeles. The singer's father was later charged and found guilty. He was sentenced to five years for voluntary manslaughter.

1990 Willie Nelson's tour bus crashed into a car in Riverdale, Canada, killing the car driver.

2001 it was reported that Spice Girl Mel B had been advised to sell her £3.5 million ($6 million) Buckinghamshire mansion because she couldn't afford to run it. The singer had told friends she was having to take out a £500,000 ($850,000) bank loan.

BORN ON THIS DAY

1928 Serge Gainsbourg, singer who had a 1969 UK No.1 single with Jane Birkin 'Je T'aime...Moi Non', the only French language chart topper. Gainsbourg died of a heart attack on March 2nd 1991.

1939 Marvin Gaye, singer/songwriter who had a 1968 US No.1 & 1969 UK No.1 single with 'I Heard It Through The Grapevine' and a 1982 US No.3 & UK No.4 single with 'Sexual Healing'. He was shot dead by his father on April 1st 1984.

1941 Leon Russell, singer/songwriter and multi-instrumentalist who has worked with Phil Spector, Bob Dylan, The Rolling Stones and Glenn Campbell. He wrote 'Delta Lady', which was a hit for Joe Cocker in 1969 and also played on The Byrds' 'Mr Tambourine Man'.

1946 Kurt Winter – guitarist with Guess Who, who had a 1970 US No.1 & UK No.19 single with 'American Woman'. He died on December 15th 1997.

1947 Emmylou Harris, country singer who released two albums with Gram Parsons, had a 1976 UK No.30 single with 'Here There And Everywhere' and a US No.37 single 'Mr Sandman'. Harris is a six times Grammy Award winner.

1952 Leon Wilkeson – bass player with Lynyrd Skynyrd, who had a 1974 US No.8 single with 'Sweet Home Alabama' and a 1982 UK No.21 single with 'Freebird'. Wilkeson died on July 27th 2001.

1953 David Robinson – drummer with The Cars, who had a 1978 UK No.3 & US No.35 single with 'My Best Friend's Girl' and a 1984 US No.3 & 1985 UK No.4 single with 'Drive'.

Serge Gainsbourg's collaboration with Jane Birkin.

1979 Jesse Carmichael – keyboard player with Maroon 5, who had a 2004 UK No.1 album with *Songs About Jane* and a 2004 US No.1 & UK No.4 single with 'She Will Be Loved'.

ON THIS DAY

1965 the first edition of new music show *Ready Steady Goes Live!* was shown on UK TV.

1965 The Who made their first radio appearance on the UK BBC's "Joe Loss Pop Show".

1967 154 Austrian Rolling Stones fans were arrested when a riot broke out at a 14,000 seater Town Hall gig after a smoke bomb was thrown onto the stage.

1971 Janis Joplin was at No.1 on the US album charts with *Pearl*.

1977 Abba were at No.1 on the UK singles chart with their fifth No.1 'Knowing Me Knowing You'. On the same day they made No.1 on the US singles chart with 'Dancing Queen', which was the group's only US No.1.

1977 Frank Sinatra scored his first-ever UK No.1 album with *Portrait Of Sinatra*, his 46th album release.

1981 CBS Records launched the "Nice Price" series of back catalogue albums in the UK. The first batch, priced at £2.99 ($5) included early albums by Bob Dylan, Santana, Billy Joel, Abba, Janis Joplin and Simon & Garfunkel.

1987 U2 kicked off their 29 date North American Joshua Tree tour at Arizona State Activity Center.

1997 Joni Mitchell was reunited with Kilauren Gibb, the daughter she gave up for adoption 32 years earlier when she was a 20-year-old struggling arts student.

1998 Rob Pilatus, one half of pop duo Milli Vanilli, was found dead in a Frankfurt Hotel room after taking a lethal combination of drugs and alcohol.

1999 The Black Crowes played a concert in Knoxville, Tennessee. Joshua Harmon, a teenager sitting in the second row, sued the band a year later for $385,000 (£226,470), claiming significant hearing loss.

2003 US soul singer Edwin Starr died, aged 61. He had had the 1970 US No.1 and UK No.3 single 'War'.

2004 Coldplay singer Chris Martin was accused of attacking a photographer after leaving a London restaurant with his wife Gwyneth Paltrow. Alessandro Copetti had been running after Paltrow's taxi and tripped. Mr Copetti said he had been taking pictures of the singer and his wife outside a restaurant when Martin kicked him from behind.

The sympathetic back-catalogue stickering campaign that was CBS 'Nice Price' series, started in 1989.

BORN ON THIS DAY

1924 Doris Day, singer and actress who had a 1956 US & UK No.1 single with 'Whatever Will Be, Will Be, (Que Sera, Sera)' plus 17 other UK Top 40 singles.

1928 Don Gibson, US country singer/songwriter who had a 1958 US No.7 single with 'Oh Lonesome Me' and a 1961 UK No.14 single with 'Sea Of Heartbreak'. 'Oh Lonesome Me' was covered by Neil Young on his *After The Gold Rush* album. Gibson died of natural causes on November 17th 2003, aged 75.

1938 Jeff Barry, songwriter. He wrote 'Tell Laura I Love Her', 'Da Doo Ron Ron', 'Be My Baby', 'Baby I Love You' and 'Do Wah Diddy Diddy.'

1941 Jan Berry – singer with Jan & Dean, who had a 1963 US No.1 & UK No.26 single with 'Surf City', which was co-written with Beach Boy Brian Wilson. Berry died on March 26th 2004 after being

in poor health from the lingering effects of brain damage from a 1966 car crash.

1943 Richard Manuel – singer, keyboardist and drummer with The Band, who had a 1969 US No.25 single with 'Up On Cripple Creek' and a 1970 UK No.16 single with 'Rag Mama Rag'. Manuel committed suicide on March 6th 1986.

1944 Tony Orlando – singer with Dawn, who had a 1971 UK & US No.1 single with 'Knock Three Times' and a 1973 US & UK No.1 single with 'Tie A Yellow Ribbon Round The Old Oak Tree'.

1949 Richard Thompson – guitarist and vocalist with Fairport Convention and solo artist. He had a 1991 UK No.32 album with *Rumour And Sigh*.

1951 Mel Schacher – bass player with Grand Funk Railroad, who had a 1974 US No.1 single with 'The Locomotion'. They were the most successful US heavy metal band of the 70s, selling over 20 million albums.

1955 Bob Deal (a.k.a. Mick Mars) – guitarist for Motley Crue, who had a 1988 UK No.23 single with 'You're All I Need' and a 1989 US No.1 album with *Dr Feelgood*.

ON THIS DAY

1956 Elvis Presley appeared on ABC-TV's *The Milton Berle Show* singing 'Heartbreak Hotel', 'Shake Rattle And Roll' and 'Blue Suede Shoes'.

1961 The Marcels started a three week run at No.1 on the US singles chart with the Rodgers and Heart song 'Blue Moon', which was also a No.1 in the UK.

1964 Bob Dylan made his first entry on the UK singles charts with 'The Times They Are A-Changin'.

1964 The Beatles had their fourth UK No.1 single with 'Can't Buy Me Love'. With advanced sales of over 2.1 million, it holds the record for the greatest advanced orders in the UK.

1966 Peter Tork opened a solo stint in Hollywood at The Troubadour. Tork had already auditioned for The Monkees, whom he would join later in the year.

1971 The Temptations scored their second US No.1 with 'Just My Imagination (Running Away With Me)', which was a No.8 hit in the UK.

1975 Steve Miller was charged with setting fire to the clothes of a friend, Benita Diorio. When police arrived at Miller's house, Diorio was putting out the flames. Miller fought with some of the policemen and was charged with resisting arrest.

1976 Johnnie Taylor started a four week run at No.1 on the US singles chart with 'Disco Lady', his tenth US Top 40 hit. The song made No.25 in the UK.

1979 Kate Bush made her concert debut at Liverpool's Empire Theatre, England.

1991 Paul McCartney recorded his unplugged session for MTV.

1993 ten years after its first release, The Bluebells had a UK No.1 single with 'Young At Heart' after it was featured on a Volkswagen TV commercial. The song was co-written by Siobhan Fahey of Bananarama.

1993 Depeche Mode went to No.1 on the UK album chart with *Songs Of Faith And Devotion*, their first UK No.1 and tenth album release.

1999 composer Lionel Bart died from cancer aged 69. Wrote 'Living Doll' for Cliff Richard, 'Little White Bull' for Tommy Steele *(left)*, and composed the musical, *Oliver*.

2001 Mariah Carey signed the richest recording deal in history. The singer signed a deal with Virgin for three albums that was worth $102 million, (£60m). The singer had sold over 120 million records worldwide, scoring 14 US No.1 singles.

BORN ON THIS DAY

1915 Muddy Waters, US blues singer and guitarist who recorded 'I Just Want To Make Love To You', 'I'm Your Hoochie Coochie Man' and 'Got My Mojo Working'. He died on April 30th 1983.

1948 Berry Oakley – bass player with The Allman Brothers Band, who had a 1973 US No.12 single with 'Ramblin Man'. Oakley was killed in a motorcycle accident on November 11th 1972.

1948 Pick Withers – drummer for Dire Straits, who had a 1985 US No.1 single with 'Money For Nothing' and a 1986 UK No.2 single with 'Walk Of Life'.

1952 Dave Hill – guitarist with Slade, who had a 1971 UK No.1 single with 'Coz I Luv You' plus five other UK No.1s and 18 Top 40 singles.

1952 Gary Moore – guitarist and vocalist with Skid Row and then Thin Lizzy, who had a 1973 UK No.6 single with 'Whisky In The Jar' and, as a solo artist, he had a 1979 UK No.8 single with 'Parisian Walkways'.

1975 Phil A. Jimenez – percussionist and vocalist for Wheatus, who had a 2001 UK No.2 single with 'Teenage Dirtbag'.

1978 Lemar Obika, UK singer who appeared on BBC TV talent show *Fame Academy* and had a 2003 UK No.2 single with 'Dance (With You)'.

ON THIS DAY

1964 The Beatles held the top five places on the US singles chart: at No.5 'Please Please Me', No.4 'I Want To Hold Your Hand', No.3 'Roll Over Beethoven', No.2 'Love Me Do' and at No.1 'Can't Buy Me Love'.

1967 Jimi Hendrix was the special guest on the first edition of BBC TV's *Dee Time*, along with Kiki Dee and Cat Stevens.

1970 Brinsley Schwarz's promotion company sent 133 UK journalists by plane to New York to see the band play live, supporting Van Morrison at the Fillmore East, at a cost of £120,000 ($204,000). The event turned into a disaster. The group planned to leave a few days before the show to rehearse, but were denied visas on a technicality. They were finally given visas on the morning of the show, and arrived hours before the concert. The plane carrying the journalists developed a mechanical fault, delaying the flight. When the journalists arrived in New York 18 hours later, they were all hung over. Brinsley Schwarz gave a underwhelming live performance, resulting in a flood of scathing reviews.

1970 Crosby, Stills, Nash & Young went to No.1 on the US album chart with *Déjà Vu*.

1976 The Sex Pistols played the first night of a residency at the El Paradiso club in Soho, London.

1987 Starship started a two week run at No.1 on the US singles chart with 'Nothin's Gonna Stop Us', which was taken from the film *Mannequin*. The song was also a No.1 in the UK.

Simon Dee braces himself for the onslaught that was Jimi Hendrix, 1967.

1987 the charity record by "Ferry Aid" was at No.1 on the UK singles chart with 'Let It Be'. The single was recorded in aid of the 1986 Zeebrugge Ferry disaster, which killed almost 200 people.

1987 U2 entered the US album chart at No.7 with *The Joshua Tree*, the highest US chart new entry for seven years.

1992 Bruce Springsteen scored his third UK No.1 album with *Human Touch*.

1992 the film soundtrack from *Wayne's World* started a two week run at No.1 on the US album chart.

1996 Take That made their final performance on *The Ivo Niehe Show* on Dutch TV, playing two songs in front of a 250 strong studio audience.

1999 The Corrs' album *Talk On Corners* went to No.1 on the UK album chart for the tenth time and they also had the No.2 position with *Forgiven, Not Forgotten*. Both albums had spent over a year on the chart.

2003 50 Cent became the bestselling artist in the US so far this year when his latest album *Get Rich or Die Tryin'* sold more than four million copies in two months.

2004 Usher was at No.1 on the US album chart with *Confessions*, the singer's second US No.1.

The immortal Muddy Waters.

BORN ON THIS DAY

1928 Tony Williams – lead vocalist with The Platters, who had a 1959 UK & US No.1 single with 'Smoke Gets In Your Eyes'. Williams died on August 14th 1992.

1929 Joe Meek, producer. He produced The Tornadoes' 1962 UK & US No.1 single 'Telstar', making them the first British act to have a No.1 in the US. He also produced hits for John Leyton and The Honeycombs. Meek shot himself dead on February 3rd 1967 after killing his landlady.

1939 Ronnie White – vocalist with The Miracles, who had a 1970 UK & US No.1 single with Smokey Robinson, 'The Tears Of A Clown'.

1942 Alan Clarke – vocalist with The Hollies, who had over 25 Top 40 hits, a 1972 US No.2 single 'Long Cool Woman (In A Black Dress)' and the 1988 UK No.1 single 'He Ain't Heavy, He's My Brother' – first released in 1969.

1950 Agnetha Faltskog – vocalist with Abba, who had a 1974 UK No.1 with 'Waterloo', which was followed by eight other UK No.1 singles and nine UK No.1 albums as well as the 1977 US No.1 single 'Dancing Queen'.

1965 Mike McCready – guitarist with Pearl Jam, who had a 1992 UK No.15 single with 'Jeremy' and a 1993 US No.1 album with *Vs.*

1973 Pharrell Williams, one half of the writing duo The Neptunes (with Chad Hugo). They produced numerous No.1 hits for Mystikal, Jay-Z, *NSYNC, Britney Spears and Nelly and released the 2003 US No.1 album *The Neptunes Present...Clones.*

ON THIS DAY

1967 hundreds of Monkees fans walked from London's Marble Arch to the US Embassy in Grosvenor Square to protest Davy Jones's planned

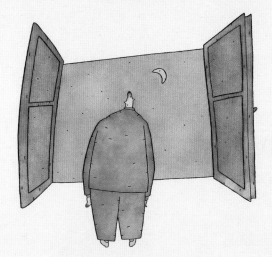

call up. He was exempted on the grounds of being responsible for supporting his father.

1968 the first date of a twice-nightly UK tour featuring Amen Corner, Gene Pitney, Status Quo, Simon Dupree & The Big Sound and Don Partridge at The Odeon Theatre, Lewisham, London.

1975 Minnie Riperton went to No.1 on the US singles chart with 'Loving You'. It was the singer's only US chart hit and a No.2 in the UK. Riperton died on July 12th 1979.

1980 Genesis scored their first UK No.1 album when *Duke* went to the top of the charts.

1980 R.E.M. played their first-ever gig, at St Mary's Episcopal Church, Athens, Georgia.

1981 Canned Heat singer Bob Hite died of a heart attack, aged 36.

1983 Danny Rapp, leader of 50s group Danny And The Juniors, committed suicide by shooting himself.

1984 Marvin Gaye's funeral took place at The Forest Lawn Cemetery, Los Angeles. The service was attended by Smokey Robinson, Stevie Wonder, Quincy Jones, Berry Gordy and other Motown singers, writers and producers.

1985 over 5,000 radio stations worldwide aired the charity single by USA for Africa 'We Are The World'. The single went on to be a No.1 in the UK, the US and most Western territories.

1985 showing on UK Channel 4 music show *The Tube* was a two hour end of series show featuring, UB40, Alison Moyet, Style Council, The Pogues, Spandau Ballet, Frankie Goes To Hollywood and Bronski Beat.

1994 Kurt Cobain of Nirvana committed suicide by shooting himself in the head at his home in Seattle. Electrician Gary Smith, who was working at Cobain's house, discovered his body three days later.

1995 Jimi Hendrix's one-time girlfriend Monika Dannerman committed suicide, two days after losing a court battle with another of the guitarist's ex-lovers.

1998 drummer Cozy Powell was killed when his car smashed into crash barriers on a motorway in Bristol, England.

1998 James went to No.1 on the UK album chart with *The Best Of James.*

1998 The Spice Girls performed their first-ever live UK concert when they appeared in front of a 9,000 strong audience in Glasgow, Scotland.

BORN ON THIS DAY

1937 Merle Haggard, US country singer/songwriter who scored 38 US country No.1s including 'Okie From Muskogee'.

1941 Brian Rankin (a.k.a. Hank Marvin) – guitarist with The Shadows, who had a 1960 UK No.1 single 'Apache' plus 28 other UK Top 40 singles as well as Marvin Welch And Farrar. As a solo artist he had the 1969 UK No.7 single 'Throw Down A Line'.

1944 Michelle Gilliam– singer with The Mamas And The Papas, who had a 1966 US No.1 and UK No.3 single with 'Monday Monday'.

1947 Tony Connor – drummer with Hot Chocolate, who had a 1975 US No.3 single with You Sexy Thing' and a 1977 UK No.1 single with 'So You Win Again', plus over 25 other Top 40 hits.

1951 Ralph Cooper – drummer with Air Supply, who had a 1980 UK No.11 single with 'All Out Of Love' and a 1981 US No.1 single with 'The One That You Love'.

1965 Frank Black – guitarist and vocalist with The Pixies, who had a 1990 UK No.28 single with 'Velouria'. Black had also been a solo artist and leads Frank Black And The Catholics.

ON THIS DAY

1960 The Everly Brothers started their first UK concert tour at London's New Victoria Theatre, supported by The Crickets.

1968 Cliff Richard sang 'Congratulations', the UK entry in the Eurovision Song Contest held at the Royal Albert Hall, London, winning second place behind the Spanish entry.

1968 Pink Floyd announced founder Syd Barrett had officially left the group. He was suffering from psychiatric disorders compounded by drug use.

1968 Simon & Garfunkel went to No.1 on the US album chart with *The Graduate*.

1974 The California Jam 1 festival took place in Ontario, California, featuring The Eagles, Black Sabbath, Deep Purple, Earth, Wind And Fire, ELP, Black Oak Arkansas and Seals & Croft. Over 200,000 fans attended.

1979 Rod Stewart married actor George Hamilton's ex-wife Alana Hamilton in Beverly Hills.

1985 UK singer/songwriter Gilbert O'Sullivan won a lawsuit against his manager Gordon Mills for unpaid royalties and was awarded (£1.2 million) $2 million.

1998 Wendy O. Williams, former singer of The Plasmatics, died from self-inflicted gunshot wounds.

2001 Dido kicked off a six date UK tour at Glasgow Barrowlands. Tickets cost £12 ($20).

2003 White Stripes went to No.1 on the UK album chart with *Elephant*, the duo's second album.

BORN ON THIS DAY

1915 Billie Holiday, (born Elinore Harris), the greatest female jazz singer of all time. She made over 100 records, worked with Count Basie and Duke Ellington and was involved in numerous arrests for drugs possession. She died on July 17th 1959 from liver failure, aged 44.

1937 Charlie Thomas – singer with The Drifters, who had a 1960 US No.1 & UK No.2 single with 'Save The Last Dance For Me'.

1947 Florian Schneider-Esleben, multi-instrumentalist with Kraftwerk, who had a 1975 US No.25 single with 'Autobahn' and a 1982 UK No.1 single 'Computer Love' / 'The Model'.

1947 Patricia Bennett – singer with The Chiffons, who had a 1963 US No.1 single with 'He's So Fine' and a 1972 UK No.4 single with 'Sweet Talkin Guy' – first issued in 1966.

1949 John Oates, singer/songwriter and guitarist with Hall And Oates, who had a 1982 US No.1 & UK No.6 single with 'Maneater'.

1960 Simon Climie, songwriter and producer who had a 1988 UK No.2 single with 'Love Changes Everything'.

ON THIS DAY

1956 The CBS Radio Network premiered the first regularly scheduled nationally broadcast rock 'n' roll show, Alan Freed's Rock 'n' Roll Dance Party.

1962 while at Ealing Jazz Club, Mick Jagger and Keith Richards met Brian Jones for the first time. Jones was calling himself Elmo Lewis and was playing guitar with Paul Jones.

1973 Diana Ross started a two week run at No.1

lady sings the blues

on the US album chart with *Lady Sings The Blues (above)*.

1975 Ritchie Blackmore quit Deep Purple to form his own band, Rainbow. Tommy Bolin replaced Blackmore in Deep Purple.

1979 Siouxsie And The Banshees played a charity gig for MENCAP, but after crowd trouble were later faced with a £2,000 ($3,400) bill for seat damage.

1979 The Doobie Brothers went to No.1 on the US album chart with *Minute By Minute*, the group's only US chart topper.

1981 Bruce Springsteen and the E Street Band kicked off their first full-scale tour in Hamburg, Germany. It was Springsteen's first tour outside North America and would take in ten countries.

1984 a record 40 British acts appeared on the US singles chart.

All the money in the world would not have saved Alice Cooper in 1988.

1985 Wham! became the first Western pop group to perform live in China, when they played at the workers' gymnasium in Beijing.

1998 American Country singer Tammy Wynette died, aged 55. She had scored 12 hit singles including 'Stand By Your Man', sold over 30 million records worldwide, married five times and once filed for bankruptcy.

1988 during a European tour, Alice Cooper accidentally hung himself in a rehearsal when a safety rope snapped, he dangled for several seconds before a roadie saved him.

2000 a tribute to Joni Mitchell was held in New York featuring performances by Elton John, Bryan Adams, Shawn Colvin, James Taylor, Cyndi Lauper, Richard Thompson, k.d. Lang and Mary Chapin Carpenter.

2000 Heinz, bass player and singer with The Tornadoes, died aged 57. The group had the Joe Meek-produced 1962 UK & US No.1 single 'Telstar', making them the first UK group to score a US No.1 single.

2002 UK *Pop Idol* runner-up Gareth Gates was at No.1 on the UK singles chart with his version of 'Unchained Melody', (making Gates the seventh act to have a Top 40 hit with the song).

2003 Avril Lavigne dominated Canada's national music awards, the Junos. She won four prizes including Best single, album and new artist.

BORN ON THIS DAY

1929 Jacques Brel, French singer/songwriter, who died of cancer on October 9th 1978. Scott Walker, Alex Harvey, Frank Sinatra and Dusty Springfield have all covered his songs.

1947 Steve Howe — guitarist with Yes, who had a 1977 UK No.7 with 'Wonderous Stories' and a 1983 US No.1 & UK No.28 single 'Owner Of A Lonely Heart', and Asia, who had a 1982 US No.4 & UK No.46 single with 'Heat Of The Moment'.

1962 Izzy Stradlin — guitarist with Guns N' Roses, who had a 1988 US No.1 & 1989 UK No.6 single with 'Sweet Child O' Mine' and a 1991 US No.1 album with *Use Your Illusion II*.

1963 Julian Lennon, singer/songwriter who had a 1991 UK No.6 single with 'Saltwater'.

1971 Darren Jessee — drummer with Ben Folds Five, who had a 1997 UK No.26 single with 'Battle Of Who Could Care Less'.

ON THIS DAY

1965 Unit Four Plus Two were at No.1 on the UK singles chart with 'Concrete And Clay'.

1967 appearing live at London's Hammersmith Odeon were Otis Redding, Sam & Dave, Eddie Floyd, Arther Conley and Booker T And The MG's.

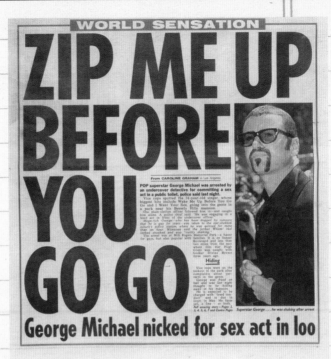

WORLD SENSATION

ZIP ME UP BEFORE YOU GO GO

George Michael nicked for sex act in loo

From CAROLINE GRAHAM in Los Angeles

POP superstar George Michael was arrested by an undercover detective for committing a sex act in a public toilet, police said last night.

Superstar George . . . he was shaking after arrest

1967 Sandie Shaw won this year's Eurovision Song Contest, held in Vienna, representing Britain with the song 'Puppet On A String'. She became the first UK female artist to win the contest.

1970 The London premiere of the movie *Woodstock* took place.

1972 written after the Bloody Sunday massacre in Northern Ireland Paul McCartney released 'Give Ireland Back To The Irish'. The song was banned by the BBC and the IBA. It made No.16 in the UK and No.21 in the US.

1977 The Damned played at the home of the New York punk scene, CBGB'S, making them the first UK punk group to play live dates in the USA.

1982 New Order's bass player Peter Hook was knocked unconscious during a riot at a gig in Rotterdam.

1985 US songwriter J. Fred Coots died. He co-wrote 'Santa Claus Is Coming To Town' and the Pat Boone US No.1 hit 'Love Letters In The Sand'.

1988 R.E.M. left IRS Records and signed with Warner Brothers Records.

1989 Roxette went to No.1 on the US singles chart with 'The Look', the duo's first US No.1 and a No.7 hit in the UK.

1994 Electrician Gary Smith, who was working at Kurt Cobain's house in Seattle, discovered Cobain's body lying on the floor in the greenhouse. Local radio station KXRX broke the news at 9.40am that the Nirvana singer and guitarist was dead. A shotgun was found next to Cobain's body.

1998 George Michael was arrested by an undercover detective at The Will Rogers Memorial Park for committing a sex act in a public toilet. He was arrested by undercover Beverly Hills police officer Marcelo Rodriguez. Michael later said, "I was followed into the restroom and this cop — well, I didn't know he was a cop at the time obviously — started playing this game. I think it's called 'I'll show you mine, you show me yours, and then when you show me yours, I'm gonna nick you!'" The singer was later fined $810 (£475) after being convicted of a "lewd act".

1998 Rolling Stones guitarist Ron Wood was rescued along with ten other passengers from a boat off the coast of Rio De Janeiro, Brazil after the engine exploded.

BORN ON THIS DAY

1932 Carl Perkins, singer/songwriter and guitarist who had a 1956 US No.2 & UK No.10 single with 'Blue Suede Shoes'. He died on January 19th 1998, aged 65.

1944 Gene Parsons – drummer with The Byrds, who had a 1965 UK & US No.1 single with 'Mr. Tambourine Man'.

1946 Les Gray – vocalist with Mud, who had a 1974 UK No.1 single with 'Tiger Feet' plus 14 other UK Top 40 singles. Gray died from throat cancer on February 21st 2004, aged 57.

1978 Rachel Stevens – vocalist with S Club 7, who had a 1999 UK No.1 single with 'Bring It All Back'. As a solo artist she had a 2003 UK No.2 single 'Sweet Dreams My LA Ex'.

1980 Albert Hammond Jr – guitarist with The Strokes, who had a 2001 UK No.14 single with 'Last Nite' and a 2001 UK No.2 album with *Is This It?*

ON THIS DAY

1956 Gene Vincent recorded the classic rock 'n' roll song 'Bebop-A-Lula'.

1965 The Rolling Stones made their live TV debut on UK TV show *Ready Steady Go!*

1966 Jeff Beck collapsed on stage during a Yardbirds gig in Marseilles, France.

1973 Queen played a showcase gig at the Marquee Club, London for their new record label EMI.

1974 Terry Jacks was at No.1 on the UK singles chart with 'Seasons In The Sun'.

1976 American folk singer/songwriter Phil Ochs hung himself at his sister's home in Queens, New York. He wrote 'There But A Fortune', which was a hit for Joan Baez.

PAUL McCARTNEY
BACK IN THE WORLD 2003

MEN ARENA
Manchester
Wed 9th April 2003

WED 09-APR-2003 8PM
LOWER TIER
BLOCK 115
ROW B   SEAT 14
WAY AHEAD
75.00   30-38497
75.00

1977 Abba went to No.1 on the US singles chart with 'Dancing Queen', the group's seventh US Top 40 hit and first No.1.

1983 David Bowie was at No.1 on the UK singles chart with 'Let's Dance', his third UK No.1.

1988 Billy Ocean started a two week run at No.1 on the US singles chart with 'Get Outta My Dreams, Get Into My Car', which was a No.3 hit in the UK.

1988 Dave Prater of soul duo Sam & Dave was killed when his car left the road and hit a tree in Syracuse, Georgia on his way to his mother's house in Ocilla. He was 50.

1989 Rolling Stone Bill Wyman announced his forthcoming marriage to 19-year-old Mandy Smith. He revealed the two had been dating for six years.

1991 record producer Martin Hannett died. He had worked with many "Manchester" groups including The Smiths, New Order, Joy Division, Happy Mondays and Magazine as well as U2 and The Psychedelic Furs.

2000 Moby started a five week run at No.1 on the UK album chart with *Play*.

2003 Paul McCartney played his first Manchester show in 24 years when he appeared at the M.E.N. Arena as part of his "Back In The World Tour 2003".

2004 a man was arrested for allegedly stalking Avril Lavigne. James Speedy, 30, from Seattle, Washington was arrested after police searched his home. He was later released on $5,000 (£2,940) bail. Mr Speedy had been under investigation since the previous summer for allegedly sending harassing letters and emails to the 19-year-old singer.

Genius at work: Phil Ochs and Joan Baez together.

BORN ON THIS DAY

1932 Nate Nelson – vocalist with The Platters, who had a 1959 UK & US No.1 single with 'Smoke Gets In Your Eyes'.

1936 Bobbie Smith – vocalist with Detroit Spinners, who had a 1980 UK No.1 & US No.2 single with 'Working My Way Back To You'.

1940 Ricky Valance, (born David Spencer). He was the first Welsh singer to score a UK No.1 with the 1960 single 'Tell Laura I Love Her'.

1947 Karl Russell – singer with The Hues Corporation, who had a 1974 US No.1 & UK No.6 single with 'Rock The Boat'.

1959 Brian Setzer – guitarist and vocalist with The Stray Cats, who had a 1980 UK No.9 single with 'Runaway Boys' and a 1983 US No.3 single with 'Stray Cat Strut'. He went on to form the Brian Setzer Orchestra.

1959 Kenneth "Babyface" Edmonds, songwriter and producer who had a 1996 US No.6 & UK No.12 single with 'This Is For The Lover In You'. He has written for and produced Boyz II Men, Whitney Houston, Bobby Brown, TLC and Toni Braxton.

1970 Mike Mushok – guitarist with Staind, who had a 2001 US No.1 album with *Break The Cycle* and a 2001 US No.7 & UK No.15 single with 'It's Been A While'.

1979 Sophie Ellis Bextor – singer with The Audience, and then with Spiller on the 2000 UK No.1 single 'Groovejet (If This Ain't Love)'. As a solo artist she had a 2001 UK No.2 single with 'Murder On The Dancefloor'.

DOWNSTAIRS SECTION ROW/BOX SEAT
10 APR 2003 15.00
PCL PRESENTS
THE WHITE STRIPES
PLUS GUESTS
Under 18's must be accompanied by an adult
www.glasgow-academy.co.uk
GLASGOW ACADEMY
121 Eglinton Street, Glasgow
THU 10 APR 2003 7:00 PM
PRICE: 15.00

ON THIS DAY

1962 The Beatles' former bass player Stuart Sutcliff died of a brain haemorrhage in an ambulance on the way to hospital, aged 22. He had lived in Hamburg after leaving The Beatles.

1965 the headmaster of a school in Wrexham, Wales asked parents not to send their children to school in corduroy trousers, like the ones worn by The Rolling Stones.

1965 British acts started a run of seven weeks at the top of the US charts when Freddie & The Dreamers went to No.1 with 'I'm Telling You Now', followed by Wayne Fontanas' 'Game Of Love', Herman's Hermits' 'Mrs Brown' and The Beatles' 'Ticket To Ride'.

1968 with his 41st single release Cliff Richard had his ninth UK No.1, 'Congratulations', the British entry in the 1968 Eurovision Song Contest.

1970 during a gig in Boston, Doors singer Jim Morrison asked the audience if "anyone wants to see my genitals". The management switched off the power and the gig was cut short.

1970 Paul McCartney issued a press statement announcing that The Beatles had split.

1976 Peter Frampton went to No.1 on the US album chart with *Frampton Comes Alive*, the biggest-selling live album in rock history.

1976 UK music weekly *The Melody Maker* reviewed a Sex Pistols' gig with the words, "I hope we shall hear no more of them".

1990 Tom Waits took Doritos Chips to court for using a "Waits" sound-alike on radio ads. The jury awarded him $2.475 million (£1.46 million) in punitive damages. Waits' comments after the case, "now by law I have what I always felt I had...a distinctive voice".

1994 over 5,000 fans attended a public memorial service for Kurt Cobain at Seattle Center's Flag Pavilion.

1998 Limp Bizkit guitarist Wes Borland married Heather McMillan. Their honeymoon was spent visiting amusement parks across the country.

1999 a charity tribute concert for the late Linda McCartney was held at the Royal Albert Hall, London. Among the performers were Paul McCartney, Chrissie Hynde, George Michael, Elvis Costello and Sinead O'Connor.

1999 TLC started a four week run at No.1 on the US singles chart with 'No Scrubs'.

2000 *NSYNC were at No.1 on the US album chart with 'No Strings Attached', their first US No.1.

Stuart Sutcliff by Stuart Sutcliff.

2001 Eminem was given two years probation and fined $3,060, (£1,800) and $6,120, (£3,600) costs after admitting carrying a concealed weapon. The charges followed an incident outside a club in Warren, Michigan the previous June when Eminem "pistol whipped" John Guerra after he saw him kissing his wife.

BORN ON THIS DAY

1946 Bob Harris, DJ and TV presenter – he presented the long-running BBC TV music show *The Old Grey Whistle Test*.

1958 Stuart Adamson – guitarist and vocalist with Skids, who had a 1979 UK No.10 single with 'Into The Valley', then Big Country, who had a 1983 UK No.10 single with 'Fields Of Fire' plus 14 other UK Top 40 singles. Adamson died on December 16th 2001.

1965 Nigel Pulsford – guitarist with Bush, who had a 1996 US No.1 & UK No.4 album with Razorblade Suitcase and a 1997 UK No.7 single with 'Swallowed'.

1966 Lisa Stansfield, singer who had a 1989 UK No.1 & US No.3 single with 'All Around The World' plus over 12 other UK Top 40 singles.

1969 Cerys Matthews – vocalist with Catatonia, who had a 1998 UK No.3 single with 'Mulder And Scully'.

1970 Delroy Pearson – singer with Five Star, who had a 1986 UK No.3 single with 'System Addict' plus 15 other UK Top 40 singles.

1987 Joss Stone, (a.k.a. Joscelyn Eve Stoker), UK singer who had a 2004 UK No.1 album with *Mind Body & Soul*.

ON THIS DAY

1956 Elvis Presley worked with the backing group The Jordanaires for the first time when he recorded the song 'I Want You, I Need You, I Love You'.

1961 Bob Dylan played his first live gig in New York at Gerde's Folk City, opening for John Lee Hooker.

1965 performing at the *New Musical Express* poll winners' concert, at London's Wembley Empire Pool, were: The Beatles, The Rolling Stones, Tom Jones, Freddie & The Dreamers, The Animals, The Kinks, Herman's Hermits, Moody Blues, Them, Cilla Black, The Seekers and Donovan.

1970 Peter Green quit Fleetwood Mac while on tour in Germany. To avoid breach of contract he agreed to finish the current tour.

Stuart Adamson of The Skids and Big Country.

1970 The Beatles started a two week run at No.1 on the US singles chart with 'Let It Be', It became the group's 19th US No.1 in six years, and was a No.2 hit in the UK.

1977 Alice Cooper played to an audience of 40,000 in Sydney, Australia – the largest crowd to attend a rock concert in the country's history.

1981 Hall And Oates started a three week run at No.1 on the US singles chart with 'Kiss On My List', the duo's second US No.1.

1986 Dave Clark's musical *Time* opened at London's Dominion Theatre, starring Cliff Richard.

1988 Cher won an Academy Award for Best actress for her work in *Moonstruck*.

1991 Paula Abdul held a press conference in to deny allegations that backing vocalist Yvete Marine had sung uncredited lead parts on Paula's *Forever Your Girl* LP.

1992 Def Leppard scored their second UK No.1 album with *Adrenalize*, the follow up to the multi-million-selling *Hysteria* album.

1994 Oasis released their first single, 'Supersonic'. It peaked at No.31 in the UK.

2001 Robbie Williams raised £165,000 ($280,500) at a charity auction. The money went to his old school in Stoke to build a performing arts block. The items sold were Robbie's personal possessions, including a toilet from a stage show, a Union Jack bikini, a pair of briefs, a Millennium jet pack and the handwritten lyrics to 'Angels', which sold for £27,000 ($45,900).

2001 Bruce Springsteen won a court battle to keep the rights to his early songs. Ronald Winter of Masquerade Music, UK, who had released the album *Before The Fame*, was found to be in breach of copyright. Springsteen was awarded more than £2 million, ($3.4 million) damages.

2003 Primal Scream played their Carling Homecoming gig at The Garage in Glasgow, Scotland.

DAMAGES: Bruce

The Boss wins £2m song row

ROCK star Bruce Springsteen yesterday won his Appeal Court battle to keep the rights to his early songs and more than £2million damages for breach of copyright.

The victory by The Boss followed his successful court battle in 1998 when he claimed those rights were stolen.

Masquerade Music, of Middlesex, and the man behind the firm, Ronald Winter, who brought out the early work in an album, Before The Fame, failed to overturn the earlier ruling.

They had claimed the trial judge was wrong to admit oral evidence as to the assignment of copyright.

SOFT GREY SOFT GREY SOFT GREY

Robbie's undergarments.

BORN ON THIS DAY

1933 Tiny Tim, singer who had a 1968 US No.17 single with 'Tiptoe Through The Tulips'. He died of a heart attack on November 29th 1996.

1944 John Kay – guitarist and vocalist for Steppenwolf, who had a 1968 US No.2 and 1969 UK No.30 single with 'Born To Be Wild'.

1950 David Cassidy, singer and actor, who had a 1972 UK No.1 single with 'How Can I Be Sure' plus nine other UK Top 40 singles and, with The Partridge Family, a 1970 US No.1 single 'I Think I Love You' and the 1972 UK No.3 single 'Breaking Up Is Hard To Do'.

1956 Alexander Briley – singer with The Village People, who had a 1978 US No.2 and 1979 UK No.1 single with 'Y.M.C.A.'.

1957 Vince Gill, US country singer who has won 17 Country Music Awards and 14 Grammy Awards. He is married to singer Amy Grant.

1978 Guy Berryman – bass player for Coldplay, who had a 2000 UK No.4 single with 'Yellow' and a 2005 world-wide No.1 album with *X&Y*.

1980 Bryan McFadden – vocalist with Westlife, who has had 12 UK No.1 singles, plus four UK No.1 albums.

ON THIS DAY

1954 Bill Haley recorded 'Rock Around The Clock'. The track was later used over the opening titles for the film *Blackboard Jungle* and went on to be a worldwide No.1 hit and the biggest-selling pop single, with sales over 25 million.

1957 "King of Skiffle" Lonnie Donegan was at No.1 on the UK singles chart with 'Cumberland Gap'.

1963 Bob Dylan performed his first major solo concert at Town Hall in New York City.

1966 Jan Berry (of Jan & Dean) was almost killed when he crashed his car into a parked truck in Los Angeles. Berry was partially paralyzed and suffered brain damage.

1966 Tom Jones went into hospital to have his tonsils removed, (there was speculation that he had a nose job).

1969 The 5th Dimension started a six week run at No.1 on the US singles chart with 'Aquarius/ Let The Sunshine In'. It made No.11 in the UK.

1973 *That'll Be The Day* premiered in London. The film featured David Essex, Ringo Starr, Keith Moon, Billy Fury and Dave Edmunds.

1975 David Bowie announced his second retirement, saying, "I've rocked my roll. It's a boring dead end, there will be no more rock 'n' roll records from me."

1975 Elton John started a two week run at No.1 on the US singles chart with 'Philadelphia

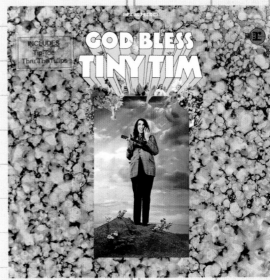

Tiny Tim, born on this day in 1933.

Freedom', his fourth US No.1. The song made No.12 in the UK.

1986 Go-Go's lead singer Belinda Carlisle married actor Morgan Mason.

1989 two DJs on Los Angeles station KLOS asked what ever happened to David Cassidy? The singer called the station and was invited onto the show. David played three songs live on air and was subsequently signed by a new record label.

1990 The Astronomical Union's Minor Planet Center announced that Asteroids 4147–4150, would be named after the four Beatles.

1993 actress Lisa Bonet filed for divorce from Lenny Kravitz.

1997 R. Kelly started a three week run at No.1 on the UK singles chart with 'I Believe I Can Fly'.

2000 Metallica filed a suit against Napster, Yale University, University of Southern California and Indiana University for copyright infringement.

HOTEL BANS WHITNEY AFTER 3-HOUR BRAWL

£20,000 damage to exclusive suite

Tongue-lashing . . . Bobby and Whitney were carpeted by hotel

Quiet retreat . . . stars go to Bel Air expecting a "good night's sleep"

Whitney Houston and Bobby Brown were counting the cost of a drunken brawl at Hollywood's Bel Air hotel on this day in 2001.

BORN ON THIS DAY

1942 Bill Conti, US singer who had a 1977 US No.1 single with 'Gonna Fly Now' (the theme from Rocky).

1943 Eve Graham – singer with The New Seekers, who had a 1972 UK No.1 and US No.7 single with 'I'd Like To Teach The World To Sing'.

1945 Lowell George – guitarist and leader of Little Feat, who had two Top 40 albums during the 70s. Their best-known songs are 'Dixie Chicken' and 'Sailin' Shoes'. He was also a one time member of Frank Zappa's Mothers Of Invention. George died from a heart attack on June 29th 1979.

1946 Al Green, soul singer who had a 1971 UK No.4 single with 'Tired Of Being Alone', a 1972 US No.1 single with 'Let's Stay Together' plus over ten other Top 40 hits.

1951 Peabo Bryson, singer who had a 1983 UK No.2 single with Roberta Flack 'Tonight I Celebrate My Love' and a 1984 US No.10 single with 'If Ever You're In My Arms Again'.

1962 Hillel Slovak – former guitarist with The Red Hot Chili Peppers, he died from a heroin overdose on June 27th 1988.

1966 Marc Ford – guitarist with The Black Crowes, who had a 1991 UK No.39 single with 'Hard To Handle', a 1991 US No.4 album with *Shake Your Money Maker* and 1992 US No.1 & UK No.2 album with *The Southern Harmony And Musical Companion*.

ON THIS DAY

1956 The UK Top 20 became The Top 30 for the first time.

1967 Nancy and Frank Sinatra were at UK No.1 on the UK singles chart with 'Somethin' Stupid', making them the only father and daughter to have a No.1 single as a team.

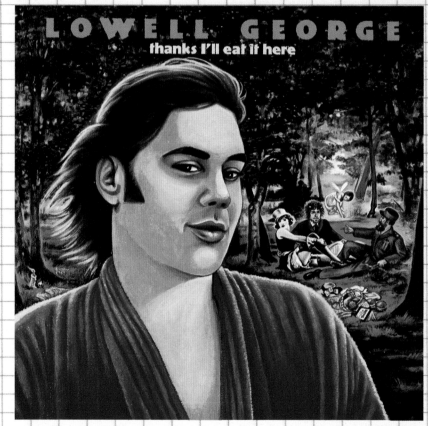

LOWELL GEORGE
thanks I'll eat it here

LONDON PALLADIUM
APRIL 13·14·15 4 perfs only
LOUIS BENJAMIN presents
THE
SUPREMES'
MARY WILSON
KAREN JACKSON & KAAREN RAGLAND
BOX OFFICE OPEN–BOOK NOW 01-437 7373
APRIL 13th & 14th at 8.0, APRIL15th at 6.15 & 8.45.

1970 appearing at Friars, Aylesbury was Genesis. The band, featuring Peter Gabriel, Mike Rutherford and Tony Banks, received £10 ($17) for the gig.

1982 Dave Crosby from Crosby, Stills, Nash & Young was arrested when police found him preparing cocaine backstage in his dressing room before a show in Dallas.

1985 USA For Africa started a four week run at No.1 in the US with 'We Are The World'.

1991 Londonbeat went to No.1 on the US singles chart with 'I've Been Thinking About You', which was a No.2 hit in the UK.

1993 the first 'Aerosmith Day' was observed in the Commonwealth of Massachusetts after the band were given their very own holiday.

1997 The Notorious B.I.G. was at No.1 on the US album charts with *Life After Death*.

2002 thieves broke into a house in Bexhill, Sussex and stole a hi-fi system and several CDs. They left albums by Madonna, Robbie Williams and Oasis but took the owner's entire collection of Showaddywaddy albums.

2003 The Beatles Apple Corp company was listed as Britain's fastest profit-growth firm with an annual profit growth of 194 percent.

BORN ON THIS DAY

1935 Loretta Lynn, country singer, who was the first woman to be named Country Music Artist Entertainer Of The Year.

1942 Tony Burrows – singer with Edison Lighthouse, who had a 1970 UK No.1 single with 'Love Grows (Where My Rosemary Goes)'. Tony holds the record for having four records in the British Top 10 at once – all under different names: Edison Lighthouse's 'Love Grows (Where My Rosemary Goes)'; White Plains' 'My Baby Loves Lovin'; The Pipkins' 'Gimme Dat Ding' and the Brotherhood of Man's 'United We Stand' – all of which were hits in both the US and UK.

1945 Ritchie Blackmore – guitarist for Deep Purple, who had a 1970 UK No.2 single with 'Black Night' and a 1973 US No.4 single 'Smoke On The Water', then Rainbow, who had a 1981 UK No.3 single with 'I Surrender'.

1948 Larry Ferguson – keyboardist with Hot Chocolate, who had a 1975 US No.3 single with 'You Sexy Thing', a 1977 UK No.1 single with 'So You Win Again' plus over 25 other Top 40 hits.

ON THIS DAY

1953 Lita Roza was at No.1 on the UK singles chart with '(How Much) Is That Doggie In The Window?'

1964 The King Bees, (featuring a young David Bowie, then David Jones), played a wedding reception at the Jack Of Clubs in London.

1967 a riot broke out at Warsaw's Palace Of Culture as The Rolling Stones made their first appearance in an Iron Curtain country. Police used tear gas in a battle with 2,000 fans.

1967 Polydor Records issued The Bee Gees' 'New York Mining Disaster 1941'. It was released with a promotional slogan announcing "The most significant talent since The Beatles". The record became a Top 20 hit in the UK & US.

Country star Loretta Lynn.

1969 the recording of 'The Ballad Of John and Yoko' took place with just two Beatles, Paul McCartney and John Lennon. Paul played bass, drums and piano with John on guitars.

1970 Creedence Clearwater Revival made their live UK debut when they played the first of two nights at The Royal Albert Hall, London.

1971 the Illinois Crime Commission issued a list of "drug-oriented records" including Jefferson Airplane's 'White Rabbit', Procol Harum's 'A Whiter Shade Of Pale' and The Beatles' 'Lucy In The Sky With Diamonds'.

1973 Led Zeppelin started a two week run at No.1 on the UK album chart with *Houses Of The Holy*, which also made No.1 in the US.

1975 after rumours that Jimmy Page, Steve Marriott, Jeff Beck and Chris Spedding were replacing Mick Taylor as guitarist in The Rolling Stones, a press release confirmed that Ron Wood would be joining the band for their forthcoming American tour.

1975 Art Garfunkel started a six week run at No.1 in the UK with the theme from the film *Watership Down*. 'Bright Eyes' went on to become the biggest-selling single of the year.

1976 Eric Faulkner of The Bay City Rollers reportedly came close to death after taking a drug overdose at their manager's house.

1976 Motown Records and Stevie Wonder announced the largest contract renewal to date, a deal worth $13 million (£7.6 million).

1978 Joy Division played at the "Stiff Test/Chiswick Challenge", at Raffters in Manchester, and was seen by future manager Rob Gretton and local journalist Tony Wilson.

1979 The Doobie Brothers went to No.1 on the US singles chart with 'What A Fool Believes', the group's second US No.1. It made No.31 in the UK.

1980 Gary Numan released "The Touring Principle", the first longform rock video to be made commercially available in the UK.

1983 Pretenders bass player Pete Farndon died from a drug overdose.

1994 Kurt Cobain was cremated in Seattle. The death certificate listed his occupation as poet/musician and his business as punk rock.

Drugs and religion: a lethal cocktail.

2003 a man was arrested and accused of making up a Bjork concert then selling tickets. Alex Conate allegedly sold tickets worth $14,000 (£8,235) after persuading a San Diego nightclub owner that Bjork had agreed to play there. He was accused of taking the money and moving to Hawaii, where he was arrested.

BORN ON THIS DAY

1939 Marty Wilde (a.k.a. Reginald Smith), singer who had a 1959 UK No.2 single with 'A Teenager In Love', plus over 10 other UK Top 40 singles.

1944 Dave Edmunds – guitarist, vocalist and producer for Love Sculpture, who had a 1968 UK No.5 single with 'Sabre Dance'. Solo he had a 1970 UK No.1 and US No.4 single with 'I Hear You Knocking' and was a member of Rockpile.

1965 Linda Perry – songwriter, producer and singer. She sung with the 4 Non Blondes, who had a 1993 UK No.2 single with 'What's Up' and a 1993 UK No. 4 album with *Bigger Better Faster More!*. Perry has also written 'Beautiful' for Christina Aguilera as well as songs for Jewel, Courtney Love, Gwen Stefani, Sugarbabes, Robbie Williams, Melissa Etheridge and Gavin Rossdale.

1966 Graeme Clark – bass player for Wet Wet Wet, who had a 1994 UK No.1 single with 'Love Is All Around' – which spent 15 weeks at No.1 – plus over 20 other UK Top 40 singles.

1967 Frankie Poullian – former bass player for The Darkness, who had a 2003 UK No.2 single with 'I Believe In A Thing Called Love' and a 2003 UK No.1 album with *Permission To Land*. He quit the band in 2005.

1968 Edward John O'Brien – guitarist with Radiohead, who had a 1997 UK No.1 & US No.21 album with *OK Computer*.

ON THIS DAY

1965 Cliff Richard was at No.1 on the UK singles chart with 'The Minute You're Gone'. It was the singer's eighth UK No.1.

1966 appearing live at the Blackpool Odeon were Jimi Hendrix, The Walker Brothers, Cat Stevens and Engelbert Humperdink. Tickets cost 5 and 10 shillings.

1972 Roberta Flack started a six week run at No.1 on the US singles chart with the Ewan MacColl song 'The First Time Ever I Saw Your Face'. It was a No.14 hit in the UK. The song was featured in the Clint Eastwood film *Play Misty For Me*.

1978 Television were forced to postpone their gig at Bristol's Colston Hall after the 12m (40ft) truck carrying their equipment was involved in a crash, killing the driver.

1982 Billy Joel spent a month in hospital after breaking his left wrist when his motorbike hit a car in Long Island, New York.

1989 American all-girl group The Bangles started a four week run at No.1 on the UK singles chart with 'Eternal Flame'.

1989 Deacon Blue were at No.1 on the UK album chart with their second album *When The World Knows Your Name*.

1989 The Fine Young Cannibals went to No.1 in the US singles chart with 'She Drives Me Crazy'.

1995 Montell Jordan started a seven week run at No.1 on the US singles chart with 'This Is How We Do It', a No.11 hit in the UK.

Milli Vanilli: crimes against music.

1996 Milli Vanilli singer Rob Pilatus was jailed for 90 days by a Los Angeles judge for three violent attacks and parole violation.

1996 the rest of Jerry Garcia's ashes were scattered near the Golden Gate Bridge in San Francisco. A small portion had been scattered in the River Ganges in India 11 days earlier. The Grateful Dead leader had died on August 9th 1995.

2001 Janet Jackson started a six week run at No.1 on the US singles chart with 'All For You'.

2001 punk pioneer Joey Ramone died after losing a long battle with lymphatic cancer. He was 49.

2003 Beyonce was sued by the Wilhemina Artist Agency who claimed she hadn't paid them the commission for her L'Oréal ads. The agency claimed the singer refused to pass on the ten percent of the $1 million (£580,000) deal that was brokered by the agency.

Radiohead promotional fairground game, hardly on a par with the Kiss Pinball machine.

BORN ON THIS DAY

1924 Henry Mancini, composer, arranger and conductor who had a 1964 UK No.10 single with 'How Soon' and a 1969 US No.1 single with 'Love Theme From Romeo and Juliet'. Mancini died on June 14th 1994.

1924 Rudy Pompilli – saxophonist with Bill Haley And His Comets, who had a 1955 UK & US No.1 single with 'Rock Around The Clock'. Pompilli died on February 5th 1976.

1935 Bobby Vinton, singer who had a 1963 US No.1 single & 1990 UK No.2 single with 'Blue Velvet' plus 29 other US Top 40 hits.

1939 Dusty Springfield, UK singer who had her first UK hit single in 1963 in the UK with 'I Only Want To Be With You', a 1966 UK No.1 & US No.4 single with 'You Don't Have To Say You Love Me' plus over 15 other UK Top 40 singles. She died on March 3rd 1999.

DUSTY SPRINGFIELD INTERNATIONAL
(APPRECIATION SOCIETY)

With Compliments

Miss LYNNE JACKSON
27 BROADWALK,
OTLEY W.YORKSHIRE
OTLEY 56235

1947 Gerry Rafferty – singer/songwriter who was part of Stealers Wheel, who had a 1973 US No.3 & UK No.8 single with 'Stuck In The Middle With You'. As a solo artist he had a 1978 UK No.3 and US No.2 single with 'Baker Street'. He was also member of the late 1960s group The Humblebums alongside Billy Connolly.

1959 Stephen Singleton – sax player with ABC, who had a 1982 UK No.4 and US No.18 single with 'The Look Of Love' plus nine other UK Top 40 singles.

1963 Little Jimmy Osmond, singer who had a 1972 UK No.1 and US No.38 single with 'Long Haired Lover From Liverpool'.

1964 Dave Pirner – vocalist and guitarist with Soul Asylum, who had a 1993 US No.5 and UK No.7 single with 'Runaway Train'.

ON THIS DAY

1956 Buddy Holly's first single 'Blue Days, Black Nights' was released.

1964 The Rolling Stones' first album was released in the UK. It went to No.1 two weeks later.

1967 Cream appeared at the *Daily Express* Record Star Show at The Empire Pool, Wembley.

1969 Desmond Dekker & The Aces were at No.1 on the UK singles chart with 'The Israelites', making Dekker the first Jamaican artist to have a UK No.1 single.

1972 The Electric Light Orchestra made their debut at The Fox and Greyhound in Croydon, England.

1977 actor David Soul from TV's *Starsky And Hutch* went to No.1 on the US singles chart with 'Don't Give Up On Us', his only US hit. The song was also No.1 in the UK.

1983 Bonnie Tyler went to No.1 on the UK chart with her debut album and only chart topper *Faster Than The Speed Of Night*.

1990 The Nelson Mandela concert took place at London's Wembley Stadium featuring Simple Minds, Neil Young, Lou Reed, Tracy Chapman and Peter Gabriel.

1993 David Lee Roth was arrested in New York's Washington Square Park for allegedly buying a $10 (£5.90) bag of marijuana.

1993 Paul McCartney headlined a concert at the

Skip Spence of Jefferson Airplane and Moby Grape.

Hollywood Bowl to celebrate Earth Day along with Ringo Starr, Don Henley and Steve Miller. He had last performed there as a member of The Beatles in 1965.

1994 on his 37th single release Prince had his first UK No.1 with 'The Most Beautiful Girl In The World'.

1997 Mark Morrison was convicted with threatening a police officer with an illegal 23,000 volt electric stun gun. The singer left Marylebone Magistrates' Court, London in tears after being warned he was likely to be sent to prison.

1999 Skip Spence, an original member of Jefferson Airplane and founding member of Moby Grape, died of lung cancer in a San Francisco hospital, aged 52. He had battled schizophrenia and alcoholism.

2003 Jerry Lee Lewis filed for divorce from his sixth wife, Kerrie McCarver Lewis. The 67-year-old singer had married Kerrie in 1984; she was the president of Lewis Enterprises Inc. fan club.

BORN ON THIS DAY

1934 Don Kirshner, producer and publisher who launched the careers of Carole King, Neil Sedaka and Harry Nilsson and was instrumental in the creation of The Monkees and The Archies.

1941 Billy Fury, UK singer who had a 1961 UK No.3 single with 'Halfway To Paradise' plus 25 other Top 40 UK singles. Fury died on January 28th 1983 of a heart attack.

1948 Jan Hammer – keyboard player with Mahavishnu Orchestra and Jeff Beck. As a solo artist he has had a 1985 US No.1 & UK No.5 single with 'Miami Vice Theme' and a 1987 UK No.2 single with 'Crockett's Theme'.

1954 Michael Sembello – guitarist and singer who had a 1983 US No.1 & UK No. 43 single with 'Maniac', as featured in the film *Flashdance*.

1955 Pete Shelley – guitarist and singer with The Buzzcocks, who had a 1978 UK No.12 single with 'Ever Fallen In Love, With Someone You Shouldn't've'.

1974 Victoria Adams of The Spice Girls, who had a 1996 UK No.1 & 1997 US No.1 single with 'Wannabe' plus eight other UK No.1 singles and a 2000 UK No.2 solo single with 'Out Of Your Mind'.

ON THIS DAY

1960 the car taking Eddie Cochran and Gene Vincent to London Airport crashed, killing 21-year-old Cochran. Vincent was also injured in the accident. Cochran's current song at the time was 'Three Steps to Heaven'.

1965 Bob Dylan's debut album *The Freewheeling Bob Dylan* was at No.1 on the UK chart.

1965 Paul McCartney spent the day shopping for furniture in Portobello Road, London disguised in a cloth cap, moustache, glasses and an overcoat.

1970 Johnny Cash played at the White House for President Nixon, who requested that he played 'A Boy Named Sue'.

1971 all four Beatles had solo singles in the UK charts: Paul McCartney with 'Another Day'; John

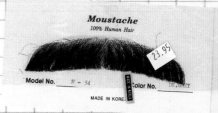

Part of McCartney's disguise from his 1965 shopping trip.

Lennon with 'Power To The People'; George Harrison with 'My Sweet Lord'; and Ringo Starr with 'It Don't Come Easy'.

1973 Pink Floyd's album *The Dark Side of the Moon* went Gold in the US. The LP went on to stay in the US chart for more than ten years, becoming the longest-charting rock record of all time.

1977 appearing at The Roundhouse, London were The Stranglers, Cherry Vanilla, The Police and The Jam.

1983 Felix Pappalardi, producer and bass player with Mountain, was shot dead by his wife Gail Collins during a jealous rage. Collins was convicted of criminally negligent homicide and sentenced to four years in prison. Pappalardi, who was 43, had produced the Cream albums *Disraeli Gears* and *Wheels of Fire*.

1994 Pink Floyd started a four week run at No.1 on the UK album chart with *The Division Bell*.

1998 Linda McCartney died after a long battle against cancer, aged 56. Linda's own range of vegetarian food products had made her a millionaire in her own right.

2004 Kurt Cobain's Mark IV-style Mosrite Gospel guitar sold for $100,000 (£58,800) at the Icons of 20th Century Music auction held in Dallas, Texas. Other items sold included Elton John and Bernie Taupin's songwriting piano ($140,000/£82,350) and a 1966 Rickenbacker guitar owned by The Byrds' Roger McGuinn ($99,000/£58,235).

BORN ON THIS DAY

1939 Glen D. Hardin – keyboardist with The Crickets, who had a 1957 US No.1 single with 'That'll Be The Day', a 1959 UK No.1 single with 'It Doesn't Matter Anymore' plus over 15 other UK Top 40 singles.

1942 Mike Vickers – multi-instrumentalist with Manfred Mann, who had a 1964 UK & US No.1 single with 'Do Wah Diddy Diddy'.

1964 Mark "Bez" Berry – percussionist and dancer with The Happy Mondays who had the 1990 UK No.5 single with 'Step On', then Black Grape, who had a 1995 UK No.8 single with 'In The Name Of The Father'.

1974 Mark Tremonti – guitarist and vocalist with Creed, who had a 2001 US No.1 & UK No.13 single with 'With Arms Wide Open' and a 2002 US No.1 album with *Weathered*.

ON THIS DAY

1953 Frankie Laine was at No.1 on the UK singles chart with 'I Believe.' The single stayed at No.1 for nine weeks.

1964 The Beatles held the UK and US No.1 position on the singles chart with 'Can't Buy Me Love'.

1969 Lulu married Bee Gee Maurice Gibb. Brother Barry was the best man. They split in 1973.

1975 four Bay City Rollers' fans were taken to hospital and 35 others required on site treatment. The fans had attempted to swim across a lake to meet their heroes during an appearance at a BBC Radio 1 fun day at Mallory Park.

1981 this year's Eurovision Song contest winners Buck's Fizz were at No.1 on the UK singles chart with their first No.1 single 'Making Your Mind Up'.

1985 Wham! became the first-ever Western pop act to have an album released in China.

1987 Aretha Franklin and George Michael started a two week run at No.1 on the US singles chart with 'I Knew You Were Waiting', which was also a No.1 in the UK.

1992 Def Leppard started a five week run at No.1 on the US album chart with *Adrenalize*.

1992 Annie Lennox went to No.1 on the UK album chart with her debut solo release *Diva*.

> "Sometimes I wish I had taken the Bob Dylan route and sang songs where my voice would not go out on me every night."
> **Kurt Cobain**

> "I shot people. I ain't gonna tell you who."
> **50 Cent**

1992 Right Said Fred had their first and only UK No.1 single with 'Deeply Dippy'. ('I'm Too Sexy' and 'Don't Talk Just Kiss' both made the Top 3).

1996 Bernard Edwards, guitarist and producer from Chic, died in a Tokyo Hotel room after complaining that he was feeling ill. He had produced ABC, Power Station and Rod Stewart.

1999 Catatonia scored their second UK No.1 album with *Equally Cursed And Blessed*. The group also had their two other albums in the Top 40 at the time.

2003 it was reported that the British share of the most played tracks on UK radio had fallen from 60 percent to 30 percent in the past five years. The chart from 2002 had only three UK acts in the Top 10, Sugarbabes, Blue and Liberty X. The most played single from 2002 was Kylie Minogue's 'Love At First Sight', which had a total of 48,486 plays on UK stations.

2005 Sports firm Reebok pulled a TV ad featuring 50 Cent after a mother whose son was shot dead complained it glamorised gun crime. The ASA had been investigating 54 other complaints from viewers over a reference to the rapper having been shot nine times.

BORN ON THIS DAY

1928 Alexis Korner *(right)*, UK blues singer and major force behind the UK early 60s R&B scene, who had a 1971 UK No.5 single with CCS 'Tap Turns On The Water'. Korner died on January 1st 1984.

1942 Alan Price – keyboardist with The Animals, who had a 1964 UK & US No.1 single with 'House Of The Rising Sun'. As a solo artist he had a 1967 UK No.4 single with 'Simon Smith And His Amazing Dancing Bear'.

1944 Bernie Worrell – keyboardist with Parliament and Funkadelic who had a 1978 US No.16 album with *One Nation Under A Groove*.

1947 Mark Volman – songwriter, vocalist and mult-instrumentalist with The Turtles, who had a 1967 US No.1 single with 'Happy Together' and a 1967 UK No.4 single with 'She'd Rather Be With Me'. As one half of duo Flo and Eddie he also worked with Frank Zappa, T. Rex and Bruce Springsteen.

ON THIS DAY

1965 the film *T.A.M.I. (Teen-Age Music International)* featuring The Rolling Stones, The Supremes, The Four Tops, James Brown, The Beach Boys and Smokey Robinson & The Miracles opened in London.

1968 John Lennon, George Harrison and their wives left the Maharishi Mahesh Yogi's ashram in Rishikesh, India two weeks before their study was complete. Ringo and Paul had already left.

1970 Eurovision Song Contest winner Dana was at No.1 on the UK singles chart with 'All Kinds Of Everything'.

1980 Blondie went to No.1 on the US singles chart with 'Call Me', which featured in the Richard Gere movie *American Gigolo*.

1980 Brian Johnson, 32-year-old singer with Geordie, joined AC/DC, replacing Bon Scott who had died after a drinks binge.

1980 for the first time ever the top five artists in the US country chart were all female: Crystal Gayle, who was at No.1; Dottie West; Debbie Boone; Emmylou Harris and Tammy Wynette.

1986 George Michael was at No.1 on the UK singles chart with 'A Different Corner', the singer's second solo No.1.

1986 Prince started a two week run at No.1 on the US singles chart with 'Kiss'. A song he wrote under the pseudonym "Christopher", 'Manic Monday', was at No.2 for The Bangles. 'Manic Monday' also made No.2 in the UK.

1988 Sonny Bono was inaugurated as the Mayor of Palm Springs.

1995 The Stone Roses played their first gig in five years when they appeared at The Rockerfella Club, Oslo, Norway.

1998 Robbie Williams started a two week run at No.1 on the UK album chart with *Life Thru A Lens*.

2000 Phil Collins won £250,000 ($425,000) in a high court case over royalties with two former members of his band. The judge ruled that they had been overpaid in error but because the two musicians had no other income they would not have to pay it back.

2002 police were investigating how tracks from the forthcoming Oasis album *Heathen Chemistry* had been illegally circulated on the Internet. They thought the person responsible had access to the Oasis private recording sessions.

2003 the oldest working musician in Britain, Conrad Leonard died aged 104. Conrad had worked with Cole Porter and Petula Clark.

Oasis seek Internet leak culprit

Oasis, the pop group whose unreleased album *Heathen Chemistry* has been illegally circulated on the Internet, said that the person responsible had access to their private recording sessions. However, the band said that the leaked tracks, which can be downloaded free of charge, were early versions, and on the new album the songs would sound much better.

An investigator has been

BORN ON THIS DAY

1939 Johnny Tillotson, US singer who had a 1960 US No.2 and 1961 UK No.1 single with 'Poetry In Motion'.

1948 Craig Frost – keyboardist with Grand Funk Railroad, who had a 1974 US No.1 single with 'The Locomotion'.

1951 Luther Vandross, soul singer who had a 1989 UK No.13 single with 'Never Too Much', first released 1983, and a US No.10 and UK No.2 single with Janet Jackson 'The Best Things In Life Are Free'. Vandross died on July 1st 2005.

1971 Mikey Welsh – bass player with Weezer, who had a 1995 UK No.12 single with 'Buddy Holly'.

ON THIS DAY

1957 Elvis Presley started an eight week run at No.1 on the US singles chart with 'All Shook Up'. It went on to be the biggest single of 1957, selling over two million copies.

1959 thirteen-year-old Dolly Parton released her first single in America, 'Puppy Love', which was later to be a hit for Donny Osmond.

1968 Deep Purple made their live debut in Tastrup, Denmark.

1970 *The New York Times* reported that Catholic and Protestant youth groups had adopted the Yellow Submarine as featured in The Beatles song as a religious symbol.

1974 MFSB featuring The Three Degrees started a two week run at No.1 on the US singles chart with 'TSOP, (The Sound Of Philadelphia)'. It made No.22 in the UK.

1979 lighting director Billy Duffy was killed in an accident during a Kate Bush concert in Southampton, England. 22-year-old Duffy fell 6m (20 ft) through an open trap door on the stage. Kate Bush held a benefit concert on May 12th with Peter Gabriel and Steve Harley at London's Hammersmith Odeon for his family.

1981 John Phillips of The Mamas And The Papas was jailed for five years after pleading guilty to drug possession charges. The sentence was suspended after 30 days. Phillips started touring the US lecturing against the dangers of taking drugs.

1985 charity record 'We Are The World' by USA For Africa was at No.1 on the UK singles chart. The all-star cast included Stevie Wonder, Tina Turner, Bruce Springsteen, Diana Ross, Bob Dylan plus the writers of the track, Michael Jackson and Lionel Richie.

1990 Janet Jackson was bestowed with a star on the Hollywood Walk Of Fame at the start of Janet Jackson Week in Los Angeles.

1991 Steve Marriott, leader of Small Faces And Humble Pie, died in a fire at his home in Essex. His work became a major influence for many 90s bands. As a child actor he played parts in *Dixon Of Dock Green* and The Artful Dodger in *Oliver*.

1992 "A Concert For Life" took place at Wembley Stadium as a tribute to Freddie Mercury and for AIDS awareness. Extreme, Bob Geldof, U2, Def Leppard, Guns N' Roses, George Michael with Queen, Elton John, Annie Lennox and David Bowie all played.

2000 Robert Plant appeared at Disney's Theater Of The Stars in Orlando, Florida to leave his hand prints outside the theatre.

2001 a memorial concert for former Small Faces and Humble Pie frontman Steve Marriott took place at the London Astoria with Peter Frampton, Midge Ure, Chris Farlowe and Humble Pie.

2002 in the dispute over who owned the rights to Nirvana's recordings Dave Grohl and Kirst Novoselic asked a Seattle Court to prove that Courtney Love was mentally unstable. They told the court that Love was "irrational, mercurial, self-centred, unmanageable, inconsistent and unpredictable". They also claimed a contract was invalid because Love was "stoned" at the time.

2002 American singer Alan Dale died. During the 1950s he had his own US TV and radio show, and also had a 1955 US No.7 single with 'Cherry Pink and Apple Blossom White'.

BORN ON THIS DAY

1936 Roy Orbison, singer/songwriter, who had a 1964 UK & US No.1 single with 'Pretty Woman' plus over 20 US & 30 UK Top 40 singles. With the Traveling Wilburys he had a 1988 UK No.21 single with 'Handle With Care'. Orbison died on December 6th 1988.

1939 Ray Peterson, US singer who had a 1960 US No.7 single with 'Tell Laura I Love Her'. He died on January 25th 2005.

1949 John Miles, singer/songwriter who had a 1976 UK No.3 single with 'Music'. He has also worked with Tina Turner.

1955 Captain Sensible, (a.k.a. Ray Burns) – singer and guitarist with The Damned, who had a 1983 UK No.3 single with 'Eloise'. As a solo artist he had a 1982 UK No.1 single with 'Happy Talk'.

1960 David Gedge – vocalist and guitarist with The Wedding Present. During 1992 they released one single every month, giving them 12 Top 30 hits and making them the only group to score more than ten new hits in one year.

1960 Steve Clark – guitarist with Def Leppard, who had a 1987 UK No.6 single with 'Animal', a 1987 worldwide No.1 album with *Hysteria* and a 1988 US No.1 single with 'Love Bites'. Clark died on January 8th 1991, aged 30 after a night of heavy alcohol consumption combined with prescription drugs.

ON THIS DAY

1956 Elvis Presley made his Las Vegas debut at the New Frontier Hotel when he opened for the Freddie Martin Orchestra and comedian Shecky Greene. The two week run was called off after only one week due to poor audience response.

1960 The Nerk Twins appeared at The Fox And Hounds in Caversham, Berkshire, England. The Nerk Twins were John Lennon and Paul McCartney, who were staying at Paul's aunt's pub.

1971 The Rolling Stones released their classic album *Sticky Fingers* in the UK. The album made No.1 in the UK and the US and was the band's first release on Atlantic Records. Andy Warhol was paid £15,000 ($25,500) for the artwork on the album sleeve, which included a working zip.

1975 Peter Ham, singer/songwriter with Badfinger, committed suicide by hanging himself. He co-wrote 'Without You', a hit for Harry Nilsson and Mariah Carey.

1976 The Ramones released their eponymous debut album. On the same day The Sex Pistols played The Nashville Rooms, London supporting The 101'ers who featured Clash vocalist Joe Strummer.

1977 Adam And The Ants made their debut at the Roxy Club, London.

1983 Dexy's Midnight Runners went to No.1 on the US singles chart with 'Come On Eileen'.

1987 Carole King sued record company owner Lou Adler for breach of contract. King claimed that she was owed over $400,000 (£235,300) in royalties. She also asked for rights to her old recordings.

1988 Roy Orbison celebrated his 52nd birthday at a Bruce Springsteen concert, during which the audience sang 'Happy Birthday' to him.

1989 Kylie Minogue was seen on British TV for the first time in the Australian soap opera *The Henderson Kids* **(right)**.

1991 founder member of The New York Dolls Johnny Thunders died of a drug overdose.

1992 George Michael announced he was donating $500,000 (£294,100) royalties from the sale of 'Don't Let The Sun Go Down On Me' to various British and American charities.

1997 club boss Paul Donavan was fined over

A rare copy of the Russian *Sticky Fingers* album.

£2,000 ($3,400) after being found guilty of tricking fans that he had singer Peter Andre appearing at his club in the West Midlands. He had in fact booked an act called Peter Andrex, a puppet who threw toilet rolls.

BORN ON THIS DAY

1942 Barbra Streisand, singer and actress who had a 1974 US No.1 & UK No.31 single with 'The Way We Were', a 1980 UK & US No.1 single with 'Woman In Love' plus over ten other UK Top 40 singles and four other US No.1s.

1945 Doug Clifford – drummer with Creedence Clearwater Revival, who had a 1969 UK No.1 and US No.2 single with 'Bad Moon Rising' plus 11 other US Top 40 singles and a 1970 US & UK No.1 album with *Cosmo's Factory*.

1947 Glenn Cornick – bass player with Jethro Tull, who had a 1969 UK No.3 and US No.11 single with 'Living In The Past'.

1960 Paula Yates, presenter on UK music TV show *The Tube*, ex-wife of Sir Bob Geldof and girlfriend of INXS singer Michael Hutchence. She died on September 17th 2000.

1963 Billy Gould – bass player with Faith No More, who had a 1993 UK No.3 and US No.4 single with 'I'm Easy'.

1982 Kelly Clarkson, winner of the US TV show *Pop Idol* who had a 2002 US No.1 single with 'A Moment Like This', a 2003 UK No.6 single with 'Miss Independent' and a 2003 US No.1 album with *Thankful*.

ON THIS DAY

1959 Buddy Holly was at No.1 in the UK with the single 'It Doesn't Matter Anymore'.

1961 Bob Dylan guested on Harry Belafonte's album *The Midnight Special* playing harmonica on the track 'Calypso King'. Dylan was paid a $50 (£29) session fee for this, his first-ever recording.

1961 Del Shannon started a four week run at No.1 on the US singles chart with 'Runaway'.

Room service at The Holiday Inn with Keith Moon.

1965 Beatles manager Brian Epstein won the "star prize" of an album when he had his letter published in music weekly *Melody Maker* informing its readers that Paul McCartney played lead guitar on 'Ticket To Ride'.

1965 Wayne Fontana And The Mindbenders went to No.1 in the US with 'Game Of Love', a No.2 hit in the UK. Wayne took his name from DJ Fontana, Elvis Presley's drummer.

1968 enjoying a wild birthday party Keith Moon, drummer of The Who, drove his Lincoln car into a Holiday Inn swimming pool.

1968 Louis Armstrong was at No.1 in the UK with the single 'What A Wonderful World/Cabaret'. At 69 years old, Armstrong became the oldest act ever to score a UK No.1.

1976 Paul *(right)* and Linda McCartney spent the evening with John Lennon at his New York Dakota apartment and watched *Saturday Night Live* on TV. The producer of the show, Lorne Michaels, made an offer on air asking The Beatles to turn up and play three songs live on the show. Lennon and McCartney thought about taking a cab to the studio, but decided they were too tired. This was the last time Lennon and McCartney were together.

1984 R.E.M. kicked off a seven date UK tour at the Tin Can Club, Birmingham, England, the band's first UK tour.

1984 Jerry Lee Lewis married wife number six, 22-year-old Kerrie McCarver.

1990 the road crew for Roger Waters discovered an unexploded World War II bomb while constructing the set for The Wall concert in Potsdamer Platz, Germany.

1995 Oasis released 'Some Might Say', which gave the band their first UK No.1 single.

2003 the first official UK download chart was compiled after EMI, Warners, Sony, BMG and Universal combined for a Digital Download day. 1.1 million tracks had been downloaded by over 150,000 computer users. The Net Parade Top 3 was: No.3, Tatu with 'All The Things She Said'; No.2, Coldplay with 'Clocks' and No.1, Christina Aguilera with 'Beautiful'.

25th April

BORN ON THIS DAY

1918 Ella Fitzgerald, US jazz singer who had a 1960 US No.27 & UK No.19 single with 'Mack The Knife'. She died on June 15th 1996.

1933 Jerry Leiber, songwriter and producer (with Stoller) for Elvis Presley, Buddy Holly, The Monkees and Cliff Richard.

1945 Bjorn Ulvaeus – guitarist and vocalist with Abba, whose first UK hit was the 1974 No.1 single 'Waterloo', followed by eight other UK No.1 singles and nine No.1 albums. They also had a 1977 US No.1 single with 'Dancing Queen'.

1945 Stu Cook – bass player with Creedence Clearwater Revival, who had a 1969 UK No.1 and US No.2 single with 'Bad Moon Rising' plus 11 other US Top 40 singles and a 1970 US & UK No.1 album with *Cosmo's Factory*.

1965 Simon Fowler – vocalist with Ocean Colour Scene, who had a 1996 UK No.4 single with 'The Day We Caught The Train' plus over 12 other Top 40 singles and a 1997 UK No.1 album with *Marchin' Already*.

1980 Jacob Underwood – singer/songwriter and guitarist with O-Town, who were winners of the US TV show *Making The Band*. They had a 2001 US No.3 single with 'All Or Nothing' and a 2001 UK No.3 single with 'Liquid Dreams'.

ON THIS DAY

1954 Johnnie Ray was at No.1 on the UK singles chart with 'Such A Night'. This was the singer's first of three UK No.1s.

1960 Elvis Presley started a four week run at No.1 on the US singles chart with 'Stuck On You', which was a No.3 hit in the UK.

1967 The Beatles recorded the theme to *Magical Mystery Tour* at Abbey Road Studios, London.

1970 The Jackson Five started a two week run at No.1 on the US singles chart with 'ABC'. It was the group's second US No.1, and it made No.8 in the UK.

1977 at a concert at the Saginaw, Michigan Civic Center, Elvis Presley made the last recordings of his life. Three songs from the show appeared on the posthumously released Presley album *Moody Blue*.

1979 The Police made their debut on BBC TV's *Top Of The Pops* performing 'Roxanne'.

1980 Stranglers singer and guitarist Hugh Cornwell was released from a London prison after serving six weeks for the possession of drugs.

1987 Madonna became the only female artist to score four UK No.1 singles when 'La Isla Bonita', went to the top of the charts.

1987 U2 started a five week run at No.1 in the US album chart with *The Joshua Tree*.

1988 Bon Jovi's manager Doc Mcgee was convicted on drug offences arising from the 1982 seizure of 18,134kg (40,000lb) of marijuana, smuggled into North Carolina from Colombia. McGee was sentenced to a five year suspended prison term and a $15,000 (£8,823) fine.

1990 the Fender Stratocaster that Jimi Hendrix used to perform the 'Star Spangled Banner' at the Woodstock Festival was auctioned off for $295,000 (£173,530).

1992 Kris Kross started an eight week run at No.1 on the US singles chart with 'Jump', which was a No.2 hit in the UK. The duo of Chris Smith and Chris Kelly were 12 and 13 when they recorded the song.

Destitute, Abba save on the travel budget by having flying lessons four at a time.

1994 Adam Horovitz of the Beastie Boys was sentenced to 200 hours of community service for attacking a TV cameraman.

1996 a pair of skin-tight trousers owned by Queen singer Freddie Mercury were sold at a pop memorabilia sale in London.

2003 in this year's *Sunday Times* Rich List, Paul McCartney was confirmed as the world's richest musician with a fortune worth over £760 million ($1,292 million). Madonna was fourth, with £227 million ($386 million), Mick Jagger was sixth with £175 million ($298 million) and Elton John seventh with £170 million ($290 million). Ozzy Osbourne became the 24th richest musician after earning an estimated £42 million ($71 million) from his TV show *The Osbournes*.

BORN ON THIS DAY

1938 Duane Eddy, guitarist who had a 1960 UK No.2 and US No.4 single with 'Because They're Young' plus over 15 other UK & US Top 40 singles.

1938 Maurice Williams, singer who had a 1960 US No.1 & 1961 UK No.14 single with The Zodiacs and 'Stay'. The song was also a hit for Jackson Browne and The Hollies.

1940 Giorgio Moroder, producer who had a 1979 US No.33 & UK No. 48 single with 'Chase' from the film *Midnight Express*. He produced Donna Summer's worldwide 1976 hit 'Love To Love You Baby' and wrote the 1984 UK No.3 single with Phil Oakey 'Together In Electric Dreams'.

1945 Tony Murray – bass guitarist with The Troggs, who had a 1966 US No.1 & UK No.2 single with 'Wild Thing'.

1945 Gary Wright – vocalist and keyboardist with Spooky Tooth and a solo artist who had a 1976 US No.2 single with 'Dream Weaver'.

1960 Roger Taylor – drummer with Duran Duran, who had a 1983 UK No.1 single with 'Is There Something I Should Know?' plus 25 other UK Top 40 singles and a 1984 US No.1 single with 'The Reflex', and Arcadia, who had a 1985 UK No.7 single with 'Election Day'.

1970 Tionne "T-Boz" Watkins – vocalist with TLC, who had a 1995 US No.1 & UK No.4 single 'Waterfalls' while the 1999 US No.1 album *Fanmail* spent 57 weeks on the UK chart.

1975 Joey Jordison – drummer with Slipknot, who had a 2001 UK No.1 album with *Iowa*.

ON THIS DAY

1964 The Beatles, Rolling Stones and The Dave Clark Five headlined the *NME* poll winners' concert at Wembley Empire Pool, London.

1966 Dusty Springfield *(left)* was at No.1 on the UK singles chart with 'You Don't Have To Say You Love Me', which was the singer's only UK No.1.

1969 Led Zeppelin played the second of two nights at The Winterland Ballroom, San Francisco in California.

1980 Blondie was at No.1 on the UK singles chart with 'Call Me', the group's fourth UK No.1.

1980 The Beat released 'Mirror In The Bathroom', the first digitally recorded single in the UK.

1982 Rod Stewart was mugged by a gunman along Hollywood's Sunset Boulevard while standing next to his car.

1982 Meat Loaf played the first of four sold-out nights at Wembley Arena, London.

1984 Mike McCartney unveiled a £40,000 ($64,000) statue of The Beatles by John Doubleday at the new £8 million Cavern Walks shopping centre. John's first wife, Cynthia, also attended.

1986 Bryan Ferry And Roxy Music started a five week run at No.1 on the UK album chart with *Street Life – 20 Greatest Hits*.

1990 New Kids On The Block's Danny Wood injured his ankle while on stage in Manchester when he tripped over a toy animal thrown on stage by a fan. He was forced to fly back to the States for treatment.

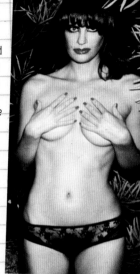

Roxy Music fan gets all hot and bothered over album release mix-up.

1994 Grace Slick pleaded guilty to pointing a shotgun at police in her California home. She claimed she was under stress because her home had burned down the previous year. She was later sentenced to 200 hours of community service.

1995 Courtney Love reportedly turned down *Playboy* magazine's $1 million (£588,000) offer for her to pose nude.

1997 Ernest Stewart, keyboard player with KC & The Sunshine Band, died of an asthma attack.

2002 TLC member Lisa Lopes was killed in a car accident in La Ceiba, Honduras, aged 30. Seven other people, including Lopes' brother and sister, who were in the Mitsubishi Montero sports utility vehicle when the crash happened, were taken to a hospital. Lopes, who was driving the car when it crashed, had spent the past month in Honduras working on various projects including a clothing line, a new solo project and a book.

ON THIS DAY

1947 Ann Peebles, US soul singer who had a 1973 US No.33 & UK No.41 single with 'I Can't Stand The Rain'.

1947 Gordon Haskell – singer/songwriter, member of King Crimson and solo artist who had a 2001 UK No.2 single with 'How Wonderful You Are' and a 2001 UK No.2 album, *Harry's Bar*.

1947 Peter Ham – vocalist and guitarist with The Iveys and Badfinger, who had a 1970 UK No.4 single with 'Come And Get It'. He committed suicide on April 23rd 1975.

1948 Kate Pierson – vocalist with The B-52's, who had a 1990 UK No.2 & US No.3 single with 'Love Shack'.

1949 Herb Murrell – vocalist with The Stylistics, who had a 1974 US No.2 single with 'You Make Me Feel Brand New', a 1975 UK No.1 single with 'Can't Give You Anything But My Love' plus 15 other UK Top 40 singles.

1951 Paul Frehley – guitarist and vocalist for Kiss, who had a 1974 US No.5 single with 'On And On' and a 1976 US No.11 album *Rock and Roll Over*, which spent 26 weeks on the chart. They also had a 1987 UK No.4 single with 'Crazy Crazy Nights'.

1959 Marco Pirroni – guitarist with Adam And The Ants, who had a 1981 UK No.1 single with 'Stand And Deliver' plus 15 other UK Top 40 singles.

1959 Sheena Easton, singer who had a 1980 UK No.3 & 1981 US No.1 single with 'Morning Train, Nine To Five'.

ON THIS DAY

1967 Sandie Shaw was at No.1 on the UK singles chart with 'Puppet On A String', her third UK No.1 and the Eurovision Song Contest winner of 1967.

1975 Pink Floyd played the last of a four night run at Los Angeles' Sports Arena. A total of 511 fans were arrested over the four nights for possession of marijuana.

1976 David Bowie was detained by customs officers on a train at the Russian/Polish Border after Nazi books and mementoes were found in his luggage.

1981 Ringo Starr married actress and one-time "Bond girl" Barbara Bach.

1985 USA For Africa started a three week run at No.1 on the US album chart with *We Are The World*.

1991 Christian singer Amy Grant started a two week run at No.1 on the US singles chart with 'Baby Baby', which was a No.2 hit in the UK.

1993 Prince issued a statement saying he was retiring from studio recordings to concentrate on films and other ventures.

1994 a man was arrested after breaking into Ace Of Base singer Jenny Berggren's home. Jenny was asleep at the time and woke up to find the man above her holding a hunting knife.

1996 Oasis played the first of two nights at Manchester's Maine Road Football Club, as a thank you to their fans. The 80,000 tickets sold out in hours.

2003 appearing at Birmingham N.I.A., England were S Club 7, Busted, Dannii Minogue, Girls Aloud, Sonique, Kym Marsh, David Sneddon and S Club 7 Juniors.

2003 US TV's *Pop Idol* winner Kelly Clarkson was at No.1 on the US album chart with *Thankful*.

2003 UK boyband Busted went to No.1 on the UK singles chart with 'You Said No'.

2003 Madonna went to No.1 on the UK album chart with *American Life*, the singer's eighth No.1 album.

BORN ON THIS DAY

1945 John Wolters – drummer with Dr. Hook, who had a 1972 UK No.2 and US No.5 single with 'Sylvia's Mother'.

1953 Kim Gordon – bass player with Sonic Youth, who had a 1993 UK No.26 single with 'Sugar Kane'.

1955 Eddie Jobson – violinist with Curved Air, who had a 1971 UK No.4 single with 'Back Street Luv', and Roxy Music, who had a 1975 UK No.2 single with 'Love Is The Drug'.

1968 Daisy Berkowitz (a.k.a. Scott Putesky) – guitarist with Marilyn Manson, who had a 1998 US No.1 album with *Mechanical Animals* and a UK No.12 single with 'The Dope Show'.

1970 Howard Donald – vocalist with Take That, who had a 1995 UK No.1 single with 'Back For Good' and seven other UK No.1 singles.

ON THIS DAY

1966 The Kinks appeared at the Mecca Ballroom, Nottingham, England.

1968 the musical "Hair" opened at the Baltimore Theater, New York. The first rock-musical, it went on to give 1,729 performances on Broadway and was made into a movie in 1979.

1973 Pink Floyd's album *Dark Side Of The Moon* went to No.1 in the US. It stayed on the chart for a record-breaking 741 weeks, selling over 20 million copies worldwide.

1979 Blondie scored their first US No.1 single with 'Heart Of Glass', which was also No.1 in the UK.

1981 former member of T. Rex, Steve Currie, was killed in a car accident on holiday in Portugal aged 34.

1990 Guns N' Roses leader Axl Rose married Erin Everly, daughter of The Everly Brothers' Don Everly at Cupid's Wedding Chapel in Las Vegas. They divorced in January 1991 after a stormy nine months of marriage.

1990 Sinead O'Connor started a six week run at No.1 on the US album chart with *I Do Not Want What I Haven't Got*.

1997 Mark Morrison was fined £750 ($1,275) after admitting threatening behaviour during an incident in Leicester city centre when he believed someone had kicked his car.

1999 the tour bus carrying The Clint Boon Experience was involved in a near-fatal accident when it was involved in a crash outside of Glasgow. Members of the band had to be airlifted to hospital.

1999 Tom Petty And The Heartbreakers received a star on the Hollywood Walk of Fame.

2000 a blaze swept through James Brown Enterprises, the office that co-ordinates the superstar's tours. Nobody was injured, but memorabilia and live tapes were destroyed in the blaze. An employee was later arrested charged with arson.

2000 Paul Atkinson was jailed for three years after being found guilty of stealing more than £25,000 ($42,500) from Rolling Stone Charlie Watts. Atkinson had been the manager of an Arabian stud farm owned by Watts.

2003 Ozzy Osbourne's son Jack was reported to be in rehab. The 17-year-old was a patient at Las Encinas Hospital in Pasadena, California.

Blondie cribs a title from the classic Herzog film.

Jesus & Mary Chain
After Show 29.4.88   ULU

BORN ON THIS DAY

1899 Duke Ellington, composer, bandleader and pianist. He worked with Louis Armstrong, Ella Fitzgerald, Dizzy Gillespie and Billie Holiday. Ellington died on May 24th 1974.

1928 Carl Gardner – singer with The Coasters, who had a 1958 US No.1 single with 'Yakety Yak' and a 1959 US No.2 and UK No.6 single with 'Charlie Brown'.

1931 Lonnie Donegan, singer who launched the skiffle craze. He had a 1960 UK No.1 single with 'My Old Man's A Dustman', plus over 30 other UK Top 40 singles. He died on November 3rd 2002.

1942 Klaus Voorman – bass player for Manfred Mann and the Plastic Ono Band. He also designed the cover for The Beatles' album Revolver.

1947 Tommy James – singer and guitarist with The Shondells, who had a 1966 US No.1 single with 'Hanky Panky' and a 1968 UK No.1 single with 'Mony Mony'.

1949 Francis Rossi – guitarist and vocalist with Status Quo, who had a 1977 UK No.3 single with 'Rockin' All Over The World' plus 50 other UK Top 75 singles since 1968.

1953 Bill Drummond, producer, A&R man, writer, musician. Joined Big In Japan in 1977 (with Holly Johnson, later of Frankie Goes To Hollywood and Ian Broudie later of The Lightning Seeds). Co-founder of Merseyside's Zoo Records. Formed KLF in the late 1980's, who had a 1991 UK No.1 single '3 AM Eternal'.

1968 Carine Wilson – singer with Wilson Phillips, who had a 1990 US No.1 & UK No.6 single with 'Hold On'. She is the daughter of Beach Boy Brian Wilson.

1979 Joanne Velda O'Meara – vocalist with S Club 7, who had a 1999 UK No.1 single with 'Bring It All Back'.

ON THIS DAY

1965 Jimmy Nicol, the drummer who stood in for Ringo Starr during a Beatles Australian tour in 1964, appeared in a London Court faced with bankruptcy and debts of £4,000 ($6,800).

1972 Roberta Flack started a five week run at No.1 on the US album chart with First Take.

1973 John Denver began a weekly live UK BBC 2 TV special, The John Denver Show.

1976 after a gig in Memphis Bruce Springsteen took a cab to Elvis Presley's Graceland and proceeded to climb over the wall. A guard took him to be another crank fan and apprehended him.

1978 P.J. Proby was sacked from his role in the London stage musical "Elvis" after repeatedly changing his lines from the script. Proby had been playing the oldest of three Presleys in the play.

1981 Elton John paid £14,000 ($23,800) for 232 "Goon Show" BBC radio scripts broadcast during the 1950s at an auction held at Christies, London.

1989 Jon Bon Jovi married childhood sweetheart Hurly on the steps of the Graceland Chapel, Las Vegas.

1992 Paula Abdul married actor Emilio Estevez. They separated in 1994.

1993 guitarist and producer Mick Ronson died of cancer. Def Leppard's Joe Elliot said of his death, "If there's a God up there why does he do this? It can only be because he's trying to put together the ultimate band."

1995 Rapper Tupac Shakur married Keisha Morris inside the Clinton Correctional Facility, where he was serving a four year jail term for sex abuse.

2001 Rod Stewart asked for wedding vows to be brought up-to-date. Stewart said "a change is needed because they've been in existence for 600 years when people used to live until they were 35".

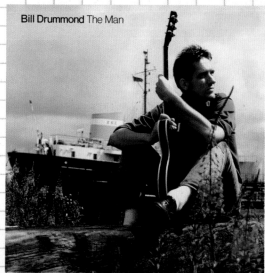

Bill Drummond, solo artist and founder of the KLF.

BORN ON THIS DAY

1933 Willie Nelson, US country singer and actor, who had a 1982 US No.5 single with 'Always On My Mind' and a 1984 UK No.17 single with 'To All The Girls I've Loved Before'. He also wrote the country classic 'Crazy' hit for Patsy Cline.

1943 Bobby Vee, US singer who had a 1961 US No.1 single & UK No.3 single with 'Take Good Care Of My Baby'.

1953 Merrill Osmond – singer with The Osmonds, who had a 1971 US No.1 single with 'One Bad Apple', a 1974 UK No.1 single with 'Love Me For A Reason' plus nine other US & UK Top 40 singles.

ON THIS DAY

1960 The Everly Brothers started a seven week run at No.1 on the UK singles chart with 'Cathy's Clown', giving Warner Bros a No.1 with their first release.

1965 Manchester group Herman's Hermits began their first US tour, supported by The Zombies.

1965 the first night of a twice-nightly UK package tour with The Yardbirds, The Kinks and Goldie And The Gingerbreads at The Adelphi Cinema, Slough, England.

1966 The Young Rascals went to No.1 on the US singles chart with 'Good Lovin'. The song had been a hit for The Olympics the year before.

1966 The Rolling Stones' fourth album *Aftermath* went to No.1 on the UK chart.

1968 BBC TV launched *The Cilla Black Show* making Cilla the first British female performer to have her own TV show. The theme song, 'Step Inside Love', was written by Paul McCartney.

1976 The Who's drummer Keith Moon paid nine cab drivers to block off both ends of a New York street so he could throw the contents of his hotel room out of the window.

1980 the film *McVicar* with Roger Daltry in the title role premiered in London.

You're My World
Cilla Black

Introducing the star of The Cilla Black Show.

1982 rock critic Lester Bangs died of a heart attack, aged 33. Bangs worked for *Rolling Stone*, *Creem* and *The Village Voice*.

1983 blues legend Muddy Waters died, aged 68. He wrote 'I Just Want To Make Love To You', 'I'm Your Hoochie Coochie Man' and 'Got My Mojo Working'.

1983 Michael Jackson started a three week run at No.1 on the US singles chart with 'Beat It', his fifth solo US No.1, which was a No.3 UK hit.

1990 Prince played a concert at Rupert's Nightclub, Minneapolis. The $100 (£58) a head ticket proceeds all went to the family of his former bodyguard Charles Huntsberry, who had died from a heart attack.

1991 Nirvana signed a deal with Geffen Records.

1999 Nazareth drummer Darrell Sweet died aged 52, after suffering a fatal heart attack before a show in New Albany, Indiana. The band had had a 1973 UK No.9 single with 'Broken Down Angel' and a 1976 US No. 8 single with 'Love Hurts'.

1999 the three former members of Spandau Ballet lost a court case against band songwriter Gary Kemp. They had claimed they were owed £1 million ($1.7 million) in lost royalties. The judge said he had become a fan of the band during the case.

2001 a light aircraft carrying Sting went off the runway as it landed in Florence. None of the four aboard – Sting, a friend and two pilots – were hurt. Brake failure was suspected.

2005 appearing at Carling Live 24 in London – The Departure, Kaiser Chiefs, Babyshambles, The Zutons and 2ManyDJs.

Cover shot for Nirvana's *Bleach* album.

Back stage demands from Demanding Divas

Cher high security room for her wigs.

Britney Spears supply of Gummie Bear soft sweets.

Shania Twain sniffer dog in case of bombs.

Janet Jackson doctor, nurse and throat specialist.

Jennifer Lopez white furniture, flowers and carpeting.

Mary J Blige first $100,000 fee paid on the night in $100 notes.

Dixie Chicks membership passes for local golf club.

Whitney Houston independent electicity supply in dressing room.

Faith Hill soundproof 'childrens room'.

Mariah Carey selection of 'live' puppy dogs.

Around the world in ... 10 songs

1 'London Calling' The Clash

2 'California Girls' The Beach Boys

3 'Spanish Stroll' Mink De Ville

4 'Back In The USSR' The Beatles

5 'China Girl' David Bowie

6 'Down Under' Men At Work

7 'Don't Cry For Me Argentina' Madonna

8 'I Love L.A.' Randy Newman

9 'New York - New York' Frank Sinatra

10 'Belfast Child' Simple Minds

The *Sunday Times* Musicians Rich List

Sir Paul McCartney – £760m

Madonna and Guy Ritchie – £215m

Sir Mick Jagger – £180m

Sir Elton John – £175m

Sting – £175m

Keith Richard – £165m

Tom Jones – £165m

Phil Collins – £130m

Eric Clapton – £120m

Ringo Starr – £115m

10 things you didn't know about ... Elvis

1 Elvis made his first ever public appearance in a talent contest at the Mississippi, Alabama Dairy Show, singing 'Old Shep'. Elvis was 10 years old at the time and came second.

2 He was fired from his job at Loew's State Theatre during 1952 after punching a fellow usher who told the manager that Elvis was getting free candy from the girl at the concession stand.

3 In 1957, Elvis was rushed to a Los Angles hospital after swallowing a porcelain cap from one of his front teeth which then lodged itself in one of his lungs.

4 Sheet metal worker Louis Balint punched Elvis at a hotel in Toledo claiming that his wife's love for the singer had caused his marriage to break up. Balint was fined $19.60 but ended up being jailed after he was unable to pay the fine.

5 In 1957, Elvis purchased the stately mansion 'Graceland' in Whitehaven, Memphis. He paid $102,500 for the property which had previously been used by the Graceland Christian Church.

6 In 1958, sales of Elvis Presley's 'Hound Dog' exceeded three million copies in the USA, becoming only the third single to do so – (Bing Crosby's 'White Christmas' and 'Rudolph The Red Nose Reindeer' by Gene Autry being the other two).

7 In 1988, Hound Dog was named the most played record of all time on American juke boxes.

8 Elvis became the first rock 'n' roll artist to be honoured by the US Postal Service with a commemorative stamp.

9 In 1997, a report showed that Elvis was the world's best selling posthumous entertainer. With world-wide sales over 1 billion, over 480 active fanclubs and an estimated 250,000 UK fans still buying his records. He died owing $3 million.

10 In 2005 Elvis was named the most successful music act of all time by Guinness World Records, having spent 2,463 weeks in the UK album and singles charts.

10 reasons not to have a night out on the town with Oasis singer Liam Gallagher

1 He caused £5,000 worth of damage when he trashed the snooker room at the Groucho Club in London. Liam was later arrested by police who thought he was a tramp.

2 In 1997, he was given a formal caution by police after admitting criminal damage following an incident with a cyclist in Camden, London. Gallagher had grabbed the rider from the window of his chauffeur-driven car and broke his Ray-bans.

3 In 2002, Liam was arrested and charged with assault after he kung-fu kicked a police officer. The incident happened at the Bayerischer hotel in Munich. The singer lost his two front teeth in the brawl and an Oasis minder was knocked out cold.

4 In 1998, Liam appeared handcuffed in a Brisbane court and was released on bail on charges of headbutting a fan during a gig in Australia.

5 In 1998, Liam and Simply Red singer Mick Hucknall were involved in a brawl at The Metropolitan Hotel, London.

6 In 1998, Liam was arrested after an alleged drunken brawl with photographer Mel Bouzac at a London pub. Bouzac had

been tipped off that Liam was in the pub wearing a Russian hat and attempted to take photos.

7 His abusive behaviour earned him a lifetime ban from airline Cathay Pacific.

8 Liam traded blows with Spandau Ballet's Tony Hadley during a gig at London's Wembley Arena.

9 In 2001, British Airways staff complained about the singer after he grabbed a stewardess' bottom, refused to stop smoking and had thrown objects around the cabin during a flight from London to Rio De Janeiro.

10 In 2001, Madame Tussaud's waxworks in London revealed that Oasis singer Liam Gallagher had come third in 'The Most Hated Characters' list of exhibits, behind Adolf Hitler and Slobodan Milosevic.

10 Record company promotional gifts

1 **Elvis Presley** Bath towel
2 **U2** Toy Trabant car
3 **Frankie Goes To Hollywood** 'Power Of Love' dildo
4 **Arrested Development** Garden hammock
5 **Inxs** Pyjamas
6 **ZZ Top** TV dinner
7 **Wet Wet Wet** Sun cream
8 **Toni Braxton** Dressing gown
9 **Kirsty McColl** Kite
10 **Beatles** Apple Records dartboard

10 Nonsense song titles

1 'De Do Do Do, De Da Da Da' – The Police
2 'Fa Fa Fa Fa Fa' – Otis Reading
3 'Ne Ne Na Na Na Na Nu Nu' – Bad Manners
4 'Ob-La-Di Ob-La-Da' – The Beatles
5 'I Do I Do I Do I Do I Do' – Abba
6 'Um Um Um Um Um Um' – Wayne Fontana and the Mindbenders
7 'Doobedood'ndoobe Doobedood'ndoobe' – Diana Ross
8 'Ba-Na-Na-Bam-Boo' – Westworld
9 'Da Doo Ron Ron' – The Crystals
10 'Na Na Na' – Cozy Powell

10 gigs you might have missed

1 1962, The Beatles played their first gig in Wales when they appeared at The Regent Dansette in Rhyl.

2 1963, appearing at The Manor House, London, The Blues By Six plus The Rolling Stones.

3 1966, 'The Bowie Showboat', a lunchtime performance from David Bowie, 'three hours of music and mime', at the Marquee Club, London, plus a top ten disco.

4 1967, The Move, Cream, Jimi Hendrix Experience and Pink Floyd on the same bill at the Tulip Bulb Auction Hall, Spalding, Lincs.

5 1971, appearing at Friars, Aylesbury, The Velvet Underground.

6 1975, Led Zeppelin – three night run at Earls Court, London.

7 1980, appearing at The Moonlight, West Hampstead, London, U2.

8 1981, appearing at The Hope & Anchor, London, Blanmange supported by Depeche Mode.

9 1988, appearing at The London School Of Economics, The Stone Roses supported by The Charlatans.

10 1993, appearing at The Wheatsheaf, Stoke On Trent, Radiohead.

10 groups with a future star in the ranks

1 The Blue Moon Boys featured Elvis Presley
2 The Manish Boys – David Bowie
3 Jimmy James and the Blue Flames – Jimi Hendrix
4 The Teen Kings – Roy Orbison
5 The Yardbirds – Jimmy Page
6 Take That – Robbie Williams
7 Them – Van Morrison
8 John's Children – Marc Bolan
9 Chain Reaction – Steve Tyler
10 The Castiles – Bruce Springsteen

Top 10 Food Songs

'Chocolate Cake' – Crowded House
'Sweets For My Sweets' – The Searchers
'Green Onions' – Booker T And The MG's
'Meat Pie Sausage Roll' – Grandad Roberts & His Son Elvis
'Peanut Butter' – The Marathons
'American Pie' – Don McLean
'Rice Is Nice' – The Lemon Pipers
'Toast' – The Streetband
'Peaches and Cream' – The Ikettes
'The Chicken Song' – Spitting Image

BORN ON THIS DAY

1930 Little Walter, blues artist. He was the first harmonica player to amplify his harp, giving it a distorted echoing sound. He died on February 15th 1968.

One of Little Walter's many harps.

1939 Judy Collins, US singer who had a 1968 US No.8 & 1970 UK No.14 single with 'Both Sides Now'.

1944 Rita Coolidge, US singer/songwriter. She was backing singer with Joe Cocker and Delaney & Bonnie, and as a solo artist she had a 1977 UK No.6 & US No.7 single with 'We're All Alone'. Rita married Kris Kristofferson in 1973.

1954 Ray Parker Jr, singer who had a 1984 US No.1 & UK No.2 single with 'Ghostbusters'.

1957 Steve Farris – guitarist with Mr. Mister, who had a 1985 US No.1 & 1986 UK No.4 single with 'Broken Wings'.

1966 Johnny Colt – bass player for The Black Crowes, who had a 1991 UK No.39 single with 'Hard To Handle', a 1991 US No.4 album with *Shake Your Money Maker* and a 1992 US No.1 & UK No.2 album with *The Southern Harmony And Musical Companion*.

1968 D'arcy Wretsky-Brown – bass player for Smashing Pumpkins, who had a 1995 US No.1 album with *Mellon Collie and the Infinite Sadness* and a 1996 UK No.7 single with 'Tonight Tonight'.

ON THIS DAY

1965 Herman's Hermits started a three week run at No.1 in the US singles chart with 'Mrs Brown You've Got A Lovely Daughter'.

1966 The Beatles played live on stage for the last time in the UK when they appeared at the *NME*

Poll Winners' concert at Wembley Empire Pool. Also on the bill were The Rolling Stones and The Who.

1967 Elvis Presley married Priscilla Beaulieu at the Las Vegas Aladdin Hotel. The couple divorced after five years of marriage on October 9th 1973.

1974 The Carpenters performed at the White House, at the request of President Nixon.

1976 Led Zeppelin started a two week run at No.1 on the US album chart with *Presence*, the group's fifth No.1 album.

1977 the "White Riot Tour" kicked off at the Roxy in London with The Clash, The Jam and the Buzzcocks.

1979 Elton John became the first pop star to perform in Israel.

1979 Rod Stewart played the first of two sold out nights at The Uptown Theatre, Chicago.

1980 Pink Floyd's single 'Another Brick In The Wall' was banned by the South African government after black children adopted the song as their anthem in protest against inferior education.

1982 Barry Manilow scored his first UK No.1 album when 'Barry Live In Britain' went to the top of the charts.

1984 Fleetwood Mac drummer and founder member Mick Fleetwood filed for bankruptcy.

1986 US songwriter and producer Hugo Peretti died, aged 70. He wrote many classic hits including, 'Twistin' The Night Away', 'Shout' and 'You Make Me Feel Brand New.'

1993 George Michael, Queen and Lisa Stansfield went to No.1 on the UK singles chart with 'The Five Live EP', which was recorded at the Freddie Mercury tribute concert.

1997 Status Quo guitarist Rick Parfit had a quadruple heart bypass operation after visiting his Harley Street doctor and complaining of chest pains.

2003 soul singer Barry White suffered a stroke while being treated for kidney failure. The singer died two months later on July 4th 2003.

2004 appearing at Carling Live 24 at venues across London were Kasabian, Franz Ferdinand, Starsailor, Feeder and Scissor Sisters.

2005 Coldplay became the first British band to have a new entry in the US Top 10 singles chart since The Beatles. Coldplay's latest single 'Speed Of Sound' entered the chart at number eight, only the second time a UK band has achieved the feat. The Beatles managed it with 'Hey Jude' in 1968.

Britney Spears, appearing at the Manchester Arena in 2004.

BORN ON THIS DAY

1904 Bing Crosby, US singer who recorded an estimated 2,600 songs in his lifetime including 'White Christmas', which was written by Irving Berlin. Crosby had 317 other hits in the USA. Died of a heart attack on a golf course in Madrid, Spain, on October 14th 1977.

1935 Link Wray, guitarist who had a 1958 US No.16 single with 'Rumble'. Wray is credited with inventing "fuzz" guitar after punching a hole in a speaker – this gave him a distorted sound.

1936 Engelbert Humperdinck, singer who had a 1967 UK No.1 and US No.4 single with 'Release Me'.

1945 Goldy McJohn – keyboardist with Steppenwolf, who had a 1968 US No.2 and 1969 UK No.30 single with 'Born To Be Wild'.

1946 Lesley Gore, singer who had a 1963 US No.1 & UK No.9 single with 'It's My Party'.

1950 Lou Gramm – vocalist with Foreigner, who had a 1985 UK & US No.1 single with 'I Want To Know What Love Is'.

1955 Jo Callis – guitarist with Human League, who had a 1981 UK No.1 & 1982 US No.1 single with 'Don't You Want Me' plus over 15 other UK Top 40 singles.

ON THIS DAY

1957 Elvis Presley recorded the Leiber And Stoller song 'Jailhouse Rock'.

1963 The Beatles were at No.1 on the UK singles chart with 'From Me To You', the group's first No.1. and the first of 11 consecutive No.1s from 11 releases.

1967 appearing at The Adelphi Theatre, Dublin, Ireland were The Beach Boys, Helen Shapiro, Simon Dupree And The Big Sound, Terry Reid and Peter Jay's Jaywalkers.

1970 one hit wonder Norman Greenbaum was at No.1 on the UK singles chart with 'Spirit In The Sky'. The song was also a No.1 hit for Doctor and the Medics in 1986 and Gareth Gates in 2003.

1972 Bruce Springsteen auditioned for CBS Records A&R man John Hammond in New York. Springsteen played a short set for him in his office and Hammond was so impressed that he arranged a real audition that night at the Gaslight Club in New York for other Columbia executives. Bruce passed the audition.

1980 Joy Division played what would be their last gig with Ian Curtis when they appeared at Birmingham University, England. Curtis committed suicide two weeks later.

1981 Scottish singer Sheena Easton started a two week run at No.1 on the US singles chart with 'Morning Train (9 To 5)'. The title of the song was changed to avoid confusion with the Dolly Parton hit '9 to 5', released in the same year.

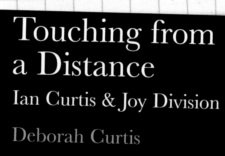

Little known UK Nirvana wearing their law suits.

1987 Cutting Crew started a two week run at No.1 on the US singles chart with '(I Just), Died In Your Arms', which was a No.4 hit in the UK.

1989 a security guard alerted the police after a man wearing a wig, fake moustache and false teeth walked into Zales Jewellers, California. Three squad cars arrived and police detained the man, who turned out to be Michael Jackson in disguise.

1989 session drummer Benny Benjamin died. One of "The Funk Brothers", he played on many Tamla Motown hits including songs for The Four Tops, Temptations, Marvin Gaye, The Supremes and Stevie Wonder. The film *Standing In The Shadows Of Motown* released in 2003 features the story of The Funk Brothers.

1991 the video for the R.E.M. song 'Losing My Religion' was banned in Ireland because its religious imagery was seen as unfit for broadcast.

1992 little-known UK band Nirvana filed a suit against the American band of the same name claiming that they had been using the name since 1968. The dispute was settled out of court in the British band's favour.

2005 36 years after they had split up, Eric Clapton joined his former Cream band mates drummer Ginger Baker and bass player Jack Bruce for the first of four sold-out nights at London's Royal Albert Hall.

Touching from a Distance

Ian Curtis & Joy Division

Deborah Curtis

'A courageous, affecting biography.' *NME*

ff

BORN ON THIS DAY

1919 Pete Seeger, US folk singer who wrote 'If I Had A Hammer', which was a hit for Peter, Paul & Mary, and 'Turn Turn Turn', which was a hit for The Byrds.

1933 James Brown, soul singer known as "Soul Brother No.1", who had a 1966 US No.8 and UK No.13 single with 'It's A Man's World', a 1986 UK No.5 single with 'Living In America' and a 1963 album with *Live At The Apollo*.

1937 Frankie Valli – singer with The Four Seasons, who had a 1976 UK & US No.1 single with 'December 1963 (Oh What A Night)'. As solo artist he had a 1978 US No.1 & UK No.3 single with 'Grease'.

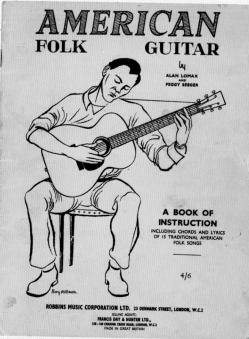

Peter Seeger could have written the book on US folk music.

1950 Mary Hopkin, singer who had a 1968 UK No.1 and US No.2 single with 'Those Were The Days', which was released on The Beatles' Apple label and was produced by Paul McCartney.

1955 Steve Jones – guitarist with the Sex Pistols, who had a 1977 UK No.2 single with 'God Save The Queen' and a 1977 UK No.1 album with *Never Mind The Bollocks, Here's The Sex Pistols*.

1972 Mark Morrison, UK singer who had a 1996 UK No.1 single with 'Return Of The Mack'.

ON THIS DAY

1965 The Beatles spent the day filming for their forthcoming film *Help!* on Salisbury Plain with the British Army's Third Tank Division.

1968 The Beach Boys opened their US tour at Singer Bowl, New York, on which the co-headliner was Maharishi Mahesh Yogi.

1969 Jimi Hendrix was arrested at Toronto airport for possession of narcotics. The guitarist was released on $10,000 (£5,882) bail.

1972 Les Harvey of Stone The Crows died after being electrocuted on stage during a gig in Swansea, Wales.

1975 Dawn started a three-week run at No.1 in the US with 'He Don't Love You, (Like I Love You)', the group's third US No.1.

1975 The Bay City Rollers started a three week run at No.1 on the UK chart with their second album *Once Upon A Star*.

1976 David Bowie played the first of six sold-out nights at Wembley, his first UK gig in three years.

1976 Paul McCartney made his first concert appearance in America in almost ten years when Wings kicked off their "Wings Over America" tour in Fort Worth, Texas. McCartney ended the tour seven weeks later with a three night run at The Forum in Los Angeles.

1986 Robert Palmer went to No.1 on the US singles chart with 'Addicted To Love', which made No.5 in the UK. Palmer originally recorded the song as a duet with Chaka Khan but due to contractual problems her voice was removed.

2001 London-based bank Coutts And Co. turned down applications from members of Oasis to open accounts on the grounds of the band's bad behaviour.

Mary Hopkin.

BORN ON THIS DAY

1942 Ronnie Bond – drummer with The Troggs, who had a 1966 US No.1 & UK No.2 single with 'Wild Thing'. Bond died on November 13th 1992.

1945 George Wadenius – guitarist for Blood, Sweat & Tears, who had a 1969 US No.12 & UK No.35 single with 'You've Made Me So Very Happy'.

1951 Bruce Day – bass player and vocalist with Santana, who had a 1970 US No.4 single with 'Black Magic Woman' and a 1977 UK No.11 single with 'She's Not There', as well as Pablo Cruise.

1951 Jackie Jackson – singer with The Jackson Five, who had a 1970 US No.1 & UK No.2 single with 'I Want You Back' and, as The Jacksons, a 1977 UK No.1 single - 'Show You The Way To Go'.

1959 Randy Travis, country singer who had a 1989 US No.3 album with *No Holdin' Back*.

1961 Jay Aston – singer with Bucks Fizz, who had a 1981 UK No.1 single with 'Making Your Mind Up' plus 12 other UK Top 40 singles.

1970 Gregg Alexander, US singer/songwriter with the New Radicals, who had a 1999 UK No.5 single with 'You Get What You Give'.

1972 Mike Dirnt – bass player with Green Day, who had a 1995 US No.2 album with *Dookie* and a 1995 UK No.7 single with 'Basket Case'.

1979 Lance Bass – singer with *NSYNC, who had a 2000 US No.1 single with 'It's Gonna Be Me' and a 1999 UK No.5 single with 'I Want You Back'.

ON THIS DAY

1956 Gene Vincent And The Blue Caps recorded 'Be Bop A Lula'.

1961 The Marcels were at No.1 on the UK singles chart with 'Blue Moon', their only UK No.1.

1963 Andy Williams started a 16 week run at No.1 on the US album chart with *Days Of Wine And Roses*.

1967 The Young Rascals started a four week run at No.1 on the US singles chart with 'Groovin'.

1967 The Jimi Hendrix Experience appeared on UK TV's *Top Of The Pops*.

1968 Mary Hopkin won her heat on the UK ITV talent show *Opportunity Knocks*. Signing with Apple Records, Paul McCartney produced her UK No.1 single 'Those Were The Days', which made No.2 in the US. She married producer Tony Visconti.

1970 four students at Kent University were killed and 11 wounded by National Guard troops at a campus demonstration protesting the escalation of the Vietnam War. The incident inspired Neil Young to compose 'Ohio', which became a hit for Crosby, Stills, Nash & Young.

1973 Led Zeppelin opened their 1973 US tour, which was billed as the "biggest and most profitable rock 'n' roll tour in the history of the United States". The group made over $3 million (£1.76 million) from the tour.

1974 Abba were at No.1 on the UK singles chart with 'Waterloo', the group's first of nine UK No.1s.

1974 Grand Funk started a two week run at No.1 on the US singles chart with their version of the Little Eva hit 'The Loco-Motion'. It was only the second time that a cover version had been a No.1 as well as the original.

1974 the film soundtrack to *The Sting* by Marvin Hamlisch started a five week run at No.1 on the US album chart.

1978 'Night Fever', the theme from the film *Saturday Night Fever* by The Bee Gees was at No.1

Kurt Cobain's place of final rest is mercifully sold off.

Madonna.

on the UK singles chart. It was the group's third No.1.

1991 25 years after her chart debut, Cher scored her first UK No.1 single with 'The Shoop Shoop Song'.

1996 Alanis Morissette started a six week run at No.1 on the UK album chart with *Jagged Little Pill*.

1996 George Michael scored his seventh UK No.1 single as a solo artist when 'Fastlove' started a three week run at the top of the chart.

1996 Mariah Carey started a two week run at No.1 on the US singles chart with 'Always Be My Baby', her 11th US No.1, and a No.3 hit in the UK.

1997 Courtney Love placed an advert in *The Seattle Times* to sell the house she had shared with Kurt Cobain. The five bedroom, four bathroom house was on the market for $3 million (£1.76 million). The carriage house where Kurt Cobain died had been knocked down.

2003 Sean Paul started a three week run at No.1 on the US singles chart with 'Get Busy', which was a No.4 hit in the UK.

2003 Madonna was at No.1 on the US album chart with *American Life*, the singer's fifth US No.1.

2004 Clement Seymour Dodd died, aged 72. He had been a producer and major force in reggae music.

BORN ON THIS DAY

1937 Johnnie Taylor, soul singer who had a 1976 US No.1 & UK No.25 single with 'Disco Lady'.

1942 Tammy Wynette, American country singer who had a 1968 US No.19 and 1975 UK No.1 single with 'Stand By Your Man'. Wynette died on April 7th 1998.

1948 Bill Ward – drummer with Black Sabbath, who had a 1970 UK No.4 single with 'Paranoid'.

1951 Rex Goh – guitarist with Air Supply, who had a 1980 UK No.11 single with 'All Out Of Love' and a 1981 US No.1 single with 'The One That You Love'.

1959 Ian McCulloch – singer with Echo & The Bunnymen, who had a 1983 UK No.8 single with 'The Cutter'.

1981 Craig David, UK singer who had a 2000 UK No.1 single with 'Fill Me In'.

ON THIS DAY

1956 Elvis Presley scored his first US No.1 single and album when 'Heartbreak Hotel' went to the top of the charts. His debut album also went to No.1.

1962 the soundtrack to *West Side Story* went to No.1 on the US album chart. It went on to spend a total of 54 weeks at the No.1 position.

1963 on a recommendation by George Harrison, Dick Rowe, Head of A&R at Decca Records (and the man who turned down The Beatles), went to see The Rolling Stones play at Crawdaddy Club, London. The band was signed to the label within a week.

1966 Manfred Mann was at No.1 on the UK singles chart with 'Pretty Flamingo'.

1968 Buffalo Springfield split up, Richie Fury formed Poco and Stephen Stills teamed up with David Crosby and Graham Nash in Crosby, Stills & Nash.

1972 the first day of the three day Bickershaw Festival, Wigan, England with The Grateful Dead, Dr. John, Donovan, The Kinks, Captain Beefheart, Hawkwind, America, Family, Country Joe MacDonald, Wishbone Ash, New Riders Of The Purple Sage, Brinsley Schwarz and the Flamin' Groovies.

1973 David Bowie scored his first UK No.1 album when *Aladdin Sane* started a five week run at the top. It featured the single 'Drive In Saturday'.

1979 The Boomtown Rats appeared at The Palladium in New York, which was the last date of a US tour.

1983 The Stranglers' 'Golden Brown' was named most performed work of 1982 at the 28th Ivor Novello Awards.

1984 Simple Minds singer Jim Kerr married Pretenders singer Chrissie Hynde in a horse drawn carriage in Central Park, New York.

1992 Radiohead released 'The Drill' EP, their first record in the UK.

1995 former Guns N' Roses drummer Steven Adler was arrested on a felony count of possession of heroin, as well as two misdemeanour drug charges.

1996 Cranberries singer Dolores O'Riordan received both a public apology and a donation of £7,500 ($12,750) to the Warchild charity from *The Sport* newspaper after they ran a story claiming she had performed a gig in Hamburg without wearing any underwear.

2000 Rod Stewart had a one hour throat operation at Cedar-Sinai Medical Center in Los Angeles to remove a growth on his thyroid. The growth turned out to be benign.

BORN ON THIS DAY

1920 Peggy Lee, singer and actress, who had a 1958 US No.8 & UK No.5 single with 'Fever'. She worked with Benny Goodman, Randy Newman and Quincy Jones. Lee died on January 21st 2002.

1942 Colin Earl – keyboard player with Mungo Jerry, who had a 1970 UK No.1 & US No.3 single with 'In The Summertime'.

1945 Bob Seger, US singer/songwriter who had a 1987 US No.1 single with 'Shakedown' from the film *Beverly Hills Cop II* and a 1995 UK No.22 single with 'We've Got Tonight'.

1950 Robbie McIntosh – drummer for the Average White Band, who had a 1975 US No.1 & UK No.6 single with 'Pick Up The Pieces'. He died on August 23rd 1974.

1967 Mark Bryan – guitarist with Hootie & The Blowfish, who had a 1995 US No.1 album *Cracked Rear View*, which sold over 15 million copies, and a 1995 UK No.50 single with 'Hold My Hand'.

1971 Chris Shiflett – guitarist with Foo Fighters, who had a 1995 UK No.5 single with 'This Is A Call' and the 2002 UK No.1 album One By One.

ON THIS DAY

1972 The Tyrannosaurus Rex double album *Prophets, Seers And Sages And The Angels Of The Ages/My People Were Fair And Had Sky In Their Hair But Now They're Content To Wear Stars On Their Brows* went to No.1 in the UK.

1973 Paul Simon set out on his first tour without Art Garfunkel, using The Jesse Dixon Singers as a back-up group.

1977 Led Zeppelin broke their own attendance record when they played in front of 76,000 people in Pontiac, Michigan.

1977 The Boomtown Rats played their first gig in England at Studio 51, London.

1978 the soundtrack to *Saturday Night Fever* started an 18-week run at No.1 on the UK album chart, and was also No.1 in the US. The album, which featured seven Bee Gee songs, went on to sell over 30 million copies worldwide.

1982 former manager of The Bay City Rollers, Tam Paton, was convicted on a charge of gross indecency with boys and was sentenced to three years in jail.

1989 former Frankie Goes To Hollywood singer Holly Johnson went to No.1 on the UK album chart with his debut solo album *Blast*.

1991 Madonna's "warts-and-all" documentary film *Truth Or Dare In Bed With Madonna* premiered in Los Angeles.

1995 Oasis scored their first UK No.1 single when 'Some Might Say' went to the top of the UK charts.

2001 Destiny's Child started a two week run at No.1 on the UK album charts with *Survivor*.

2004 a sale at Christies in London became the most successful pop auction in the company's history after Beatles memorabilia sold for a record £788,643 ($1,340,693). The auction included a leather collar worn by John Lennon, which sold for £117,250 ($199,325). A signed copy of a management deal with The Beatles and manager Brian Epstein sold for £122,850 ($208,845). A Vox Kensington guitar used by Lennon and Harrison went for £100,000 (£170,000). Also sold were a coloured felt-pen drawing by Lennon (£10,000/$17,000), a letter with his signature (£5,500/$9,350), and a pen-and-ink drawing called "Happy Fish" (£9,500/$16,150).

The Rats, trapped in Studio 51. Bob aims to make their poverty history.

BORN ON THIS DAY

1939 Jimmy Ruffin, singer who had a 1974 UK No.4 single with 'What Becomes Of The Broken-Hearted'.

1943 Rick Westwood – guitarist with Brian Poole & The Tremeloes, who had a 1967 UK No.1 & US No.11 single with 'Silence Is Golden'.

1943 Thelma Houston, US soul singer who had a 1977 US No.1 & UK No.13 single with 'Don't Leave Me This Way'.

1946 Jerry Nolan – drummer with The New York Dolls, who had the 1973 album *New York Dolls*. He died of a stroke on January 14th 1992.

1948 Pete Wingfield, UK singer and producer who had a 1975 UK No.7 and US No.15 single with 'Eighteen With A Bullet'.

1949 Keith (a.k.a. James Keefer), US singer who had a 1967 US No.7 and UK No.24 single with '98.6'.

1969 Eagle Eye Cherry, singer/songwriter who had a 1998 UK No.6 single with 'Save Tonight'.

ON THIS DAY

1966 The Mamas and the Papas started a three week run at No.1 on the US singles chart with 'Monday Monday', which made No.3 in the UK. The group was reported as saying they all hated the song – except for its writer John Phillips.

The actual half dollar that inspired 50 Cent's name.

1972 Reginald Dwight changed his name by deed poll to Elton Hercules John.

1972 The Rolling Stones released *Exile on Main Street* **(left)**, the second album on their own label.

1977 The Eagles went to No.1 on the US singles chart with 'Hotel California', the group's fourth US No.1 which made No.8 in the UK.

1978 90,000 tickets were sold in eight hours for Bob Dylan's forthcoming London dates.

1983 Paul Weller unveiled his new group Style Council at an anti-nuclear benefit gig in London.

1988 Terence Trent D'arby went to No.1 on the US singles chart with 'Wishing Well', which was a No.4 hit in the UK.

1998 Eddie Rabbitt, US singer/songwriter, died of lung cancer. He had had a 1981 US No.1 & UK No.53 single with 'I Love A Rainy Night'. Elvis, Dr. Hook and Tom Jones all recorded his songs.

2000 Britney Spears went to No.1 on the UK singles chart with 'Oops! I Did It Again'.

2003 50 Cent was sued by a US surgeon over an unpaid medical bill. The doctor claimed 50 Cent and his friend turned up at a hospital with multiple gunshot wounds in 2000, but said the rapper never paid the $34,000, (£20,000) he owed for treatment despite being asked for it several times.

BORN ON THIS DAY

1911 Robert Johnson *(right)*, blues singer and guitarist. He influenced Muddy Waters, Elmore James, Eric Clapton (Cream covered his song 'Crossroads') and The Rolling Stones (who covered 'Love In Vain'). Johnson died on August 16th 1938.

1940 Ricky Nelson, US singer who had a 1958 US No.1 with 'Poor Little Fool', a 1961 UK No.2 single with 'Hello Mary Lou' plus over 30 US Top 40 hit singles. He played himself on his parents' US TV show *The Adventures Of Ozzie And Harriet*. he died on December 31st 1985.

1943 Toni Tennille – singer with Captain & Tennille, who had a 1980 US No.1 & UK No.7 single with 'Do That To Me One More Time'.

1947 Rick Derringer, producer, guitarist and vocalist with The McCoys, who had a 1965 US No.1 & UK No.5 single with 'Hang On Sloopy' and the Edgar Winter Group, who had a 1973 US No.1 & UK No.18 single with 'Frankenstein'.

1951 Chris Frantz – drummer with Talking Heads, who had a 1983 US No.9 single with 'Burning Down The House' and a 1985 UK No.6 single with 'Road To Nowhere'.

1951 Philip Bailey – singer with Earth, Wind And Fire, who had a 1975 US No.1 single with 'Shining Star' and a 1981 UK No.3 single with 'Let's Groove'. As a solo artist he had a 1985 UK No.1 single with 'Easy Lover', which was a duet with Phil Collins.

1955 Alex Van Halen – drummer with Van Halen, who had a 1984 US No.1 & UK No.7 single with 'Jump'.

1964 Dave Rowntree – drummer with Blur, who had a 1994 UK No.1 album with *Park Life*, which spent over two years on the UK chart, a 1995 UK No.1 single with 'Country House' and over 12 other UK Top 40 singles.

1972 Darren Hayes – singer with Savage Garden, who had a 1998 US No.1 & UK Top 5 single with 'Truly Madly Deeply'. As a solo artist he had a 2002 UK No.8 single with 'Insatiable'.

1975 Enrique Iglesias, singer who had a 2000 US No.1 single with 'Be With You' and a 2002 UK No.1 & US No.3 single with 'Hero'.

1985 Matt Jay – bass player with Busted, who had a 2003 UK No.1 single with 'You Said No' and a 2002 UK No.2 album with *Busted*.

ON THIS DAY

1955 Tony Bennett was at No.1 on the UK singles chart with 'Stranger In Paradise', the US singer's only UK No.1.

1964 The Beatles had held the No.1 position on the US singles chart for 14 weeks with three No.1s in succession: 'I Want To Hold Your Hand' for seven weeks, 'She Loves You' for two weeks and 'Can't Buy Me Love' for five weeks.

1967 Gerry And The Pacemakers announced they were splitting up, recognizing that they could no longer keep pace with the rapidly changing UK rock scene.

1976 Abba scored their third UK No.1 single with 'Fernando'. Also on this day Abba started a nine week run at No.1 on the UK album chart with their *Greatest Hits* album.

1976 BBC Radio 1 DJ Johnny Walker announced he was quitting the station after being told he must pretend to like The Bay City Rollers.

1976 former lead singer of the Lovin' Spoonful John Sebastian went to No.1 on the US singles chart with 'Welcome Back', which was taken from the US TV show *Welcome Back Kotter*.

1982 Neil Bogart died of cancer at the age of 39. Bogart was responsible for the development of Casablanca Records, working with Donna Summer, The Village People, Kiss and Joan Jett.

1982 Vangelis went to No.1 on the US singles chart with 'Chariots Of Fire', his only US No.1 and a No.12 hit in the UK.

1993 Aerosmith entered the US album chart at No.1 with *Get A Grip*.

1993 Mark Knopfler received an honorary music doctorate from the University of Newcastle-upon-Tyne, England.

1996 a Los Angeles judge ruled against Tommy Lee and wife Pamela Anderson in their bid to keep *Penthouse* magazine from publishing still photos from an X-rated home movie that was stolen from their home.

1999 Ricky Martin went to No.1 on the US singles chart with 'Livin' La Vida Loca', which was also a UK No.1.

BORN ON THIS DAY

1914 Hank Snow, US country singer known as "The Singing Ranger" who released over 100 albums. He died on December 20th 1999.

1937 Dave Prater – singer and part of duo Sam & Dave, who had a 1967 US No.2 & UK No.24 single with 'Soul Man'.

1937 Sonny Curtis – guitarist and vocalist with The Crickets, who had a 1957 US No.1 single with 'That'll Be The Day', a 1959 UK No.1 single with 'It Doesn't Matter Anymore' plus over 15 other UK Top 40 singles.

1943 Tommy Roe, singer who had a 1969 UK & US No.1 single with 'Dizzy' plus ten other US Top 40 hits. 'Dizzy' was also a hit for Vic Reeves *(right)* and The Wonder Stuff in 1991.

1944 Richie Furay – guitarist and vocalist with Buffalo Springfield, who had a 1967 US No.17 single with 'For What Its Worth', Poco, who had a 1979 US No.17 single with 'Crazy Love' and Souther Hillman, Furay Band, who had a 1974 US No.27 single with 'Fallin' In Love'.

1949 Billy Joel, singer/songwriter who had a 1980 US No.1 single with 'It's Still Rock And Roll To Me', a 1983 UK No.1 single with 'Uptown Girl' plus over 20 other US & UK Top 40 singles.

1962 Dave Gahan – singer with Depeche Mode, who had a 1984 UK No.4 single with 'People Are People' plus over 25 other UK Top 40 singles.

1962 Paul Heaton – singer and guitarist who was part of The Housemartins, who had a 1986 UK No.1 single with 'Caravan Of Love', then The Beautiful South, who had a 1990 UK No.1 single with 'A Little Time' plus over 15 other UK Top 40 singles.

ON THIS DAY

1959 UK music paper *Melody Maker* introduced a "Juke Box Top 20" chart compiled from 200 juke boxes around the UK.

1964 appearing at The Rhodes Centre, Bishop's Gate, England were Gene Vincent and The Shouts. The poster advertised that the first 50 girls to arrive at the venue would be admitted free, while tickets cost six shillings and sixpence ($0.91c).

1964 Chuck Berry began his first-ever UK tour at The Astoria Theatre, London, supported by The Animals, The Swinging Blue Jeans, Karl Denver and The Nashville Teens.

1964 Louis Armstrong went to No.1 on the US singles chart with 'Hello Dolly', which was a No.4 hit in the UK. The record ended The Beatles' 14 week run at No.1 on the chart.

1965 Bob Dylan played the first of two sold-out nights at London's Royal Albert Hall.

1973 Mick Jagger added $150,000 (£88,235) of his own money to the $350,000 (£205,882) raised by The Rolling Stones' January benefit concert for victims of the Nicaraguan earthquake.

1974 Bruce Springsteen played at Boston's Harvard Square Theater, which inspired *Rolling Stone* critic John Landau to write, "I have seen rock 'n' roll's future and his name is Bruce Springsteen."

1978 Fee Waybill of The Tube broke a leg after falling from the stage at the Hammersmith Odeon, London while wielding a chain saw during the band's set.

1980 'I Don't Like Mondays' by The Boomtown Rats won Best pop song and Outstanding British lyric at the 25th Ivor Novello Awards. Supertramp's 'The Logical Song' won Best song.

1987 Starship started a four week run at No.1 on the UK singles chart with 'Nothing's Gonna Stop Us Now', as featured in the film *Mannequin*. It was also a No.1 in the US.

1998 Jimmy Page appeared on the TV show *Saturday Night Live* with rapper Sean "Puffy" Combs and performed 'Come With Me' from the Godzilla movie soundtrack. The song sampled the guitar riff from Led Zeppelin's 'Kashmir'.

1999 The Backstreet Boys scored their first UK No.1 single with 'I Want It That Way', their eighth UK Top 10 hit.

Bob Dylan 40 years later.

BORN ON THIS DAY

1920 Bert Weedon, guitarist who had a 1959 UK No.10 single with 'Guitar Boogie Shuffle'. He also published the *Play In A Day* guitar tutor. Weedon worked with Tommy Steele, Cliff Richard, Frank Sinatra and Tony Bennett.

1935 Larry Williams, US singer who had a 1957 US No.5 & UK No. 21 single with 'Short Fat Mannie'. The Beatles and The Jam covered his songs. Williams died from gunshot wounds on January 2nd 1980, aged 45.

Bert Weedon does the Boogie Shuffle.

1938 Henry Fambrough – vocalist with Detroit Spinners, who had a 1980 UK No.1 & US No.2 single with 'Working My Way Back To You'.

1941 Danny Rapp – vocalist with Danny & The Juniors, who had a 1958 US No.1 & UK No.3 single with 'At The Hop'. Rapp shot himself dead on April 5th 1983.

1946 Donovan, singer/songwriter who had a 1966 US No.1 & 1967 UK No.2 single with 'Sunshine Superman'.

1946 Graham Gouldman – guitarist and singer with The High Spots, The Crevattes and 10CC, who had a 1975 UK No.1 & US No.2 single with 'I'm Not In Love' plus ten other UK Top 30 hits including two No.1s. Gouldman also wrote hits for Herman's Hermits, The Hollies and The Yardbirds.

1947 Dave Mason – guitarist with Traffic, who had a 1967 UK No.2 single with 'Hole In My Shoe'. As a solo artist he had a 1977 US No.12 single with 'We Just Disagree'. He has worked with Eric Clapton, Delaney & Bonnie and George Harrison.

1952 Sly Dunbar, session drummer. As part of duo Sly And Robbie he has worked with Peter Tosh, Robert Palmer, Jimmy Cliff, Grace Jones and Joe Cocker.

1957 John Ritchie (a.k.a. Sid Vicious) – bass player for the Sex Pistols, who had a 1977 UK No.2 single with 'God Save The Queen' and a 1977 UK No.1 album *Nevermind The Bollocks, Here's The Sex Pistols*. He died on February 2nd 1979.

1960 Bono – vocalist and guitarist with U2. The group's first UK Top 10 was the 1984 No.3 single 'Pride, In The Name Of Love', and have since scored over 25 other UK Top 40 hit singles. The band also had a 1987 worldwide No.1 album with *The Joshua Tree* plus five other UK No.1 albums including the 2000 release *All That You Can't Leave Behind*.

ON THIS DAY

1967 Mick Jagger and Keith Richards appeared at Chichester Crown Court, Sussex charged with being in possession of drugs. They elected to go to trial pleading not guilty and were granted £1,000 ($1,700) bail.

1969 Frank Sinatra's version of 'My Way' entered the British Top 10 for the first time. Over the next three years it re-entered the Top 50 singles chart eight times.

1969 The Moody Blues started a two week run at No.1 on the UK album chart with *On The Threshold Of A Dream*, their first No.1 album.

1969 The Turtles gave a special performance at the White House as guests of Tricia Nixon. Stories circulated concerning members of the group allegedly snorting cocaine off Abraham Lincoln's desk.

1974 The Who sold out Madison Square Gardens, New York for four nights by selling 80,000 tickets.

1975 Stevie Wonder played in front of 125,000 fans at a free concert near the Washington Monument to celebrate Human Kindness Day.

1986 Falco was at No.1 on the UK singles chart with 'Rock Me Amadeus'. Falco became the first-ever Austrian act to score a UK and US No.1 hit.

1986 The Pet Shop Boys went to No.1 on the US singles chart with 'West End Girls', the duo's first US No.1. It was also a No.1 in the UK.

1994 Rapper Tupac Shakur began serving a 15 day county jail term for attacking director Allen Hughes on a video set.

1999 country singer/songwriter Shel Silverstein died of a heart attack, aged 57. He wrote 'A Boy Named Sue' for Johnny Cash and 'Sylvia's Mother' for Dr. Hook.

2000 Bobby Brown was arrested at Newark airport, New Jersey for breaking his probation order. He'd been wanted in Florida since 1999 when his probation officer reported that a urine test proved positive for cocaine use.

STONES: 'A STRONG, SWEET SMELL OF INCENSE'

Story of girl in a fur-skin rug

BORN ON THIS DAY

1888 Irving Berlin, composer of many pop, stage show and film hits. He emigrated from Siberia to New York as a child. He was the composer of 'White Christmas' and 'Let's Face The Music and Dance'. He died on September 22nd 1989.

1941 Eric Burdon – vocalist with The Animals, who had a 1964 UK & US No.1 single with 'House Of The Rising Sun'.

1943 Les Chadwick – guitarist and bass guitarist with Gerry And The Pacemakers, who had a 1963 UK No.1 single with 'You'll Never Walk Alone' and a 1965 US No.6 single with 'Ferry Across The Mersey'.

1947 Butch Trucks – drummer with The Allman Brothers Band, who had a 1973 US No.12 single with 'Ramblin Man'.

1974 Ryan Adams, singer/songwriter who had a 2001 UK No.53 single with 'New York, New York'.

1983 Holly Valance, singer and actress, who had a 2002 UK No.1 single with 'Kiss Kiss'.

ON THIS DAY

1963 The Beatles started a 30 week run at No.1 on the UK album charts with their debut album *Please Please Me*, making it the longest running No.1 album by a group ever. The band's follow up *With The Beatles* replaced it at the top on December 7th 1963 and stayed there for 21 weeks.

1964 while on a UK tour, The Rolling Stones were refused lunch at The Grand Hotel, Bristol, which is where they were staying, because they were not wearing jackets and ties.

1965 Roger Miller was at No.1 on the UK singles chart with 'King Of The Road'. It was the singer's only UK No.1. The Proclaimers had a UK No.9 hit with their version of the song in 1990.

1967 The Bee Gees made their BBC TV *Top Of The Pops* debut performing 'New York Mining Disaster'.

1970 the triple soundtrack album *Woodstock* was released in the US, going Gold within two weeks.

1972 John Lennon appeared on the US television *Dick Cavett Show*, claiming he was under surveillance from the FBI.

1979 appearing at Cobo Arena, Detroit was Rod Stewart *(left)* on his "Blondes Have More Fun" tour. Tickets cost $12.50 (£7.35).

1981 Bob Marley died of lung cancer and a brain tumour, aged 36. He had scored the 1981 UK No.8 single 'No Woman No Cry' plus over ten other UK Top 40 singles. In 1990, February 6th was proclaimed a national holiday in Jamaica to commemorate his birth.

1985 UK producer and keyboard player Paul Hardcastle was at No.1 on the UK singles chart with '19'. The title referred to the average age of American soldiers in the Vietnam War.

1991 Roxette scored their fourth US No.1 single with 'Joyride', which was inspired by an interview with Paul McCartney – who said that writing songs with John Lennon had been like a joyride.

2001 The Black Crowes and Oasis kicked off "The Tour of Brotherly Love", a joint North American tour, at The Joint in Las Vegas.

2004 US songwriter John Whitehead was killed by a gunman. He co-wrote 'Back Stabbers' for the O'Jays and as part of duo McFadden & Whitehead wrote and sang 'Ain't No Stopping Us Now', which sold more than eight million copies and was nominated for a Grammy Award.

The Rolling Stones release a protest single under a pseudonym!

BORN ON THIS DAY

1928 Burt Bacharach, songwriter. With Hal David he wrote, 'Close To You', '24 Hours From Tulsa', 'Make It Easy On Yourself', 'Magic Moments' and 'I Say A Little Prayer'. They also won two Oscars for the film score *Butch Cassidy And The Sundance Kid* and for 'Raindrops Keep Fallin' On My Head'.

1942 Ian Dury, singer/ songwriter, poet and actor who had a 1979 UK No.1 single with 'Hit Me With Your Rhythm Stick'. He died on March 27th 2000, aged 57.

1944 Billy Swan, US singer who had a 1974 US No.1 & 1975 UK No.6 single with 'I Can Help'.

1946 Ian McLagan – keyboardist with Small Faces, who had a 1967 UK No.3 & US No.17 single with 'Itchycoo Park' and a 1968 UK No.1 album with *Ogden's Nut Gone Flake*. As Faces they had a 1971 UK No.6 & US No.17 single with 'Stay With Me'. McLagan has also been part of The Rolling Stones' touring band.

1948 Steve Winwood *(left)* – vocalist and keyboard player with the Spencer Davis Group, who had a 1966 UK No.1 single with 'Keep On Running', Traffic, who had a 1967 UK No.2 single with 'Hole In My Shoe' and Blind Faith, who had a 1969 UK & US No.1 self titled album. As a solo artist he had a 1986 US No.1 & UK No.1 single with 'Higher Love'.

Ivor bestowed his award on Led Zeppelin in 1977.

ON THIS DAY

1958 The Everly Brothers started a four week run at No.1 in the US with 'All I Have To Do Is Dream'. The song was written in 15 minutes!

1963 Bob Dylan walked out of rehearsals for the US TV *Ed Sullivan Show* after being told he couldn't perform 'Talking John Birch Society Blues' due to it mocking the military.

1964 The Beach Boys started a four week run at No.1 on the US album chart with Beach Boys Concert, the group's first US No.1.

1965 The Rolling Stones recorded '(I Can't Get No) Satisfaction' at RCA Hollywood studios. Guitarist Keith Richards came up with the guitar riff in the middle of the night a week earlier. It gave the band their first No.1 single in the US.

1968 Jimi Hendrix was arrested by police on his way to Toronto for possession of hashish and heroin.

1971 Mick Jagger married Bianca Macias at St Tropez Town Hall. The couple separated in 1977.

1977 Led Zeppelin received the Outstanding contribution to British music at the second Ivor Novello Awards.

1983 Meat Loaf filed for bankruptcy with debts of over $1 million (£588,000).

1986 Joe Strummer of The Clash was banned from driving after being convicted of drink driving.

1996 17-year-old Bernadette O'Brien died the day after being injured "body surfing" at the Smashing Pumpkins gig at The Point, Dublin.

1996 Hootie & the Blowfish went to No.1 on the US album chart with *Fairweather Johnson*.

2000 thieves stole the gates to Strawberry Fields, the Merseyside landmark immortalized by The Beatles' song. The 3m (10ft) high iron gates were later found at local scrap metal dealers.

2001 Travis played a gig at singer Fran Healy's local primary school at Weston Park, Crouch End, London. The 150 crowd paid a £1 ($1.7) entry fee to the summer fete.

2003 Jimi Hendrix Experience bass player Noel Redding died, aged 57, at his home in Ireland.

BORN ON THIS DAY

1933 Mike Stoller, songwriter and producer (with Leiber) for Elvis Presley, Buddy Holly, The Monkees and Cliff Richard.

1941 Ritchie Valens, US singer who had a 1958 US No.2 and 1959 UK No.29 single with 'Donna'. He died on February 3rd 1959.

1943 Mary Wells, singer who had a 1964 US No.1 & UK No.5 single with 'My Guy', which was written by Smokey Robinson. Wells died of cancer on July 26th 1992.

1945 Magic Dick – harmonica player with The J. Geils Band, who had a 1982 US No.1 & UK No.3 single with 'Centerfold'.

1947 Overend Watts – bass player for Mott The Hoople, who had a 1972 UK No.3 and US No.37 single with 'All The Young Dudes'.

1950 Stevie Wonder, singer/songwriter and multi-instrumentalist. He had a 1963 US No.1 single with 'Fingertips', over 40 other US & UK Top 40 singles and a 1976 US No.1 double album with *Songs In The Key Of Life*.

1951 Paul Thompson *(right)* – drummer for Roxy Music, who had a 1972 UK No.4 single with 'Virginia Plain' plus 15 other UK Top 40 singles.

1966 Darius Rucker – vocalist and guitarist for Hootie & The Blowfish, who had a 1995 US No.1 album with *Cracked Rear View*, which sold over 15 million copies, and a 1995 UK No.50 single with 'Hold My Hand'.

1979 Michael Madden – bass player for Maroon 5, who had a 2004 UK No.1 album with *Songs About Jane* and a 2004 UK No.4 single with 'She Will Be Loved'.

The Supremes, the only thing 'standard' about them were their Motown press shots.

ON THIS DAY

1967 The Monkees' second album *More Of The Monkees* went to No.1 on the UK charts for one week. In 1967 only four albums reached No.1 on the UK charts: *The Sound Of Music*, *Sgt Pepper's Lonely Hearts Club Band* and The Monkees' first and second albums.

1967 The Supremes scored their tenth US No.1 single with 'The Happening', which was a No.6 hit in the UK. It was the last single to be released by The Supremes, as from now on the group were known as Diana Ross And The Supremes.

1968 John Lennon and Paul McCartney gave a series of interviews to help launch Apple Corps in the US.

1971 on his 21st birthday Stevie Wonder received all his childhood earnings. Despite having earned $30 million (£17.6 million) so far, he'd received only $1 million (£588,000).

1974 43 people were arrested and more than 50 were injured after youths started throwing bottles outside a Jackson Five concert at the RFK stadium in Washington D.C.

1979 David Lee Roth from Van Halen collapsed on stage during a concert in Spokane, Washington.

1989 Bon Jovi went to No.1 on the US singles chart with 'I'll Be There For You', the group's fourth US No.1 and a No.18 hit in the UK.

2000 former Happy Monday's singer Shaun Ryder's Volkswagen Corrado was found abandoned after being stolen and used as the getaway car in an armed robbery on Harry Ramsden's fish and chip restaurant in Manchester, England. £7,000 ($11,900) cash was taken in the robbery.

BORN ON THIS DAY

1936 Bobby Darin, singer who had a 1959 US & UK No.1 single with 'Mack The Knife' plus 20 other US Top 40 hits. He died on December 20th 1973.

1943 Jack Bruce – bass player and vocalist for the Graham Bond Organisation, John Mayall's Bluesbreakers, Manfred Mann, Cream, who had a 1967 UK No.11 single with 'I Feel Free' and a 1968 US No.5 single with 'Sunshine Of Your Love', and West, Bruce & Laing.

1946 Gene Cornish – guitarist with The Young Rascals, who had a 1967 US No.1 and UK No.8 single with 'Groovin'.

1946 Lek LecKenby – guitarist with Herman's Hermits, who had a 1964 UK No.1 single with 'I'm Into Something Good' and a 1965 US No.1 single with 'Mrs Brown You've Got A Lovely Daughter'. He died on June 4th 1994.

1947 Al Ciner – guitarist with Three Dog Night, who had a 1970 UK No.3 & US No.1 single with 'Mamma Told Me Not To Come'.

1952 David Byrne – singer for Talking Heads, who had a 1983 US No.9 single with 'Burning Down The House' and a 1985 UK No.6 single with 'Road To Nowhere'. As a solo artist he had a 2002 UK No. 2 single with X-Press, 'Lazy'.

1963 Fabrice Morvan – singer with Milli Vanilli, who had a 1989 US No.1 & UK No.2 single with 'Girl I'm Gonna Miss You'.

1971 Danny Wood – singer with New Kids On The Block, who had a 1989 UK No.1 single with 'You Got It, The Right Stuff' and a 1990 US No.1 single with 'Step By Step'.

1973 Natalie Appleton – singer with All Saints, who had a 1998 UK No.1 and US No.4 single with 'Never Ever'.

APOLLO THEATRE, Glasgow

M.C.P. presents—

The Kinks + The AK Band

Plus Support

Thursday, 14th May 1981

Evening 7-30

STALLS
£3 75

Z 35

MANCHESTER A. B. Cooper (Printers) Ltd.

No Cameras or Recording Equipment. No Ticket exchanged nor money refunded. Official Programmes sold only in the Theatre.

To be retained.

1973 Shanice, US female singer who had a 1992 US & UK No.2 single with 'I Love Your Smile'.

ON THIS DAY

1957 Elvis Presley was rushed to a Los Angeles hospital after swallowing a porcelain cap from one of his front teeth, which then lodged itself in one of his lungs.

1969 Fairport Convention's van crashed on the way home from a gig in Birmingham *(right)* killing drummer Martin Lamble, Richard Thompson's girlfriend and clothes designer Jeannie Franklyn.

1977 Leo Sayer went to No.1 on the US singles chart with 'When I Need You', the singer's second US No.1 and also a No.1 in the UK.

1983 Spandau Ballet scored their first and only UK No.1 album with *True*.

1988 Gloria Estefan and Miami Sound Machine started a two week run at No.1 on the US singles chart with 'Anything For You', which was a No.10 hit in the UK.

1988 Led Zeppelin reunited for the Atlantic Records 40th anniversary party in New York, appearing with the son of John Bonham, Jason, on drums.

1990 appearing live at the Mayflower, Glasgow was Lenny Kravitz on his first UK tour.

1993 four "Super Hero" costumes worn by the group Kiss sold at a sale at Christies, London for £20,000 ($34,000).

1994 Stiltskin were at No.1 on the UK singles chart with the song 'Inside', which was used on a TV jeans commercial.

1997 Mark Morrison was jailed after threatening a police officer with an electric stun gun. He was also ordered to pay £350 ($595) costs.

1998 George Michael was fined $810 (£476) after being convicted of a "lewd act" in a Los Angeles lavatory. The Los Angeles court also ordered him to undergo psychological counselling and carry out 80 hours community service.

2003 lawyers for Britney Spears and the Skechers footwear company settled a dispute out of court over a deal for the pop star to market a line of roller skates and accessories. Spears had filed a $1.5 million (£880,000) breach of agreement lawsuit against Skechers in December, claiming that the company failed to pay her adequately. Skechers had responded with a $10 million (£5.88 million) lawsuit, accusing Spears of fraud and breach of the agreement she signed in January 2002.

Fairport drummer dies in M1 crash

FAIRPORT CONVENTION drummer Martin Lamble, and an American girl known as Jeannie The Tailor were killed when the group's van overturned and crashed on the M1 at Mill Hill on Monday morning.

The group were on the way back to London after a gig at Mother's Club in Birmingham.

Martin (l) and Jeannie Franklyn, girl friend of Fairport guitarist Richard Thompson, both died instantly. Group members, Thompson, Simon Nicol and Tyger Hutchings were all taken to hospital in Stanmore with cuts and bruises. Richard suffered cracked ribs in the crash. Road manager Harvey Bramham was also seriously injured. Singer Sandy Denny escaped injury because she was not travelling in the group bus. She had made the journey from Birmingham with boyfriend Trevor Lucas.

LAMBLE: died instantly.

BORN ON THIS DAY

1932 Baba Oje – rapper with Arrested Development, who had a 1992 UK No.2 and US No.8 single with 'People Everyday'.

1944 Ian Amey (a.k.a. Tich) – guitarist with Dave Dee, Dozy, Beaky, Mick & Tich, who had a 1968 UK No.1 single with 'Legend Of Xanadu'.

1948 Brian Eno – synthesizer player with Roxy Music, who had a 1972 UK No.4 single with 'Virginia Plain', producer for U2 and solo artist.

1948 Gary Thain – bass player for the Keef Hartley Band and Uriah Heep. He died of a drug overdose on March 19th 1976, aged 28.

1951 Dennis Fredericksen – vocalist for Toto, who had a 1983 US No.1 & UK No.3 single with 'Africa'.

1953 Mike Oldfield, multi-instrumentalist. His album *Tubular Bells* was the first album released on the Virgin record label in 1973 and went on to sell over ten million copies.

The actual Wonderwall itself.

ON THIS DAY

1945 the first album chart was introduced in the US. The albums were a collection of 78rpm singles.

1959 Elvis Presley was at No.1 on the UK singles chart with his fourth No.1 'A Fool Such As I/I Need Your Love Tonight'.

1967

The Jimi Hendrix Experience played two shows in Berlin, West Germany.

1968 George Harrison and Ringo Starr attended the premiere of *Wonderwall* at the Cannes Film Festival.

1971 Crosby, Stills, Nash & Young scored their second US No.1 album with *4 Way Street*.

1974 Frank Zappa and his wife announced the birth of their third child, a boy named Ahmet Rodan after the Japanese movie monster who lived off a steady diet of 707 aircraft.

1976 The Rolling Stones went to No.1 on the US album chart with *Black And Blue*, the group's sixth US No.1 album.

1981 Public Image Ltd performed a show at New York's Ritz Club posing behind a video screen while the music was played from tapes. They were showered with missiles and booed off stage.

1982 Asia went to No.1 on the US album chart with their self-titled album. It spent a total of nine weeks at No.1.

1982 Stevie Wonder and Paul McCartney started a seven week run at No.1 on the US singles chart with 'Ebony And Ivory'. The song gave McCartney his 24th US No.1 as a songwriter and was also a No.1 in the UK.

1991 Manic Street Preachers guitarist Richey Edwards carved "4 real" into his arm with a razor blade while being interviewed by music paper *NME*.

1992 Barbara Lee of The Chiffons died. The band scored the 1963 US No.1 single 'He's So Fine'.

1993 Janet Jackson started an eight week run at No.1 on the US singles chart with 'That's The Way Love Goes', her sixth US No.1 and a No.2 hit in the UK.

1997 Courtney Love sold the Seattle mansion she shared with Kurt Cobain.

Brian Eno invents early laptop and iPod device!

A local family purchased the house in the Denny Blaine area for $3 million (£1.76 million).

1997 Oasis attempted to exert censorship over the Internet. The group was working with Sony to put an end to unofficial websites carrying lyrics, soundfiles and photographs.

1998 Frank Sinatra died aged 82. He had his first hit in 1940 and went on to have over 25 US & UK Top 40 singles, including the 1969 UK No.5 single 'My Way'.

2000 it was reported that Britney Spears had been crowned the queen of America's fastest growing youth movement, the teenage celibates. Spears told a German magazine that she intended to abstain from sex until her wedding night.

2002 Jamiroquai played their Carling Homecoming gig at the Ealing Broadway Boulevard, London.

2002 Jamiroquai singer Jay Kay claimed he was assaulted at the premiere of *Star Wars, Episode II: Attack Of The Clones* in London. The singer suffered facial injuries during an incident with a photographer after the star-studded event.

2003 June Carter Cash, country singer and wife of Johnny Cash died aged 73. She had had hits with Johnny Cash including 'If I Were A Carpenter'.

BORN ON THIS DAY

1939 Pervis Jackson – vocalist for Detroit Spinners, who had a 1980 UK No.1 & US No.2 single with 'Working My Way Back To You'.

1944 Billy Cobham, jazz drummer who worked with Miles Davis, Mahavishnu Orchestra, James Brown, Santana and played on the soundtrack to the film *Shaft*.

1946 Robert Fripp – guitarist with King Crimson, who had a 1969 UK No.5 album with *In The Court Of The Crimson King*.

Gentleman Robert Fripp.

1947 Barbara Lee – vocalist with The Chiffons, who had a 1963 US No.1 single with 'He's So Fine'. She died on May 15th 1992.

1947 Darrell Sweet – drummer with Nazareth, who had a 1973 UK No.9 single with 'Broken Down Angel' and a 1976 US No. 8 single with 'Love Hurts'. He died on April 30th 1999 after suffering a fatal heart attack before a show in New Albany, Indiana.

1951 Jonathan Richman – guitarist with The Modern Lovers, who had a 1977 UK No.5 single with 'Egyptian Reggae' and a 1977 UK No.11 with 'Roadrunner'.

1953 Richard Page – vocalist and bass player with Mr. Mister, who had a 1985 US No.1 & 1986 UK No.4 single with 'Broken Wings'.

1965 Chris Novoselic – bass player with Nirvana, who had a 1991 UK No.7 & 1992 US No.6 single with 'Smells Like Teen Spirit', taken from the 1991 album *Nevermind* which spent over two years on the UK chart and made US No.1 album in 1992.

1966 Janet Jackson, singer who had a 1986 US No.1 & UK No.10 single with 'When I Think Of You' plus six other US No.1s and over 20 UK Top 40 singles.

1970 Gabrielle, singer who had a 1993 UK No.1 single with 'Dreams' and over 10 other UK Top 20 singles plus a 2000 UK No.1 album with *Rise*.

ON THIS DAY

1962 B. Bumble And The Stingers were at No.1 on the UK singles chart with 'Nut Rocker', which was an instrumental based on Tchaikovsky's Nutcracker Suite.

1964 Mary Wells started a two week run at No.1 on the US singles chart with 'My Guy', which made No.5 in the UK.

1966 The Beach Boys' album *Pet Sounds* was released in the US.

1966 The Castiles (featuring Bruce Springsteen) record two songs co-written by Bruce at the Bricktown Studio in New Jersey. Only five copies of the record were pressed.

1969 Jack Casady of Jefferson Airplane was arrested for possession of marijuana and received a two and a half year suspended sentence.

1969 Pete Townshend spent the night in a US jail for assaulting a man at The Fillmore East. What Townshend didn't know was the man who jumped onto the stage was a plainclothes policeman trying to warn the audience that a fire had broken out. The Who guitarist was later fined £30 ($51) for the offence.

1970 Crosby, Stills, Nash & Young went to No.1 on the US album chart with *Deja Vu*.

1970 The England World Cup Squad were at No.1 on the UK singles chart with 'Back Home'.

1974 Brian May collapsed in New York while Queen were on a US tour and was flown back to England suffering from hepatitis.

1976 Patti Smith made her UK debut at The Roundhouse, London.

1986 Elvis Costello married The Pogues bass player Caitlin O'Riordan in Dublin.

1999 Boyzone scored their sixth UK No.1 single with 'You Needed Me', making them the act with the most UK Top 5 hits of the 90s.

2004 band Keane started a four week run at No.1 on the UK album chart with their debut release *Hopes and Fears*.

BORN ON THIS DAY

1942 Taj Mahal, US multi-instrumentalist, composer of film soundtracks and member of The Rising Sons with Ry Cooder.

1941 Malcolm Hale – guitarist and vocalist with Spanky And Our Gang, who had a 1967 US No.9 single with 'Sunday Will Never Be The Same Again'. Hale died on October 31st 1968 of carbon monoxide poisoning due to a faulty heater.

1944 Jesse Winchester, Canadian folk singer/songwriter who had a 1981 US No.32 single with 'Say What'.

1953 George Johnson – guitarist and vocalist and one half of the duo Brothers Johnson, who had a 1980 US No.4 & UK No.6 single with 'Stomp'.

1961 Enya Ni Bhraonain – vocalist with Clannad, who had a 1982 UK No.5 single with 'Harry's Game'. As a solo artist she had a 1988 UK No.1 single with 'Orinoco Flow', eight other UK Top 40 singles and a 2001 US No.2 album with *A Day Without Rain*.

1970 Jordan Knight – singer with New Kids On The Block, who had a 1989 UK No.1 single with 'You Got It, The Right Stuff' and a 1990 US No.1 single with 'Step By Step'. As a solo artist he had a 1999 UK No.5 single with 'Give It To You'.

1971 Vernie Bennett – singer with Eternal, who had a 1997 UK No.1 single with 'I Wanna Be The Only One'.

1974 Andrea Corr – singer with The Corrs, who had a 1998 UK No.3 single with 'What Can I Do' and *Talk On Corners* was the bestselling UK album of 1998.

ON THIS DAY

1963 the first Monterey Folk Festival was held and featured Joan Baez, Bob Dylan and Peter, Paul & Mary.

1964 Bob Dylan made his official UK live debut when he appeared at the Royal Festival Hall, London.

The late Sharon Sheeley.

1967 The Tremeloes were at No.1 on the UK singles chart with 'Silence Is Golden', the group's only UK No.1.

1975 Elton John was awarded a Platinum record for sales of a million copies of the LP *Captain Fantastic And The Brown Dirt Cowboy*, the first album ever to be certified Platinum on the day of its release.

1986 Spitting Image started a three week run at No.1 on the UK singles chart with 'The Chicken Song'. *Spitting Image* had become the "must see" Sunday night TV show; it mocked politicians and public figures.

1986 Whitney Houston started a three week run at No.1 in the US with 'Greatest Love Of All', the singer's third US No.1 and a No.8 hit in the UK.

1996 Kevin Gilbert, multi-instrumentalist and songwriter, died of accidental asphyxiation. He had been a member of Giraffe, worked with Sheryl Crow and co-wrote the 1994 UK No.4 hit 'All I Want To Do'.

2002 Sharon Sheeley, US songwriter, died aged 62. Her hits included 'Poor Little Fool', a US No.1 for Ricky Nelson in 1958, and the 1959 hit for Eddie Cochran 'Somethin' Else'. Sheeley had survived the car crash that killed Cochran in 1960.

Peter, Paul & Mary enjoy a nice day at the park before the Monterey Folk Festival.

BORN ON THIS DAY

1911 Joe Turner, US blues songwriter who wrote 'Shake Rattle and Roll' and 'Sweet Sixteen.' He died on November 23rd 1985.

1912 Perry Como, singer and TV presenter who had a 1957 US No.1 single with 'Round And Round', 15 US and over 25 UK chart hits and a 1958 UK No.1 single with 'Magic Moments'. He died on May 12th 2001.

1942 Albert Hammond, singer/songwriter who had a 1972 US No.5 single with 'It Never Rains In Southern California' and a 1973 UK No.19 single with 'Free Electric Band'.

1949 Rick Wakeman – keyboardist with Strawbs and Yes. As a solo artist he had a 1974 UK No.1 album with *Journey To The Centre Of The Earth*.

1952 George Strait, country singer whose 1992 album *Pure Country* spent 40 weeks on the US chart. He also had a 2001 No. 9 US album with *The Road Less Travelled*.

1953 Butch Tavares – vocalist, keyboardist and harmonica player for Tavares, who had a 1976 UK No.4 and US No.15 single with 'Heaven Must Be Missing An Angel'.

1957 Michael Cretu, songwriter and multi-instrumentalist of Enigma, who had a 1991 UK No.1 & US No.5 single with 'Sadness Part 1'.

1958 Toyah, UK singer who had a

1981 UK No.8 single with 'I Want To Be Free'.

1969 Martika, singer who had a 1989 US No.1 & UK No.5 single with 'Toy Soldiers'. The song was sampled by Eminem in his 2005 song of the same name.

ON THIS DAY

1967 John Lennon and Paul McCartney sang backing vocals on The Rolling Stones' track 'We Love You' during a recording session at Olympic Studios, London.

1968 appearing at The Northern California Rock Festival in Santa Clara were Grateful Dead, The Doors, The Steve Miller Band and Jefferson Airplane.

1974 Ray Stevens started a three week run at No.1 on the US singles chart with the novelty song 'The Streak'. It was also a No.1 in the UK.

1975 five times married US country singer Tammy Wynette was at No.1 on the UK singles chart with 'Stand By Your Man'.

1980 Joy Division singer Ian Curtis hung himself at the age of 23, with Iggy Pop's 'The Idiot' playing on his turntable. The singer left a note that said, "At this very moment, I wish I were dead. I just can't cope anymore."

1984 Simple Minds were at No.1 on the US singles chart with 'Don't You Forget About Me', which was taken from the film

The Breakfast Club. The song made No.7 in the UK.

1991 R.E.M. went to No.1 on the US album chart with *Out Of Time*.

1993 in Glasgow, Scotland four bands were appearing at one venue: Sister Lovers, 18 Wheeler, Boyfriend and Oasis. After seeing Oasis Creation Records boss Alan Mcgee declared, "I've found the greatest rock 'n' roll band since The Beatles."

1993 Michael Bolton played the first of four sold-out nights at Wembley Arena, London.

1997 Blur won the year's Music Industry Soccer Six – pop's equivalent of the FA Cup. The band's win at Fulham FC's ground Craven Cottage saw them beating off competition from Robbie Williams, My Life Story and The Prodigy.

2000 Madonna's boyfriend Guy Ritchie was arrested after attacking a fan outside the superstar's London home. Ritchie was said to have kicked and punched a male fan after the couple returned home from a night out.

2003 The Isley Brothers were at No.1 on the US album chart with *Body Kiss*, the group's first US No.1 in over 30 years.

2004 Clint Warwick, the original bass player with The Moody Blues, died from liver disease at the age of 63. Clint left the band in 1966 after playing on their only number one hit 'Go Now'.

R.E.M. men out of time.

BORN ON THIS DAY

1932 Alma Cogan, UK singer who had a 1955 UK No.1 single with 'Dreamboat' plus 20 other UK Top 40 hits. She was the youngest female to top the charts during the 50s. Alma died of stomach cancer on October 26th 1966.

1945 Pete Townshend – guitarist and vocalist with The Who, who had a 1965 UK No.2 single with 'My Generation', a 1967 US No.9 single with 'I Can See For Miles' plus over 20 other UK Top 40 hit singles, 16 US Top 40 singles and rock opera albums *Tommy* and *Quadrophenia*.

1948 Tom Scott –saxophonist with the L.A. Express who worked with Joni Mitchell, Carole King and Steely Dan. He is also a composer of film soundtracks and TV shows.

1949 Dusty Hill – bass player for ZZ Top, who had a 1984 US No.8 and 1985 UK No.16 single with 'Legs'.

1952 Grace Jones, singer and model who had a 1985 UK No.12 single with 'Slave To The Rhythm'.

1952 Jeffrey Hyman (a.k.a. Joey Ramone) – vocalist with The Ramones, who had a 1977 UK No.22 single with 'Sheena Is A Punk Rocker'. He died on April 15th 2001.

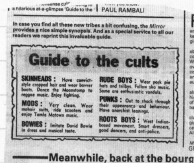

1970 Attrell "Prince Be" Cordes – vocalist and keyboardist with PM Dawn, who had a 1991 US No.1 & UK No.3 single with 'Set Adrift On Memory Bliss'.

1972 Jenny Berggren – vocalist with Ace Of Base, who had a 1993 UK No.1 single with 'All That She Wants' and a 1994 US No.1 single with 'The Sign'.

ON THIS DAY

1958 the soundtrack to *South Pacific* went to No.1 on the US album chart.

1968 Johnny Cash appeared live on stage at The Odeon, Newcastle, England.

1973 Stevie Wonder went to No.1 on the US singles chart with 'You Are The Sunshine Of My Life'. It was his third US No.1 and a No.7 hit in the UK.

1976 Stones guitarist Keith Richards crashed his car near Newport Pagnell, England, after falling asleep at the wheel. Marijuana and cocaine were found in his car, resulting in another fine.

1978 Dire Straits released their first major label single 'Sultans Of Swing', which was recorded on a £120 ($205) budget.

1979 Eric Clapton held a party at his Surrey house, celebrating his recent marriage to Patti Boyd. Clapton set up a small stage in the garden and as the evening progressed Paul McCartney, George Harrison and Ringo Starr ended up jamming together along with Clapton, Ginger Baker and Mick Jagger. The all-star band ran through old Little Richard and Eddie Cochran songs.

1979 Supertramp went to No.1 on the US album chart with *Breakfast In America*, the group's only US No.1.

1980 Ringo Starr and his future wife were involved in a car crash less than half a mile from where Marc Bolan was killed. The car was a write-off but Starr and Bach were not seriously injured.

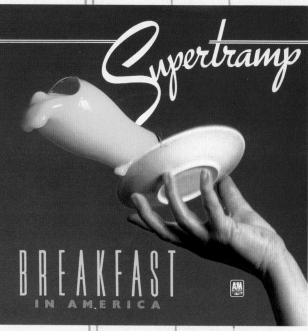

1981 Sting was named Songwriter of the year at the 26th Ivor Novello Awards.

1984 Bob Marley And The Wailers started a 12-week run at No.1 in the UK with the compilation album *Legend*, released to commemorate the third anniversary of Marley's death.

1988 James Brown was arrested for the fifth time in 12 months, following a car chase near his home. Brown was charged with assault, resisting arrest and being in charge of illegal weapons. He was given a six year jail sentence.

1990 Madonna started a three week run at No.1 on the US singles chart with 'Vogue'. Originally planned as a B-side, it became the singer's eighth US No.1 and was also a No.1 in the UK.

2001 Mike Sammes, founder of The Mike Sammes Singers, died aged 73. He had worked with Tom Jones, Cliff Richard and featured on The Beatles' 'I Am The Walrus' and 'The Long And Winding Road'.

BORN ON THIS DAY

1942 Jill Jackson – vocalist with Paul & Paula, who had a 1963 US No.1 & UK No.8 single with 'Hey Paula'.

1944 Joe Cocker, singer who had a 1968 UK No.1 single with 'With A Little Help From My Friends' plus eight other UK Top 40 singles and a 1982 US No.1 single with Jennifer Warnes 'Up Where We Belong'.

1946 Cherilyn Sarkasian, a.k.a. Cher, part of Sonny & Cher, who had a 1965 UK & US No.1 single with 'I Got You Babe'. Solo she had three US No.1s in the 1970s including the 1971 US No.1 single 'Gypsys, Tramps and Thieves'. She had a 1991 UK No.1 single 'The Shoop Shoop Song', and the 1998 UK No.1 & 1999 US No.1 single with 'Believe' plus over 15 other UK Top 40 singles.

1947 Steve Currie – bass player with T. Rex, who had a 1971 UK No.1 single with 'Hot Love' plus over 20 other UK Top 40 singles. Currie died on April 28th 1981.

1958 Jane Wieldin – guitarist and vocalist with The Go-Go's, who had a 1982 US No.2 single with 'We Got The Beat' and a 1982 UK No.47 single with 'Our Lips Our Sealed'. As a solo artist she had a 1988 UK No.12 single with 'Rush Hour'.

1961 Nick Heyward – guitarist and vocalist with Haircut 100, who had a 1982 UK No.3 single with 'Love Plus One'. Now a solo artist.

ON THIS DAY

1957 Andy Williams was at No.1 in the UK with 'Butterfly', the US singer's only UK No.1 and the first of 40 hit singles from 1957 until 2002 on the UK chart.

1967 The Beatles' new album

Rock 'n' Roll

with

"Vernon and the GI's"

1977 and Wales' kings of rock and roll reach 199 on the pop chart.

Sgt Pepper's Lonely Hearts Club Band had a preview on Kenny Everett's radio programme "Where It's At". The BBC had announced a ban on the track 'A Day In The Life', saying it could promote drug use.

1967 The Young Rascals started a two week run at No.1 on the US singles chart with 'Groovin', which made No.8 in the UK. The group named themselves after a US comedy TV show.

1968 on BBC 2 TV a short play, *The Pistol Shot*, featured a young dancer called David Bowie.

1972 T. Rex was at No.1 on the UK singles chart with 'Metal Guru', the group's fourth No.1. They also had the UK No.1 album with *Bolan Boogie*.

1978 *The Buddy Holly Story* film was premiered in Holly's home town of Lubbock, Texas.

1989 'Ferry 'Cross The Mersey' by Ferry Aid started a three week run at No.1 on the UK singles chart. The song was recorded to raise funds for the Hillsbourgh Football victims. Gerry Marsden, Paul McCartney, Holly Johnson and The Christians all featured on the recording.

1989 Paula Abdul started a two week run at No.1 on the US singles chart with 'Forever Your Girl', her second US No.1 and a No.24 hit in the UK.

1995 Don Henley married model Sharon Summerall. Guests included Billy Joel, Randy Newman, Sheryl Crow, Sting, Jackson Browne and Bruce Springsteen.

1995 Robson Green and Jerome Flynn started a seven week run at No.1 on the UK singles chart with their versions of 'Unchained Melody/(There'll Be Blue Birds Over) The White Cliffs Of Dover'. This was the third time that 'Unchained Melody' had been a hit.

1997 U2 cause traffic chaos in Kansas City, Missouri *(below)* after they paid for traffic control to close down five lanes to shoot the video for 'Last Night On Earth'. The following day a Cadillac crashed into a plate glass window to avoid a cameraman.

1998 Tommy Lee from Motley Crue was jailed for six months after being found guilty of spousal abuse.

2003 soul singer James Brown was pardoned for his past crimes in the US state of South Carolina. Brown had served a two-and-a-half-year prison term after an arrest on drug and assault charges in 1988. He was granted a pardon by the State Department of Probation, Parole and Pardon Services. Brown sang 'God Bless America' after the decision.

U2's highway to hell!

Freeway to go: U2's pesky video shoot

U2 caused traffic chaos in Kansas City, Missouri last Tuesday (May 20) when they closed down the freeway system to shoot the video for a forthcoming single, 'Last Night On Earth'. The band paid for traffic control to close five interstate roads which carry 100,000 cars daily to the downtown area of town.

Kansas City Police spokesperson Russ Dykstra said the video shoot went off without incident but detour roads set up to provide traffic with alternative routes into the city were blocked by serious accidents.

"A trailer jack-knifed on a detour route and as a consequence of that we had one multi-car collision and one separate incident; we also suffered a power cut on another detour road," he said.

The permit for the video shoot was approved by the state on May 17 but details were not released to the public until the day before filming was due to start.

On Wednesday (21) they continued filming on local downtown streets. At one point in the day, a Cadillac crashed into a plate glass window to avoid cameramen.

"I can't believe the stupidity of it," Mike Right, Vice President of Public Affairs for the AAA Auto Club of Missouri told the *Kansas City Star.*

"They close down an interstate highway that serves downtown Kansas City for a music video? I've never heard of such a thing."

Kansas City Mayor Emanuel Cleaver took a different approach to the disruption, telling the *Star* that a video from a popular rock band would give the city a lot of free publicity. "I'd never heard of U2 until they came to the city to do a concert, but this

provides an opportunity for us to put our city on display throughout the world," he said.

The video depicts the progress of an airborne disease as it lays waste to a city. A band spokeswoman told *NME* they wanted to film in Kansas because of its unique skyline.

In 1987, U2 narrowly escaped arrest after they brought traffic chaos to Los Angeles during the shooting of the 'Where The Streets Have No Name' video.

BORN ON THIS DAY

1941 Ronald Isley – singer with The Isley Brothers, who had a 1968 UK No.3 single with 'This Old Heart Of Mine' and a 1969 US No.2 single with 'It's Your Thing'.

1943 Hilton Valentine – guitarist with The Animals, who had a 1964 UK & US No.1 single with 'House Of The Rising Sun'.

1943 John Dalton – bass player for The Kinks, who had a 1964 UK No.1 & US No.7 with 'You Really Got Me', a 1967 UK No.2 single with 'Waterloo Sunset' plus 19 other UK Top 40 singles.

1943 Vincent Crane – keyboardist with The Crazy World Of Arthur Brown, who had a 1968 UK No.1 and US No.12 single with 'Fire', and Atomic Rooster, who had a 1971 UK No.4 single with 'The Devil's Answer'. He died on February 14th 1989.

1948 Leo Sayer, UK singer who had a 1977 UK & US No.1 single with 'When I Need You', the Chrysalis record label's first No.1, plus 13 other UK Top 40 singles.

1955 Stan Lynch – drummer with Tom Petty And The Heartbreakers, who had a 1980 US No.15 single with 'Refugee' and a 1989 UK No.28 single with 'I Won't Back Down'.

1964 Martin Blunt – bass player for The Charlatans, who had a 1990 UK No.9 single with 'The Only One I Know', a 1996 UK No.3 single with 'One To Another' plus three UK No.1 albums.

1972 The Notorious B.I.G., US rapper who had a 1995 UK No.34 single with 'One More Chance' and a 1997 US No.1 single with 'Hypnotize'. He was gunned down and killed on the streets of Los Angeles on March 9th 1997, aged 24.

ON THIS DAY

1955 Eddie Calvert was at No.1 in the UK with 'Cherry Pink and Apple Blossom White'. The song had also been a No.1 for Perez Prado the same year.

1966 The Mamas And The Papas went to No.1 on the US album chart with *If You Can Believe Your Eyes And Ears*.

1974 two would-be concert promoters were arrested by police in America on fraud charges in connection with selling mail order tickets for a forthcoming Elten John show (Elten with an E and not an O). Police took away over $12,000 (£7,058) in cheques.

1977 Rod Stewart was at No.1 on the UK singles chart with the double A-side 'I Don't Want To Talk About It/First Cut Is The Deepest'.

PROMOTION

BUSTED

THE DATES

MAY 2003

Fri 21st	BLACKPOOL OPERA HOUSE
Thu 22nd	HULL ARENA
Fri 23rd	NOTTINGHAM ROYAL CENTRE
Sat 24th	HALLAM FM ARENA, SHEFFIELD
Sun 25th	LIVERPOOL EMPIRE
Mon 26th	GLASGOW ARMADILLO
Wed 28th	BRIGHTON CENTRE
Thu 29th	BIRMINGHAM NIA ACADEMY
Fri 30th	WEMBLEY ARENA
Sat 31st	NEWCASTLE TELEWEST ARENA

JUNE 2003

Sun 1st	CARDIFF INT. ARENA

Please check with venue or ticket hotline for latest details

TICKET PRICE £18.50, £22.50
(AGENCY & CREDIT CARD BOOKINGS SUBJECT TO BOOKING FEE)

1980 five Jimi Hendrix Gold discs were stolen from The Electric Ladyland Studios, California.

1980 Joe Strummer of The Clash was arrested at a much troubled gig in Hamburg, Germany after smashing his guitar over the head of a member of the audience. He was released after an alcohol test proved negative.

1983 David Bowie went to No.1 on the US singles chart with 'Let's Dance', his second US No.1 and also a No.1 in the UK.

1988 Prince got his first UK No.1 album with *Lovesexy*.

1988 Wet Wet Wet and Billy Bragg were at No.1 on the UK singles chart with 'With A Little Help From My Friends' and 'She's Leaving Home', two Beatles songs recorded for the Childline charity.

Wet Wet Wet: less wet, more greasy.

1995 Hootie & the Blowfish started a four week run at No.1 in the US with *Cracked Rear View*. The album went on to sell over 15 million copies.

2000 Whitney Houston started a two-week run at No.1 on the UK album chart with *The Greatest Hits*.

2000 Billie Piper went to No.1 on the UK singles chart with 'Day & Night'.

2003 Mariah Carey hit back at Eminem's threats to sample the slushy voicemail messages she left on his mobile. Carey described the rapper as "a little girl" saying it's "like dealing with a girlfriend in 7th grade", and he shouldn't do it because it'll get him in a bit of trouble with her lawyers.

BORN ON THIS DAY

1950 Bernie Taupin, Elton John's long-time songwriting partner. They first met in 1967 after both responded to an ad by Liberty Records seeking new talent in UK music weekly the *New Music Express*. As well as working with Elton John for over 30 years other acts including Rod Stewart, Cher, The Motels, John Waite, Starship and Alice Cooper have all recorded songs written by Taupin.

1954 Jerry Dammers – keyboard player, songwriter with The Specials who had the 1981 UK No.1 single 'Ghost Town'. Dammers was the driving force behind the 1988 'Nelson Mandela 70th Birthday Tribute' concert at Wembley Stadium.

1955 Iva Davis – singer, songwriter with Australian group Icehouse who had the 1983 UK No.17 single 'Hey Little Girl' and the 1988 US No.8 single 'Electric Blue'. The group's 1988 album *Man of Colours* set an Australian record for the biggest selling Australian group album of all time on the domestic market. Now works as a solo artist.

1959 Steven Morrissey – vocalist with The Smiths, who had a 1984 UK No.10 single with 'Heaven Knows I'm Miserable Now' plus over 15 other UK Top 40 singles and the 1985 UK No.1 album *Meat Is Murder*. As a solo artist he had a 1988 UK No.5 single with 'Suedehead' plus over 15 other UK Top 40 singles.

Madame Tussauds' popular (but perhaps a little crass) 'Touch J-Lo's Bum' feature.

1967 Dan Roberts – bass player for Crash Test Dummies, who had a 1994 UK No.2 & US No.4 single with 'Mmm Mmm Mmm Mmm'.

ON THIS DAY

1961 Ernie K-Doe went to No.1 on the US singles chart with 'Mother In Law'.

1964 The Beatles scored their second US No.1 album with *The Beatles' Second Album*. It displaced *Meet The Beatles!* from the top of the charts.

1966 16-year-old Bruce Springsteen and his band The Castilles recorded their first and only track, 'That's What You Get' in New Jersey.

1968 Gary Puckett And The Union Gap were at No.1 on the UK singles chart with 'Young Girl'.

1970 this week's UK Top 5 singles were: No.5, 'Daughter Of Darkness', Tom Jones; No.4, 'Question', The Moody Blues; No.3, 'Yellow River', Christie; No.2, 'Spirit In The Sky', Norman Greenbaum and No.1, 'Back Home', The England World Cup Squad.

1976 The Rolling Stones played at Earl's Court in London.

1976 Wings started a five week run at No.1 on the US singles chart with 'Silly Love Songs', McCartney's fifth US No.1 since leaving The Beatles. It made No.2 in the UK.

1980 Adam And The Ants appeared live at the Electric Ballroom, London.

1989 rap group Public Enemy fired one of its members, Professor Griff, after he made anti-Semitic remarks in the *Washington Post*.

Adam Ant: no longer a Prince Charming.

1991 Wil Sin from The Shamen drowned when he was pulled under by strong currents while taking a break from filming the group's new video in Tenerife.

1993 Ace Of Base started a three week run at No.1 in the UK with the single 'All That She Wants'.

1999 Tim McGraw was at No.1 on the US album chart with *A Place In The Sun*.

2000 Robbie Williams set up a children's charity with the cash he earned from a deal with Pepsi. The trust, "Give It Sum", boasted £2 million ($3.4 million) seed money. Beneficiaries would include UNICEF and Jeans For Genes.

2000 Travis swept the board at the Ivor Novello awards. Singer Fran Healy won two awards for Best contemporary song for the single 'Why Does It Always Rain On Me?' and Songwriter of the year for the Travis album *The Man Who*.

2002 Adam Ant appeared at The Old Bailey in London charged with possession of an imitation firearm. Ant (a.k.a. Stuart Goddard) had been arrested in January after an altercation at The Prince of Wales pub in London when a bouncer refused to let him in.

2002 all the members from Alien Ant Farm were hospitalized after their tour bus was involved in a crash in Spain. The band's driver was killed.

2003 a new model of J-Lo was unveiled at Madame Tussauds in London. The waxwork cost £52,000 ($88,400) to make.

2003 soul singer Ruben Studdard won the second series of talent show *American Idol* after 24 million viewers voted in the final. Studdard beat fellow finalist Clay Aiken in a tense live showdown.

BORN ON THIS DAY

1934 Robert Moog, who invented the Moog synthesizer in 1964.

1943 Norman Johnson – singer with Chairmen Of The Board, who had a 1970 UK & US No.3 single with 'Give Me Just A Little More Time'.

1944 Ramon "Tiki" Fulwood – drummer with Parliament and Funkadelic who had a 1978 US No.16 album with *One Nation Under A Groove*.

1946 Daniel Klein – bass player with the J. Geils Band, who had a 1982 US No.1 & UK No.3 single with 'Centrefold'.

1947 Bill Hunt – French horn player for the Electric Light Orchestra, who had a 1979 UK No.3 & US No.4 single with 'Don't Bring Me Down' plus 26 other Top 40 hits.

1953 Rick Fenn – guitarist with 10CC, who had a 1975 UK No.1 & US No.2 single with 'I'm Not In Love' plus ten other UK Top 30 hits including two No.1s.

1967 Philip James Selway – drummer for Radiohead, who had a 1997 UK No.1 & US No.21 album with *OK Computer*.

1972 Maxwell, US male singer who had a 1997 UK No.27 single with 'Sumthin' Sumthin' The Mantra' and a 2001 US No.1 album with *Now*.

Students Union

Manchester University
Students Union
Tel (0161) 275 2930

SJM CONCERTS presents

THE WANNADIES

+ Special Guests
FRIDAY 23rd MAY 1997
Doors 7.30 p.m.   **£7 (Advance)**
UNRESERVED

Retain This Portion   Conditions Overleaf

00213

1974 Jewel Kilcher, US singer/songwriter who had a 1995 US No.5 album with *Pieces Of You* and a 1997 US No.3 single with You Were Meant For Me'.

1974 Richard Jones – bass player with Stereophonics, who had a 2001 UK No.1 album with *Just Enough Education To Perform*.

ON THIS DAY

1960 The Everly Brothers started a five week run at No.1 on the US singles chart with 'Cathy's Clown', which spent seven weeks at No.1 in the UK.

1964 Ella Fitzgerald became the first artist to have a hit with a Beatles cover when 'Can't Buy Me Love' entered the UK chart.

1970 the Grateful Dead played their first gig outside the US at "The Hollywood Rock Music Festival" in Newcastle-Under-Lyme, England.

1974 George Harrison announced the launch of his own record label, Dark Horse.

1975 Led Zeppelin started a three night run at Earl's Court, London. Tickets cost £1 ($1.70) and £2.50 ($4.25).

1979 due to a record company dispute, Tom Petty was forced to file for bankruptcy owing $575,000 (£338,235). A long-running battle with his record company followed.

1980 Saxon and Tygers Of Pan Tang kicked off a 22 date UK tour at Bristol Coliston Hall. Tickets were £2.00–3.00 ($3.40–5).

1982 the UK Musicians Union moved a resolution to ban synthesizers and rhythm machines from sessions and live concerts fearing that their use would put musicians out of work.

1987 The Beastie Boys and Run-DMC opened their UK tour in London.

1991 New Kids On The Block played the first of five nights at Birmingham's NEC.

1992 a statement issued by Freddie Mercury's attorneys stated that Mercury had bequeathed the majority of his estate (£10 million/$17 million) to his long-time friend Mary Austin.

1998 Mariah Carey went to No.1 on the US singles chart with 'My All'.

2000 Noel Gallagher walked out on his band Oasis during a European tour. The move was put down to a series of bust-ups with his brother Liam.

2002 Cliff Richard announced plans to launch a new wine "Vida Nova". 27,000 bottles of the Portuguese red from the grapes of his 25 acre estate would sell at £8.99 ($15.28) a bottle.

2002 winners at the 47th Ivor Novello awards included, Dido, Songwriter of the year; Best song, U2, 'Walk On' and Kylie Minogue won the Dance award, Most performed work and Best international hit for 'Can't Get You Out Of My Head'.

Kylie Minogue: 2002's award-winning dance act, the non-waxwork version, that is.

BORN ON THIS DAY

1941 Bob Dylan, (a.k.a. Robert Zimmerman), singer/songwriter. He has released over 40 albums since 1964, and was a major influence on The Beatles and Rolling Stones during the 60s. He had a 1965 US No.2 single with 'Like A Rolling Stone' and a 1969 UK No.5 single with 'Lay Lady Lay'.

1942 Derek Quinn – guitarist with Freddie & The Dreamers, who had a 1963 UK No.3 single with 'You Were Made For Me' and a 1965 US No.1 single with 'I'm Telling You Now'.

1947 Albert Bouchard, drummer and vocalist for Blue Oyster Cult, who had a 1976 US No.12 and 1978 UK No.16 single with 'Don't Fear The Reaper'.

1947 Cynthia "Plaster" Caster, a groupie who became famous for making plaster casts of rock star's penises. Clients include Jimi Hendrix and members from MC5, Television, The Kinks and various road managers.

1962 Gene Anthony Ray, Leroy in TV's *Fame*. He was axed from the show in 1984 after his mother was jailed for running a drug ring. He died on November 19th 2003.

1969 Rich Robinson – guitarist with The Black Crowes, who had a 1991 UK No.39 single with 'Hard To Handle' and a 1992 US No.1 & UK No.2 album with *The Southern Harmony And Musical Companion*.

Leeds Univents backstage Pass

ROBERT PALMER

Tuesday 24th May 1983

ON THIS DAY

1956 the first Eurovision Song Contest was held in Lugano, Switzerland. The event was the brainchild of Marcel Baisoncon of the European Broadcasting Union. Seven countries participated and they were each allowed two songs. Both Luxembourg and the winner Switzerland used the same singer for both. Switzerland won with 'Refrain' by Lys Assia.

1962 Elvis Presley was at No.1 on the UK singles chart with 'Good Luck Charm', his 11th UK No.1 single.

1963 Elmore James, US blues guitarist and singer, died of a heart attack aged 45. He wrote 'Shake Your Money Maker', which was covered by Fleetwood Mac in 1968. He influenced Jimi Hendrix, BB King and Keith Richards.

1969 Bob Dylan scored his fourth No.1 UK album with *Nashville Skyline*.

1969 tonight on BBC TV's *33 & A Third Revolutions Per Monkee* guests included Fats Domino, Jerry Lee Lewis, Little Richard and Julie Driscoll, along with all four members of The Monkees.

1969 The Beatles with Billy Preston started a five week run at No.1 on the US singles chart with 'Get Back', the group's 17th US No.1.

1975 Earth, Wind And Fire went to No.1 on the US singles chart with 'Shining Star', the group's first and only US No.1.

1980 Genesis fans turning up at the Roxy Club box office in Los Angeles to buy tickets for a forthcoming gig were surprised to find the band members Collins, Banks and Rutherford selling the tickets themselves.

1982 The Clash kicked off a 12 date UK tour at Leeds University.

1997 Hanson started a three week run at No.1 on the US singles chart with 'MMMBop', the brothers first US No.1. It was also a No.1 in the UK.

1997 The Spice Girls went to No.1 on the US album chart with *Spice*, making them only the third all-girl group to do so after The Supremes and The Go-Go's.

1999 Freddie Mercury was featured on a new set of millennium stamps issued by the Royal Mail.

2000 a New York Judge told Pretenders singer Chrissie Hynde that if she wanted her March arrest for protesting the sale of leather goods in a Gap store dismissed, she'd better keep her nose clean for the next six months.

2000 Andrea and Sharon Corr both collapsed in the midday sun while shooting their new video in the Mojave Desert in California. The pair were treated in hospital for heat exhaustion.

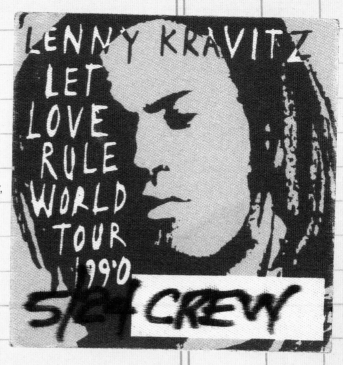

BORN ON THIS DAY

1921 Hal David, US songwriter, pianist and arranger. With Burt Bacharach he wrote many classic songs including, 'Close To You', '24 Hours From Tulsa', 'Make It Easy On Yourself', 'Magic Moments' and 'I Say A Little Prayer'. They won two Oscars for the film score *Butch Cassidy And The Sundance Kid* and 'Raindrops Keep Fallin' On My Head'.

1926 Miles Davis, jazz trumpeter and composer who had a 1959 album with *Kind of Blue*. He was a major influence on jazz music. Davis died on September 28th 1991.

1936 Donnie Elbert, US soul singer who had a 1972 US No.22 & UK No.11 single with 'I Can't Help Myself'. He died on January 26th 1989.

1947 Mitchell Margo – singer with The Tokens, who had a 1961 US No.1 & UK No.11 single with 'The Lion Sleeps Tonight'.

1948 Klaus Meine – singer with The Scorpions, who had a 1991 UK No.2 single with 'Wind Of Change'.

1950 Robert Steinhardt – violin and string player and vocalist with Kansas, who had a 1978 US No.3 single with 'Dust In The Wind' and a UK No.59 single with 'Carry On Wayward Son'.

1958 Paul Weller – singer and guitarist with The Jam, who had a 1980 UK No.1 single with 'Going Underground' plus over 15 other UK Top 40 singles, and Style Council, who had a 1983 UK No.3 single with 'Long Hot Summer' plus 14 other UK Top 40 singles. As a solo artist he had a 1995 UK No.7 single with 'The Changing Man'.

1975 Lauryn Hill – singer with The Fugees, who had a 1996 UK No.1 single with 'Killing Me Softly'. As a solo artist she had a 1998 UK No.3 single with 'Doo Wop, That Thing'.

ON THIS DAY

1965 blues artist Sonny Boy Williamson died in his sleep. Van Morrison, The Who, The Animals, Yardbirds and Moody Blues all covered his songs.

1967 Procol Harum's 'A Whiter Shade Of Pale' entered the UK chart for the first time. It went on to top the charts.

1968 Simon & Garfunkel scored their second US No.1 album with *Bookends*.

1973 Carole King played a concert in New York's Central Park, which attracted an audience of 100,000.

1978 after seeing The Hype (U2) playing at the Project Arts Centre, Dublin, Paul McGuinness became their manager.

1985 Dire Straits scored their second UK No.1 album with *Brothers In Arms*, which was also No.1 in the US and 24 other countries. It went on to sell over 20 million copies worldwide.

1985 Wham! started a two week run at No.1 on the US singles chart with 'Everything She Wants'.

1992 Khalil Rountree, tour manager of Boyz II Men, was killed by gunfire after a scuffle in an elevator on the 26th floor of a hotel in Chicago. Their assistant tour manager was also injured.

1995 the earliest known recording of Mick Jagger and Keith Richards, from 1961, was sold at Christies in London for £50,250 ($85,425).

1997 a report showed that Elvis Presley was the world's bestselling posthumous entertainer with worldwide sales of over one billion, over 480 fanclubs and an estimated 250,000 UK fans who still buy his records. Ironically he had died owing $3 million (£1.76 million).

2002 30 Eminem fans were hurt after a crowd surge at a gig in Washington D.C. Five people were taken to hospital, and one man suffered a heart attack.

Paul Weller (left) in The Jam.

BORN ON THIS DAY

1904 George Formby, UK singing comedian and ukulele player. He made over 20 films and his best-known song is 'Leaning On A Lamp Post'. He was made an OBE in 1946 and died on March 6th 1961. Formby influenced George Harrison.

1942 Ray Ennis – guitarist and singer with Swinging Blue Jeans, who had a 1964 UK No.2 and US No.24 single with 'Hippy Hippy Shake'.

1943 Levon Helm – drummer for The Band, who had a 1969 US No.25 single with 'Up On Cripple Creek' and a 1970 UK No.16 single with 'Rag Mama Rag'.

1948 Stevie Nicks – singer with Fleetwood Mac, who had a 1987 UK No.5 single with 'Little Lies' and a 1977 US No.1 single 'Dreams', which was taken from the worldwide No.1 album *Rumours*.

1949 Mick Ronson – guitarist and producer. He was a member of Mott The Hoople, who had a 1972 UK No.3 single 'All The Young Dudes', and worked with David Bowie on the 1974 UK No.5 single 'Rebel Rebel'. Ronson died on April 28th 1993.

1962 Acker Bilk went to No.1 on the US singles chart with 'Stranger On The Shore'. It became a million seller in the UK, making No.2 on the charts.

1964 Lenny Kravitz, singer and guitarist who had a 1993 UK No.1 album with *Are You Gonna Go My Way?* and a 1999 UK No.1 single with 'Fly Away'.

1972 Alan White – drummer with Oasis (he replaced Tony McCarroll in 1995), who had a 1996 UK No.1 single with 'Don't Look Back In Anger'. He was sacked from the band in 2004.

ON THIS DAY

1969 John and Yoko began an eight-day "bed-in" at the Hotel La Reine Elizabeth, Montreal, Canada. They were promoting world peace.

1972 at the point of splitting up David Bowie offered Mott The Hoople two of his new songs 'Suffragette City', which they turned down and 'All The Young Dudes', which they recorded.

1972 the first day of the four day festival "The Great Western Express" near Lincoln featured The Faces, Joe Cocker, Humble Pie, Slade, The Groundhogs, Ry Cooder, Don Mclean, Brewers Droop plus a special appearance by Monty Python.

1973 the Edgar Winter Group went to No.1 on the US singles chart with 'Frankenstein', the band's only US No.1. It reached No.18 in the UK. The group featured ex-McCoys guitarist Rick Derringer.

The Edgar Winter Group enjoy some studio time.

1974 tragedy struck at a David Cassidy concert at London's White City when over 1,000 fans had to be treated by first aid workers due to the frenzied excitement. One fan, Bernadette Whelan, died from heart failure four days later.

1978 at 5.30 on Irish TV a programme called *Youngline* was broadcast, a series for young people highlighting their interests. On this day it featured a new Irish band called U2 (alias Hype).

1979 the first day of the two day Loch Lomond Festival started with The Stranglers, Dr Feelgood, Skids, Third World and The Dickies. On day two were AWB, Buzzcocks, Rockpile and The Boomtown Rats, who played 'I Don't Like Mondays' for the first time live.

1990 for the first time ever the top five positions in the US singles chart were held by female artists: Madonna was at No.1 with 'Vogue'; Heart were at No.2, Sinead O'Connor was at No.3, Wilson Phillips at No.4 and Janet Jackson was at No.5.

1994 Michael Jackson married Lisa Marie Presley, daughter of Elvis. The couple divorced in 1995.

1996 a fire at the home of Eric Clapton caused over £1.5 million ($2.55 million) worth of damage. Firemen arrived on the scene to find Clapton braving the blaze to save his collection of guitars.

2002 the first episode of *At Home With The Osbournes* was shown on MTV in the UK.

BORN ON THIS DAY

1935 Rudy Lewis – singer with The Drifters, who had a 1960 US No.1 & UK No.2 single with 'Save The Last Dance For Me'. He died on May 10th 1964.

1956 Neil Finn– guitarist and vocalist with Split Enz, who had a 1980 UK No.12 single with 'I Got You', Crowded House, who had a 1992 UK No.7 single with 'Weather With You', and The Finn Brothers.

1957 Eddie Harsch – keyboardist with The Black Crowes, who had a 1991 UK No.39 single with 'Hard To Handle' and a 1992 US No.1 & UK No.2 album with *The Southern Harmony And Musical Companion*.

1957 Siouxsie Sioux – singer with Siouxsie And The Banshees, who had a 1983 UK No.3 single with 'Dear Prudence' plus over 15 other UK Top 40 singles', and The Creatures, who had a 1983 UK No.14 single with 'Right Now'.

1971 Lisa "Left-Eye" Lopes – vocalist with TLC, who had a 1995 US No.1 & UK No.4 single with 'Waterfalls' and a 1999 US No.1 album with *Fanmail*, which also spent 57 weeks on the UK chart. Lisa was killed in a car accident on April 26th 2002.

1975 Andre 3000, (a.k.a. Andre Benjamin) – US rapper and member of Outkast, who had a 2001 US No.1 & UK No.2 single with 'Ms Jackson'.

ON THIS DAY

1957 Buddy Holly & The Crickets released their first record, 'That'll Be The Day'. It went on to be a UK No.1 and US No.3 hit.

1964 11 boys were suspended from a school in Coventry, England for having Mick Jagger hair cuts.

1965 Sandie Shaw was at No.1 on the UK singles chart with 'Long Live Love'.

1967 to celebrate Cilla Black's birthday her manager Brian Epstein organized illuminated greetings at London's Piccadilly Circus and sites in Manchester, Bristol and Birmingham.

1977 singer/songwriter Declan McManus made his "live" debut at the Nashville in London as Elvis Costello.

1977 the Sex Pistols' single 'God Save The Queen' was released. Banned by TV, radio and high street shops, pressing plant workers refused to handle the record. It sold 200,000 copies in one week and made No.2 on the UK charts.

1983 The Smiths were at No.1 on the UK independent chart with their debut single 'Hand In Glove'.

1989 Cliff Richard *(top)* released his 100th single 'The Best Of Me', which became his 26th Top 3 UK hit.

Split Enz dress up in order to meet the future in-laws!

1990 The Stone Roses played at Spike Island, Widnes, Cheshire to a capacity crowd of 30,000.

1997 Oasis singer Liam Gallagher was left with cuts and bruises after a scuffle with a youth at the Tower Thistle Hotel in East London. Members of the band had been drinking at the bar when the fight broke out.

1999 at the Ivor Novello Songwriting Awards Rod Stewart won a Lifetime achievement award, Robbie Williams and Guy Chambers won Songwriters of the year and Chrissie Hynde won Outstanding contribution to British music.

2000 Paula Yates was awarded £400,000 ($680,000) in an out-of-court settlement from her boyfriend Michael Hutchence's fortune. Hutchence had died in 1997.

2001 Christina Aguilera, Lil' Kim, Mya and Pink started a five week run at No.1 on the US singles chart with 'Lady Marmalade'.

BORN ON THIS DAY

1917 Papa John Creech – violinist with Jefferson Airplane and Hot Tuna. Died in 1994 aged 76.

1943 Tony Mansfield – drummer with Billy J. Kramer And The Dakotas, who had a 1964 UK No.1 & US No.7 single with 'Little Children'.

1944 Billy Vera, US singer who had a 1987 US No.1 single with The Beaters, 'At This Moment', which was featured in the US TV show *Family Ties*.

1944 Gladys Knight – singer with The Pips, who had a 1973 US No.1 single with 'Midnight Train To Georgia', a 1975 UK No.4 single with 'The Way We Were' plus 20 other UK Top 40 singles.

1945 John Fogerty – guitarist and vocalist with Creedence Clearwater Revival *(right)*, who had a 1969 UK No.1 and US No.2 single with 'Bad Moon Rising' plus ten other US Top 30 hits and a 1970 US & UK No.1 album with *Cosmo's Factory*. He has also worked as a solo artist and been a member of The Blue Ridge Rangers.

1949 Wendy O Williams – singer with The Plasmatics, a New York punk band who had the 1980 UK No. 55 single 'Butcher Baby'. She died from self-inflicted gunshot wounds on April 6th 1998.

1962 Roland Gift – vocalist with Fine Young Cannibals, who had a 1989 US No.1 & UK No.5 single with 'She Drives Me Crazy'.

1968 Kylie Minogue, singer and actress, who had a 1988 UK No.1 single with 'I Should Be So Lucky' plus over 20 other UK Top 40 hit singles.

A/C PRODUCTIONS Presents

✸ IN CONCERT

CREEDENCE CLEARWATER REVIVAL

PLUS

BOOKER T. & The M.G.s

SAT. JAN 31
8:30 P.M.
OAKLAND COLISEUM

TICKETS ON SALE

| COLISEUM BOX OFFICE | SHERMAN - CLAY OAKLAND | DOWNTOWN CENTER BOX OFFICE S.F. | SAN JOSE BOX OFFICE | PALO ALTO BOX OFFICE |

MACY'S, TICKETRON, COMPUTICKET & COLISEUM AGENCIES

ON THIS DAY

1964 The BBC received over 8,000 postal applications for tickets for The Rolling Stones' appearance on *Juke Box Dury*.

1966 Herb Alpert And The Tijuana Brass went to No.1 on the US album chart with *What Now My Love?*

1966 Percy Sledge started a two week run at No.1 on the US singles chart with 'When A Man Loves A Woman'. It made No.4 on the UK chart and No.2 when reissued in 1987.

1969 Mick Jagger and Marian Faithfull were arrested at their London home and charged with possession of cannabis. They were released on £50 ($85) bail.

1977 appearing at London's Hammersmith Odeon were Blondie with support band Television making their live UK debut.

1977 Sting, Stewart Copeland and Andy Summers played together for the first time when they performed as part of Mike Howlett's band, Strontium 90, at the Circus Hippodrome, Paris.

1982 promoter Bill Graham staged a special Vietnam Veterans benefit concert in San Francisco starring The Jefferson Starship, the Grateful Dead and Country Joe.

1983 actress and singer Irene Cara started a six week run at No.1 on the US singles chart with 'Flashdance...What A Feeling'. Taken from the film *Flashdance*, it was a No.2 hit in the UK. Irene had also appeared in TV's *Roots* and *The Next Generation*.

1983 the four day "US Festival 83" was held in California, featuring The Clash, U2, David Bowie, The Pretenders, Van Halen, Stray Cats, Men At Work, Judas Priest, Stevie Nicks and Ozzy Osbourne. Over 750,000 fans attended.

1990 Mitch Mitchell, former drummer with Jimi Hendrix, took out a High Court action against *Private Eye* over an allegedly defamatory item.

1996 Depeche Mode singer Dave Gahan was rushed to Cedars-Sinai Hospital, Los Angeles after an apparent drug overdose. The singer was later arrested for possession of cocaine and heroin.

2000 Britney Spears was at No.1 on the US album chart with Oops!...I Did It Again.

2000 Sonique started a three week run at No.1 on the UK singles chart with 'It Feels So Good'.

2005 appearing at Carling Live 24 in Manchester were I am Kloot, Doves, Elbow, The Coral, Chemical Brothers and Ian Brown.

BORN ON THIS DAY

1941 Roy Crewsdon – guitarist for Freddie & The Dreamers, who had a 1963 UK No.3 single with 'You Were made For Me' and a 1965 US No.1 single with 'I'm Telling You Now'.

1945 Gary Brooker – vocalist and keyboardist with Procol Harum, who had a 1967 UK No.1 and US No.5 single with 'A Whiter Shade Of Pale'.

1955 Mike Porcaro – bass player with Toto, who had a 1983 US No.1 & UK No.3 single with 'Africa'.

1958 Marie Fredriksson – singer for Roxette, who had a 1990 US No.1 & UK No.3 single with 'It Must Have Been Love'.

1959 Mel Gaynor – drummer with Simple Minds, who had a 1985 US No.1 single with 'Don't You, Forget About Me', a 1989 UK No.1 single with 'Belfast Child' plus over 20 other UK Top 40 singles.

1967 Noel Gallagher – guitarist with Oasis, first hit in 1994 with UK No.31 single 'Supersonic', 1996 UK No.1 single with 'Don't Look Back In Anger' and a 1994 UK No.1 album *Definitely Maybe*, which was the fastest-selling UK debut album ever.

1975 Melanie Brown, a.k.a. Mel B and Scary Spice, singer with The Spice Girls, who had a 1996 UK No.1 & 1997 US No.1 single with 'Wannabe' plus eight other UK No.1 singles. As a solo artist she had a 1998 UK No.1 single with 'I Want You Back'.

ON THIS DAY

1942 Bing Crosby recorded the Irving Berlin song 'White Christmas'. It went on to become the biggest-selling single of all time with sales of over 30 million. (It was overtaken by the 1997 Elton John version of 'Candle In The Wind'.)

1961 Ricky Nelson started a two week run at No.1 on the US singles chart with 'Travellin' Man'. Sam

Cooke had turned the song down. The B-side was the Gene Pitney song 'Hello Mary Lou', which became a double A-side UK No.1.

1965 Bob Dylan's album *Bring It All Back Home* was at No.1 on the UK charts.

1965 The Beach Boys started a two week run at No.1 on the US singles chart with 'Help Me Rhonda', the group's second US No.1. It only reached No.27 on the UK chart.

Brown Sugar / Bitch / Let It Rock

The Rolling Stones

The Rolling Stones at No.1 again, this time with 'Brown Sugar'.

1967 appearing live at the Tulip Bulb Auction Hall in Spalding, Lincs, England, were The Move, Cream, Jimi Hendrix Experience, Zoot Money and Pink Floyd. Tickets cost £1 ($1.70).

1971 The Rolling Stones started a two week run at No.1 on the US singles chart with 'Brown Sugar'. It was the band's sixth US No.1.

1975 fans rioted when The Osmonds appeared at London's Wembley Pool.

1976 Diana Ross started a two week run No.1 on the US singles chart with 'Love Hangover', her fourth US No.1. The song made No.10 in the UK.

1977 new Manchester band Warsaw (later to become Joy Division) made their live debut supporting the Buzzcocks at The Electric Circus, Manchester.

1992 concerned that some pupils were overly identifying with Freddie Mercury, the Sacred Heart School in Clifton, New Jersey decided not to sing 'We Are The Champions' at their Graduation Ceremony.

1992 the FBI recovered 44 nude photographs of Madonna that had been stolen from fashion photographer Steven Meisel.

1997 US singer/songwriter Jeff Buckley disappeared after taking a swim in the Mississippi River. His body was found on June 4th after being spotted by a passenger on a tourist riverboat.

2001 The Eagles made their first-ever visit to Russia, appearing at SC Olymisky in Moscow.

2002 Australian actress and singer Natalie Imbruglia became the new face of L'Oreal when she signed a deal worth £100,000 ($170,000) with the French cosmetics manufacturer.

BORN ON THIS DAY

1944 Lenny Davidson – guitarist and vocalist with The Dave Clark Five, who had a 1964 UK No.1 single with 'Glad All Over', a 1965 US No.1 single with 'Over And Over' plus 15 other UK Top 15 singles.

1955 Nicky "Topper" Headon – drummer with The Clash, who had a 1979 UK No.11 single with 'London Calling', a 1982 US No 8 single with 'Rock The Casbah', a 1991 UK No.1 single with 'Should I Stay Or Should I Go' (first released in 1982) plus 15 other UK Top 40 singles.

1964 Tom Morello – guitarist with Rage Against The Machine, who had a 1996 US No.1 album with *Evil Empire*, and Audioslave.

1968 Tim Burgess – vocalist with The Charlatans, who had a 1990 UK No.9 single with 'The Only One I Know', a 1996 UK No.3 single with 'One To Another' plus three UK No.1 albums.

ON THIS DAY

1964 The Beatles went to No.1 on the US singles chart with 'Love Me Do', the group's fourth US No.1 in five months.

1966 Dolly Parton married Carl Dean in Catoosa County, Georgia.

1970 Ray Stevens went to No.1 on the US singles chart with 'Everything Is Beautiful'. The former DJ had a string of novelty hits, including 'Jeremiah

Peabody's Poly Unsaturated Quick Dissolving Fast Acting Pleasant Tasting Green & Purple Pill'.

1972 Roxy Music played their first major live show when they appeared at The Great Western Express Festival in Lincolnshire.

1974 Bernadette Whelan, a 14-year-old David Cassidy fan, died of heart failure four days after attending a concert of his. Over 1,000 other fans had to be given first aid during the White City Stadium show in London.

1980 Carl Radle, bass player with Derek And The Dominoes, died of kidney failure aged 38. He had also worked with George Harrison and Delaney & Bonnie.

1987 Adam Horovitz from The Beastie Boys was arrested while on tour after a beer can hit a fan during a disturbance in Liverpool.

1987 David Bowie kicked off his 87 date Glass Spider world tour at the Feynoord Stadium, Rotterdam, Holland.

1988 Leonard Cohen played the first of three sold-out nights at London's Royal Albert Hall.

1990 As a protest against the *Valdez* oil spill, Midnight Oil played a concert in front of Exxon's offices in 6th Avenue in New York City. The police had to close down the surrounding streets.

1992 Paul Simon married singer Edie Brickell.

1992 The Black Crowes went to No.1 on the US album chart with *The Southern Harmony And Musical Companion*.

1996 Alan Whitaker from Penzance appeared on the UK TV quiz show *Mastermind*, his specialist subject being the Sex Pistols. He won a place in the semi-final of the show answering all but one of the 18 questions correctly.

2003 record producer Mickie Most died, aged 64. Member of The Most Brothers during the late 50s he had also produced hits for The Animals, Herman's Hermits, Lulu and Jeff Beck. He ran his own label, RAK, in the 70s and had hits with Hot Chocolate, Suzi Quatro and Mud.

BORN ON THIS DAY

1938 Peter Yarrow – singer and guitarist with Peter, Paul & Mary, who had a 1969 US No.1 & 1970 UK No.1 single with 'Leaving On A Jet Plane'.

1947 Junior Campbell – keyboardist, guitarist and vocalist with Marmalade, who had a 1969 UK No.1 single with 'Ob-La-Di Ob-La-Da'.

1948 John Bonham – drummer with Led Zeppelin, who had a 1969 US No.4 single with 'Whole Lotta Love'. The band's fourth album, released in 1971 featuring the rock classic 'Stairway To Heaven', has sold over 11 million copies. Bonham died on October 25th 1980 after choking on his own vomit.

1952 Karl Bartos – keyboardist and percussionist with Kraftwerk, who had a 1975 US No.25 single with 'Autobahn' and a 1982 UK No.1 single with 'Computer Love / The Model'.

1964 MC Darryl "D" McDaniels – rapper with Run-DMC, who had a 1986 UK No.8 single with Aerosmith 'Walk This Way' and a 1998 UK No.1 single with 'It's Like That'.

1965 Steve White – drummer with Style Council, who had a 1983 UK No.3 single with 'Long Hot Summer' plus 14 other UK Top 40 singles.

ON THIS DAY

1961 Chuck Berry opened Berry Park, an amusement complex near St Louis. The park had its own zoo, golf course and ferris wheel.

1965 Marianne Faithfull became a resident guest on BBC2 TV's *Gadzooks! It's The In Crowd*.

1969 The Plastic Ono Band recorded 'Give Peace A Chance' during a "bed-in" at the Hotel La Reine in Montreal, Canada.

1971 36 Grateful Dead fans were medically treated after unknowingly drinking LSD-laced cider at a gig in the US.

The Sex Pistols' new single wasn't well received by the powers-that-be.

1976 The Who gave themselves a place in *The Guinness Book Of Records* as the loudest performance of a rock band, at 120 decibels, when they played at Charlton Athletic football ground.

1977 The Patti Smith group started a nine night residency at New York's CBGB's.

1977 the BBC announced a ban on the new Sex Pistols single 'God Save The Queen' saying it was "in gross bad taste". The IBA issued a warning to all radio stations saying that playing the single would be in breach of Section 4:1:A of the Broadcasting Act. The single reached No.2 on the UK chart.

1980 Lipps Inc went to No.1 on the US singles chart with 'Funkytown', a UK No.2 hit.

1980 Paul McCartney went to No.1 on the UK album chart with *McCartney II*.

1980 'The Theme From M*A*S*H* (Suicide Is Painless)' was at No.1 on the UK singles chart ten years after it was first recorded.

1982 The Rolling Stones played at the 100 Club, Oxford St, London, to a sold-out crowd of 400 people.

1982 R.E.M. signed a five album deal with I.R.S. Records, an independent label based in California.

1989 David Bowie's Tin Machine made their live debut at the International Music Awards, New York.

1998 Geri Halliwell announced she had quit the Spice Girls, saying, "This is because of differences between us. I am sure the group will continue to be successful and I wish them all the best."

2003 UK police announced that thousands of people at this year's pop festivals would be subjected to a computerized drug test. Fans would be asked to provide swab samples from their hands, which would be inserted into a drug detection machine. It was to be a voluntary test but anyone refusing could be searched by anti-drug officers.

JUST THE TICKET

BORN ON THIS DAY

1934 Pat Boone, US singer who had a 1956 UK No.1 single with 'I'll Be Home', a 1957 US No.1 single with 'Love Letters In The Sand' plus over 30 other UK Top 40 hit singles.

1947 Ron Wood – guitarist with the Jeff Beck Group, The Faces, who had a 1972 UK No.6 & US No.17 single with 'Stay With Me', and The Rolling Stones, whom he joined in 1975 – they had a 1978 US No.1 & UK No.3 single with 'Miss You'.

1950 Charlene, singer who had a 1982 UK No.1 & US No.3 single with 'I've Never Been To Me'.

1959 Alan Wilder – keyboardist and drummer with Depeche Mode, who had a 1984 UK No.4 single with 'People Are People' plus over 25 other UK Top 40 singles.

1960 Simon Gallup – bass player with The Cure, who had a 1989 US No.2 single 'Love Song', a 1992 UK No.6 single 'Friday I'm In Love' plus over 20 other UK Top 40 singles.

1974 Alanis Morissette, singer/songwriter who had a 1996 US No.4 & UK No.11 single with 'Ironic' from her *Jagged Little Pill* album, which has sold more than 27 million copies making it the best-ever selling record by a female performer.

ON THIS DAY

1959 *Juke Box Jury* started on BBC TV with a Saturday night slot hosted by David Jacobs.

1961 Elvis Presley was at No.1 on the UK singles chart with 'Surrender', his eighth UK No.1.

1963 Lesley Gore started a two week run at No.1 on the US singles chart with the Quincy Jones produced 'It's My Party', which was a No.9 hit in the UK. The song was also a UK No.1 for Dave Stewart and Barbara Gaskin in 1981.

1964 The Rolling Stones arrived on BA flight 505 at Kennedy Airport for their debut US tour.

1968 Simon & Garfunkel went to No.1 on the US singles chart with 'Mrs Robinson'. Featured in the Dustin Hoffman and Ann Bancroft film *The Graduate*, the song was also a UK hit for the Lemonheads in 1992.

1971 the two room shack in Tupelo, Mississippi where Elvis Presley was born on January 8th 1935 was opened to the public as a tourist attraction.

1972 the first day of recording took place at Abbey Road Studios on what would become Pink Floyd's *Dark Side Of The Moon* album.

1973 former Soft Machine drummer Robert Wyatt broke his spine after attempting to leave a party by climbing down a drainpipe and then falling three storeys. It left Wyatt permanently crippled and confined to a wheelchair.

1974 UK music weekly *NME* published its 100 great albums with: No.3, The Beach Boys' *Pet Sounds*; No.2, Bob Dylan's *Blonde On Blonde* and The Beatles' *Sgt Pepper* at No.1.

1975 The Rolling Stones kicked off their biggest-ever US tour, 45 shows in 26 cities, at Louisiana State University.

1981 the first issue of *Kerrang!* magazine was published as a special bi-weekly music paper. On the front cover was AC/DC with features on Motorhead, Girlschool and Saxon.

1985 Prince And The Revolution started a three week run at No.1 on the US album chart with *Around The World In A Day*.

1991 David Ruffin of The Temptations died of a drug overdose. The group had had a 1971 US No.1 & UK No. 8 single with 'Just My Imagination' and reissued 'My Girl' to reach UK No.2 in 1992. As a solo artist Ruffin had had a 1975 US No.9 & UK No.10 single with 'Walk Away From Love'.

1991 Seal started a three week run at No.1 on the UK album charts with his self-titled debut LP.

1991 Sting appeared on the first airing of a new Soviet TV rock show, called *Rock Steady*.

1996 'Three Lions', the official song of the England Football team, by Baddiel And Skinner and The Lightning Seeds went to No.1 on the UK singles chart.

1997 Spice Girl Baby Spice arrived back in the UK in a wheelchair after breaking her ankle during a Turkish TV show.

2000 the film *Honest*, starring three of the All Saints, was pulled by cinemas after a disastrous showing at the box office. The three singers played sisters who turn to crime in the late 60s.

2003 Staind were at No.1 on the US album chart with *14 Shades Of Gray*, the US band's second No.1 and a No.16 hit in the UK.

BORN ON THIS DAY

1924 Maurice Kinn, who launched the *New Musical Express* in 1953. The music weekly instigated the first charts based on record sales. Kinn died on August 3rd 2000.

1941 Charlie Watts – drummer for The Rolling Stones, who had a 1965 UK & US No.1 single 'Satisfaction' and over 35 UK & US Top 40 singles and albums. Watts also does occasional gigs with Charlie Watts And His Big Band.

1944 Marvin Hamlisch, pianist and composer who had a 1974 US No.1 album with *The Sting* and a US No.3 single with 'The Entertainer'. He won a 1973 Grammy for *The Way We Were*.

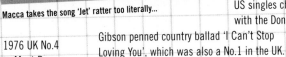

Macca takes the song 'Jet' ratter too literally...

1950 Chubby Tavares – singer with Tavares, who had a 1976 UK No.4 and US No.15 single with 'Heaven Must Be Missing An Angel'.

1959 Michael Steele – bass player and vocalist with The Bangles, who had a 1986 UK No.2 single with the Prince song 'Manic Monday' and a 1986 US No.1 single with 'Walk Like An Egyptian'.

1960 Tony Hadley – vocalist with Spandau Ballet, who had a 1983 UK No.1 and US No.4 single with 'True' plus 16 other UK Top 40 hits.

1976 Tim Rice-Oxley – piano player with Keane, who had a 2004 UK No.1 album with *Hopes And Fears*.

1980 Fabrizio Moreti – drummer with The Strokes, who had a 2001 UK No. 14 single with 'Last Nite'.

ON THIS DAY

1957 Johnnie Ray was at No.1 on the UK singles chart with 'Yes Tonight, Josephine', the US singer's third and final UK No.1.

1962 Owen Gray's 'Twist Baby' became the first single released on UK-based Island Records. The label became home to such acts as Free, Traffic, Jethro Tull, Nick Drake, Bob Marley and U2.

1962 Ray Charles started a five week run at No.1 on the US singles chart with the Don Gibson penned country ballad 'I Can't Stop Loving You', which was also a No.1 in the UK.

1964 The Rolling Stones made their US TV debut on *The Les Crane Show*.

1966 Frank Sinatra was at No.1 on the UK singles chart with 'Strangers In The Night', the singer's second UK No.1.

1967 David Bowie released his self-titled debut album, which didn't make the charts.

1973 The Electric Light Orchestra began their first US tour, a 40 date trek, in San Diego, California.

1976 Wings set a new world record when they performed in front of 67,100 fans in Seattle, the largest attendance for an indoor crowd.

1981 Prince made his live British debut at The Lyceum Ballroom, London, (he did not play in the UK again for five years).

1984 Wham! had their first UK No.1 with 'Wake Me Up Before You Go Go', inspired by a note Andrew Ridgeley left lying in his bedroom.

1989 Rolling Stone Bill Wyman secretly married 19-year-old Mandy Smith. Wyman's 28-year-old son was best man and all the other Stones attended. (The marriage lasted 17 months.)

1995 Stone Roses' John Squire smashed his collarbone in a cycling accident, causing the band to pull out of major gigs.

2002 it was reported that Paul McCartney had thrown his fiancée Heather Mills' engagement ring out of a hotel window during a row. Guards at Miami's Turnberry Isle Resort combed the grounds using metal detectors and later found the £15,000 ($25,500) ring.

2003 a painting of Kylie Minogue wearing gold hotpants caused tempers to fray among drivers in Brighton. Artist Simon Etheridge put up the almost life-size picture in his own Art Asylum gallery as part of a festival and since then motorists had caused regular traffic hold-ups as they stopped to take a second look.

MACCA THROWS FIANCEE'S RING OUT OF HOTEL WINDOW

...And responds in a fit of pique!

3rd June

BORN ON THIS DAY

1943 Michael Clarke – drummer with The Flying Burrito Brothers and The Byrds, who had a 1965 US & UK No.1 single with 'Mr. Tambourine Man'. Clarke died of liver failure on December 19th 1993.

1946 Ian Hunter – vocalist and guitarist with Mott The Hoople, who had a 1972 UK No.3 single with 'All The Young Dudes'. As a solo artist he had a 1975 UK No.14 single with 'Once Bitten Twice Shy' and also wrote the book *Diary Of A Rock 'n' Roll Star*.

1946 John Paul Jones – bass player, keyboardist and producer for Led Zeppelin, who had a 1969 US No.4 single with 'Whole Lotta Love'. The band's fourth album, which was released in 1971 and featured the rock classic 'Stairway To Heaven', has sold over 11 million copies. Jones has also worked with R.E.M.

1947 Mickey Finn – percussionist with T. Rex, who had a 1971 UK No.1 single with 'Hot Love' plus over 20 other UK Top 40 singles. Finn died on January 11th 2002.

1950 Suzi Quatro – vocalist and bass player who had a 1973 UK No.1 single with 'Can The Can', ten other UK Top 40 singles and a 1979 US No.4 single with Chris Norman, 'Stumblin' In'.

1951 Deniece Williams, US singer who had a 1978 US No.1 & UK No.3 single with Johnny Mathis 'Too Much Too Little Too Late' and a 1984 US No.1 & UK No.2 single with 'Let's Hear It For The Boy'. She also worked as a backing singer with Stevie Wonder's group Wonderlove.

1962 David Cole – member, writer and producer with C&C Music Factory, who had a 1991 UK No.4 single with 'Things That Make You Go Hmmm...' and a 1991 US No.1 single with 'Gonna Make You Sweat'. He also produced Mariah Carey, Whitney Houston and Aretha Franklin. Cole died January 24th 1995.

1974 Kelly Jones – vocalist and guitarist with Stereophonics, who had a 2001 UK No.1 album with *Just Enough Education To Perform*.

ON THIS DAY

1964 Ringo Starr collapsed during a photo session suffering from acute tonsillitis just days before a Beatles world tour was about to start. Session drummer Jimmy Nichol replaced Ringo and became a Beatle for 11 days.

1967 Aretha Franklin went to No.1 on the US singles chart with her version of the Otis Redding hit 'Respect'. It made No.10 on the UK chart. Aretha scored her first UK No.1 20 years later with 'Knew You Were Waiting' with George Michael.

Famous for 11 days: Jimmie Nichol.

Aretha accepts that 'The Godmother Of Soul' does not pack the same punch as James Brown's title.

1970 The Kinks' Ray Davies was forced to make a 9,656km (6,000 mile) round trip from New York to London to record one word in a song. Davies had to change the word 'Coca-Cola' to 'Cherry Cola' on the band's forthcoming single 'Lola' due to an advertising ban.

1972 Jethro Tull started a two week run at No.1 on the US album chart with *Thick As A Brick*.

2001 Shaggy started a four week run at No.1 on the UK singles chart with 'Angel'. His album *Hot Shot* also went to No.1 on the UK album chart on this day.

2001 Staind started a three week run at No.1 on the US album chart with *Break The Cycle*.

2002 appearing at The Queen's Jubilee concert at Buckingham Palace were Paul McCartney, Sting, Elton John, Cliff Richard, Phil Collins, Brian May, Ozzy Osbourne, The Corrs, Brian Wilson, Annie Lennox, Tom Jones, Eric Clapton, Will Young, Atomic Kitten and S Club 7.

2003 a grandfather who set up his own pirate radio station in Wakefield, Yorkshire was under investigation by local broadcasting authorities. The man, known as Ricky Rock, erected a 9.75m (32ft) transmitter in his garden and had been playing hits by The Beach Boys, The Beatles and Elvis Presley. Ricky said he set the station up because "talentless boy bands and dance music" featured on local stations did not cater to the tastes of his generation.

BORN ON THIS DAY

1940 Cliff Bennett – singer with Cliff Bennett And The Rebel Rousers, who had a 1966 UK No.6 single with 'Got To Get You Into My Life'.

1944 Roger Ball – saxophonist and keyboardist with Average White Band, who had a 1975 US No.1 and UK No.6 single with 'Pick Up The Pieces'.

1945 Gordon Waller – guitarist and singer and one half of duo Peter & Gordon, who had a 1964 UK & US No.1 single with 'A World Without Love'.

1952 Jimmy McCulloch – guitarist with Thunderclap Newman, who had a 1969 UK No.1 single with 'Something In The Air'. He also worked with Wings, John Entwistle, Stone The Crows and The Bluesbreakers. McCulloch died on September 27th 1979.

ON THIS DAY

1942 Capitol Records was launched by Glenn Wallichs, the man who invented the art of record promotion by sending copies of new releases to disc jockeys.

1967 appearing live at The Saville Theatre London were Procol Harum, the Jimi Hendrix Experience and Denny Laine.

1969 Tommy Roe was at No.1 on the UK singles chart with 'Dizzy'. The song was also a UK No.1 for Vic Reeves and Wonder Stuff in 1991.

1975 The Rolling Stones became the first rock band to receive royalties for sales of their records in Russia.

1976 live recordings were made of performances from Blondie, Mink DeVille, Talking Heads, Laughing Dogs and Tuff Darts. These were released as *Live At CBGB'S New York*.

1983 The Police started a four week run at No.1 in the UK with 'Every Breath You Take', the group's fifth and final No.1 single.

1985 Elton John began a legal battle with Dick James Music, seeking the rights to early songs and recordings plus damages estimated at more than £30 million ($51 million). The singer lost a six-month court battle to recover the copyright to 169 songs. However, the court ordered Dick James to cough up millions in unpaid royalties.

1986 "A Conspiracy Of Hope" two week US tour started, featuring U2, Sting, Lou Reed, Bryan Adams and Peter Gabriel.

1992 Iron Maiden played a gig at the Oval pub, Norwich, England before 400 fans as The Nodding Donkeys. It was a thank you to the pub's landlord, Chris Hiles.

1992 Smokey Robinson's half sister, Rose Ella Jones' filed a suit against Smokey claiming she

had been cheated out of royalty payments from songs written during the 80s.

1993 Kurt Cobain was arrested after a dispute at his house in Seattle. The disagreement allegedly concerned Cobain's collection of firearms.

1994 Oasis was on the front cover of this week's UK music weekly *NME*, the band's first-ever front cover.

1994 Wet Wet Wet started a 15 week run at No.1 on the UK singles chart with 'Love Is All Around'. Written by Reg Presley of The Troggs the song was a former Top 10 for his band in 1967.

2000 a teenage Sisqo fan was shot in the leg at a concert by the R&B star in Phoenix, Arizona when violence erupted after punters began objecting to parking fees of $30 (£17.60) at the venue.

2000 Eminem started an eight week run at No.1 on the US album chart with his debut release *The Marshall Mathers LP*.

2004 Nathan Moore, former singer with Brother Beyond and Worlds Apart, appeared at Highbury Corner magistrate's court and pleaded guilty to a charge of kerb crawling in central London. Moore had been arrested in the Kings Cross area after he approached a woman he thought was a prostitute and requested a sexual favour. He then rode away on his moped before being arrested.

BORN ON THIS DAY

1941 Floyd Butler – vocalist with The Friends Of Distinction, who had a 1969 US No.3 single with 'Grazing In The Grass'. Died on April 29th 1990.

1946 Freddie Stone – guitarist with Sly And The Family Stone, who had a 1971 US No.1 & 1972 UK No.15 single with 'Family Affair'.

1947 Tom Evans – guitarist, bass player and vocalist with Badfinger, who had a 1970 UK No.4 and US No.7 single with 'Come And Get It'. Evans committed suicide on November 23rd 1983.

1954 Nicko McBrain – drummer with Iron Maiden, who had a 1991 UK No.1 single with 'Bring Your Daughter To The Slaughter'.

1956 Richard Butler – vocalist with Psychedelic Furs, who had a 1986 UK No.18 single with 'Pretty In Pink'.

1971 Mark Wahlberg – singer with New Kids On The Block. As a solo artist he had a 1991 US No.1 single with 'Good Vibrations'.

ON THIS DAY

1956 Elvis Presley appeared on ABC-TV's *Milton Berle Show*, and while singing 'Hound Dog' performed his suggestive "gyrating" movements for the first time. The media went mad!

1961 Roy Orbison went to No.1 on the US chart with 'Running Scared', also a No.9 hit in the UK.

1964 The Rolling Stones played their first-ever live date in the US when they appeared at the Swing Auditorium, San Bernardino, California.

1965 the soundtrack album to *The Sound of Music* started a ten week run at No.1 on the UK chart. It returned to the top of the charts on no less than 11 other occasions, spending over 380 weeks on the chart.

1966 at the Marquee Club, London was "The Bowie Showboat", a lunchtime performance from David Bowie, "three hours of music and mime", plus a Top Ten disco. Admission was 3 shillings, ($0.42c).

1971 Grand Funk Railroad smashed the record held by The Beatles when they sold out Shea Stadium in 72 hours.

1971 Paul McCartney's second solo album *Ram* started a two week run at No.1 on the UK chart. It featured the US No.1 single 'Uncle Albert/Admiral Halsey'.

1974 Sly Stone married Kathy Silva on stage during a gig at Madison Square Gardens. (They separated four months later.)

1976 appearing at Celtic Football Club were The Who, The Sensational Alex Harvey Band, Little Feat, Outlaws and Streetwalkers. Tickets cost £4 ($7).

1977 Alice Cooper's boa constrictor, a co-star of his live act, suffered a fatal bite from a rat it was being fed for breakfast. Cooper held auditions for a replacement and a snake named "Angel" got the gig.

1979 blues legend Muddy Waters (aged 64), married Marva Jean Brooks on her 25th birthday.

Lock up your daughters, it's Nicko McBrain.

Metropolis Music Presents

Pixies

BRIXTON ACADEMY
Saturday 5th June 2004
Doors 7:00pm
Tickets £25.00 Advance
(Subject To Booking Fee)

**STALLS
STANDING**

0999

1988 The Pet Shop Boys played their debut live show when they appeared at London's Piccadilly Theatre as part of an Anti Section 28 Benefit concert.

1990 Bobby Brown played the first of eight sold-out nights at London's Wembley Arena.

1993 Mariah Carey married the President of Sony Music, Tommy Mottola, in Manhattan. Guests included Billy Joel, Bruce Springsteen, Barbra Streisand and Ozzy Osbourne. (The couple separated in 1997.)

1997 ex-Small Faces, The Faces and leader of Slim Chance Ronnie Lane died, aged 51, after a 20 year battle with multiple sclerosis.

1997 Noel Gallagher married Meg Matthews at the Little Church Of The West in Las Vegas, (where Elvis married Priscilla). The Oasis guitarist divorced Matthews in 2001.

2004 US guitarist Robert Quine was found dead of an apparent heroin overdose. He had worked with Richard Hell And The Voidoids, who had a 1977 album with *Blank Generation*, featuring the track 'Love Comes In Spurts' as well as Lou Reed, Brian Eno, Lloyd Cole and They Might Be Giants.

BORN ON THIS DAY

1936 Levi Stubbs – vocalist with The Four Tops, who had a 1965 US No.1 single with 'I Can't Help Myself' and a 1967 UK No.6 single with 'Standing In The Shadows of Love'.

1939 Gary U.S. Bonds, singer who had a 1961 US No.1 single with 'Quarter To Three' and a 1981 UK No.43 single with 'This Little Girl'.

1944 Clarence White – guitarist with The Byrds, who had a 1965 UK & US No.1 single with 'Mr. Tambourine Man'. He died on July 14th 1973.

1944 Peter Albin – bass player with the Janis Joplin band Big Brother And The Holding Company, who had a 1971 US No.1 single with 'Me And Bobby McGee' and a 1971 US No.1 album with *Pearl*.

1960 Steve Vai – guitarist with Frank Zappa, David Lee Roth and Whitesnake, who had a 1987 US No.1 & UK No.9 single with 'Here I Go Again'. As a solo artist he has released eight albums.

1970 James Shaffer – guitarist with Korn, who had a 1998 UK No.23 single with 'Got The Life' and a 1998 US No.1 album with *Follow The Leader*.

ON THIS DAY

1962 the first Beatles recording session took place at Abbey Road Studios, recording four tracks, one of which was 'Love Me Do'. The four musicians received payments for the session of £7.10 ($12.07) each.

1966 Roy Orbison's first wife, Claudette, was killed when a truck pulled out of a side road and collided with the motorbike that she and her

Genius Stubbs on gardening leave.

husband were riding on. She was 25.

1970 appearing at this year's Buxton Festival in Derbyshire, England were Colosseum, Taste, Atomic Rooster, Matthews Southern Comfort, Brinsley Schwartz, the Strawbs and Daddy Longlegs.

1971 John & Yoko jammed live on stage with Frank Zappa at The Filmore East in New York.

1979 Def Leppard played at Crookes Workingman's Club in Sheffield. The gig was reviewed in UK music paper *Sounds*, which led to a recording contract with Phonogram Records.

1982 at the start of the US "Peace Week" Tom Petty, Crosby, Stills & Nash, Bob Dylan, Stevie Wonder, Stevie Nicks and Jackson Browne all appeared at The Rose Bowl, Pasadena, California to a crowd of 85,000 fans.

1986 A&R man Dick Rowe died of diabetes. Rowe became famous for not signing The Beatles to Decca records and made the classic quote "Nobody cares about guitar groups anymore". He did, however, sign The Rolling Stones to Decca.

1987 Kim Wilde went to No.1 on the US singles chart with 'You Keep Me Hanging On', which was a No.2 hit in the UK. The song had been a 1966 hit for The Supremes.

The late Dave Rowberry.

1987 Whitney Houston had her second UK No.1 single with 'I Wanna Dance with Somebody (Who Loves Me)'.

1993 a re-formed Velvet Underground played at Wembley Arena, London.

1996 inventor William Palmer died. He had invented the magnetic tape recorder. Before this music had been cut direct to record.

1998 Boyzone scored their third UK No.1 album with *Where We Belong*. It was also the first time in chart history that both the No.1 positions were by Irish acts, with B*Witched at the top of the singles chart.

1999 Australian filmmaker Baz Luhrmann went to No.1 on the UK singles chart with 'Everybody's Free To Wear Sunscreen'.

1999 plans were announced for Elvis Presley to tour the UK almost 23 years after his death with a virtual version of the "King" performing with a live orchestra and members of his band.

2002 Dee Dee Ramone, guitarist with The Ramones, died in Los Angeles of a drug overdose, aged 49.

2003 keyboard player with The Animals Dave Rowberry died, aged 62. The band had had a 1964 UK & US No.1 single with 'House Of The Rising Sun'.

2003 a High Court judge in London ruled that rap lyrics should be treated as a foreign language after admitting that he was unsure of the meaning of "shizzle my nizzle" and "mish mish man". 'The court battle was over a copyright issue between the Ant'ill Mob and the Heartless Crew, who had used the lyrics on a remix.

BORN ON THIS DAY

1917 Dean Martin, actor and singer, who had a 1956 UK & US No.1 single with 'Memories Are Made Of This' plus over 15 other UK Top 40 singles. He died December 25th 1995.

1940 Tom Jones, singer who had a 1965 UK No.1 and US No.10 single with 'It's Not Unusual' plus over 20 other UK and US Top 40 hit singles.

1957 Paddy Mcaloon – guitarist and vocalist with Prefab Sprout, who had a 1988 UK No.7 single with 'The King Of Rock 'N' Roll'.

1958 Prince Rogers Nelson (T.A.F.K.A.P), singer and guitarist who had a 1984 US No.1 & UK No.4 single with 'When Doves Cry', a 1994 UK No.1 single with 'The Most Beautiful Girl In The World' plus over 40 other Top 40 singles.

1967 Dave Navarro – guitarist with Red Hot Chili Peppers, who had a 1992 UK No.26 single with 'Under The Bridge'.

1985 Charlie Simpson – guitarist and vocalist with Busted, who had a 2003 UK No.1 single with 'You Said No' and a 2002 UK No.2 album with *Busted*.

ON THIS DAY

1963 The Rolling Stones made their UK TV debut when they appeared on *Thank Your Lucky Stars*.

1969 supergroup Blind Faith, featuring Eric Clapton, Ginger Baker and Steve Winwood, made their live debut at a free concert in London's Hyde Park.

1975 Elton John's album *Captain Fantastic And The Brown Dirt Cowboys* went to No.1 on the US album chart, the first album ever to enter the US chart at No.1.

1975 John Denver went to No.1 on the US singles chart with 'Thank God I'm A Country Boy', the singer's third US No.1.

1977 Led Zeppelin played the first of six sold out nights at Madison Square Garden, New York.

1979 Blondie performed 'Sunday Girl' on UK TV show *Top Of The Pops*.

1980 appearing at The Summer Of 80, Crystal Palace were Bob Marley And The Wailers, AWB, Joe Jackson and The Q-Tips.

1983 Shawn Michelle Stevens became wife number five for Jerry Lee Lewis.

1985 The Smiths played the first date of a US tour at Chicago's Aragon Ballroom.

1986 Madonna went to No.1 on the US singles chart with 'Live To Tell', her third US No.1 single and a No.2 hit in the UK.

1990 The Black Crowes played their debut UK gig at the Marquee, London.

1995 Radiohead's Johnny Greenwood was admitted to hospital after his ear was leaking blood. The problem was diagnosed as his arm movement from continuous guitar playing.

1997 Noel Gallagher played a five song set at the Tibet Freedom Concert, Downing Stadium, New York. U2, Patti Smith and Radiohead also appeared at the concert.

1998 songwriter Wally Gold died aged 70. He wrote 'It's My Party', a hit for Lesley Gore, and 'It's Now or Never', a hit for Elvis Presley. He had been a member of the late 50s group The Four Esquires, and also produced Kansas and Gene Pitney.

1999 Backstreet Boys were at No.1 on the US album chart with *Millennium*, the US boyband's first No.1 album.

2002 Liam Howlett of The Prodigy married former All Saints singer Natalie Appleton at a ceremony in Les Adrets, France. Guests included Liam and Noel Gallagher and former Eurythmic Dave Stewart.

2002 Virgin Records announced they had dropped Victoria Beckham after her debut solo album, which cost over £3 million ($5.1 million) to make, had sold only 50,000 copies.

BORN ON THIS DAY

1940 Nancy Sinatra, singer and actress who had a 1966 UK & US No.1 single 'These Boots Are Made For Walking'. With her father Frank she scored the 1967 UK No.1 single 'Somethin' Stupid', making them the only father and daughter to have a No.1 single as a team.

1944 Boz Scaggs – singer and member of The Marksmen with Steve Miller and The Wigs. As a solo artist he had a 1976 US No.3 single with 'Lowdown' and a 1977 US No.11 and UK No.13 single with 'Lido Shuffle'.

1960 Mick Hucknall, singer/songwriter with Simply Red, who had a 1986 US No.1 & UK No.2 single with 'Holding Back The Years', a 1995 UK No.1 single with 'Fairground', a 1991 UK No.8 single with 'Stars' and a worldwide No.1 1991 album with *Stars*.

1962 Nick Rhodes – keyboardist with Duran Duran, who had a 1983 UK No.1 single with 'Is There Something I Should Know?' plus 25 other UK Top 40 singles and a 1984 US No.1 single with 'The Reflex', then Arcadia, who had a 1985 UK No.7 single with 'Election Day'.

1965 Rob Pilatus – vocalist with Milli Vanilli, who had a 1989 US No.1 & UK No.2 single with 'Girl I'm Gonna Miss You'. He died of a drug and alcohol overdose on April 2nd 1998.

ON THIS DAY

1954 US record labels started to supply radio stations with 45rpm discs for the first time, replacing the 78rpm records.

1967 Procol Harum were at No.1 on the UK singles chart with 'A Whiter Shade Of Pale', the group's only UK No.1.

1967 The Beatles' *Sgt Peppers Lonely Hearts Club Band* went to No.1 in the UK. Costing £25,000 ($42,500) to produce the album was recorded over 700 hours of studio time. It was also the first album to print the lyrics on the sleeve. The album spent 27 weeks at No.1 on the UK chart.

1969 founder member of The Rolling Stones Brian Jones announced that he was leaving the group, saying that he no longer saw "eye to eye" with the rest of the band.

1974 Bill Wyman became the first Rolling Stone to release a solo album with *Monkey Grip*. It made No.39 in the UK and No.99 in the US.

1974 Dolly Parton was at No.1 on the US country chart with 'I Will Always Love You'. Written by Parton it was later a worldwide hit for Whitney Houston in 1992.

1974 Paul McCartney and Wings went to No.1 on the US singles chart with 'Band On The Run', his third solo US No.1 and a No.3 hit in the UK.

1991 Bruce Springsteen married Patti Scialfa at their Beverley Hills home.

2001 appearing at the Milton Keynes Bowl, England were AC/DC, The Offspring, Queens Of The Stone Age and Megadeth. Tickets cost £28.50 ($48.45).

2002 Jennifer Lopez separated from her second husband, dancer Cris Judd, after nine months of marriage.

2003 Led Zeppelin were at No.1 on the US album chart with *How The West Was Won*, the band's seventh US No.1.

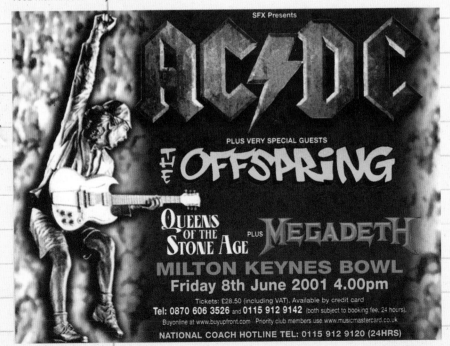

SFX Presents

AC/DC

PLUS VERY SPECIAL GUESTS

THE OFFSPRING

QUEENS OF THE STONE AGE PLUS **MEGADETH**

MILTON KEYNES BOWL

Friday 8th June 2001 4.00pm

Tickets: £28.50 (including VAT). Available by credit card
Tel: 0870 606 3526 and 0115 912 9142 (both subject to booking fee, 24 hours).
Buyonline at www.buyupfront.com Priority club members use www.musicmastercard.co.uk

NATIONAL COACH HOTLINE TEL: 0115 912 9120 (24HRS)

APOLLO THEATRE, GLASGOW

HARVEY GOLDSMITH ENTERTAINMENTS
presents

THE WHO

Friday, 8th June, 1979
at 7.30 p.m.

STALLS

No. 31 **SS**

No Support
TICKET £5.00
TO BE RETAINED
TICKETS CANNOT BE EXCHANGED

BORN ON THIS DAY

1891 Cole Porter, US singer and composer. He wrote countless classic songs, including 'Night And Day', 'I Get A Kick Out Of You' and 'Ev'ry Time We Say Goodbye'. Died October 15th 1964.

1915 guitarist Les Paul, inventor of the Gibson Les Paul guitar who also had a 1953 UK No.7 single with 'Vaya Con Dios' and the US No.7 single 'Hummingbird' with May Ford featuring his multi-layered recording techniques. He also pioneered "close miking" and echo delay recording. He broke his right arm in a car accident and had it set at an angle so he could still play guitar.

1929 Johnny Ace, R&B singer, Billboard's "most played artist of 1955". He died playing Russian roulette backstage at a gig on December 25th 1954.

1934 Jackie Wilson, US soul singer who scored 24 US Top 40 hits during the late 50s and 60s. He also had a 1986 UK No.1 single with the reissued 'Reet Petite'. Van Morrison wrote 'Jackie Wilson Said' about him, which was covered by Dexy's Midnight Runners. Wilson suffered a heart attack on stage at a New Jersey Club in 1975 and was in a coma until he died on January 21st 1984.

1941 Jon Lord – keyboardist for Deep Purple, who had a 1970 UK No.2 single with 'Black Night' and a 1973 US No.4 single with 'Smoke On The Water'.

1947 Mitch Mitchell – drummer with the Jimi Hendrix Experience, who had a 1967 UK No.3 single with 'Purple Haze' and a 1970 UK No.1 single with 'Voodoo Chile'. Mitchell had been in the ITV's *Ready Steady Go!* house band.

1949 George Bunnell – bass player with Strawberry Alarm Clock *(top)*, who had a 1967 US No.1 single with 'Incense And Peppermints'.

ON THIS DAY

1972 Columbia Records boss John Hammond signed New Jersey singer/songwriter Bruce Springsteen.

1978 Siouxsie And The Banshees signed to Polydor Records.

1984 Cyndi Lauper started a two week run at No.1 on the US singles chart with 'Time After Time', which was a No.3 hit in the UK.

1990 MC Hammer's album *Please Hammer Don't Hurt 'Em* started a record-breaking 21 week stay at the top of the US album charts, making it the longest uninterrupted stay at the top since the album charts started.

1990 the mansion owned by the group Five Star was repossessed by bailiffs after non-payment of the mortgage. The group had achieved 15 Top 20 hits over five years.

1990 Wilson Phillips went to No.1 on the US singles chart with 'Hold On'. 25 years earlier to the day Wendy and Carnies' father Beach Boy Brian had been at No.1 with 'Help Me Rhonda'.

1990 Englandneworder started a two week run at No.1 on the UK singles chart with 'World In Motion'.

1994 after an argument TLC singer Left Eye set fire to her boyfriend's Atlanta mansion, worth $2 million (£1.176 million), burning it to the ground. She was charged with arson and fined $10,000 (£5,882) with five years probation.

2000 Sinead O'Connor announced that she was a lesbian. The mother of two told the American magazine *Curve* that she had been in the closet for years saying "I am a lesbian. I haven't been very open about that, I've gone out with blokes because I haven't necessarily been terribly comfortable about being a lesbian."

strawberry alarm clock
THE WORLD IN A SEA SHELL

2003 Former Boyzone frontman Ronan Keating raised more than £100,000 ($170,000) for cancer during a 23 day walk from the Giant's Causeway in County Antrim to Kinsale in County Cork. He visited 610 towns along the way, walking an average of 32km (20 miles) each day.

> "It was a bit rough...but the Bronx is everything I am."
> **Jennifer Lopez**

BORN ON THIS DAY

1910 Chester Burnett, (a.k.a. "Howlin Wolf"), blues singer and guitarist, who had a 1956 hit with 'Smoke Stack Lightning'. He died from cancer on January 10th 1976.

1922 Judy Garland, singer and actress. She played Dorothy in the 1939 film *Wizard Of Oz* and sang 'Over The Rainbow' in the film. The song was voted Song of the century in a 2001 poll published in America. She had a 1961 US No.1 comeback album with *Judy At Carnegie Hall*. She died June 22nd 1969 of a barbiturate overdose.

ASGARD presents

THE JAYHAWKS

Plus Guests

The Shepherds Bush Empire

Tuesday 10th June 1997

Doors: 7:00pm

Tickets: £11.00 in advance *1997*

DOWNSTAIRS STANDING   0760

1941 Shirley Owens – singer with The Shirelles, who had a 1961 US No.1 & UK No.4 single with 'Will You Love Me Tomorrow'.

1961 Kim Deal – guitarist and vocalist with the Pixies, who had a 1990 UK No.28 single 'Velouria', and The Breeders, who had a 1993 UK No.40 with 'Cannonball' EP.

1964 Jimmy Chamberlin – drummer with Smashing Pumpkins, who had a 1995 US No.1 album with *Mellon Collie And The Infinite Sadness* and a 1996 UK No.7 single with 'Tonight Tonight'.

1973 Faith Evans, US female singer who had a 1997 US & UK No.1 single with Puff Daddy 'I'll Be Missing You' and a 2000 UK No.26 single with Whitney Houston 'Heartbreak Hotel'.

ON THIS DAY

1966 Steve Marriott of The Small Faces collapsed while performing on UK TV show *Ready Steady Go!* The group were forced to cancel the following week's gigs.

1972 Elvis Presley played his first-ever concert in New York. The four shows were recorded and became the album *Elvis* as recorded at Madison Square Garden.

1972 Sammy Davis Jr started a three week run at No.1 on the US singles chart with 'Candy Man', his only US No.1. The song was taken from the film *Willy Wonka And The Chocolate Factory*.

1972 The Rolling Stones' double album *Exile On Main Street* went to No.1 on the UK chart.

1974 The Who began a four night sold-out run at Madison Square Garden.

1977 Joe Strummer and Nicky Headon from The Clash were each fined £5 ($8.50) by a London court for spray-painting "The Clash" on a wall.

1978 John Travolta and Olivia Newton John went to No.1 on the US singles chart with 'You're The One That I Want', which was also No.1 in the UK.

1982 Addi Harris from The Shirelles died of a heart attack after a show in Atlanta. The group had had a 1961 US No.1 & UK No.4 single with 'Will You Love Me Tomorrow'.

1983 Chris Sievey of UK group The Freshies released the first computer game single. When played on a Sinclair ZX 81 computer via a record deck the lyrics of the song came onto the screen.

1986 Jerry Garcia of Grateful Dead went into a five day diabetic coma, resulting in the band withdrawing from their current tour.

1988 the first of two nights at Earl's Court, London with George Michael. Tickets cost £14.50 ($25) and £12.50 ($21.25)

1989 Bette Midler went to No.1 on the US singles chart with 'Wind Beneath My Wings', which was taken from the film *Beaches*. The song was a No.5 hit in the UK.

1989 Jason Donovan was at No.1 on the UK singles chart with his version of 'Sealed With A Kiss', a hit for Brian Hyland in 1962.

1989 Madonna's 'Express Yourself' became her 18th UK Top 5 hit, a new record for a female artist.

1991 Temptation Eddie Kendricks was arrested while attending the funeral of David Ruffin in Detroit on charges of owing $26,000 ($15,294) in child support.

1997 INXS kicked off a seven date UK tour at Aberdeen Exhibition Centre. Tickets cost £17.50 ($30).

2003 Kym Mathers, the ex-wife of rapper Eminem, was arrested and released pending further investigation in St. Clair Shores, Michigan for driving with a revoked licence. Two Ziploc bags containing a "white powdery substance" were found in the glove box of the white Cadillac.

2004 Ray Charles died, aged 73. Glaucoma had rendered Charles blind at the age of six. He had had the 1962 UK & US No.1 single 'I Can't Stop Loving You' plus over 30 US Top 40 singles.

BORN ON THIS DAY

1940 Joseph DiNicola – vocalist with Joey And The Starlighters, who had a 1962 US No.1 single with 'Peppermint Twist, Part 1'. Jimi Hendrix was a member of the band during 1964.

1947 Glenn Leonard – vocalist with The Temptations, who had a 1971 UK No.8 single with 'Just My Imagination' and the reissued 'My Girl' was a UK No.2 in 1992.

1949 Frank Beard – drummer with ZZ Top, who had a 1984 US No.8 & 1985 UK No.16 single with 'Legs'.

1951 Lynsey De Paul, singer/songwriter, who had a 1972 UK No.5 single with 'Sugar Me'. She became the first woman to win an Ivor Novello Songwriting Award.

ON THIS DAY

1949 Hank Williams made his debut at the "Grand Ole Opry" in Nashville and received an unprecedented total of six encores.

1966 The Rolling Stones started a two week run at No.1 on the US singles chart with 'Paint It Black', the group's third US No.1 single. It was also a No.1 in the UK.

1967 in music weekly *Melody Maker*'s ads pages was the following ad: "Freaky lead guitarist, bass and drummer wanted for Marc Bolan's new group. Also any other astral flyers like with car's amplification and that which never grows in window boxes, phone Wimbledon 0697." Tyrannosaurus Rex was born...

1969 The Beatles were at No.1 on the UK singles chart with 'The Ballad Of John And Yoko', the group's 17th UK No.1.

1977 Joe Strummer and Topper Headon were detained overnight in prison in Newcastle upon Tyne having failed to appear at Morpeth Magistrates on May 21st to answer a charge relating to the theft of a Holiday Inn pillowcase. They were both fined £100 ($170).

1977 as Britain celebrated the Queen's Silver Jubilee The Sex Pistols reached No.2 on the singles chart with 'God Save The Queen'.

1977 KC & The Sunshine Band became only the second group after The Jackson Five to achieve four US No.1s when 'I'm Your Boogie Man' went to the top of the charts.

1988 Nelson Mandela's 70th birthday tribute took place at Wembley Stadium, London featuring Whitney Houston, Phil Collins, Dire Straits, Stevie Wonder, Tracy Chapman, George Michael, Eric Clapton, UB40, The Eurythmics and Simple Minds. It was broadcast live on BBC 2 to 40 different countries with an estimated audience of 1 billion.

1997 Mick Hucknall *(left)* received a Master of Science Degree at UMIST, Manchester for his fundraising work following an IRA bombing the previous year.

2002 Sir Paul McCartney married Heather Mills at St Salvator Church, Ireland *(above)*. Guests included Ringo Starr, Dave Gilmour, Jools Holland and Chrissie Hynde. Heather walked down the aisle clutching a bouquet of 11 "McCartney" roses.

2003 Adam Ant was arrested after going berserk and stripping off in a London cafe. The former 80s star had thrown stones at neighbours' homes, smashing windows, before going to the nearby cafe.

BIG BASH: Massive marquees are erected at Castle Leslie – but Macca's local Irish family members are not invited

WITH THIS RINGO I THEE WED
Starr turn for Macca

EX-BEATLE Ringo Starr will read a moving poem for Paul McCartney and Heather Mills at their wedding on Tuesday.

Drummer Ringo is expected to fly in from the States today to put the finishing touches to his lines which will feature some words from Beatles classic All You Need is Love.

The song, written by McCartney with John Lennon, is believed to be Macca's favourite Beatles number. And Ringo's fresh version is guaranteed to have the guests in tears.

Simply honoured

UMIST

BORN ON THIS DAY

1941 Chick Corea, jazz musician who worked with Miles Davis, Stanley Clarke and Bobby McFerrin.

1941 Roy Harper *(right with Jimmy Page)*, UK folk singer/songwriter, who had a 1977 UK No.25 album with *Bullinamingvase*. Led Zeppelin wrote the tribute 'Hat's Off To Roy Harper', which featured on the band's third album.

1943 Reg Presley – vocalist with The Troggs, who had a 1966 US No.1 & UK No.2 single with 'Wild Thing'. Presley wrote 'Love Is All Around', which had 15 weeks at UK No.1 for Wet Wet Wet.

1944 Harold Cowart – bass player for John Fred & His Playboy Band, who had a 1968 US No.1 & UK No.3 single with 'Judy In Disguise'.

1951 Brad Delp – guitarist and vocalist with Boston, who had a 1977 UK No.22 single with 'More Than A Feeling' and a 1986 US No.1 single with 'Amanda'.

1951 Bun E. Carlos – drummer with Cheap Trick, who had a 1979 UK No.29 & US No.17 single with 'I Want You To Want Me' and a 1988 US No.1 single with 'The Flame'.

1952 Pete Fardon – bass player with The Pretenders, who had a 1980 UK No.1 single with 'Brass In Pocket'. He died of a drug overdose on April 14th 1983.

1959 John Linnell – accordian player and keyboardist for They Might Be Giants, who had a 1990 UK No.6 single with 'Birdhouse In Your Soul'.

ON THIS DAY

1965 The Beatles were included in the Queen's Birthday Honours List to each receive the MBE. Protests poured into Buckingham Palace. MP Hector Dupuis said, "British Royalty has put me on the same level as a bunch of vulgar numbskulls."

1965 The Supremes scored their fifth consecutive US No.1 single when 'Back In My Arms Again' went to the top of the charts.

1966 the Dave Clark Five made a record twelfth appearance on US TV's *Ed Sullivan Show*.

1976 on this week's UK singles chart were: No.5, J.J. Barrie, 'No Charge'; No.4, Our Kid, 'You Just Might See Me Cry'; No.3, Wings, 'Silly Love Songs'; No.2, The Real Thing, 'You To Me Are Everything' and No.1 The Wurzels' 'Combine Harvester'.

1978 playing live around the UK were: Dire Straits at Erics, Liverpool, The Thompson Twins at The Limit in Sheffield and The Jam at King George's Hall, Blackburn.

1982 Bruce Springsteen, James Taylor, Jackson Browne, Linda Ronstadt and Gary "US" Bonds all appeared at a rally for nuclear disarmament in Central Park, New York to over 450,000 fans.

1989 The Elvis Presley Autoland Museum opened at Graceland. The museum contained over 20 cars which were owned by Presley.

1993 UB40 had their third UK No.1 single with '(I Can't Help), Falling In Love With You'.

1999 it was reported that Oasis had paid Gary Glitter £200,000 ($340,000) as an out-of-court settlement after being accused of using the Gary Glitter lyric, 'Hello, hello, it's good to be back' in the song 'Hello'.

2002 the man who is credited with discovering Britney Spears was celebrating after selling his record company Zomba to BMG Music. Clive Calder started Zomba in 1975 and had hits with Billy Ocean, Sam Fox and Tight Fit. BMG paid $2 billon (£1.176 million) for the company.

2005 Michael Jackson was cleared of all charges of child abuse by a jury of eight women and four men at the end of a 16 week hearing in Santa Maria, California. Jackson was found not guilty of all ten charges including abusing a 13-year-old boy, conspiracy to kidnap and supplying alcohol to a minor to assist with a felony.

BORN ON THIS DAY

1949 Dennis Locorriere – guitarist with Dr. Hook, who had a 1972 US No.5 & UK No.2 single with 'Sylvia's Mother' plus nine other US Top 40 hits.

1968 David Gray, singer/songwriter. His *White Ladder* was the second-biggest-selling UK album of 2001. He also had a 2000 UK No.5 single with 'Babylon'.

1957 Rolf Brendel – drummer with Nena, who had a 1984 UK No.1 & US No.2 single with '99 Red Balloons'.

1968 Deneice Pearson – singer with Five Star, who had a 1986 UK No.3 single with 'System Addict' plus 15 other UK Top 40 singles.

ON THIS DAY

1968 Cream released the single 'Anyone For Tennis'. It didn't chart.

1970 The Beatles started a two week run at No.1 on the US singles chart with 'The Long And Winding Road', the group's 20th US No.1. The album *Let It Be* started a four week run at No.1 the US album chart on the same day.

1972 Clyde McPhatter, original lead vocalist with The Drifters, died of a heart attack in New York.

1975 John Lennon made his last-ever TV appearance, on the US show *Salute To Sir Lew Grade*, performing 'Slippin And Slidin' and 'Imagine'.

1981 Smokey Robinson was at No.1 on the UK singles chart with 'Being With You'.

1992 Billy Ray Cyrus started a 17 week run at No.1 on the US album chart with *Some Gave All*.

1995 Alanis Morissette released *Jagged Little Pill*, which went on to sell over 15 million copies worldwide and made her the first female Canadian to score a US No.1 album.

2000 37-year-old Susan E. Santodonato collapsed and died of a heart attack outside New York radio station Star 105.7 after a Britney Spears impersonator left the building. A crowd had gathered after a DJ claimed Britney Spears was in the studio.

2000 Bobby Brown admitted he was an alcoholic, saying, "I have a disease, I am an addict, I am an alcoholic." The singer made the admission while appearing in a Florida court.

2003 former East 17 member Brian Harvey was cleared of drugs charges *(above)* after the prosecution's key witness refused to give evidence and left the UK for Spain. Harvey had been arrested after a *News Of The World* investigation and charged with possessing and supplying cocaine.

2003 the elder statesmen of music were rewarded in this year's Queen's Birthday Honours List for their services to music. Sting was awarded a CBE, Gerry Marsden an MBE, Errol Brown an MBE and Pink Floyd's Dave Gilmour a CBE.

Pop star's drug trial collapses

By Adam Sherwin
Media Reporter

BRIAN HARVEY, the former East 17 pop musician, was cleared of drugs charges yesterday after the prosecution's key witness refused to give evidence and left the country.

An investigation by the *News of the World* had resulted in Harvey, 27, being arrested and charged with possessing and supplying cocaine.

The court was told that Kemal Zorba, who had been paid £15,000 by the newspaper, refused to attend court and was believed to be in Spain.

Judge Gareth Hawkesworth formally entered not guilty verdicts and told Mr Harvey: 'You leave this court without a stain on your character.'

The Judge criticised the *News of the World* after being told that Zorba had left the country with the money he had been paid by the newspaper. 'May this be a salutary lesson to the proprietors of that newspaper,' he said.

His comments came after the collapse last week of the trial of five men charged with conspiring to kidnap Victoria Beckham and her children. The Crown Prosecution Service decided a key witness in that case was unreliable because he was a convicted liar who had been paid by the *News of the World*.

Mr Harvey's solicitor called for an investigation into the decision by the CPS to pursue the matter.

The newspaper is owned by News International, parent company of *The Times*.

Grumpy Clapton vows revenge on his barber.

BORN ON THIS DAY

1945 Rod Argent – keyboard player with The Zombies, who had a 1964 UK No.12 single with 'She's Not There', and Argent, who had a 1972 UK No.5 single with 'Hold Your Head Up'. Rod is also a TV/film composer.

1949 Alan White – drummer for Plastic Ono Band, who had a 1970 UK No.5 single with 'Instant Karma', and Yes, who had a 1977 UK No.7 single with 'Wonderous Stories'.

1949 Jim Lea – bass player, pianist and violinist for Slade, who had a 1971 UK No.1 single with 'Coz I Luv You' plus five other UK No.1 hits and 18 UK Top 40 hit singles.

1958 Nick Van Ede – vocalist for Cutting Crew, who had a 1987 US No.1 & 1986 UK No.4 single with 'I Just Died In Your Arms Tonight'.

1961 Boy George, (a.k.a. George O'Dowd) – DJ and singer with Culture Club, who had a 1983 UK No.1 & 1984 US No.1 single with 'Karma Chameleon'. As a solo artist he had a 1987 UK No.1 single with 'Everything I Own'.

ON THIS DAY

1953 Elvis Presley graduated from IC Hulmes High School in Memphis. His graduation photo shows him to have a split curl in the middle of his forehead, which was to become his trademark.

1961 country singer Patsy Cline was involved in a near fatal car crash in Nashville. She sustained head injuries after being thrown through the windscreen.

1964 12-year-old Carol Dryden was discovered by a railway worker packed in a tea chest on a station platform addressed to The Beatles.

1970 Derek & The Dominoes played their first gig when they appeared at London's Lyceum.

1974 Ray Stevens was at No.1 on the UK singles

Rod Argent shares the spoils of success with Russ Ballard.

chart with 'The Streak', a song based on the latest British craze of running naked in a public place.

1980 Billy Joel started a six week run at No.1 on the US album chart with *Glass Houses*, his second US No.1 album.

1984 a model of Boy George was unveiled at Madame Tussaud's Waxworks in London on his 23rd birthday.

1986 Bob Geldof was named in the Queen's Birthday Honours List, receiving an honorary knighthood in recognition of his humanitarian activities.

1986 Patti Labelle and Michael McDonald started a three week run at No.1 on the US singles chart with 'On My Own'.

1986 Queen scored their fifth UK No.1 album with *A Kind Of Magic*, featuring the single 'One Vision'.

1986 three fans died during an Ozzy Osbourne gig at Long Beach Arena, California after falling from a balcony.

1989 Pete De Freitas, drummer with Echo And The Bunnymen, was killed when his motorbike collided with a car.

1994 composer Henry Mancini died aged 64. He had written the 1969 US No.1 single 'Love Theme from Romeo And Juliet' as well as many TV and film themes, including the 'Theme From *The Pink Panther*'.

1995 Irish guitarist Rory Gallagher died after a chest infection set in following a liver transplant.

1997 Puff Daddy and Faith Evans started an 11 week run at No.1 on the US singles chart with 'I'll Be Missing You', a tribute to the late Notorious B.I.G. It was also a No.1 in the UK.

2000 Noel Gallagher from Oasis was voted into first place in *Melody Maker*'s annual "Uncoolest People in Rock" survey. Marilyn Manson came second and Robbie Williams was voted third.

2002 during a UK visit Michael Jackson made a tour of Parliament and was shown the monarch's throne in the House of Lords. Whenever Jackson went outside he called for an umbrella to shield his face from the sun.

2002 former East 17 singer Brian Harvey was jailed for 56 days at the High Court London after breaching an injunction taken out by his estranged wife.

2002 Mick Jagger became a Sir when he was knighted in the Queen's Birthday Honours List.

Patsy Cline, queen of country.

BORN ON THIS DAY

1933 Waylon Jennings, US country singer who had a 1980 US No.21 single with 'Theme From *The Dukes Of Hazzard*'. He also had country No.1 hits and played bass with Buddy Holly in 1959. Jennings died on February 13th 2002.

1941 Harry Nilsson, US singer/songwriter who had a 1972 UK & US No.1 single with his version of the Badfinger song 'Without You' and a 1969 US No.6 single with 'Everybody's Talkin' from the film *Midnight Cowboy*. The Monkees, Three Dog Night and The Ronettes all covered his songs. He died on January 15th 1994.

1943 Johnny Halliday, the "French Elvis" and a major star in Europe. Jimmy Page, Peter Frampton and Foreigner's Mick Jones have all played on his records.

1943 Muff Winwood – bass player with The Spencer Davis Group, who had a 1966 UK No.1 single with 'Keep On Running'. He has also been a producer and head of A&R for Sony Records.

1946 Noddy Holder – guitarist and vocalist for Slade, who had a 1971 UK No.1 single with 'Coz I Luv You' plus five other UK No.1 singles and 18 UK Top 40 hits as well as three No.1 albums.

1966 Michael Britt – guitarist with Lonestar, who had a 2000 US No.1 & UK No. 21 single with 'Amazed'.

1981 Billy Martin – guitarist with Good Charlotte, who had a 2002 US No.7 album with *The Young And The Hopeless* and a 2003 UK No.6 single with 'Girls and Boys'.

ON THIS DAY

1958 ITV's pop show *Oh Boy* was broadcast for the first time in the UK.

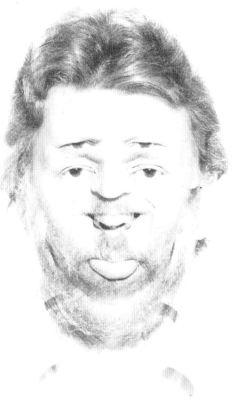

Nilsson demonstrates the sheer power of his drug intake.

1963 Kyu Sakamoto started a three week run at No.1 on the US singles chart with 'Sukiyaki', the first-ever Japanese song to do so. It made No.6 on the UK chart in 1963 and was also a No.10 UK single for Kenny Ball in the same year.

1965 Bob Dylan recorded his first "electric" hit, 'Like A Rolling Stone'.

1974 Abba's debut album *Waterloo* entered the UK chart for the first time, peaking at No.28.

1977 the Sex Pistols held a party on a boat sailing down the River Thames. They performed 'Anarchy In The UK' outside The Houses Of Parliament and members from the party were arrested when the boat docked later that day.

1978 appearing live around the UK: at Hull University, Jonathan Richman & The Modern Lovers, Racing Cars appeared at Poole Arts Centre and Bob Dylan played the first of six sold-out nights at London's Earl's Court.

1982 Pete Farndon, bass player with The Pretenders, was fired from the group. He went on to form a group with Topper Headon from The Clash. He was found dead in his bath on April 14th 1983.

1985 Dire Straits started a nine week run at No.1 on the US album chart with *Brothers In Arms*.

1986 U2 and Sting headlined a concert in New Jersey celebrating 25 years of Amnesty International.

DYLAN PLAYS SIX AT EARLS COURT

1988 during Bruce Springsteen's stay in Rome during a world tour paparazzi took a shot of Bruce in his underpants sharing an intimate moment with his backing singer Patti Scialfa. The picture confirmed the rumour that Bruce and Patti are having an affair.

1989 Nirvana's debut album *Bleach* was released in the US. The title came from a poster "Bleach Your Works", urging drug users to bleach their needles.

2002 a rare autographed copy of The Beatles' album *Sgt Pepper's Lonely Hearts Club Band* sold at auction for £34,000 ($57,800), more than five times the estimated price.

2003 Metallica were at No.1 on the US album chart with *St Anger*, the band's fourth US No.1 and a No.3 hit in the UK.

BORN ON THIS DAY

1941 Lamont Dozier, producer and songwriter (part of Holland/Dozier/Holland), who wrote for Motown, The Supremes, The Four Tops, Marvin Gaye, Martha Reeves & The Vandellas, Freda Payne and Chairmen Of The Board.

1946 Ian Matthews – singer with Fairport Convention and Matthews Southern Comfort, who had a 1970 UK No.1 & 1971 US No.23 single with 'Woodstock'. He has since had a varied career as a solo artist.

1954 Gerry Roberts – guitarist with The Boomtown Rats, who had a 1979 UK No.1 single with 'I Don't Like Mondays' plus ten other UK Top 40 hit singles.

1971 Tupac Amaru Shakur – rapper who had a 1996 US No.1 single with 'How Do U Want It/California Love' and a 1996 UK No.6 single with 'California Love'. He died from bullet wounds on September 13th 1996.

ON THIS DAY

1962 The Konrads (featuring Dave Jay later to become David Bowie), made their live debut when they played at Bromley Technical School in Kent, England.

1964 The Rolling Stones paid £1,500 ($2,500) in return air fares from America back to the UK to honour a booking made a year earlier for £100 ($170) at Magdalen College Oxford.

1967 the three day Monterey Pop Festival in California began. All the proceeds went to charity and the artists agreed to perform for free. The "Summer of Love" was born. The festival saw the first major US appearances by The Who, Jimi Hendrix and Janis Joplin. Also on the bill were: The Byrds, Grateful Dead, Otis Redding, Simon & Garfunkel, The Steve Miller Band, Canned Heat, The Mamas And The Papas, Jefferson Airplane, Buffalo Springfield and The Electric Flag. Tickets cost $3.50–6.50 (£2–3.80).

1970 Mungo Jerry was at No.1 on the UK singles chart with 'In The Summertime'. It was the bestselling single of 1970 and a hit in 26 other countries.

1973 Suzi Quatro had her first UK No.1 single with 'Can The Can'. 10CC were at No.2 with 'Rubber Bullets' and Fleetwood Mac at No.3 with 'Albatross'.

1982 Pretenders guitarist James Honeyman-Scott died following sustained cocaine and heroin addiction.

1984 Frankie Goes To Hollywood had their second UK No.1 single with 'Two Tribes'. It stayed at No.1 for nine weeks making F.G.T.H. the first band to have their first two singles go to No.1.

1988 Vince Neil of Motley Crue married mud wrestler Sharisse Rudell.

1989 the first day of the three day Glastonbury Festival with Van Morrison, Elvis Costello, Throwing Muses, Pixies, All About Eve, Hot House Flowers, The Waterboys, Suzanne Vega and Fairground Attraction. Tickets cost £28 ($48).

1990 Roxette started a two week run at No.1 on the US singles chart with 'It Must Have Been Love', taken from the film *Pretty Woman*. It became the duo's third US No.1 and a No.3 hit in the UK.

1999 singer turned politician Screaming Lord Sutch was found dead after hanging himself. He was 58.

2000 on the first night of his "Up in Smoke" tour in Chula Vista, Snoop Dogg's tour bus was stopped at the Temecula border checkpoint, San Diego after the border patrol smelled marijuana wafting from the bus. One arrest was made.

2002 46 years after his first hit, Elvis Presley started a four week run at No.1 on the UK singles chart with 'A Little Less Conversation' (Elvis vs JXL), giving Elvis a total of 18 UK No.1 singles – the most by any artist in chart history. This also set a new record for the longest span of No.1 hits with 44 years, 11 months and 9 days. His first No.1 was 'All Shook Up' in 1957.

Jimi Hendrix plays Monterey, 1967.

BORN ON THIS DAY

1930 Cliff Gallup – guitarist with Gene Vincent And The Blue Caps, who had a 1956 US No.7 & UK No.16 single with 'Be-Bop-A-Lula'. Gallup died of a heart attack on October 9th 1988.

1942 Norman Kuhlke – drummer with The Swinging Blue Jeans, who had a 1964 UK No.2 and US No.24 single with 'Hippy Hippy Shake'.

Paul Young (the other one) shows why 'Every Day hurts'.

1946 Barry Manilow, US singer/songwriter who had a 1975 US No.1 & UK No.11 single with 'Mandy' and also wrote 'Could It Be Magic' and 'Copacabana'. He has scored over 25 US Top 40 singles.

1947 Glenn Buxton – guitarist with the Alice Cooper Band, who had a 1972 UK No.1 and US No.7 single with 'School's Out'. He died October 19th 1997.

1947 Greg Rolie – keyboardist and vocalist for Santana, who had a 1970 US No.4 single with 'Black Magic Woman' and a 1977 UK No.11 single with 'She's Not There'.

1947 Paul Young – singer with Sad Café, who had a 1979 UK No.3 single with 'Every Day Hurts', and Mike And The Mechanics, who had a 1989 UK No.2 single with 'The Living Years'. Young died on July 15th 2000.

1969 Kevin Thornton – singer with Color Me Bad, who had a 1991 UK No.1 single with 'I Wanna Sex You Up' and a 1991 US No.1 single with 'I Adore Mi Amor'.

ON THIS DAY

1954 the first edition of UK music paper *Record Mirror* was published.

1965 Elvis Presley was at No.1 in the UK with 'Crying In The Chapel', his 15th UK No.1 single.

1966 guitarist Peter Green joined John Mayall's Bluesbreakers.

1972 Don McLean had his first UK No.1 single with 'Vincent'. The song was written about the 19th-century artist Van Gogh. The song is played daily at the Van Gogh Museum in Amsterdam.

1972 The Rolling Stones' album *Exile On Main Street* started a four week run at the top of the US charts.

1976 Ian Dury played his last gig with Kilburn And The High Roads before starting his solo career. The show at The Assembly Hall, Walthamstow also had the Sex Pistols and The Stranglers on the bill.

1978 Andy Gibb started a seven week run at No.1 on the US singles chart with 'Shadow Dancing'. The single made No.42 in the UK.

1978 from the film *Grease*, 'You're The One That I Want' by John Travolta and Olivia Newton-John started a nine week run at No.1 on the UK singles chart.

1979 Anita Ward was at No.1 on the UK singles chart with 'Ring My Bell'.

1985 The Crowd were at No.1 in the UK with 'You'll Never Walk Alone'. The single was recorded to raise funds for The Bradford City Football disaster that had killed over 50 people.

1989 New Kids On The Block went to No.1 on the US singles chart with 'I'll Be Loving You Forever', the group's first US No.1. It was a No.5 hit in the UK.

1999 a teenage girl was crushed to death during a gig by Hole at the Hultsfred Festival, Sweden.

2000 it was reported that sales of pirate music CDs had now exceeded more than 500 million a year and accounted for one in every five sold. The Phonographic Industry estimated it was costing the music industry £3 billion ($5.1 billion) in lost sales.

2001 Travis started a four week run at No.1 on the UK album chart with *The Invisible Band*.

BORN ON THIS DAY

1942 Paul McCartney – singer and guitarist with The Beatles and solo artist. He is also the most successful rock composer of all time. The Beatles scored 21 US No.1 & 17 UK No.1 singles and McCartney has scored over 30 US & UK solo Top 40 hit singles.

1942 Carl Radle – bass player with Derek & The Dominoes, who had a 1972 UK No.7 single with 'Layla'. He also worked with George Harrison and Delaney & Bonnie. Radle died of kidney failure on June 30th 1980, aged 38.

1953 Jerome Smith – guitarist with KC & The Sunshine Band, who had a 1975 US No.1 single with 'Get Down Tonight' and a 1983 UK No.1 single with 'Give It Up'. He died on August 2nd 2000 after being crushed by a bulldozer he was operating.

1957 Tom Bailey – vocalist and keyboardist with The Thompson Twins, who had a 1984 UK No.2 single with 'You Take Me Up' and a 1984 US No.3 single with 'Hold Me Now'.

1961 Alison Moyet – singer with Yazoo, who had a 1982 UK No.2 single with 'Only You'. As a solo artist she had a 1985 UK No.2 single with 'That Ole Devil Called Love'.

1965 Twiggy Ramirez – bass player with Marilyn Manson, who had a 1998 US No.1 album with *Mechanical Animals* and a UK No.12 single with 'The Dope Show'.

1971 Nathan Morris – vocalist with Boyz II Men, who had a 1992 US & UK No.1 single with 'End Of The Road'.

ON THIS DAY

1955 Jimmy Young was at No.1 on the UK singles chart with 'Unchained Melody'. Young scored another ten Top 40 singles and went on to become one of the UK's favourite radio DJs.

1966 this week's UK singles chart: No.5, Percy Sledge, 'When A Man Loves A Woman'; No.4, The Mersey's, 'Sorrow'; No.3, The Mamas And The Papas, 'Monday Monday'; No.2, The Beatles, 'Paperback Writer' and No.1, Frank Sinatra, 'Strangers In The Night'.

1974 Peter Hoorelbeke, drummer with US band Rare Earth, was arrested after a concert for throwing his drum sticks into the crowd.

1977 appearing at Friars, Aylesbury, England were Tom Petty And The Heartbreakers.

1977 Fleetwood Mac went to No.1 on the US singles chart with 'Dreams', the group's first and only US No.1. It made No.24 in the UK.

1983 Swiss band Yello released the first three-dimensional picture disc, complete with 3D glasses.

1988 Rick Astley went to No.1 on the US singles chart with 'Together Forever', his second US No.1 and a No.2 hit in the UK.

1994 The Beastie Boys entered the US album chart at No.1 with *Ill Communication*.

1997 the first of two nights at Oakland Coliseum, San Francisco with U2 supported by Oasis.

2000 rapper Nate Dogg was arrested for allegedly kidnapping his girlfriend from her mother's house, holding her against her will, assaulting her and setting a car on fire. All charges were later dismissed.

2002 U2 lost a bid to prevent the demolition of Hanover Quay Studio in Dublin. Over 8,000 fans signed an online petition to preserve the studio, where the group recorded *All That You Can't Leave Behind* and some of their *Pop* album.

2003 *Pop Idol* creator Simon Fuller became the first British music manager since The Beatles' Brian Epstein to hold the top three positions in the US singles chart. Fuller, who steered the Spice Girls and S Club 7 to success, was in charge of bestselling artists Clay Aiken and Ruben Studdard, together with the *American Idol 2* Final 10. During 2003 Fuller sold more than ten million records around the world and has had 96 No.1 singles and 79 top-placed albums in both the US and UK during his career. He was named in the latest *Sunday Times* Rich List as the 359th wealthiest person in the UK with assets of £90 million ($153 million).

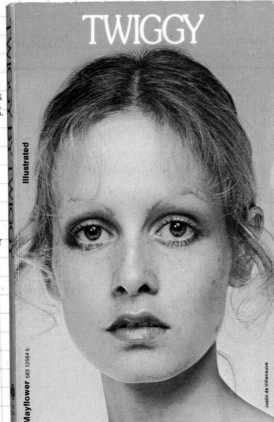

TWIGGY

Illustrated

Mayflower 583 125646

Justin de Villeneuve

Join Marilyn Manson and watch your pretty face go to pot!

BORN ON THIS DAY

1936 Tommy Devito – singer and guitarist with The Four Seasons, who had a 1976 UK & US No.1 single with 'December 1963, Oh What A Night'.

WILTSHIRE GAZETTE AND HERALD, THURSDAY, JUNE 23, 1966.

WILTS ATHLETIC CHAMPIONSHIPS

Junior men
100 yards: 1 M. Drake (Marlborough) 10.4sec., 2 K. Hall (Swindon), 3 J. Worthington (Marlborough).
220 yards: 1 M. Drake (Marlborough) 22.8secs., 2 J. Worthington (Marlborough), 3 K. Hall (Swindon).
440 yards: 1 N. Grist (Trowbridge) 51.7sec. (record), 2 D. Lyall (Calne), 3 C. Darby (Bradford-on-Avon).
880 yards: 1 N. Grist (Trowbridge) 2min. 1.9sec., 2 S. Barnes (Swindon).
One mile: 1 J. Bednarski (Swindon) 4min. 26sec. (record), 2 J. Glague (Marlborough), 3 P. Wright (Marlborough).
Long jump: 1 M. Phillips (Marlborough) 20ft. 6¾in., 2 P. Millard (Swindon), 3 A. Oruston (Marlborough).
Triple jump: 1 P. Millard (Swindon) 40ft. 5in., 2 A. Oruston (Marlborough).
Javelin: 1 G. Rudkin (Marlborough) 146ft. 10in., 2 S. Barnes (Swindon) 3 D. Arthur (Marlborough).
Discus: 1 C. Cox (Marlborough) 125ft. 5in., 2 M. Wood (Marlborough).
Shot: 1 M. Wood (Marlborough) 40ft. 2¼in. 2 C. Cox (Marlborough).

M. R. Drake, of Marlborough College, winner of the junior 100 yards at the Wiltshire championships on Saturday.

Nick Drake: singer, songwriter and accomplished junior athlete.

1948 Nick Drake, UK singer/songwriter, who had the 1972 album *Pink Moon*. Drake committed suicide on November 25th 1974, aged 26.

1951 Ann Wilson – vocalist for Heart, who had a 1987 US No.1 & UK No.3 single with 'Alone'.

1960 Dennis Fuller – vocalist with The London Boys, who had a 1989 UK No.2 single with 'London Nights.' He was killed in a car crash with London Boy partner Edem Ephraim on January 21st 1996.

1963 Paula Abdul – singer and dancer who had a 1990 US No.1 & UK No.2 single with 'Opposites Attract' plus five other US No.1 singles. Her 1989 album *Forever Your Girl* spent ten weeks as US No.1. She is currently judge on the *American Idol* TV show.

1970 Brian Welch – guitarist for Korn, who had a 1998 UK No.23 single with 'Got The Life' and a 1998 US No.1 album with Follow The Leader.

ON THIS DAY

1965 appearing at The Uxbridge Blues Festival were The Who, Cliff Bennett & The Rebel Rousers, Zoot Money and Marianne Faithfull.

1965 The Four Tops went to No.1 on the US singles chart with 'I Can't Help Myself'.

1967 in an interview with *Life* magazine Paul McCartney admitted that he had taken the drug LSD.

1971 Carole King started a five week run at No.1 on the US singles chart with 'It's Too Late/I Feel The Earth Move'. Both songs were from the album *Tapestry*, which also topped the US charts on this day.

1974 The Delinquents, a band featuring Mick Jones (later of The Clash), made their debut at the Students' Union bar, Queen Elizabeth College, Kensington.

1976 future Smiths singer Steve Morrissey had a letter published in this week's music magazine *Record Mirror And Disc* **(right)** asking the editor why the paper had not included any stories on the Sex Pistols.

Don't mention it

DEAR MAILMAN, I went to see the Sex Pistols at Manchester and they are the most exciting rock band to emerge since the New York Dolls. It puzzles me why bands like them don't get a mention in Record Mirror.
Steve Morrissey, Stretford, Manchester
● There you go, one free mention and that's yer lot.

Master

1977 Paul Cook from the Sex Pistols was beaten up by six men wielding knives and iron bars outside Shepherd's Bush underground station. Cook required 15 stitches to a head wound.

MAM proudly presents
DAVID BOWIE
IN CONCERT *with support*
The Apollo
Renfield Street, Glasgow
Monday, 19th June, 1978
at 7.30 p.m.
Ticket **£6.00** inc. VAT
STALLS **T**
No re-admission
For conditions see reverse
To be retained and produced on demand
N° 18

1980 Donna Summer became the first act to be signed by David Geffen to his new Geffen Record label.

1987 Guns N' Roses made their UK live debut playing the first of three nights at the Marquee Club, London.

1990 Prince started a 12 night sold-out run at London's Wembley Arena.

1992 the "Greenpeace Stop Sellafield" campaign concert took place at G-Mex in Manchester with U2, Big Audio Dynamite II, Public Enemy and Kraftwerk.

1993 Tina Turner went to No.1 on the UK album chart with *What's Love Got To Do With It?*

2000 it was announced that Eminem was to be immortalized in animation, with a new cartoon series that would be hosted on a new website. 26 weekly "webisodes" would be broadcast on the site, featuring Eminem providing all the voices.

2003 G-Man from So Solid Crew was jailed for four years for possessing a loaded handgun. The 24-year-old, real name Jason Phillips, dumped a loaded gun during a police chase in London the previous November. He'd always denied it, as well as denying knowing anything about 11 other bullets that were found in a flat in South London. The jury in London's Southwark Crown Court heard evidence that DNA found on the weapon matched his, and found him guilty.

BORN ON THIS DAY

1924 Chet Atkins, guitarist, who had a 1960 UK No.46 single with 'Teensville'. He recorded over 100 albums during his career and was a major influence on George Harrison and Mark Knopfler. Atkins died on June 30th 2001, aged 77.

1936 Mickie Most, record producer who was a member of The Most Brothers during the late 50s. He produced hits for The Animals, Herman's Hermits, Lulu and Jeff Beck. He ran his own label, RAK, in the 70s and had hits with Hot Chocolate, Suzi Quatro and Mud. Most died on May 30th 2003, aged 67.

1936 Billy Guy — singer with The Coasters, who had a 1958 US No.1 single with 'Yakety Yak' and a 1959 UK No.6 single with 'Charlie Brown'.

1937 Jerry Keller, singer/songwriter who had a 1959 UK No.1 and US No.14 single with 'Here Comes Summer'.

1942 Brian Wilson — vocalist, pianist, bass player and songwriter with The Beach Boys, who had a 1966 UK & US No.1 single with 'Good Vibrations' plus over 25 other UK Top 40 singles and a 1966 classic album with *Pet Sounds*. He toured the long-lost *Smile* album in 2004.

1949 Lionel Richie — vocalist and keyboardist with The Commodores, who had a 1978 UK & US No.1 single with 'Three Times A Lady'. As a solo artist he had a 1984 UK & US No.1 single with 'Hello' plus over ten other UK Top 40 hit singles.

1953 Alan Longmuir — bass player with the Bay City Rollers, who had a 1975 UK No.1 single with 'Bye Bye Baby' plus 11 other UK Top 20 singles and a 1976 US No.1 single with 'Saturday Night'.

1960 John Taylor — bass player for Duran Duran, who had a 1983 UK No.1 single with 'Is There Something I Should Know?' plus 25 other UK Top 40 singles, and a 1984 US No.1 single with 'The Reflex', and The Power Station, who had a 1985 UK No.14 single with 'Some Like It Hot'.

1966 Stone Gossard — guitarist with Pearl Jam, who had a 1992 UK No.15 single with 'Jeremy' and a 1993 US No.1 album with *Vs.*

ON THIS DAY

1969 David Bowie recorded 'Space Oddity' at Trident Studios, London.

1969 the first day of a three day Festival in Newport, California, featuring: Ike And Tina Turner, Marvin Gaye, Creedence Clearwater Revival, The Byrds, The Rascals, Steppenwolf, the Jimi Hendrix Experience, Janis Joplin, Johnny Winter, Eric Burdon and Love. A three day ticket cost $15 (£8.80).

1974 appearing at Knebworth Park, England were Led Zeppelin, Van Morrison, The Mahavishnu Orchestra and The Doobie Brothers. A special PA system was used, claiming to be the best-ever used for an outside event. It weighed 12 tons and needed five technicians.

1981 'Stars On 45', a medley of Beatles songs set to a disco beat, went to No.1 on the US singles chart. It was the start of a flood of 'Stars On' hits including Stars on Stevie Wonder, punk songs, Status Quo and Chas & Dave.

1986 acts appearing at the fourth annual Prince's Trust Rock Gala *(below)* included Phil Collins, Dire Straits, Tina Turner and Elton John.

1992 Mariah Carey scored her sixth US No.1 single with 'I'll Be There', which was a No.2 hit in the UK. The song was also a US No.1 for The Jackson Five in 1970.

1995 Jeff Buckley played the first night of an UK tour at The Queen's Hall, Edinburgh.

1997 Lawrence Payton of The Four Tops died from liver cancer, aged 59. The group had had a 1965 US No.1 single with 'I Can't Help Myself' and a 1967 UK No.6 single with 'Standing In The Shadows Of Love'.

1998 Baddiel And Skinner and the Lightning Seeds started a three week run at No.1 on the UK singles chart with '3 Lions 98'.

1998 appearing at Ozzfest, Milton Keynes Bowl, England were Black Sabbath, Foo Fighters, Korn, Pantera, Soulfly, Slayer, Fear Factory, Coal Chamber, Life of Agony, Limp Bizkit, Entombed, Human Waste Project, Neurosis and Pitchshifter.

2000 The Ronettes were awarded $2.6 million (£1.5 million) in "back earnings" from Phil Spector. New York judge Paula Omansky ruled that the legendary producer had cheated them out of royalties.

2004 Velvet Revolver were at No.1 on the US album chart with *Contraband*.

BORN ON THIS DAY

1936 O.C. Smith, singer who had a 1968 US No.1 single with 'Little Green Apples' and a 1968 UK No.2 single with 'The Son Of Hickory Holler's Tramp'. He died on November 23rd 2001.

1944 Ray Davies – guitarist and vocalist with The Kinks, who had a 1964 UK No.1 & US No.7 single with 'You Really Got Me', a 1967 UK No.2 single with 'Waterloo Sunset' plus 19 other UK Top 40 singles. The band also had a 1983 US No.6 single with 'Come Dancing'.

1944 Miguel Vicens – bass player with Los Bravos, the first Spanish rock band to have a UK and US hit single. 'Black Is Black' reached No.2 in the UK and No.4 in the US in 1966.

1945 Chris Britton – guitarist with The Troggs, who had a 1966 US No.1 & UK No.2 single with 'Wild Thing'.

1948 Joey Molland – guitarist and vocalist with Badfinger, who had a 1970 UK No.4 and US No.7 single with 'Come And Get It'.

1949 Greg Munford, Strawberry Alarm Clock, who had a 1967 US No.1 single with 'Incense And Peppermints'.

1950 Joey Kramer – drummer with Aerosmith, who had a 1989 UK No.3 single with 'Love In An Elevator' and a 1998 US No.1 single with 'I Don't Want To Miss A Thing'.

1953 Nils Lofgren – guitarist, pianist and vocalist with Grin and the E Street Band. As a solo artist he had a 1976 UK No.8 album with *Cry Tough*.

1959 Marcella Detroit – vocalist with Shakespear's Sister, who had a 1992 UK No.1 single with 'Stay'. She has also worked with Eric Clapton.

ON THIS DAY

1966 guitarist Jimmy Page made his live debut with The Yardbirds at the Marquee Club, London.

1966 The Rolling Stones sued 14 hotels over a booking ban in New York, claiming that the ban was violating civil rights laws.

1966 Tom Jones needed 14 stitches in his forehead after his Jaguar was involved in a car crash in Marble Arch, London.

1975 appearing live on stage to 120,000 fans at Wembley Stadium, London were Elton John, The Beach Boys, Joe Walsh, Rufus and The Eagles. Tickets cost £3.50 ($5.95).

1975 Captain And Tennille started a four week run at No.1 on the US singles chart with the Neil Sedaka song 'Love Will Keep Us Together'.

1975 guitarist Ritchie Blackmore quit Deep Purple to form his own group Rainbow.

Jimmy Page with his Yardbirds.

1977 Johnny Rotten was attacked in a brawl outside Dingwalls in Camden, London.

1979 Angus MacLise, Velvet Underground's first drummer, died aged 34. He had quit the band in 1965.

1980 Bert Kaempfert died, aged 56. He produced Beatles' recordings while they were working in Germany. Both Sinatra and Presley covered his songs 'Strangers In The Night' and 'Wooden Heart'.

1980 The Stranglers were arrested by police after a concert at Nice University for allegedly starting a riot.

1985 this was the first day of this year's Glastonbury Festival with Aswad, The Boomtown Rats, Clannad, The Colour Field, Ian Dury, King, The Pogues, Midnight Oil, Thompson Twins, Misty In Roots and Maria Muldaur. A three day ticket cost £16 ($27).

1988 the UK leg of Bruce Springsteen's "Tunnel Of Love Express" was at Aston Villa Football Club, Birmingham, England.

1992 The Orb released 'Blue Room'. The single had a duration of 39 minutes and 58 seconds, two seconds shorter than the maximum permitted for a single under UK chart rules.

2000 39-year-old Karen McNeil, who claimed that she was the wife of Axl Rose and that she communicated with him telepathically, was jailed for one year for stalking the singer.

BORN ON THIS DAY

1936 Kris Kristofferson, singer/songwriter and actor who wrote 'Me And Bobby McGee' and 'Help Me Make It Through The Night'. His film roles include *A Star Is Born* with Barbra Streisand.

1944 Peter Asher – singer and guitarist with Peter & Gordon, who had a 1964 UK & US No.1 single with 'World Without Love', which was written by Lennon And McCartney. Asher was a producer and Head of Apple Records in the late 60s.

Jeff Beck without his Yardbirds.

1947 Howard Kaylan – singer with The Turtles, who had a 1967 US No.1 single with 'Happy Together' and a 1967 UK No.4 single with 'She'd Rather Be With Me'. As Flo and Eddie they worked with Frank Zappa, T. Rex and Bruce Springsteen.

1948 Todd Rundgren – guitarist, vocalist and producer. He was part of Nazz and Utopia and as a solo artist had a 1972 US No.16 & 1973 UK No.36 single with 'I Saw The Light'. He produced Meat Loaf's *Bat Out Of Hell* album.

1949 Alan Osmond – singer with The Osmonds, who had a 1971 US No.1 single with 'One Bad Apple', a 1974 UK No.1 single with 'Love Me For A Reason' plus nine other US & UK Top 40 singles.

1953 Cyndi Lauper, singer who had a 1984 US No.1 single with 'Time After Time' and a UK No.2 single with 'Girls Just Want To Have Fun'.

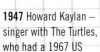

1971 Glastonbury toilets, so much more advanced than the current ones.

ON THIS DAY

1963 13-year-old Stevie Wonder first entered the US singles chart as Little Stevie Wonder with 'Fingertips Parts One and Two'.

1968 Herb Alpert started a four week run at No.1 on the US singles chart with 'This Guy's In Love With You'. It was his first No.1 plus first No.1 for the A&M label and the writers Bacharach and David's first chart topper. The song was a No.3 hit in the UK.

1968 The Jeff Beck group featuring Rod Stewart made their US debut at the Fillmore East, New York.

1968 the Otis Redding album *Dock Of The Bay* went to No.1 in the UK. (Redding was killed in a plane crash on December 10th 1967.)

1969 singer and actress Judy Garland died of a barbiturate overdose. She had played Dorothy in the 1939 film *Wizard Of Oz*, singing 'Over The Rainbow' in the film.

1971 appearing at the second Glastonbury Festival were Melanie, Quintessence, The Edgar Broughton Band, Pink Fairies, Terry Reid, Gong, David Bowie, Hawkwind, Arthur Brown, Brinsley Schwarz, Fairport Convention and Family.

1980 Don McLean had his second UK No.1 single with the Roy Orbison song 'Crying'.

1981 Mark Chapman pleaded guilty to the charge of murdering John Lennon in 1980.

1985 Bryan Adams started a two week run at No.1 on the US singles chart with 'Heaven', his first No.1 single. It made No.35 in the UK. The song had been featured in the film *Night In Heaven*.

1985 appearing at "The Longest Day", Milton Keynes Bowl, Milton Keynes were U2, Faith Brothers, Spear Of Destiny, Billy Bragg, The Ramones and R.E.M.

Morleigh gets dressed up for The Edge.

1992 Kurt Cobain was rushed to hospital after a gig in Belfast suffering from acute stomach pains brought on by ulcers.

1992 three members of MC Hammer's tour crew were wounded in a drive-in shooting incident. Three days later Joseph Mack, a dancer in Hammer's entourage, was shot on stage during a concert in Nevada.

2000 Mick Jagger was ordered to reveal his financial worth and income to a New York court in his child support battle with the mother of his last child, Brazilian model Luciana Morad.

2002 U2 guitarist "The Edge" married his girlfriend of ten years, Morleigh Steinberg, in Eze in the south of France. The couple first met when she was a belly dancer on the band's Zoo TV tour. Guests included Bono, Dave Stewart and Lenny Kravitz.

BORN ON THIS DAY

1929 June Carter Cash, country singer and wife of Johnny Cash. She died on May 15th 2003, aged 73.

1940 Adam Faith, singer and actor who had a 1959 UK No.1 single with 'What Do You Want' plus over 20 other UK Top 40 singles. His acting roles included the TV series *Love Hurts*. Faith died on March 8th 2003.

1940 Stu Sutcliffe – bass player for The Beatles 1960–61. He stayed in Hamburg until his death on April 10th 1962, of a brain haemorrhage in an ambulance on the way to hospital, aged 22.

1965 Paul "Bonehead" Arthurs – guitarist for Oasis, whose first single 'Supersonic' was a 1994 UK No.31. The band also had a 1996 UK No.1 single with 'Don't Look Back In Anger' and the 1994 UK No.1 album *Definitely Maybe* was the fastest-selling UK debut album ever. Arthurs left Oasis in August 1999.

1981 Anthony Costa – singer with Blue, who had a 2002 UK No.1 single with 'If You Come Back'.

ON THIS DAY

1957 Lonnie Donegan was at No.1 on the UK singles chart with 'Gamblin' Man/Putting On The Style', the singer's second UK No.1.

1960 Eddie Cochran was at No.1 in the UK with the single 'Three Steps To Heaven'.

1962 Ray Charles started a 14 week run at No.1 on the US album chart with *Modern Sounds In Country And Western Music*.

1962 the film soundtrack to *West Side Story* went to No.1 on the UK charts for the first time. It spent a total of 13 weeks at No.1 on seven different occasions.

1966 The Beatles had their tenth consecutive UK No.1 single with 'Paperback Writer'.

1970 Chubby Checker was arrested in Niagara Falls after police discovered marijuana and other drugs in his car.

1973 10CC were at No.1 on the UK singles chart with 'Rubber Bullets', the first of three UK No.1s. (The band also had a No.1 as Hotlegs.)

1973 George Harrison started a five week run at No.1 on the US album chart with *Living In The Material World*, his second US No.1.

Cooper, cooped up in hospital.

1975 during his "Welcome To My Nightmare" tour in Vancouver Alice Cooper fell from the stage and broke six ribs.

1984 Duran Duran started a two week run at No.1 on the US singles chart with 'The Reflex', the group's first US No.1 and also a No.1 in the UK.

1989 George Michael received the Silver Clef Award for Outstanding achievements to British music.

1990 13-year-old Keith Sorrentino filed a $500,000 (£294,118) lawsuit against Madonna, claiming he suffered nightmares and bed-wetting problems after an incident outside Madonna's home when she allegedly flung him to the ground.

1990 Buddy Holly's Gibson acoustic guitar sold for £139,658 ($237,419) in a Sotheby's auction. The guitar was in a tooled leather case made by Holly himself.

1990 Elton John had his first UK solo No.1 single with 'Sacrifice/Healing Hands', after achieving over 40 previous Top 75 singles.

1995 drummer Alan White made his live debut with Oasis at Glastonbury Festival. Ex-Take That member Robbie Williams appeared on stage with the band.

2000 The Experience Music Project was unveiled in Seattle by Paul Allen, co-founder of Microsoft. The £150 ($255) museum contained over 80,000 items of Hendrix memorabilia, including a smashed guitar from the 1967 Monterey Pop Festival.

2002 The top pop earners from US sales during 2001 were listed by *Rolling Stone* magazine as: Madonna at No.5 with £29.1 million ($49.5 million); Dave Matthews Band *(below)* at No.4 with £31 million ($52.7 million); The Beatles at No.3 with £34.2 million ($58 million); Dr. Dre at No.2 with £37.1 million ($63 million) and, top of the list, U2 with £44.2 million ($75 million).

2002 Nelly started a seven week run at No.1 on the US singles chart with 'Hot In Here'.

BORN ON THIS DAY

1944 Arthur Brown, singer who had a 1968 UK No.1 and US No.12 single with 'Fire' with The Crazy World Of Arthur Brown.

1944 Jeff Beck – guitarist with Screaming Lord Sutch then The Yardbirds, who had a 1965 UK No.3 & US No.6 single with 'For Your Love', then Rod Stewart. As a solo artist he had a 1967 UK No.14 single with 'Hi-Ho Silver Lining' and a 1975 solo album with *Blow By Blow*. As part of The Honeydrippers (with Jimmy Page, Robert Plant And Nile Rodgers), he had a 1984 US No.3 single with 'Sea Of Love'.

1944 Mick Fleetwood – drummer with Fleetwood Mac, who had a 1987 UK No.5 single with 'Little Lies' and 1977 US No.1 single with 'Dreams' from the worldwide No.1 album *Rumours*.

1945 Colin Blunstone – singer with The Zombies, who had a 1964 UK No.12 single with 'She's Not There'. As a solo artist he had a 1981 UK No.13 single with 'What Becomes Of The Broken Hearted?'

1949 John Illsley – bass player with Dire Straits, who had a 1985 US No.1 single with 'Money For Nothing', a 1986 UK No.2 single with 'Walk Of Life' and a 1985 worldwide No.1 album with *Brothers In Arms*.

1957 Jeff Cease – guitarist with The Black Crowes, who had a 1991 UK No.39 single with 'Hard To Handle' and a 1992 US No.1 & UK No.2 album with *The Southern Harmony And Musical Companion*.

1961 Curt Smith – vocalist and bassist with Tears For Fears, who had a 1985 US No.1 & UK No.2 single with 'Everybody Wants To Rule The World' plus over 12 other UK Top 40 singles.

1970 Glenn Medeiros, singer who had a 1988 UK No.1 single with 'Nothing's Gonna Change My Love For You' and a 1990 US No.1 single with 'She Ain't Worth It'.

ON THIS DAY

1965 John Lennon's second book of poetry and drawings, *A Spaniard In The Works*, was published.

1965 The Hollies were at No.1 on the UK singles chart with 'I'm Alive', the group's first of two UK No.1s and over 25 other Top 40 singles.

1966 The Rolling Stones kicked off their fifth North American tour at the Manning Bowl, Lynn, Massachusetts. The support acts were The McCoys and The Standells.

1967 The Monkees went to No.1 on the US album charts with *Headquarters*, the group's second chart topper.

1969 The UK Top 5 singles this week were: No.5, 'Living In The Past', Jethro Tull; No.4, 'Time Is Tight', Booker T And The MG's; No.3, 'Dizzy', Tommy Roe; No.2, 'Oh Happy Day', Edwin Hawkins Singers and No.1, 'The Ballad Of John And Yoko', The Beatles.

1972 appearing at the Guildford City Hall, England was David Bowie on his "Ziggy Stardust" world tour.

1978 appearing at Knebworth Park were Genesis, Jefferson Starship, Jeff Beck, Tom Petty And The Heartbreakers, Devo, Brand X and The Atlanta Rhythm Section. Tickets cost £6 ($10).

1988 UB40 bass player Earl Falconer was sent to prison for six months, with a further 12 suspended, after admitting to causing his brother's death in a car accident.

1989 Paul McCartney scored his seventh UK No.1 solo album with *Flowers In The Dirt*, which featured the single 'My Brave Face'.

1990 New Kids On The Block's Donnie Wahlberg fell through an unlocked trapdoor mid-concert in Saratoga Springs. He escaped with minor injuries.

SAD LOVERS & GIANTS

FRIDAY 24 JUNE
THE CASTLE
452 Finchley Rd. London NW11
(Finchley Rd. Tube)

1992 Donny Osmond started a year long run in the musical "Joseph And The Amazing Technicolor Dreamcoat" in Toronto, Canada.

2001 Blink 182 scored their second US No.1 album with *Take Off Your...*

2003 A man who had been deported from Sweden for stalking Abba singer Agnetha Faltskog was arrested near the singer's island retreat. Gert van der Graaf had been the singer's boyfriend from 1997 to 1999, but had been issued a restraining order, barring him from seeing or talking to her, in 2000.

2004 a Fender Stratocaster that Eric Clapton nicknamed "Blackie" sold at a Christie's auction for $959,500 (£564,412) in New York, making it the most expensive guitar in the world. The proceeds of the sale went towards Clapton's Crossroads addiction clinic, which he founded in 1998.

2004 Carling Live Taste of the Summer, The Barfly, Islington, North London.

BORN ON THIS DAY

1935 Eddie Floyd, soul singer who had a 1966 US No.28 & 1967 UK No.19 single with 'Knock On Wood'. He also wrote '634-5789' for Wilson Pickett.

1939 Harold Melvin, pianist and vocalist who had a 1972 US No.3 & 1974 UK No.9 single with 'If You Don't Know Me By Now'. He died on March 24th 1997.

1940 Clint Warwick – bass guitarist with The Moody Blues, who had a 1965 UK No.1 & US No.10 single with 'Go Now'. Warwick left the band in 1966. He died from liver disease on May 18th 2004.

1945 Carly Simon, singer/songwriter who had a 1973 UK No.3 and US No.1 single with 'You're So Vain' and a 1974 US No.5 single with James Taylor 'Mockingbird'.

1946 Allen Lanier – guitarist and keyboardist with Blue Oyster Cult, who had a 1976 US No.12 & 1978 UK No.16 single with 'Don't Fear The Reaper'.

1952 Tim Finn – vocalist and pianist with Split Enz, who had a 1980 UK No.12 single with 'I Got You', and Crowded House, who had a 1992 UK No.7 single with 'Weather With You'. He has also been a solo artist and member of the Finn Brothers.

1963 George Michael – singer/songwriter with Wham!, who had a 1984 UK & US No.1 single with 'Wake Me Up Before You Go Go'. His first solo No.1 single was the 1984 UK & US 'Careless Whisper'. He has had seven other UK & US No.1 singles and over ten other UK Top 40 hits.

ON THIS DAY

1964 Roy Orbison was at No.1 on the UK singles chart with 'It's Over', his second UK No.1.

1966 appearing at The Hollywood Bowl were The Beach Boys, The Byrds, Love, Captain Beefheart, The Lovin' Spoonful and Percy Sledge.

1967 40 million people saw The Beatles perform 'All You Need Is Love', live via satellite as part of the TV global link up *Our World*. Mick Jagger, Keith Richards, Eric Clapton, Graham Nash, Keith Moon and Gary Leeds provided backing vocals.

1969 The Hollies recorded 'He Ain't Heavy, He's My Brother'. Elton John played piano on the session.

1977 *The Muppet Show* album by The Muppets went to No.1 on the UK album chart.

1983 the film soundtrack to *Flashdance* started a two week run at No.1 on the US album chart.

1983 The Police scored their fourth UK No.1 album with *Synchronicity*, which was also No.1 in the US. It featured the singles 'Every Breath You Take' and 'Wrapped Around Your Finger'.

1987 songwriter Boudleaux Bryant died. He had written, with his wife Felice, The Everly Brothers' hits 'Bye Bye Love', 'All I Have To Do Is Dream', 'Wake Up Little Susie' and 'Raining In My Heart',

a hit for Buddy Holly.
Other acts to record their songs include Bob Dylan, The Beatles, Tony Bennett, Simon & Garfunkel, Sarah Vaughan, the Grateful Dead, Dolly Parton, Elvis Presley, The Beach Boys, Roy Orbison, Elvis Costello, Count Basie, Dean Martin, Ruth Brown, Cher, R.E.M. and Ray Charles.

1988 Debbie Gibson went to No.1 on the US singles chart with 'Foolish Beat', making Debbie the youngest female to write, produce and record a US No.1 single. It was a No.9 hit in the UK.

1994 five people attending this year's Glastonbury Festival were shot and injured when a lone madman pulled a gun and started shooting.

2000 Eminem went to No.1 on the UK album chart with *The Marshall Mathers LP*.

2004 appearing at this year's three day Glastonbury Festival were Wilco, Nelly Furtado, Elbow, Groove Armada, PJ Harvey, Kings of Leon, Oasis, Scissor Sisters, Starsailor, Black Eyed Peas, Paul McCartney, Joss Stone, Morrissey and Muse.

BORN ON THIS DAY

1910 Elvis Presley's manager Colonel Tom Parker. Before working in the music business he ran a troupe of dancing chickens. He died on January 21st 1997.

1940 Billy Davis Jr, singer who had a 1977 US No.1 & UK No.7 single with 'You Don't Have To Be A Star'. He was also a member of The 5th Dimension.

1942 Larry Taylor – bass player for Canned Heat, who had a 1970 UK No.2 & US No.26 single with 'Let's Work Together'.

1955 Mick Jones *(below)* – guitarist and vocalist with The Clash, who had a 1979 UK No. 11 single with 'London Calling', a 1982 US No.8 single with 'Rock The Casbah', a 1991 UK No.1 single with 'Should I Stay Or Should I Go?', first released 1982, and 15 other UK Top 40 singles. He was also part of Big Audio Dynamite, who had a 1986 UK No.11 single with 'e=mc2'.

1956 Chris Isaak, singer/songwriter and actor who had a 1990 UK No.10 & 1991 US No.6 single with 'Wicked Game'.

1961 Terri Nunn – vocalist with Berlin, who had a 1986 UK & US No.1 single with 'Take My Breath Away'.

1969 Colin Greenwood – bass player for Radiohead, who had a 1997 UK No.1 & US No.21 album with *OK Computer*.

1969 Mark Decloedt – drummer with EMF, who had a 1990 UK No.3 & 1991 US No.1 single with 'Unbelievable'.

"Come on Bonzo, you MUST be able to find the drugs, I've made it really easy for you."

ON THIS DAY

1965 The Byrds went to No.1 on the US singles chart with their version of Bob Dylan's 'Mr Tambourine Man'. Only Roger McGuinn from the band featured on the track. Drummer Hal Blaine, who played on the song, also played on Simon and Garfunkel's 'Bridge Over Troubled Water'.

1973 Keith Richards and Anita Pallenberg were arrested on drugs and gun charges *(above)*.

1974 Cher divorced Sonny Bono after ten years of marriage.

1977 Elvis Presley made his last-ever live stage appearance when he appeared at the Market Square Arena in Indianapolis.

1981 Bob Dylan played the first of five nights in London during his current European tour.

1988 Bros were at No.1 on the UK singles chart with 'I Owe You Nothing', the group's only UK No.1 single.

1993 Jamiroquai started a three week run at No.1 on the UK album chart with *Emergency On Planet Earth*.

1999 Elton John was reported to be in talks with a City finance house to secure a £25 million ($42.5 million) loan, using his back catalogue of hits as security. It had been reported that Elton had been spending £250,000 ($425,000) a week on credit cards.

2000 Britney Spears' hometown of Kentwood, Louisiana announced that a new museum, due to open early next year, would include a section including fan mail, platinum records and genuine items of the singer's clothing.

2002 Billy Joel checked out of a Connecticut hospital known for treating substance abuse.

2003 the *Sun* newspaper reported that Gareth Gates' mum had moved into his flat to curb the *Pop Idol* star's wild behaviour. Wendy Gates was said to be furious after her son had been spotted on a string of benders.

BORN ON THIS DAY

1935 Doc Pomus, US songwriter who wrote many early 60s hits with Mort Shuman including, 'Sweets For My Sweet', 'Teenager In Love' and 'Save The Last Dance For Me.' He died on February 26th 1991.

1944 Bruce Johnson – vocalist and guitarist with The Beach Boys, who had a 1966 UK & US No.1 single with 'Good Vibrations', plus over 25 other US and UK Top 40 singles.

1951 Gilson Lavis – drummer for Squeeze, who had a 1979 UK No.2 single with 'Up The Junction'.

1962 Michael Ball, singer who had a 1989 UK No.2 single with 'Love Changes Everything'.

ON THIS DAY

1885 Chichester Bell and Charles Tainter applied for a patent on their invention, the gramophone.

1964 Peter & Gordon went to No.1 on the US singles chart with the Lennon And McCartney song 'A World Without Love', which was also a No.1 in the UK. Peter Asher went on to become James Taylor and Linda Ronstadt's manager.

1967 Mick Jagger was found guilty of illegal possession of two drugs found in his jacket at a party given by Keith Richards. He was remanded overnight at Lewes jail, then bailed for £7,000 ($11,900).

1968 Elvis Presley made his famed comeback special, known as the "Burbank Sessions".

1969 appearing at Exeter University Summer Ball, England were The Moody Blues, Colosseum, Bob Kerr's Whoopee Band and Orange Bicycle.

1970 The Jackson Five started a two week run at No.1 on the US singles chart with 'The Love You Save', the group's third No.1 of the year. It made No.7 in the UK.

1970 appearing at The Bath Festival of Blues and Progressive Music were Led Zeppelin, The Byrds and Jefferson Airplane. Tickets cost £2.10s.

The many faces of The Ox.

1987 Whitney Houston became the first women in US history to enter the album chart at No.1 with *Whitney*. She also became the first woman to top the singles chart with four consecutive releases when 'I Wanna Dance With Somebody' hit No.1.

1988 The Fat Boys filed a $5 million (£2.94 million) lawsuit against The Miller Beer Company following a TV commercial featuring three overweight rappers clad in Fat Boys-style Davy Crockett hats.

1989 Tom Jones was awarded a star on the Hollywood Walk Of Fame.

1991 Carlos Santana was arrested at Houston Airport when officials found cannabis in his luggage.

1994 Aerosmith became the first major band to let fans download a full new track free from the Internet.

1996 during a free concert by The Fugees in Harlem a man started to fire shots from a gun, injuring 22 people.

1997 appearing at the three day Glastonbury Festival were Radiohead, Cast, The Bluetones, Manson, The Chemical Brothers, Ash, The Seahorses, Smashing Pumpkins, The Prodigy, Beck, Sheryl Crow, Sting, Dodgy, Travis, Ray Davies, Kula Shaker and Steve Winwood.

1998 after spending 30 weeks on the UK album chart The Corrs went to No.1 with *Talk On Corners*.

2002 on the eve of a new American tour John Entwistle (aka The Ox), bass player with The Who, died of a heart attack in his Las Vegas hotel room.

2003 rapper Mystikal pleaded guilty to charges that he forced his hairstylist to perform sex acts on him and two bodyguards. Mystikal, (real name Michael Tyler), had been charged with aggravated rape. He agreed to plead guilty and was sentenced to five years' probation.

2004 UK singer Mike Skinner scored his first UK No.1 album when The Streets' album *A Grand Don't Come For Free* went to the top of the charts.

BORN ON THIS DAY

1943 Bobby Harrison — drummer with Procol Harum, who had a 1967 UK No.1 & US No.5 single with 'A Whiter Shade Of Pale'.

1948 John Martyn, UK singer/songwriter and guitarist who had a 1973 album *Solid Air*.

1959 Clint Boon — keyboardist with Inspiral Carpets, who had a 1990 UK No.14 single with 'This Is How It Feels'. He is part of The Clint Boon Experience.

1963 Andy Couson — bass player with All About Eve, who had a 1988 UK No.10 single with 'Martha's Harbour', The Mission and The Lucy Nation.

1963 Beverley Craven, singer who had a 1991 UK No.3 single with 'Promise Me' and a 1991 UK No.3 self-titled album.

1971 Ray Slijngaard — vocalist with 2 Unlimited, who had a 1993 UK No.1 single with 'No Limit'.

ON THIS DAY

1966 The Small Faces appeared live at the Marquee Club in Wardour Street, London. Admission cost 7s 6d, ($1.05).

1969 Henry Mancini started a two week run at No.1 on the US singles chart with 'Love Theme from Romeo And Juliet'.

Left: John Martyn.

Right: A fun day out at the Bath Festival of Blues.

George Michael and Andrew Ridgeley bid farewell to their fans.

1969 appearing at the Bath Festival Of Blues were Fleetwood Mac, John Mayall, Ten Years After, Led Zeppelin, Nice, Chicken Shack, Keef Hartley, Blodwyn Pig and Taste. The DJ was John Peel and tickets cost 22s 6d.

1975 The Eagles started a five week run at No.1 on the US album chart with *One Of These Nights*.

1975 Wings went to No.1 on the UK chart with the album *Venus And Mars*, which featured the US No.1 single 'Listen What The Man Said'.

1977 Elton John achieved a life-long ambition when he became the Chairman of Watford Football Club.

1983 appearing at The Murrayfield Stadium, Edinburgh was David Bowie on the "Serious Moonlight" tour.

1985 Sister Sledge was at No.1 on the UK singles chart with 'Frankie', the sisters' only UK No.1.

BATH FESTIVAL OF BLUES
RECREATION GROUND

THIS SATURDAY
JUNE 28th
FEATURING:

FLEETWOOD MAC
JOHN MAYALL • TEN YEARS AFTER
LED ZEPPELIN • NICE

CHICKEN SHACK • JON HISEMAN'S COLOSSEUM
MICK ABRAHAMS' BLODWYN PIG • KEEF HARTLEY
GROUP THERAPY • LIVERPOOL SCENE • TASTE
SAVOY BROWN'S BLUES BAND • CHAMPION JACK DUPREE
CLOUDS • BABYLON • PRINCIPAL EDWARD'S
MAGIC THEATRE • DEEP BLUES BAND • JUST BEFORE DAWN
D.J. **JOHN PEEL**

REFRESHMENTS & HOT SNACKS WILL BE AVAILABLE ALL DAY	In case of bad weather there will be a substantial amount of undercover accommodation	IN ADVANCE All day 18/6. Eve. only 14/6 ON DAY All day 22/6. Eve. only 16/6

TICKETS OBTAINABLE FROM BATH FESTIVAL BOX OFFICE,
ABBEY CHAMBERS, ABBEY CHURCHYARD, BATH, SOMERSET

1986 Wham! were at No.1 on the UK singles chart with their fourth and final UK No.1 'The Edge Of Heaven'. Also on this day Wham! played their farewell concert in front of 80,000 fans at Wembley Stadium, London.

1993 The Manic Street Preachers played a sold-out gig at the Marquee Club, London.

1996 appearing at The Royal Albert Hall, London was Bert Bacharach. Oasis guitarist Noel Gallagher joined him on stage for a version of 'This Guy's In Love With You'.

1997 Puff Daddy and Faith Evans started a three-week run at No.1 on the UK singles chart with 'I'll Be Missing You'.

1997 Radiohead went to No.1 on the UK album chart with their third album *OK Computer*.

2004 Beastie Boys were at No.1 on the US album chart with *To The 5 Boroughs*, the rappers' fourth US No.1.

BORN ON THIS DAY

1945 Little Eva, US singer. She had been a babysitter for Carole King and Gerry Goffin, who asked her to record a song they had just written, which gave her the 1962 US No.1 & UK No.2 single 'The Loco-Motion'. She died on April 10th 2003.

1948 Derv and Lincoln Gordon (twins) — vocalist and guitarist respectively with The Equals, who had a 1968 UK No.1 & US No.32 single with 'Baby Come Back'.

1948 Ian Paice — drummer with Deep Purple, who had a 1970 UK No.2 single with 'Black Night'.

1953 Colin Hay — singer and guitarist with Men At Work, who had a 1983 UK and US No.1 single with 'Down Under'.

1964 Stedman Pearson — singer with Five Star, who had a 1986 UK No.3 single with 'System Addict' plus 14 other UK Top 40 singles.

1978 Nicole Scherzinger — singer with Eden's Crush, who had a 2001 US No.8 single with 'Get Over Yourself'.

ON THIS DAY

1961 Del Shannon was at No.1 on the UK singles chart with 'Runaway'. It was his only UK No.1 but the first of 14 UK Top 40 hits.

1967 Keith Richard was found guilty of allowing his house to be used for the illegal smoking of cannabis. He was sentenced to one year in jail and a £500 ($850) fine. Mick Jagger was also fined £100 ($170) and given three months in jail on drug charges.

1968 a free concert was held in Hyde Park, London with Pink Floyd, Jethro Tull and T. Rex.

1968 The Small Faces started a six week run at No.1 on the UK album chart with *Ogden's Nut Gone Flake*, a concept album with a round cover designed to look like a tobacco tin.

1978 Peter Frampton broke his arm and cracked several ribs when he was involved in a car crash in the Bahamas.

1979 Lowell George **(left)** of Little Feat was found dead of a heart attack in a motel in Arlington.

1985 David Bowie and Mick Jagger recorded 'Dancing In The Street' for the forthcoming "Live Aid" fund-raising event.

1985 John Lennon's 1965 Rolls-Royce Phantom V limousine, with psychedelic paintwork, sold for a record sum of $3,006,385, (£1,768,462) at a Sotheby's auction in New York.

1985 U2 played in front of 55,000 fans at Croke Park, Dublin.

1988 *The Guardian* newspaper reported that many music CDs would fade and distort over the next few years due to manufacturing faults,

JACKO'S 50ft PLUNGE AT GIG

By RICHARD SIMPSON

MICHAEL Jackson suffered severe bruising after plunging 50 feet when a bridge collapsed during a spectacular concert.

Millions of telly viewers across Europe saw him fall as he sang his Number One hit Earthsong.

The star was standing in the middle of a three-section bridge when it was raised high above the 70,000 fans in the audience.

As the gig at Munich's Olympic stadium drew to a close on Sun-

day night, the bridge's central section was lowered to its original position. But it failed to lock into place and plunged on to the stage, carrying Jacko with it.

The singer, 39, who landed on his chest, was treated in hospital for cuts, bruised ribs and legs, an injured ankle and shock.

His spokesman said: "Fortu-

nately the bridge fell straight — otherwise it would have been much more serious.

"If you can imagine a lift falling at speed, it was like that.

"Michael took quite an impact. He's got a lot of bruising."

The gig, which also starred Boyzone and All Saints, raised £1million for Nelson Mandela Children's Fund and the Red Cross.

Jacko is due to fly back to the U.S. today.

sending shock-waves through the music industry.

1988 appearing at the Moore Theatre, Seattle were Nirvana, Mudhoney and Tad.

1996 it was reported that US record company bosses were considering random drug tests for popstars similar to those carried out on athletes, to try and reduce the drug death toll in the industry.

1999 Michael Jackson suffered severe bruising after falling over 15m (50ft) when a bridge collapsed during a concert at Munich's Olympic stadium. Jacko was singing 'Earth Song' at the time of the accident.

2000 eight men were trampled to death during Pearl Jam's performance at The Roskilde festival, near Copenhagen. Police said the victims had all slipped or fallen in the mud in front of the stage.

2000 Eminem's mother went to court claiming defamation of character in a $10 million (£5.8 million) civil suit, after taking exception to the line "My mother smokes more dope than I do" from her son's single 'My Name Is'.

2003 Destiny's Child singer Beyonce started a five week run at No.1 on the UK album chart with *Dangerously In Love*, which was also a US No.1.

2004 Courtney Love was reprimanded by Los Angeles judge Melissa Jackson for turning up five hours late to a hearing. Love pleaded guilty to a single charge of disorderly conduct and was given a discharge, on condition she paid the victim's medical bills, joined a drug programme and stayed out of trouble.

BORN ON THIS DAY

1943 Florence Ballard – vocalist with The Supremes, who had a 1964 US & UK No.1 single with 'Baby Love' plus 11 other US No.1 singles. She died February 21st 1976.

1944 Glenn Shorrock – vocalist with Australian group Little River Band, who had a 1978 US No.3 single with 'Reminiscing' plus 12 other US Top 40 singles.

1951 Andy Scott – guitarist and vocalist with Sweet, who had a 1973 UK No.1 single with 'Blockbuster', plus 14 other UK Top 40 singles.

1951 Stanley Clarke, jazz bass player who has worked with Chick Corea, Santana, Keith Richards, Quincy Jones and Paul McCartney.

1983 Cheryl Tweedy – singer with Girls Aloud, who had a 2002 UK No.1 single ' with 'Sound Of The Underground'.

ON THIS DAY

1966 The Beatles played the first of three concerts at the Nippon Budokan Hall, Japan.

1973 George Harrison knocked Paul McCartney's 'My Love' from the top of the US singles chart with 'Give Me Love, Give Me Peace On Earth'. His second US No.1, it reached No.8 in the UK.

1973 Slade were at No.1 on the UK singles chart with 'Skweeze Me Pleeze Me', the group's fifth UK No.1.

1975 Cher married Greg Allman four days after divorcing Sonny Bono. They split after ten days, followed by a three-year on-and-off marriage.

1976 police raided the home of Neil Diamond searching for drugs – they found less than one ounce (28g) of marijuana.

Andy Scott in 'tough exterior' glam-pop pose.

1976 Stuart Goddard (Adam Ant), placed the following ad in the classified section of the Melody Maker, "Beat on a bass, with the B-Sides". Andy Warren answered the ad and they went on to form Adam And The Ants.

1977 Marvel Comics launched a comic book based on the rock group Kiss.

1978 United Artists released the Buzzcocks single 'Love You More'. At 1 minute 29 seconds it was the second shortest single ever released. (Maurice Williams And The Zodiacs 1960 hit 'Stay' was the shortest hit at one minute 28 seconds.)

1979 Tubeway Army started a five week run at No.1 on the UK singles chart with 'Are Friends Electric?'

1979 one hit wonder Anita Ward started a two week run at No.1 on the US singles chart with 'Ring My Bell', which was also a UK No.1.

1984 Huey Lewis & The News went to No.1 on the US album chart with *Sports*.

1989 police were called in to control over 4,000 Bobby Brown fans trying to see him at the HMV Record store in London's Oxford Street. Six fans were hospitalized and one had to be given the kiss of life.

1989 The Stone Roses played at Leeds Polytechnic. The gig almost didn't take place after a security man wouldn't let singer Ian Brown into the gig.

1990 police raided Chuck Berry's estate and seized homemade porn videos, drugs and guns.

1990 Miles Davis played the first of two nights at London's Hammersmith Odeon.

1995 Garth Brooks was given a star on Hollywood's Walk Of Fame. The country singer buried the master tapes of his *Hits* album under the star.

2001 American guitarist and producer Chet Atkins died in Nashville, aged 77. He had recorded over 100 albums during his career and been a major influence on George Harrison and Mark Knopfler.

2001 Beach Boys member Al Jardine went to court in a bid to sue his former band mates, claiming he had been frozen out of the Beach Boys. The $4 million (£2.35 million) suit was filed against Mike Love, Brian Wilson, the Carl Wilson Trust and Brother Records Incorporated in a New York Superior Court. In 1998 a US judge temporarily barred Jardine from performing under the name "Beach Boys Family And Friends" after representations from Mike Love and Brother Records. Jardine lost the case in 2003.

Chet Atkins, backdoor bluegrass.

LIGGERS' DELIGHT

The Doors, Matrix Club, San Francisco, March 1967.

Holiday Inn letterhead

LONDON CALLING
SAFE EUROPEAN HOME
GUNS OF BRIXTON (PS)
TRAIN IN VAIN
CAREER OPP
MAG 7
CAR JAMMING
BANKROBBER
KNOW YOUR RIGHTS
GARAGELAND
POLICE AND THIEVES
CLASH CITY ROCKERS
BRAND NEW CAD
SPANISH BOMBS
RADIO CLASH
CASBAH
SOMEBODY GOT MURDERED
CLAMPDOWN
ARMAGIDEON
POLICE ON MY BACK
STRAIGHT TO HELL
SHOULD I STAY
FOUGHT THE LAW

The Clash, Ashbury Park, New Jersey, May 1982.

Let's Spend the night Together
Hang onto Yourself
Ziggy Stardust
Changes
The Supermen
Five Years
The Width of A Circle
Life on Mars?
John, I'm Only Dancing
Moonage Daydream
The Jean Genie
Suffragette City
Rock 'n' Roll Suicide

David Bowie, Ziggy Stardust tour, December 1972.

Monkey Island Hotel letterhead

I FEEL FINE
SHE'S A WOMAN
IF I NEED SOMEONE (PAUL)
ACT NATURALLY (R)
NOWHERE MAN (J)
BABY'S IN BLACK (George to cover)
YESTERDAY (all)
HELP
WE CAN WORK IT OUT (Mai)
DAY TRIPPER
I'M DOWN

The Beatles, Odeon Cinema, Glasgow, 1965.

Hey Jimi
God save the...
Sgt Pepper
SPANISH CASTLE MAGIC
WATCHTOWER
Machine Gun
Lover Man
freedom
Red House
Dolly Dagger
Midnight Lightning
Foxy Lady
Message to love
Hey Baby
Ezy Rider
Hey Joe
Haze
Chile
In from the storm

Jimi Hendrix, Isle of Wight, August 1970.

BREED
DRAIN YOU
ANEURYSM
SCHOOL
SLIVER
IN BLOOM
COME AS YOU ARE
LITHIUM
ABOUT A GIRL
TOURETTES
POLLY
LOUNGE ACT
MORE THAN A FEELING
FERN SPIRIT
ON A PLAIN
NEGATIVE CREEP
BEEN A SON
ALL APOLOGIES
D LOVE
DUMB
STAY AWAY
TERRITORIAL PISSINGS
STAR SPANG.
LED DANIVER

Nirvana, Reading Festival, August 1992.

---

ibis letterhead

INDEPENDENCE DAY
BORN IN USA
BADLANDS
OUT IN THE STREEET
SEEDS
JOHNNY 99
DARKNESS
THE RIVER
WORKING ON THE HIGHWAY
TRAPPED
PROVE IT ALL NIGHT
GLORY DAYS
PROMISED LAND
MY HOMETOWN
THUNDER ROAD
COVER ME
DANCING IN THE DARK
HUNGRY HEART
CADILLAC RANCH
BECAUSE THE NIGHT
I'M ON FIRE
PINK CADILLAC
ROSALITA
CAN'T HELP FALLING IN LOVE

BORN TO RUN
BOBBY JEAN
TWO HEARTS

RAMROD
TWIST AND SHOUT

Bruce Springsteen, Wembley, London, July 1985.

SHE BELONGS TO ME
FOURTH TIME AROUND
JOHANNA
BABY BLUE
DESOLATION ROW
JUST LIKE A WOMAN
TAMBOURINE MAN
TELL ME MOMMA
I DON'T BELIEVE YOU
BABY LET ME FOLLOW YOU DOWN
TOM THUMB
LEOPARD SKIN PILL BOX HAT
ONE TOO MANY MORNINGS
THIN MAN
ROLLING STONE

Bob Dylan, Free Trade Hall, May 1966.

Gramercy Park Hotel letterhead

Led Zeppelin, Earl's Court, May 1975.

PARIS........TUES.

ZOO STATION
FLY
REAL THING
MYSTERIOUS WAYS
ONE
END OF THE WORLD
WILD HORSES
ARMS AROUND THE WORLD
ANGEL OF HARLEM
SATELLITE OF LOVE
BAD
ALL I WANT IS YOU
BULLET THE BLUE SKY
RUNNING TO STAND STILL
STREETS
PRIDE
STILL HAVEN'T FOUND
DESIRE
ULTRAVIOLET
WITH OR WITHOUT YOU
LOVE IS BLINDNESS

U2, Zoo TV tour, 1992.

BORN ON THIS DAY

1915 Willie Dixon, blues singer and guitarist who wrote classic songs including: 'You Shook Me', I Can't Quit You Baby' and 'Little Red Rooster'. He was a major influence on The Rolling Stones and Led Zeppelin. Dixon died on January 29th 1992.

1939 Delaney Bramlett – singer and guitarist with Delaney & Bonnie, who had a 1971 US No.13 single with 'Never Ending Song Of Love'. He also worked with Eric Clapton during the early 70s.

1945 Deborah Harry – singer for Blondie, who had five UK No.1 singles including the 1979 UK & US No.1 single 'Heart Of Glass' as well as a 1978 worldwide No.1 album with *Parallel Lines*.

1951 Fred Schneider – vocalist with The B-52s, who had a 1990 UK No.2 & US No.3 single with 'Love Shack'.

1963 Roddy Bottum – keyboardist with Faith No More, who had a 1993 UK No.3 and US No.4 single with 'I'm Easy'.

1971 Missy Elliott - US singer, rapper and songwriter who had a 1998 UK No.1 single with Melanie B, 'I Want You Back'. 2001 album *Miss E…So Addictive*.

ON THIS DAY

1956 Elvis Presley appeared on NBC-TV's *The Steve Allen Show* and performed 'Hound Dog'…to a live hound dog.

1962 appearing live at The Cavern Club, Liverpool were Gene Vincent and the up and coming local group The Beatles.

1969 John Lennon, Yoko Ono and family were involved in a car accident in Scotland. Both John and Yoko needed hospital treatment.

1972 Neil Diamond went to No.1 on the US singles chart with 'Song Sung Blue', his second US No.1 and a No.14 hit in the UK.

1973 appearing at Earl's Court, London were Slade and The Sensational Alex Harvey Band. Tickets cost £1–2 ($1.70–3.40). Special Slade trains were running from Brighton, Bristol, Birmingham and Manchester to take fans to the show.

1975 10cc were at No.1 on the UK singles chart with 'I'm Not In Love'.

1981 Rushton Moreve, bass player with Steppenwolf, was killed in a car crash in Los Angeles. The band had had a 1968 US No.2 and 1969 UK No.30 single with 'Born To Be Wild'.

1983 Bon Jovi signed to Phonogram's Mercury Records.

1989 Prince scored his second UK No.1 album with *Batman*.

Noddy Holder: "2 tickets to Birmingham, please."

1989 appearing at the Rock Torhout Festival, Torhout, Belgium were Lou Reed, Joe Jackson, Elvis Costello, The Robert Cray Band, Nick Cave And The Bad Seeds, Tanita Tikaram, Pixies, R.E.M. and Texas.

1995 DJ Wolfman Jack died of a heart attack. He had been the master of ceremonies for the rock 'n' roll generation of the 60s on radio, and later on television during the 70s.

1999 Guy Mitchell, US singer, died aged 72. He had had a 1957 UK & US No.1 single with 'Singing The Blues' plus over ten other UK Top 40 singles.

2001 Rolling Stone Ron Wood was commissioned to paint a group portrait of diners who were regulars at the West End London restaurant The Ivy. Elton John and Pet Shop Boy Neil Tennant were two pop stars to be included in the portrait.

2001 Usher started a four week run at No.1 on the US singles chart with 'U Remind Me'.

2002 six postage stamps designed by Sir Paul McCartney went on sale in the Isle Of Man. Proceeds from their sale went to the Adopt-A-Minefield charity.

Woody misunderstood what being a 'painter and decorator' is all about.

BORN ON THIS DAY

1940 Paul Williams – vocalist with The Temptations, who had a 1971 US No.1 & UK No.8 single with 'Just My Imagination' and the reissued 'My Girl', which was a UK No.2 in 1992. Williams died on August 17th 1973 after shooting himself.

1949 Roy Bittan – keyboardist with E Street Band, who had a 1984 US No.2 & 1985 UK No.4 single with 'Dancing In The Dark'.

1952 Johnny Colla – guitarist and saxophonist with Huey Lewis & The News, who had a 1985 US No.1 & UK No.11 single with 'The Power Of Love'.

1954 Pete Briquette – bass player and vocalist with The Boomtown Rats, who had a 1979 UK No.1 single with 'I Don't Like Mondays' plus ten other UK Top 40 singles.

1961 Paul Geary – drummer with Extreme, who had a 1991 US No.1 & UK No.2 single with 'More Than Words'.

1983 Michelle Branch, US singer/songwriter and guitarist who had a 2002 UK No.18 single with 'Everywhere', a 2002 US No.5 & UK No.16 with Santana 'The Game Of Love' and a 2003 US No.2 album with *Hotel Paper*.

ON THIS DAY

1962 Jimi Hendrix was honourably discharged from the 101st Airborne Paratroopers after breaking his ankle during his 26th and final parachute jump.

1963 UK record companies increased the price of records, making singles 6 shillings and 8d, ($0.93) and albums £1 and 12 shillings ($4.48).

1966 Frank Sinatra went to No.1 on the US singles chart with 'Strangers In The Night'. The song was taken from the film *A Man Could Get Killed* and was also a No.1 in the UK.

1967 The Beatles started a 15 week run at No.1 on the US album chart with *Sgt Pepper's Lonely Hearts Club Band*, the group's tenth US chart topper.

1969 Thunderclap Newman were at No.1 on the UK singles chart with the Pete Townshend produced 'Something In The Air'.

1973 Roxy Music's synthesizer player Brian Eno quit after personality clashes with main man Bryan Ferry.

1977 Bill Conti went to No.1 on the US singles chart with 'Gonna Fly Now' (the theme from *Rocky*).

1980 Bob Weir and Mickey Hart from the Grateful Dead were arrested on suspicion of starting a riot at the San Diego Sports Arena after they tried to interfere in a drugs bust.

1980 Sheena Easton was featured in the BBC TV series *Big Time*, recording her first single and undergoing the marketing process as a new artist.

1981 Bruce Springsteen played the first of six nights at the new Brendan Byrne Arena, New Jersey.

1982 Nicky Headon of The Clash was remanded on bail, charged with stealing a bus stop worth £30 ($51) from London's Fulham Road.

1983 Rod Stewart was at No.1 on the UK singles chart with 'Baby Jane', his sixth UK No.1.

1988 Tracy Chapman started a three-week run at No.1 on the UK album chart with her self-titled debut LP. Helped by her performance at the Nelson Mandela's 70th Birthday Tribute Concert at Wembley Stadium, the album also made No.1 in the US.

1991 Axl Rose caused a riot to break out after leaping into the crowd to remove a camera from a fan at the Riverpoint Amphitheatre, Maryland Heights. Over 50 people were injured and 15 fans were arrested.

2001 Liverpool Airport at Speke was renamed John Lennon Airport. Yoko Ono was present to unveil a new logo that included the late Beatle's famous self-portrait and the words "Above Us Only Sky", taken from his *Imagine* album.

Brian Eno predicts the entire U2 stage set some 20 years before 'Zoo TV'.

Sunday
2nd July 1967
TWO PERFORMANCES
in order of appearance

JIMMY POWELL and THE DIMENSIONS
JOHN MAYALL'S BLUESBREAKERS
THE JEFF BECK GROUP

intermission

CREAM

Resident compere: Rick Dane

BORN ON THIS DAY

1929 David Lynch — vocalist with The Platters, who had a 1959 UK & US No.1 single with 'Smoke Gets In Your Eyes'. He died of cancer on January 2nd 1981.

1940 Fontella Bass, singer and pianist who had a 1965 US No.4 and UK No.11 single with 'Rescue Me'.

1943 Judith Durham — vocalist with The Seekers, who had a 1965 UK No.1 single with 'I'll Never Find Another You'.

1957 Laura Branigan, singer who had a 1984 US No.4 & UK No.5 single with 'Self Control'. She died of a brain aneurysm on August 26th 2004.

1960 Vince Clarke — keyboardist with Depeche Mode, who had a 1981 UK No.8 single with 'Just Can't Get Enough', Yazoo, who had a 1982 UK No.2 single with 'Only You', and Erasure, who had a 1992 UK No.1 single with 'Abba-Esque EP', plus over 20 other UK Top 40 singles.

ON THIS DAY

1969 Rolling Stone Brian Jones drowned while under the influence of drugs and alcohol after taking a midnight swim in his pool, aged 27. His body was found at the bottom of the pool by his Swedish girlfriend Anna Wohlin.

1970 the three day Atlanta Pop Festival took place, featuring: The Allman Brothers Band, Jimi Hendrix, Jethro Tull, Johnny Winter, Mountain, Procol Harum and Rare Earth. Over 200,000 fans attended the festival.

1971 Jim Morrison was found dead in a bathtub in Paris. The cause of death was given as a heart attack. On the 25th anniversary of his death an estimated 15,000 fans gathered at Pere Lachaise Cemetery in Paris to pay their respects.

1973 on the last night of a 60 date tour David Bowie announced that he was about to retire from live performing, although it eventually transpired that it was "Ziggy Stardust" the stage persona retiring, not Bowie himself.

1973 Laurens Hammond, the inventor of the Hammond organ, died aged 73. The Hammond was used by many rock artists including Procol Harum, Keith Emerson, Led Zeppelin, The Allman Brothers and The Faces.

1975 the lead singer from Three Dog Night, Chuck Negron, was arrested at his Louisville hotel room on the opening night of the band's tour and charged with possession of cocaine.

1976 Beach Boy Brian Wilson played his first live show with the band in seven years when they appeared at the Anaheim Stadium, California.

1982 The Human League started a three week run at No.1 on the US singles chart with 'Don't You Want Me', which was also a UK No.1.

2002 a session violinist serenaded a High Court judge during a copyright battle worth an estimated £100,000 ($170,000). The case was over the rights to The Bluebells' version of 'Young At Heart'. Bobby Valentino won his case to be recognized as joint owner of the song.

2002 Sir Elton John *(above)* became the first person to be made an honorary doctorate from the Royal Academy Of Music.

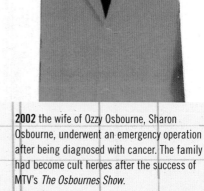

2002 the wife of Ozzy Osbourne, Sharon Osbourne, underwent an emergency operation after being diagnosed with cancer. The family had become cult heroes after the success of MTV's *The Osbournes Show*.

2002 three diners at a newly opened Britney Spears-owned restaurant suffered food poisoning. The three students, who had eaten wild striped bass at the New York restaurant, made official complaints and vowed never to eat there again.

2003 Libertines singer Pete Doherty was arrested after breaking into band member Carl Barat's flat and stealing a laptop computer and a guitar.

BORN ON THIS DAY

1938 Bill Withers, singer/songwriter who had a 1972 US No.1 single with 'Lean On Me' and a 1988 UK No.4 single with 'Lovely Day' (the song was first released in 1978).

3G RK   Friday, July 5, 2002   9

U.S. CALLERS JEER AT GEORGE ON LIVE TV

By DOMINIC MOHAN and BRIAN FLYNN

NEW YORK POST   200 YEARS   25 CENTS

POP PERV'S 9/11 SLUR

ANGRY Americans jeered and heckled George Michael yesterday as he spoke on a live talk show to defend his controversial single.

The ex-Wham! star, 39, took part in a hastily-arranged phone interview on US news channel CNN in a last-ditch bid to rescue his reputation.

George gets 'shot' down on TV.

1940 Dave Rowberry – keyboardist with The Animals, who had a 1964 UK & US No.1 single with 'House Of The Rising Sun'. He died on June 6th 2003.

1943 Alan Wilson – guitarist, harmonica player and vocalist with Canned Heat, who had a 1979 UK No.2 and US No.26 single with 'Let's Work Together'. Wilson died on September 3rd 1970.

1948 Jeremy Spencer – guitarist with Fleetwood Mac, who had a 1969 UK No.1 single with 'Albatross'. He left the band during a 1971 US tour saying he was going out to buy a newspaper. He was found two days later in LA at the Children of God "headquarters" with his hair shaved off.

1954 John Waite – singer with The Babys, who had a 1977 US No.13 & UK No.45 single with 'Isn't It Time?' As a solo artist he had a 1984 US No.1 & UK No.9 single with 'Missing You'.

Death of Barry White ends a Pavarotti duet

Maurice Chittenden

THE soul singer Barry White, who died on Friday, had been planning to record a musical duet with Luciano Pavarotti, the opera singer, as part of a comeback album.

White, who was 58, had been preparing to lay down tracks for an album of duets before he went into hospital last September after suffering kidney failure. He also had a stroke in May.

The velvet-voiced baritone had hoped to re-record one of his biggest hits, You're the First, the Last, My Everything, with the Italian tenor.

Music insiders believe the sight of the so-called "walrus of love" duetting with the colossus of opera would have provided an instant hit.

The two singers of matching physique had previously paired up for the song — with Pavarotti singing the lyrics in Italian — for a charity concert in the tenor's home town of Modena two years ago.

White has since signed to make the duets record with the Def Jam label, previously best known for hip-hop artists who have largely replaced soul music in the charts.

White intended to record a series of songs with other artists including James Brown, the self-proclaimed godfather of soul, Luther Vandross, one of White's favourite singers, and Earth, Wind & Fire, a group with whom he had planned to tour.

He died at Cedars-Sinai medical centre in Los Angeles where he had been undergo-

ing dialysis. Yesterday tributes continued to pour in for the Texas-born singer whose recordings were used by bachelors over candlelit dinners in the 1970s before beckoning their women to the bedroom. His voice has been described as sounding like a rich chocolate cake.

When he addressed the Oxford Union debating society two years ago, the father

White: planned a comeback

of eight shattered his own myth by telling students that he did not make love to anybody's music, even his own. "When I hear music, it attracts me away from what I'm doing," he said.

But his fans will have none of it. As one, calling herself only Cuzin Addie, said in a message posted on a fan website yesterday: "Never has any one music artist touched me the way he did. Every one of his songs holds a memory for me. Every one. From my first marriage to my last divorce."

ON THIS DAY

1958 The Everly Brothers held the UK No.1 position with 'All I Have To Do Is Dream'. It was the duo's first No.1 single.

1964 The Beach Boys started a two week run at No.1 on the US singles chart with 'I Get Around'. The group's first No.1. it was a No.7 hit in the UK.

1964 The Rolling Stones appeared on *Juke Box Jury*, making it the only time the show had five panellists rather than four.

1968 Elvis Presley donated a Rolls Royce to a Hollywood women's charity, which raised $35,000 (£20,600).

Soul Love Machine Barry White passed away on this day in 2003.

1969 appearing at the two day Atlanta Pop Festival were Janis Joplin, Led Zeppelin, Johnny Winter, Delaney & Bonnie, Creedence Clearwater Revival, Canned Heat, Joe Cocker, Blood, Sweat & Tears and Paul Butterfield.

1973 Slade's drummer Don Powell was badly injured in a car crash in which his girlfriend was killed.

1976 appearing live at London's Roundhouse were The Ramones, The Stranglers and The Flamin' Groovies. Tickets cost £1.60 ($2.70).

1976 The Clash made their live debut supporting the Sex Pistols at the Black Swan, Sheffield.

1982 Ozzy Osbourne married Sharon Arden, the daughter of music business manager Don Arden.

1985 Dire Straits played the first of ten consecutive nights at London's Wembley Arena.

1990 Paul Stanley from Kiss sustained neck and back injuries when he was involved in a car crash in New Jersey.

1993 the Smashing Pumpkins played an acoustic show at the strip club Raymond's Revue Bar in Soho, London.

1999 Victoria "Posh Spice" Adams married footballer David Beckham at Luttrellstown Castle, Ireland. The couple signed a deal worth £1 million ($1.7 million) for *OK* magazine to have the exclusive picture rights.

2002 George Michael took part in a live phone interview on US news channel CNN, defending his single 'Shoot The Dog'. Americans were upset by the controversial video, which showed President Bush in bed with Prime Minister Tony Blair.

2003 Barry White, soul singer and producer, died from kidney failure, aged 58.

2004 New York band Scissor Sisters went to No.1 on the UK album chart with their self-titled album.

BORN ON THIS DAY

1920 Smiley Lewis, R&B singer/songwriter who wrote 'One Night', which was covered by Elvis Presley, and 'I Hear You Knocking', which was a 1955 US No.2 for Gale Storm and a UK No.1 & US No.2 for Dave Edmunds in 1970. Lewis died on October 20th 1966.

1943 Robbie Robertson – guitarist and vocalist with The Band, who had a 1969 US No.25 single with 'Up On Cripple Creek' and a 1970 UK No.16 single with 'Rag Mama Rag'. As a solo artist he had a 1988 UK No.15 single with 'Somewhere Down The Crazy River'.

1946 Michael Monarch – guitarist with Steppenwolf, who had a 1968 US No.2 and 1969 UK No.30 single with Born To Be Wild'.

1948 Cassie Gaines, backing singer with Lynyrd Skynyrd. She was killed in a plane crash on October 20th 1977 with two other members of the band.

1950 Huey Lewis – actor and singer with Huey Lewis & The News, who had a 1985 UK No.11 & US No.1 single with 'The Power Of Love'.

1959 Marc Cohn, US singer/songwriter who had a 1991 UK No. 22 single with 'Walking In Memphis'.

1979 Shane Filan – vocalist with Westlife, who have scored 12 UK No.1 singles, their first UK being in 1999 with 'Swear It Again', plus four UK No.1 albums.

ON THIS DAY

1954 working together for the first time in a recording studio were Scotty Moore, Bill Black and Elvis Presley. Fooling around during a break they came up with an uptempo version of 'That's All Right'. Producer Sam Phillips had them repeat the jam and recorded it. It became Presley's first release on Sun Records.

1966 on the recommendation of Keith Richards' girlfriend, The Animals' Chas Chandler went to see Jimi Hendrix play at The Cafe Wha? in New York. Chandler suggested that Hendrix should go to England.

1969 The Rolling Stones gave a free concert in London's Hyde Park before an audience of 250,000, as a tribute to Brian Jones, who had died two days earlier. Mick Jagger read an extract from Percy Bysshe Shelley's 'Adonais' and released 3,500 butterflies. It was also guitarist Mick Taylor's live debut with the Stones.

1975 appearing at The Knebworth Festival were Pink Floyd, Captain Beefheart, Steve Miller and Roy Harper.

1978 pressing of the new album by The Rolling Stones, *Some Girls*, was halted at EMI's pressing plant after complaints from celebrities, including Lucille Ball, who were featured in mock advertisements on the album sleeve.

1982 Sun Records' musical director Bill Justis died, aged 56. He had the 1957 US No.2 single 'Raunchy' and also worked with Johnny Cash, Elvis Presley and Jerry Lee Lewis.

1986 Billy Ocean went to No.1 on the US singles chart with 'There'll Be Sad Songs (To Make You Cry)' which was a No.12 hit in the UK.

1986 Janet Jackson started a two week run at No.1 on the US album chart with *Control*.

1999 The Eurythmics announced their first world tour for more than ten years, stating that all profits would be given to charity. The duo made the announcement from the Greenpeace boat *Rainbow Warrior*, which was moored on the River Thames.

2002 it was reported that Dr. Dre had become the richest music star after earning £62 million ($105.4 million) in the last year – £37 million ($63 million) from his own earnings plus £25 million ($42.5 million) from his record label Aftermath.

2003 the *Daily Star* ran a front page story claiming that Manic Street Preachers guitarist Richey Edwards' body had been found. Fishermen in an angling contest discovered bones half buried in mud on the riverbank near Avonmouth. Edwards disappeared in February 1995 after his car was found at a service station at the Seven Bridge – a well-known suicide spot.

ROCK SUPERSTAR'S SKELETON FOUND

THE skeleton of Manic Street Preachers' star Richey Edwards was found last night – eight years after his mystery disappearance.
Full story: Page 7

BORN ON THIS DAY

1925 Bill Haley, singer and guitarist who had a 1955 UK & US No.1 single with 'Rock Around The Clock'. He was known as the "first rock 'n' roll star". Haley died on February 9th 1981.

1937 Gene Chandler, soul singer who had a 1962 US No.1 single with 'Duke Of Earl' and a 1979 UK No.11 single with 'Get Down.

1939 Jet Harris – guitarist with The Shadows, who had a 1963 UK No.1 single with 'Foot Tapper' plus 28 other UK Top 40 singles.

1945 Rik Elswit – guitarist with Dr. Hook, who had a 1972 US No.5 & UK No.2 single with 'Sylvia's Mother' plus nine other US Top 40 hits.

1952 David Smith – singer with The Real Thing, who had a 1976 UK No.1 single with 'You To Me Are Everything'.

1959 John Keeble – drummer with Spandau Ballet, who had a 1983 UK No.1 single with 'True' plus 16 other UK Top 40 singles.

PAN books G687

With eight pages of photographs from the film

THE BEATLES IN THEIR FIRST FAB FILM!

A HARD DAY'S NIGHT

Also starring WILFRID BRAMBELL. Produced by Walter Shenson, directed by Richard Lester. A United Artists release.

A novel by JOHN BURKE based on the original screenplay by ALUN OWEN

2/6

The star guests bid for Sir Elton's sandals

A PAIR of Sir Elton John's sandals were set to become the most expensive shoes in history when they went under the hammer last night.

Offers starting at £20,000 were invited for the Salvatore Ferragamo sandals at a charity ball held by the musician. Made from black satin, each shoe features a horse-shoe-shaped brooch by Chopard consisting of 480 diamonds and weighing five carats. The brooches can be detached and worn separately.

Organisers were optimistic the shoes would fetch more than the £29,800 paid in 1999 for a Swarovski-crystal studded pair once owned by Marilyn Monroe.

Among those thought to be interested in bidding were Elle Macpherson, Naomi Campbell Anastacia and Victoria Beckham.

At the event were actress Kate Winslet and husband Jim Threapleton, taking a night off from looking after their eight-month-old baby Mia.

They were among 480 guests invited to the £1,000-a-ticket auction at Woodside – Elton's mansion in Windsor.

The event, which is held every year, raises money for his Aids Foundation.

1969 Michael Grant – keyboard player with Musical Youth, who had a 1982 UK No.1 single with 'Pass The Dutchie'.

1976 50 Cent (a.k.a. Curtis Jackson), US rapper who had a 2003 US No.1 single with 'In Da Club'. His debut album, *Get Rich Or Die Tryin*, was named the biggest-selling US album in 2003, going platinum six times over.

ON THIS DAY

1957 John Lennon and Paul McCartney met for the first time at The Woolton Church Parish Fete where The Quarry Men were appearing. Apparently John Lennon was impressed that McCartney could tune a guitar.

1963 James Brown went to No.2 on the US album chart with *Live At The Apollo*. The album spent a total of 33 weeks on the chart.

1964 The Beatles' *A Hard Day's Night* premiered at The Pavilion, London.

1968 Woburn Music Festival, Woburn Abbey, Bedfordshire took place, featuring: Donovan, Fleetwood Mac, Pentangle, the Jimi Hendrix Experience, Alexis Korner, Family and T. Rex. The two day tickets were priced at £2 ($3.40).

1971 band leader, singer and trumpet player Louis Armstrong died. He had had a 1964 US No.1 single with 'Hello Dolly!' and a 1968 UK No.1 single with 'What A Wonderful World'.

1973 Queen released their debut single 'Keep Yourself Alive' in the UK.

1974 The Hues Corporation went to No.1 on the US singles chart with 'Rock The Boat', a No. 6 hit in the UK.

1975 Keith Richards was arrested by the highway patrol in Arkansas on charges of reckless driving and possessing an offensive weapon – an 18cm (7in) hunting knife.

1976 The Damned made their London debut supporting the Sex Pistols at the 100 Club.

1979 soul singer and producer Van McCoy died, aged 38. He had scored a US No.1 & UK No.2 single with 'The Hustle' in 1975 and produced Gladys Knight and Aretha Franklin.

1992 David Gates from Gateshead, Northumberland was given one year's probation after being convicted of stealing guitars from the back of a van belonging to The Bay City Rollers.

1996 'Three Lions' (the official song of The England Football team) by Baddiel And Skinner and The Lightning Seeds was at No.1 on the UK singles chart.

1997 The Prodigy went to No.1 on the US album chart with *The Fat Of The Land*.

2001 a pair of Sir Elton John's sandals were set to become the most expensive shoes in history when they went under the hammer for charity. Offers over £20,000 were invited for the Salvatore Ferragamo sandals to raise funds for Elton's Aid Trust.

2002 George Harrison's widow Olivia put the couple's home up for sale for £20 million ($34 million) saying she couldn't bear to live with the memories of the attack by schizophrenic Michael Abram who broke into the house in 1999.

BORN ON THIS DAY

1928 Mary Ford, singer who had a 1953 UK No.7 single with Les Paul, 'Vaya Con Dios'. Ford died from cancer on September 30th 1977.

1932 Joe Zawinul, pianist with the Miles Davis Band and Weather Report, who had a 1976 single with 'Birdland' and a 1977 album with *Heavy Weather*.

1933 J.J. Barrie, one hit wonder with 1976 UK No.1 single 'No Charge'.

1940 Richard Starkey (a.k.a. Ringo Starr) – drummer and vocalist with The Beatles. The Beatles scored 21 US No.1 & 17 UK No.1 singles. As a solo artist he had a 1974 US No.1 & UK No.4 single with 'You're Sixteen' plus nine other US Top 40 hits.

1950 David Hodo – vocalist with The Village People, who had a 1978 US No.2 & 1979 UK No.1 single with 'YMCA'.

1962 Mark White – bass player with The Spin Doctors, who had a 1993 UK No.3 & US No.7 single with 'Two Princes'.

1963 Vonda Shepard, US singer/songwriter who had a 1998 UK No.10 single with 'Searchin' My Soul', which featured in TV show *Ally McBeal*.

ON THIS DAY

1957 on his tenth UK single release, Elvis Presley scored his first UK No.1 single - 'All Shook Up'.

1962 David Rose And His Orchestra went to No.1 on the US singles chart with 'The Stripper'.

1963 The Rolling Stones made their debut on ITV's *Thank Your Lucky Stars*, performing 'Come On'.

1966 The Kinks were at No.1 on the UK chart with 'Sunny Afternoon', the group's third UK No.1.

1971 26-year-old pop star Bjorn Ulvaeus and his 21-year-old fiancée Agnetha Faltskog were married in Verum, Sweden. 3,000 fans arrived and in the chaos a police horse stepped on the bride's foot.

1973 Billy Preston started a two week run at No.1 on the US singles chart with 'Will It Go Round In Circles', his first of two US chart toppers.

1979 The Boomtown Rats made a personal appearance at the opening of the new Virgin Megastore in London.

1980 Led Zeppelin played their last-ever concert when they appeared in West Berlin at the end of a European tour. The set included 'Black Dog', 'Rock and Roll', 'Kashmir', 'Trampled Underfoot' and 'Stairway To Heaven'. They finished the show with 'Whole Lotta Love'.

1984 Bruce Springsteen went to No.1 on the US album chart with *Born In The USA*. It went on to spend a total of 139 weeks on the chart.

1984 Prince started a five week run at No.1 on the US singles chart with 'When Doves Cry', his first US No.1. It went on to sell over two million copies, and made No.4 in the UK.

1989 it was announced that for the first time compact discs were outselling vinyl albums.

1990 The Rolling Stones played the last of three sold-out nights at Wembley Stadium, London as part of the band's "Urban Jungle" tour.

1999 it was reported that to attract young people to their mobile vans UK ice cream sellers would start to play pop hits as music instead of the traditional chimes. Spice Girls and Oasis hits would be the first to be played.

2000 Bobby Brown was released from jail. The singer was released early from the North Broward Detention Centre after receiving a ten day reprieve for good behaviour.

2000 Eminem's wife, Kymberly Mathers, was hospitalized after she slit her wrists. She had become upset after seeing her husband's live show, in which he used a naked doll called Kim.

2001 appearing at this year's T In The Park festival, Scotland were Stereophonics, David Gray, The Dandy Warhols, The Proclaimers, Paul Weller, Texas, Coldplay, Beck, Toploader, Ash, Starsailor, Nelly Furtado, James and Muse. Weekend tickets cost £64 ($108.80).

2001 Corr's member Sharon Corr married barrister Gavin Bonner at St John's Church, Cratloe, Co. Clare.

2001 appearing at South Park, Oxford, England were Radiohead and Beck.

2003 it was reported that Britney Spears had made $500,000 (£294,118) profit after selling her five bedroom home in Los Angeles. The singer had paid $1.8 million for the house two years previously and sold it for $2.3 million.

BORN ON THIS DAY

1944 Jai Johnny Johanson – drummer with The Allman Brothers Band, who had a 1973 US No.12 single with 'Ramblin Man'.

1955 Russell Christian – vocalist with The Christians, who had a 1988 UK No.8 single with 'Harvest For The World'.

1960 Andy Fletcher – bass player and synth player for Depeche Mode, who had a 1984 UK No.4 single with 'People Are People' plus over 25 other UK Top 40 singles.

1963 Joan Osborne, singer/songwriter who had a 1996 UK No.6 single with 'One Of Us'.

1970 Beck David Campbell, a.k.a. Beck, singer/songwriter who had a 1994 UK No.15 single with 'Loser' and the 1996 album *Odelay*, which spent 51 weeks on the UK charts.

ON THIS DAY

1967 *Melody Maker* ran a front page comment condemning a three month jail sentence given to Mick Jagger for possession of Benzedrine tablets.

1967 The Monkees began a 29 date tour, with the Jimi Hendrix Experience as support act. Hendrix was dropped after eight shows, being told his act was not suitable for their teenybopper audience.

1969 Marianne Faithfull collapsed on the set of *Ned Kelly*

TLC, chasing waterfalls.

after taking a drug overdose. She was admitted to a Sydney hospital. She was later dropped from the movie.

1970 The Everly Brothers Show started an eleven week prime time slot on ABC-TV in the US.

1971 a minor riot occurred during a Mott The Hoople gig at the Royal Albert Hall, London. Some fans were injured and two boxes were damaged, causing a temporary ban on rock gigs. The group paid £1,467 ($2,494) for damages to property.

1972 Bill Withers started a three week run at No.1 on the US singles chart with 'Lean On Me', his only No.1 hit. It made No.18 in the UK.

1972 Donny Osmond was at No.1 on the UK singles chart with his version of the Paul Anka song 'Puppy Love'. It was the first of three solo No.1s for Donny.

1978 Gerry Rafferty's album *City To City* went to

Nigel Martin-Smith and the death of pop.

No.1 on the US chart knocking off *Saturday Night Fever*, which had been at the top of the charts for almost six months.

1978 Joe Strummer and Paul Simonon from The Clash were arrested for being drunk and disorderly after a gig at the Apollo in Glasgow. Both were fined.

1979 the B-52s made their UK live debut at London's Lyceum Ballroom, supported by The Tourists.

1989 The Fine Young Cannibals scored their second US No.1 with 'Good Thing'.

1995 TLC started a seven week run at No.1 on the US singles chart with 'Waterfalls', the group's second US No.1 and a No.4 hit in the UK.

1999 Take That's ex-manager Nigel Martin Smith started a new business, as an undertaker. It was reported that he was unhappy with a service he had used so he decided to buy a local funeral firm in Manchester.

2001 Alicia Keys went to No.1 on the US chart with her debut album *Songs In A Minor*.

2002 Michael Jackson spoke out against the music industry's treatment of artists, alleging that the business was rife with racism. Speaking at a civil rights meeting in New York, Jackson claimed there was a "conspiracy" among record companies, especially towards black artists. A spokesman for Jackson's record label said the remarks were "ludicrous, spiteful and hurtful".

BORN ON THIS DAY

1946 Bon Scott – vocalist with AC/DC, who had a 1980 UK No.36 single with 'Whole Lotta Rosie' and a 1980 UK No.1 & US No.14 album with *Back in Black*, which sold over ten million copies. Scott died on February 20th 1980. He was found dead in the backseat of a friend's car. The coroner's report stated he had "drunk himself to death".

1959 Jim Kerr – vocalist with Simple Minds, who had a 1985 US No.1 single with 'Don't You, Forget About Me', a 1989 UK No.1 single with 'Belfast Child' plus over 20 other UK Top 40 singles.

1959 Marc Almond – singer with Soft Cell, who had a 1981 UK No.1 single with 'Tainted Love'. As a solo artist he had a 1989 UK No.1 single with Gene Pitney 'Something's Gotten Hold Of My Heart'.

1965 Courtney Love – guitarist and vocalist with Babes In Toyland and Hole, who had a 1995 UK No.16 single with 'Doll Parts'. She is also a solo artist. She married Kurt Cobain from Nirvana on February 24th 1992.

1975 Jack White (a.k.a. John Gillis) – guitarist and vocalist with The White Stripes, who had a 2003 UK No.1 album with *Elephant*.

ON THIS DAY

1955 Bill Haley And His Comets went to No.1 on the US singles chart with '(We're Gonna) Rock Around The Clock'. The song stayed at No.1 for eight weeks and became one of the biggest-selling singles of all time.

1966 Rod Allen, bass player with The Fortunes, was taken to hospital after being injured when fans pulled him from the stage during a gig at The Starlight Rooms in Lincoln.

1972 Paul McCartney and Wings kicked off a 26

Simple Minds.

date tour appearing at the French town Chateauvillon. The band travelled on a double-decker London bus with psychedelic interior.

1974 Crosby, Stills, Nash & Young kicked off a reunion tour in Seattle in front of 15,000 fans.

1977 Elvis Costello quit his day job at Elizabeth Arden Cosmetics to become a full-time musician.

1983 The Police started an eight week run at No.1 on the US singles chart with 'Every Breath You Take', which was also No.1 in the UK.

1983 Wham! went to No.1 on the UK album chart with their debut release *Fantastic!*, which went on to spend 116 weeks on the chart.

1989 New Edition's production manager was charged with criminal homicide after allegedly shooting the support acts security man after they had run over their stage time.

1999 a statement was issued by Jerry Hall's lawyers saying that she had formally agreed to separate from husband Mick Jagger after more than 20 years of marriage.

1999 Elton John had a pacemaker fitted in an operation at a London hospital following reports about his ill health. Sir Elton was forced to cancel a series of concerts.

2002 The Charlatans played their Carling Homecoming gig at the Debating Hall, Manchester.

2004 David Bowie was forced to cancel a string of European shows after emergency heart surgery.

Jerry Hall painted by Paul Benney.

BORN ON THIS DAY

1944 John "Beaky" Dymond – guitarist with Dave Dee, Dozy, Beaky, Mick And Tich, who had a 1968 UK No.1 single with 'Legend Of Xanadu'.

1947 Arlo Guthrie, singer/songwriter who had a 1967 album with *Alice's Restaurant* and a 1972 US No.18 single with 'The City Of New Orleans'. He is the son of folk singer Woody Guthrie.

1949 Dave Smalley – bass player with The Young Rascals, who had a 1967 US No.1 and UK No.8 single with 'Groovin', and The Raspberries, who had a 1972 US No.5 single with 'Go All The Way'.

1954 Neil Tennant – vocalist with Pet Shop Boys, who had a 1986 UK & US No.1 single with 'West End Girls' plus three other UK No.1 singles and over 20 UK Top 40 hits. He was once the editor of music paper *Smash Hits*.

1970 Jason Orange – vocalist with Take That, who had a 1995 UK No.1 single with 'Back For Good' plus seven other UK No.1 singles.

1980 Jessica Simpson, singer who had a 2000 UK No.7 single with 'I Wanna Love You Forever'. She featured on MTV's *Newlyweds* show with her husband, ex-98° member Nick Lachey.

ON THIS DAY

1954 Sam Phillips took an acetate recording of Elvis Presley singing 'That's All Right' to Memphis radio station WHBQ DJ Dewey Phillips. He played the song just after 9.30pm and the phone lines lit up asking the DJ to play the song again.

1961 Bobby Lewis started a seven week run at No.1 on the US singles chart with 'Tossin' and Turnin', which made it the longest-running No.1 single of 61.

1964 200,000 Liverpudlians took to the streets to celebrate The Beatles' return to Liverpool for the northern premiere of *A Hard Day's Night*.

1965 The Rolling Stones started a four week run at No.1 on the US singles chart with '(I Can't Get No) Satisfaction', the group's first US No.1.

Elton and the original Blue!

1968 Eric Clapton announced that Cream would break up after their current tour. They re-formed in 2005.

1968 The Nice were banned from appearing at London's Royal Albert Hall after burning an American flag on stage.

1969 the funeral of Rolling Stone Brian Jones took place at Hatherley Road Parish Church, Cheltenham. Canon Hugh Evan Hopkins read Jones' own epitaph, "Please don't judge me too harshly".

1974 David Bowie played the first of five dates at The Tower Theatre in Philadelphia. The recordings of the gigs made up the *David Live* album, which was released later that year.

1979 Chuck Berry was sentenced to five months in jail after being found guilty of tax evasion.

1980 Bob Marley And The Wailers began what would be Marley's last-ever UK tour when they appeared in Dublin, Ireland.

1989 David F. Pearsall, aged 18, from New Jersey, was charged with theft after stealing a guitar at a concert in Riverfront Park belonging to Richie Sambora of Bon Jovi.

2002 UK boy band Blue were taken to court by a group who said they had the name first. The band had been issued with a writ by Scottish group Blue, who had a UK No.18 hit in 1977. The band collaborated with Elton John on his hit 'Sorry Seem To Be The Hardest Word' in 2004.

Beaky

Real name: John Dymond.
Born: Amesbury, July 10, 1944.
Hair: Brown. Eyes: Blue.
Height: 5 ft. 11 in.
Weight: 10 st.

It happened four years ago! Dave Dee, Dozy, Beaky, Mick and Tich invaded the British pop charts. They took Britain by storm – and, overnight, they left the tag of a small-time group to become one of Britain's best-loved groups.

BORN ON THIS DAY

1951 Bonnie Pointer – singer with The Pointer Sisters, who had a 1984 UK No.2 & US No.5 single with 'Automatic'.

1954 Benny DeFranco – guitarist with The DeFranco Family, who had a 1973 US No.3 single with 'Heartbeat – It's A Lovebeat', which was the biggest-selling US single of 1973. Modelled on The Osmonds, the group featured ten-year-old singer Tony DeFranco.

1959 Richie Sambora – guitarist with Bon Jovi, who had a 1987 US No.1 & UK No.4 single with 'Livin' On A Prayer'.

1959 Susanne Vega, singer/songwriter who had a 1990 UK No.2 single 'Tom's Diner', with DNA.

1966 Mel – singer and one half of duo Mel & Kim, who had a 1987 UK No.1 single with 'Respectable'.

1975 Lil' Kim (Kimberly Jones), US singer who had a 1997 UK No.11 single with 'Not Tonight' and a 2001 US & UK No.1 single with Christina Aguilera, Mya and Pink – 'Lady Marmalade'.

ON THIS DAY

1969 Space Oddity by David Bowie *(right)* was released in the UK for the first time.

1970 the soundtrack album Woodstock started a four week run at No.1 on the US album chart.

1970 Three Dog Night started a two-week run at No.1 in the US with their version of the Randy Newman song 'Mamma Told Me Not To Come'. It was a No.3 hit in the UK.

1977 the opening night of The Vortex Club, Wardour Street, London saw Siouxsie, Adam And The Ants, The Slits and Sham 69 playing.

1981 The Specials had their second and final UK No.1 single with 'Ghost Town'.

1987 Heart started a three week run at No.1 on the US singles chart with 'Alone', which was a No.3 hit in the UK.

1992 a range of eight ties designed by Jerry Garcia *(right)* of The Grateful Dead went on sale in the US. President Bill Clinton bought a set, and the collection grossed $10 million (£5.88 million) in the US by the end of the year.

1993 appearing at Finsbury Park, London were Neil Young with Booker T And The MG's, Pearl Jam and James. Tickets cost £22.50 ($38.25).

1996 Jonathan Melvoin from the Smashing Pumpkins died from a drug overdose, aged 34.

1998 Billie went to No.1 on the UK singles chart with 'Because We Want To'. The 15-year-old made chart history by becoming the second-youngest female to score a No.1; Helen Shapiro was the youngest at 14 with the 1961 No.1 single 'You Don't Know'.

1999 Ricky Martin started a three week run at No.1 on the UK singles chart with 'Livin' La Vida Loca'.

2002 the funeral of The Who's bass player John Entwistle took place at a church in The Cotswolds. More than 200 mourners filed into the 12th-century church of St Edward in Stow-on-the-Wold.

2004 UK band McFly went to No.1 on the UK album chart with *Room On The 3rd Floor*.

DAVID BOWIE PLAYS *Stylophone* ON 'SPACE ODDITY'

'PLAY ALONG WITH THE GROUPS'

The greatest CRAZE since the YO-YO . . . the fantastic STYLOPHONE used by DAVID BOWIE in 'SPACE ODDITY' has created this new and wonderfully exciting craze. This is how it works.

The STYLOPHONE is a pocket electronic organ with a completely new concept in sound . . . it's so easy, a baby could learn to play it in fifteen minutes. All you do is put on your favourite record and play along with the group of your choice. The exciting sounds you make together will be unbelievable. Go along NOW to your local music or record shop and try one out. Take home a STYLOPHONE today and play with the groups TONIGHT.

IT'S ALL HAPPENING, THE CRAZE HAS BEGUN, EVERYBODY'S PLAYING THE STYLO-PHONE

If you have any difficulty in obtaining a STYLOPHONE — rush to the nearest phone and complain to:—
Dubreq Studios
276/281 Cricklewood
Broadway, N.W.2
Tel.: 01-452-0047/9456

BORN ON THIS DAY

1943 Christine McVie — keyboardist and vocalist with Chicken Shack then Fleetwood Mac, who had a 1987 UK No.5 single with 'Little Lies' and a 1977 US No.1 single with 'Dreams', taken from the worldwide No.1 album *Rumours*.

1949 John Wetton — bass player and vocalist with King Crimson, U.K. Uriah Heep, Roxy Music then Asia, who had a 1982 US No.4 & UK No.46 single with 'Heat Of The Moment'.

1950 Eric Carr — drummer with Kiss, who had a 1974 US No.5 single 'On And On'. Their 1976 US No.11 album *Rock and Roll Over* spent 26 weeks on the chart. They also had a 1987 UK No.4 single with 'Crazy Crazy Nights'. Carr died November 24th 1991.

1952 Liz Mitchell — singer with Boney M, who had a 1978 UK No.1 & US No.30 single with 'Rivers Of Babylon'.

1962 Dan Murphy — guitarist with Soul Asylum, who had a 1993 US No.5 and UK No.7 single with 'Runaway Train'.

1977 Dominic Howard, drummer with Muse, who had a 2003 UK No.1 album with *Absolution* and a 2003 UK No.8 single with 'Time Is Running Out'.

ON THIS DAY

1954 19-year-old Elvis Presley signed a contract with Sun Records. He also gave in his notice at his day job at The Crown Electric Company.

1962 Ray Charles was at No.1 on the UK singles chart with 'I Can't Stop Loving You'.

1962 The Rolling Stones made their live debut at the Marquee Jazz Club, London with Dick Taylor on bass and Mick Avory on drums. The band were billed as Mick Jagger And The Rolling Stones and were paid £20 ($34) for the gig.

1968 Monkee Mickey Dolenz married Samantha Juste, who he'd met when working in the UK on the BBC TV show *Top Of The Pops*.

ONE NIGHT ONLY
THE TOURISTS
THURSDAY 12th JULY at 9.30
Tickets £3

1969 one-hit wonders Zager And Evans started a six week run at No.1 in the US with 'In The Year 2525 (Exordium And Terminus)'. The song was also a No.1 in the UK.

1979 US singer/songwriter Minnie Riperton died of cancer, aged 31. The Stevie Wonder- produced 'Loving You' gave Minnie a US No.1 single in 1975.

1980 appearing at The Moonlight, West Hampstead, London was U2. Tickets cost £1.50 ($2.50).

1980 Olivia Newton-John and the Electric Light Orchestra had the UK No.1 single with 'Xanadu', which was taken from the film of the same name. It gave Olivia Newton-John her third UK No.1 single.

1983 ex-Traffic member Chris Wood died of liver failure.

1986 Boy George, his friend Marilyn and several others were arrested in London for possession of drugs.

1986 Simply Red scored their first US No.1 single with 'Holding Back The Years', which was a No.2 hit in the UK.

1988 Michael Jackson arrived in the UK for his first-ever solo appearances. He performed a total of eight nights to 794,000 people, grossing just under £13 million ($22 million).

1996 Smashing Pumpkins drummer Jimmy Chamberlain was charged with drug possession after the death of the band's keyboard player Jonathan Melvoin in his New York hotel room.

1999 Limp Bizkit were at No.1 on the US album chart with *Significant Other*, the band's first US No.1.

2003 appearing at this year's two-day T In The Park festival, Scotland were R.E.M., The White Stripes, Idlewind, The Cardigans, The Proclaimers, The Music, The Charlatans, Coldplay, Supergrass, The Darkness, Turin Brakes, The Coral and Feeder.

The multi talented Chris Wood outside Island Records.

BORN ON THIS DAY

1942 Roger McGuinn – guitarist and vocalist with The Byrds, who had a 1965 US & UK No.1 single with 'Mr. Tambourine Man'. Roger was the only member of The Byrds to play on the hit – the other musicians were session players.

1942 Stephen Jo Bladd – drummer with The J. Geils Band, who had a 1982 US No.1 & UK No.3 single with 'Centerfold'.

1961 Lawrence Donegan – bass player with Lloyd Cole And The Commotions, who had a 1985 UK No.19 single with 'Brand New Friend'.

ON THIS DAY

1963 The Rolling Stones played their first-ever gig outside London when they appeared at The Alcove Club, Middlesborough, Yorkshire. They were supporting The Hollies.

1964 The Animals went to No.1 on the UK singles chart with 'House Of The Rising Sun'. This was the first No.1 to have a playing time of more than four minutes.

1965 Paul McCartney was presented with five Ivor Novello Awards at a lunch party at The Savoy, London. John Lennon refused to attend and Paul was 40 minutes late because he'd forgotten about the engagement.

1969 over 100 US radio stations banned The Beatles' new single 'The Balled Of John And Yoko' due to the line 'Christ, you know it ain't easy', calling it offensive.

1974 Elton John started a two-week run at No.1 on the UK album chart with *Caribou*, his third No.1 album and also a No.1 in the US.

1974 George McCrae started a two week run at

No.1 on the US singles chart with 'Rock Your Baby', his only US No.1 and a No.1 in the UK.

1976 the first issue of UK punk fanzine *Sniffin' Glue* was published, with features on The Stranglers, Ramones and Blue Oyster Cult. It was edited by former bank clerk Mark Perry.

1985 at 12.01 Status Quo started the "Live Aid" extravaganza, which was held between Wembley Stadium, London and The JFK Stadium, Philadelphia. The cream of the world's biggest rock stars took part in the worldwide event, raising over £40 million ($68 million). TV pictures were beamed to over 1.5 billion people in 160 countries, making it the biggest broadcast ever known.

1985 Duran Duran became the first artists to have a No.1 on the US singles chart with a James Bond theme when 'A View To A Kill' went to the top of the charts.

1985 Elton John resigned with MCA Records in America. His five album deal was worth $8 million (£4.7 million), making it the biggest advance in history at the time.

1985 Tears For Fears went to No.1 on the US album chart with *Songs From The Big Chair*.

1990 Curtis Mayfield was badly injured after a strong gust of wind blew a lighting rig on him during an outside concert in Brooklyn, New York.

1991 Bryan Adams went to No.1 on the UK singles chart with 'Everything I Do I Do It For You', taken from the film *Robin Hood Prince Of Thieves*. It stayed at No.1 for a record-breaking 16 weeks, and was also No.1 in the US and 16 other countries.

1991 The Everly Brothers Foundation

bought 32.4 hectares (80 acres) of land in the brothers' home town, with plans to build a theme park and museum in honour of the duo.

Simon and Garfunkle rip off an old Tears For Fears sleeve (see 28th August.)

1996 over 2,000 guitar players set a new world record for the largest "jam" ever when they all played 'Heartbreak Hotel' for 75 minutes.

1997 Red Hot Chili Peppers singer Anthony Kiedis underwent five hours of hospital surgery after being involved in a motorbike accident.

1997 The Spice Girls went to No.1 on the US album chart with *Spice*.

2002 Fatboy Slim brought the Brighton area to a standstill when he threw a free beach party. Organizers had expected 60,000 fans to attend but over 250,000 turned up, causing chaos on the roads with traffic jams over 16km (10 miles) long. Fatboy Slim spent £100,000 ($170,000) of his own money supporting the event after a sponsor pulled out.

2004 Arthur "Killer" Kane, bassist for the New York Dolls, died in Los Angeles due to complications from leukaemia. Kane, 55, was a founding member of the legendary 1970s band.

Invite one F. B. Slim and you can't get a place on the beach anywhere.

BORN ON THIS DAY

1912 Woody Guthrie, US folk singer. He was a major influence on Bob Dylan and American folk music – the 70s film *Bound For Glory* is based on his life. He died on October 3rd 1967.

1966 Ellen Reid – keyboardist for Crash Test Dummies, who had a 1994 UK No.2 & US No.4 single with 'Mmm Mmm Mmm Mmm'.

1971 Nick McCabe – guitarist with The Verve, who had a 1997 UK No.1 single with 'The Drugs Don't Work'.

1975 Taboo – MC with the Black Eyed Peas, (2003 UK No.1 single 'Where Is The Love').

1978 Ruben Studdard, singer and winner of the second series of *American Idol* who had a 2003 US No.2 single with 'Flying Without Wings'.

ON THIS DAY

1962 The Beatles played their first gig in Wales when they appeared at The Regent Dansette in Rhyl. Tickets cost five shillings, ($0.70).

1964 The Rolling Stones were at No.1 on the UK singles chart with 'It's All Over Now', the band's first UK No.1.

1967 The Who began their first US tour as support band to Herman's Hermits.

1971 appearing at the UK Lincoln Folk Festival were The Byrds, James Taylor, Steeleye Span, Tom Paxton and The Incredible String Band. Tickets cost £2.00 ($3.40).

1973 Clarence White of The Byrds was killed by a drunk driver while he was loading equipment after a gig in Palmdale, California.

1973 during a concert at the John Wayne Theater in Hollywood, California, Phil Everly smashed his guitar and stormed off stage. Don finished the set by himself and announced that The Everly Brothers had split.

1977 appearing at The Garden, Penzance, Cornwall were Elvis Costello *(left)* And The Attractions. They were making their live debut supporting Wayne County.

1979 Donna Summer scored her third No.1 US single when 'Bad Girls' hit the top. The album of the same name also started a five week run at No.1.

KENNEDY STREET ENTERPRISES & HARVEY GOLDSMITH ENTERTAINMENTS
In Association With Piccadilly Radio

Present

DAVID BOWIE

PLUS SPECIAL GUESTS
AT
MANCHESTER CITY FOOTBALL GROUND
MAINE ROAD, MANCHESTER
ON TUESDAY, 14th JULY 1987

Gates open 3.00 p.m.
Show commences 5.00 p.m.   Show finishes 10.00 p.m.

ADMIT THROUGH TURNSTILES 29 – 54

TICKET £15.00
Subject to Booking Fee

Nº 06865

Secretary

To be retained. (See plan and conditions on back)

1980 Allen Klein, ex-manager of The Beatles and The Rolling Stones, began serving a two month prison sentence for falsifying tax returns.

1982 Pink Floyd's The Wall had its movie premiere in London.

1986 Madonna was at No.1 on the UK singles chart with her second No.1 'Papa Don't Preach'. Madonna also had the UK No.1 album with *True Blue*.

1989 at The Peach Festival, South Carolina, 432 guitarists broke the world record for the most guitar players appearing in unison for the longest period of time, when they performed 'Louie Louie' for 30 minutes.

1997 Walkers Spice Girls Crisps went on sale in the UK. Over 16 million bags were sold by the end of the year.

2000 Five became the latest pop idols to call for the legalization of cannabis. J and Richie told *Sky* magazine that the drug should no longer be outlawed, "No one who smokes a spliff goes out and starts fights like someone who's been drinking".

2003 plans for Sting to write an official anthem for Tuscany came under fire by locals, who insisted the job should go to an Italian and not a foreigner. The British pop star owned a house in Tuscany and had been nominated to compose the anthem by Franco Banchi, who lived nearby.

BORN ON THIS DAY

1946 Linda Ronstadt, US singer/songwriter who had a 1975 US No.1 single with 'You're No Good', a 1989 UK No.2 single with Aaron Neville, 'Don't Know Much' plus over 15 other US Top 40 hits.

1948 Artimus Pyle – drummer with Lynyrd Skynyrd, who had a 1974 US No.8 single with 'Sweet Home Alabama' and a 1982 UK No.21 single with 'Freebird'.

1949 Trevor Horn – vocalist and producer with Buggles, who had a 1979 UK No.1 single with 'Video Killed The Radio Star', and Yes (1980–81). He also produced three UK No.1s for Frankie Goes To Hollywood – 'Relax', 'Two Tribes', & 'The Power Of Love'.

1952 Johnny Thunders (a.k.a. John Genzale) – guitarist and vocalist for The New York Dolls, who had a 1973 album with *New York Dolls*. He died of a drug overdose on April 23rd 1991.

1953 Alicia Bridges, US singer who had a 1978 US No.5 & UK No.32 single with 'I Love The Night Life'.

1956 Ian Curtis – vocalist with Joy Division, who had a 1980 UK No.13 single with 'Love Will Tear Us Apart'. Curtis committed suicide on May 18th 1980 by hanging himself.

ON THIS DAY

1956 The Teenagers featuring Frankie Lymon were at No.1 on the UK singles chart with 'Why Do Fools Fall In Love'. The song was a No.6 hit in the US.

New York Dolls decide on the new 'Darkness' image for their second album.

1958 John Lennon's mother Julia was killed when she was knocked down by a car driven by an off-duty policeman.

1965 this week's US Top 3 singles were: No.3 The Byrds, 'Mr. Tambourine Man'; No.2 The Four Tops, 'I Can't Help Myself' and at No.1 The Rolling Stones with '(I Can't Get No) Satisfaction'.

1972 Elton John started a five week run at No.1 on the US album chart with *Honky Chateau*, his first US chart topper.

1973 appearing at The Great Western Express festival at White City, London were The Edgar Winter Group, Sly & The Family Stone, Canned Heat, Lindisfarne and The Kinks. Ray Davies of The Kinks announced from the stage that he was sick of the whole thing and was retiring. He then walked into the local hospital and collapsed.

1978 appearing at Blackbushe Aerodrome, Surrey was Bob Dylan with special guests Eric Clapton, Joan Armatrading and Graham Parker.

1985 nude photos of Madonna taken in 1977 appeared in this month's *Playboy* and *Penthouse* magazines.

1989 Simply Red scored their second US No.1 single with 'If You Don't Know Me By Now', which had been a 1973 UK hit for Harold Melvin And The Blue Notes.

1998 Aerosmith were forced to cancel a forthcoming US tour after Joey Kramer was involved in a freak accident. The drummer's car set on fire and was completely destroyed as he was filling up with petrol. Kramer was admitted to hospital with second degree burns.

2000 Happy Mondays singer Shaun Ryder was reprimanded by a Manchester judge after he turned up a day late in court to give evidence. Ryder told the court he had been on a bender. A man was cleared of dangerous driving and assaulting Ryder.

2004 appearing at the Carling Live Sessions at the Barfly, Islington, North London, Razorlight

CARLINGLIVE.COM

BORN ON THIS DAY

1940 Tony Jackson — bass guitarist and vocalist with The Searchers, who had a 1964 UK No.1 & US No.13 single with 'Needles And Pins'. Jackson died on August 18th 2003.

1941 Desmond Dekker, singer who had a 1969 UK No.1 & US No.9 single with 'Israelites'.

1947 Thomas Boggs — drummer with The Box Tops, who had a 1967 US No.1 & UK No.5 single with 'The Letter'.

1952 Stewart Copeland of Curved Air, who had a 1971 UK No.4 single with 'Back Street Luv', and Police, who had a 1983 UK & US No.1 single with 'Every Breath You Take' plus four other UK No.1 singles.

ON THIS DAY

1966 Tommy James & The Shondells started a two week run at No.1 on the US singles chart with 'Hanky Panky', a song first recorded by The Raindrops. It made No.38 in the UK.

1972 Smokey Robinson made his last appearance with The Miracles at a concert in Washington D.C.

1977 Barry Manilow went to No.1 on the US album chart with *Barry Manilow Live*, the singer's only US chart topper.

1977 Shaun Cassidy went to No.1 on the US singles chart with 'Da Doo Ron Ron', his only US No.1. Shaun is the half brother of David Cassidy.

1981 US singer/songwriter Harry Chapin was killed when a tractor-trailer crashed into the car he was driving.

1986 Dolly Parton's theme park Dollywood opened in Tennessee.

Robbie Williams entertains a guest!

1988 Steve Cayter, a road crew technician with Def Leppard, died of a brain haemorrhage on stage before an American show at the Alpine Valley Music Theater.

1993 this was the first of the three day Phoenix festival featuring Sonic Youth, Faith No More, The Black Crowes, Julian Cope, Pop Will Eat Itself, Radiohead, Living Colour, Manic Street Preachers and Pulp. Tickets cost £49 ($83).

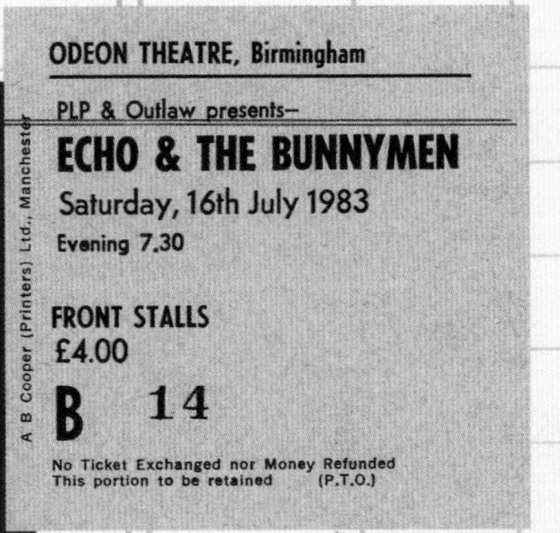

ODEON THEATRE, Birmingham

PLP & Outlaw presents—

ECHO & THE BUNNYMEN

Saturday, 16th July 1983

Evening 7.30

FRONT STALLS
£4.00

B   14

No Ticket Exchanged nor Money Refunded
This portion to be retained   (P.T.O.)

A B Cooper (Printers) Ltd., Manchester

1994 the film soundtrack to *The Lion King* started a nine week run at No.1 on the US album chart.

1995 Osmonds member Wayne Osmond underwent a brain tumour operation at Duke University Medical Center, North Carolina.

1996 John Panozzo, drummer with Styx, died from cirrhosis of the liver, aged 48.

2000 Coldplay went to No.1 on the UK album chart with their debut release *Parachutes*.

2000 Matchbox 20 went to No.1 on the US singles chart with 'Bent'.

2000 The Corrs presented a petition to the European Commission demanding legislation to end piracy on the Internet. The Manic Street Preachers and The Spice Girls also added their names to the petition.

2001 Robbie Williams started a two week run at No.1 on the UK singles chart with 'Eternity/The Road To Mandalay'.

BORN ON THIS DAY

1941 Spencer Davis, guitarist who had a 1966 UK No.1 single with 'Keep On Running' and a 1967 US No.7 single with 'Gimme Some Lovin'.

1949 Geezer Butler – bass player with Black Sabbath, who had a 1970 UK No.4 single with 'Paranoid'.

1949 Mick Tucker – drummer with Sweet, who had a 1973 UK No.1 single with 'Blockbuster' plus 14 other UK Top 40 singles. He died of leukaemia on February 14th 2002.

1949 Mike Vale – bass guitarist with Tommy James & The Shondells, who had a 1966 US No.1 single with 'Hanky Panky' and a 1968 UK No.1 single with 'Mony Mony'.

1952 Chet McCracken – drummer for The Doobie Brothers, who had a 1979 US No.1 single with 'What A Fool Believes' and a 1993 UK No.7 single with 'Long Train Runnin'.

1971 Jarrett Cordes, DJ Minutemix of PM Dawn, who had a 1991 US No.1 & UK No.3 single with 'Set Adrift On Memory Bliss'.

1982 Natasha Hamilton – vocalist with Atomic Kitten, who had a 2000 UK No.1 single with 'Whole Again'.

Spencer of Spencer Davies Group.

ON THIS DAY

1961 Motown records released the first Supremes single, 'Buttered Popcorn/Who's Loving You'.

1968 the animated film *Yellow Submarine* premiered at The London Pavilion. The Beatles made a cameo appearance in the film but didn't supply their own voices for the characters.

1972 a bomb exploded under The Rolling Stones' equipment van in Montreal – this was believed to be the work of French separatists. Angry fans also rioted, throwing bottles and rocks, after 3,000 tickets turned out to be fake.

1974 The Moody Blues opened what they claimed was the first "Quadraphonic" surround sound recording studio in the world.

1975 Bob Marley And The Wailers played the first of two nights at The Lyceum, London. Both nights were recorded for the November released "live" album, which featured the single 'No Woman No Cry'.

1978 Simple Minds made their live debut at The Satellite Club, Glasgow, Scotland.

1982 Irene Cara was at No.1 on the UK singles chart with 'Fame', which was taken from the film and TV series of the same name.

1987 The Ozzy Osbourne Band started a 16 week tour of US prisons.

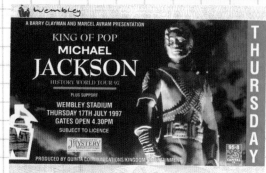

1992 the first night of a tour by Guns N' Roses, Metallica and Faith No More opened in Washington D.C.

1993 U2 scored their fifth UK No.1 album with *Zooropa*.

1995 Robbie Williams left Take That. The group had scored six UK No.1 singles with Robbie in the group.

1996 Chas Chandler died aged 57 at Newcastle General Hospital, England, where he was undergoing tests related to an aortic aneurysm. He had been bass player with The Animals and manager of Jimi Hendrix and Slade.

1999 it was reported that Will Smith had become the highest-paid black actor, demanding $20 million (£11.76 million) a film.

1999 Drummer Kevin Wilkinson hung himself at home, aged 41. He had worked with China Crisis, Howard Jones, Holly & The Italians, Squeeze and The Waterboys.

2003 Several of Hong Kong's biggest music stars and industry figures were arrested as part of an investigation into corruption in the music industry. This followed allegations that chart positions and music awards had been rigged.

BORN ON THIS DAY

1938 Ian Stewart – keyboard player for The Rolling Stones. He died of a heart attack in his doctor's waiting room on December 12th 1985.

1939 Dion Dimucci, singer who had a 1961 US No.1 & UK No.11 single with 'Runaround Sue'.

1941 Martha Reeves, soul singer who had a

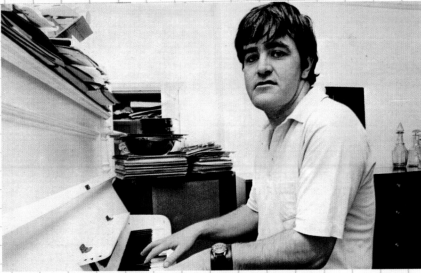

Ian Stewart, not initially welcome in the Stones as he may have upstaged Jagger's good looks.

1964 US No.2 & 1969 UK No.4 single with The Vandellas' 'Dancing In The Street' plus ten US and six UK other Top 40 singles.

1945 Danny McCullock – guitarist with The Animals, who had a 1964 UK & US No.1 single with 'House Of The Rising Sun'.

1949 Wally Bryson – guitarist with The Young Rascals, who had a 1967 US No.1 and UK No.8 single with 'Groovin' and guitarist and singer/songwriter with The Raspberries, who had a 1972 US No.5 single with 'Go All The Way'.

1950 Glenn Hughes – singer with The Village People, who had a 1978 US No.2 & 1979 UK No.1 single with 'YMCA'. Hughes died March 4th 2001.

1962 Jack Irons – drummer for Pearl Jam, who had a 1992 UK No.15 single with 'Jeremy' and a 1993 US No.1 album with *Vs*.

1975 Daron Malakian – guitarist with System Of A Down, who had a 2001 US No.1 & UK No.13 album with *Toxicity*.

ON THIS DAY

1953 truck driver Elvis Presley made his first-ever recording when he paid $4 (£2.35) at the Memphis recording service singing two songs, 'My Happiness' and 'That's When Your Heartaches Begin'.

1960 Brenda Lee went to No.1 on the US singles chart with 'I'm Sorry'. Seeking publicity the 4ft 11in tall singer was once billed as a 32-year-old midget and had the nickname Little Miss Dynamite.

1964 The Four Seasons started a two week run at No.1 on the US singles chart with 'Rag Doll'. It was the group's fourth No.1 and made No.2 on the UK chart.

1966 Bobby Fuller, leader of The Bobby Fuller Four, was found dead in his car in Los Angeles, aged 22. Fuller died mysteriously from gasoline asphyxiation while parked outside his apartment. Police labelled it a suicide, but the possibility of foul play has always been mentioned.

1970 BBC Radio 1 DJ Kenny Everett was sacked after he joked on air that the wife of the conservative transport minister Mary Peyton had "crammed a fiver into the examiner's hand" when taking her driving test.

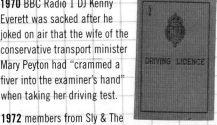

"Mr Everett, your driving licence, please."

1972 members from Sly & The Family Stone were arrested after police found 0.9kg (2lb) of marijuana in the group's motor home.

1978 Def Leppard made their live debut at Westfield School, Sheffield, England in front of 150 students.

1988 Nico (of Velvet Underground) died of a brain haemorrhage after falling off her bicycle while on holiday in Ibiza.

1991 Whitney Houston married ex-New Edition singer Bobby Brown at her New Jersey estate.

1991 the first night of the "Lollapalooza" tour at The Compton Terrace, Phoenix featured Living Colour, Siouxsie And The Banshees, Jane's Addiction, Nine Inch Nails, the Henry Rollins Band and The Butthole Surfers.

1994 Cranberries singer Dolores O'Riordan married ex-Duran Duran manager Don Burton.

1998 Another Level went to No.1 on the UK singles chart with 'Freak Me'.

1998 The Beastie Boys went to No.1 on the UK album chart with *Hello Nasty*. It was only the second rap album to make No.1 in the UK, the first being Wu-Tang Clan with *Wu-Tang Clan Forever* in 1997.

BORN ON THIS DAY

1946 Allan Gorrie – bass player and vocalist with the Average White Band, who had a 1975 US No.1 & UK No.6 single with 'Pick Up The Pieces'.

The Grateful Dead.

1947 Brian May – guitarist with Queen, who had a 1975 UK No.1 single with 'Bohemian Rhapsody', which also reached No.1 in 1991, plus over 40 other UK Top 40 singles. The band also enjoyed a 1980 US No.1 single with Crazy Little Thing Called Love'. As a solo artist May had a 1992 UK No.5 single with 'Too Much Love Will Kill You'.

1947 Bernie Leadon – guitarist with The Eagles. He quit the band in January 1976.

1947 Keith Godchaux – keyboardist and vocalist with the Grateful Dead, who recorded the classic 1970 album *Workingman's Dead*. He died after being involved in a car crash on July 23rd 1979.

1952 Allen Collins – guitarist with Lynyrd Skynyrd, who had a 1974 US No.8 single with 'Sweet Home Alabama' and a 1982 UK No.21 single with 'Freebird'. Collins died on January 23rd 1990 aged 37.

ON THIS DAY

1954 Sun Records released the first Elvis Presley single 'That's All Right/Blue Moon Of Kentucky', which made the local Memphis chart.

1958 the manager of The Drifters, George Treadwell, sacked the entire group and hired the unknown Ben E. King and The Five Crowns as their replacements.

1967 The Beatles were at No.1 on the UK singles chart with 'All You Need Is Love'.

1975 the Bay City Rollers were at No.1 on the UK singles chart with 'Give A Little Love', the group's second and final UK No.1.

1980 Queen scored their third UK No.1 album with *The Game*, which featured the single 'Another One Bites The Dust'.

1986 Genesis went to No.1 on the US singles chart with 'Invisible Touch'. The band's former lead singer, Peter Gabriel, was at No.2 with 'Sledgehammer'.

1987 Bruce Springsteen played his first-ever

show behind the Iron Curtain when he appeared in East Berlin in front of 180,000 people. The show was broadcast on East German TV.

1989 after large amounts of money were found in his cell, James Brown was moved from a minimum security prison to a medium security jail.

1991 Steven Adler, ex-drummer with Guns N' Roses, filed a suit in the Los Angeles county court alleging that he was fraudulently removed from the group and that the band introduced him to hard drugs.

1996 The Spice Girls made their debut on UK TV music show *Top Of The Pops*.

Tim Westwood in hokum Hollywood-style shoot out scare!

1999 BBC Radio 1 DJ Tim Westwood was shot by a gunman who sprayed bullets at Westwood's car in Kensington, London. A statement the following day said he was recovering in a London hospital.

2001 Wu Tang Clan rapper ODB was sentenced to spend between two and four years behind bars after being found guilty of drug possession. He was arrested in July 1999 when police found cocaine and marijuana in his car after he was pulled over for driving through a red light.

BORN ON THIS DAY

1945 John Lodge – bass player and vocalist with The Moody Blues, who had a 1965 UK No.1 & US No.10 single with 'Go Now' and 1968 UK No.19 & 1972 US No.2 single with 'Nights In White Satin'.

1945 Kim Carnes, US female singer who had a 1981 US No.1 & UK No.10 single with 'Betty Davis Eyes'.

1947 Carlos Santana – guitarist with Santana, who had a 1977 UK No.11 single with 'She's Not There' and a 1999 US No.1 single with 'Smooth', which spent 11 weeks at No.1 and was also No.1 in the UK. Santana won eight Grammys in the 2000 awards.

1956 Paul Cook – drummer with the Sex Pistols, who had a 1977 UK No.2 single with 'God Save The Queen' and a 1977 UK No.1 album with *Never Mind The Bollocks, Here's The Sex Pistols.*

Paul Cook.

1958 Michael McNeil – keyboardist for Simple Minds, who had a 1985 US No.1 single with 'Don't You, Forget About Me', a 1989 UK No.1 single with 'Belfast Child' plus over 20 other UK Top 40 singles.

1964 Chris Cornell – singer and guitarist with Soundgarden, who had a 1994 US No.1 & UK No. 4 album *Superunknown* and the 1994 UK No.12 single 'Black Hole Sun'. Now a solo artist.

ON THIS DAY

1954 The Blue Moon Boys made their live debut appearing on a flatbed truck outside a new drug store in Memphis. The band line up was Elvis Presley, Scotty Moore and Bill Black.

1963 Jan & Dean started a two week run at No.1 on the US singles chart with 'Surf City', which was written by Beach Boy Brian Wilson and had the Beach Boys on backing vocals. The single made No.26 in the UK.

1968 Cream started a four week run at No.1 on the US album chart with *Wheels Of Fire* **(right)**.

1968 Hugh Masekela started a two week run at No.1 on the US singles chart with 'Grazing In The Grass'.

1971 The Carpenters' show *Make Your Own Kind Of Music* started a six week run on NBC-TV.

1973 TV talent show *Opportunity Knocks* winners Peters And Lee were at No.1 on the UK singles chart with their first single 'Welcome Home'.

1974 David Bowie appeared at New York's Madison Square Gardens.

1974 appearing at Knebworth Park, England were Tim Buckley, The Sensational Alex Harvey Band , Mahavishnu Orchestra, Van Morrison, The Doobie Brothers and The Allman Brothers Band.

1976 the Buzzcocks made their live debut supporting the Sex Pistols and The Damned at The Lesser Free Trade Hall, Manchester. In the audience were future Smiths' singer Morrissey, Bernard Sumner and Peter Hook, who went on to form Joy Division, and Mark E. Smith who went on to form The Fall. Tickets for the night cost £1 ($1.70).

1977 Gary Kellgren, studio engineer at the Los Angeles Record Plant studio, drowned in a Hollywood swimming pool. He had worked with John Lennon, George Harrison, Jimi Hendrix, Barbra Streisand and Rod Stewart.

1986 the film based on the life of Sex Pistol Sid Vicious, *Sid And Nancy*, premiered in London.

1991 EMF went to No.1 on the US singles chart with 'Unbelievable'. The song had spent 14 weeks on the chart before reaching the top.

1995 Public Enemy's Flavor Flav broke both his arms when he was involved in a motorcycle accident in Milan.

1996 Gary Barlow scored his first UK No.1 hit single when 'Forever Love' went to the top of the charts for one week.

1999 church groups in middle America claimed that pictures of Britney Spears printed in *Rolling Stone* magazine encouraged child pornography. The shots showed Britney in her bedroom with not many clothes on.

2003 a tooth said to have been pulled out of Elvis Presley's mouth after an injury failed to sell on the auction site eBay. The tooth had been put on a ten day sale with a reserve price of £64,100 ($108,970). The tooth was also accompanied by some of the singer's hair.

BORN ON THIS DAY

1942 Kim Fowley, singer and producer who worked with The Murmaids, PJ Proby, The Beach Boys, The Runaways, Frank Zappa, Slade and Family. He produced the 1962 B. Bumble And The Stingers' UK No.1 'Nut Rocker'.

1946 Barry Whitwam – drummer with Herman's Hermits, who had a 1964 UK No.1 single with 'I'm Into Something Good' and a 1965 US No.1 single with 'Mrs Brown You've Got A Lovely Daughter'.

1947 Cat Stevens, singer/songwriter who had a 1967 UK No.2 single with 'Matthew And Son' and a 1972 UK No.9 & US No.6 single with 'Morning Has Broken'. He also wrote 'The First Cut Is The Deepest', which has been covered by P.P. Arnold, Rod Stewart and Sheryl Crow. Stevens converted to the Muslim religion in 1977 and changed his name to Yusuf Islam.

1955 Howie Epstein – bass player with Tom Petty And The Heartbreakers, who had a 1988 UK No.28 single with 'I Won't Back Down'.

1961 Jim Martin – guitarist for Faith No More, who had a 1993 UK No.3 and US No.4 single with 'I'm Easy'.

1974 Terry Caldwell – backing vocalist with East 17, who had a 1994 UK No.1 single with 'Stay Another Day' plus over 15 other UK Top 40 singles.

ON THIS DAY

1961 The Everly Brothers were at No.1 on the UK singles chart with 'Temptation'. The song was the duo's fourth UK No.1.

1973 Jim Croce started a two week run at No.1 on the US singles chart with 'Bad, Bad Leroy Brown'. Croce was killed in a plane crash three months later.

1973 appearing at this year's Buxton Festival in Derbyshire, England were Canned Heat, Chuck Berry, Nazareth, Edgar Broughton Band, Groundhogs, Sensational Alex Harvey Band, Medicine Head, Brewers Droop, Roy Wood and Wizard.

1977 the Sex Pistols made their debut on UK show *Top Of The Pops*.

1990 Roger Waters' "The Wall" extravaganza took place at the Berlin Wall in Potzdamer Platz, Berlin. Over 200,000 people attended and the event was broadcast live throughout the world. Van Morrison, Bryan Adams, Joni Mitchell and others also took part.

1994 Oasis played their first-ever American show as part of the New Music Seminar at Wetlands in New York.

1996 Alanis Morissette started a second run at No.1 on the UK album chart with *Jagged Little Pill*, which stayed at the top for eight weeks.

1996 the tour bus that was carrying the members of Terrorvision inadvertently ran over sleeping festival fan Daniel Duffy as he lay in his tent. He broke his hip.

2002 producer Gus Dudgeon was killed in a car accident. His wife, Sheila, also died in the accident. Dudgeon was best known for his work with Elton John but he also produced David Bowie, The Beach Boys, Zombies, Kiki Dee, Strawbs, XTC and Joan Armatrading.

2003 Coldplay singer Chris Martin *(right)* was charged with malicious damage in Australia after he allegedly attacked a photographer's car. Martin admitted he had lost his temper due to the constant harassment by the journalist, who had taken pictures of him surfing at Seven Mile Beach. Consequently Martin smashed his windscreen and let the air out of his tyres.

2004 Composer Jerry Goldsmith died after a long battle with cancer, aged 75. He had created the

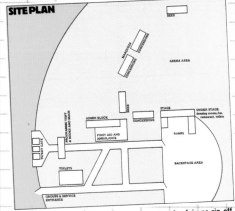

Buxton Festival: one stage, plenty of toilets, no fun fair, no rip-off prices. Those were the days.

music for scores of classic movies and television shows including *Star Trek*, *Planet Of The Apes*, *The Man From U.N.C.L.E.* and *Dr. Kildare.*

BORN ON THIS DAY

1941 George Clinton, founder of Parliament/Funkadelic, who had a 1978 US No.16 album with *One Nation Under A Groove*. He also had a 1994 UK No.22 single with 'Bop Gun'.

1944 Estelle Bennett – singer with The Ronettes, who had a 1963 US No.4 & UK No.4 single with 'Be My Baby'.

1944 Ric Davis – vocalist and keyboardist with Supertramp, who had a 1979 UK No.7 & US No.6 single with 'The Logical Song' and a 1979 US No.1 & UK No.3 album *Breakfast In America*.

1947 Don Henley – drummer and vocalist with The Eagles, who had a 1977 US No.1 & UK No.8 single with 'Hotel California' plus five US No.1 albums. The bands' *Greatest Hits 1971–1975* is the second biggest-selling album in the world with sales over 30 million. As a solo artist he had a 1985 US No.5 & UK No.12 single with 'The Boys of Summer'.

1967 Pat Badger – bass player with Extreme, who had a 1991 US No.1 & UK No.2 single with 'More Than Words'.

1973 Daniel Jones – guitarist and keyboard player with Savage Garden, who had a 1998 US No.1 & UK No.4 single with 'Truly Madly Deeply'.

ON THIS DAY

1965 Mick Jagger, Brian Jones and Bill Wyman were each fined £5 ($8.50) at East Ham Magistrates Court, London after being found guilty of insulting behaviour at a Romford Road service station, where they had urinated against a wall.

1967 this week's UK Top 5 singles were: No.5, 'A Whiter Shade Of Pale', Procol Harum; No.4, 'She'd Rather Be With Me', The Turtles; No.3, 'It Must Be Him', Vikki Car'; No.2, 'Alternate Title', The Monkees and No.1, 'All You Need Is Love', The Beatles.

1969 Aretha Franklin was arrested for causing a disturbance in a Detroit parking lot.

1972 Paul and Linda McCartney were arrested in Sweden for possession of drugs.

1977 Stiff Records released *My Aim Is True*, the debut album from Elvis Costello.

1979 Little Richard, now known as the Reverend Richard Pennman, told his congregation about the evils of rock 'n' roll music, declaring, "If God can save an old homosexual like me, he can save anybody".

1989 former actress Martika started a two week run at No.1 on the US singles chart with 'Toy Soldiers', which was a No.5 hit in the UK.

1989 Courtney Love married her first husband James Moreland, the singer with LA band Leaving Trains.

1989 Simply Red scored their first UK No.1 album with their third release *A New Flame*.

1989 the soundtrack album *Batman* by Prince started a six week run at No.1 on the US album chart.

1999 Simple Minds closed their official fan club due to dwindling membership.

2001 Destiny's Child went back to No.1 on the UK album chart for the second time with *Survivor*.

2004 legendary French singer and guitarist Sacha Distel died after a long battle with deteriorating health. He had had a 1970 UK No.10 single with 'Raindrops Keep Falling On My Head'.

2004 singer/songwriter and producer Arthur Crier died of heart failure. A member of The Chimes he had worked with Little Eva, Gene Pitney, The Four Tops, The Temptations, Ben E. King, Johnny Nash and The Coasters.

STALLS   ROW   C   SEAT   30

CCE PRESENTS
BRIAN WILSON
NO SUPPORT
CARLING APOLLO MANCHESTER
£ 0.00 STOCKPORT ROAD MANCHESTER
SC   THU 22-JUL-04 19:45
£ 0.00
21-33602 COMP   SFA600 22JUL4 16:03

No Exchange   No Refund   www.cclive.co.uk

FIVE

plus a host of special guests

CARDIFF CASTLE
SATURDAY 22 JULY
TICKETS £25.00 (MAX 6 PER PERSON)
TICKETS DIRECT - 08705 40 50 40
CARDIFF ARENA & TICKETLINE

LONDON HYDE PARK
SUNDAY 23 JULY
TICKETS £27.50 (MAX 6 PER PERSON)
CALL: 020 7420 1000/7734 8932/7344 4040
www.tickets-online.co.uk

BORN ON THIS DAY

1945 Dino Danelli – drummer with The Young Rascals, who had a 1967 US No.1 & UK No.8 single with 'Groovin'.

1946 Andy Mackay – sax and woodwind player for Roxy Music, who had a 1972 UK No.4 single with 'Virgina Plain' and 15 other UK Top 40 singles.

1947 David Essex, singer and actor, who had a 1974 UK No.1 single with 'Gonna Make You A Star', 18 other UK Top 40 singles and a 1974 US No.5 single with 'Rock On'.

1947 Tony Joe White, singer/songwriter who had a 1969 US No.8 single with 'Polk Salad Annie' and a 1970 UK No.22 single with 'Groupie Girl'. He also wrote 'Steamy Windows', which was a UK No.13 single for Tina Turner.

1950 Blair Thorton – guitarist with Bachman Turner Overdrive, who had a 1974 US No.1 & UK No.2 single with 'You Ain't Seen Nothing Yet'.

1952 Janis Siegel – singer with Manhattan Transfer, who had a 1977 UK No.1 with 'Chanson D'amour' and a 1981 US No.7 single with 'Boy From New York City'.

1961 Martin Gore – keyboardist with Depeche Mode, who had a 1984 UK No.4 single with 'People Are People', over 25 other UK Top 40 singles and a 1990 US No.8 single with 'Enjoy The Silence'.

1964 Tim Kellett – keyboardist and trumpet player for Simply Red, who had a 1986 US No.1 & UK No.2 single with 'Holding Back The Years', and Olive, who had a 1997 UK No.1 single with 'You're Not Alone'.

1965 Slash – guitarist with Guns N' Roses, who had a 1988 US No.1 & 1989 UK No.6 single with 'Sweet Child O' Mine' and a 1991 US & UK No.1 album with *Use Your Illusion II*, and Velvet Revolver, who had a 2004 US No.1 album with *Contraband*.

1970 Sam Watters – vocalist with Color Me Bad, who had a 1991 UK No.1 single with 'I Wanna Sex You Up' and a 1991 US No.1 single with 'I Adore Mi Amor'.

1973 Fran Healy – vocalist and guitarist with Travis, who had a 1999 UK No.1 album with *The Man Who* and a 1999 UK No.10 single with 'Why Does It Always Rain On Me?'.

1980 Steve "Stevo 32" Jocz – drummer with Sum 41, who had a 2001 UK No.13 single with 'In Too Deep'.

ON THIS DAY

1964 The Beatles were at No.1 on the UK singles chart with 'A Hard Day's Night', the group's fifth UK No.1.

1966 Frank Sinatra went to No.1 on the US album chart with *Strangers In The Night*.

1969 The Rolling Stones were at No.1 on the UK singles chart with 'Honky Tonk Women', the group's eighth UK No.1.

1977 Led Zeppelin drummer John Bonham and group manager Peter Grant were charged with assault after a fight broke out backstage during a US concert with employees of the promoter.

1979 keyboard player with the Grateful Dead Keith Godchaux died after being involved in a car accident, aged 32.

1980 Cliff Richard received his OBE from the Queen at Buckingham Palace.

1983 Paul Young had his first UK No.1 single with his version of the Marvin Gaye song 'Wherever I Lay My Hat, (That's My Home)'.

THE
NASH VILLE
ROOM

Fri. 21 £1.50
PSYCHEDELIC FURS
The Subliminal Squad

Sat. 22 £1.50
JOY DIVISION
+ Support

Sun. 23 £1.25
SELECTOR
+ The Beat

Mon. 24 £1
RAMBOW
+ The Trendies

Tues. 25 £1
RAMBOW
+ The Jukes

Thurs. 27 £1.25
COWBOYS INTERNATIONAL
+ Support
**CORNER CROMWELL ROAD
NORTH END ROAD, W.14**
Adjacent West Kensington Tube
Tel. 01-603 6071

1983 The Police went to No.1 on the US album chart with *Synchronicity*. The album spent a total of 17 weeks at No.1.

1988 after 49 weeks on the US album chart, Def Leppard's *Hysteria* went to the No.1 position.

1988 Richard Marx went to No.1 on the US singles chart with 'Hold On To The Nights', his first US No.1 single.

1992 Chicago received their own star on the Hollywood Walk of Fame.

1995 two R.E.M. fans died at Dublin's Slane Castle gig. One drowned in the River Boyne and the other was allegedly pushed from a bridge.

1996 Rob Collins, keyboard player with The Charlatans, died in a car crash, aged 29.

2000 Farrah Franklin left Destiny's Child after only five months with the group. The remaining trio of Beyonce, Kelly and Michelle said that Farrah was not kicked out but had all agreed that Farrah and Destiny's Child should part ways.

2003 James Brown announced his separation from his fourth wife using an advertisement featuring the Disney character Goofy. The 70-year-old placed the notice in *Variety* magazine. It featured a picture of himself, his wife Tomi Rae and their two-year-old son, James Joseph Brown II, posing with Goofy at Walt Disney World.

BORN ON THIS DAY

1941 Barbara Love – singer with The Friends Of Distinction, who had a 1969 US No.3 single with 'Grazing In The Grass'.

1942 Heinz Burt – bass player for The Tornados, who had a 1962 UK & US No.1 single with 'Telstar'. It was the first major hit from a UK act on the American chart. Burt died on April 7th 2000.

1947 Alan Whitehead – drummer for Marmalade *(right)*, who had a 1969 UK No.1 single with 'Ob-La-Di Ob-La-Da' and a 1970 US No.10 single with 'Reflections Of My Life'.

1951 Lynval Golding – guitarist with The Specials, who had a 1981 UK No.1 single with 'Ghost Town'.

1961 Gary Cherone – vocalist with Extreme, who had a 1991 US No.1 & UK No.2 single with 'More Than Words'.

1970 Jennifer Lopez, singer and actress who had a 2001 UK No.1 single with 'Love Don't Cost A Thing' and a 2001 US No.1 single with 'I'm Real'.

ON THIS DAY

1965 The Byrds were at No.1 on the UK singles chart with their version of the Bob Dylan song 'Mr. Tambourine Man'.

1967 all four Beatles and their manager Brian Epstein signed a petition printed in *The Times* newspaper calling for the legalization of marijuana.

1971 The Raiders went to No.1 on the US singles chart with 'Indian Reservation'.

1972 Bobby Ramirez, drummer with Edgar Winters White Trash, was killed in a brawl in a Chicago bar, which began after comments were made about the length of his hair.

1976 appearing at Cardiff Castle, Cardiff, Wales were Status Quo, The Strawbs, Hawkwind, Curved Air and Budgie.

1977 Donna Summer was at No.1 on the UK singles chart with 'I Feel Love'.

1978 the Robert Stigwood film *Sgt Pepper's Lonely Hearts Club Band* was released, featuring The Bee Gees and Peter Frampton.

1980 Peter Sellers, actor and singer, died of a heart attack. He had had a 1956 UK No.9 single with 'Ying Tong Song' with The Goons, a 1960 UK No.4 single with 'Goodness Gracious Me' with Sophia Loren and a 1965 UK No.14 single with 'A Hard Day's Night'.

1982 Survivor started a six week run at No.1 on the US singles chart with 'Eye Of The Tiger', taken from the film *Rocky III*. It was also No.1 in the UK.

1984 the father of Aretha Franklin, the Rev. C.L. Franklin, died. Franklin had been in a coma since 1979, after being shot by burglars.

1993 U2 started a two week run at No.1 on the US album chart with *Zooropa*.

1993 UB40 started a seven week run at No.1 on the US singles chart with 'Can't Help Falling In Love'. On the same day they also went to No.1 on the UK album chart with *Promises And Lies*.

1995 Pink Floyd were at No.1 on the US album chart with *Pulse*, the band's fifth US No.1.

1997 Liam Gallagher was given a formal caution by police after admitting criminal damage following an incident with a cyclist in Camden, London. Gallagher had grabbed the rider from the window of his chauffeur driven car and broken his Ray-bans.

2000 Ronan Keating was at No.1 on the UK singles chart with 'Life Is A Roller Coaster'. *NSYNC had the US No.1 with 'It's Gonna Be Me'.

2002 A garden centre was sued over claims it killed a collection of the late singer Freddie Mercury's prized koi fish. Mercury's former partner, Mary Austin who inherited the Japanese koi collection claimed 84 fish died when the electricity powering a temporary pond was accidentally turned off by a worker from Clifton Nurseries, of Maida Vale, West London. At the time of Mercury's death he had amassed one of the best collections of the fish in the UK. One koi can be worth £250,000.

2003 Ozzy Osbourne's long-standing tour manager, Bobby Thompson, was found dead in his Detroit hotel room. Thompson had been battling throat cancer.

BORN ON THIS DAY

1941 Manuel Charlton – guitarist for Nazareth, who had a 1973 UK No.9 single with 'Broken Down Angel' and a 1976 US No.8 single with 'Love Hurts'.

1942 Bruce Woodley – vocalist with The Seekers, who had a 1965 UK No.1 & US No.5 single with 'I'll Never Find Another You'.

1943 Jim McCarty – drummer with The Yardbirds, who had a 1965 UK No.3 & US No.6 single with 'For Your Love'.

1944 Tom Dawes – guitarist with Cyrkle, who had a 1966 US No.2 single with 'Red Rubber Ball'. The band was signed by Brian Epstein and supported The Beatles on their 1966 US tour.

The Cyrkle in, guess what, a circle.

1946 Jose "Chepito" Areas – percussionist with Santana, who had a 1970 US No.4 single with 'Black Magic Woman' and a 1977 UK No.11 single with 'She's Not There'.

1951 Verdine White – bass player and vocalist with Earth, Wind And Fire, who had a 1975 US No.1 single with 'Shining Star' and a 1981 UK No.3 single with 'Let's Groove'.

1958 Thurston Moore – guitarist and vocalist for Sonic Youth, who had a 1993 UK No.26 single with 'Sugar Kane'.

ON THIS DAY

1963 Cilla Black made a recording test for EMI Records after George Martin had spotted her while at a Gerry And The Pacemakers gig in Liverpool.

1964 The Beatles' third album *A Hard Day's Night* started a 21 week run at the top of the UK charts.

1965 Bob Dylan went "electric" at The Newport Folk Festival and was booed off stage.

1969 Neil Young appeared with Crosby, Stills & Nash for the first time at a concert at New York's Fillmore East.

1970 The Carpenters started a four week run at No.1 on the US singles chart with '(They Long To Be) Close To You'. It was the first of three US No.1s and 17 other Top 40 hits for them.

1971 T. Rex were at No.1 on the UK singles chart with 'Get It On', the group's second UK No.1.

Bob Dylan presents his Shane McGowan impersonation (with teeth).

1976 Elton John and Kiki Dee were at No.1 on the UK singles chart with 'Don't Go Breaking My Heart'. It was Elton's first UK No.1 after 16 Top 40 hits.

1987 Madonna had her fifth UK No.1 single with the title track from her 1987 film *Who's That Girl?*

1990 Bruce Springsteen became a father when Patti Sciafa gave birth to a baby boy, Evan James.

1995 country singer Charlie Rich died. His 1974 song 'The Most Beautiful Girl' made No.2 in the UK and 'Behind Closed Doors' was a No.1 country hit.

1998 Jamiroquai went to No.1 on the UK singles chart with 'Deeper Under Ground', their 13th hit and first UK No.1.

1999 This year's Woodstock Festival ended with riots and 120 people were arrested. Three people died during the three day festival in separate incidents and many were hospitalized after drinking polluted water.

2002 two former members of Destiny's Child settled out of court over the lyrics to 'Survivor', which they claimed were libellous. LeToya Luckett and LaTavia Roberson, who left the group in 2000, said that the song broke an agreement that stopped both sides making "any public comment of a disparaging nature concerning one another". The line that they were suing over said, "You thought that I'd be stressed without you, but I'm chillin.' You thought I wouldn't sell without you, sold nine million."

2003 Erik Braunn from US band Iron Butterfly died, aged 52.

BORN ON THIS DAY

1941 Neil Landon – singer with The Flowerpot Men, who had a 1967 UK No.4 single with 'Let's Go To San Francisco', and The Ivy League, who had a 1965 UK No.3 single with 'Tossing and Turning'.

1941 Bobby Hebb, US singer who had a 1966 US No.2 and UK No.12 single with 'Sunny'.

1941 Darlene Love – singer with The Crystals, who had a 1962 US No.1 single with 'He's A Rebel' and a 1963 UK No.2 single with 'Then He Kissed Me'.

1942 Dobie Gray – singer who had a 1965 US No.13 and UK No.25 single with 'The In Crowd' and a 1973 US No.5 single with 'Drift Away'.

1943 Mick Jagger – singer with The Rolling Stones, who had a 1969 UK & US No.1 single with 'Honky Tonk Women' and over 35 UK & US Top 40 singles and albums. As a solo artist he had a 1985 UK No.1 single with David Bowie 'Dancing In The Street'.

1949 Roger Taylor – drummer and vocalist with Queen, who had a 1975 UK No.1 single with 'Bohemian Rhapsody', which also made UK No.1 in 1991, plus over 40 other UK Top 40 singles. The band also had a 1980 US No.1 single with 'Crazy Little Thing Called Love'. He went on to form The Cross.

1980 Dave "Brown Sound" Baksh – guitarist and songwriter with Sum 41, who had a 2001 UK No.13 single with 'In Too Deep'.

1967 Tim Barnwell, a.k.a. DJ Headliner – member of Arrested Development, who had a 1992 US No.8 & UK No.2 single with 'People Everyday'.

ON THIS DAY

1962 Frank Ifield was at No.1 on the UK singles chart with 'I Remember You'. This was the singer's first of four UK No.1s.

1968 The Jackson Five signed a one year contract with Motown Records.

1974 graffiti artists were hired to spray paint sites in London to promote The Rolling Stones' new single 'It's Only Rock 'n' Roll' *(above)*.

1975 The Eagles started a five week run at No.1 on the US album chart with *One Of These Nights*.

1975 Van McCoy And The Soul City went to No.1 on the US singles chart with 'The Hustle', his only US chart hit. The song was a No.3 hit in the UK.

1977 Elvis Costello was arrested as he performed outside a CBS Records sales conference at The London Hilton Hotel and was fined £5 ($8.50).

1977 Led Zeppelin cut short a US tour after Robert Plant's 6-year-old son Karac died unexpectedly.

1980 appearing at the Monsters Of Rock festival, Donington Park, England were Rainbow, Judas Priest, Scorpions, Saxon, April Wine and Riot. Tickets cost £7.50 ($12.75).

1986 Peter Gabriel went to No.1 on the US singles chart with 'Sledgehammer', which was a No.4 hit in the UK. On the same day the film soundtrack to *Top Gun* went to No.1 on the US album chart.

1990 Brent Mydland from the Grateful Dead was found dead on the floor of his home, aged 38, from a drug overdose.

1992 Motown artist Mary Wells died of cancer. She had had a 1964 US No.1 & UK No.5 single with 'My Guy'.

1997 it was reported that eight people who had attended this year's Glastonbury Festival had been admitted to hospital after contracting the e-coli bug, which had claimed the lives of 22 people in Scotland earlier in the year.

1997 Puff Daddy and Faith Evans went back to No.1 on the UK singles chart for another three weeks with 'I'll Be Missing You'.

2000 Oasis were booed off stage during a show at the Paleo Festival in Switzerland after singer Liam Gallagher had insulted the 35,000 strong audience.

2001 Sir Paul McCartney announced his engagement to Heather Mills *(left)*, the anti-landmine campaigner and former model.

BORN ON THIS DAY

1944 Bobbie Gentry, US singer who had a 1967 US No.1 single with 'Ode To Billie Joe' and a 1969 UK No.1 single with 'I'll Never Fall In Love Again'.

1947 Andy McMaster – singer/songwriter and multi-instrumentalist with Motors, who had a 1978 UK No.4 single with 'Airport'.

1950 Michael Vaughn – guitarist with Paper Lace, who had a 1974 UK No.1 single with 'Billy Don't Be A Hero' and a 1974 US No.1 single with 'The Night Chicago Died'.

1953 Suzi Carr – singer with Will To Power, who had a 1989 UK No.6 single with 'Baby I Love Your Way/Freebird'.

1960 Conway Savage – bass player with Nick Cave And The Bad Seeds, who had a 1996 UK No.36 single with PJ Harvey 'Henry Lee'.

1962 Karl Mueller – bass player with Soul Asylum, who had a 1993 US No.5 and UK No.7 single with 'Runaway Train'.

ON THIS DAY

1958 fans of rock 'n' roll music were warned that tuning into music on the car radio can cost more money. Researchers from the Esso gas company said the rhythm of rock 'n' roll can cause the driver to be foot heavy on the pedal, making them waste fuel.

1968 Bee Gee Robin Gibb collapsed as the group were about to set out on their first US tour, suffering from nervous exhaustion.

1974 John Denver started a two week run at No.1 on the US singles chart with 'Annie's Song', the singer's second US No.1. The song was a tribute to his wife and was written in ten minutes while he was on a ski lift.

1974 Wings started a seven week run at No.1 on the UK album chart with *Band On The Run*, which featured the title track, 'Jet' and the US hit 'Helen Wheels'. The album sold over six million copies worldwide.

1976 after a four year legal fight, John Lennon was awarded his Green card, allowing him permanent residence in the US.

Expensive American car entertainment.

1976 Bruce Springsteen sued his manager Mike Appel for fraud and breach of trust. The case dragged on for a year, halting Springsteen's career. An out-of-court settlement was reached the following year.

1984 Roger Taylor from Duran Duran married Giovanna Cantonne in Naples, Italy.

1985 Paul Young went to No.1 on the US singles chart with his version of the Daryl Hall song 'Every Time You Go Away'.

1986 Queen became the first Western act since Louis Armstrong in 1964 to perform in Eastern Europe when they played at Budapest's Nepstadion, Hungary. The gig was filmed and released as *Queen Magic* in Budapest.

1987 U2 filmed their video 'Where the Streets Have No Name' on the rooftop of a building in LA, causing traffic chaos below.

1989 Michael Jackson sued the *Daily Mirror* for libel after they printed a less than flattering colour photo of the ever-changing singer on the front page.

1991 Bryan Adams started a seven week run at No.1 on the US singles chart with '(Everything I Do) I Do It For You'. Jesus Jones was at No.2 with 'Right Here, Right Now'.

1996 The Spice Girls scored their first No.1 UK single with 'Wannabe'. It stayed at the top for seven weeks and on the chart for 24.

1997 Jason Caulfield and James Hunt, roadies with Primal Scream, were both arrested for possessing drugs during a festival in Tullinge, Sweden.

1997 the Soundtrack album *Men In Black* started a two week run at No.1 on the US album chart.

2001 bass player with Lynyrd Skynyrd Leon Wilkeson died. The band had had a 1974 US No.8 single with 'Sweet Home Alabama' and a 1982 UK No.21 single with 'Freebird'.

2002 Mariah Carey checked herself into an undisclosed hospital suffering from "extreme exhaustion". The singer cancelled all public appearances, including her headlining appearance at the MTV 20th birthday party. Her record company denied tabloid reports that Carey tried to commit suicide, saying she did have cuts on her body but the injuries were unintentional after breaking some dishes and glasses.

BORN ON THIS DAY

1938 George Cummings – steel guitarist with Dr. Hook, who had a 1972 US No.5 & UK No.2 single with 'Sylvia's Mother' plus nine other US Top 40 hits.

1944 Mike Bloomfield – guitarist and member of the Paul Butterfield Band and Electric Flag. He played on Dylan's album *Highway 61 Revisited*. Bloomfield died on February 15th 1981.

1945 Rick Wright – keyboardist with Pink Floyd, who had a 1973 US No.1 & UK No.2 album with *Dark Side Of The Moon*, which spent a record breaking 741 weeks on the US chart.

1949 Peter Doyle – singer with The New Seekers, who had a 1972 UK No.1 & US No.7 single with 'I'd Like To Teach The World To Sing'. Doyle died on October 13th 2001.

1949 Simon Kirke – drummer for Free, who had a 1971 UK No.2 & US No.4 single with 'All Right Now', and Bad Company, who had a 1974 UK No.15 and US No.5 single with 'Can't Get Enough'.

1949 Steve Took – percussionist with T. Rex, who had a 1971 UK No.1 single with 'Hot Love' plus over 20 other UK Top 40 singles. He died on October 27th 1980.

ON THIS DAY

1954 the first press interview with 19-year-old Elvis Presley was published in the *Memphis Press-Scimitar*.

1966 Chris Farlowe And The Thunderbirds were at No.1 on the UK singles chart with the Jagger and Richards song 'Out Of Time'.

A SHOW FOR THE ENTIRE FAMILY

MR. DYNAMITE

JAMES BROWN

N.Y. APOLLO Theatre

THUR. JULY 28 8:00 P.M.

GUARANTEED SELL-OUT...COME EARLY!

1966 James Brown appeared at The Apollo Theatre, New York.

1969 police in Moscow reported that thousands of public phone booths had been vandalized after thieves were stealing parts of the phones to convert their acoustic guitars to electric. A feature in a Russian youth magazine had shown details on how to do this.

1979 'I Don't Like Mondays', a song inspired by a true-life shooting incident, gave The Boomtown Rats their second UK No.1 single.

1980 appearing at the Dalymount Festival in Dublin were The Police, U2 and Squeeze.

1990 Elton John started a five week run at No.1 on the UK album chart with *Sleeping With The Past*, his fifth No.1 album.

1990 Partners In Kryme started a four week run at No.1 with 'Turtle Power', which was the first rap chart topper in the UK.

1991 an estimated 2,000 youths rioted after an MC Hammer concert in Penticton, Canada. Almost 100 arrests were made.

1996 Marge Ganser from The Shangri-Las died of breast cancer. The group scored over ten hits during the 60s, including the 1964 US No.1 'Leader Of The Pack'.

2002 Dave Matthews Band went to No.1 on the US album chart with *Busted Stuff*.

2003 The wine Sir Cliff Richard made from his Algarve estate started a UK supermarket battle. Fans were asking all the stores when the wine would go on sale. The Tesco chain said they would be the first, in fact but the Waitrose shops had been selling the £8.49 ($14.44) a bottle red for the past week.

Sir Cliff's red wine causes a scramble

By Valerie Elliott
Consumer Editor

THE popularity of the wine Sir Cliff Richard makes from his Algarve estate has started a supermarket battle.

The second vintage of Vida Nova, or new life, red wine from the grapes of his 25-acre estate near Albufeira has caused much excitement with fans asking for months when the bottles are to go on sale.

Tesco said yesterday that the wine would go on sale this Thursday on Tesco.com "weeks ahead of every other British retailer". Waitrose, however, has been selling the wine via Waitrose Direct for a week and in selected branches since the end of last week. Single bottles are priced at £8.49.

A Tesco spokesman admitted that he must have been given false information but said that the company still expected the wine to sell as fast as the latest Harry Potter.

Stocks in Britain are limited, because a proportion of the wine, said to be more elegant than last year's, stays in Portugal to be served at leading restaurants in the Algarve. Sir Cliff also has his own allocation for his homes, including the Barbados mansion where Tony Blair and his family are to spend their summer holidays.

The wine is a blend of two Portuguese grapes, trincadeira and aragones, with shiraz.

BORN ON THIS DAY

1946 Neal Doughty – keyboardist with REO Speedwagon, who had a 1981 US No.1 & UK No.7 single with 'Keep On Loving You'.

1953 Geddy Lee – bass player and vocalist with Rush, who had a 1980 UK No.13 single with 'Spirit Of Radio' and a 1982 US No.21 single with 'New World Man'.

1956 Patti Sciafa – singer with the Bruce Springsteen Band and also Mrs Springsteen.

1959 John Sykes –guitarist with Thin Lizzy, Whitesnake, who had a 1987 US No.1 & UK No.9 single with 'Here I Go Again', and Tygers Of Pan Tang.

1972 Simon Jones – bass player for The Verve, who had a 1997 UK No.1 single with 'The Drugs Don't Work'.

1973 Wanya Morris – singer with Boyz II Men, who had a 1992 US & UK No.1 single with 'End Of The Road'.

Geddy Lee, steady girls.

ON THIS DAY

1963 Elvis Presley was at No.1 on the UK singles chart with '(You're The) Devil In Disguise'. It was his 14th UK No.1.

1966 Eric Clapton, Jack Bruce and Ginger Baker made their live debut as Cream at The Twisted Wheel, Manchester.

1966 Bob Dylan suffered a broken neck vertebra when he crashed his Triumph 55 motorbike near his home in Woodstock, New York.

1967 The Doors started a three week run at No.1 on the US singles chart with 'Light My Fire'. The group's first US No.1, it only reached No.49 on the UK chart. When it was reissued in 1991 it made No.7 in the UK.

1968 Gram Parsons left The Byrds on the eve of a tour of South Africa, refusing to play to segregated audiences.

1968 the first recording session of The Beatles' seven minute epic 'Hey Jude', a song written about John's son Julian, took place.

1972 Screaming Lord Sutch was arrested in London after jumping from a bus in Downing Street with four nude women to publicize forthcoming gigs.

1972 UK singer/songwriter Gilbert O'Sullivan started a five week run at No.1 on the US singles chart with 'Alone Again, (Naturally)'. It was his only US No.1. The follow-up, 'Claire', made No.2.

1973 Led Zeppelin lost $180,000 (£105,882) in cash when a thief made off with their safety deposit box from two Madison Square Garden concerts.

1974 Mamas And The Papas singer Cass Elliot died from a heart attack after choking on her own vomit. She was staying at Harry Nillson's London flat when she died.

1978 Prince appeared on the US charts for the first time with 'Soft and Wet'.

1978 the film soundtrack to _Grease_ went to No.1 on the US album chart.

Sutch a rarity

SUTCH: would you vote for this man?

Gary Merrin

1980 David Bowie starred in the stage play of The Elephant Man, in Denver, Colorado.

1981 on the day of the wedding between Prince Charles and Lady Diana a bunch of records were released relating to the event: 'Lady D' by Typically Tropical; 'Charley's Angels' by Mini & The Metros and 'Diana' by Mike Berry. They all failed to reach the charts.

1982 Andy Taylor from Duran Duran married the group's hairdresser, Tracey Wilson, during a US tour.

1982 The Asgard Hotel in Dublin, owned by Thin Lizzy's Phil Lynott, was completely destroyed by fire.

1987 Michigan state governor James Blanchard declared an annual statewide Four Tops Day, honouring the group for its contribution to American music.

2001 Atomic Kitten started a two week run at No.1 on the UK singles chart with their version of the 1989 Bangles hit 'Eternal Flame'.

2001 Destiny's Child started a two week run at No.1 on the US singles chart with 'Bootylicious'.

2004 keyboard player Huby Heard died from heart problems. He had been a member of Billy Preston's The God Squad and also worked with Teddy Pendergrass and Ray Charles.

BORN ON THIS DAY

1941 Paul Anka, singer who had a 1957 UK & US No.1 single with 'Diana'. The single sold over nine million copies worldwide. He wrote many classic songs including: 'It Doesn't Matter Anymore', 'Puppy Love' and the lyrics to 'My Way'.

1946 Jeffrey Hammond-Hammond – bass player for Jethro Tull, who had a 1969 UK No.3 & US No.11 single with 'Living In The Past'.

1949 Andy Scott – guitarist for Sweet, who had a 1973 UK No.1 single with 'Blockbuster' plus 14 other UK Top 40 singles.

1949 Hugh Nicholson – guitarist and songwriter for Marmalade, who had a 1969 UK No.1 single with 'Ob-La-Di Ob-La-Da'.

1958 Kate Bush, singer/songwriter who had a 1978 UK No.1 single with 'Wuthering Heights' plus over 20 other UK Top 40 singles.

1968 Sean Moore – drummer with Manic Street Preachers, who had a 1996 UK No.2 single with 'A Design For Life' plus two UK No.1 singles.

A very young Ms Bush.

ON THIS DAY

1966 The Troggs started a two week run at No.1 on the US singles chart with 'Wild Thing'. The group's singer Reg Presley saw Wet Wet Wet enjoy 15 weeks at No.1 on the UK singles chart in 1994 with his song 'Love Is All Around'.

1966 *Datebook* published Maureen Cleave's interview with John Lennon in which he said "We're bigger than Jesus now". US Christians reacted with outrage, organizing "Beatle bonfires" during which they burned the group's records.

1970 Jimi Hendrix appeared at The Magical Gardens in Mauii, Hawaii.

1977 The Bee Gees' younger brother Andy Gibb started a four week run at No.1 on the US singles chart with 'I Just Wanna Be Your Everything'. It was the first of three US No.1s for him, and made No.26 in the UK.

1986 Boy George was fined £250 ($425) by a London court for possession of heroin.

1988 Gary Glitter appeared in a full-page ad in the *NME*. He was pictured holding a very large tub of skin rejuvenating cream. The heading was, "The things people do to keep hold of their young persons' railcard".

1988 Steve Winwood started a four week run at No.1 on the US singles chart with 'Roll With It', which was a No.53 hit in the UK.

1991 a police officer was forced to tear up a traffic ticket given to the limousine that Axl Rose was travelling in after it made an illegal turn. Rose threatened to pull that night's gig if the ticket was issued.

1995 appearing at the National Bowl, Milton Keynes, England, were R.E.M., Sleeper, The Cranberries and Radiohead.

1998 Jamiroquai were at No.1 in the UK chart with 'Deeper Underground'. Brandy and Monica held the US No.1 position with 'The Boy Is Mine'.

2000 nine Pearl Jam fans were killed at this year's Roskilde festival in Denmark during the band's set. The victims, all men and aged between 17 and 28, were trampled to death close to the stage. Police said the deaths happened in muddy and rainy conditions when the crowd pressed and crushed the victims against the open-air stage. Members of the group told the crowd to move back because people were being pressed up against the stage.

2003 Jim O'Neill, chairman of the Professional Association of Teachers, warned that children were being put under pressure to grow up too soon by pop stars who use a sexy image. "Kylie Minogue might be a great singer but in many of these things you can see more of her bottom than you hear of her voice," said Mr O'Neill.

BORN ON THIS DAY

1946 Gary Lewis, singer who had a 1965 US No.1 single with the Playboys, 'This Diamond Ring' plus 11 other US Top 40 hits.

1947 Karl Green – guitarist with Herman's Hermits, who had a 1964 UK No.1 single with 'I'm Into Something Good' and a 1965 US No.1 single with 'Mrs Brown You've Got A Lovely Daughter'.

1951 Carlo Karges – guitarist with Nena, who had a 1984 UK No.1 & US No.2 single with '99 Red Balloons'.

1958 Bill Berry – drummer with R.E.M., who had a 1991 UK No.6 & US No.10 single 'Shiny Happy People', over 20 Top 40 UK singles and a 1992 UK No.1 & US No.2 album with *Automatic For The People*. Berry quit the band in 1997.

1963 Norman Cook – DJ and bass player. He was a member of the Housemartins, who had a 1986 UK No.1 single with 'Caravan Of Love', Beats International, who had a 1990 UK No.1 with 'Dub Be Good To Me', and Freak Power, who had the 1995 UK No.3 with 'Turn On Tune In Cop Out'. A.K.A. Pizzaman and Fatboy Slim, he had a 1999 UK No.1 single with 'Praise You'.

1964 Jim Corr – guitarist and vocalist with The Corrs, who had a 1998 UK No.3 single with 'What Can I Do?' while *Talk On Corners* was the bestselling UK album of 1998.

1978 Will Champion – drummer with Coldplay, who had a 2000 UK No.4 single with 'Yellow' and the 2005 worldwide No.1 album *X&Y*.

Bill Berry, no relation to Chuck.

ON THIS DAY

1959 Cliff Richard was at No.1 on the UK singles chart with 'Living Doll', the singer's first of 14 UK No.1s.

1964 country singer Jim Reeves was killed in a plane crash when his aircraft, which was flying from Arkansas to Nashville, crashed in thick fog. 41-year-old Reeves was the first country singer to cross over into the pop market – he had had a 1960 US No.2 single with 'He'll Have To Go' and a 1966 UK No.1 single with 'Distant Drums'.

1968 Tommy James & The Shondells were at No.1 on the UK singles chart with 'Mony Mony'. The song was also a hit for Billy Idol in 1987.

1969 Elvis Presley kicked off a four week run at the Las Vegas International Hotel (his first live show since 1961). He reportedly netted $1.5 million (£880,000) for the shows. On the menu at the hotel was an Elvis special, polk salad with corn muffins and honey.

1971 James Taylor went to No.1 on the US singles chart with the Carole King song 'You Got A Friend'. Taylor scored nine other solo US Top 40 hits during the 70s.

1971 a security guard was stabbed to death during a concert by The Who at New York's Forest Hill Stadium.

1976 George Benson started a two week run at No.1 on the US album chart with *Breezin*.

1980 Jon Phillips of The Mamas And The Papas was apprehended by FBI narcotics agents for possession of cocaine. He was later sentenced to 250 hours community service giving anti-drug lectures.

1985 The Eurythmics had the No.1 position on the UK singles chart with 'There Must Be An Angel, (Playing With My Heart)'. Paul Young had the US No.1 with 'Everytime You Go Away'.

1998 Beastie Boys were at No.1 on the US album chart with *Hello Nasty*, the band's third US No.1 album.

1999 Christina Aguilera scored her first US No.1 single with 'Genie In A Bottle', which was also a No.1 in the UK.

2000 eighties pop maestro Mike Stock was declared bankrupt. Mike, who was one third of 80s hit factory Stock, Aitken and Waterman, had been involved in several court battles over copyright issues.

2001 BBC producer John Walters died, aged 63. Walters had produced and worked with Radio 1 DJ John Peel.

Mike 'Stocks and Shares' Stock, and the perils of pop success.

STAIRWAY TO HEAVEN

BORN ON THIS DAY

1942 Jerry Garcia – guitarist and vocalist with Grateful Dead, who had a 1970 album *Workingman's Dead* plus over 25 other albums. He died on August 9th 1995.

1946 Boz Burrell – bass player with King Crimson and Bad Company, who had a 1974 UK No.15 & US No.5 single with 'Can't Get Enough'.

1951 Jaco Pastorius – bass player for Weather Report, who had a 1976 single with 'Birdland' and a 1977 album *Heavy Weather*. He also worked with Joni Mitchell. Pastorius died September 21st 1987.

1959 Joe Elliott – vocalist with Def Leppard, who had a 1987 UK No.6 single with 'Animal' and a 1987 worldwide No.1 album with *Hysteria*. The band also had a 1988 US No.1 single with 'Love Bites'.

1963 Artis Ivey Jr (a.k.a. Coolio), rapper who had a 1995 US & UK No.1 single with 'Gangsta's Paradise'.

ON THIS DAY

1960 Aretha Franklin made her first recordings for CBS Records.

1963 the first *Beatles Monthly* was published, a magazine devoted to the group. It continued until 1969 and at its peak was selling 350,000 copies a month.

Two anonymous lucky winners of the 'Win A Guitar' competition in the first *Beatles Monthly* magazine.

1964 US singer Johnny Burnette was killed in a boating accident on Clear Lake, California, aged 30. He had had the 1961 US No.8 & UK No.3 single 'Your Sixteen'.

1964 The Beatles scored their fifth US No.1 single in seven months when 'A Hard Day's Night' went to the top of the charts. The group had now spent 17 weeks at the No.1 position in this year.

1969 the three day Atlantic City Pop Festival took place with BB King, Janis Joplin, Santana, Joni Mitchell, Three Dog Night, Dr. John, Procol Harum, Arthur Brown, Little Richard and Canned Heat. Tickets cost $13 (£7.60).

1971 The Concert For Bangladesh took place, organized by George Harrison to aid victims of famine and war in Bangladesh. Also playing were Bob Dylan, Ringo Starr, Billy Preston, Eric Clapton, Ravi Shankar and members from Badfinger.

1971 *The Sonny & Cher Comedy Hour* started on prime time American TV.

1980 Def Leppard made their US Live debut when they appeared at the New York City concert opening for AC/DC.

1987 Los Lobos were at No.1 on the UK singles chart with their version of the Ritchie Valens song 'La Bamba', which was also a No.1 hit in the US. The song was the title track from the film based on Ritchie Valens, who died in the same plane crash that killed Buddy Holly.

1987 MTV Europe was launched. The first video played was 'Money For Nothing' by Dire Straits, which contained the appropriate line "I Want My MTV".

2000 Liverpool music store Rushworth and Dreaper closed down after 150 years of trading. The store had become famous after supplying The Beatles and other Liverpool groups with musical instruments.

2002 a new book, *Show The Girl The Door*, written by a former tour manager disclosed some strange demands by female acts. It revealed that Shania Twain travelled with a sniffer dog in case of bombs. Jennifer Lopez liked her dressing room to be all white, including carpets, flowers and furniture. Cher had high security rooms for her wigs. Janet Jackson had a full medical team on standby, including a doctor, nurse and throat specialist, and Britney Spears would demand her favourite Gummie Bear soft sweets.

BORN ON THIS DAY

1937 Garth Hudson – organ player for The Band, who had a 1969 US No.25 single with 'Up On Cripple Creek' and a 1970 UK No.16 single with 'Rag Mama Rag'.

1939 Edward Patten – vocalist with The Pips, who had a 1973 US No.1 single with 'Midnight Train To Georgia' and a 1975 UK No.4 single with Gladys Knight, 'The Way We Were'.

1941 Doris Coley – vocalist with The Shirelles, who had a 1961 US No.1 & UK No.4 single with 'Will You Love Me Tomorrow?' She died on February 5th 2000.

1949 Fat Larry – singer with Fat Larry's Band, who had a 1982 UK No.2 single with 'Zoom'. He died on December 5th 1987.

1951 Andrew Gold – singer/songwriter. As a solo artist he had a 1977 US No.7 single with 'Lonely Boy' and a 1978 UK No.5 single with 'Never Let Her Slip Away'. As a member of Wax, he had a 1987 UK No.12 single with 'Bridge To Your Heart'.

ON THIS DAY

1957 the official Elvis Presley Fan Club was launched in the UK.

1960 Johnny Kidd And The Pirates were at No.1 on the UK singles chart with 'Shakin' All Over'. It was their only UK No.1.

1971 Creedence Clearwater Revival kicked off a ten date US tour at the Assembly Center, Tulsa.

1973 The Mamas And The Papas filed a lawsuit against their record label Dunhill for $9 million (£5.3 million) in unpaid royalties.

1975 The Eagles went to No.1 on the US singles chart with 'One Of These Nights', the group's second US No.1 single and the first to chart in the UK, where it made No.23.

1977 The Who bought Shepperton Film Studios for £350,000 ($595,000).

1983 James Jamerson, Motown Records session player, died of a heart attack, aged 45. One of "The Funk Brothers" he had played on many Motown hits by The Temptations, Marvin Gaye, The Four Tops and Martha And The Vandellas.

1986 Peter Cetera started a two week run at No.1 on the US charts with the theme from the film *Karate Kid II*, 'The Glory Of Love'. It made No.3 in the UK.

1986 Chris de Burgh was at No.1 in the UK with 'The Lady In Red'. It was his first No.1 after 24 single releases.

1987 David Martin, bass player with Sam The Sham & The Pharaohs, died of a heart attack. The band had the 1965 US No.2 & UK No.11 single 'Wooly Bully'.

1991 Rick James and his girlfriend Tanya Hijazi were arrested in Hollywood, charged with assault with a deadly weapon, aggravated mayhem, torture, false imprisonment and forcible oral copulation. James was released on $1 million (£0.6 million) bail.

The initial copy of *Mojo* (then *Mojo Navigator*) was a mere zerox fanzine.

1998 *Mojo* magazine published the results from a nationwide survey asking, "Who is your favourite recording artist of all time?" Fifth place was Elton John, fourth Queen, third Frank Sinatra, second Elvis Presley and first The Beatles.

2000 Jerome Smith from KC & The Sunshine Band died after being crushed by a bulldozer he was operating.

2001 New Orleans International Airport was renamed Louis Armstrong Airport in honour of the legendary jazz musician.

2004 Eric Clapton bought a 50% share in the historic gentleman's outfitters Cordings to save it from closure after the store, based in London since 1839, had run into financial difficulties. The guitarist said he had been fond of the shop since a window display caught his eye when he was 16, and has become a regular shopper there.

BORN ON THIS DAY

1926 Tony Bennett, singer who had a 1955 UK No.1 single with 'Stranger In Paradise' and a 1965 UK No.25 single with 'I Left My Heart In San Francisco'.

BY THE DOORS

TOUCH ME

85 CENTS
NIPPER MUSIC COMPANY, INC.
DISTRIBUTED BY MUSIC SALES CORPORATION
33 WEST 60TH STREET
NEW YORK 10023

the Doors

1941 Beverly Lee – singer with The Shirelles, who had a 1961 US No.1 & UK No.4 single with 'Will You Love Me Tomorrow?'

1946 John York – bass player and vocalist with The Byrds, who had a 1965 UK & US No.1 single with 'Mr. Tambourine Man'.

1951 John Graham – guitarist with Earth, Wind And Fire, who had a 1975 US No.1 single with 'Shining Star' and a 1981 UK No.3 single with 'Let's Groove'.

1956 Kirk Brandon – singer and guitarist for Spear Of Destiny, who had a 1987 UK No.14 single with 'Never Take Me Alive', and Theatre Of Hate, who had a 1982 UK No.40 single with 'Do You Believe In The Westworld?'

1963 James Hetfield – singer and guitarist with Metallica, who had a 1991 UK No.5 single with 'Enter Sandman'.

1966 Dean Sams – keyboardist with Lonestar, who had a 2000 US No.1 & UK No.21 single with 'Amazed'.

1971 Deirdre Roper a.k.a. Spinderella, singer with Salt-N-Pepa, who had a 1991 UK No.2 single with 'Let's Talk About Sex'.

ON THIS DAY

1968 The Doors started a two week run at No.1 on the US singles chart with 'Hello I Love You', the group's second US No.1 and a No.15 hit in the UK.

1971 Paul McCartney announced the formation of his new group Wings, with his wife Linda and ex-Moody Blues member Denny Laine.

1974 headlining at The Schaefer Festival, New York was Anne Murray – the opening act was Bruce Springsteen's E Street Band.

1974 Bad Company went to No.1 on the US album chart with their self-titled debut album.

1985 'Drive' by The Cars was re-released, following its use during "Live Aid", with all royalties going to the Band Aid trust.

1985 Madonna scored her first UK No.1 single with 'Into The Groove'. The track was taken from the movie *Desperately Seeking Susan*, which featured the singer and actress Rosanna Arquette.

1985 Tears For Fears started a three week run at No.1 on the US singles chart with 'Shout', the duo's second US No.1.

1986 *News Of The World* printed an exclusive interview with 16-year-old model Mandy Smith who revealed she'd been having an affair with Rolling Stone Bill Wyman for the past two and a half years.

1996 Los Del Rio started a 14 week run at No.1 on the US singles chart with 'Macarena', which was a No.2 hit in the UK.

2000 Maurice Kinn died, aged 76. The UK publisher launched the *New Musical Express* in 1953, which instigated the first charts based on record sales, and organized the annual *NME* poll winners concerts.

2001 co-founder of US group The 5th Dimension Ron Townson died of kidney failure, aged 68. The group had had the 1969 US No.1 & UK No.11 single 'Aquarius'.

2003 UK band The Coral scored their first UK No.1 album with *Magic And Medicine*.

BORN ON THIS DAY

1901 Louis Armstrong, singer, bandleader and trumpet player who had a 1964 US No.1 single with 'Hello Dolly!' and a 1968 UK No.1 single with 'What A Wonderful World'. Armstrong died on July 6th 1971.

marquee

90 Wardour St., W1   01-437 6603

OPEN EVERY NIGHT FROM 7.00 p.m. to 11.00 p.m.
REDUCED ADMISSION FOR STUDENTS AND MEMBERS

Thurs., 4th Aug. (Adm. 80p)
THE BUZZCOCKS
Wire & Ian Fleming

Fri., 5th Aug. (Adm. 76p)
RADIO STARS
Plus guests & Ian Fleming

Sat., 6th Aug. (Adm. 75p)
Free admission with this ad. before 8 p.m.
X RAY SPECS
Plus support & Ian Fleming

Sun., 7th Aug. (Adm. £1)
Live Recording of . . .
MARQUEE MYSTERY BAND
Plus friends & Nick Leigh
(Please ring for details)

Mon., 8th Aug. (Adm. 75p)
THE BOYS
Plus support & D.J.

Tues., 9th Aug.
(See Panel below)

Wed., 10th Aug. (Adm. 80p)
CHELSEA
Plus support & Ian Fleming

Thurs., 11th Aug. (Adm. 90p)
EDGAR BROUGHTON'S CHILDERMASS
Al & Ian Fleming

Hamburgers and other hot and cold snacks are available

TUESDAY, 9th AUGUST.
(Admission 70p)
RICO
Major Wiley and D.J.
READING ROCK '77
AUGUST BANK HOLIDAY WEEKEND. SEE PAGE 7

1936 Elsberry Hobbs – vocalist with The Drifters, who had a 1960 US No.1 & UK No.2 single with 'Save The Last Dance For Me'.

1940 Larry Knechtel – guitarist and keyboardist for Bread, who had a 1970 US No.1 & UK No.5 single with 'Make It With You'.

1952 Marie Ni Bhraonain – vocalist with Clannad, who had a 1982 UK No.5 single with 'Harry's Game'.

ON THIS DAY

1958 Billboard introduced "The Hot 100 Singles Chart". Ricky Nelson was at No.1 with 'Poor Little Fool'.

1963 UK music weekly *New Musical Express* reported that The Beatles could score their first US hit with 'From Me To You' as the single was "bubbling under" at No.116.

1966 The Troggs were at No.1 on the UK singles chart with 'With A Girl Like You', the group's only UK No.1 single.

1967 a female Monkees fan stowed away on the band's plane between shows in Minneapolis and St. Louis. The girl's father threatened to bring charges against the group for transporting a minor across state lines.

1968 the two day Newport Pop Festival took place in California with Canned Heat, Sonny & Cher, Steppenwolf, The Byrds, Grateful Dead, Tiny Tim, Iron Butterfly and Jefferson Airplane. Over 100,000 fans attended the festival.

1979 a benefit concert was held to raise money for the widow of Little Feat's Lowell George who died from a heart attack in June of this year. Members of his band plus Jackson Browne, Emmylou Harris and Bonnie Raitt all helped to raise over $230,000, (£110,000).

1980 John Lennon began recording what would become his final album *Double Fantasy* at The Hit Factory, New York.

MARIAH HIRES PRIVATE EYE TO SPY ON HER EX

1984 Prince started a 24 week run at the top of the US album charts with *Purple Rain*. It went on to sell over ten million copies.

1990 during a New Kids On The Block concert in Montreal, Canada three armed robbers stole souvenir sales proceeds valued at $260,000 (£152,941).

1990 Mariah Carey started a four week run at No.1 on the US singles chart with her debut single 'Vision Of Love', a No.9 hit in the UK.

1996 Oasis roadie James Hunter was crushed to death between a fork-lift truck and a lorry during the band's shows at Balloch Country Park, Loch Lomond in Scotland.

1999 appearing at The Paramount Theatre, Denver was Britney Spears with UK support group Steps.

2001 the *News Of The World* reported that Mariah Carey had hired a private eye to spy on her ex-husband, record boss Tommy Mottola. Investigator Jack Palladino told the paper that Mariah believed her ex-husband was conducting a smear campaign against her.

2002 Bruce Springsteen scored his fifth UK No.1 album with The Rising, which was also No.1 in the US.

THE RED COW

Thursday, August 4
WINDOW
Adm. Free

Friday, August 5
JOHNNY DUCANN BAND
(ex Atomic Rooster)
Adm. Free

Saturday, August 6
THE POLICE
Adm. 60p

Sunday, August 7
HEAD OVER HEELS
Adm. Free

Wednesday, August 10
PRAIRIE OYSTER
Adm. Free

Hammersmith Road, W.6

BORN ON THIS DAY

1941 Airto Moreira – drummer with Weather Report, who had a 1976 single with 'Birdland' and a 1977 album with *Heavy Weather*.

1942 Rick Huxley – guitarist with Dave Clark Five, who had a 1964 UK No.1 single with 'Glad All Over', a 1965 US No.1 single with 'Over And Over' plus over 15 other UK Top 40 singles.

1946 Jimmy Webb, US singer/songwriter who wrote the 1968 hit for Richard Harris 'MacArthur Park' plus 'Galverston' for Glen Campbell and 'Up Up and Away' for The 5th Dimension.

1947 Gregory Leskiw – guitarist with Guess Who, who had a 1970 US No.1 & UK No.19 single with 'American Woman'.

1959 Pete Burns – singer for Mystery Girls and Dead Or Alive, who had a 1985 UK No.1 single with 'You Spin Me Round, Like A Record'.

1960 Stuart Croxford –keyboardist for Kajagoogoo, who had a 1983 UK No.1 single with 'Too Shy'.

1975 Dan Hipgrave – guitarist with Toploader, who had a 2000 UK No.7 single with 'Dancing In The Moonlight'.

ON THIS DAY

1956 Doris Day was at No.1 on the UK singles chart with 'Whatever Will Be, Will Be', the singer and actress' second UK No.1 single.

1968 country guitarist Luther Perkins died in a fire. He had worked with Johnny Cash, Jerry Lee Lewis and The Carter Family.

1972 Aerosmith signed to CBS Records for $125,000 (£73,529) after record company boss Clive Davis saw them play at Max's Kansas City Club, New York.

1975 Kim Fowley formed the first-ever all-female heavy rock band, The Runaways. Joan Jett was one of the members.

1975 The Beatles released their seventh studio album, Revolver.

1975 Robert Plant and his wife were badly injured in a car crash while on holiday in Rhodes.

1978 The Rolling Stones went to No.1 on the US singles chart with 'Miss You', the group's eighth US No.1 single and a No.3 hit in the UK.

1979 Def Leppard signed to Phonogram records with an advance of £120,000 pounds ($180,000) giving them a 10% royalty on 100% of sales for the first two years.

1981 Olivia Newton-John was awarded a Gold Star on Hollywood Boulevard.

1983 David Crosby, from Crosby, Stills & Nash, was sentenced to five years in jail in Texas for cocaine and firearms offences. Crosby had slept through most of his trial.

1984 Bruce Springsteen played the first of ten nights at the Meadowlands in New Jersey to mark the homecoming of his "Born in the U.S.A." Tour.

1986 Michael Rudetsky, keyboard player with Culture Club, was found dead at Boy George's Hampstead home.

1989 Prince was at No.1 on the US singles chart with 'Batdance', which was taken from the *Batman* movie.

1992 Jeff Porcaro of Toto died, aged 38, of a heart attack, caused by an allergic reaction to lawn pesticides.

1993 Randy Hobbs, bass player with Edgar Winter And Motrose, was found dead in his hotel room in Dayton, Ohio from a drug overdose, aged 45.

1995 Take That played the first of ten sold-out nights at The Nynex Arena, Manchester (the shows were without Robbie Williams who had just quit the group). Take That were also at UK No.1 on the UK singles chart with 'Never Forget'.

1996 it was reported that UK TV music show *Top Of The Pops* had hit rock bottom with its lowest audience ever, only two and a half million viewers. In its heyday the show attracted 17 million.

2000 police were called to Gary Glitter's West London home when a crowd gathered outside and started to shout abuse at the former pop star, who was currently back in London to attend to business affairs before heading abroad again.

2001 David Gray returned to the No.1 position on the UK album chart with *White Ladder*.

Top Thirty Singles

1	(1)	I FEEL LOVE .... Donna Summer, GTO
2	(2)	MA BAKER .... Boney M, Atlantic
3	(5)	ANGELO .... Brotherhood Of Man, Pye
4	(4)	PRETTY VACANT .... Sex Pistols, Virgin
5	(4)	FANFARE FOR THE COMMON MAN
		Emerson, Lake and Palmer, Atlantic
6	(3)	SO YOU WIN AGAIN
		Hot Chocolate, RAK
7	(13)	WE'RE ALL ALONE
		Rita Coolidge, A & M
8	(23)	FLOAT ON .... Floaters, ABC

STRANGLERS: Following up the success of 'Peaches' (still in, at 32) with 'Something Better Change'

9	(25)	YOU GOT WHAT IT TAKES
		Showaddywaddy, Arista
10	(7)	BABY DON'T CHANGE YOUR MIND
		Gladys Knight and the Pips, Buddah
11	(21)	EASY .... Commodores, Motown
12	(9)	OH LORI .... Alessi, A & M
13	(8)	SLOW DOWN .... John Miles, Decca
14	(16)	ROADRUNNER ONCE, ROADRUNNER TWICE .... Jonathan Richman, Beserkley
15	(19)	IT'S YOUR LIFE .... Smokie, RAK
16	(24)	ALL AROUND THE WORLD
		Jam, Polydor
17	(17)	THE CRUNCH ...... Rah Band, Good Earth
18	(35)	EXODUS
		Bob Marley and the Wailers, Island
19	(—)	SOMETHING BETTER CHANGE
		Stranglers, United Artists
20	(10)	SAM .... Olivia Newton-John, EMI
21	(14)	FEEL THE NEED
		Detroit Emeralds, Atlantic
22	(11)	PEACHES .... Stranglers, United Artists
23	(—)	PROVE IT .... Television, Elektra
24	(18)	ONE STEP AWAY .... Tavares, Capitol
25	(—)	THAT'S WHAT FRIENDS ARE FOR
		Deniece Williams, CBS
26	(—)	NIGHTS ON BROADWAY
		Candi Staton, Warner Bros.
27	(15)	DREAMS .... Fleetwood Mac, Warner Bros.
28	(29)	ROCKY MOUNTAIN WAY
		Joe Walsh, ABC
29	(—)	DO WHAT YOU WANNA DO
		T-Connection, TK
30	(—)	I KNEW THE BRIDE
		Dave Edmunds, Swan Song

■ The Melody Maker chart is used by the Daily Mirror, The Sun, Daily Telegraph, Sunday People, News Of The World; scores of evening and weekly newspapers throughout Britain; and quoted in papers all over the world.

Top Thirty Albums

1	(2)	A STAR IS BORN .... Soundtrack, CBS
2	(1)	THE JOHNNY MATHIS COLLECTION
		CBS
3	(10)	I REMEMBER YESTERDAY
		Donna Summer, GTO
4	(5)	LOVE AT THE GREEK
		Neil Diamond, CBS
5	(4)	HOTEL CALIFORNIA .... Eagles, Asylum
6	(3)	THE MUPPET SHOW .... Muppets, Pye
7	(9)	RUMOURS Fleetwood Mac, Warner Bros
8	(7)	GOING FOR THE ONE .... Yes, Atlantic

TANGERINE DREAM: still weaving that magic as 'Sorcerer' enters at number 17.

9	(7)	STRANGLERS IV (RATTUS NORVEGI-CUS) .... Stranglers, United Artists
10	(6)	ARRIVAL .... Abba, Epic
11	(12)	STEVE WINWOOD .... Island
12	(11)	EXODUS
		Bob Marley and the Wailers, Island
13	(13)	DECEPTIVE BENDS .... 10cc, Mercury
14	(18)	20 ALL TIME GREATS
		Connie Francis, Polydor
15	(14)	WORKS
		Emerson, Lake and Palmer, Atlantic
16	(19)	A NEW WORLD RECORD
		Electric Light Orchestra, Jet
17	(—)	SORCERER .... Tangerine Dream, MCA
18	(22)	ON STAGE .... Rainbow, Polydor
19	(—)	LOVE IN THE AIR AGE
		Be-Bop Deluxe, EMI
20	(15)	BEST OF MAMAS AND PAPAS ... Arcade
21	(16)	BEATLES AT THE HOLLYWOOD BOWL
		EMI
22	(15)	IN FLIGHT George Benson, Warner Bros
23	(28)	CSN ... Crosby, Stills and Nash, Atlantic
24	(30)	ABBA'S GREATEST HITS .... Epic
25	(20)	I'M IN YOU ... Peter Frampton, A & M
	(—)	LITTLE QUEEN .... Heart, Portrait
27	(—)	STREISAND SUPERMAN
		Barbra Streisand, CBS
28	(22)	AMERICAN STARS 'N' BARS
		Neil Young, Reprise
29	(—)	FACE TO FACE
		Steve Harley and Cockney Rebel, EMI
30	(—)	ANIMALS .... Pink Floyd, Harvest

Two titles tied for 25th position

BORN ON THIS DAY

1929 Mike Elliot – saxophonist with The Foundations, who had a 1967 UK No.1 single with 'Baby Now That I've Found You' and a 1969 US No.3 single with 'Build Me Up A Buttercup'.

1938 Isaac Hayes, singer/songwriter who had a 1971 US No.1 & UK No.4 single with 'Theme From *Shaft*' and a 1998 UK No.2 single as Chef (from *South Park*), 'Chocolate Salty Balls'.

1952 Pat McDonald – guitarist, harmonica player and vocalist with Timbuk 3, who had a 1987 UK No.21 single with 'The Future's So Bright, I Gotta Wear Shades'.

1972 Geri Halliwell, Ginger Spice – singer with The Spice Girls, who had a 1996 UK No.1 & 1997 US No.1 single with 'Wannabe' plus seven other No.1 singles. She left the band on June 7th 1998 and her first solo No.1 was the 1999 'Mi Chico Latino'.

ON THIS DAY

1964 Rod Stewart made his TV debut on The Beat Room as a member of The Hoochie Coochie Men.

1965 Decca Records released The Small Faces debut single 'Whatcha Gonna Do About It?' It peaked at No.14 on the UK chart.

Small Faces, big hits.

1973 Stevie Wonder was seriously injured when his car crashed into a truck, leaving him in a coma for four days. The accident also left him without any sense of smell.

1977 this week's UK Top 5 singles were: No.5, 'Fanfare For The Common Man', ELP; No.4, 'Pretty Vacant', the Sex Pistols; No.3, 'Angelo', Brotherhood Of Man; No.2, 'Ma Baker', Boney M and No.1, 'I Feel Love', Donna Summer.

1983 *The Very Best Of The Beach Boys* went to No.1 on the UK album chart.

1988 *Appetite For Destruction*, Guns N' Roses' debut album, went to No.1 in the US, after spending 57 weeks on the chart and selling over five million copies.

1988 Yazz And The Plastic Population started a five week run at No.1 on the UK singles chart with 'The Only Way Is Up'.

1989 Adam Clayton of U2 was arrested in The Blue Light Inn car park in Dublin for marijuana possession and intent to supply the drug to another person. His conviction was waived in exchange for paying £25,000 ($42,500) to the Dublin Woman's Aid Centre.

1990 Ace Of Base made their live debut when they played in Gothenburg, Sweden.

1994 Lisa Loeb started a three week run at No.1 on the US singles chart with 'Stay, (I Missed You)', which was a No.6 hit in the UK.

1994 Manic Street Preachers guitarist Richey Edwards booked into a private clinic to be treated for nervous exhaustion.

2000 former Boyzone member Ronan Keating started a two week run at No.1 on the UK album chart with his debut release *Ronan*.

2000 Robbie Williams went to No.1 on the UK singles chart with 'Rock DJ'.

2001 Whitney Houston became one of the highest-paid musicians in the world after signing a new deal with Arista Records said to be worth more than $100 million (£59 million).

2002 a report by 560 UK undertakers said bereaved families were preferring pop songs to hymns at funerals. 'Wind Beneath My Wings' by Bette Midler was the most requested song, along with Robbie Williams' 'Angels', Whitney Houston's 'I Will Always Love You' and Elton John's 'Candle In The Wind.' Queen's 'Another One Bites The Dust' was one of the more unusual songs to be chosen.

BORN ON THIS DAY

1925 Felice Bryant, songwriter who, with her husband Boudleaux, wrote The Everly Brothers' hits 'Bye Bye Love', 'All I Have To Do Is Dream', 'Wake Up Little Susie' as well as 'Raining In My Heart' – which was a hit for Buddy Holly. She died on April 22nd 2003.

1936 Charles Pope – singer with The Tams, who had a 1971 UK No.1 single with 'Hey Girl Don't Bother Me'. He died on March 16th 1996.

1945 Kerry Chater – guitarist and bass guitarist with Gary Puckett And The Union Gap, who had a 1968 UK No.1 & UK No.2 single with 'Young Girl'.

1950 Rodney Crowell, country guitarist and songwriter who worked with Emmylou Harris. Acts who covered his songs include Bob Seger, Willie Nelson and Carlene Carter.

1952 Andy Fraser – bass player with John Mayall's Bluesbreakers and then joined Free when he was aged 16. Free had a 1970 UK No.2 & US No.4 single with 'All Right Now'. Ted Nugent, Robert Palmer and Joe Cocker have all covered songs written by Fraser.

1958 Bruce Dickinson – vocalist with Iron Maiden, who had a 1982 UK No.1 album with The *Number Of The Beast* and a UK No.1 single in 1991 with 'Bring Your Daughter To The Slaughter'.

1965 Raul Malo – vocalist with The Mavericks, a US country rock group, who had a 1998 UK No.4 single with 'Dance The Night Away'.

ON THIS DAY

1957 The Quarry Men made their debut at Liverpool's Cavern Club, without guitarist Paul McCartney who was away on a Scout trip.

1965 Herman's Hermits went to No.1 on the US singles chart with 'I'm Henry VIII, I Am'. The single was only released in the US. The singer from the group, Peter Noone, once interviewed Elvis Presley for UK music paper *New Musical Express*.

1971 The Bee Gees started a four week run at No.1 on the US singles chart with 'How Can You Mend A Broken Heart?' It was the group's tenth US hit and first No.1.

1974 Peter Wolf from The J. Geils Band married actress Faye Dunaway in Beverly Hills.

1976 Elton John and Kiki Dee were at No.1 on the US singles chart with 'Don't Go Breaking My Heart'. This gave Elton his sixth US No.1 and was also his first UK No.1 single.

1979 Led Zeppelin played their last-ever UK show when they appeared at Knebworth Park.

1982 Fleetwood Mac started a five week run at No.1 on the US album chart with Mirage. It was the band's third US No.1.

1982 *Kids From Fame* by The Kids Of Fame started an eight week run at No.1 on the UK album chart.

1984 US soul singer Esther Phillips died from liver failure. She had a 1975 US No.20 & UK No.6 single with 'What A Difference A Day Makes'.

1997 Garth Brooks played to the largest crowd ever to attend a concert in New York's Central Park. An estimated one million people saw the live show, with an additional 14.6 million viewing live on HBO.

2001 harmonica player Larry Adler *(right)* died, aged 87. He was known for his original collaborations with George Gershwin, Kate Bush, Sting and Vaughan Williams as well as his own virtuoso performances.

2002 three members of Oasis were injured when the taxi they were travelling in was involved in a crash during a US tour in Indianapolis. Noel Gallagher *(below)*, Andy Bell and Jay Darlington were all taken to hospital and treated for cuts and bruises.

BORN ON THIS DAY

1927 Andy Warhol, pop artist and producer and the founder of the Pop Art movement. He produced and managed The Velvet Underground, designed the 1967 *Velvet Underground And Nico* "peeled banana" album cover and The Rolling Stones' *Sticky Fingers* album cover. He died on February 22nd 1987 after a gall bladder operation.

1933 Joe Tex, US soul singer who had a 1965 US No.5 single with 'Hold On To What You've Got' and a 1977 UK No.2 single with 'Ain't Gonna Bump No More, With No Big Fat Woman'. Tex died on August 12th 1982, aged 49.

1949 Airrion Love – vocalist with The Stylistics, who had a 1975 US No.1 single with 'You Make Me Feel Brand New', a 1975 UK No.1 single with 'Can't Give You Anything But My Love' plus 15 other UK Top 40 singles.

1961 Paul Jackson – bass player with T'Pau, who had a 1987 UK No.1 single with 'China In Your Hand' and a 1987 US No.4 single with 'Heart And Soul'.

1961 The Edge (a.k.a. Dave Evans) – guitarist with U2, who scored five consecutive US No.1s plus 25 UK top 40 singles. The 1987 worldwide No.1 album *The Joshua Tree* was the first CD album to sell over a million.

1973 Scott Stapp – vocalist with Creed, who had a 2001 US No.1 & UK No.13 single with 'With Arms Wide Open' and a 2002 US No.1 album with *Weathered*.

1976 Joshua Chasez – vocalist with *NSYNC, who had a 2000 US No.1 single with 'It's Gonna Be Me' and a 1999 UK No.5 single with 'I Want You Back'.

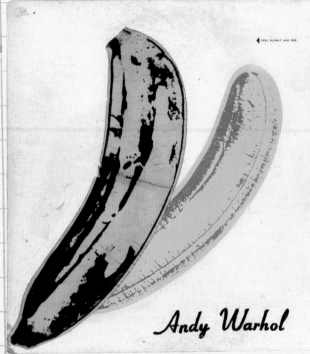

Andy Warhol

ON THIS DAY

1960 16-year-old Brian Hyland went to No.1 on the US singles chart with 'Itsy Bitsy Teeny Weeny Yellow Polka Dot Bikini', a No.8 in the UK. It was also a UK No.1 for Bombalurina featuring TV presenter Timmy Mallett in 1990.

1963 The Searchers were at No.1 on the UK singles chart with 'Sweets For My Sweet', the group's first of three UK No.1s.

1964 a single by The Young World Singers called 'Ringo For President' was released in the US.

1966 in response to John Lennon's remark about The Beatles being bigger than Jesus, the South African Broadcasting Corporation banned all Beatles records.

1970 Janis Joplin bought a headstone for the grave of her greatest influence, Bessie Smith, at the Mont Lawn Cemetery in Philadelphia. (Smith died in 1937, after being refused admission to a whites only hospital.)

Bigger than The Beatles?

1980 The Greater London Council banned The Plasmatics from blowing a car up on stage during their UK live debut at London's Hammersmith Odeon.

1983 Harold Melvin and members from The Bluenotes were arrested in Atlantic City on charges of cocaine possession.

1991 appearing at The Jericho Tavern, Oxford were On A Friday (soon to be renamed Radiohead).

1992 a riot broke out during a Guns N' Roses and Metallica gig at Montreal stadium when Metallica's show was cut short after singer James Hetfield was injured by pyrotechnics.

1998 The Spice Girls had the UK No.1 single with 'Viva Forever', Brandy and Monica were at No.1 on the US singles chart with 'The Boy Is Mine.'

BORN ON THIS DAY

1939 Billy Henderson – vocalist with the Detroit Spinners, who had a 1980 UK No.1 & US No.2 single with 'Working My Way Back To You'.

1946 John Parry – drummer with Bonzo Dog Doo Dah Band, who had a 1968 UK No.5 single with 'I'm The Urban Spaceman'.

1954 Bruce Thomas – bass guitarist for Elvis Costello And The Attractions, who had a 1979 UK No.2 single with 'Oliver's Army'.

1955 Benjamin Orr – bass guitarist and vocalist for The Cars, who had a 1978 UK No.3 single with 'My Best Friend's Girl' and a 1985 UK No.4 single with 'Drive'. Orr died on October 3rd 2000.

1963 Whitney Houston, singer who had a 1985 UK & US No.1 single with 'Saving All My Love For You', a 1992 UK & US No.1 single with 'I Will Always Love You' plus nine other US No.1s and 20 UK Top 40 singles – including four No.1s.

ON THIS DAY

1953 Mantovani and his Orchestra were at No.1 on the UK singles chart with 'Song From The Moulin Rouge'.

1958 Cliff Richard started a four week residency at Butlins Holiday Camp in Clacton-On-Sea, Essex, as Cliff Richard And The Drifters.

1963 the first-ever edition of *Ready, Steady, Go!* was shown on UK TV. Introduced by Keith Fordyce and 19-year-old Cathy McGowan, the first show featured The Searchers, Jet Harris, Pat Boone, Billy Fury and Brian Poole & The Tremeloes. The final show was in December 1966, after 175 episodes.

1967 Scott McKenzie was at No.1 on the UK singles chart with 'San Francisco (Be Sure To Wear Some Flowers In Your Hair)'. It was the singer's only UK Top 40 hit.

1969 Jethro Tull scored their only UK No.1 album with their second release *Stand Up*.

1975 The Bee Gees started a two week run at No.1 on the US singles chart with 'Jive Talkin', the group's second US No.1. The song made No.5 in the UK.

1975 Typically Tropical was at No.1 on the UK singles chart with 'Barbados'.

1980 AC/DC scored their first UK No.1 album with *Back In Black*.

Cathy McGowan, ready to go.

Cliff Richard's support act gets the Butlins crowd going!

1986 Queen gave what would be their last-ever live performance when they appeared at Knebworth Festival.

1994 during an Oasis gig at The Riverside in Newcastle upon Tyne Noel Gallagher was hit in the face by a man who had jumped on the stage. Noel refused to carry on and a mob of 300 people attacked the band's bus as they were leaving.

1995 Jerry Garcia, guitarist and singer from the Grateful Dead, died of a heart attack, aged 53.

1999 manager Bob Herbert was killed in a car crash in Windsor. Herbert was behind the formation of The Spice Girls and Five and had managed Bros during the 80s.

2003 Nicky Byrne of Westlife married the daughter of Irish Prime Minister Bertie Ahern in France.

BORN ON THIS DAY

1909 Leo Fender, inventor of The Telecaster and Stratocaster guitars. He died on March 21st 1991.

1928 Jimmy Dean, singer who had a 1961 US No.1 & UK No.2 single with 'Big Bad John'. He went on to present a prime time variety show on US TV.

1940 Bobby Hatfield – singer with The Righteous Brothers, who had a 1965 UK & US No.1 single with 'You've Lost That Lovin' Feelin' and a 1990 UK No.1 single 'Unchained Melody' – it was first released in 1965. Hatfield died on November 5th 2003.

1943 James Griffin – vocalist and guitarist with Bread, who had a 1970 US No.1 & UK No.5 single with 'Make It With You'.

1947 Ian Anderson – vocalist and flautist for Jethro Tull, who had a 1969 UK No.3 and US No.11 single with 'Living In The Past'.

1947 Ronnie Spector (a.k.a. Veronica Bennett) – singer with The Ronettes, who had a 1963 US No.2 & UK No.4 single with 'Be My Baby'. She married producer Phil Spector in 1967. They divorced in 1974.

1948 Patti Austin, singer who had a 1983 US No.1 & UK No.11 single with James Ingram, 'Baby Come To Me'.

1961 Jon Farriss – drummer and vocalist with INXS, who had a 1988 UK No.2 & US No.1 single with 'Need You Tonight'.

ON THIS DAY

1959 four male members of The Platters were arrested after a gig in Cincinnati after being found with four 19-year-old women (three of them white), in various stages of undress. The scandal resulted in radio stations across the US removing Platters records from their playlists.

1963 13-year-old Little Stevie Wonder started a three week run at No.1 on the US singles chart with 'Fingertips part II', making him the youngest singer to top the charts.

1963 on UK TV the 100th edition of *Thank Your Lucky Stars* was broadcast, with Cliff Richard, The Shadows, Searchers, Brian Poole & The Tremeloes, Billy J. Kramer & The Dakotas and Alma Cogan.

1964 Mick Jagger was fined £32 ($54) in Liverpool for driving without insurance and breaking the speed limit.

1968 Cream started a four week run at No.1 on the US album chart with *Wheels Of Fire*.

1972 Paul and Linda McCartney were arrested and fined £800 ($1,360) for possession of cannabis in a drugs bust after a concert in Gothenburg, Sweden.

1974 Roberta Flack went to No.1 on the US singles chart with 'Feel Like Makin' Love', the singer's third US No.1.

1985 Simon Le Bon from Duran Duran was airlifted to safety when his boat, Drum, overturned while racing off the English coast.

2001 Toploader guitarist Dan Hipgrave married TV presenter Gail Porter at an Edinburgh registry office.

2002 Lisa Marie Presley married actor Nicolas Cage at a resort in Hawaii. The marriage was Presley's third. She was married previously to musician Danny Keough and pop star Michael Jackson. Cage filed for divorce four months later.

THANK YOUR LUCKY STARS

THE ROLLING STONES
THE TORNADOS
BRIAN POOLE and the TREMELOES
JET HARRIS and TONY MEEHAN
EDEN KANE
HEINZ
BILLY FURY

BORN ON THIS DAY

1942 Mike Hugg – drummer with Manfred Mann, who had a 1964 UK & US No.1 single with 'Do Wah Diddy Diddy'.

1949 Eric Carmen – singer with The Young Rascals, who had a 1967 US No.1 and UK No.8 single with 'Groovin', then The Raspberries, who had a 1972 US No.5 single with 'Go All The Way'. As a solo artist he had a 1976 US No.2 single with 'All By Myself'.

1950 Erik Braunn – guitarist with Iron Butterfly, who had a 1968 US No.14 single with 'In-A-Gadda-Da-Vida'. Braunn died on July 25th 2003, aged 52.

1954 Bryan Bassett – guitarist with Wild Cherry, who had a 1976 US No.1 & UK No.7 single with 'Play That Funky Music'.

1955 Joe Jackson, singer/songwriter who had a 1980 UK No.5 single with 'It's Different For Girls'.

ON THIS DAY

1962 Neil Sedaka started a two week run at No.1 on the US singles chart with 'Breaking Up Is Hard To Do', his first US No.1 as a solo artist. The song was a No.7 hit on the UK chart.

1967 appearing at the Seventh National Jazz, Pop, Ballads and Blues festival at The Royal Windsor Racecourse, England were The Small Faces, The Move, Marmalade, Paul Jones, Pink Floyd, Amen Corner, Donovan, Zoot Money, Cream, Jeff Beck, John Mayall, Peter Green's Fleetwood Mac and The Crazy World Of Arthur Brown. An advance three day ticket cost £2 ($3.40).

1969 350 special guests were invited to see Motown Records' new signing, The Jackson Five, play at The Daisy Club in Beverly Hills.

1979 The Knack started a five week run at No.1 on the US album chart with *Get The Knack*.

1984 Ray Parker Jr started a three week run at No.1 on the US singles chart with the theme from the film *Ghostbusters*. Parker had been a session guitarist for Stevie Wonder and Marvin Gaye. The song was a No.2 hit in the UK.

Eric Carmen in pane.

1989 three members of the LL Cool J crew were arrested and charged with raping a 15-year-old girl. The incident took place after a concert when the girl had won a backstage pass on a radio contest.

1999 four music festivals took place in Cornwall for the full solar eclipse. James, The Levellers, Van Morrison, Kula Shaker and the Happy Mondays were all appearing at various events.

1999 Kiss arrived on Hollywood Boulevard to unveil their own star on The Walk Of Fame. The band had released over 30 albums and sold over 80 million records worldwide.

2000 Madonna gave birth to a baby boy, Rocco Ritchie, at The Cedars-Sinai Hospital, Beverly Hills.

2001 appearing at the Ozzfest at PNC Bank Arts Center, New Jersey were Black Sabbath, Linkin Park, Slipknot and Marilyn Manson.

2002 Bruce Springsteen started a two week run at No.1 on the US album chart with *The Rising*, the singer's fifth US No.1. It was also No.1 in the UK.

BORN ON THIS DAY

1941 Craig Douglas, singer who had a 1959 UK No.1 single with 'Only Sixteen' plus nine other UK Top 40 hits.

1949 Mark Knopfler – guitarist and vocalist with Dire Straits, who had a 1985 US No.1 single with 'Money For Nothing', a 1986 UK No.2 single with 'Walk Of Life' and a 1985 worldwide No.1 album with *Brothers In Arms*. More recently Knopfler has produced solo work and also been a part of the Notting Hillbillies.

1951 August Darnell – vocalist with Kid Creole And The Coconuts, who had a 1982 UK No.2 single with 'Annie I'm Not Your Daddy'.

1953 Jerry Speiser – drummer with Men At Work, who had a 1983 UK & US No.1 single with 'Down Under'.

1958 Jurgen Dehmel – bass player for Nena, who had a 1984 UK No.1 & US No.2 single with '99 Red Balloons'.

1961 Roy Hay – guitarist and vocalist with Culture Club, who had a 1983 UK No.1 & 1984 US No.1 single with 'Karma Chameleon' plus seven other UK Top 10 singles.

1963 Sir Mix-A-Lot, US rapper who had a 1992 US No.1 single 'Baby Got Back'. The song was a No.56 hit in the UK.

ON THIS DAY

1964 The Beatles' first film *A Hard Day's Night* opened in 500 American cinemas to rave reviews.

1967 the Jimi Hendrix Experience appeared at The Ambassador Theater, Washington D.C.

1970 Derek & the Dominoes appeared at the Speakeasy, London.

1971 John and Yoko donated £1,000 ($1,700) to the Clyde Shipbuilders Scottish Union fighting fund, who were refusing to stop work at the Glasgow site after being made redundant.

1972 Alice Cooper was at No.1 on the UK singles chart with 'School's Out'. The song was a No.7 hit in the US.

1977 Henri Padovani, guitarist with The Police, quit the group after nine months leaving them as the trio of Sting, Andy Summers and Stewart Copeland. The band went on to sell over five million singles and have five successive albums enter the UK chart at No.1.

1978 The Commodores started a two week run at No.1 on the US singles chart with 'Three Times A Lady'. It was also No.1 in the UK and became Motown's biggest British-selling single.

1984 as The Olympic Games came to a close, Lionel Richie performed 'All Night Long' live from Los Angeles.

1985 Kyu Sakamoto was killed in a plane crash. He had had a 1963 US No.1 & UK No.6 single with 'Sukiyaki', the first-ever Japanese act to have a US No.1.

1986 Prince started a run of five nights at Wembley Arena, London. It was his first UK show for five years.

1994 Woodstock '94 was held in Saugerties, New York, attended by over 350,000 fans. The festival featured Green Day, Nine Inch Nails, Aerosmith and the Red Hot Chili Peppers. Tickets cost $135.00, (£89.00).

1996 The Spice Girls were at No.1 on the UK singles chart with 'Wannabe' while Los Del Rio were at No.1 on the US singles chart with 'Macarena'.

2001 Alicia Keys went to No.1 on the US singles chart with 'Fallin'.

2001 So Solid Crew scored their first UK No.1 single with '21 Seconds'.

2003 Lee Ryan from Blue was arrested while driving a Porsche around central London and was charged with drink driving. Ryan had spent the night knocking back drinks at Browns nightclub in Covent Garden with his cousin and a record company executive. After annoying others in the club with rowdiness and his cousin's throwing up in the VIP area, bouncers threw Lee out. Lee opted to drive his £60,000 ($102,000) Porsche. Officers pulled the star over just after 4am on Tower Bridge Road and breath tests showed him to be twice over the legal drinking limit.

BORN ON THIS DAY

1949 Cliff Fish – bass player with Paper Lace, who had a 1974 UK No.1 single with 'Billy Don't Be A Hero' and a 1974 US No.1 single with 'The Night Chicago Died'.

1951 Dan Fogelberg, US singer/songwriter who created the 1979 album *Phoenix*. He also worked with Joe Walsh, Jackson Browne and Randy Newman.

1958 Feargal Sharkey – singer with the Undertones, who had a 1980 UK No.9 single with 'My Perfect Cousin'. As a solo artist he had a 1985 UK No.1 single with 'A Good Heart', written by Maria McKee. Moved into the business side of the music industry, working as an A&R manager for Polydor and then as a member of the UK Radio Authority.

1959 Mark Nevin – singer/songwriter with Fairground Attraction, who had a 1988 UK No.1 single with 'Perfect'.

1982 LeAnn Rimes, singer who had a 1997 US No.3 & 1998 UK No.7 single with 'How Do I Live?' The song spent 30 weeks on the UK Top 40 singles chart, making it the first record to do so since 'Relax' by Frankie Goes To Hollywood.

ON THIS DAY

1964 Manfred Mann was at No.1 on the UK singles chart with 'Do Wah Diddy Diddy', the band's first of three UK No.1s.

1965 Jefferson Airplane made their live debut at San Francisco's Matrix Club.

1965 Mike Smith of the Dave Clark Five was pulled off stage by fans at a concert in Chicago. He broke two ribs.

A typical day in the busy life of *Peter Andre*, pop star.

August 13, 1996.

- **7am** Wake up in a Bangkok hotel and do a few morning exercises
- **8am** Bolt down breakfast
- **8.30am** Interviews with Thai press
- **11am** Photo shoot for Thai magazines
- **1pm** Press interview while eating lunch
- **2pm** Another photo shoot
- **4pm** Zip round Bangkok to record three radio interviews
- **6pm** Two record signings at HMV
- **8pm** Soundcheck for gig tonight
- **9pm** Bolt down some dinner
- **10pm** Back to venue to prepare and warm-up for gig
- **11pm** Give a blinding gig
- **12.30am** Back to hotel to shower and change
- **1am** Off to a club to party
- **4am** Back to hotel to push up a few zzzzs before alarm goes off at...
- **7am** Brrrrring!

Words: Susie Bona. Photos: Mike Prior

1966 Lovin' Spoonful started a three week run at No.1 on the US singles chart with 'Summer In The City', which made No.8 in the UK.

1966 *Revolver*, The Beatles' seventh album release in three years, started a seven week run at No.1 in the UK.

1971 John Lennon flew from Heathrow Airport to New York. He never set foot on British soil again.

1971 sax player King Curtis Ousley was stabbed to death by a vagrant on the front steps of his New York home. Ousley had worked with John Lennon and also played on The Coasters' 'Yakety Yak'.

1975 Bruce Springsteen and the E Street Band started a five-night run at New York's Bottom Line Club.

1976 The Clash played a private gig for the press at Chalk Farm rehearsal studios, London.

1977 Bachman Turner Overdrive split up. Their UK hit 'You Ain't Seen Nothing Yet' made No.2 in November 1974.

1982 soul singer Joe Tex died of a heart attack, aged 49. He had had nine US Top 40 hits, including the 1972 US No.2 single 'I Gotcha'.

1983 KC & The Sunshine Band were at No.1 on the UK singles chart with 'Give It Up'.

1994 members from Oasis and The Verve were arrested after smashing up a hotel bar and breaking into a church to steal communion wine. Both bands had been appearing at Hulsfred Festival in Sweden.

1999 ex-Guns N' Roses member Slash was arrested, accused of assaulting his girlfriend at his Sunset Boulevard recording studio by Los Angeles County sheriff's deputies. He was released on bail.

2000 Melanie C went to No.1 on the UK singles chart with 'I Turn To You'.

2002 Adam Ant pleaded guilty to threatening drinkers at The Prince Of Wales Pub in London in January of this year. The former 80s star had returned to the bar with a starting pistol after being refused entry. He had also thrown a car alternator through the window of the pub.

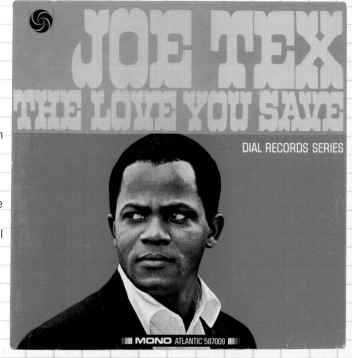

JOE TEX
THE LOVE YOU SAVE

DIAL RECORDS SERIES

MONO ATLANTIC 587009

BORN ON THIS DAY

1941 David Crosby – singer/songwriter and guitarist, member of The Byrds and Crosby, Stills, Nash & Young. The latter had a 1969 UK No.17 single with 'Marrakesh Express', a 1970 US No.11 single with 'Woodstock' and a 1970 US No.1 album with *Déjà vu*. Crosby also had a 1975 US No.6 solo album with *Wind On The Water*.

1946 Larry Graham – bass player for Sly & The Family Stone, who had a 1971 US No.1 & 1972 UK No.15 single with 'Family Affair'. He went on to form Graham Central Station.

1947 George Newsome – drummer with the Climax Blues Band, who had a 1976 UK No.10 and 1977 US No.3 single with 'Couldn't Get It Right'.

1956 Sharon Bryant – singer with Atlantic Starr, who had a 1987 US No.1 & UK No.3 single with 'Always'.

1965 Mark Collins – guitarist with The Charlatans, who had a 1990 UK No.9 single with 'The Only One I Know', a 1996 UK No.3 single with 'One To Another' plus three UK No.1 albums.

1974 Ana Matronic (a.k.a. Ana Lynch) – vocalist for Scissor Sisters who had a 2004 UK No.1 self-titled album and a 2004 UK No.12 single with 'Laura'.

ON THIS DAY

1958 Elvis Presley's mother Gladys died. At her funeral two days later Presley was so overcome with grief he was unable to stand and had to be supported. Over 500 police were at the service to keep the gigantic crowd at bay.

1962 unhappy with drummer Pete Best's role in The Beatles, Brian Epstein and the other three members decided to sack him. Best played his last gig the following night at The Cavern, Liverpool.

1965 Sonny And Cher started a three week run at No.1 on the US singles chart with 'I Got You Babe'. Sunny Bono had also written 'Needles and Pins', a UK No.1 in 1964. Sonny was killed in a skiing accident on January 5th 1998.

1968 'Fire' by The Crazy World Of Arthur Brown was at No.1 on the UK singles chart. Brown would perform the song with his hat set alight!

1970 Stephen Stills was arrested on suspected drugs charges while staying at a San Diego Hotel after being found crawling along a corridor in an incoherent state. He was freed on $2,500 (£1,470) bail.

1970 this was the first day of the three day UK Yorkshire Folk, Blues & Jazz Festival at Krumlin, Yorkshire, featuring Atomic Rooster, Pink Floyd, The Kinks, Elton John, Mungo Jerry, Yes, Alan Price, Georgie Fame, Juicy Lucy, Pretty Things and The Groundhogs. Weekend tickets cost £3 ($5).

1971 The Moody Blues went to No.1 on the UK chart with their sixth album, *Every Good Boy Deserves A Favour*.

1976 funded by a £400 ($680) loan 'So It Goes' by Nick Lowe became the first record released on Stiff Records. Lowe played all the instruments and the single cost £45 ($76) to record.

1985 Michael Jackson outbid Yoko Ono and Paul McCartney to secure the ATV Music Publishing catalogue. At $47.5 million (£28 million) he gained the rights to more than 250 songs written by Lennon and McCartney.

1992 Tony Williams, lead singer with The Platters, died in his sleep, aged 64.

1993 Freddie Mercury had his first solo UK No.1 single with 'Living On My Own'.

1999 Ronan Keating had the UK No.1 single with 'When You Say Nothing At All'.

2002 Dave Williams, lead singer of US heavy rock band Drowning Pool, was found dead on the band's tour bus during Ozzy Osbourne's Ozzfest tour in Manassas, Virginia. The band's debut album, *Sinner*, had sold over one million copies in the US since its release in June 2001.

2003 One True Voice, the boyband formed from the ITV1 pop talent show *Popstars: The Rivals*, split up. The group were formed alongside Girls Aloud after winning their places in the series. One True Voice were later voted Britain's worst group in a poll, just a day after their tour was cancelled due to poor ticket sales.

> "People should be very free with sex, but they should draw the line at goats."
> **Elton John**

BORN ON THIS DAY

1933 Bill Pinkney – singer with The Drifters, who had a 1960 US No.1 & UK No.2 single with 'Save The Last Dance For Me'.

1938 "Stix" Nesbert Hooper – drummer with The Crusaders, who had a 1979 UK No.5 & US No.36 single with 'Street Life'.

1950 Tommy Aldridge – drummer with Whitesnake, who had a 1987 US No.1 & UK No.9 single with 'Here I Go Again'.

1967 MCA (a.k.a. Adam Yauch) – vocalist, rapper and bass player for the Beastie Boys, who had a 1987 UK No.11 single with 'You Gotta Fight For Your Right To Party'.

ON THIS DAY

1964 actor and singer Dean Martin *(above)* went to No.1 on the US singles chart with 'Everybody Loves Somebody'. The song was a No.11 hit in the UK.

1965 The Beatles set a new world record for the largest attendance at a pop concert when they played in front of 55,600 fans at Shea Stadium, New York.

1969 Woodstock Festival was held on Max Yasgur's 600 acre (243 hectare) farm in Bethel outside New York. Attended by over 400,000 people, the free event featured: Jimi Hendrix; Joe Cocker; Crosby, Stills, Nash & Young; Santana; The Who; Creedence Clearwater Revival; Grateful Dead; Janis Joplin; The Band; Canned Heat; Joan Baez; Melanie; Ten Years After; Sly & The Family Stone; Johnny Winter; Jefferson Airplane; Ravi Shankar; Country Joe And The Fish; Blood, Sweat & Tears and Arlo Guthrie. During the three days there were three deaths, two births and four miscarriages. Joni Mitchell was booked to appear but had to pull out due to being booked for a TV show. It was she who wrote the song 'Woodstock'.

1981 Diana Ross and Lionel Richie started a nine week run at No.1 on the US singles chart with 'Endless Love', a No.7 in the UK. The song was the title from a film starring Brooke Shields.

1987 Michael Jackson had his third UK No.1 with the single 'I Can't Stop Loving You', a duet with Siedah Garrett.

1991 Paul Simon played a free concert in New York's Central Park before an audience of three quarters of a million people.

1992 Boyz II Men started a 13 week run at No.1 on the US singles chart with 'End Of The Road', the group's first US No.1. Taken from the Eddie Murphy film *Boomerang*, it broke the 36-year-old record held by Elvis for the longest run at No.1.

1995 the hotel owned by U2, The Clarence, was damaged by a fire that took over three hours to control. The Kitchen nightclub in the same building was affected and had to be evacuated.

2002 a memorial to John Lennon was unveiled in the remote Scottish village of Durness, where Lennon had spent his holidays from age seven to fifteen. The lyrics from 'In My Life' had been inscribed on three stones.

2004 Rolling Stones drummer Charlie Watts was being treated for throat cancer.

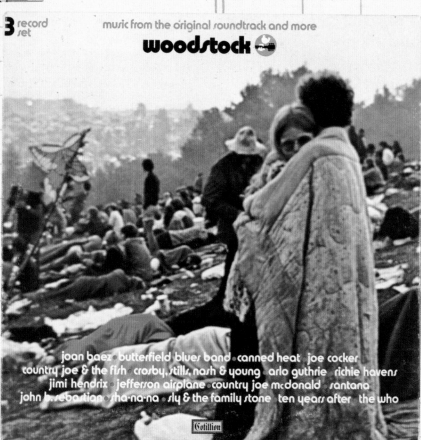

3 record set

music from the original soundtrack and more

woodstock

joan baez · butterfield blues band · canned heat · joe cocker country joe & the fish · crosby, stills, nash & young · arlo guthrie · richie havens jimi hendrix · jefferson airplane · country joe mcdonald · santana john b. sebastian · sha-na-na · sly & the family stone · ten years after · the who

Cotillion

BORN ON THIS DAY

1915 Al Hibbler, singer who had a 1955 UK No.2 & US No.3 single with 'Unchained Melody'.

1946 Gordon Fleet – drummer for The Easybeats, who had a 1966 UK No.6 & 1967 US No.16 single with 'Friday On My Mind'.

1953 James Taylor – singer with Kool & The Gang, who had a 1981 US No.1 & UK No.7 single with 'Celebration', a 1984 UK No.2 single with 'Joanna' and over 15 other Top 40 hits.

1957 Tim Farriss – guitarist with INXS, who had a 1988 UK No.2 & US No.1 single with 'Need You Tonight'.

1958 Madonna (a.k.a. Madonna Louise Ciccone), singer and actress, whose first hit was the 1984 UK No.6 single 'Holiday'. She also had a 1984 US No.1 with 'Like A Virgin', her first UK No.1 was the 1985 'Into The Groove' and she's had six other UK No.1s, over ten US No.1 singles and over 30 other Top 40 hits.

1968 LL Cool J, rapper and actor who had a 1995 US No.3 single with 'Hey Lover', a 1997 UK No.1 single with 'Ain't Nobody' and a 2000 US No.1 album with *G.O.A.T.*

1972 Emily Erwin – singer and banjo player with Dixie Chicks, who had a 1999 UK No.26 single with 'There's Your Trouble' and a 1999 US No.1 album with *Fly*.

ON THIS DAY

1938 blues musician Robert Johnson died. He had influenced Muddy Waters, Elmore James, Eric Clapton and The Rolling Stones.

1962 Little Stevie Wonder, aged 12, released his first single 'I Call It Pretty Music (But The Old People Call It The Blues)'. The track featured Marvin Gaye on drums.

1968 The Jackson Five made their formal debut with Diana Ross And The Supremes at the Great Western Forum, California.

1970 this week's UK Top 5 singles were: No.5, Free, 'All Right Now'; No.4, Shirley Bassey, 'Something'; No.3, Hotlegs, 'Neanderthal Man'; No.2, The Kinks, 'Lola' and No.1, Elvis Presley, 'The Wonder Of You'.

1975 singer Peter Gabriel announced he was leaving Genesis to go solo.

1976 Cliff Richard set out on a tour of Russia, starting with a night at the Hall Of The October Revolution in Leningrad.

1977 Elvis Presley was found dead, lying on the floor in his bathroom, by his girlfriend Ginger Alden. Presley had been seated on the toilet reading *The Scientific Search For Jesus*. He died of heart failure at the age of 42.

1983 singer/songwriter Paul Simon married actress Carrie Fisher.

1985 Madonna married actor Sean Penn in Malibu. She filed for divorce the following year.

1997 on the 20th anniversary of Elvis Presley's death over 30,000 fans descended on Memphis Tennessee for a ten minute mourning circuit, circling his grave. A poll found that almost a third of the fans were keeping an eye out for him in the crowd.

Peter Gabriel leaves Genesis for a young lady.

1997 appearing at the two-day V97 festival in Chelmsford and Leeds were Blur, The Prodigy, Beck, Kula Shaker, Dodgy, Foo Fighters, Placebo, James and Ash. Weekend tickets cost £50 ($85).

BORN ON THIS DAY

1947 Gary Talley – guitarist with The Box Tops, who had a 1967 US No.1 & UK No.5 single with 'The Letter'.

1953 Kevin Rowland – singer/songwriter and guitarist with Dexy's Midnight Runners, who had a 1982 UK No.1 & 1983 US No.1 single with 'Come On Eileen'. As a solo artist he had a 1986 UK No.13 single with 'Because Of You'.

1958 Belinda Carlisle – vocalist for The Go-Go's, who had a 1982 US No.2 single with 'We Got The Beat' and a 1982 UK No.47 single with 'Our Lips Are Sealed'. As a solo artist she had a 1987 US & UK No.1 single with 'Heaven Is A Place On Earth'.

1964 Maria McKee – vocalist for Lone Justice, who had a 1987 UK No.45 single with 'I Found Out'. As a solo artist she had a 1990 UK No.1 single with 'Show Me Heaven'.

1965 Steve Gorman – drummer with The Black Crowes, who had a 1991 UK No.39 single with 'Hard To Handle'.

1969 Donnie Wahlberg – singer with New Kids On The Block, who had a 1989 UK No.1 single with 'You Got It, The Right Stuff' and a 1990 US No.1 single with 'Step By Step'.

1977 Claire Richards – vocalist with Steps, who had a 1998 UK No.1 single with 'Heartbeat/Tragedy'.

ON THIS DAY

1960 The Beatles arrived in Hamburg, Germany to start a residency at The Indra Club and then moved on to The Kaiserkeller Club, where they made a total of 106 appearances.

1965 The Byrds were forced to cancel a concert during their UK tour at The Guildhall, Portsmouth when only 250 of the 4,000 tickets had been sold.

1968 The Doors started a four week run at No.1 on the US album chart with *Waiting For The Sun*.

1968 The Rascals (formally the Young Rascals), started a five week run at No.1 on the US singles chart with 'People Got To Be Free'. The group had 13 US Top 40 hits.

1971 Johnny Cash played the first of three nights at The Kings Hall, Belle Vue, Manchester.

1973 former Temptations singer Paul Williams was found dead in his car after shooting himself. Williams owed $80,000 (£47,060) in taxes and his celebrity boutique business had failed.

1974 Eric Clapton started a four week run at No.1 on the US album chart with *461 Ocean Boulevard*, which was a No.3 hit in the UK.

1974 UK group Paper Lace scored their only US No.1 single with 'The Night Chicago Died'. The song was a No.3 hit in the UK.

1986 Madonna was at No.1 on the US singles chart with 'Papa Don't Preach', her fourth US No.1 and also a No.1 in the UK. Also on this day Madonna went to No.1 on the US album chart with *True Blue*.

Kevin Rowland puts in his Punk Rock dues in 'The Killjoys'.

1995 Depeche Mode singer Dave Gahan was rushed to Cedars-Sinai Medical Center after an apparent suicide attempt. Police had found him at his Los Angeles home with a 5cm (2in) laceration on his wrist.

1998 Carlos Santana received a star on the Hollywood Walk Of Fame.

1999 Former Bay City Rollers drummer Derek Longmuir appeared at the Edinburgh Sheriff Court accused of child porn and drugs offences. Longmuir, 48, denied the charges. He was later sentenced to 300 hours community service.

2002 appearing at the UK festival V2002 in Chelmsford were Travis, Alanis Morissette, Nickelback, Supergrass, Elvis Costello, The Bluetones, Mull Historical Society, Badly Drawn Boy and The Chemical Brothers.

2003 Eva Cassidy started a two week run at No.1 on the UK album chart with *American Tune*, the US singer's third UK No.1 album.

BORN ON THIS DAY

1930 Johnny Preston, US singer who had a 1960 US & UK No.1 single with 'Running Bear'.

1944 Carl Wayne – vocalist with The Move, who had a 1969 UK No.1 single with 'Blackberry Way'. He died on August 31st 2004.

1945 Nona Hendryx – singer with Labelle, who had a 1975 US No.1 & UK No.17 single with 'Lady Marmalade'.

1945 Barbara Harris – singer with The Toys, who had a 1965 US No. 2 & UK No.5 single with 'A Lover's Concerto'.

1950 Dennis Elliott – drummer for Foreigner, who had a 1985 UK & US No.1 single with 'I Want To Know What Love Is'.

1951 John Rees – bass player with Men At Work, who had a 1983 UK & US No.1 single with 'Down Under'.

1952 Patrick Swayze, actor and singer who had a 1988 US No.3 & UK No.17 single with Wendy Fraser, 'She's Like The Wind'.

ON THIS DAY

1958 The Kalin Twins were at No.1 on the UK singles chart with 'When'. The brothers became the first twins to score a No.1 record.

1960 The Beatles played their first date outside the UK when they opened at the Indra Club, Hamburg.

1962 Ringo Starr made his debut with The Beatles at the Horticultural Society Dance, Birkenhead.

1969 Mick Jagger was accidentally shot in the hand on set during filming of *Ned Kelly* in Australia.

1973 Diana Ross scored her second US No.1 single with 'Touch Me In The Morning'.

1976 *Variety* reported that Marvin Gaye faced two consecutive five day prison terms in Los Angeles county jail for contempt of court after failing to pay alimony and child support.

1977 The Police made their live debut as a three piece band when they played at Rebecca's, Birmingham.

1979 appearing at Wembley Stadium were AC/DC, Nils Lofgren, The Stranglers and The Who.

1979 Nick Lowe married Johnny Cash's stepdaughter, Carlene Carter, in Los Angeles.

1982 Liverpool named four streets after the Fab Four, John Lennon Drive, Paul McCartney Way, George Harrison Close and Ringo Starr Drive.

1983 appearing at New York's Shea Stadium were headline act, The Police, Joan Jett And The Blackhearts and R.E.M. (the latter's biggest gig to date).

1984 George Michael was at No.1 on the UK singles chart with his first solo single 'Careless Whisper'. It made George the first person to reach No.1 as a solo artist and a member of a band in the same year and gave Epic Records UK their first UK million seller.

1984 Nick Rhodes from Duran Duran married American model Julie Anne at Marylebone registry office, London.

1992 Kurt Cobain became a father when his wife Courtney Love gave birth to a daughter, Frances Bean.

2003, Tony Jackson, bass player with The Searchers, died of cirrhosis of the liver. The band had had a 1964 UK No.1 & US No.13 single with 'Needles And Pins'.

Marvin Gaye plays a round of 'Here My Dear', the new divorce game!

BORN ON THIS DAY

1940 Ginger Baker – drummer with Cream, who had a 1966 UK No.11 single with 'I Feel Free' and a 1968 US No.5 single with 'Sunshine of your Love', and Ginger Baker's Air Force.

1940 Johnny Nash, singer who had a 1972 US No.1 single with 'I Can See Clearly Now' and a 1975 UK No.1 single with 'Tears On My Pillow'.

1940 Roger Cook, songwriter and vocalist. As a member of Blue Mink he had a 1970 UK No.3 single with 'Melting Pot'. He has had more than 80 Top 30 hits, including 'Something's Gotten Hold Of My Heart', 'Long Cool Woman In A Black Dress', 'You've Got Your Troubles' and 'I'd Like To Teach The World To Sing'.

1943 Billy J. Kramer – singer with Billy J. Kramer And The Dakotas, who had a 1964 UK No.1 & US No.7 single with 'Little Children'.

1945 Ian Gillan *(right)* – vocalist for Deep Purple, who had a 1970 UK No.2 single with 'Black Night' and a 1973 US No.4 single with 'Smoke On The Water'.

1951 John Deacon – bass player and vocalist for Queen, who had a 1975 UK No.1 single with 'Bohemian Rhapsody', which was also UK No.1 in 1991, plus over 40 other UK Top 40 singles and a 1980 US No.1 single with 'Crazy Little Thing Called Love'.

1980 Darius Danesh, singer and 2001 UK TV's *Popstars* contestant who became famous for his rendition of Britney Spears' 'Baby One More Time'. He had a 2002 UK No.1 single with 'Colourblind'.

ON THIS DAY

1964 The Rolling Stones played the first of six nights at The New Theatre Ballroom, Guernsey. The group were also told on this day that British United Airways had banned the group from flying with them.

1967 The Beatles scored their 14th US No.1 single with 'All You Need Is Love'. Mick Jagger, Keith Richards, Eric Clapton, Keith Moon, Graham Nash, Marianne Faithfull and Walker Brother Gary Leeds all sang backing vocals on the track.

1973 actor and singer Kris Kristofferson married singer Rita Coolidge in Malibu, California.

1974 Prince Charles' favourite 70s group, The Three Degrees, were at No.1 on the UK singles chart with 'When Will I See You Again?', the group's only UK No.1.

1977 the Sex Pistols started an undercover UK tour as The Spots (an acronym for "Sex Pistols on tour secretly").

1978 The Commodores started a five week run at No.1 on the UK singles chart with 'Three Times A Lady'.

1988 'Hound Dog' by Elvis Presley was named the most played record of all time on American jukeboxes.

1989 Bros appeared at a sold-out Wembley Arena, London.

1999 a TV ad featuring the late Linda McCartney urging a boycott of fishing was banned by the Advertising Clearance Centre.

1999 Lauryn Hill won New artist of the year and Album of the year at the US Source Hip Hop Music Awards in Los Angeles. R. Kelly won R&B artist of the year; DMX won artist of the year and Solo and live performer of the year.

2001 American soul singer Betty Everett died, aged 61. She had had a 1964 US No.6 single with 'The Shoop Shoop Song (It's In His Kiss)'.

2003 a man from Nottinghamshire who sent threatening emails to S Club singer Tina Barrett was jailed for six months. 41-year-old Steven Hindley had showered the singer with roses, chocolates and teddy bears. But when his messages were ignored he began to make threats to the band, including a potential sniper attack. One email begged Miss Barrett to visit him at his home, claiming he was the victim of a brain tumour and had just three weeks to live.

2000 appearing at this year's V2000 festival, Staffordshire were Richard Ashcroft, Paul Weller, James, Toploader, Moby, Beth Orton, Joe Strummer, Feeder, The Dandy Warhols and Coldplay.

Telephone
Hoylake 1136.

Brookside.
Heron Road.
Meols,
Ches.

19th. August, 1961

Mr. P. Best, Mr.
8, Hymans Green,
Liverpool 12.

Dear Mr. Best,

　　　　Will you let me have your terms for the services of the Beetles to play at Hoylake Y.M.C.A. from the 8-0 P.m. till 11-0 P.m., and if xxxxx you are available on Friday, the 8th. Sept. next.

　　　　As I am going away from home in two days time, I would appreciate it if you could let me have this information by return. You can get me on the phone at the above no. on Monday or Tuesday mornings.

　　　　We have other dates, but this is the present urgent one as I wish to fix it before going away.

Yours faithfully,

Chas. K. Tranter.

BORN ON THIS DAY

1924 Jim Reeves, US country singer. He was the first country singer to cross over into the pop market and had a 1960 US No.2 single with 'He'll Have To Go' and a 1966 UK No.1 single with 'Distant Drums'. Reeves was killed in a plane crash on July 31st 1964 when the single engine aircraft flying from Arkansas to Nashville crashed in thick fog.

1931 Paul Robi – singer with The Platters, who had a UK & US No.1 single with 'Smoke Gets In Your Eyes'. He died of cancer on February 1st 1989.

1946 Ralf Hutter – Kraftwerk, who had a 1982 UK No.1 single with 'Computer Love/The Model'.

1947 James Pankow – trombone player for Chicago, who had a 1976 UK & US No.1 single with 'If You Leave Me Now'.

1948 Robert Plant – vocalist with Led Zeppelin, who had a 1969 US No.4 single with 'Whole Lotta Love'. The band's fourth album, released in 1971, featured the rock classic 'Stairway To Heaven' and has sold over 11 million copies. As a solo artist Plant had a 1983 UK No.11 single with 'Big Log'. As a member of The Honeydrippers (alongside Jimmy Page, Jeff Beck and Nile Rodgers), he had a 1984 US No.3 single with 'Sea Of Love'.

1949 Phil Lynott – bass player and vocalist with Thin Lizzy, who had a 1973 UK No.6 single with

Page and Plant's cottage in Wales where they recorded much of *Led Zepellin III*.

'Whisky In The Jar', a 1976 UK No.8 single with 'The Boys Are Back In Town' plus eight UK Top 10 albums. Lynott died on January 4th 1986.

1952 Doug Fieger – vocalist with The Knack, who had a 1979 US No.1 & UK No.6 single with 'My Sharona'.

1971 Fred Durst – vocalist with Limp Bizkit, who had a 2001 UK No.1 single with 'Rollin' and a 2000 US & UK No.1 album with *Chocolate Starfish And The Hotdog Flavored Water*.

ON THIS DAY

1955 Bo Diddley appeared at the Apollo Theater, Harlem.

1963 The Rolling Stones appeared at The Star & Garter Hotel, Windsor.

1965 Andrew Loog Oldham launched the Immediate Label, home of The Small Faces, Nice and Chris Farlowe.

1968 the University of Tennessee reported that a guinea pig subjected to days of rock music played at 120 decibels had suffered acute hearing damage.

1977 setting off to probe Jupiter and Saturn, Voyager 1 launched from Earth. The space craft had a disk with recordings of sounds and images of Earth designed to portray the diversity of life and culture on the planet. The Chuck Berry song 'Johnny B. Goode' was one of the examples of Earth music on the disk.

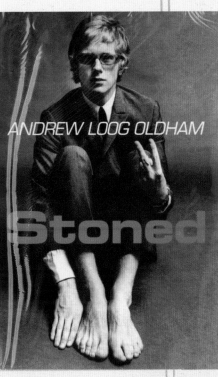

ANDREW LOOG OLDHAM

Stoned

1986 Rick Allen, drummer with Def Leppard, made his first live appearance with the band at Donington after losing an arm in a car accident. Allen had a special modified drum kit built for him.

1988 Steve Winwood went to No.1 on the US album chart with *Roll With It*.

1988 two rock fans died while "slam dancing" as Guns N' Roses played at the Monsters Of Rock Festival, Castle Donington.

1990 Aerosmith appeared at the Marquee Club, London. Jimmy Page joined the band on stage for a blues jam.

1992 a US doctor filed a $35 million (£20.6 million) lawsuit against the Southwest Bell phone company, alleging that his wife died because he could not reach 911 due to all lines being jammed by the huge demand for Garth Brooks concert tickets.

1997 BBC TV aired the documentary *Oasis: Right Here, Right Now*, which included the group talking about their troublesome last year plus performances of three new songs.

2000 Craig David started a two week run at No.1 on the UK album chart with his debut release *Born To Do It*. Janet Jackson went to No.1 on the US singles chart with 'Doesn't Really Matter' while Nelly started a five week run at No.1 on the US album chart with *Country Grammar*.

BORN ON THIS DAY

1904 big band leader Count Basie. He worked with Frank Sinatra as well as his own band. He died on April 26th 1984.

1938 Kenny Rogers, singer/songwriter, who had a 1977 UK No.1 single with 'Lucille', a 1980 US No.1 & UK No.12 single with 'Lady' plus 15 other US Top 40 hits.

1941 Tom Coster – keyboard player with Santana, who had a 1970 US No.4 single with 'Black Magic Woman' and a 1977 UK No.11 single with 'She's Not There'.

1952 Joe Strummer – guitarist and vocalist with The Clash, who had a 1979 UK No.11 single with 'London Calling', a 1982 US No.8 single with 'Rock The Casbah, a 1991 UK No.1 single 'Should I Stay Or Should I Go?' (first released 1982) and 15 other UK Top 40 singles. He was also a member of Joe Strummer & The Mescaleros. Strummer died on December 22nd 2002.

1957 Budgie – drummer with Siouxsie And The Banshees, who had a 1983 UK No.3 single with 'Dear Prudence' plus over 15 other UK Top 40 singles. As part of The Creatures he had a 1983 UK No.14 single with 'Right Now'.

1957 Kim Sledge – singer for Sister Sledge, who had a 1979 US No.2 single 'We Are Family' and a 1985 UK No.1 with 'Frankie'.

1971 Liam Howlett – keyboardist for The Prodigy, who had a 1996 UK No.1 single with 'Firestarter' and a 1997 UK & US No.1 album with *The Fat Of The Land*.

ON THIS DAY

1965 The Rolling Stones started a three week run at No.1 on the US album chart with *Out Of Our Heads*, the group's first US chart topper.

1968 Tommy James & The Shondells returned to the UK No.1 position for the second time with the single 'Mony Mony'.

1971 appearing at the Tregye Festival, Truro were Arthur Brown's Kingdom Come, Hawkwind, Duster Bennett, Brewers Droop, Indian Summer, Graphite and, second from the bottom on the bill, Queen. Tickets cost £1.25 ($2).

1972 Jack Casady of Jefferson Airplane was arrested after a fight broke out on stage during a concert. The police had been called "pigs", Grace Slick was "maced" and another group member injured at the show in Akron.

1983 Ramones guitarist Johnny Ramone had a four hour brain surgery operation after being found unconscious in a New York Street, where he had been involved in a fight.

1997 ex-Stone Roses drummer Alan Wren was jailed for seven days after being rude to a top Manchester magistrate. He was before the court due to having no car insurance and lost his temper after being quizzed about his earnings.

2003 Madame Tussauds in London opened an interactive *Pop Idol* display with a speaking waxwork of judge Simon Cowell. It made comments such as: "That was extraordinary. Unfortunately, extraordinarily bad." "Do you really think that you could become a Pop Idol? Well, then, you're deaf."

Joe Strummer proves that not all punk bands had to be ugly.

out of our heads THE ROLLING STONES*

DECCA

BORN ON THIS DAY

1920 John Lee Hooker, blues singer and guitarist, who had a 1951 US million-selling album with *I'm In The Mood*, a 1964 UK No.23 single with 'Dimples' and a 1989 album with *The Healer*. He died on June 21st 2001.

1945 Ron Dante – singer for The Archies, who had a 1969 US & UK No.1 single with 'Sugar Sugar', and Cufflinks, who had a 1969 UK No.4 single with 'Tracy'.

1958 Ian Mitchell – guitarist with the Bay City Rollers, who had a 1975 UK No.1 single with 'Bye Bye Baby', plus 11 other UK Top 20 singles, and a 1976 US No.1 single with 'Saturday Night'.

1961 Debbie Peterson – drummer with The Bangles, who had a 1986 UK No.2 single with the Prince song 'Manic Monday' and a 1986 US No.1 single with 'Walk Like An Egyptian'.

1961 Roland Orzabal – singer/songwriter with Tears For Fears, who had a 1985 US No.1 & UK No.2 single with 'Everybody Wants To Rule The World' plus over 12 other UK Top 40 singles.

1963 Tori Amos, singer/songwriter who had a 1994 UK No.4 single with 'Cornflake Girl' and a 1992 album with *Little Earthquakes*.

1972 Paul Doucette – drummer with Matchbox 20, who had a 1998 UK No.38 single with 'Push' and a 2000 US No.1 single with 'Bent'.

1973 Howie D – singer with the Backstreet Boys, who had a 1997 US No.2 single with 'Quit Playing Games With My Heart' and a 1999 UK No.1 single with 'I Want It That Way'.

ON THIS DAY

1962 a lunchtime session at The Cavern Club, Liverpool became the first TV appearance of The Beatles as it was recorded by Granada TV. (The programme was shown on October 17th 1962).

1964 The Supremes started a two week run at No.1 on the US singles chart with 'Where Did Our Love Go', their first No.1. It made No.3 in the UK.

1966 New York teenagers Carol Hopkins and Susan Richmond climbed out onto the ledge on the second floor of a city hotel and threatened to jump unless they could get to meet The Beatles. Police managed to talk them down.

1970 Bread went to No.1 on the US singles chart with 'Make It With You', the group's only No.1 hit. The song made No.5 in the UK.

1970 Creedence Clearwater Revival started a nine week run at No.1 on the US album chart with *Cosmo's Factory*, the group's second US chart topper.

1978 Sex Pistol Sid Vicious made his last live stage appearance when he appeared with Rat Scabies, Glen Matlock and Nancy Spungen at London's Electric Ballroom. In the audience were Elvis Costello, Blondie, Joan Jett, The Slits and Captain Sensible.

1980 appearing at the 20th National Rock Festival in Reading were Iron Maiden, Whitesnake, Def Leppard, UFO, Gillan, Budgie, Pat Travers Band and Rory Gallagher. Advance tickets were £12.50 ($21.25).

1997 U2 played the first of two sold-out nights at Wembley Stadium on their Pop Mart tour.

2003 Kjell Henning Bjoernestad, a Norwegian Elvis Presley impersonator, set a world record by singing the rock 'n' roll legend's hits non-stop for over 26 hours. The previous record was set by British Elvis fan Gary Jay, who sang for 25 hours, 33 minutes and 30 seconds.

2003 appearing at this year's Carling Weekend: Reading and Leeds festival were Blur, Beck, The White Stripes, Linkin Park, Doves, The Streets, The Libertines, The Darkness, Junior Senior, The Sleepy Jackson, Metallica, System Of A Down, Sum 41, Primal Scream, Good Charlotte, Yeah Yeah Yeahs, Elbow and The Thrills.

BORN ON THIS DAY

1936 Rudy Lewis – singer with The Drifters, who had a 1960 US No.1 & UK No.2 single with 'Save The Last Dance For Me'. Lewis died on May 20th 1964.

1947 Keith Moon – drummer for The Who, who had a 1965 UK No.2 single with 'My Generation', plus over 20 other Top 40 hits, a 1967 US No.9 single with 'I Can See For Miles' and also recorded the rock opera albums *Tommy* and *Quadrophenia*. Moon died on September 7th 1978.

1949 Rick Springfield, singer/songwriter who had a 1981 US No.1 & UK No.43 single with 'Jessie's Girl'.

1951 Jimi Jamison – vocalist with Cobra then Survivor, who had a 1982 US & UK No.1 single with 'Eye Of The Tiger'.

1959 Edwyn Collins – singer/songwriter with Orange Juice, who had a 1983 UK No.8 single with 'Rip It Up'. As a solo artist he had a 1995 UK No.4 single with 'A Girl Like You'.

1962 Shaun Ryder – vocalist with Happy Mondays, who had a 1990 UK No.5 single with 'Step On', and Black Grape, who had a 1995 UK No.8 single with 'In The Name Of The Father'.

1978 Julian Casablancas – guitarist and vocalist with The Strokes, who had a 2001 UK No.14 single with 'Last Nite'.

1979 Richard Neville – vocalist with Five, who had a 1998 UK No.2 single with 'Everybody Get Up' and a 1999 UK No.1 single with 'Keep On Movin'.

ON THIS DAY

1962 John Lennon married Cynthia Powell at Liverpool's Mount Pleasant register office. He then played a gig that night with The Beatles at Liverpool's Riverpark Ballroom.

1965 security guards at a Manchester TV studio hosed down 200 Rolling Stones fans who broke down barriers while waiting for the band to arrive for a performance.

1969 Johnny Cash started a four week run at No.1 on the US album chart with *Johnny Cash At San Quentin*.

1969 The Rolling Stones started a four week run at No.1 on the US singles chart with 'Honky Tonk Women', the group's fifth US No.1. It was also No.1 in the UK.

1970 Lou Reed and the Velvet Underground performed together for the last time at the New York Club "Max's Kansas City".

Richard Neville's 1968 book showing just how long-lasting his looks were!

1971 Diana Ross was at No.1 on the UK singles chart 'I'm Still Waiting', the singer's first solo UK No.1.

1980 David Bowie was at No.1 on the UK singles chart with 'Ashes To Ashes', his second UK No.1.

1980 The Heatwave Festival, Toronto took place with Talking Heads, Elvis Costello, The B-52s, The Pretenders, Rockpile and The Rumour. Tickets cost $30 (£17.65). With only 50,000 people attending, the festival lost over $1 million (£0.6 million).

1986 Boris Gardiner started a three week run at No.1 on the UK singles chart with 'I Wanna Wake Up With You'.

1986 Sigue Sigue Sputnik came up with an idea to sell advertising space between the tracks on their forthcoming new album.

1991 the re-formed Dire Straits kicked off a two year, 300 date world tour in Dublin.

1996 the father of Noel and Liam from Oasis, Tommy Gallagher, was jailed for one month by a Manchester Court for driving while disqualified.

2003 Lee Ryan of boyband Blue was banned from driving for 18 months after admitting drink driving. Ryan was also ordered to pay a £2,250 ($3,825) fine at Tower Bridge magistrate's court, London.

WINDSOR 4 STARTS 23 AUG. '75

BORN ON THIS DAY

1944 Jim Capaldi – drummer and vocalist for Traffic, who had a 1967 UK No.2 single with 'Hole In My Shoe'. As a solo artist he had a 1975 UK No.4 single with 'Love Hurts'. Capaldi died of stomach cancer on January 28th 2005, aged 60.

1945 Malcolm "Molly" Duncan, sax and flute player for the Average White Band, who had a 1975 US No.1 & UK No.6 single with 'Pick Up The Pieces'.

1948 Jean-Michel Jarre, French instrumentalist who had a 1977 UK No.4 single with 'Oxygene Part IV'.

1956 Matt Aitken, part of the Stock, Aitken and Waterman production team who produced over ten UK No.1 singles.

Jim Capaldi about to start a vow of silence.

ON THIS DAY

1963 Stevie Wonder became the first artist ever to score a US No.1 album and single in the same week. Wonder was at No.1 on the album chart with *Little Stevie Wonder/The 12-Year-old Genius* and had the No.1 single 'Fingertips part 2'. This was also the first-ever live recording to make No.1.

1967 17-year-old Bruce Springsteen joined a group called Earth.

1977 singer/songwriter Waylon Jennings was arrested and charged with possession of cocaine. Jennings had recently been named an honorary police chief.

1979 celebrating 30 years in show business, BB King played at the Roxy Club, Sunset strip, Los Angeles.

1981 Mark Chapman was given a 20 year jail sentence for the murder of John Lennon.

1983 the fifth wife of Jerry Lee Lewis, Shawn Michelle Stevens, was found dead at their Mississippi home after a methadone overdose.

1985 Huey Lewis & The News started a two week run at No.1 on the US singles chart with a song featured in the hit movie *Back To The Future*, 'The Power Of Love'.

1991 Lenny Kravitz was at No.2 in the US singles chart with 'It Ain't Over Till It's Over'. It was held off the No.1 position by Bryan Adams' 'Everything I Do'.

1991 Metallica scored their first UK No.1 album with their self-titled LP.

1995 Pulp singer Jarvis Cocker presented this week's UK TV Music show *Top Of The Pops*. Guests included Oasis, Blur, Bjork and The Charlatans.

1996 Liam Gallagher failed to turn up for the recording of the Oasis MTV unplugged session at London's Royal Festival Hall in front of 400 fans. He later sat in the audience and watched the show with his brother Noel taking over on vocals.

1998 Gene Page, producer and keyboardist, died after a long illness. He had worked with Barbra Streisand, Barry White, The Righteous Brothers, Dobie Gray and Bob & Earl. He also produced Whitney Houston's 'Greatest Love of All' and Roberta Flack's 'Tonight I Celebrate My Love'.

2001 appearing at this year's Carling Weekend: Reading and Leeds Festival were Travis, Eminem, Eels, Green Day, Marilyn Manson, PJ Harvey, Manic Street Preachers, Weezer, Iggy Pop, Queens Of The Stone Age, The Cult, Frank Black, The Strokes,

Supergrass, Ash, Stephen Malkmus and Mercury Rev. The three day tickets cost £80 ($136).

2004 Al Dvorin, the announcer who popularized the phrase "Elvis has left the building", died in a crash on his way home from an Elvis convention in California. Dvorin, aged 81, was in a car driven by long-time Elvis photographer Ed Bonja. He was never paid for recordings of his words, and was bitter towards the multi-million pound Elvis Presley Enterprises. In the early 1970s, Presley's manager asked Dvorin to inform fans at a gig that Presley would not be appearing for an encore. He took the stage and announced: "Ladies and gentlemen, Elvis has left the building. Thank you and goodnight."

BORN ON THIS DAY

1918 Leonard Bernstein, composer, pianist and conductor. He composed music for *West Side Story* and *On The Waterfront* and conducted the New York Philharmonic Orchestra aged 25. He died on October 14th 1990.

1949 Gene Simmons – bass player and vocalist for Kiss, who had a 1974 US No.5 single 'On And On', a 1976 US No.11 album *Rock And Roll Over*, which spent 26 weeks on the chart, and a 1987 UK No.4 single with 'Crazy Crazy Nights'.

1950 Willy DeVille – singer with Mink DeVille, who had a 1977 UK No.20 single with 'Spanish Stroll'.

1951 James Warren – vocalist and bass player for The Korgis, who had a 1980 UK No.5 single with 'Everybody's Got To Learn Sometime'.

1951 Rob Halford – singer with Judas Priest, who had a 1980 UK No.12 single with 'Living After Midnight'.

1955 Elvis Costello – singer/songwriter who had a 1979 UK No.2 single with The Attractions, 'Oliver's Army', 1979 UK No.2 album *Armed Forces* spent 28 weeks on the chart. Plus over 15 other UK Top 40 hits and 13 US Top 40 albums.

1961 Billy Ray Cyrus, US singer who had a 1992 UK No.3 single with 'Achy Breaky Heart'. He also enjoyed a 17 week run at No.1 on the US album chart in 1992 with *Some Gave All*.

1962 Vivian Campbell – guitarist with Dio, Whitesnake and Def Leppard whom he joined in 1992. Had the 1995 UK No.2 single 'When Love And Hate Collide'.

ON THIS DAY

1957 Paul Anka was at No.1 in the UK with 'Diana', his only UK No.1 as a solo artist.

1960 The Shadows were at No.1 on the UK singles chart with 'Apache'. It was the first of five UK No.1s for the group.

1962 Little Eva went to No.1 on the US singles chart with 'The Locomotion'.

1970 Elton John made his US live debut when he kicked off a 17 date tour at the Troubadour in Los Angeles.

1973 Donny Osmond was at No.1 on the UK singles chart with 'Young Love'.

1979 25 years after his first UK No.1 single, Cliff Richard had his tenth chart topper with 'We Don't Talk Anymore'.

1979 The Knack started a five week run at No.1 on the US singles chart with 'My Sharona', the group's only US chart topper. It made No.6 in the UK.

1993 Snoop Doggy Dogg was released on $1 million (£0.6 million) bail after being accused of being involved with the murder of a member of the By Yerself gang during a shooting in Los Angeles. He was acquitted of the charges in 1996.

1994 Jimmy Page and Robert Plant recorded their MTV unplugged set at London's television centre.

1997 a deranged man, who had escaped from a mental institution near Helsinki, Finland, had planned to set fire to the stage that Michael Jackson was performing from. However he was arrested before he was able to light the gasoline he had put on the stage.

2000 appearing at this year's Carling Weekend: Reading and Leeds Festival were Oasis, Primal Scream, Foo Fighters, The Bluetones, Muse, Eminem, Beck, Stereophonics, Blink 182, Slipknot, Placebo, Pulp, Rage Against The Machine, Gomez, Limp Bizkit, Embrace and The Wannadies. Tickets cost £33 ($56).

2001 US singer and actress Aaliyah was killed in a plane crash in the Bahamas, aged 22. The small Cessna plane crashed a few minutes after take off, killing everyone on board with the exception of four passengers who were pulled from the wreckage but later died. Aaliyah had been filming a video for her latest release, 'Rock The Boat', on the island.

BORN ON THIS DAY

1941 Chris Curtis – drummer for The Searchers, who had a 1964 UK No.1 single with 'Needles And Pins' and a 1964 US No.3 single with 'Love Potion Number Nine'.

1948 Brian Duffy (a.k.a. Jet Black) – drummer with The Stranglers, who had a 1982 UK No.2 single with 'Golden Brown' and over 20 other Top 40 hits.

1950 Bill and Dick Cowsill – singer/songwriters and guitarists with The Cowsills, who had a 1967 US No.2 single with 'The Rain, The Park & Other Things' and a 1969 US No.2 single with the theme from *Hair*. TV's *Partridge Family* was based on the Cowsill family.

1954 Michael Chetwood – keyboardist for T'Pau, who had a 1987 UK No.1 single with 'China In Your Hand' and a 1987 US No.4 single with 'Heart And Soul'.

1966 Dan Vickrey – guitarist with Counting Crows, who had a 1994 UK No.28 single with 'Mr Jones' and a 1996 US No.1 album with *Recovering The Satellites*.

1969 Adrian Young – drummer with No Doubt, who had a 1997 UK No.1 single with 'Don't Speak' and a 1997 No.1 US album with *Tragic Kingdom*.

ON THIS DAY

1965 Sonny And Cher were at No.1 on the UK singles chart with 'I Got You Babe', the duo's only UK No.1.

1967 Mick Jagger and Marianne Faithfull joined up with The Beatles in Bangor, North Wales to seek guidance from Maharishi Mahesh Yogi.

1970 appearing over three days at the third Isle Of Wight Festival were Bob Dylan, Joan Baez, Joni Mitchell, Jimi Hendrix, (his last-ever UK appearance), Donovan, Jethro Tull, Miles Davis, Arrival, Cactus, Family, Taste, Mungo Jerry, ELP, The Doors, The Who, Spirit, The Moody Blues, Chicago, Procol Harum, Sly & The Family Stone

and Free. Weekend tickets cost £3 ($5).

1973 10CC made their live debut at the Palace Lido, Isle of Man at the start of a UK tour.

1977 appearing at the three day UK 17th Reading Festival were Uriah Heep, Thin Lizzy, The Sensational Alex Harvey Band, Eddie & the Hot Rods, Golden Earring, Aerosmith, The Doobie Brothers, Hawkwind, Racing Cars, John Miles, Graham Parker, The Enid, No Dice and Frankie Miller's Full House. A three day ticket cost £7.95 ($13.50).

1978 Frankie Valli went to No.1 on the US singles chart with the Barry Gibb song 'Grease'. It went on to sell over two million in the States. The song was a No.3 hit in the UK.

1993 a double-sided acetate of The Beatles performing live at The Cavern in Liverpool sold for £16,500 ($28,050) at Christies, London. This set a world record price for a recording.

1995 Seal went to No.1 on the US singles chart with 'Kiss From A Rose', which was taken from the film *Batman Forever*.

2004 US cinematographer David Myers died after suffering a stroke. He had worked on various music films including *Woodstock*, *Elvis On Tour*, *The Last Waltz*, *The Grateful Dead Movie*, *Mad Dogs & Englishmen* and *Cracked Actor: A Film About David Bowie*.

2005 appearing at this year's Carling Weekend: Reading and Leeds Festivals were Iron Maiden, The Killers, Pixies, Foo Fighters, Razorlight, Kasabian, Queens of the Stone Age and Kings of Leon.

BORN ON THIS DAY

1942 B.J. Thomas, singer/songwriter who had a 1970 US No.1 & UK No.38 single with 'Raindrops Keep Falling On My Head'.

1942 Daryl Dragon – keyboardist for Captain & Tennille, who had a 1980 US No.1 & UK No.7 single with 'Do That To Me One More Time'.

1953 Alex Lifeson – guitarist for Rush, who had a 1980 UK No.13 single with 'Spirit Of Radio' and a 1982 US No.21 single with 'New World Man'.

1956 Glen Matlock – bass player with Sex Pistols (early and reformed) and the Rich Kids, who had a 1978 UK No.24 single with 'Rich Kids'.

Alex Lifeson and a nosey drummer.

1970 Tony Kanal – bass player with No Doubt, who had a 1997 UK No.1 single with 'Don't Speak' and a 1997 No.1 US album with *Tragic Kingdom*.

ON THIS DAY

1964 The Honeycombs were at No.1 on the UK singles chart with 'Have I The Right?', the group's only UK No.1.

1965 The Beatles met Elvis Presley for the first and only time when they went to his house in Bel Air, California. Elvis played a bass guitar and sang as he jammed with The Beatles, with McCartney playing piano. Apparently John Lennon upset Elvis by asking him why he didn't go back to making rock 'n' roll records.

1966 The Beach Boys' 'God Only Knows' reached No.2 on the UK singles chart.

1967 The Beatles' manager Brian Epstein was found dead locked in the bedroom at his London home. A coroner's inquest concluded that Epstein died from an overdose of the sleeping pill Carbitrol. Jimi Hendrix, who was set to appear at London's Saville Theatre that evening, cancelled the gig as a mark of respect.

1977 The Floaters were at No.1 in the UK with the single 'Float On'.

1988 'Monkey' gave George Michael his eighth US No.1 single of the 80s, a record beaten only by Michael Jackson.

1988 Kylie Minogue started a four week run at No.1 on the UK album chart with her debut LP *Kylie*.

1990 blues guitarist Stevie Ray Vaughan was killed when the helicopter he was travelling in collided with a ski slope. Vaughan came to prominence on David Bowie's hit 'Let's Dance'. Three members of Eric Clapton's entourage were also killed in the accident.

2004 winners at this year's *Kerrang!* awards included: The Darkness for Best British band and Best live band; Best band on the planet award went to Metallica. Green Day were inducted into the *Kerrang!* Hall of Fame, Best album went to Muse for *Absolution*.

2004 appearing at this year's Carling Weekend: Reading and Leeds festivals were Green Day, The Darkness, The Hives, The White Stripes, Morrissey, Franz Ferdinand, 50 Cent, Supergrass, The Streets, The Offspring and The Libertines.

AUGUST 26-30 1970 Weekend £3
ISLE OF WIGHT FESTIVAL

Friday 20/- August 28th

Chicago
Family
Taste
Arrival
Melanie
Voices of East Harlem
Cactus
Procol Harum
Tony Joe White
Lighthouse

Saturday 35/- August 29th

Doors Who
Ten Years After
Joni Mitchell
Sly and the Family Stone
Cat Mother
Free
John Sebastian
Emmerson, Lake & Palmer
Mungo Jerry
Spirit
Miles Davies

Sunday 40/- August 30th

Jimi Hendrix Experience
Jethro Tull
Joan Baez
Leonard Cohen & The Army
Richie Havens
Moody Blues
Pentangle
Ralph McTell
Good News
Donovan & The Open Road

BORN ON THIS DAY

1939 Clem Cattini – drummer for The Tornados, who had a 1962 UK & US No.1 single 'Telstar'. This was the first major hit from a UK act on the American chart.

1943 Ann "Honey" Lantree – drummer for The Honeycombs, who had a 1964 UK No.1 & US No.5 single with 'Have I The Right?'

1943 David Soul, actor and singer who had a 1977 UK & US No.1 single with 'Don't Give Up On Us'.

1948 Danny Seraphine – drummer for Chicago, who had a 1976 UK & US No.1 single with 'If You Leave Me Now'.

1949 Hugh Cornwell – guitarist and vocalist with The Stranglers, who had a 1982 UK No.2 single with 'Golden Brown' and over 20 other Top 40 hits.

1951 Wayne Osmond – singer with The Osmonds, who had a 1971 US No.1 single with 'One Bad Apple', a 1971 US 1974 UK No.1 single with 'Love Me For A Reason' plus nine other US & UK Top 40 singles.

1965 Shania Twain (a.k.a. Eilleen Regina Edwards), Canadian singer who had the biggest-selling UK album of 1999 with *Come On Over* – it has sold over 34 million copies worldwide. She also had the 1999 UK No.3 single 'That Don't Impress Me Much'.

ON THIS DAY

1964 after playing a show at Forest Hills Tennis Stadium, New York The Beatles met with Bob Dylan for the first time. It was today in The Delmorico Hotel in New York that Dylan introduced the Fab Four to marijuana.

1965 The Who appeared at The Matrix Club, Coventry, England.

1967 appearing at The Hastings Stadium Festival Of Music were The Kinks, Dave Dee, Beaky, Mick & Tich and The Crazy World Of Arthur Brown. Tickets cost 10 shillings, ($1.38).

The Stranglers' Hugh Cornwell.

1968 Simon & Garfunkel started a five week run at No.1 on the UK album chart with *Bookends*.

1968 The Beach Boys were at No.1 on the UK singles chart with 'Do It Again', the group's second and final UK No.1.

1978 The Rolling Stones released the double A-sided single 'Beast Of Burden/When The Whip Comes Down' in the US.

Simon and Garfunkle perfect their 80s teen image, (see 13 July).

1981 producer Guy Stevens died of a heart attack. He had worked with Mott The Hoople, Free and The Clash.

1988 Kylie Minogue set a new UK record when her debut album *Kylie* became the biggest-selling album by a female artist in Britain, with sales of almost two million.

1993 Billy Joel started a three week run at No.1 on the US album chart with *River Of Dreams*.

1997 singer Gina G. was taken ill during a flight from London to Glasgow when she suffered an allergic reaction to a flu treatment and had to be rushed to hospital upon landing at Glasgow airport.

1998 Geri Halliwell announced that she was selling off her Spice Girls clothes in a charity auction. The PVC catsuit she used to wear was up for £5,000 ($8,500), knee high boots were up for £1,200 ($2,040) and the Union Jack dress she wore to the Brit Awards was up for £8,000 ($13,600).

TEARS FOR FEARS
Songs From The Big Chair

BORN ON THIS DAY

1924 Dinah Washington, US singer who had a 1959 US No.8 single with 'What A Diff'rence A Day Makes' and a 1961 UK No.35 single with 'September In The Rain'. She died on December 14th 1963.

1942 Sterling Morrison – guitarist with Velvet Underground, who had a 1968 song 'White Light, White Heat'. Morrison died of cancer on August 30th 1995.

1953 Rick Downey – drummer with Blue Oyster Cult, who had a 1978 UK No.16 single with 'Don't Fear The Reaper'.

1958 Michael Jackson – singer with The Jackson Five, who had a 1970 US No.1 & UK No.2 single with 'I Want You Back' and, as The Jacksons, a 1977 UK No.1 single with 'Show You The Way To Go'. As a solo artist he had a 1983 UK & US No.1 single with 'Billie Jean' and 11 other US No.1s and 40 UK Top 40 singles.

1959 Eddi Reader – singer/songwriter for Fairground Attraction, who had a 1988 UK No.1 single with 'Perfect'. As a solo artist she had a 1994 UK No.33 single with 'Patience of Angels'.

1975 Kyle Cook – guitarist with Matchbox 20, who had a 1998 UK No.38 single with 'Push' and a 2000 US No.1 single with 'Bent'.

ON THIS DAY

1966 The Beatles played their final live concert when they appeared at San Francisco's Candlestick Park to 25,000 fans. The last song they played was a version of Little Richards' 'Long Tall Sally'.

Patti Smith: 'Get 'em on' shout the fans.

1970 Edwin Starr started a three week run at No.1 on the US singles chart with 'War', his only No.1. It was a No.3 in the UK.

1976 blues artist Jimmy Reed died in San Francisco, aged 50. He was a major influence on The Rolling Stones.

1978 this was the first night of a four date UK tour by the Patti Smith Group at The City Hall, Newcastle, with special guests The Pop Group. Tickets cost £1.50 ($2.55) and £3 ($5).

1981 Aneka was at No.1 on the UK singles chart with 'Japanese Boy', the Scottish singer's only Top 40 hit.

1981 The two day Rock on the Tyne festival began in Gateshead, England, featuring Ian Dury, Elvis Costello, U2, Rory Gallagher, Doll By Doll, Wang Chung, Becket. Dr Feelgood, The Gingers Nutters featuring Ginger Baker, Trimmer and Jenkins and Lindisfarne.

1986 a dress worn by Kim Wilde was sold at Christies for £400 ($680).

1987 Def Leppard scored their first UK No.1 album with *Hysteria*, which also became No.1 on the US chart in July the following year after spending 49 weeks working its way to the top.

1987 Lee Marvin, actor and singer, died. He had had a 1970 UK No.1 single with 'Wand'rin Star', taken from the film *Paint Your Wagon*.

1987 Los Lobos started a three week run at No.1 on the US singles chart with 'La Bamba', which was also a No.1 hit in the UK. The song was taken from the film about the life of Ritchie Valens.

1987 Rick Astley's debut hit 'Never Gonna Give You Up' started a five week run at No.1 on the UK singles chart and became the biggest-selling single of 1987.

1992 U2 became the second act ever (Billy Joel was the first) to play at The Yankee Stadium, New York during their sold-out Zoo TV tour.

2003 winners at this year's MTV Video Music Awards held in New York included: Missy Elliot, Video of the year for 'Work It'; Viewers' choice award, 'Lifestyles Of The Rich And Famous' by Good Charlotte; Rap video went to 50 Cent for 'In Da Club' and Pop video went to Justin Timberlake for 'Cry Me A River'. Madonna stunned a packed Radio City Hall audience by passionately kissing Britney Spears and Christina Aguilera during a racy version of 'Like A Virgin'.

ROUNDHAY PARK LEEDS

BCC PROUDLY PRESENT

MICHAEL JACKSON

PLUS SUPPORT

PEPSI

GATE 2

MONDAY 29 AUGUST 1988
(SUBJECT TO LICENCE)

DOORS OPEN AT 5 PM.
ISSUED SUBJECT TO CONDITIONS ON REVERSE
NO ALCOHOL, BOTTLES OR TINS PERMITTED
SITE MANAGEMENT BY KENNEDY STREET
TICKET PRICE SUBJECT TO BOOKING FEE

TO BE RETAINED

TICKETS £16.50

006757

BORN ON THIS DAY

1935 John Phillips – singer/songwriter with The Mamas And The Papas, who had a 1966 US No.1 and UK No.3 single with 'Monday Monday'. Phillips died of heart failure, aged 65, on March 18th 2001.

1939 John Robert Parker Ravenscroft (a.k.a. John Peel), BBC radio DJ and TV presenter. He was BBC radio's longest-serving DJ and the first to introduce The Ramones, Roxy Music, The Smiths and The Fall. He founded Dandelion Records in 1969. Peel died of a heart attack on October 25th 2004.

1941 John McNally – guitarist with The Searchers, who had a 1964 UK No.1 single with 'Needles And Pins' and a 1964 US No.3 single with 'Love Potion Number Nine'.

1950 Micky Moody – guitarist with Juicy Lucy, who had a 1970 UK No.14 single with 'Who Do You Love?', and Whitesnake, who had a 1987 US No.1 & UK No.9 single with 'Here I Go Again'.

1954 Ronald Beitle – drummer for Wild Cherry, who had a 1976 US No.1 & UK No.7 single with 'Play That Funky Music'.

ON THIS DAY

1969 two weeks after the Woodstock Festival, the second Isle of Wight Festival took place. Over 150,000 turned up over the two days to see Bob Dylan, The Band, Blodwyn Pig, Blonde On Blonde, Bonzo Dog Dooh Dah Band, Edgar Broughton Band, Joe Cocker, Aynsley Dunbar, Family, Fat Mattress, Julie Felix, Free, Gypsy, Richie Havens,

John Peel: 'Get 'em on' shout the fans.

The Moody Blues, The Nice, Tom Paxton, Pentangle, The Pretty Things, Third Ear Band and The Who. Tickets cost 25 shillings ($3.00). Celebrities who attended included Keith Richards, Charlie Watts, John and Yoko, George Harrison, Ringo Starr, Jane Fonda, Liz Taylor and Richard Burton.

1969 one-hit wonders Zager And Evans were at No.1 on the UK singles chart with 'In The Year 2525'.

1969 the three day Texas Pop Festival took place featuring Janis Joplin, Led Zeppelin, Sam & Dave, Santana, Johnny Winter, Grand Funk Railroad, Delaney & Bonnie, Nazz, Spirit, BB King, Canned Heat and Chicago. Over 120,000 fans attended the festival.

1975 KC & The Sunshine Band went to No.1 on the US singles chart with 'Get Down Tonight', the group's first of five No.1s. The song made No.21 in the UK.

1975 Paul Kossoff, guitarist with Free and Back Street Crawler "died" for 35 minutes in hospital.

He actually died on March 19th 1976 of heart failure, after a history of drug abuse.

1975 Rod Stewart had his fifth UK No.1 album when *Atlantic Crossing* started a five week run at the top of the charts.

1988 Bruce Springsteen's wife Julianne filed for a divorce after newspapers published photos of Springsteen and backing singer Patti Scialfa together (the couple married in 1991).

1989 Billy Joel fired his manager and former brother-in-law, Frank Weber, after an audit revealed discrepancies. Joel took him to court and sued for $90 million (£53 million).

1989 Izzy Stradlin from Guns N' Roses was arrested for making a public disturbance on a US air flight after urinating on the floor, verbally abusing a stewardess and smoking in the non-smoking section of the aircraft.

1997 members from The Wu-Tang Clan were arrested after the alleged assault on a record promotions manager following a show in Chicago.

1997 The Notorious B.I.G., featuring Puff Daddy And Mase, went to No.1 on the US singles chart with 'Mo Money Mo Problems', a No.6 hit in the UK.

1999 appearing at the Chastain Park Amphitheatre, Atlanta, R.E.M. and Wilco.

2003 Sam Phillips the founder of Sun Records and studio died. Phillips changed the face of American music recording Elvis Presley, Carl Perkins, Ike Turner, B.B. King and Jerry Lee Lewis.

BORN ON THIS DAY

1939 Jerry Allison – drummer for The Crickets, who had a 1957 US No.1 single with 'That'll Be The Day', a 1959 UK No.1 single 'It Doesn't Matter Anymore'.

1945 Van Morrison, Irish singer/songwriter and former member of Them, who had a 1965 UK No.2 single with 'Here Comes The Night'. As a solo artist he had a 1970 UK No. 32 album with *Moondance* plus over 15 other UK Top 40 albums.

1957 Gina Schock – drummer for The Go-Go's, who had a 1982 US No.2 single with 'We Got The Beat'.

1957 Glenn Tilbrook – guitarist and vocalist with Squeeze, who had a 1979 UK No.2 single with 'Up The Junction'.

1966 Peter Cunnah – vocalist with D:Ream, who had a 1994 UK No.1 single with 'Things Can Only Get Better'.

1970 Debbie Gibson, singer who had a 1988 US No.1 & UK No.9 single with 'Foolish Beat'.

1977 Del Marquis, (a.k.a Derek Gruen) – guitarist with Scissor Sisters, who had a 2004 UK No.1 self-titled album and a 2004 UK No.12 single with 'Laura'.

ON THIS DAY

1963 the girl trio Angels started a three week run at No.1 on the US singles chart with 'My Boyfriend's Back'. The writers of the song, Bob Feldman, Jerry Goldstein and Richard Gottehrer, were a trio of Brooklyn songwriter/producers who went on to write the hits 'Sorrow' and have the 1965 US No.11 single as The Strangeloves with 'I Want Candy'.

1965 Sonny And Cher arrived in the UK for their first promotional visit.

1968 appearing at the first Isle Of White Festival, held over two days, were The Move, The Pretty Things, The Crazy World Of Arthur Brown, Orange Bicycle, Jefferson Airplane, Fairport Convention and T. Rex. Tickets cost 25 shillings, ($3.00).

1971 Jagger, Richards, Wyman and Watts from The Rolling Stones, plus Brian Jones' father, filed a high court writ against ex-managers Oldham and Easton, claiming they made a secret deal with Decca in 1963 to deprive the group of royalties.

1974 Traffic made their last live performance at the annual UK Reading Festival.

1976 George Harrison was found guilty of "subconscious plagiarism" of the Ronnie Mack song 'He's So Fine' when writing 'My Sweet Lord', which meant earnings from the song had to go to Mack's estate. The Chiffons then recorded their own version of 'My Sweet Lord'.

1980 Karen Carpenter married real estate developer Thomas Burris in Beverly Hills.

1985 *Brothers In Arms* by Dire Straits started a nine week run at No.1 in the US album charts. The album also topped the charts in 25 other countries and went on to sell over 20 million worldwide.

1986 Bob Geldof married TV presenter Paula Yates.

1991 appearing at London's Wembley Stadium were Guns N' Roses, Skid Row and Nine Inch Nails.

1994 Aaliyah and R. Kelly secretly married at the Sheraton Gateway Suites in Rosemont. Aaliyah never admitted being married, though a magazine published a copy of the marriage certificate. She was only 15 at the time, so the marriage was later annulled.

2002 NASA announced that Lance Bass, singer with *NSYNC, was to become the first celebrity astronaut. His $23.8 million (£14 million) place on a Russian Soyuz module would make him the youngest person, at 23 years of age, to go into orbit. Bass ended up not taking part in the flight after failing to pay for his $20 million ticket on the craft.

2003 The Darkness started a four week run at No.1 on the UK chart with *Permission To Land*, the UK band's debut album.

2004 singer Carl Wayne died of cancer. He had been a member of Carl Wayne And The Vikings and The Move, and also worked with The Hollies and the Electric Light Orchestra.

2004 appearing at the Carling Academy, Glasgow, Velvet Revolver.

BORN ON THIS DAY

1947 Barry Gibb – singer/songwriter and producer with The Bee Gees, who had a 1967 UK No.1 single with 'Massachusetts', a 1978 UK & US No.1 single with 'Night Fever' plus over 30 other UK Top 40 singles and nine US No.1s over four decades.

1950 Peter Hewson – singer with Chicory Tip, who had a 1972 UK No.1 single with 'Son Of My Father' – claimed to be the first UK No.1 single to feature a synthesizer.

1955 Bruce Foxton – bass player and vocalist with The Jam, who had a 1980 UK No.1 single with 'Going Underground' plus 14 other UK Top 40 singles.

1957 Gloria Estefan, singer who had a 1984 UK No.6 single with 'Dr Beat' plus over 20 other UK Top 40 hits and a 1988 US No.1 single with 'Anything For You'.

1976 Babydaddy (a.k.a. Scot Hofman) – bass player with Scissor Sisters, who had a 2004 UK No.1 self-titled album and a 2004 UK No.12 single with 'Laura'.

ON THIS DAY

1955 after complaints from his neighbours, rock 'n' roll fan Sidney Adams was fined £3 and 10 shillings by a London Court after he played Bill Haley's 'Shake Rattle and Roll' all day long at full volume.

1956 Elvis Presley was at No.2 on the US charts with 'Hound Dog'. He was held off the top spot by The Platters' 'My Prayer'.

1957 this was the start of "The Biggest Show Of Stars" package tour, at Brooklyn Paramount featuring Buddy Holly & The Crickets, The Drifters, The Everly Brothers and Frankie Lymon. On some dates white artists were unable to play because of segregation laws.

1962 Tommy Roe went to No.1 on the US singles chart with 'Sheila', which was a No.3 hit in the UK.

1969 after his headline performance at the Isle Of Wight Festival Bob Dylan went to stay the night with John Lennon at his Tittenhurst Park house.

1973 Rod Stewart had his third No.1 UK album when *Sing It Again* started a three week run at No.1.

1974 The Osmonds were at No.1 on the UK singles chart with 'Love Me For A Reason', the group's only UK No.1.

1979 appearing at The Edinburgh Rock Festival were Van Morrison, Talking Heads, Squeeze, The Undertones, Steele Pulse and The Chieftains. Tickets were £6 ($10).

1979 U2 released their very first record in Ireland, an EP titled 'U2-3'.

1980 Stevie Wonder played the first of six sold-out nights at Wembley Arena, London.

1983 lead guitarist with The Clash, Mick Jones, was fired by the other three members of the group, who claimed he had drifted apart from the original idea of the group.

1984 after a 25 year career Tina Turner had her first solo No.1 in the US with 'What's Love Got To Do With It?'

1990 The Cure broadcast a four hour pirate radio show from a secret London location to premiere their latest album *Mixed Up*.

1996 Kim Wilde married actor Hal Fowler, whom she met while working on the West End musical "Tommy".

2000 All five Spice Girls had places in a new list of the UK Top 20 earning celebrity directors. The girls' own companies were all listed with profits of £6 million ($10 million) each. The companies were Monsta Productions (Emma), Moody Productions (Posh), Red Girl Productions (Mel C), Moneyspider Productions (Mel B) and Geri Productions.

2002 Atomic Kitten started a four week run at No.1 on the UK singles chart with their version of the Blondie hit 'The Tide Is High'.

2002 Coldplay scored their second UK No.1 album with *A Rush Of Blood To The Head*.

2004 Babyshambles frontman – and former Libertine – Pete Doherty was given a suspended four month jail sentence after admitting possession of a flick knife. The singer was found with the weapon by police as he drove to his home in London in June.

Fleetwood Mac

Barry Dickins and Rod MacSween for I.T.B.
in association with Capital Radio
Present

Behind the Mask Tour

TURNSTILE B

plus
Special Guests

Tickets £20.00

GATES OPEN at 1.30 p.m.
SHOW STARTS at 5.30 p.m.

Saturday
1st September 1990
(SUBJECT TO LICENCE)

No alcohol, bottles or cans permitted

Issued subject to conditions on reverse

TICKET Nº 002916

TO BE RETAINED

BORN ON THIS DAY

1925 Hugo Montenegro, composer who had a 1968 UK No.1 & US No.2 single with 'The Good The Bad And The Ugly', taken from the soundtrack to the Clint Eastwood spaghetti Western film of the same name. He died on February 6th 1981.

1925 Russ Conway, pianist and composer who had a 1959 UK No.1 single with 'Side Saddle', plus 17 other UK Top 40 hits. He died on November 16th 2000.

1943 Rosalind Ashford – vocalist with The Vandellas, who had a 1962 US No.2 & 1969 UK No.4 single with 'Dancing In The Street', and Ashford & Simpson, who had a 1985 UK No.3 single, 'Solid'.

1951 Mik Kaminski – violinist for the Electric Light Orchestra, who had a 1979 UK No.3 & US No.4 single with 'Don't Bring Me Down' plus 26 other Top 40 hits.

1957 Steve Porcaro, keyboard player with Toto, who had a 1983 US No.1 & UK No.3 single, 'Africa'.

1958 Fritz McIntyre – keyboard player with Simply Red, who had a 1986 US No.1 & UK No.2 single with 'Holding Back The Years'.

1959 Paul Deakin – drummer with The Mavericks, US country rock group, who had a 1998 UK No.4 single with 'Dance The Night Away'.

1975 Tony Thompson – singer with Hi-Five, who had a 1991 US No.1 & UK No.43 single with 'I Like The Way (The Kissing Game)'.

ON THIS DAY

1965 appearing at London's Marquee Club were Steampacket with Long John Baldry, Rod Stewart, Julie Driscoll and The Brian Auger Trinity.

Russ keeps those hands together and concentrates on the film.

1970 Led Zeppelin appeared at the Oakland Stadium, Oakland, California.

1971 the Grateful Dead's former manager was arrested after disappearing with over $70,000 (£41,176) of the band's money.

1972 Rod Stewart was at No.1 on the UK singles chart with 'You Wear It Well', his second UK No.1.

1987 David Bowie played Madison Square Garden, New York on the Glass Spider world tour.

1988 the "Human Rights Now!" world tour kicked off at Wembley Stadium, London with Sting, Bruce Springsteen, Peter Gabriel, Tracy Chapman and Youssu n'dour, taking in five continents and claiming to be the most ambitious rock tour in history.

1989 Ozzy Osbourne was charged with threatening to kill his wife Sharon. He was released on the condition that he immediately went into detox. The case was latter dropped when the couple decide to reconcile.

1990 Black Sabbath kicked off a 14 date UK tour at The Royal Court Liverpool.

1995 Michael Jackson went to No.1 on the US singles chart with a song written by R. Kelly, 'You Are Not Alone', which was also a No.1 in the UK.

2001 Jennifer Lopez was at No.1 on the US singles chart with 'I'm Real'.

2001 Slipknot went to No.1 on the UK album chart with *Iowa*.

2002 Burglars raided the London home of Icelandic singer Bjork. Thieves broke into Bjork's luxury flat in Maida Vale, London and stole valuable recording equipment. The 36-year-old singer was asleep in the flat at the time.

U.F.O. Festival

MOVE Saturday

PINK FLOYD Friday & Saturday

ARTHUR BROWN Friday

TOMORROW with KEITH WEST Friday

SOFT MACHINE Saturday

DENNY LAINE Saturday

ALSO: **THE NACK, FAIRPORT CONVENTION, FILMS** Friday & Saturday, 10 p.m.–6 a.m. at the ROUNDHOUSE OPEN TO THE PUBLIC FRIDAY (25/-. UFO Members 15/-) MEMBERS (15/-) and GUESTS (25/-) only SATURDAY FOR THE BENEFIT OF RELEASE

Festival fever on this day in 1967.

3rd September

BORN ON THIS DAY

1934 blues guitarist Freddie King. Eric Clapton covered his 'Have You Ever Loved A Woman?' on the *Layla* album. King died on December 27th 1976 of heart trouble and ulcers, aged 42.

1942 Al Jardine – guitarist and vocalist with The Beach Boys, who had a 1966 UK & US No.1 single with 'Good Vibrations' plus over 25 other UK Top 40 singles.

1944 Gary Leeds – drummer with The Walker Brothers, who had a 1966 UK No.1 & US No.13 single with 'The Sun Ain't Gonna Shine Anymore'.

1948 Donald Brewer – drummer with Grand Funk Railroad, who had a 1974 US No.1 single with 'The Locomotion'. They were the most successful US heavy metal band of the 70s, selling over 20 million albums.

1973 Jennifer Paige, US singer who had a 1998 UK No.4 single with 'Crush'.

1973 David Mead, US singer/songwriter who had a 2001 UK radio airplay hit with 'Girl On The Roof'.

1980 Jay "Cone" McCaslin – bass player for Sum 41, who had a 2001 UK No.13 single with 'In Too Deep'.

ON THIS DAY

1965 a Rolling Stones gig in Dublin ended in a riot after 30 fans jumped onto the stage. Mick Jagger was knocked to the floor as the rest of the band fled the stage.

1966 Donovan went to No.1 on the US singles chart with 'Sunshine Superman'. The song made No.2 in the UK.

1968 Jimi Hendrix appeared at the Balboa Stadium, San Diego, California.

1970 Al Wilson, guitar player with Canned Heat, was found dead at fellow band member Bob Hite's garden in Topanga Canyon, Los Angeles, aged 27.

1970 it was reported that the Bob Dylan bootleg album *Great White Wonder* had sold over 350,000 copies.

1977 Elvis Presley had his 17th UK No.1 single with 'Way Down'.

1982 the three day US Festival in San Bernardino, California took place featuring Tom Petty, Fleetwood Mac, The Police, The Cars, Talking Heads, Ramones, B-52s, The English Beat, Gang Of Four, Grateful Dead, Pat Benatar and Jackson Browne. The festival was bankrolled by Steven Wozniak, Apple Computers' founder. Tickets cost $37.50 (£22).

1983 The Eurythmics went to No.1 on the US singles chart with 'Sweet Dreams (Are Made Of This)'.

1983 UB40 had their first UK No.1 with a cover of the Neil Diamond song 'Red Red Wine'.

1988 Rick Astley was at No.1 on the UK singles chart with 'Never Gonna Give You Up'.

1991 Ike Turner was released from prison having served 18 months of a four year prison term. (Ike had been arrested ten other times and in an interview with *Variety* he claimed to have spent over $11 million [£6.5 million] on cocaine).

The Animated Egg
I Said, She Said, Ah Cid-Sippin' And Trippin', Sock It My Way-That's How It Is-And Others

1967 saw the release of an album said to be "possibly more influential than Sgt Pepper".

2000 Madonna started a four week run at No.1 on the US singles chart with 'Music'.

2000 Robbie Williams started a three week run at No.1 on the UK album chart with *Sing When You're Winning*.

2002 The Rolling Stones' 40th anniversary "Licks" tour kicked off at the Fleet Center, Boston. Tickets for the best seats cost $224 (£118). The world tour would see the band playing to over 2.5 million fans over the course of 100 shows.

2003 Libertines singer Pete Doherty was sentenced to six months in jail after being found guilty of burglary and drug possession charges. His sentence was reduced to two months on appeal.

2004 songwriter and producer Billy Davis died in New York after a long illness. He co-wrote Jackie Wilson's, 'Reet Petite' and the jingle 'I'd Like To Buy The World A Coke'. Aretha Franklin, James Brown, Marvin Gaye, The Supremes and Gladys Knight all recorded his songs.

The sun is shining for Gary Walker.

BORN ON THIS DAY

1942 Merald "Bubba" Knight – vocalist with The Pips, who had a 1973 US No.1 single with 'Midnight Train To Georgia' and a 1975 UK No.4 single with Gladys Knight, 'The Way We Were'.

1951 Martin Chambers – drummer with The Pretenders, who had a 1980 UK No.1 single with 'Brass In Pocket' and a 1983 US No.5 single with 'Back On The Chain Gang'.

1971 Ty Longley – guitarist with Great White. The band had a 1989 US hit with a cover of Ian Hunter's 'Once Bitten, Twice Shy'. Longley was killed on February 20th 2003 along with 100 fans after pyrotechnics ignited a club during a gig in West Warwick, Rhode Island.

1981 Beyonce – singer with Destiny's Child, who had a 2000 US No.1 single with 'Say My Name' and a 2001 US & UK No.1 single and album *Survivor* and a 2003 US & UK No.1 single with 'Crazy In Love' from the world-wide No.1 album *Dangerously In Love*.

The Who and their mounting shopping list.

ON THIS DAY

1961 The Highwaymen started a two week run at No.1 on the US singles chart with 'Michael', which also made No.1 in the UK. The group was made up of five university students.

1962 The Beatles' first proper recording session at London's Abbey Road studios took place. They recorded 'Love Me Do'. (Producer George Martin had them return the next day to re-record the track using session drummer Andy White.)

1965 The Who had their van stolen, containing over £5,000 ($8,500) worth of equipment, outside the Battersea Dogs' home. The band was inside the home at the time buying a guard dog. The van was later recovered.

1968 The Bee Gees had their second UK No.1 single with 'I've Gotta Get A Message To You'.

1971 taken from the album *Ram*, Paul and Linda McCartney went to No.1 on the US singles chart with the US-only released 'Uncle Albert/Admiral Halsey', Paul's first solo No.1.

1972 concessionaire Francisco Caruso was killed during a Wishbone Ash concert in Texas after refusing to give a fan a free sandwich.

1976 Fleetwood Mac went to No.1 on the US album chart with their self-titled album, the group's first of three No.1 albums.

1976 The Bee Gees went to No.1 on the US singles chart with 'You Should Be Dancing', the group's third US No.1. The song made No.5 in the UK.

1976 the Sex Pistols made their television debut when they appeared on the Granada TV programme *So It Goes*.

1982 Survivor was at No.1 on the UK singles chart with the theme from the film *Rocky III*, 'Eye Of The Tiger'.

1982 The Steve Miller Band started a two week run at No.2 on the US singles chart with 'Abracadabra', the group's third US No.1. It was a No.2 hit in the UK.

1984 U2 played the first of six nights at Sydney Entertainment Centre, Australia.

1995 Blur, Oasis, Radiohead, Paul Weller, Manic Street Preachers, Stone Roses and others all recorded tracks for the *War Child* charity album, which was released five days later. All profits went to children caught up in the war in former Yugoslavia.

1996 Oasis created outrage at the MTV awards. During the band's performance of 'Champagne Supernova' at New York's Radio City Hall Liam spat on stage and threw a beer into the crowd.

Rare War Child Christmas Cards, this one by Thom Yorke.

BORN ON THIS DAY

1936 Willie Woods – guitarist with Junior Walker And The All Stars, who had a 1969 US No.4 single with 'What Does It Take, To Win Your Love'. Woods died of lung cancer on May 27th 1997.

1939 John Stewart – singer/songwriter with The Kingston Trio. As a solo artist he had a 1979 US No.5 single with 'Gold'. He also wrote The Monkees' hit 'Daydream Believer'.

1945 Al Stewart, singer/songwriter who had a 1977 UK No.31 & US No.8 single with 'Year Of The Cat'.

1946 Buddy Miles – drummer with The Ink Spots, Wilson Pickett, Electric Flag and Jimi Hendrix. Featured on the 1970 Hendrix album *Band Of Gypsies*.

1946 Freddie Mercury *(right)* – singer/ songwriter for Queen, who had a 1975 UK No.1 single with 'Bohemian Rhapsody', also UK No.1 in 1991, plus over 40 other UK Top 40 singles. The band also had a 1980 US No.1 single with 'Crazy Little Thing Called Love'. As a solo artist Mercury had a 1987 UK No.4 single with 'The Great Pretender'. He died of bronchio-pneumonia on January 24th 1991 aged 45, just one day after he publicly announced he was HIV positive.

1946 Loudon Wainwright III, US singer/songwriter who had a 1973 US No.17 single with 'Dead Skunk'. He once appeared in TV's M.A.S.H. He is the father of Rufus Wainwright.

1968 Brad Wilk – drummer with Rage Against The Machine, who had a 1996 US No.1 album with *Evil Empire*.

ON THIS DAY

1963 The Rolling Stones kicked off their fourth UK tour at The Astoria, London. It was a 32 date package tour with Mike Berry And The Innocents, The Mojos, Simon Scott and The Leroys.

1964 The Animals started a three week run at No.1 on the US singles chart with 'House Of The Rising Sun'. When first released the record company printed the time of the song at three minutes, feeling that the real time of four minutes was too long for radio DJ's to play.

1965 Sonny And Cher made their first live UK appearance when they appeared at the 100 Club in London.

1966 John Lennon started filming in Germany on his role as Private Gripweed in *How I Won The War*.

1969 The Stooges made their New York debut at The Pavilion supporting MC5.

1978 Joe Negroni from Frankie Lymon & The Teenagers died of a brain haemorrhage. The band had had a 1956 UK No.1 & US No.6 single with 'Why Do Fools Fall In Love?'

1981 Soft Cell were at No.1 on the UK singles chart with their version of 'Tainted Love'. (First recorded by Gloria Jones in the mid 1960s.)

1987 Ian Asbury of The Cult was arrested after a show in Vancouver ended in a riot. Staff at the concert claimed they were assaulted by Asbury, who spent the night in the cells.

1990 Charley Charles, the ex-Ian Dury And The Blockheads drummer, died of cancer.

1992 Kylie Minogue went to No.1 on the UK album chart with her *Greatest Hits* compilation LP.

McCartney's wife wins libel damages

By A Correspondent

HEATHER MILLS, Sir Paul McCartney's wife, accepted £50,000 libel damages yester- been vindicated." All of the money had been donated to a charity founded by Miss Mills for innocent landmine victims.

Miss Mills — Lady McCart-

1994 Oasis appeared live at the Hacienda, Manchester to celebrate the launch of their debut album *Definitely Maybe*. Tickets cost £7 ($12).

1998 Aerosmith scored their first US No.1 single with the Diane Warren-penned song 'I Don't Want To Miss A Thing'.

1998 the Manic Street Preachers scored their first UK No.1 single with 'If You Tolerate This Your Children Will Be Next', the group's 19th hit. This made the band the first Welsh act to have a No.1 single since Shakin' Stevens in 1985.

1999 after spending 58 weeks on the chart Shania Twain went to No.1 on the UK album chart with *Come On Over*. It gave the Canadian singer the biggest-selling UK album of the year.

2002 Heather Mills, Sir Paul McCartney's wife, accepted £50,000 ($85,000) libel damages over an article in the *Sunday Mirror*. The paper had suggested that Mills had acted dishonestly over cash collected for an earthquake appeal.

2004 The Libertines went to No.1 on the UK album chart with their self-titled second album.

STALLS GEN-AD   136   9

SJM CONCERTS PRESENTS
PJ HARVEY
PLUS SPECIAL GUESTS
CARLING APOLLO
17.50 STOCKPORT ROAD, MANCHESTER
SO 2.75   SUN 05-SEP-04 19:30
20.25   31868

www.cclive.co.uk   No Exchange   No Refund

BORN ON THIS DAY

1925 Jimmy Reed, blues singer who had a 1964 UK No.45 single with 'Shame Shame Shame'. He also wrote 'Big Boss Man' and 'Bright Lights Big City' and was a major influence on The Rolling Stones. Elvis Presley covered his 'Baby, What You Want Me To Do?' Reed died on August 29th 1976.

1944 Roger Waters – vocalist and bass player with Pink Floyd, who had a 1973 US No.1 & UK No.2 album with *Dark Side Of The Moon*, which spent a record breaking 741 weeks on the US chart. He left the band in 1985.

1969 Marc Anthony, US singer/songwriter, who had a 2000 US No.2 single with 'You Sang To Me'.

1969 Paddy Boom (a.k.a. Patrick Seacor) – drummer with Scissor Sisters, who had a 2004 UK No.1 self-titled album and a 2004 UK No.12 single with 'Laura'.

1971 Delores O'Riordan – singer with The Cranberries, who had a 1994 UK No.14 single with 'Linger'. The 1993 album *Everybody Else Is Doing It So Why Can't We* spent 86 weeks on the UK chart.

1980 Kerry Katona – singer with Atomic Kitten, who had a 2000 UK No.1 single with 'Whole Again'. She left the group in 2001.

ON THIS DAY

1957 the first flexi-disc was produced and used in a promotion for a Nestle chocolate bar.

1963 Cilla Black signed a management contract with Beatles' manager Brian Epstein.

1967 Engelbert Humperdinck was at No.1 on the UK singles chart with 'The Last Waltz', the singer's second and final UK No.1.

1970 Jimi Hendrix made his final live appearance when he appeared at the Isle Of Fehmarn in Germany.

1974 The 101 All Stars (formed by Joe Strummer of The Clash) made their debut at The Telegraph, Brixton Hill, London.

1975 Glen Campbell started a two week run at No.1 on the US singles chart with 'Rhinestone Cowboy', his first No.1 after 13 Top 40 hits. It made No.4 in the UK.

1976 Fleetwood Mac went to No.1 on the US album chart for the first time with their album *Fleetwood Mac*.

1980 U2 appeared at The Fiesta Suite, Plymouth, England.

1980 The Jam was at No.1 on the UK singles chart with

'Start', the group's second UK No.1.

1986 all-girl group Bananarama went to No.1 on the US singles chart with 'Venus'. The song had also been a No.1 for Dutch group Shocking Blue in 1970.

1988 2,000 items of Elton John's personal memorabilia including his boa feathers, 'Pinball Wizard' boots and hundreds of pairs of spectacles were auctioned at Sotheby's in London.

1990 Tom Fogerty, guitarist with Creedence Clearwater Revival, died, aged 49, due to complications from AIDS, which he acquired during a blood transfusion.

1994 Session piano player Nicky Hopkins died. He had worked with The Rolling Stones, Jeff Beck, The Beatles, The Who, Small Faces and Screaming Lord Sutch.

1997 Elton John recorded a new version of 'Candle In The Wind' after performing the song live at Diana, Princess of Wales' funeral. A record 31.5 million across Britain watched Elton play the special tribute to Diana.

2001 Earth, Wind And Fire announced that their forthcoming 30th anniversary American tour would be sponsored by Viagra.

2004 Jamiroquai singer Jay Kay was banned from driving for six months after being clocked driving at more than 100mph (161kmph).

2005 Carling Live Presents Limp Bizkit at Finsbury Park, London.

Elton flogs off his riches yet again.

BORN ON THIS DAY

1936 Buddy Holly – singer with The Crickets, who had a 1957 US No.1 with 'That'll Be The Day', a 1959 UK No.1 single with 'It Doesn't Matter Anymore' plus over 15 other UK Top 40 singles. Holly influenced The Beatles and The Rolling Stones. He was killed in a plane crash on February 3rd 1959.

1949 Gloria Gaynor, singer who had a 1979 UK & US No.1 single with 'I Will Survive'.

1951 Chrissie Hynde – guitarist and vocalist with The Pretenders, who had a 1980 UK No.1 single with 'Brass In Pocket' plus over ten other UK Top 40 singles. As a solo artist she had a 1985 UK No.1 single 'I Got You Babe' with UB40.

1954 Benmont Tench – keyboard player for Tom Petty & The Heartbreakers, who had a 1989 UK No.28 single with 'I Won't Back Down'.

1969 Jean-Benoit Dunckel – keyboard player for Air, who had a 1998 UK No.6 album with *Moon Safari*. It spent over a year on the UK chart.

ON THIS DAY

1959 Craig Douglas was at No.1 on the UK singles chart with his version of the Sam Cooke hit 'Only Sixteen'.

1968 The Doors appeared at The Roundhouse, London. The night was filmed by Granada TV. The band also scored their only US No.1 album on this day with *Waiting For The Sun*.

1972 David Bowie appeared live at The Top Rank, Hanley, Stoke on Trent.

1973 The Rolling Stones kicked off a nine date UK tour at the Empire Pool, London. Tickets cost £2.20 ($3.75).

1975 Rod Stewart was at No.1 on the UK singles chart with his version of the Sutherland Brothers' song, 'Sailing'. The song had been featured in the BBC TV series about HMS *Ark Royal*.

A DANCE

will be held at the

VILLAGE HALL, IRBY

to be held on

Friday, 7th September 1962

The Beatles and the Courting Group

8·0 p.m. till 11·30 p.m.

TICKETS—7/6 each

1976 Abba was at No.1 on the UK singles chart with 'Dancing Queen', the group's fourth UK No.1.

1985 David Bowie and Mick Jagger were at No.1 on the UK singles chart with their version of the Martha Reeves And The Vandellas' 1964 hit 'Dancing In The Street'. The song had been recorded as part of the Live Aid charity appeal.

1985 John Parr started a two week run at No.1 on the US singles chart with 'St Elmo's Fire', which was taken from the film of the same name. The song was a No.6 hit in the UK.

1985 Ringo Starr became the first Beatle to be a grandfather when his son Zak and wife Sarah had a daughter, Tatia Jayne.

1991 Gloria Estefan was awarded damages of $5 million ($2.9 million) for the injuries she sustained when her tour bus was involved in an accident.

1991 Motley Crue signed a record deal for which they were guaranteed $22.5 million (£13.25 million).

Motley Crue's advance (extract).

1996 Bon Jovi drummer Tico Torres married model Eva Herzigova.

2001 Michael Jackson was reunited on stage with The Jackson Five at the 30th Anniversary Celebration in New York City's Madison Square Garden. It ended Jackson's 11 year hiatus from performing in the US. Eminem, Whitney Houston, Gladys Knight, Britney Spears and Destiny's Child all appeared to celebrate the 30th anniversary of Jackson's singing career.

2003 singer/songwriter Warren Zevon died. He once worked as The Everly brothers band leader and went on to record over five solo albums and had a 1978 US No.21 single with 'Werewolves Of London'.

2003 Black Eyed Peas started a seven week run at No.1 on the UK singles chart with 'Where Is The Love?'

BORN ON THIS DAY

1897 Jimmie Rodgers, the first country music star, singer/ songwriter. He sold over 12 million records. He was also the first person to be elected into the Country Music Hall Of Fame. He had a 1957 US No.1 single with 'Honeycomb' plus over ten other US Top 40 hits. Rodgers died on May 26th 1933.

1925 Peter Sellers, actor and singer who had a 1956 UK No.9 single, 'Ying Tong Song', with The Goons, a 1960 UK No.4 single, 'Goodness Gracious Me', with Sophia Loren and a 1965 UK No.14 single with 'A Hard Day's Night'. Sellers died of a heart attack on July 24th 1980.

1932 Patsy Cline, US country singer who had a 1961 US No.19 single with 'Crazy'. She was killed in a plane crash on March 5th 1963.

1960 David Steele – bass player with Fine Young Cannibals, who had a 1989 UK No.5 single with 'She Drives Me Crazy', and The Beat, who had a 1983 US No.1 & UK No.3 single with 'Can't Get Used To Losing You'.

1975 Richard Hughes – drummer with Keane, who had a 2004 UK No.1 album with *Hopes And Fears*.

1979 Pink (a.k.a Alicia Moore) *(right)* US singer, who had a 2001 UK No.2 single with 'Get The Party Started' and a 2001 US & UK No.1 single with Christina Aguilera, Lil' Kim and Mya, 'Lady Marmalade'.

ON THIS DAY

1957 'Reet Petite' by Jackie Wilson was released for the first time going on to be a UK No 6 hit, re-released 29 years later in 1986 it became a UK No.1.

1968 The Beatles performed 'Hey Jude' on the UK ITV *Frost On Sunday* programme in front of an invited audience.

1973 Marvin Gaye started a two week run at No.1 on the US singles chart with 'Let's Get It On', his second US No.1. It only reached No.31 in the UK.

1973 The Allman Brothers Band started a five week run at No.1 on the US albumalbum chart with *Brothers And Sisters*, the group's only US No.1.

1978 Keith Moon, drummer with The Who, died of an overdose of heminevrin prescribed to combat alcoholism. A post-mortem confirmed there were 32 tablets in his system, 26 were undissolved. Moon had attended a party the night before that was organized by Paul McCartney for the launch of *The Buddy Holly Story* movie.

1980 Kiss played the first of two sold-out nights at London's Wembley Arena.

1984 Stevie Wonder had his first UK No.1 with 'I Just Called To Say I Love You', which was taken from the film *Lady In Red*. It was 18 years after Wonder's chart debut in 1966. The

song stayed at No.1 for six weeks.

1990 Jon Bon Jovi went to No.1 on the US singles chart with 'Blaze Of Glory', which was taken from the film *Young Guns II*. It was a No.2 in the UK.

1993 Kurt Cobain and Courtney Love appeared on stage together at a show in Hollywood. They performed 'Penny Royal Tea', a song they had written together.

1995 R.E.M. kicked off an 18 date US tour at the Miami Arena, Miami, Florida with Radiohead as support band.

1997 29 years after forming, Led Zeppelin released their first-ever single in the UK to promote their reissued back catalogue. 'Whole Lotta Love' had been recorded in 1969 and was featured on their second album.

1997 Derek Taylor *(above)*, the publicist for The Beatles, died aged 67. He had been responsible for many of the legends surrounding their career and had also worked with The Beach Boys and The Byrds.

2002 Iron Maiden singer Bruce Dickinson *(right)* started his new job as an airline pilot. The heavy metal singer qualified as a £35,000 ($59,500) a year first officer with Gatwick-based airline Astraeus.

BORN ON THIS DAY

1940 Joe Negroni – singer with Frankie Lymon & The Teenagers, who had a 1956 UK No.1 & US No.6 single with 'Why Do Fools Fall In Love?' He died on September 5th 1978.

1941 Otis Redding, US soul singer who had a 1968 US No.1 & UK No.3 single with 'Sittin' On, The Dock Of The Bay' plus ten other UK Top 40 singles. Redding was killed in a plane crash on December 10th 1967.

1945 Doug Ingle – vocalist and keyboardist with Iron Butterfly, who had a 1968 US No.14 single with 'In-A-Gadda-Da-Vida'.

1946 Billy Preston – songwriter, keyboardist and singer who had a 1973 US No.1 single with 'Will It Go Round In Circles?', a 1978 UK No.2 single with Syreeta 'With You I'm Born Again' and a 1969 US & UK No.1 single 'Get Back' with The Beatles.

1946 Bruce Palmer – bass player with Buffalo Springfield, who had a 1967 US No.17 single with 'For What It's Worth'. He died of a heart attack on October 4th 2004.

1952 Dave Stewart – producer, songwriter, guitarist and keyboardist with Longdancer, The Tourists, who had a 1979 UK No.4 single with 'I Only Want To Be With You' and Eurythmics, who had a 1983 US No.1 & UK No.2 single with 'Sweet Dreams' and a 1985 UK No.1 single with 'There Must Be An Angel'.

1970 Macy Gray (a.k.a. Natalie McIntyre), US singer who had a 1999 UK No.6 single with 'I Try' and a 1999 US No.4 album with *How Life Is*.

ON THIS DAY

1965 the *Hollywood Reporter* ran an advertisement "Madness, folk & roll, musicians singers wanted for acting roles in new T.V. show, parts for 4 insane boys". With the four selected The Monkees were born.

1965 The Rolling Stones were at No.1 in the UK

This is it—the big line-up of d-j's (most of them ex-pirates) signed for the BBC's swinging Radio 1 pop station which goes into operation on 247 metres, medium wave, on September 30. At the far back (bespectacled) is Robin Scott, controller of Radio 1 and the alternative light programme, Radio 2. Left to right (top row) are: TONY BLACKBURN, JIMMY YOUNG, KENNY EVERETT, DUNCAN JOHNSON, DAVID RIDER, DAVE CASH, PETE BRADY, DAVID SYMONDS. Centre row: BOB HOLNESS, TERRY WOGAN, BARRY ALLDIS, MIKE LENNOX, KEITH SKUES, CHRIS DENNING, JOHNNY MORGAN. Bottom row: PETE MURRAY, ED STEWART, PETE DRUMMOND, ALAN FREEMAN, MIKE RAVEN, MIKE AHERN and JOHN PEEL.

ale Friday, week ending September 9, 1967   *On sale Friday, week ending September 9, 1967*

with '(I Can't Get No) Satisfaction', giving them their fourth UK No.1 single.

1972 Jim Croce started a five week run at No.1 on the US album chart with *You Don't Mess Around With Jim*.

1972 Slade were at No.1 on the UK singles chart with 'Mama Weer All Crazee Now', the group's third UK No.1.

1977 David Bowie appeared on Marc Bolan's ITV show *Marc*, singing a duet with Bolan. After the show Bowie and Bolan recorded some demos together, which were never finished as Bolan was killed in a car crash one week later.

1978 A Taste Of Honey started a three week run at No.1 on the US singles chart with 'Boogie Oogie Oogie', which was a No.3 hit in the UK.

1978 appearing at Knebworth Park were Frank Zappa, The Tubes, Peter Gabriel, The Boomtown Rats, Rockpile and Wilko Johnson's Solid Senders. Tickets cost £5.50 ($9.35).

1978 Boney M scored their first UK No.1 album when Night Flight To Venus started a four week run at the top.

1980 The Allman Brothers Band kicked of a UK tour at Manchester's Apollo Theatre.

1989 appearing at the Cabaret Metro, Chicago was Sonic Youth supported by Nirvana.

1989 Italian-based group Black Box started a six week run at No.1 on the UK singles chart with 'Ride On Time'.

1989 New Kids On The Block scored their second US No.1 single with 'Hangin' Tough', a No.1 in the UK in 1990. The group also went to No.1 on the US album chart with *Hangin' Tough*.

1992 Nirvana's bass player Chris Novoselic knocked himself unconscious during the MTV Music And Video Awards – he was hit on the head by his guitar after throwing it "skywards".

1995 Coolio started a three week run at No.1 on the US singles chart with 'Gangsta's Paradise', which was based on Stevie Wonder's 'Pastime Paradise'. The song also made No.1 in the UK.

2001 Aaliyah went to No.1 on the US album chart with her self-titled album.

BORN ON THIS DAY

1898 Waldo Semon, inventor. Semon invented vinyl in 1926, which was used to make LP and 45rpm records. He died on May 26th 1998, aged 100.

1939 Cynthia Lennon, first wife of John Lennon. The couple divorced on November 8th 1968.

1945 Jose Feliciano, singer/songwriter and guitarist who was born blind. He had a 1968 US No.3 & UK No.6 single with 'Light My Fire'.

1946 Danny Hutton – vocalist with Three Dog Night, who had a 1970 UK No.3 & US No.1 single with 'Mamma Told Me Not To Come'.

1949 Barrie Barlow – drummer with Jethro Tull, who had a 1969 UK No.3 single with 'Living In The Past'.

1950 Don Powell – drummer with Slade, who had a 1971 UK No.1 single with 'Coz I Luv You' plus five other UK No.1 singles and 18 Top 40 hits.

1950 Joe Perry – guitarist for Aerosmith, who had a 1989 UK No.13 single with 'Love In An Elevator' and a 1998 US No.1 single with 'I Don't Want To Miss A Thing'.

1956 Johnnie "Fingers" Moylett – keyboardist with The Boomtown Rats, who had a 1979 UK No.1 single with 'I Don't Like Mondays' plus ten other UK Top 40 hits.

1957 Carol Decker – vocalist with T'Pau, who had a 1987 UK No.1 single with 'China In Your Hand' and a 1987 US No.4 single with 'Heart And Soul'.

1957 Siobhan Fahey – singer with Bananarama, who had a 1984 UK No.3 single with 'Robert De Niro's Waiting' plus over 20 other UK Top 40 singles and a 1986 US No.1 single with 'Venus', and Shakespear's Sister, who had a 1992 UK No.1 single with 'Stay'.

ON THIS DAY

1962 The BBC banned the Bobby "Boris" Pickett And The Crypt-Kickers single 'Monster Mash', saying it was offensive. The single became a UK No.3 hit over ten years later in 1973.

1963 during a chance meeting between The Rolling Stones and Paul McCartney and John Lennon at Studio 51 jazz club in London, the duo played the Stones a partly finished song, 'I Wanna Be Your Man'. The Stones liked and later recorded it.

1964 The Kinks' third single, 'You Really Got Me', was at No.1 on the UK singles chart. Future Led Zeppelin founder, guitarist Jimmy Page, played tambourine on the track.

1964 Rod Stewart recorded his first single, a version of Willie Dixon's 'Good Morning Little School Girl'. Future Led Zeppelin bass player John Paul Jones played on the session.

1966 The Supremes started a two week run at No.1 on the US singles chart with 'You Can't Hurry Love', the group's sixth US No.1. It made No.3 in the UK and gave Phil Collins a UK No.1 in 1982.

1968 The Beatles were at No.1 on the UK singles chart with 'Hey Jude', the group's 15th UK No.1 and the longest chart topper ever, at seven minutes ten seconds. The single was the first release on the group's Apple Records label.

1974 The New York Dolls split up. The influential American band made just two albums.

1979 The Police appeared live at The Assembly Rooms, Derby, England.

1983 former guitarist with Stevie Wonder, Michael Sembello, started a two week run at No.1 on the US singles chart with 'Maniac', which was featured in the film *Flashdance*. The song was a No.43 hit in the UK.

1984 Iron Maiden kicked off a 24 date UK tour at The Apollo, Glasgow.

1988 Guns N' Roses started a two week run at No.1 on the US singles chart with 'Sweet Child O' Mine', the group's first US No.1. It was a No.24 hit in the UK.

1988 Phil Collins was at No.1 on the UK singles chart with 'A Groovy Kind Of Love', which was also a hit for the Mindbenders in 1966.

1992 Slash from Guns N' Roses married actress and model Renee Suran.

1997 an electric chair that was used in Alcatraz and once owned by Andy Warhol was sold for £4,800 ($8,160) at an auction in Bristol. Warhol used to sit in the chair and watch horror movies.

2001 Jamiroquai singer Jay Kay pleaded not guilty to assault charges after being accused of hitting a photographer and destroying camera equipment outside a London nightclub. Photographer Dennis Gill alleged that Jay Kay punched him and destroyed equipment worth £250 ($425) outside the Attica nightclub in London's West End. The case was adjourned until October 2001.

> "I'm a rotten guitar player if I'm standing still."
> **Angus Young, AC/DC**

BORN ON THIS DAY

1940 Bernie Dwyer – drummer with Freddie & The Dreamers, who had a 1963 UK No.3 single with 'You Were Made For Me' and a 1965 US No.1 single with 'I'm Telling You Now'.

1943 Mickey Hart – percussionist with the Grateful Dead, who had a 1970 album *Workingman's Dead*.

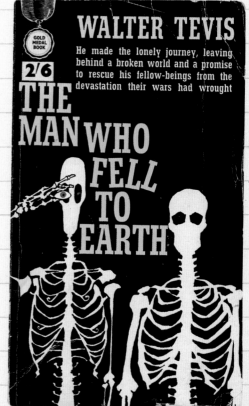

1957 Jon Moss– drummer with Culture Club, who had a 1983 UK No.1 & 1984 US No.1 single with 'Karma Chameleon' plus seven other UK Top 10 singles.

1958 Mick Talbot – keyboardist with Style Council, who had a 1983 UK No.3 single with 'Long Hot Summer' plus 14 other UK Top 40 singles, and Merton Parkers, who had a 1979 UK No.40 single with 'You Need Wheels'.

1965 Moby (a.k.a. Richard Hall) – singer, producer who had a 1991 UK No.10 single with 'Go' and a 2000 UK No.1 album with Play which became the biggest-selling UK indie album of 2000, going Platinum in over 20 countries.

1967 Harry Connick Jr, singer and actor who had a 1991 UK No.32 single with 'It Had To Be You, Recipe For Love'.

1971 Richard Ashcroft – guitarist and vocalist for The Verve, who had a 1997 UK No.1 single with 'The Drugs Don't Work' and a 1997 UK No.1 album Urban Hymns, which spent over 100 weeks on the UK chart. As a solo artist he had a 2000 UK No.3 single with 'A Song For The Lovers' and a 2000 UK No.1 album with Alone With Everybody.

1977 Jonny Buckland – guitarist with Coldplay, who had a 2000 UK No.4 single with 'Yellow' and the 2005 worldwide No.1 album *X&Y*.

1977 Ludacris (a.k.a. Chris Bridges), rapper who had a 2001 UK No.10 single with Missy Elliott, 'One Minute Man' and a 2002 US No.3 album with *Word Of Mouf*.

ON THIS DAY

1960 Nancy Sinatra married American teen idol Tommy Sands.

1961 Judy Garland started a 13 week run at No.1 on the US album chart with *Judy At Carnegie Hall*.

1964 a 16-year-old youth won a Mick Jagger impersonation contest at The Town Hall, Greenwich. The winner turned out to be Mick's younger brother Chris Jagger.

1968 Larry Graham, bass player from Sly & The Family Stone, was busted for cannabis possession as the band arrived in London at the start of a UK tour.

1971 Donny Osmond started a three week run at No.1 on the US singles chart with 'Go Away Little Girl', his only US solo chart topper. The song had also been a No.1 for Steve Lawrence in 1963.

1971 the animated *Jackson Five* series premiered on ABC-TV.

1977 David Bowie recorded a guest appearance on Bing Crosby's Merrie Olde Christmas TV show, duetting with Crosby on 'The Little Drummer Boy'. The track became a hit five years later.

1982 John Cougar started a nine week run at No.1 on the US album chart with *American Fool*.

1987 Level 42's 'It's Over' became the first CD video single to go on sale in the UK. It contained 20 minutes of music and five minutes of video (which remained unseen until CDV players went on sale).

2003 Jennifer Lopez and Ben Affleck postponed their wedding, blaming the media frenzy surrounding it. The pair had tried to keep the precise location of their wedding secret, but following a series of leaks the media had pinpointed a private estate in Santa Barbara.

2004 lyricist Fred Ebb died of a heart attack. He co-wrote the classic tracks 'New York, New York' and 'Chicago'.

Bowie stands next to Crosby!

BORN ON THIS DAY

1940 Tony Bellamy – guitarist, pianist and vocalist with Redbone, who had a 1971 UK No.2 & US No.21 single with 'The Witch Queen Of New Orleans'.

1943 Maria Muldaur, singer/songwriter who had a 1974 US No.6 & UK No.21 single with 'Midnight At The Oasis'.

1944 Barry White, soul singer and producer who had a 1974 UK No.1 single with 'You're The First The Last My Everything' and a 1974 US No.1 single with 'Can't Get Enough Of Your Love, Babe'. White died from kidney failure on July 4th 2003, aged 58.

1944 Colin Young – vocalist with The Foundations, who had a 1967 UK No.1 single with 'Baby Now That I've Found You' and a 1969 US No.3 single with 'Build Me Up A Buttercup'.

1952 Gerry Beckley – singer/songwriter and guitarist with America, who had a 1972 US No.1 & UK No.3 single with 'Horse With No Name'.

1956 Brian Robertson – guitarist with Thin Lizzy, who had a 1973 UK No.6 single with 'Whisky In The Jar', and Motorhead.

1966 Ben Folds – vocalist and pianist with Ben Folds Five, who had a 1997 UK No.26 single with 'Battle Of Who Could Care Less'.

ON THIS DAY

1954 the first 'teen idol' Frank Sinatra was at No.1 on the UK singles chart with 'Three Coins In The Fountain'. It was Sinatra's first UK No.1.

1963 The Beatles were at No.1 on the UK singles chart with 'She Loves You', the group's second No.1.

1966 the first episode of *The Monkees* TV show was broadcast in the US on NBC.

1970 Creedence Clearwater Revival scored their first UK No.1 album with *Cosmo's Factory*. The

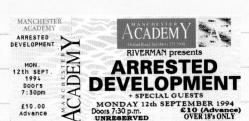

MANCHESTER ACADEMY
ARRESTED DEVELOPMENT
MON. 12th SEPT. 1994
Doors 7:30pm
£10.00 Advance
00554

RIVERMAN presents
ARRESTED DEVELOPMENT
+ SPECIAL GUESTS
MONDAY 12th SEPTEMBER 1994
Doors 7:30 p.m.   £10 (Advance)
UNRESERVED   OVER 18's ONLY
00554
Retain This Portion   Conditions Overleaf

album was also a US No.1, where it sold over three million copies.

1970 Smokey Robinson And The Miracles were at No.1 on the UK singles chart with 'The Tears Of A Clown'.

1972 The Faces appeared at New York's Madison Square Garden.

1981 Meat Loaf went to No.1 on the UK album chart with *Dead Ringer*.

1986 P.I.L. guitarist John McGeoch needed 40 stitches in his face after a wine bottle was thrown at the stage during a gig in Vienna.

1987 Michael Jackson started a five week run at No.1 on the UK album chart with his follow up to the *Thriller* album, *Bad*. It also stayed at No.1 on the US chart for six weeks.

1987 the soundtrack album *La Bamba*, featuring Los Lobos, started a two week run at No.1 on the US album chart.

1988 Pogues singer Shane MacGowan was admitted to a Dublin hospital suffering from nervous exhaustion.

1990 Stevie Nicks and Christine McVie from

Fleetwood Mac announced they were leaving the band at the end of their current tour.

1995 INXS singer Michael Hutchence pleaded guilty to punching photographer Jim Bennett outside a London hotel. He was fined £400 ($680) and ordered to pay £1,875 ($3,188) costs.

1997 Abba's producer Stig Anderson died of a heart attack.

2003 Johnny Cash *(below)*, singer/songwriter, died of respiratory failure aged 71. He had had a 1969 US No.2 & UK No.4 single with 'A Boy Named Sue' plus 11 other US Top 40 singles. He had also had the Johnny Cash US TV show in late 60s/early 70s.

2004 Natasha Bedingfield went to No.1 on the UK album chart with her debut release *Unwritten*.

2004 drummer Kenny Buttrey died in Nashville. He had worked with Neil Young, Area Code 615, Barefoot Jerry, Bob Dylan and Jimmy Buffett.

13th September

BORN ON THIS DAY

1939 Dave Quincy – sax player with Manfred Mann, who had a 1964 UK & US No.1 single with 'Do Wah Diddy Diddy'.

1941 David Clayton-Thomas – vocalist with Blood, Sweat & Tears, who had a 1969 US No.12 & UK No.35 single with 'You've Made Me So Very Happy'.

1944 Peter Cetera – vocalist and bass guitarist with Chicago, who had a 1976 US & UK No.1 single with 'If You Leave Me Now'. As a solo artist he had a 1986 US No.1 & UK No.3 single with 'Glory Of Love'.

1952 Don Was (a.k.a. Don Fagenson), producer, songwriter and bass player with Was (Not Was), who had a 1992 UK No.4 single with 'Shake Your Head'.

1952 Randy Jones – singer with The Village People, who had a 1978 US No.2 & 1979 UK No.1 single with 'YMCA'.

1977 Fiona Apple, US singer/songwriter who had a 1996 album with *Tidal*.

1983 James Bourne – singer/songwriter and guitarist with Busted, who had a 2003 UK No.1 single with 'You Said No' and a 2002 UK No.2 album with *Busted*.

ON THIS DAY

1955 Little Richard recorded the classic song 'Tutti Frutti' for the Speciality label in Los Angeles.

1958 Cliff Richard made his British TV debut on Jack Good's *Oh Boy*, performing 'Move It'.

1960 the Federal Communications Act in the USA was amended to outlaw payments of cash or gifts in exchange for airplay of records.

1963 while driving down from Scotland in The Hollies' van, guitarist Graham Nash checked to see if the door was locked. It wasn't and he fell out as the van was travelling at 40mph (64kmph). He escaped with minor injuries.

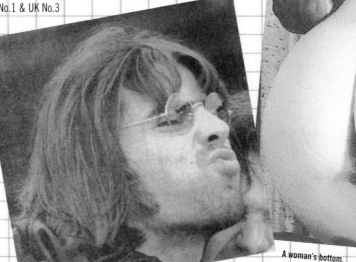

Liam Gallagher.

A woman's bottom.

1965 the Paul McCartney-penned song 'Yesterday' was released as a Beatles single in the US. It went on to top the charts.

1969 John and Yoko flew to Toronto with the Plastic Ono Band to perform live at the Rock & Roll Revival Show with The Doors, Chuck Berry and Little Richard.

1980 Jackson Browne scored his only US No.1 album with *Hold Out*.

1986 Berlin took No.1 on the US singles chart with 'Take My Breath Away'. On the B-side was The Righteous Brothers' 'You've Lost That Lovin' Feelin''. Both songs featured in the film *Top Gun*.

1996 both Noel and Liam Gallagher arrived back in the UK on separate flights from the US amid rumours that Oasis were splitting. A statement from the record company said there would be no live gigs but the band would continue to record.

1996 rap star Tupac Amaru Shakur died after being shot six days earlier when he was driving through Las Vegas. 13 bullets were fired into his BMW and the incident was blamed on East and West Coast gang wars.

1997 Mariah Carey started a three week run at No.1 on the US singles chart with 'Honey', her 12th US No.1 and third single to debut at No.1. It was a No.3 hit in the UK.

1997 The Verve scored their first UK No.1 single with 'The Drugs Don't Work'.

2003 US store Wal-Mart was refusing to stock *Permission To Land*, the No.1 album by UK rock group The Darkness, because the sleeve featured a woman's bottom *(above)*.

2003 Michael Jackson held a charity party for 500 guests at his Neverland ranch in Santa Ynes, Santa Barbara County. Tickets cost $5,000 (£2,941).

BORN ON THIS DAY

1946 Pete Agnew – bass player for Nazareth, who had a 1973 UK No.9 single with 'Broken Down Angel' and a 1976 US No.8 single with 'Love Hurts'.

1949 Steve Gaines – guitarist with Lynyrd Skynyrd, who had a 1974 US No.8 single with 'Sweet Home Alabama' and a 1982 UK No.21 single with 'Freebird'. Gaines died in a plane crash on October 20th 1977.

1950 Paul Kossoff – guitarist with Free, who had a 1970 UK No.2 & US No.4 single with 'All Right Now', and Back Street Crawler. Kossoff died on March 19th 1976.

1954 Barry Cowsill – bass player with The Cowsills, who had a 1967 US No.2 single with 'The Rain, The Park & Other Things' and a 1969 US No.2 single with the theme from *Hair*. TV's *Partridge Family* was based on the Cowsill family.

1955 Steve Berlin – sax and keyboard player for Los Lobos, who had a 1987 UK & US No.1 single with 'La Bamba'.

1959 Morten Harket – vocalist with A-Ha, who had a 1985 US No.1 single with 'Take On Me' and a 1986 UK No.1 single with 'The Sun Always Shines On TV'.

ON THIS DAY

1966 Otis Redding appeared at The Orchid Ballroom, Purley, Surrey, England. Tickets cost 10 shillings ($1.40).

1968 while he was on tour in the UK Roy Orbison's house in Nashville burnt down. His two eldest sons both died in the blaze.

1968 the first episode of *The Archies* was aired on US TV. The following year *The Archies* started an eight week run at No.1 on the UK singles chart with 'Sugar Sugar', and became the longest-running one hit wonder in the UK.

1970 Stevie Wonder married Syreeta Wright, a former secretary at Motown Records.

1974 appearing live at Wembley Stadium, London were Crosby, Stills, Nash & Young with Joni Mitchell.

1974 Eric Clapton scored a US No.1 with his version of the Bob Marley song 'I Shot The Sheriff'.

1974 Mike Oldfields' second album *Hergest Ridge* started a three week run at No.1 on the UK chart.

1974 Stevie Wonder started a two week run at No.1 on the US album chart with *Fulfillingness First Finale*, his second US No.1.

1989 Perez Prado died of a stroke. He had the US & UK 1955 No.1 single 'Cherry Pink & Apple Blossom White'.

1991 Paul Young **(left)** went to No.1 on the UK album chart with *From Time To Time – The Singles Collection*, his third UK No.1 LP.

1991 Paula Abdul scored her sixth US No.1 single with 'The Promise Of A New Day', a No.52 hit in the UK.

1994 US singer Steve Earle was sentenced to one year in jail after being found guilty of possession of crack cocaine.

1995 the lyrics to The Beatles song 'Getting Better', handwritten by Paul McCartney, sold for £161,000 ($272,700) at a Sotheby's auction in London.

1997 over 2,000 fans watched Pete Townshend unveil an English Heritage blue plaque at 23 Brook Street, Mayfair, London to mark where Jimi Hendrix had lived 1968–9. Hendrix was the first pop star to be awarded with such a plaque.

1999 it was reported that George Michael was being sued for $10 million (£6 million) by the policeman who arrested the singer in a public lavatory. Marcelo Rodriguez claimed he was mocked in the video Outside, which had left him with "severe injury and shock to his nervous system and person, and great mental and physical pain and suffering".

1999 The Strokes made their live debut at The Spiral in New York.

2003 Mary J. Blige was at No.1 on the US album chart with *Love & Life*, the singer's second US No.1.

BORN ON THIS DAY

1941 Les Braid – bass player with The Swinging Blue Jeans, who had a 1964 UK No.2 single with 'Hippy Hippy Shake'.

1956 Jaki Graham, soul singer who had a 1985 UK No.5 single with 'Could It Be I'm Falling In Love?'

1960 Michel Dorge – drummer with the Crash Test Dummies, who had a 1994 UK No.2 & US No.4 single with 'Mmm Mmm Mmm Mmm'.

1976 Ivette Sosa – singer with Popstars Eden's Crush, who had a 2001 US No.8 single with 'Get Over Yourself'.

1976 KG – singer with MN8, who had a 1995 UK No.2 single with 'I've Got A Little Something For You'.

ON THIS DAY

1956 Elvis Presley started a five week run at No.1 on the US singles charts with 'Don't Be Cruel'.

1962 The Four Seasons started a five week run at No.1 on the US singles chart with 'Sherry'. The song made No.8 in the UK. They became the first American group to have three No.1s in succession.

1966 The Small Faces were at No.1 on the UK singles chart with 'All Or Nothing'.

U2 concert caused deafness

Paris: A 34-year-old man who lost his hearing after standing too close to a loudspeaker at a concert by the Irish rock band U2 in Marseilles in 1993 has been awarded more than £20,000 (Ben Macintyre writes). A court in the city ruled the promoter was negligent after hearing that the man circumvented security barriers to get near to a giant speaker.

1970 appearing at The Marquee, London were Black Sabbath and The Dog That Bit People.

1979 Led Zeppelin scored their sixth US No.1 album when *In Through The Out Door* started a seven week run at the top of the charts.

1984 Frankie Goes To Hollywood's *(left)* 'Relax' became the longest-running chart hit since Engelbert Humperdink's 'Release Me'. 'Relax' spent 43 weeks on the UK singles chart.

1990 George Michael scored his second UK No.1 solo album with his second release *Listen Without Prejudice Vol.1*.

1990 New Kids On The Block's business manager had his briefcase, containing $100,000 (£58,800), stolen from a hotel in Hollywood.

1990 The Steve Miller Band had a UK No.1 with 'The Joker' 16 years after its first release.

1996 Pearl Jam went to No.1 on the US album chart with *No Code*.

1997 a 34-year-old man was awarded more than £20,000 ($34,000) by a French court after he lost his hearing when he stood too close to loudspeakers at a U2 concert in 1993.

2002 Dixie Chicks started a two week run at No.1 on the US album chart with *Home*.

2003 Abba tribute acts overtook Elvis impersonators in the battle of British covers of singers, according to a survey. The Swedish group jumped from third most tributed act in 2001 to top in 2002 with imitators like Abba

Chapter 21 of this epic and influential tome describes the effects of standing too close to speakers and the detriment to hearing. There are also passages about ensuing blindness too.

Fever and Voulez Vous putting on Abba shows. Elvis dropped to number two while the Beatles dropped to three. The Performing Right Society carried out the research.

2004 Ramones guitarist Johnny Ramone (a.k.a. John Cummings) died in Los Angeles of prostate cancer. He had been a founding member of the Ramones and was a major influence on many punk and 90s bands.

BORN ON THIS DAY

1925 BB King, US modern blues guitarist who had a 1964 US No.34 single with 'Rock Me Baby' and a 1989 UK No.6 single with U2, 'When Love Comes To Town'. King had been a major influence on Eric Clapton.

1942 Bernie Calvert – bass player with The Hollies, who had a 1972 US No.2 single with 'Long Cool Woman In A Black Dress' and a 1988 UK No.1 single 'He Ain't Heavy, He's My Brother', which was first released in 1969.

1944 Betty Kelly – singer with Martha And The Vandellas, who had a 1964 US No.2 & 1969 UK No.4 single with 'Dancing In The Street'.

1948 Kenny Jones – drummer with Small Faces, who had a 1967 UK No.3 single with 'Itchycoo Park' and a 1968 UK No.1 album with *Ogden's Nut Gone Flake*, and The Faces, who had a 1972 UK No.6 single 'Stay With Me'. He was also drummer for The Who after Keith Moon – the band had a 1981 UK No.9 single with 'You Better You Bet'.

1950 David Bellamy – singer/songwriter and guitarist with the Bellamy Brothers, who had a 1976 US No.1 single with 'Let Your Love Flow' and a 1979 UK No.3 single with 'If I Said You Had A Beautiful Body Would You Hold It Against Me?'

1963 Richard Marx, singer/songwriter who had a 1989 US No.1 & UK No.2 single with 'Right Here Waiting' and a 1992 UK No.3 single with 'Hazard'.

1976 Tina Barrett – vocalist with S Club 7, who had a 1999 UK No.1 single with 'Bring It All Back'.

1984 Katie Melua, UK singer/songwriter who had a 2004 UK No.1 album with *Call Off The Search*.

ON THIS DAY

1966 The Who appeared at the Odeon, Derby, England.

1970 Led Zeppelin won the Best group category in the *Melody Maker* readers' poll. It was the first time for eight years that it hadn't been The Beatles.

1970 Jimi Hendrix joined Eric Burdon on stage at Ronnie Scott's jazz club in London for what would become Jimi's last public appearance.

1972 Rod Stewart had his second UK No.1 album with *Never A Dull Moment*.

1977 29-year-old former T. Rex singer Marc Bolan was killed when the car that was being driven by his girlfriend, Gloria Jones, left the road and hit a tree in Barnes, London. Miss Jones broke her jaw. The couple were on the way to Bolan's home in Richmond after a night out. A local man who witnessed the smash said, "When I arrived a girl was lying on the bonnet and a man with long dark curly hair was stretched out in the road – there was a hell of a mess."

1978 Blondie *(left)* appeared live on stage at London's Hammersmith Odeon. Tickets cost £1.50–3 ($2.50–5).

1979 the first rap single was released, The Sugarhill Gang's 'Rapper's Delight'.

1983 The Smiths appeared at The Moles Club, Bath.

1988 former Clash drummer Topper Headon was released from jail after serving ten months of a 15 month sentence on a narcotics charge.

1989 Gloria Estefan went to No.1 on the US singles chart with 'Don't Wanna Lose You', which was a No.6 hit in the UK.

1995 appearing at The Whisky A Go-Go, Los Angeles was Kara's Flowers (later to become Maroon 5).

1996 21-year-old Ricardo Lopez was found dead in his Hollywood apartment after committing suicide. Before his death Ricardo had mailed an acid bomb to singer Bjork's management.

1998 at a Sotheby's auction a notebook belonging to Beatles' roadie Mal Evans containing the lyrics to 'Hey Jude' sold for £111, 500 ($189,550), a two-tone denim jacket belonging to John Lennon fetched £9,200 (15,640) and the Union Jack dress worn by Ginger Spice went for £41,320 ($70,244).

2004 Weather Girls singer Izora Armstead died, aged 62, of heart failure at a hospital in San Leandro, East San Francisco. She was also a member of Two Tons O' Fun and featured on four Sylvester albums, including *(You Make Me Feel) Mighty Real*.

BORN ON THIS DAY

1923 Hank Williams, US country singer/songwriter who scored 36 Top 10 country hits including 'Your Cheating Heart' and 'Hey Good Lookin'. Williams was found dead on January 1st 1953 in the back of a Cadillac after his driver was stopped for speeding. The police officer had noticed that Williams looked dead.

1933 Jeanine Deckers, "The Singing Nun" who had a 1963 US No.1 & UK No.7 single with 'Dominique'. She died on March 31st 1985 of an overdose of sleeping pills taken in a suicide pact with a friend.

1939 Lamonte McLemore – singer with The 5th Dimension, who had a 1969 US No.1 & UK No.11 single with 'Aquarius'.

1950 Fee Waybill – vocalist with The Tubes, who had a 1977 UK No.28 single with 'White Punks On Dope' and a 1983 US No.10 single with 'She's A Beauty'.

Fee Waybill auditions for Frankenstein's Monster!

1962 Baz Luhrmann, Australian filmmaker who had a 1999 UK No.1 single with 'Everybody's Free To Wear Sunscreen'.

1969 Keith Flint – vocalist for The Prodigy, who had a 1996 UK No.1 single with 'Firestarter' and a 1997 UK & US No.1 album with *The Fat Of The Land*.

1973 Anastacia, US singer who had a 2000 UK No.6 single with 'I'm Outta Love' and a 2000 UK No.1 album with *Not That Kind*.

1976 Maile Misajon – singer with Popstar's Eden's Crush, who had a 2001 US No.8 single with 'Get Over Yourself'.

ON THIS DAY

1931 the first 33 and a third LP players were launched by RCA Victor at the Savoy Plaza Hotel in New York.

1964 police arrived at a Rolling Stones gig at the ABC Theatre in Carlisle after a trouble broke out with the 4,000 fans at the concert.

1976 the Sex Pistols played a gig for the inmates at Chelmsford Prison, Essex.

1977 *20 Golden Greats* by Diana Ross And The Supremes started a seven week run at No.1 on the UK album chart.

1983 Paul Young scored his first UK No.1 album with his debut release *No Parlez*. The album returned to the top of the charts on four other occasions, spending a total of 119 weeks on the chart.

1991 4.2 million copies of Guns N' Roses' *Use Your Illusion I* and *Use Your Illusion II* were simultaneously released for retail sale, the largest ship out in pop history in the US.

1991 Rob Tyner, former lead singer with the Detroit band MC5, died of heart failure.

1994 Boyz II Men started a two week run at No.1 on the US album chart with *II*.

1994 Whigfield started a four week run at No.1 in the UK with the single 'Saturday Night'.

1996 a bomb was found at a South London sorting office addressed to singer Bjork. Police in Miami had alerted the post office after finding the body of Ricardo Lopez, who had made a video of himself making the bomb and then killing himself.

1998 a 19-year-old man was taken off a plane in Denver after harassing members of Hootie & The Blowfish, who were travelling in the first class section of the plane.

1999 singer Frankie Vaughan died, aged 71. During the 50s he scored 20 UK Top 30 singles including the No.2 'Green Door'. He was made an OBE in 1965.

2000 Paula Yates *(right)* was found dead in bed from a suspected drug overdose. Yates had presented the long-running UK music TV show *The Tube* during the 80s, married Bob Geldof and, most recently, was the girlfriend of INXS singer Michael Hutchence who was found dead in his hotel suite in Sydney on November 22nd 1997, aged 37.

BORN ON THIS DAY

1933 Jimmie Rodgers, singer who had a 1957 US No.1 & UK No.30 single with 'Honeycomb'.

1939 Frankie Avalon, singer who had a 1959 US No.1 & UK No.16 single with 'Venus'.

1946 Alan King — guitarist and vocalist with Ace, who had a 1974 UK No.20 single with 'How Long?'

1950 Mike Hossack — drummer with The Doobie Brothers, who had a 1979 US No.1 single with 'What A Fool Believes' and a 1993 UK No.7 single with 'Long Train Runnin'.

1952 Douglas Colvin (a.k.a. Dee Dee Ramone) — bass player with the Ramones, who had a 1977 UK No.22 single with 'Sheena Is A Punk Rocker'. He died of a drug overdose on June 6th 2002.

1961 Martin Beedle — drummer with Cutting Crew, who had a 1987 US No.1 & 1986 UK No.4

Toyah resurrects her career.

single with '(I Just) Died In Your Arms'.

1962 Joanne Catherall — vocalist with The Human League, who had a 1981 UK No.1 & 1982 US No.1 single with 'Don't You Want Me?' plus over 15 other UK Top 40 singles.

1967 Ricky Bell — singer with New Edition, who had a 1983 UK No.1 single with 'Candy Girl', and Bell Biv DeVoe, who had a 1990 US No.3 single with 'Do Me!'.

ON THIS DAY

1961 Bobby Vee started a two week run at No.1 on the US singles chart with 'Take Good Care Of My Baby'. The song reached No.3 in the UK charts.

1970 Jimi Hendrix was pronounced dead on arrival at St. Mary Abbot's Hospital, London, after choking on his own vomit. Hendrix had left the message "I need help bad, man" on his manager's answer phone earlier that night.

1971 The Who scored their first No.1 UK album with *Who's Next*, their sixth LP release.

1972 appearing at The Oval, London were The Who, Mott The Hoople, The Faces and Atomic Rooster.

1976 one hit wonders Wild Cherry started a three week run at No.1 on the US singles chart with 'Play That Funky Music'. The song started life as a B-side and was also the group's only hit in the UK, making No.7.

1980 appearing at The Rainbow, London were Gang Of Four, Toyah, Au Pairs, Chelsea, XTC and The Police.

1981 Gary Numan took off on a round the world trip in a single-engine Cessna plane. The attempt ended when he was forced to land in

India where local police arrested him.

1982 the seven minute epic by Dire Straits, 'Private Investigations', went to No.2 in the UK singles chart. It was held off No.1 by Survivor's 'Eye Of The Tiger'.

1983 Kiss appeared without their make-up for the first time during an interview on MTV.

1984 David Bowie won Video of the year for 'China Girl' at the first MTV Video Awards.

1993 Garth Brooks went to No.1 on the US album chart with, *In Pieces*. The album spent 25 weeks on the chart and sold over 6 million copies. The album peaked at No.2 on the UK chart.

1993 Meat Loaf went to No.1 on the UK album chart for the first of five times with *Bat Out Of Hell II*.

2002 James Brown was being sued by his own daughters for more than £650,000 ($1,105,000) of song royalties they said were owed. Deanna Brown Thomas, who works at a South Carolina radio station, and Dr Yamma Brown Lumar, a Texas physician, said Brown had withheld royalties on 25 co-written songs because of a family grudge. The lawsuit claimed that Brown had held a grudge against his daughters since 1998, when Ms Thomas had her father committed to a psychiatric hospital to be treated for addiction to painkillers.

2003 The Beautiful South played their Carling Homecoming gig at The Wellington Club, Hull, England.

BORN ON THIS DAY

1931 Brook Benton, soul singer who had a 1959 UK No.28 single with 'Endlessly' and a 1979 US No.4 single with 'Rainy Night In Georgia'. He died on April 9th 1998.

1934 Brian Epstein, Beatles' manager and manager of other Liverpool acts. Epstein died of an accidental overdose of brandy and barbiturates on August 27th 1967.

1935 Nick Massi – singer with The Four Seasons, who had a 1976 UK & US No.1 single with 'December 1963, Oh What A Night'. Massi died on December 24th 2000.

1940 Bill Medley – singer with The Righteous Brothers, who had a 1965 UK & US No.1 single with 'You've Lost That Lovin' Feelin'.

1943 Cass Elliott, singer who had a 1966 US No.1 & UK No.3 single with 'Monday Monday'. Elliot was staying at Harry Nilsson's flat in London when she died from a heart attack on July 29th 1974.

1945 Freda Payne, US soul singer who had a 1970 US No.3 & UK No.1 single with 'Band Of Gold'.

1946 John Coghlan – drummer with Status Quo, who had a 1977 UK No.3 single with 'Rockin' All Over The World' plus 50 other UK Top 75 singles since 1968. Coghlan left the group in 1982.

1947 Lol Creme – vocalist and guitarist with 10CC, who had a 1975 UK No.1 & US No.2 single with 'I'm Not In Love' plus ten other UK Top 30 hits, and Godley & Creme, who had a 1981 UK No.3 single with 'Under Your Thumb'. Creme is now a video producer.

1951 Daniel Lanois, producer and singer/songwriter who produced Peter Gabriel's *So*, U2's *Joshua Tree* as well as Brian Eno and Bob Dylan. Lanois also created the 1990 solo album *Acadie*.

1952 Nile Rodgers – lead guitarist and producer with Chic, who had a 1978 US No.1 & UK No.7 single with 'Le Freak', and The Honeydrippers (with Jimmy Page, Jeff Beck and Robert Plant), who had a 1984 US No.3 single with 'Sea Of Love'. Rodgers also produced Diana Ross, Sister Sledge and David Bowie.

Glastonbury album in pre-supermarket festival days.

1963 Jarvis Cocker – vocalist with Pulp, who had a 1995 UK No.2 single with 'Common People'.

1977 Ryan Dusick – drummer with Maroon 5, who had a 2004 UK No.1 album with *Songs About Jane* and a 2004 US No.1 & UK No.4 single with 'She Will Be Loved'.

ON THIS DAY

1960 Chubby Checker went to No.1 on the US singles chart with 'The Twist'. It was a No.14 hit in the UK in 1962 and a version with The Fat Boys made No.2 in the UK in 1988.

1969 Creedence Clearwater Revival scored their only UK No.1 single with 'Bad Moon Rising'. Also on this day the group started a four week run at No.1 on the US album chart with *Green River*.

1970 The first UK Glastonbury Festival took place featuring Marc Bolan, Ian Anderson, Keith Christmas, Quintessence, Stackridge, Al Stewart, Amazing Blondel and Sam Apple Pie.

1970 Diana Ross started a three week run at No.1 on the US singles chart with 'Ain't No Mountain High Enough'. It was the singer's first solo No.1 since leaving The Supremes, and was a No.6 in the UK.

1973 country rock singer/songwriter and one time member of The Byrds and The Flying Burrito Brothers, Gram Parsons, died of a heroin overdose, aged 26. He had also had a 1974 solo album with *Grievous Angel*.

1975 Queen signed a management deal with Elton John's manager John Reid.

1981 Simon & Garfunkel reunited for a concert in New York's Central Park. Over 400,000 fans attended the show and the performance was recorded for a record and video release.

1990 Kylie Minogue's 'Better The Devil You Know' gave producers Stock, Aitken and Waterman their 100th UK chart entry.

1995 PM Dawn's DJ JC Eternal was arrested on charges of sexual assault and child abuse after an alleged affair with his 14-year-old cousin. He was released on $10,000 (£5,880) bail.

1998 Robbie Williams scored his first solo UK No.1 single with 'Millennium'.

2003 police were investigating reports that Paul McCartney scuffled with a photographer when the singer went to see magician David Blaine, who was in a plastic box dangling over the River Thames. Standard said one of its photographers had clashed with McCartney.

BORN ON THIS DAY

1946 Michael Oldroyd – guitar and vocals with Manfred Mann's Earth Band, who had a 1978 UK No.6 single with 'Davy's On The Road Again'.

1949 Chuck and John Panozzo – bass player and drummer with Styx, who had a 1979 US No.1 & 1980 UK No.6 single with 'Babe'. John Panozzo died on July 16th 1996.

1959 Alannah Currie – vocalist and sax player with The Thompson Twins, who had a 1984 UK No.2 single with 'You Take Me Up' and a 1984 US No.3 single with 'Hold Me Now'.

1960 David Hemmingway – drummer with the Housemartins, who had a 1986 UK No.1 single with 'Caravan Of Love', and The Beautiful South, who had a 1990 UK No.1 single with 'A Little Time' plus over 15 other UK Top 40 singles.

1966 Nuno Bettencourt – guitarist with Extreme, who had a 1991 US No.1 & UK No.2 single with 'More Than Words'.

1967 Matthew and Gunnar Nelson, US singers and twin sons of 60s singer Ricky Nelson. They had a 1990 US No.1 & UK No.54 single with 'Can't Live Without Your Love and Affection'.

1979 Rick Woolstenhulme – drummer with Lifehouse, who had a 2001 US No.10 & UK No.25 single with 'Hanging By A Moment'.

ON THIS DAY

1969 based on the comic-book TV series *Archie And His Friends*, The Archies started a four week run at No.1 on the US singles chart with 'Sugar Sugar'. It also became the longest-running one hit wonder in the UK after spending eight weeks at the top of the charts.

1969 Blind Faith started a two week run at No.1 on the UK chart with their self-titled debut album. The only release from the Eric Clapton, Ginger Baker, Steve Winwood and Rick Grech line-up, it also made No.1 in the US. The band's only UK gig was Hyde Park on June 7th 1969.

Manfred Mann's Earth Band and a tree.

1969 the *Melody Maker* readers' poll results were published. Eric Clapton won Best musician, Bob Dylan Best male singer and Best album for *Nashville Skyline*, Best group went to The Beatles, Best single was Simon & Garfunkel's 'The Boxer' and Janis Joplin won Best female singer.

1970 The Rolling Stones' live album *Get Your Ya-Yas Out* started a two week run at No.1 on the UK chart, recorded at New York's Madison Square Garden.

1972 Paul and Linda McCartney were arrested for the second time in four weeks for possession of cannabis, this time at their Scottish farmhouse.

1973 on his way to perform his second concert of the day singer/songwriter Jim Croce was killed with five others when his chartered aircraft hit a tree on take off in Louisiana.

1975 'Fame' gave David Bowie his first No.1 in the US. The song was co-written with John Lennon.

1975 The Bay City Rollers made their US TV debut when they appeared on the *Saturday Night Variety Show*.

1976 the first of the two night 100 Club Punk Festival, Oxford St, London, featuring The Sex Pistols, The Clash, Sub Way Sect, Suzie (spelling on the poster) And The Banshees, the Buzzcocks, Vibrators and Stinky Toys. Admission was £1.50 ($2.50).

1976 the *Captain & Tennille Musical Variety Show* premiered on ABC TV in the US.

1980 Kate Bush scored her first UK No.1 album with *Never For Ever*.

1980 Queen started a five week run at No.1 on the US album chart with *The Game*, the group's only US No.1 album.

1986 Huey Lewis & The News started a three week run at No.1 on the US singles chart with 'Stuck With You', which was a No.12 hit in the UK.

1993 The Charlatans keyboard player Rob Collins was sentenced to eight months imprisonment for his part in a robbery.

1997 The *Daily Mirror* ran a front page story "Ban this sick stunt" referring to 'Sorted for E's & Whizz', the new single from Pulp.

1999 Christina Aguilera was at No.1 on the US album chart with her self-titled debut album.

BORN ON THIS DAY

1923 Jimmy Young, UK singer and BBC radio DJ who had a 1955 UK No.1 single with 'Unchained Melody' plus ten other UK Top 40 hit singles.

1934 Leonard Cohen, singer/songwriter and poet who had a 1968 UK No.13 & US No. 83 album with *Songs Of Leonard Cohen*.

1947 Don Felder – guitarist with The Eagles, who had a 1977 US No.1 & UK No.8 single with 'Hotel California' plus five US No.1 albums. Their *Greatest Hits 1971–1975* is the 2nd biggest-selling album in the world with sales of over 30 million.

1967 Faith Hill, country singer who had a 1993 US country No.1 with 'Wild One' and a 1998 UK No.13 single with 'This Kiss'. She is married to Tim McGraw.

1967 Tyler Stewart – drummer with Barenaked Ladies, who had a 1998 US No.1 & UK No.5 single with 'One Week'.

1972 David Silveria – drummer with Korn, who had a 1998 UK No.23 single with 'Got The Life' and a 1998 US No.1 album with *Follow The Leader*.

1972 Liam Gallagher –vocalist for Oasis, whose first single was the 1994 UK No.31 single 'Supersonic'. The band also had a 1996 UK No.1 single with 'Don't Look Back In Anger' and a 1994 UK No.1 album with *Definitely Maybe*, which was the fastest selling UK debut album ever.

1977 Sam Rivers – bass player with Limp Bizkit, who had a 2001 UK No.1 single with 'Rollin' and a US & UK No.1 album with *Chocolate Starfish And The Hotdog Flavored Water*.

ON THIS DAY

1961 21-year-old singer/songwriter Bob Dylan recorded his debut album in one day. The studio bill was $400 (£235).

1963 Bobby Vinton started a three week run at No.1 on the US singles chart with 'Blue Velvet'. The single became a hit in the UK 27 years later when it reached No.2.

1968 Jeannie C. Riley went to No.1 on the US singles chart with 'Harper Valley PTA'. Jeannie

Dylan has spent the rest of his days trying to better this debut album.

won a Grammy for the Best female country singer of 1968.

1968 Madame Tussaud's Waxworks, London gave The Beatles their fifth image change of clothes and hair in four years.

1970 Freda Payne was at No.1 on the UK singles chart with 'Band Of Gold', the singer's only UK No.1.

1971 the first edition of the new BBC TV music show *The Old Grey Whistle Test* was aired. The show featured film clips of Jimi Hendrix from Monterey Festival playing 'Wild Thing', Bob Dylan playing 'Maggies Farm' plus America and Lesley Duncan performing "live" in the studio.

1974 Barry White went to No.1 on the US singles chart with 'Can't Get Enough Of Your Love Baby', the singer's first and only US solo chart topper. It made No.8 in the UK.

1974 Carl Douglas was at No.1 on the UK singles chart with 'Kung Fu Fighting', which was also a US No.1.

1980 Bob Marley collapsed while jogging in New York's Central Park. After hospital tests he was diagnosed as having cancer.

1985 Madonna scored her first UK No.1 album with *Like A Virgin* ten months after its release.

1985 with the help of an innovative animated video, which received heavy MTV exposure, 'Money For Nothing' gave Dire Straits their first US No.1 single.

1986 The *National Inquirer* magazine featured a picture of Michael Jackson in an oxygen chamber with a story claiming that Jackson had a bizarre plan to live until he was 150 years old.

1992 Parlophone Records released 'Creep' by Radiohead. The single didn't chart but featured in the majority of critics' lists at the end of the year.

1996 R.E.M. went to No.1 on the UK album chart with *New Adventures In Hi-Fi*.

1996 the Fugees scored their second UK No.1 single with 'Ready Or Not'.

BORN ON THIS DAY

1949 David Coverdale – vocalist with Deep Purple and Whitesnake, who had a 1987 US No.1 & UK No.9 single with 'Here I Go Again'.

1953 Richard Fairbrass – singer with Right Said Fred, who had a 1991 US No.1 & UK No.2 single with 'I'm Too Sexy' and a 1993 UK No.1 album with *Up*.

1956 Debby Boone, singer and daughter of 50s singer Pat Boone. She had ten weeks at No.1 on the US singles chart with 'You Light Up My Life' in 1977. This was the longest stay at the top since Guy Mitchell's 'Singing The Blues'. The song was a No.48 hit in the UK.

1957 Nick Cave – singer/songwriter with Birthday Party then Nick Cave And The Bad Seeds, who had a 1995 UK No.11 single with Kylie Minogue, 'Where The Wild Roses Grow' and a 1996 UK No.36 single with PJ Harvey, 'Henry Lee'.

1960 Joan Jett – singer, songwriter and guitarist with all girl band The Runaways. Then he had a 1982 US No.1 & UK No.4 single 'I Love Rock 'n' Roll' with Joan Jett and the Blackhearts.

1975 Mystikal (a.k.a. Michael Tyler), US rapper who had a 2001 US No.1 & UK No.7 single with 'Stutter'.

1982 Billie, UK singer and actress who had a 1998 UK No.1 single with 'Because We Want To'.

ON THIS DAY

1964 Herman's Hermits were at No.1 on the UK singles chart with 'I'm Into Something Good', the group's only UK No.1.

Def Leppard in early Sheffield times.

1965 San Francisco band The Great Society, featuring Grace Slick, made their live debut at The Coffee Gallery, North Beach, California.

1966 Jim Reeves was at No.1 on the UK singles chart with 'Distant Drums'. It was the singer's only UK No.1 of 20 UK Top 40 hits.

1969 *The Music Scene*, a new weekly TV show, aired on ABC in the US for the first time. Stevie Wonder, Crosby, Stills, Nash & Young, Tom Jones, Cass Elliot, James Brown, Janis Joplin and Sly & The Family Stone were all booked to appear on the show.

1974 *The Sonny Bono Comedy Revue* was shown for the first time on ABC-TV.

1979 Jackson Browne, Chaka Khan, Bruce Springsteen, Bonnie Raitt and Tom Petty appeared at Madison Square Garden, New York for two anti-nuclear benefit shows.

1981 composer Harry Warren died, aged 88. He wrote over 400 songs including 'I Only Have Eyes For You', which was a hit for The Flamingos and Art Garfunkel.

1984 former lead singer of the Babies, John Waite went to No.1 on the US singles chart with 'Missing You'.

1986 The Smiths signed to EMI Records in the UK for £1 million ($1.7 million).

1990 Garth Brooks' album *No Fences* entered the US album chart. It went on to become the biggest-selling country album of all time and sold over 13 million copies in the first five years of release.

1991 Bryan Adams made chart history when '(Everything I Do) I Do It For You' had its 12th consecutive week as the UK No.1.

1992 during a US tour Def Leppard were forced to cancel two shows when their sound equipment truck was found abandoned after the driver had attempted to rob a store. The driver was later charged with possessing drugs and criminal damage.

1999 Diana Ross was arrested on Concorde after an incident at Heathrow Airport. The singer claimed that a female security guard had touched her breasts when being frisked and Ross retaliated by rubbing her hands down the security guard.

23rd September

BORN ON THIS DAY

1930 Ray Charles, singer/songwriter who had a 1962 UK & US No.1 single with 'I Can't Stop Loving You' plus over 30 US Top 40 singles. Charles died on June 10th 2004, aged 73.

1939 Roy Buchanan, US guitarist. He first worked with Dale Hawkins then was offered the job as Brian Jones' replacement with The Rolling Stones. He hung himself in a police cell after being arrested for drunkenness on August 14th 1988.

1943 Julio Iglesias, singer who had a 1981 UK No.1 single with 'Begin The Beguine'. The Spanish singer has sold over 100 million albums.

1943 Steve Boone – bass player with The Lovin' Spoonful, who had a 1966 US No.1 & UK No.8 single with 'Summer In The City'.

1943 Toni Basil, US singer, actress and dancer who had a 1982 US No.1 & UK No.2 single with 'Mickey'.

1949 Bruce Springsteen, US singer/songwriter who had a 1975 US No.3 & UK No.17 album *Born To Run*, a 1985 US No.2 & UK No.4 single with 'Dancing In The Dark', and the 1994 UK No.2 single with 'Streets of Philadelphia' plus over 15 other UK Top 40 singles and six US No.1 albums.

ON THIS DAY

1957 The Crickets went to No.1 on the US singles chart with 'That'll Be The Day'.

1961 The Shadows' debut album *Shadows* started a four week run at No.1 on the UK charts.

1965 The Walker Brothers were at No.1 on the UK singles chart with 'Make It Easy On Yourself'. It was the trio's first of two UK No.1s.

1966 the "Rolling Stones 66" 12 date UK tour began at the Royal Albert Hall, London. The band was supported by The Yardbirds, Ike and Tina Turner and Peter Jay And The New Jaywalkers.

1967 making their UK live debut, The Mothers Of Invention appeared at the Royal Albert Hall, London.

1967 The Box Tops started a four week run at No.1 on the US singles chart with 'The Letter'. It made No.5 in the UK.

1969 the *Northern Star* newspaper of Northern Illinois University ran a story claiming that Paul McCartney had been killed in a car crash in 1966 and had been replaced by a lookalike. Russell Gibb of WKNR-FM in Detroit picked up on the claim and the story went worldwide. By late October 1969 the hoax was well entrenched, so McCartney came out of seclusion at his Scottish farm to deny the story.

1989 Milli Vanilli started a two week run at No.1 on the US singles chart with 'Girl I'm Gonna Miss You', the duo's second US No.1 and a No.2 hit in the UK. Also today the duo went to No.1 on the US album chart with *Girl You Know It's True*.

1995 Shaggy scored his second No.1 UK single when 'Boombastic' went to the top of the charts for one week.

2001 Jay-Z started a three week run at No.1 on the US album chart with *The Blueprint*.

2001 Kylie Minogue started a five week run at No.1 on the UK singles chart with 'Can't Get You Out Of My Head'. The song was co-written by former Mud guitarist Rob Davis.

2001 Macy Gray went to No.1 on the UK album chart with *The Id*.

2002 musical winners at this year's Oscars included Sting, who won Best musical performance for *Sting In Tuscany...All This Time*, and the Best reality TV show went to *The Osbournes*.

2004 Slipknot's Corey Taylor issued a statement denying he was dead. Rumours started after a shock jock in Des Moines broadcast the announcement that the singer had died of a drug overdose, which then became a fatal car crash.

BORN ON THIS DAY

1933 Mel Taylor – drummer with The Ventures, who had a 1960 US No.2 & UK No.8 single with 'Walk, Don't Run'. Taylor died of lung cancer on August 11th 1996.

1942 Gerry Marsden – singer with Gerry And The Pacemakers, who had a 1963 UK No.1 single with 'You'll Never Walk Alone' and a 1965 US No.6 single with 'Ferry Across The Mersey'.

1942 Linda McCartney, wife of Paul, photographer, member of Wings and animal rights campaigner. She died of cancer on April 17th 1998.

1971 Marty Cintron III – singer and guitarist with No Mercy, who had a 1997 UK No.2 single with 'Where Do You Go?'

1971 Peter Salisbury – drummer with The Verve, who had a 1997 UK No.1 single with 'The Drugs Don't Work'.

ON THIS DAY

1961 John Leyton was at No.1 on the UK singles chart with 'Johnny Remember Me'. It was the UK singer's only UK No.1.

1965 The Rolling Stones kicked of a 24 date UK tour at The Astoria, London with The Spencer Davis Group supporting.

1966 Jimi Hendrix arrived in London with manager Chas Chandler on a flight from New York with only the clothes he was wearing, having sold his other belongings to pay a hotel bill in New York.

1975 Rod Stewart had the UK No.1 single with 'Sailing'.

1980 the "Son Of Stiff UK Tour" kicked off in London with Tenpole Tudor, Any Trouble, Joe King Carrasco, The Equators and Dirty Looks.

1983 Billy Joel went to No.1 on the US singles chart with 'Tell Her About It', his second US No.1 and a No.4 hit in the UK.

1983 UB40 scored their first UK No.1 album with *Labour Of Love*.

1984 Culture Club had their second UK No.1 single with 'Karma Chameleon', staying at the top of the charts for six weeks.

1988 Bobby McFerrin started a two week run at No.1 on the US singles chart with 'Don't Worry Be Happy', the first *a cappella* record to be a No.1. The song was a No.2 in the UK.

1988 The Hollies were at No.1 on the UK singles chart with 'He Ain't Heavy He's My Brother' after the track was used on a UK TV beer commercial. The song was originally a hit in 1969.

1991 The Black Crowes kicked off a 14 date UK tour at Bristol Colston Hall.

1995 The Charlatans were arrested by 24 armed police after a flight to New York. The band were accused of trying to disrupt the plane's flight path and passengers complained of the group being drunk, spitting and interfering with in-flight TV sets.

1997 Barry Loukaitis was convicted of shooting and killing two pupils and a teacher at a school in Washington. His defence team claimed he had copied scenes from Pearl Jam's video 'Jeremy'.

2000 Mariah Carey and Westlife started a two week run at No.1 on the UK singles chart with their version of the Phil Collins hit 'Against All Odds'.

2003 Singer/ songwriter Matthew Jay died, aged 24, after falling from a seventh storey window in London. He had released the 2001 album *Draw* and toured with The Doves, Stereophonics, Dido and Starsailor.

BORN ON THIS DAY

1943 Gary Alexander – guitarist and vocalist with The Association, who had a 1967 US No.1 single with 'Windy'.

1945 Onnie McIntyre – guitarist and vocalist with Average White Band, who had a 1975 US No.1 & UK No.6 single with 'Pick Up The Pieces'.

1946 Bryan MacLean – guitarist with Love, who had a 1966 US No.33 single with '7 And 7 Is' and a 1968 UK No.24 album with *Forever Changes*. He died of a heart attack on December 25th 1998.

1955 Zucchro (a.k.a. Adelmo Fornaciari), Italian singer who had a 1991 UK No.4 with Paul Young, 'Senza Una Donna'.

1968 Will Smith – actor and singer with DJ Jazzy Jeff & The Fresh Prince, who had a 1993 UK No.1 single with 'Boom! Shake The Room'. As a solo artist he had a 1997 UK No.1 single with 'Men In Black'.

1975 Declan Donnelly – singer with PJ & Duncan, who had a 1994 UK No.9 single with 'Let's Get Ready To Rhumble'. He is now a TV presenter.

ON THIS DAY

1965 The Beatles' cartoon series premiered on ABC-TV in the US. The first story was titled "I Want To Hold Your Hand" and had the group exploring the ocean floor in a diving bell where they met a lovesick octopus.

1968 Welsh singer Mary Hopkins was at No.1 on the UK singles chart with 'Those Were The Days'. Hopkins was signed to The Beatles' Apple label after appearing on UK TV talent show *Opportunity Knocks*.

1970 the first episode of *The Partridge Family* was shown on US TV, featuring Shirley Jones, David Cassidy, Susan Dey and Danny Bonaduce.

1971 appearing at Friars, Aylesbury, England were David Bowie and America.

1971 Deep Purple went to No.1 on the UK chart with their third album *Fireball*.

1975 Jackie Wilson had a heart attack while performing live on stage at the Latin Casino, New Jersey. He lapsed into a coma, suffering severe brain damage (he died on January 21st 1984). Van Morrison wrote 'Jackie Wilson Said' in his honour, which was also covered by Dexy's Midnight Runners.

1976 Wings played a charity concert in St. Mark's Square, Venice to raise funds for the historic city. The night was a success but the weight of the equipment used by the group caused more damage to the square.

1980 John Bonham, drummer with Led Zeppelin, died aged 32 after a heavy drinking session. "Bonzo" was found dead at guitarist Jimmy Page's house of what was described as asphyxiation after inhaling his own vomit (he had drunk 40 shots in four hours).

1992 two fans were stabbed and 20 arrests were made after trouble broke out at an Ozzy Osbourne gig in Oklahoma City. The sale of alcohol at the concert was blamed for the incident.

1993 Nirvana went to No.1 on the UK album chart with *In Utero*, the band's first UK No.1 album.

1995 Courtney Love was given a one year prison sentence suspended for two years, fined $1,000 (£700) and ordered to attend an anger management course after being found guilty of assaulting Bikini Kill singer Kathleen Nanna.

1996 Charlie Watts was the second Rolling Stone to become a grandfather when his daughter Seraphina gave birth to a baby girl.

1999 Liam Gallagher was stopped by customs officials at Heathrow airport and made to pay £1,300 ($2,210) after not declaring a fur coat he had bought in America.

2003 singer/songwriter Robert Palmer *(left)* died of a heart attack, aged 54. He had been a member of Vinegar Joe and as a solo artist had a 1986 US No.1 & UK No.5 single with 'Addicted To Love'.

SPIN DOCTORS

Saturday 25th September
MANCHESTER ACADEMY

Sunday 26th September
GLASGOW BARROWLANDS

Tuesday 28th September
WOLVERHAMPTON CIVIC HALL

Thursday 7th October
BRIXTON ACADEMY

GET A LIFE. GET TO A GIG. GET AN XL

BORN ON THIS DAY

1926 Julie London, singer who had a 1956 US No.9 & UK No.22 single with 'Cry Me A River'. London died on October 18th 2000.

1943 Georgie Fame, singer/songwriter who had a 1965 UK No.1 single with 'Yeh Yeh' and a 1968 UK No.1 single with 'The Ballad Of Bonnie And Clyde'.

1945 Bryan Ferry – vocalist and keyboardist for Roxy Music, who had a 1972 UK No.4 single with 'Virginia Plain' plus 15 other UK Top 40 singles. As a solo artist he had a 1976 UK No.4 single with 'Let's Stick Together'.

1947 Lynn Anderson, singer who had a 1970 US No.3 & 1971 UK No.3 single with 'Rose Garden'.

1948 Olivia Newton-John, singer and actress who had a 1978 UK & US No.1 single with John Travolta, 'You're The One That I Want', a 1980 UK No.1 single with ELO 'Xanadu' and a 1981 US No.1 & UK solo No.7 single with 'Physical'.

1954 Cesar Rosas – singer/songwriter and guitarist with Los Lobos, who had a 1987 UK & US No.1 single with 'La Bamba'.

1954 Craig Chaquico – songwriter and guitarist for Jefferson Starship, who had a 1987 UK & US No.1 single with 'Nothing's Gonna Stop Us'.

1962 Tracey Thorn – singer with Everything But The Girl, who had a 1995 UK No.3 & 1996 US No.2 single with 'Missing'.

1965 Cindy Herron – singer with En Vogue, who had a 1992 US No.2 & UK No.4 single with 'My Lovin'.

1967 Radio Times *in hard drug competition!*

Win a portable transistor in 'CRACK THE CLUE'

A musical crossword broadcast on Radio 1 (247)— the swinging new BBC radio service.

Winners every week! *Listen* for the 3 clues broadcast twice daily (Monday-Friday). *Write* your answers on the entry form which will appear every week in Radio Times. *Results* for each weekly competition will be broadcast on Saturdays.

Prizes! High-quality transistor portables to be won every week!

Full Details and entry form for the first of the weekly 'Crack the Clue' competitions are in this week's Radio Times dated Sept. 28.

Ask your newsagent to reserve your RADIO TIMES. Every Thursday—8d.

A BBC Publication.

1972 Shawn Stockman – singer with Boyz II Men, who had a 1992 US & UK No.1 single with 'End Of The Road'.

ON THIS DAY

1961 The Greenbriar Boys started a two week residency at Gerde's Folk Club in New York. The opening act was Bob Dylan.

1964 Roy Orbison started a three week run at No.1 on the US singles chart with 'Oh Pretty Woman'.

1968 Rolling Stone Brian Jones was fined £50 ($85), with 100 guineas cost, after being found guilty of possession of cannabis.

1969 The Beatles released their final studio album *Abbey Road* in the UK.

1981 Genesis scored their second UK No.1 album with *Adacab*.

1981 The Go-Go's started a six week run at No.1 on the US album chart with *Beauty And The Beat*.

1987 Michael Jackson started a six week run at No.1 on the US album chart with *Bad*.

1987 Whitney Houston started a two week run at No.1 on the US singles chart with 'Didn't We Almost Have It All'.

1992 Belinda Carlisle went to No.1 on the UK album chart with *The Best Of Belinda Volume 1.*

1996 Charlie Watts was the second Rolling Stone to become a grandfather when his daughter Seraphina gave birth to a baby girl.

1997 the Irish independent radio commission placed a ban on radio stations playing any songs by Eurovision Song Contest winner Dana, as it was seen to be giving her an unfair advantage during the current election campaign.

1998 Melanie B featuring Missy Elliott went to No.1 on the UK singles chart with 'I Want You Back'.

1999 Leftfield went to No.1 on the UK album chart with *Rhythm And Stealth*.

2004 Green Day scored their first UK No.1 album with *American Idiot*, the band's seventh release.

Stones star Charlie is grandpop

ROLLING Stone Charlie Watts has become a grandad after his daughter Seraphina had a baby girl. Friends said the 55-year-old drummer was "thrilled and delighted." Seraphina, 28, and baby Charlotte Antoinette are doing fine. Charlie's Stones pal Mick Jagger is already a grandad — his daughter Jade has two children.

BORN ON THIS DAY

1943 Randy Bachman – guitarist and vocalist for Guess Who, who had a 1970 US No.1 & UK No.19 single with 'American Woman', and Bachman Turner Overdrive, who had a 1974 US No.1 & UK No.2 single with 'You Ain't Seen Nothing Yet'.

1947 Meat Loaf (a.k.a. Marvin Lee Aday), singer who had a 1993 UK & US No.1 single with 'I'd Do Anything For Love, But I Won't Do That' and a record breaking 1978 album *Bat Out Of Hell*, which spent 457 weeks on the UK album chart.

1953 Greg Ham – multi-instrumentalist with Men At Work, who had a 1983 UK and US No.1 single with 'Down Under'.

1953 Robbie Shakespeare, session bass player. As part of Sly And Robbie he has worked with Peter Tosh, Robert Palmer, Jimmy Cliff, Grace Jones and Joe Cocker.

1958 Shaun Cassidy, singer and actor who had a 1977 US No.1 single with 'Da Doo Ron Ron'. Shaun is the half brother of David Cassidy.

1967 Brett Anderson – vocalist with Suede, who had a 1994 UK No.3 single with 'Stay Together'.

1970 Mark Calderon – vocalist with Color Me Bad, who had a 1991 UK No.1 single with 'I Wanna Sex You Up' and a 1991 US No.1 single with 'I Adore Mi Amor'.

1984 Avril Lavigne – singer who had a 2002 US & UK No.3 single with 'Complicated' and a 2002 US No.2 & UK No.1 album with *Let Go*. Lavigne is the youngest girl to top the charts —she was 17 years and three months old.

ON THIS DAY

1964 The Beach Boys made their TV debut on *The Ed Sullivan Show*.

1972 Rory Storm, singer from UK 60s group Rory Storm & The Hurricanes, died, aged 32, after taking an overdose of sleeping pills in a suicide pact with his mother. Ringo Starr played drums with Storm before joining The Beatles.

1973 *Rolling Stone* magazine reported that Carlos Santana, who was now a disciple of Sri Chinmoy, had the name of Devadip, which means "The lamp of the light of the supreme".

1978 Eric Clapton sponsored a West Bromwich Albion UEFA cup tie against Galatasarey of Turkey. Eric also presented each player with a gold copy of his latest album *Slowhand*.

1979 former Thunderclap Newman and Wings guitarist Jimmy McCullough died, aged 26.

1980 David Bowie scored his fourth UK No.1 album with *Scary Monsters And Supercreeps*.

1986 Lionel Richie started a two run at No.1 on the US album chart with *Dancing On The Ceiling*.

1986 Metallica's tour bus crashed as it was travelling between Stockholm and Copenhagen. Bass player Cliff Burton was found crushed to death under the bus after being thrown out of the bus window. Two of the band's roadies were pinned under the bus for three hours until the fire department rescued them.

1987 Dolly Parton's TV show *Dolly* was shown for the first time on American network ABC.

1990 Dee Dee Ramone of the Ramones was arrested for possessing marijuana during a drug bust in New York's Greenwich Village.

1990 Marvin Gaye's name was added to Hollywood Boulevard's "Walkway Of Fame" in Los Angeles.

1998 The Manic Street Preachers scored their first UK No.1 album with their fifth album *This Is My Truth, Tell Me Yours*.

2003 a BBC 6 Music programme reported on the backstage requirements of artists. Limp Bizkit insist that all the lamps in their rooms be dimmable, while Mariah Carey will only have bendy straws. Van Halen insist that backstage celery is trimmed and not peeled. The Red Hot Chili Peppers ask for a meditation room and a selection of aromatherapy candles. Barry Manilow requests that the air temperature in the auditorium be kept at a regular 18°C (65°F).

BORN ON THIS DAY

1902 Ed Sullivan, TV host who also led The Ed Sullivan Singers And Orchestra. He introduced The Beatles and other UK acts to America via his Ed Sullivan TV Show. Sullivan died on October 13th 1974.

1938 Benjamin Earl Nelson (also known as Ben E. King) – singer with The Drifters, who had a 1960 US No.1 & UK No.2 single with 'Save The Last Dance For Me'. Ben also had a 1987 UK No.1 solo single with 'Stand By Me', which was first released in 1961.

1943 Nick Nicholas – bass player with Steppenwolf, who had a 1969 US No.2 & UK No.30 single with 'Born To Be Wild'.

1946 Helen Shapiro, singer who had a 1961 UK No.1 single with 'Walking Back To Happiness'.

1953 Jim Diamond, singer/songwriter who had a solo 1984 UK No.1 single with 'I Should Have Known Better'. He formed PHD, who had a 1982 UK No.3 single with 'I Won't Let You Down'.

1960 Jennifer Rush, singer who had a 1985 UK No.1 single with 'The Power Of Love'.

1966 Kenny Wilson (a.k.a. Ginger Fish) – drummer with Marilyn Manson, who had a 1998 US No.1 album with *Mechanical Animals* and a UK No.12 single with 'The Dope Show'.

Kate Bush

Hounds Of Love

1987 Hilary Duff, US singer and actress, star of the *Lizzie McGuire* TV show she also had a 2003 US No.1 album with *Metamorphosis*.

ON THIS DAY

1968 DJ Dewey Phillips died. He was the first DJ to play an Elvis record on the radio.

1968 The Beatles started a nine week run at No.1 on the US singles chart with 'Hey Jude'. The Paul McCartney song, written about Lennon's son Julian, gave the group their 16th US No.1 and the biggest seller of 1968.

1974 Bad Company went to No.1 on the US album chart with their self-titled debut album.

1974 Canadian singer Andy Kim went to No.1 on the US singles chart with 'Rock Me Gently', his only US No.1. It made No.2 in the UK. Kim was the co-writer of The Archies' 'Sugar Sugar'.

1976 A&M Records sued George Harrison for $6 million (£3.5 million) over non-delivery of a new album after he missed the deadline by two months.

1980 The Police were at No.1 on the UK singles chart with 'Don't Stand So Close To Me', the group's third No.1.

1985 Kate Bush scored her second UK No.1 album with *Hounds Of Love*.

1991 Bryan Adams was awarded the Order of Canada and the Order of British Columbia.

1991 Garth Brooks went to No.1 on the US album chart with *Ropin' The Wind*. The album spent a total of 18 weeks at the No.1 position and 70 weeks on the chart, eventually selling over 11 million copies.

1991 Guns N' Roses released two albums, *Use Your Illusion I* and *Use Your Illusion II*, which debuted at No.1 and No.2 on the UK album chart.

1991 jazz trumpeter and composer Miles Davis *(right)* died of a stroke and pneumonia. Davis was a major influence on jazz music and created the classic 1959 album *Kind of Blue*.

1994 Bobby Brown witnessed a fatal drive-by shooting in Roxbury. His sister's fiancé was killed in the incident.

1997 LeAnn Rimes went to No.1 on the US album chart with *You Light Up My Life, Inspirational Songs*.

2002 Madonna was voted the greatest female singer of all time by 750,000 music fans in a VH1 poll. But critics and music fans were unhappy with the position of Kylie Minogue, who was voted into second place beating Diana Ross, (12th) and Annie Lennox (14th).

2004 producer Phil Spector was charged with the murder of actress Lana Clarkson in an unsealed indictment. Spector was in attendance at a Los Angeles court as the indictment about the slaying of 40-year-old Clarkson was read. He remained free on $1 million (£0.6 million) bail.

29th September

BORN ON THIS DAY

1907 Gene Autry, America's singing cowboy. During his career he scored 25 successive Top 10 country hits. Autry died on October 2nd 1998, aged 91.

1935 Jerry Lee Lewis, singer who had a 1958 UK No.1 & US No.1 single with 'Great Balls Of Fire' and a 1957 multi-million seller 'Whole Lotta Shakin' Goin' On'.

1939 Tommy Boyce, singer/songwriter who had a 1968 US No.8 single with Bobby Hart, 'I Wonder What She's Doing Tonite?' He also wrote 'Last Train To Clarksville', 'I'm Not Your Stepping Stone' and 'Scooby-Doo Where Are You?' Boyce sold over 40 million records. He committed suicide on November 23rd 1994.

1943 Manuel Fernandez – organ player for Los Bravos, who had a 1966 UK No.2 & US No.4 single with 'Black Is Black'. They were the first Spanish rock band to have a UK and US hit single.

1948 Mark Farner – guitarist and vocalist with Grand Funk Railroad, who had a 1974 US No.1 single with 'The Locomotion'. The band was the most successful US heavy metal band of the 70s, selling over 20 million albums.

1957 Mari Wilson, UK singer who had a 1982 UK No.8 single with 'Just What I Always Wanted'.

1968 Matt and Luke Goss – singer and drummer respectively for Bros, who had a 1988 UK No.1 single with 'I Owe You Nothing' plus ten other UK Top 40 singles.

1981 Suzanne Shaw – singer with *Popstars* winners Hear'Say, who had a 2001 UK No.1 single with 'Pure and Simple'.

ON THIS DAY

1956 Bill Haley had five songs in the UK Top 30, 'Rockin Through The Rye', 'Saints Rock 'n' Roll', 'Rock Around The Clock', 'Razzle Dazzle' and 'See You Later Alligator'.

1960 Ricky Valance was at No.1 on the UK singles chart with 'Tell Laura I Love Her'.

1963 the first night of a 30 date UK tour featuring The Everly Brothers, Bo Diddley, The Rolling Stones, Mickie Most and The Flintstones kicked off at the New Vic, London. The acts played two shows each night.

1971 Gilbert O'Sullivan made his live debut at London's Royal Albert Hall. Also on the bill were Sweet, Dave Edmunds' Rockpile and Ashton Gardner & Dyke.

1973 Grand Funk went to No.1 on the US singles chart with 'We're An American Band', the group's first of two US chart toppers.

1976 enjoying his own birthday celebrations singer Jerry Lee Lewis accidentally shot his bass player Norman Owens in the chest while blasting holes in an office door. Owens survived but sued his boss.

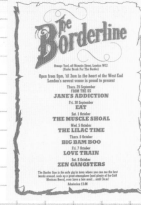

1979 The Police had their first UK No.1 single with 'Message In A Bottle'.

1980 appearing at the Rainbow, London was Elvis Costello supported by The Stray Cats.

1984 Prince And The Revolution started a two week run at No.1 on the US singles chart with 'Let's Go Crazy', Prince's second US No.1 and a No.7 hit in the UK.

1989 while travelling on his motorbike from Los Angeles Bruce Springsteen called in at Matt's Saloon in Prescott, Arizona and jammed with the house band for an hour. He also donated $100,000 (£58,824) to a barmaid's hospital bill.

1990 Maria McKee was at No.1 in the UK with 'Show Me Heaven', a song featured in the film *Days Of Thunder*.

1990 Nelson went to No.1 on the US singles chart with '(Can't Live Without Your) Love and Affection'. The duo were the twin sons of 50s singer Ricky Nelson.

2003 John Mayer was at No.1 on the US album chart with *Heavier Things*.

2004 Keith Moon's five piece drum kit, custom-made for The Who drummer in 1968, sold for £120,000 ($204,000) in London to an American collector.

BORN ON THIS DAY

1933 Cissy Houston, soul singer and mother of Whitney Houston. She was a member of Sweet Inspirations, The Drinkard Singers (with Dionne Warwick) and back-up singer with Elvis Presley, Aretha Franklin, Chaka Khan and Luther Vandross.

1935 Johnny Mathis, singer who had a 1976 UK No.1 single with 'When A Child Is Born' plus ten other UK Top 40 singles, a 1978 US No.1 single with 'Too Much Too Little, Too Late' and over 15 other Top 40 singles. His *Greatest Hits* album spent over nine years on the US chart.

1942 Frankie Lymon – singer with Frankie Lymon & the Teenagers, who had a 1956 UK No.1 & US No.6 single with 'Why Do Fools Fall In Love?' Lymon died from a drug overdose on February 28th 1968, aged 25.

1942 Gus Dudgeon, producer. He is best known for his work with Elton John. He also produced David Bowie, The Beach Boys, Zombies, Kiki Dee, Strawbs, XTC and Joan Armatrading. Dudgeon was killed in a car accident on July 21st 2002. His wife, Sheila, was also killed in the accident.

1943 Marilyn McCoo, singer who had a 1977 US No.1 & UK No.7 single with 'You Don't Have To Be A Star'. She was also a member of The 5th Dimension.

1946 Sylvia Peterson – singer with The Chiffons, who had a 1963 US No.1 single with 'He's So Fine' and a 1972 UK No.4 single with 'Sweet Talking Guy', which was first released in 1966.

1947 Marc Bolan – guitarist and singer/songwriter with T. Rex, who had a 1971 UK No.1 single with 'Hot Love' plus over 20 other UK Top 40 singles and a 1972 US No.10 single with 'Bang A Gong (Get It On)'. Bolan was killed in a car accident on September 16th 1977.

ON THIS DAY

1965 EMI Records launched its budget price "Music For Pleasure" label, selling the albums in grocery stores for 12/6d each.

1967 BBC Radio 1 was launched in the UK and ex-Radio Caroline DJ Tony Blackburn was the first DJ on air. The Move's 'Flowers In The Rain' was the first record played.

1969 Christine Hinton, the girlfriend of Dave Crosby, was killed in a car crash near San Francisco.

1972 David Cassidy was at No.1 on the UK singles chart with 'How Can I Be Sure?', his first of two UK No.1s.

1974 police were called to a Lynyrd Skynyd and Blue Oyster Cult concert after a fight broke out between two sound engineers. The Skynyrd engineer claimed that the sound had been deliberately turned off during the band's set.

1977 Mary Ford died from cancer after being in a diabetic coma for 54 days. She had the 1957 UK No.7 single 'Vaya Con Dios' with Les Paul.

1978 John Travolta and Olivia Newton-John had their second UK No.1 from the film *Grease* with 'Summer Nights'.

1984 the music division of Thorn EMI, once said to be the greatest recording organization in the world, reported a worldwide loss of almost £5 million ($8.5 million) during the last six months.

1989 Tina Turner scored her first solo UK No.1 album with *Foreign Affair*.

1992 US singer Steve Earle was arrested in Nashville after he failed to report for jury service.

1993 Kate Pierson from The B-52s was charged with criminal mischief and trespassing during an anti-fur protest at Vogue's New York City offices.

1995 Mariah Carey made chart history when she started an eight week run at No.1 on the US singles chart with 'Fantasy'. It made her the first female act to enter the chart in pole position.

1999 Chris de Burgh's website was closed down after countless obscene messages were being posted on the visitors' guest book. One message consisted entirely of two four-letter words repeated 3,500 times.

MUSICAL ANAGRAMS

PHILIPS

BF 1600
304 137 BF

45

MONO
▽

A

Campbell,
Connelly

℗ 1967

304 137 1F

LONESOME ROAD (2.27)
(Shilkret/Austin)
THE WONDER WHO?
Arranged by Herb Bernstein
Produced and directed by
Bob Crewe

ALL RIGHTS OF THE RECORD PRODUCER AND OF THE OWNER OF THE WORK REPRODUCED RESERVED. COPYING, PUBLIC PERFORMANCE AND BROADCASTING OF THIS RECORD PROHIBITED

Anthony Kiedis Is a thin donkey

Sir Paul McCartney Musical carpentry

Barry Manilow Library woman

Natalie Imbruglia Ta! I am a nubile girl

Mariah Carey A creamy hair

Marilyn Manson My norm anal sin.

Courtney Love You not clever

Kelly Osbourne One bulky loser

Lisa Stansfield A daft silliness

Elvis Aaron Presley Seen alive? Sorry, pal!

Whitney Houston Shut it now, honey!

Robbie Williams I warm millions

Tori Amos I'm a torso

Eminem The Real Slim Shady Elementary, idle mishmash

Heather McCartney Hatchet mercenary

Justin Timberlake I'm a jerk, but listen

Gordon Sumner Grunted minor songs

James Brown Mr Jawbones

Thom Yorke OK to rhyme

Madonna And moan

Michael Jackson Manacle his jock

Brian Wilson Slow in brain

Carlos Santana Carnal sonatas

Chris Rea Rich arse

Damon Albarn Dan Abnormal

Christina Aguilera It is a raunchier gal

Michael Bolton I'm the local nob

Bono No B.O.!

Emma Bunton/Baby Spice Bumpy bimbo nets an ace

Kate Bush Shut beak

Belinda Carlisle Call dire lesbian

Eric Clapton Narcoleptic

Celine Dion No, I decline

Bob Dylan Nobby Lad

David Essex Sex advised

Gloria Estefan Large fat nose

George Michael I come, he gargle!

Bette Midler Diet? Tremble!

Kylie Minogue I like 'em young

Alanis Morissette It's nasal, tiresome

Dolly Parton Play not, Lord

Axl Rose Oral sex `

Britney Spears Nip yer breasts

Bruce Springsteen Bursting presence

Rod Stewart Two red rats

BAM CARUSO
INTERNATIONAL

STEREO
Copyright
Control

NRICO 30
9176 3421-0

SIDE ONE

RODUCED BY
BERNARD
GAZDA

RABBI JOSEPH GORDAN

"COMPETITION"
(J. Jordan)

FOR ONE NIGHT ONLY

FILLMORE AUDITORIUM
1805 Geary St. San Francisco
TUES. JULY 26th
From 9:00 p.m. to 1:00 a.m.
DANCE and SHOW
"My Girl"   "Don't Look
"Since I Lost   Back"
My Baby"   "Its Growing"
THE
"Not Too Proud To Beg"
TEMPTATIONS
.....and their.....
ORCHESTRA
"Get Ready"   "Far-away"

DEAD KENNEDYS
the BAGS
ALLEY CATS
1839 GEARY BLVD. S.F.
OCT. 6   10

THE RAMONES
Santa Cruz Civic

BENNY LEVIN AND RUSSELL CLARK
PROUDLY PRESENT
FOR IMPACT TALENT ASSOCIATES LTD
THE FIRST NEW ZEALAND APPEARANCE OF
the PHENOMENAL
LITTLE FEAT
HAILED BY MICK JAGGER AND JIMMY PAGE AS:
"THE GREAT AMERICAN ROCK BAND OF THE '70's"
LOWELL GEORGE · VOCALS, GUITAR   BILL PAYNE · PIANO
KEN GRADNEY · BASS   RICHIE HAYWARD · DRUMS
SAM CLAYTON · PERCUSSION   PAUL BARRERE · GUITAR
IN PERSON
ONE CONCERT ONLY
CHRISTCHURCH TOWN HALL   TUES. JULY 6TH 8.30 p.m.

HOWLIN' WOLF
BIG BROTHER HOLDING
AVALON BALLROOM SAN FRANCISCO

Bob DYLAN
DEC. 5
IN CONCERT-8:30 P.M.
WILSON HI. SCHOOL
PRESENTED BY THE GOLDEN BEAR

THE ROLLING STONES

RTL
ZERO
"UN CONCERT DANS LE PARC"
BOB DYLAN
SANTANA
JOAN BAEZ
PARIS
PARC DE SCEAUX
DIMANCHE 1er JUILLET 1984
LOCATION : 3 FNAC, CLEMENTINE

THE BEATLES. LONDON PALLADIUM
ROYAL COMMAND PERFORMANCE 1963

JIMI HENDRIX
EXPERIENCE
JOSHUA LIGHT SHOW
BILL GRAHAM'S
FILLMORE EAST
SECOND AVENUE & SIXTH STREET
ONE NIGHT ONLY
FRIDAY MAY 10
TWO SHOWS 8:00 P.M. & 11:30 P.M.

TUXEDOMOON
MINIMAL MAN
SOUND OF SEX
FEB 19 THU 9:00PM Victoria Theater 2961 16TH ST NR MISSION
R.R.Z. 864-1639

MOBY GRAPE
AVALON

BORN ON THIS DAY

1930 Richard Harris, actor and singer who had a 1968 US & UK No.4 single with 'MacArthur Park'.

1935 Julie Andrews, singer and actress who had a 1965 UK & US No.1 album with *The Sound Of Music*, which spent 382 weeks on the UK chart.

1944 Scott McKenzie, singer who had a 1967 UK No.1 & US No.4 single with 'San Francisco, Be Sure To Wear Some Flowers In Your Hair'. He also auditioned for The Monkees.

1945 Donny Hathaway, US soul singer who had a 1972 UK No.29 single with Roberta Flack, 'Where Is The Love?' and a 1978 US No.2 single with 'The Closer I Get'. Hathaway committed suicide by falling from a 15th floor hotel window on January 13th 1979.

1947 Rob Davis – guitarist for Mud, who had a 1974 UK No.1 single with 'Tiger Feet' plus 14 other UK Top 40 singles. He co-wrote 'Can't Get You Out Of My Head', the 2001 UK No.1 hit for Kylie Minogue.

1948 Cub Koda – guitarist for Brownsville Station, who had a 1973 US No.3 UK No.27 single with 'Smokin' In The Boys Room'. Koda died on July 5th 2000.

1974 Keith Duffy – vocalist with Boyzone, who had a 1996 UK No.1 single with 'Words'.

ON THIS DAY

1966 Jimi Hendrix appeared live for the first time in the UK when he jammed with Cream at their gig at London Polytechnic.

1967 the first edition of BBC Radio 1s "Top Gear" was aired. It was presented by John Peel and Pete Drummond with The Move, Traffic, Pink Floyd, Tim Rose and Tomorrow featuring Keith West.

1970 Jimi Hendrix was buried at The Greenwood Cemetery at the Dunlop Baptist Church, Seattle. Among the mourners were Miles Davis, Eric Burdon, Johnny Winter and members of Derek And The Dominoes.

1973 The Simon Park Orchestra were at No.1 on the UK singles chart with 'Eye Level', which was taken from the ITV series *Van Der Valk*. It was the first TV theme to become a No.1 in the UK.

1975 drummer Al Jackson was murdered after he confronted an intruder in his home. Jackson had worked with Booker T And The MGs and Al Green.

1977 Elton John became the first musician to be honoured in New York City's Madison Square Hall Of Fame.

1977 Meco started a two week run at No.1 on the US singles chart with a disco version of 'Star Wars Theme'. He had other hits with his versions of 'Close Encounters', 'Wizard Of Oz' and 'Empire Strikes Back'.

1981 The Pretenders were forced to cancel the last leg

Ms. Dynamite realises she needs a bigger mantelpiece after sweeping the board at the MOBOs.

of a US tour when drummer Martin Chambers put his hand through a window pane, cutting tendons and arteries.

1982 John Cougar went to No.1 on both the US album and singles chart with the album *American Fool* and the single 'Jack And Diane'.

1983 the Swedish post office issued an Abba stamp.

1983 a David Bowie world convention was held at The Cunard Hotel in London. The event had the largest collection of Bowie merchandise ever assembled. Tickets cost £6.90 ($11.73).

1988 Bon Jovi scored their first UK No.1 album with their fourth release *New Jersey*.

1999 singer Lena Zavoroni died, aged 35, after a long battle against anorexia. She was discovered on TV talent show *Opportunity Knocks* and in 1974 became the youngest British singer to earn a silver disc with 'Ma He's Making Eyes At Me'.

2004 Ms Dynamite was arrested over allegations of assault after an incident at a restaurant in Central London. Ms Dynamite (real name Niomi McLean-Daley) was arrested in connection with the allegation after voluntarily attending a police station. She was later released on bail.

2004 the Lord Mayor of Melbourne officially opened AC/DC Lane after veteran rockers AC/DC. The Lord Mayor erected the sign to cheers and bagpipes playing the band's song 'Long Way To The Top'. The City of Melbourne had extra copies of the sign made, in anticipation of fans stealing them.

SUNDAY
AT THE
SAVILLE
OCTOBER 1: 6 p.m. & 8.30 p.m.
PINK FLOYD
TOMORROW
featuring **KEITH WEST**
INCREDIBLE STRING BAND
Special guest : **TIM ROSE**
BOOK: TEM 4011
A NEMS PRESENTATION
in association with Brian Morrison Agency

BORN ON THIS DAY

1945 Don McLean, singer/songwriter who had a 1971 US & 1972 UK No.1 single with 'American Pie', which was inspired by the death of Buddy Holly.

1950 Mike Rutherford – guitarist with Genesis, who had a 1986 US No.1 single with 'Invisible Touch', a 1992 UK No.7 single with 'I Can't Dance' and six UK No.1 albums, and Mike And The Mechanics, who had a 1989 US No.1 & UK No.2 single with 'The Living Years'.

1951 Sting – singer/songwriter and bass player with The Police, who had a 1983 UK & US No.1 single with 'Every Breath You Take' plus four other UK No.1 singles. As a solo artist Sting had a 1990 UK No.15 single with 'Englishman In New York' plus over 15 other UK Top 40 singles.

1952 John Otway – singer and guitarist who had a 1977 UK No.27 single 'Really Free', with Wild Willy Barrett and a 2002 UK No.7 single with 'Bunsen Burner'.

1955 Phil Oakey – singer with Human League, who had a 1981 UK No.1 & 1982 US No.1 single with 'Don't You Want Me?' plus over 15 other UK Top 40 singles.

Rock City
BACK STAGE PASS
SHOW: U2
DATE: 2/10/81
AUTHORISED BY: Various

1969 Badly Drawn Boy (a.k.a Damon Gough), singer/songwriter who had a 2002 album with _Have You Fed The Fish?_

1971 Tiffany, singer who had a 1987 US No.1 & 1988 UK No.1 single with 'I Think We're Alone Now'.

ON THIS DAY

1971 Rod Stewart started a five week run at No.1 on the US singles chart with 'Maggie May/Reason To Believe', his first solo No.1. His album _Every_

Picture Tells A Story also started a four week run on this day at No.1 on both the US and UK charts.

1972 Led Zeppelin **_(above)_** played the first of two sold-out nights at Budokan Hall, Tokyo, Japan.

1977 the body of Elvis Presley and his mother Gladys were moved from the cemetery where they were buried to Graceland after an unsuccessful attempt was made to bodysnatch the coffin.

1980 Leaveil Degree from the soul group The Whispers started a two year prison sentence in Boron, California for his part in a diamond robbery.

1982 John Cougar started a four week run at No.1 on the US singles chart with 'Jack and Diane', his first US No.1. It was a No.25 hit in the UK.

1982 Musical Youth were at No.1 on the UK singles chart with 'Pass The Dutchie'. The song was originally called 'Pass The Kutchie', but this was changed to avoid the song being banned for its drug reference.

1983 Abba singer Agnetha Faltskog was taken to hospital suffering from concussion after being involved in a car crash in Skane, Sweden.

1983 Welsh singer Bonnie Tyler was at No.1 on the US singles chart with the Jim Steinman written and produced 'Total Eclipse Of The Heart'. It was also a No.1 in the UK.

1995 Oasis released their second album _(What's The Story) Morning Glory_. It entered the UK chart at No.1.

1996 a Pearl Jam show in Hartford, Connecticut ended in a riot when mass fighting broke out among the 30,000 strong crowd.

2002 Robbie Williams signed the most lucrative British record deal in history when he signed with EMI records for £80 million ($136 million). Asked what he was going to do with money Robbie said, "I'm going to count it all."

2002 Carling Live presents – David Bowie at the Carling Apollo, Hammersmith, London.

2003 police were called to a suspected burglary at the Los Angeles house of Courtney Love's former boyfriend and ex-manager Jim Barber. Ms Love was picked up in the street outside and detained. Shortly after her arrest, Ms Love was taken to hospital with a suspected drug overdose.

BORN ON THIS DAY

1938 Eddie Cochran, singer and guitarist who had a 1958 US No. 8 single 'Summertime Blues', and a 1960 UK No.1 single 'Three Steps To Heaven'. He was killed in a car crash on April 17th 1960, aged 21.

1941 Ernest Evans "Chubby Checker", singer who had a 1960 US.No.1 & UK No.14 single with 'The Twist' and a 1962 UK No.2 single with 'Let's Twist Again'. 'The Twist' is the only song to go to No.1 on the US singles charts twice – once in 1960 and again in 1962.

1947 Lindsey Buckingham – guitarist and vocalist with Fleetwood Mac, who had a 1987 UK No.5 single with 'Little Lies' and a 1977 US No.1 single 'Dreams' from worldwide No.1 album *Rumours*.

1954 Stevie Ray Vaughan, guitarist – he was killed in a helicopter crash on August 27th 1990. His family successfully sued the operators of the company for allowing an unqualified pilot to fly in fog and were awarded $2 million (£1.2 million). Vaughan played guitar on David Bowies *Let's Dance* album

ROYAL ALBERT HALL, OCT. 3
RIK & JOHN GUNNELL IN ASSOCIATION WITH HAROLD DAVISON & TITO BURNS
PRESENT THE ONLY APPEARANCE IN ENGLAND OF

JAMES BROWN
AND HIS 18 PIECE AMERICAN BAND
PLUS THE J.B. DANCERS
TWO PERFORMANCES—6.30 p.m. and 9.0 p.m.
TICKETS 30/-, 25/-, 20/-, 15/-, 10/-, 5/- BOX OFFICE : KEN 8212 and Agencies

1962 Tommy Lee – drummer with Motley Crue, who had a 1988 UK No.23 single with 'You're All I Need' and a 1989 US No.1 album with *Dr. Feelgood*.

1969 Gwen Stefani – vocalist with No Doubt, who had a 1997 UK No.1 single with 'Don't Speak' and a 1997 No.1 US album with *Tragic Kingdom*. As a solo artist she had the 2005 US No.1 single with 'Hollaback Girl' from the 2004 worldwide Top 5 album *Love, Angel, Music, Baby*.

1971 Kevin Richardson – singer with Backstreet Boys, who had a 1997 US No.2 single with 'Quit Playing Games With My Heart' and a 1999 UK No.1 single with 'I Want It That Way'.

1978 Jake Shears (a.k.a. Jason Sellards) – vocalist with Scissor Sisters, who had a 2004 UK No.1 self-titled album and a 2004 UK No.12 single with 'Laura'.

ON THIS DAY

1945 Elvis Presley made his first-ever public appearance in a talent contest at the Mississippi, Alabama Dairy Show, singing 'Old Shep'. Elvis was ten years old at the time and came second.

1967 singer/songwriter Woody Guthrie died after suffering from Huntington's Chorea disease. He was a major influence on Bob Dylan and American folk music. The 70s film *Bound For Glory* is based on his life.

1978 the members of Aerosmith bailed 30 fans out of jail after they were arrested for smoking pot during an Aerosmith concert at Fort Wayne Coliseum.

1980 BBC TV aired *The Police In The East* documentary, featuring The Police on tour.

1987 M/A/R/S were at No.1 on the UK singles chart with 'Pump Up The Volume'.

1992 Sinead O'Connor ripped up a photograph of Pope John Paul II on the US TV show *Saturday Night Live* in a protest at abortion laws. The incident happened as Sinead ended her live performance and out of nowhere produced a photograph of Pope John Paul II. There was stunned silence in the studio and the station went to a commercial. NBC was fined $2.5 million (£1.5 million) by the Federal Communications Commission.

1999 Akio Morita, the founder of Sony Electronics, died, aged 78. The 1979 Sony Walkman transformed both Sony and consumers across the world.

1999 Tom Jones went to No.1 on the UK album chart with *Reload*, making the singer the oldest artist to score a No.1 album with new material.

2000 John Lennon's assassin Mark Chapman was denied parole after serving 20 years in prison. Chapman was interviewed for 50 minutes by parole board members, who concluded that releasing Chapman would "deprecate the seriousness of the crime".

2000 The Cars' lead singer and bass player Benjamin Orr died of cancer at the age of 44.

BORN ON THIS DAY

1942 Helen Reddy, singer who had a 1975 US No.1 & UK No.5 single with 'Angie Baby'. It was a song that Cher turned down.

1944 Patti Labelle, singer who had a 1975 US No.1 & UK No.17 single with 'Lady Marmalade' and a 1986 US No.1 & UK No.2 single with Michael McDonald, 'On My Own'.

1959 Chris Lowe – keyboardist with the Pet Shop Boys, who had a 1986 UK & US No.1 single with 'West End Girls' plus three other UK No.1 singles and over 20 other UK Top 40 singles.

1961 Jon Secada, US singer who had a 1992 UK No. 5 single with 'Just Another Day'.

1984 Katina Sergeevna – singer with Tatu, who had a 2003 UK No.1 single with 'All The Things She Said'.

ON THIS DAY

1961 Bob Dylan played a showcase at New York's Carnegie Hall to 53 people.

1962 The Tornados were at No.1 on the UK singles chart with the instrumental 'Telstar'.

1965 Johnny Cash was arrested crossing the Mexican border into El Paso, Texas after customs officials found hundreds of pills in his guitar case. He received a suspended jail sentence and a $1,000 (£588) fine.

1969 Creedence Clearwater Revival started a four week run at No.1 on the US album chart with *Green River*, the group's first US chart topper.

1969 The Beatles' *Abbey Road* album went to No.1 on the UK chart. It was the last recording from the group and featured the George Harrison songs 'Something' and 'Here Comes The Sun'.

1970 US singer Janis Joplin was found dead at the Landmark Hotel, Hollywood after an accidental heroin overdose. She had had a 1971 US No.1 single with 'Me And Bobby McGee' and a 1971 US No.1 album with *Pearl*.

1973 the BBC broadcast the 500th edition of *Top Of The Pops*. Slade, Gary Glitter and The Osmonds all appeared on the show.

1975 Pink Floyd went to No.1 on the UK album chart with *Wish You Were Here*, which featured a tribute to ex-member Syd Barratt, 'Shine On You Crazy Diamond'. The album was also No.1 in the US.

1980 Carly Simon collapsed on stage during a show in Pittsburgh suffering from nervous exhaustion.

1980 Queen started a three week run at No.1 on the US singles chart with 'Another One Bites The Dust'.

Janie Hendrix.

1982 The Smiths made their live debut at the Ritz in Manchester, England.

1986 Paul Simon started a five week run at No.1 on the UK album chart with *Graceland*.

1991 Blur kicked off a 13 date UK tour at Middlesborough Town Hall.

1999 it was reported that Jimi Hendrix's sister Janie was planning to exhume his body and move it to a pay-to-view mausoleum. Other plans for the site included a chance for fans to buy one of the burial plots around the guitarist's new resting place.

2000 Craig David picked up the awards for Best R&B act, Best UK newcomer and Best UK single for 'Fill Me In' at the Mobo Awards.

2003 The Darkness kicked off a 15 date UK tour at Stoke, Keele University.

BORN ON THIS DAY

1942 Richard Street – singer with The Temptations, who had a 1971 US No.1 & UK No.8 single with 'Just My Imagination' and the reissued 'My Girl' was a UK No.2 in 1992.

1943 Steve Miller – singer and guitarist who had a 1974 US No.1 & 1990 UK No.1 single with 'The Joker'.

1947 Brian Johnson – singer with Geordie, who had a 1973 UK No.6 single with 'Because Of You', AC/DC (he joined AC/DC in 1980 after the death of Bon Scott), who had a 1980 UK No.36 single with 'Whole Lotta Rosie' and a UK No.1 & US No.4 album with *Back In Black* – it sold over ten million copies.

1949 Brian Connolly – vocalist with Sweet, who had a 1973 UK No.1 single with 'Blockbuster' plus 14 other UK Top 40 singles. Connolly died of kidney and liver failure on February 10th 1997.

1954 Bob Geldof – singer with The Boomtown Rats, who had a 1979 UK No.1 single with 'I Don't Like Mondays' plus ten other UK Top 40 singles. He was also the organizer of Band Aid and Live8.

1955 Russell Craig Mael – singer with Sparks, who had a 1974 UK No.2 single with 'This Town Ain't Big Enough For The Both Of Us'.

1961 David Bryson – guitarist with Counting Crows, who had a 1994 UK No.28 single with 'Mr Jones' and a 1996 US No.1 album with *Recovering The Satellites*.

1978 James Burgon Valentine – vocalist and guitarist with Maroon 5, who had a 2004 UK No.1 album with *Songs About Jane* and a 2004 US No.1 & UK No.4 single with 'She Will Be Loved'.

ON THIS DAY

1958 Cliff Richard And The Shadows played their first gig together at the Victoria Hall, Hanley, England.

1966 Jimi Hendrix, drummer Mitch Mitchell and bass player Noel Redding played together for the first time. As a result the Jimi Hendrix Experience was formed.

1974 Mike Oldfields' *Tubular Bells* went to No.1 for the first time on the UK album chart 15 months after it was first released. It went on to sell over ten million copies worldwide.

1974 Olivia Newton-John started a two week run at No.1 on the US singles chart with 'I Honestly Love You', the singer's first of five US chart toppers.

1980 UK music weekly *NME* had Joy Division's 'She's Lost Control' as single of the week.

1985 Midge Ure was at No.1 on the UK singles chart with 'If I Was'. It was the former Ultravox and Slik singer's only solo No.1.

1987 ex-Smiths guitarist Johnny Marr began rehearsals with The Pretenders in preparation for the band supporting U2 in America.

1991 Bryan Adams scored his first UK No.1 album with *Waking Up The Neighbours*.

MANIC STREET PREACHERS

OCTOBER 1994

Wednesday 5th
GLASGOW BARROWLANDS
031 557 6969

Thursday 6th
NEWCASTLE UNIVERSITY
091 232 8402

Friday 7th
NORWICH UEA
0603 505401

Saturday 8th
WOLVERHAMPTON CIVIC HALL
0902 312030

Monday 10th
CAMBRIDGE CORN EXCHANGE
0223 357851

Tuesday 11th
LEICESTER DE MONTFORT UNIVERSITY
0533 555576. C.C. 0602 483456

Wednesday 12th
PORTSMOUTH GUILDHALL
0705 824355

Thursday 13th
MANCHESTER ACADEMY
061 839 0858 / 061 834 5104

Saturday 15th
SHEFFIELD OCTAGON
0742 753300

Sunday 16th
LEEDS TOWN & COUNTRY
0532 442999

Monday 17th
NOTTINGHAM ROCK CITY
0602 412544

Tuesday 18th
EXETER UNIVERSITY
0222 230130

Thursday 20th
CARDIFF ASTORIA

New Album 'The Holy Bible' Out Now

1991 Guns N' Roses started a two week run at No.1 on the US album chart with *Use Your Illusion II*.

1992 Eddie Kendricks of The Temptations died of lung cancer one year after having a lung removed.

1996 'Breakfast At Tiffany's' by Deep Blue Something was at No.1 on the UK singles chart for one week.

1999 Roger Daltrey announced that The Who were reforming, and their first performance would be in Las Vegas on October 29th. The show was also being planned to be broadcast live on the Internet.

1999 Travis kicked off a 20 date sold-out UK tour at Barrowlands, Glasgow.

2000 *Top Of The Pops* issued a Top 40 chart based on singles that had spent the longest time on the UK chart. No.3 was 'My Way', Frank Sinatra; No.2 'She Loves You', The Beatles and No.1 'Relax', Frankie Goes To Hollywood.

2003 Dido started a four week run at No.1 on the UK album chart with *Life For Rent*, the UK singer's second No.1 album.

BORN ON THIS DAY

1948 Millie Small, singer who had a 1964 US & UK No.2 single with 'My Boy Lollipop'.

1949 Bobby Farrell – singer with Boney M, who had a 1978 UK No.1 & US No.30 single with 'Rivers Of Babylon'.

1949 Thomas McClary – guitarist with The Commodores, who had a 1978 UK & US No.1 single with 'Three Times A Lady'.

1951 David Hidalgo – singer and guitarist with Los Lobos, who had a 1987 UK & US No.1 single with 'La Bamba'.

1951 Gavin Sutherland – singer and bass guitarist with the Sutherland Brothers, who had a 1976 UK No.5 single with 'Arms Of Mary'. He also wrote the million seller 'Sailing', which was a No.1 for Rod Stewart in 1975.

1960 Richard Jobson – singer with The Skids, who had a 1979 UK No.10 single with 'Into The Valley', then the Armoury Show. He is now an occasional TV presenter and film writer and director.

1961 Tim Burgess – drummer with T'Pau, who had a 1987 UK No.1 single with 'China In Your Hand' and a 1987 US No.4 single with 'Heart and Soul'.

ON THIS DAY

1959 Jerry Keller was at No.1 on the UK singles chart with 'Here Comes Summer'.

1963 The Yardbirds appeared at Studio 51, Leicester Square, London.

1964 The Beatles spent the afternoon recording 'Eight Days A Week' at Abbey Road Studios. Late evening was spent at The Ad Lib Club, London partying with The Ronettes and Mick Jagger.

Elvis attempts a fine Tanita Tikaram impersonation.

1967 The Jimi Hendrix Experience recorded a session for the UK BBC radio show "Top Gear". Stevie Wonder, who was also appearing, jammed with Hendrix.

1970 The US Top 5 singles were: No.5, 'All Right Now' by Free; No.4, 'Ain't No Mountain High Enough', Diana Ross; No.3, 'Candida', Dawn; No.2, 'I'll Be There', Jackson Five and No.1, 'Cracklin' Rose' by Neil Diamond.

1973 Cher started a two week run at No.1 on the US singles chart with 'Half-Breed', the singer's second US No.1. It was not a hit in the UK.

1973 Slade scored their second UK No.1 album when *Sladest* started a three week run at the top.

1978 Johnny O'Keefe, Australia's "King of rock 'n' roll" died. He co-wrote and had the 1958 hit with, 'Real Wild Child', which was covered by Iggy Pop in 1986.

1980 The Bee Gees sued their record company Polygram and the band's manager Robert Stigwood for $200m (£118m) for fraud.

1984 David Bowie scored his sixth UK No.1 album with *Tonight*, which featured the single 'Blue Jean'.

1996 Celine Dion was at No.1 on the US album chart with *Falling Into You*.

1998 a music industry poll was published by London magazine *Time Out*, naming the top stars from the past 30 years: No.5 was Marvin Gaye, No.4 James Brown, No.3 Bob Marley, No.2 The Beatles and No.1 went to David Bowie.

1999 winners at the Mobo Awards included: Kele Le Roc, Best newcomer and Best single; Shanks & Bigfoot, Best dance act, TLC won Best video for 'No Scrubs', Lauryn Hill, Best international act and Tina Turner won a Lifetime achievement award.

2000 rapper Busta Rhymes was sentenced to five years probation by Manhattan Supreme Court after pleading guilty to a gun possession charge.

2002 Mick Jagger donated £100,000 ($170,000) to his old Grammar school in Dartford to help pay for a music director and buy musical instruments. The new centre was also named after Mick Jagger.

2002 Elvis Presley started a three week run at No.1 on the US album chart with *Elvis 30 #1 Hits*.

BORN ON THIS DAY

1927 Al Martino, singer, who had a 1952 US & UK No.1 single with 'Here In My Heart', the first No.1 in the *NME* singles chart, and a 1963 US No.3 with 'I Love You Because'.

1941 Martin Murray – guitarist with The Honeycombs, who had a 1964 UK No.1 single with 'Have I The Right?'

1945 Kevin Godley – drummer and singer/songwriter with 10CC, who had a 1975 UK No.1 & US No.2 single with 'I'm Not In Love' plus ten other UK Top 30 hits including two No.1s. As part of Godley And Creme he had a 1981 UK No.3 single with 'Under Your Thumb'. He is now a video producer.

1951 John Cougar Mellencamp, singer/songwriter who had a 1982 US No.1 & UK No.25 single with 'Jack and Diane' and a 1982 US No.1 album with *American Fool*.

1953 Tico Torres – drummer with Bon Jovi, who had a 1987 US No.1 & UK No.4 single with 'Livin' On A Prayer'.

1959 Simon Cowell, record executive and producer, as well as a judge on TV shows. He is notorious for his uncompromisingly harsh and controversial criticism of *Pop Idol* and *American Idol* contestants.

1967 Toni Braxton, US singer, who had a 1996 US No.1 & UK No.2 single with 'Un-Break My Heart'.

1968 Thom Yorke – vocalist, guitarist and keyboardist with Radiohead, who had a 1997 UK No.1 & US No.21 album with *OK Computer* and a 1998 UK No.5 single with 'No Surprises'.

1969 Leeroy Thornhill, dancer with The Prodigy, who had a 1996 UK No.1 single with 'Firestarter' and a 1997 UK & US No.1 album with *The Fat Of The Land*.

ON THIS DAY

1961 appearing at Withita Forum, Kansas were The Platters, Del Shannon, The Drifters, Brook Benton, and U.S. Bonds. Tickets cost $2–3 (£1.20–1.75).

1966 Johnny Kidd was killed, aged 27, in a car crash while on tour in Radcliffe, Manchester. He had had the 1960 UK No.1 single 'Shakin' All Over'.

1966 Smiley Lewis, New Orleans R&B singer, died of stomach cancer. He wrote 'One Night', which was covered by Elvis Presley, and 'I Hear You Knocking', which was a 1955 US No.2 for Gale Storm and a UK No.1 & US No.2 for Dave Edmunds.'

1967 Cass Elliot from The Mamas And The Papas spent the night in a London jail after being accused of stealing a TV from a hotel. A concert appearance had to be cancelled as a result.

1975 the New York Supreme Court voted by a two to one majority to reverse John Lennon's deportation order.

1978 *Billboard* magazine reported that Marvin Gaye had twice filed bankruptcy papers earlier in the year, having debts of $7 million (£4 million).

1978 the *Grease* soundtrack started a 13 week run at No.1 on the UK chart.

1982 Led Zeppelin's Jimmy Page was given a 12 month conditional discharge after being found guilty of possessing cocaine.

1989 Janet Jackson scored her second US No.1 single with 'Miss You Much'. It stayed at the top for four weeks but was a No.22 hit in the UK.

1995 Alanis Morissette went to No.1 on the US album chart with *Jagged Little Pill*. The album went on to become the biggest-selling album ever by a female artist, with sales over 27 million.

1999 it was reported that Lauryn Hill was being sued by four musicians who claimed they worked with the singer on her *Miseducation* album. The musicians were seeking unpaid royalties as co-writers and producers.

1999 winners at the Irish Hot Press Awards included: The Corrs for Best Irish band; Andrea Corr won Best female singer; Divine Comedy won Best Irish band; the band's singer, Neil Hannon, won Best male singer and Westlife won Best pop act.

BORN ON THIS DAY

1934 Doc Green – vocalist with The Drifters, who had a 1960 US No.1 & UK No.2 single with 'Save The Last Dance For Me'.

1940 George Bellamy – guitarist with The Tornados, who had a 1962 UK & US No.1 single with 'Telstar'. It was the first major hit from a UK act on the American chart.

1945 Butch Rillera – drummer with Redbone, who had a 1971 UK No.2 & US No.21 single with 'The Witch Queen Of New Orleans'.

1945 Ray Royer – guitarist with Procol Harum, who had a 1967 UK No.1 & US No.5 single with 'A Whiter Shade Of Pale'.

1947 Tony Wilson – bass player with Hot Chocolate, who had a 1975 US No.3 single with 'You Sexy Thing', a 1977 UK No.1 single with 'So You Win Again' plus over 25 other Top 40 hits.

1949 Hamish Stewart – guitarist and singer with Average White Band, who had a 1975 US No.1 & UK No.6 single with 'Pick Up The Pieces'. Now solo.

1951 John Cummings (a.k.a. Johnny Ramone) – guitarist with the Ramones, who had a 1977 UK No.22 single with 'Sheena Is A Punk Rocker'. He died in Los Angeles of prostate cancer on September 15th 2004.

1967 Teddy Riley – singer with Blackstreet, who had a 1996 UK No.9 & US No.1 with 'No Diggity', featuring Dr. Dre.

ON THIS DAY

1964 Roy Orbison was at No.1 on the UK singles chart with 'Oh Pretty Woman', his third UK No.1.

1964 Ringo Starr took his driving test in Enfield, London. He passed first time.

1965 The Who appeared at The City Hall, Perth, Scotland.

1969 appearing at The Coventry Theatre, England was Humble Pie supported by David Bowie.

1977 David Soul was at No.1 on the UK singles chart with 'Silver Lady', his second UK No.1 single.

1980 Bob Marley collapsed on stage during a concert in Pittsburgh. This became the last time he ever appeared on stage performing.

1987 the three members from ZZ Top made advance return bookings for seats on the first passenger flight to the Moon. (The three are still waiting for confirmation of the flight.)

1987 Guns N' Roses played the last night of a five date UK tour when they appeared at London's Hammersmith Odeon.

1988 Def Leppard were at No.1 in the US singles chart with 'Love Bites'.

1988 on their 12th single release U2 scored their first UK No.1 with 'Desire'. The track was taken from the album *Rattle And Hum*.

1992 The US Postal Service issued a set of commemorative stamps to celebrate pop music legends. The stamps included Elvis Presley, Bill Haley, Buddy Holly, Otis Redding, Ritchie Valens, Clyde McPhatter and Dinah Washington.

1997 Robbie Williams appeared at The Royal Court, Liverpool.

2000 All Saints went to No.1 on the UK singles chart with 'Black Coffee'.

2000 Christina Aguilera started a four week run at No.1 on the US singles chart with 'Come On Over Baby'.

2000 Radiohead started a two week run at No.1 on the UK album chart with *Kid A*.

2003 Coldplay singer Chris Martin asked Australian police to drop a charge of malicious damage after allegedly attacking a photographer's car. Martin was charged in July for breaking a windscreen with a rock after being photographed surfing. Martin did not appear in court at Byron Bay, New South Wales, when his lawyer, Megan Cusack, asked for the charge to be dropped.

BORN ON THIS DAY

1940 John Lennon – singer/songwriter and guitarist with The Beatles. The Beatles sold over 20 million singles worldwide from 1962–70 and scored more UK & US No.1 albums than any other group. 1967's *Sgt Pepper's* is the UK's biggest-selling album ever. Lennon was shot dead on December 8th 1980. In 1990 'Imagine' was played simultaneously in 130 countries to commemorate what would have been Lennon's 50th birthday.

1944 John Entwistle – bass player with The Who, who had a 1965 UK No.2 single with 'My Generation' plus over 20 other UK Top 40 hits, 16 US Top 40 singles and the rock opera albums *Tommy* and *Quadrophenia*. Entwistle died in Las Vegas on June 27th 2002.

1948 Jackson Browne, US singer/songwriter who had a 1978 UK No.12 single with 'Stay', a 1978 UK No. 28 album *Running On Empty* and a 1982 US No.7 single with 'Somebody's Baby'.

1970 Polly Harvey (a.k.a. PJ Harvey *below*), singer/songwriter and guitarist who had a 1993 UK No.27 single with '50ft Queenie'.

ON THIS DAY

1958 Eddie Cochran recorded the classic song 'C'mon Everybody', which was a 1959 UK No.6 single and a 1979 hit for the Sex Pistols.

1961 Ray Charles started a two week run at No.1 on the US singles chart with 'Hit The Road Jack', a No.6 hit in the UK.

1965 The Beatles started a four week run at No.1 on the US singles chart

with the Paul McCartney ballad 'Yesterday'. This gave the group their tenth US No.1. The track was never released as a single in the UK.

1971 Rod Stewart was at No.1 on the UK singles chart with 'Maggie May' (it was first released as a B-side). This was the first of six UK No.1s for Stewart.

1973 Elvis Presley and Priscilla divorced after six years of marriage. Priscilla was awarded property worth $725,000 (£426,470) and $4,200 (£2,470) a month support.

1975 Sean Taro Ono Lennon was born, the only child of John Lennon by Yoko Ono. John Lennon retired for five years to become a househusband.

1978 The Human League appeared at Sheffield University, England.

1978 Jacques Brel, French singer/songwriter, died of cancer. Scott Walker, Alex Harvey, Frank Sinatra and Dusty Springfield have all covered his songs.

1984 *Thomas The Tank Engine And Friends*, narrated by Ringo Starr, was shown for the first time on British TV.

1990 The Stone Roses were each fined £3,000 ($5,100) after being found guilty of criminal damage at their former record company's offices.

Odds On!

Scarily enough, it's already that time of year when people are speculating as to who will top the charts come Crimbo '99. The lovely people at Ladbrokes, the betting specialists, believe the gift is strong with them, and kindly divulged who they believed were the hot favourites and rather sad cold pilchards for the final singles chart of the millennium! Surprise, surprise, the Spice Girls are hot favourites again (and they haven't even definitely got a record out!)

The runners and riders are:

Spice Girls	3/1	Robbie	12/1
B*Witched	3/1	Vengaboys	16/1
Steps	7/1	Geri	25/1
Westlife	7/1	Mel C	33/1
Boyzone	7/1	Mel G	40/1
S Club	12/1	Emma	66/1
		Posh and Becks duet	100/1

Please note that the odds are subject to change and you must be at aged 18 or over to place a bet.

1993 Nirvana entered the US album chart at No.1 with *In Utero*.

1999 Ladbrokes released the betting odds for the final UK singles chart of the millennium *(left)*. Spice Girls and B*Witched at 3 to 1, Steps, Westlife & Boyzone at 7 to 1, Robbie Williams 12 to 1 and a Posh Spice and David Beckham duet at 100 to 1!

2001 a man wrecked a $300,000 (£176,470) sports car owned by hip-hop star Missy Elliott after losing control of the vehicle and crashing into a traffic sign and a tree. Joseph Johnson had taken the Lamborghini Diablo away from the garage where it was stored without permission for a late night spin. He was later sentenced to three years in jail and ordered to pay $170,000 (£100,000) for the car and $1,975 (£1,162) for curb repairs at the site of the accident.

2003 Ambrose Kappos, 37, of New York was charged with three counts of stalking and harassing singer Sheryl Crow. He was arrested after being accused of sneaking into New York's Hammerstein Ballroom then trying to get into Crow's limousine when she left the venue. Mr Kappos' brother said he was harmless but "infatuated" with the singer.

BORN ON THIS DAY

1952 Sharon Osbourne, wife of Ozzy and star of MTV's *The Osbournes* TV show. She is also a judge on UK TV show The *X Factor*.

1955 David Lee Roth – vocalist for Van Halen, who had a 1984 US No.1 & UK No.7 single with 'Jump'. As a solo artist he had a 1988 UK No.27 single with 'Just Like Paradise'.

1955 Midge Ure – guitarist and vocalist with Slik, who had a 1976 UK No.1 with 'Forever And Ever', Rich Kids, who had a 1978 UK No.24 with 'Rich Kids', and Ultravox, who had a 1981 UK No.2 with 'Vienna. He co-wrote the Band Aid 1985 UK No.1 'Do They Know It's Christmas?' As a solo artist he had a 1985 UK No.1 with 'If I Was'.

1959 Kirsty MacColl, singer/songwriter who had a 1985 UK No.7 single with 'A New England' and a 1987 UK No.2 single with The Pogues, 'Fairytale Of New York'. She was killed in a boating accident on December 18th 2000.

1961 Martin Kemp – bass player with Spandau Ballet, who had a 1983 UK No.1 single with 'True' plus 16 other UK Top 40 singles. More recently he became an actor, roles have included playing Reggie Kray in *The Krays* and Steve Owen in UK soap *Eastenders*.

ON THIS DAY

1902 the Gibson Mandolin guitar company was formed. Gibson's first electric guitar the ES-150 was produced in 1936, and in 1946 Gibson introduced the P-90 single coil pickup, which was eventually used on the first Les Paul model made in 1952.

1963 appearing at The Gaumont, Wolverhampton, England were Little Richard, The Everly Brothers, Bo Diddley, The Rolling Stones, Micky Most, The Flintstones and Bob Bain.

1970 The Carpenters were at No.2 on the US singles chart with 'We've Only Just Begun'. The song was originally written for a TV commercial advertising a bank.

1970 Black Sabbath were at No.1 on the UK chart with their second album *Paranoid*. The album is regarded as one of the classic heavy metal albums.

1970 Neil Diamond went to No.1 on the US singles chart with 'Cracklin' Rosie', his first No.1 as an artist. Diamond wrote the 1966 No.1 hit 'I'm A Believer' for The Monkees.

1976 the Sex Pistols recorded a version of 'Anarchy In The UK' at Lansdowne Studios, London.

1978 Joe Perry and Steve Tyler from Aerosmith were injured after a cherry bomb was thrown on stage during a gig in Philadelphia. The group performed behind a cyclone fence for the rest of the tour.

1979 Fleetwood Mac were awarded a star on Hollywood's Walk Of Fame.

1980 the funeral of Led Zeppelin's drummer John Bonham took place in Rushnock, Hereford, England.

1983 the first night on Wham!'s "Club Fantastic" tour kicked off in Aberdeen, Scotland.

1987 Whitesnake went to No.1 on the US singles chart with 'Here I Go Again', a No.9 hit in the UK in 1987.

1992 Garth Brooks went to No.1 on the US album chart with *The Chase*. The album spent 35 weeks on the chart and sold over 6 million copies.

1992 R.E.M. scored their second UK No.1 album with *Automatic For The People*, which featured the singles 'Drive', 'Everybody Hurts', 'Man On The Moon' and 'The Sidewinder Sleeps Tonight'.

1999 a charity auction selling Elvis's belongings was held at The Grand Hotel, Las Vegas. His wristwatch sold for $32,500 (£19,117), a cigar box fetched $25,000 (£14,706), an autographed baseball sold for $19,000 (£11,176) and a 1956 Lincoln Continental sold for $250,000 (£147,059).

1999 teenager Christina Aguilera went to No.1 on the UK singles chart with 'Genie In A Bottle'.

2000 Britney Spears made her UK live debut when she played the first of three sold-out nights at London's Wembley Arena.

Britainy Spears

TEEN IDOL STORMS UK

BORN ON THIS DAY

1946 Gary Mallaber – drummer with the Steve Miller Band, who had a 1974 US No.1 & 1990 UK No.1 single with 'The Joker'.

1949 Daryl Hall – singer/songwriter with Hall And Oates, who had a 1982 US No.1 & UK No.6 single with 'Maneater' plus five other US No.1s. As a solo artist Hall had a 1986 UK No.28 single with 'Dreamtime'.

1950 Andrew Woolfolk, sax player with Earth, Wind And Fire, who had a 1975 US No.1 single with 'Shining Star' and a 1981 UK No.3 single with 'Let's Groove'.

1957 Blair Cunningham – drummer with Haircut 100, who had a 1982 UK No.3 single with 'Love Plus One'.

1973 Brendan Brown – guitarist and vocalist with Wheatus, who had a 2001 UK No.2 single with 'Teenage Dirtbag'.

ON THIS DAY

1960 Aretha Franklin made her stage debut at the Village Vanguard, New York.

1962 'Love Me Do' gave The Beatles their first appearance on the UK singles chart.

1965 Gerry Marsden married his former fan club secretary Pauline Behan.

1967 The Bee Gees were at No.1 on the UK singles chart with 'Massachusetts', the group's first of five UK No.1s.

1969 one-hit wonders Jane Birkin and Serge Gainsbourg were at No.1 on the UK singles chart with 'Je T'aime Moi Non', the only French language chart topper ever.

1974 John Denver was at No.1 on the UK singles chart with 'Annie's Song'.

BBC claims Michael barred film

By Mark Benham and Adam Sherwin

GEORGE MICHAEL refused to let the BBC screen footage of his appearance at the NetAid concert because he was not happy with his performance, the corporation claimed last night. The performer's manager, Andy Stephens, denied that the star totally refused permission for the footage to be broadcast.

"We are obviously hoping to be included in any subsequent rebroadcasts."

The BBC claimed that the singer banned a screening on television on Saturday night and on last night's highlights.

Michael was one of a score of high-profile acts who appeared at shows in London,

take to the stage, and at one point Ronan Keating, the Boyzone singer, was sent on to talk to the crowd. Michael finally joined about 50 dancers and gospel singers to sing his hit song, *Fast Love*, but the sound was noticeably muffled and the audience's enthusiasm appeared to wane.

Michael: "technical difficulties" at NetAid

1975 Neil Sedaka started a three week run at No.1 on the US singles chart with 'Bad Blood', his third No.1. The song featured Elton John on backing vocals.

1976 Dutch group Pussycat was at No.1 on the UK singles chart with 'Mississippi'.

1978 appearing at The Pavilion, Hemel Hempstead were Siouxsie And The Banshees supported by Spizz Oil and The Human League.

1979 Whitesnake kicked off a 19 date UK tour at the Portsmouth Guildhall.

1986 Janet Jackson started a two week run at No.1 on the US singles chart with 'When I Think Of You', her first US No.1 and a No.10 hit in the UK.

1986 Madonna was at No.1 on the UK singles chart with 'True Blue', her third UK No.1.

1988 Ringo Starr and his wife Barbara started treatment for alcohol abuse in Tucson, Arizona.

1997 Elton John went to No.1 on the US singles chart with his worldwide charity hit 'Candle In The Wind 1997'. It was his eighth US No.1 single.

1997 The Verve started a four week run at No.1 on the UK album chart with *Urban Hymns*.

1999 Deborah Rowe, the wife of Michael Jackson, filed for divorce after three years of marriage. The couple met when Rowe was working as a nurse at his plastic surgeon's office.

1999 George Michael refused to let BBC TV screen footage of his appearance at the Netaid concert because he was not happy with his performance.

1999 Motley Crue drummer Tommy Lee was released on $5,000 (£2,941) bail after facing charges relating to a riot at a gig in North Carolina in 1997. Lee allegedly incited the crowd to attack a guard and had also poured a drink over his head.

2003 the studio session for Elvis Presley's debut single 'That's All Right' was voted the most pivotal moment in rock history by *Mojo* magazine readers. Bob Dylan's switch from acoustic to electric guitars in 1965 came second, and The Clash's debut single 'White Riot' in 1977 was voted third.

Elvis examines his pivotal moment.

BORN ON THIS DAY

1935 Luciano Pavarotti, Italian singer who had a 1990 UK No.2 single with 'Nessun Dorma' and a 1990 UK No.1 album with *The Essential Pavarotti*, which spent 72 weeks on the UK chart.

1935 Sam Moore – singer with Sam & Dave, who had a 1964 UK No.24 & 1967 US No.2 single with 'Soul Man'.

1942 Melvin Franklin – singer with The Temptations, who had a 1971 US No.1 & UK No.8 single with 'Just My Imagination' and the reissued 'My Girl' was a UK No.2 in 1992. Franklin died on February 23rd 1995.

1948 Rick Parfitt – vocalist and guitarist with Status Quo, who had a 1977 UK No.3 single with 'Rockin' All Over The World' plus over 50 other UK Top 75 singles.

1966 Brian Kennedy, Irish singer/songwriter who has worked with the Van Morrison Band. As a solo artist Kennedy had a 1996 UK No.27 single with 'Life, Love and Happiness'.

1969 Martie Seidel – singer with Dixie Chicks, who had a 1999 UK No.26 single with 'There's Your Trouble' and a 1999 US No.1 album with *Wide Open Space*.

ON THIS DAY

1957 during an Australian tour Little Richard publicly renounced rock 'n' roll and embraced God, telling a story of dreaming of his own damnation after praying to God when one of the engines on a plane he was on caught fire.

1968 Big Brother And The Holding Company went to No.1 on the US album chart with their album *Cheap Thrills*.

1969 a DJ on Detroits WKNR radio station received a phone call that indicated if you play The Beatles' 'Strawberry Fields Forever' backwards you can hear John Lennon say the words "I buried Paul". This added to the worldwide rumour that Paul McCartney was dead.

1971 Gene Vincent died from a perforated ulcer, aged 36. He had had a 1956 US No.7 & UK No.16 single with 'Be-Bop-A-Lula'.

1974 Olivia Newton-John went to No.1 on the US album chart with *If You Love Me, Let Me Know*.

1974 the Bay City Rollers went to No.1 on the UK album chart with their debut album *Rollin*.

1975 Rod Stewart And The Faces made their final live appearance when they played at Nassau Coliseum, Long Island.

World premiere of *How I Won the War* on this day in 1967.

1978 while living at the Chelsea Hotel in New York Sid Vicious called the police to say that someone had stabbed his girlfriend Nancy Spungen. He was arrested and charged with murder and placed in the detox unit of a New York prison.

1982 appearing at Shea Stadium, New York was The Who supported by The Clash.

1985 Jennifer Rush was at No.1 on the UK singles chart with 'The Power Of Love'. The song stayed at No.1 for five weeks and became the biggest-selling single of the year.

1991 Simply Reds' fourth album *Stars* went to No.1 on the UK chart for the first of five times. It featured the singles 'Thrill Me', 'For Your Babies' and the title track 'Stars'.

1992 Tupac Shakur was released from prison pending an appeal for sexual assault on $1.4 million (£0.8 million) bail.

1997 singer/songwriter John Denver was killed when the light aircraft he was piloting crashed into Monterey Bay, California. He was 53.

1997 the Backstreet Boys were forced to cancel a show in Madrid after over 7,000 fans arrived for the 5,000 capacity show. More than 300 young girls had to be treated after fainting in the heat.

1999 Adrian Young, drummer with No Doubt, proposed to his girlfriend during a gig in San Francisco. Young came on to the stage before the band's encore and got down on bended knee with a ring. His girlfriend Nina accepted.

1999 six stamps honouring The Bee Gees were issued by the island of their birth, The Isle Of Man. Their mother had run a local post office on the island.

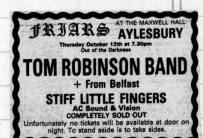

BORN ON THIS DAY

1935 Barry McGuire, US singer who had a 1965 US No.1 & UK No.3 single with 'Eve Of Destruction'.

1938 Marv Johnson, US singer, who had a 1960 US No.9 single with 'I Love The Way You Love' and a 1969 UK No.10 single with 'I'll Pick A Rose For My Rose'. Johnson died on May 16th 1993.

1946 Richard Carpenter – keyboardist and vocalist with The Carpenters, who had a 1973 UK No.2 single with 'Yesterday Once More' and a 1970 US No.1 & UK No.6 single with 'Close To You'.

1947 Chris De Burgh, singer/songwriter who had a 1986 UK No.1 single with 'The Lady In Red'.

1953 Tito Jackson – singer with The Jackson Five, who had a 1970 US No.1 & UK No.2 single with 'I Want You Back' and, as The Jacksons, a 1977 UK No.1 single with 'Show You The Way To Go'.

ON THIS DAY

1955 Buddy & Bob (Buddy Holly) opened for Elvis Presley at the "Big D Jamboree", held at Lubbock's Cotton Club, Texas. Nashville talent scout Eddie Crandall was in audience and arranged for Holly to audition and record demos for the Decca US label.

1961 a charity evening was held to raise funds for St. John's ambulance brigade at Liverpool's Albany Cinema with Ken Dodd and The Beatles.

1965 Jimi Hendrix signed his first recording contract.

He received $1 (58p) and a 1% royalty on all of his recordings.

1966 appearing at the launch of London's Roundhouse venue were Pink Floyd (who were paid £15/$25.50) and Soft Machine. Legend has it that L.S.D.-coated sugarcubes were given away as prizes.

1966 The Four Tops started a two week run at No.1 on the US singles chart with 'Reach Out And I'll Be There'. It was the group's second US No.1 and their first No.1 in the UK.

1968 Led Zeppelin made their live debut when they appeared at Surrey University, England.

1972 Lieutenant Pigeon was at No.1 on the UK singles chart with 'Mouldy Old Dough'. Keyboard player Rob Woodward had his mum play piano on the single, making them the only mother and son act to score a UK No.1.

1973 Keith Richards was found guilty of trafficking cannabis by a Nice court and was given a one year suspended sentence and a 5,000 franc (£520.60) fine. He was also banned from entering France for two years.

1976 the Sex Pistols signed to EMI records for £40,000 ($68,000). The contract was terminated three months later with the label stopping

Menswear, currently residing in the 'where are they now?' file.

Rob Woodward dreams of the kind of success Menswear would have.

production of the 'Anarchy In The UK' single and deleting it from its catalogue. EMI later issued a statement saying it felt unable to promote The Sex Pistols' records in view of the adverse publicity generated over the last few months.

1977 Debby Boone started a ten week run at No.1 on the US singles chart with 'You Light Up My Life', the longest stay at the top since Guy Mitchell's 'Singing The Blues'. The song made No.48 in the UK.

1979 Abba played their first concert in North America when they appeared in Vancouver.

1988 Bon Jovi started a four week run at No.1 on the US album chart with *New Jersey*.

1988 UB40 went to No.1 on the US singles chart with their version of the Neil Diamond song 'Red Red Wine'. It was also a No.1 hit in the UK.

1994 R.E.M. entered the US album chart at No.1 with *Monster*.

2000 guitarist, singer and producer Dave Edmunds had a triple heart bypass operation. The 56-year-old Welsh rocker had the operation at LA's Cedars-Sinai Hospital.

BORN ON THIS DAY

1923 Bert Kaempfert, songwriter and producer who had a 1961 US No.1 single with 'Wonderland By Night'. Presley and Sinatra covered his songs, and he also produced the first recorded Beatles session. Kaempfert died on June 21st 1980.

1937 Emile Ford, US singer who had a 1959 UK No.1 single with The Checkmates, 'What Do You Want To Make Those Eyes At Me For?'

1938 Nico – singer with Velvet Underground, who had a 1968 song with 'White Light, White Heat'. She died on July 18th 1988.

1943 Fred Turner – bass player with Bachman Turner Overdrive, who had a 1974 US No.1 & UK No.2 single with 'You Ain't Seen Nothing Yet'.

1947 Bob Weir – guitarist with the Grateful Dead, who had a 1970 album with *Workingman's Dead*.

1959 Gary Kemp – guitarist and keyboardist with Spandau Ballet, who had a 1983 UK No.1 single 'True' plus 16 other UK Top 40 singles.

1962 Michael Balzary (a.k.a. Flea) – guitarist with Red Hot Chili Peppers, who had a 1994 UK No.9 single with 'Give It Away', a 1992 UK No.26 single with 'Under The Bridge' and a 2002 UK No.1 album with *By The Way*.

1969 Wendy Wilson – singer with Wilson Phillips, who had a 1990 US No.1 & UK No.6 single with 'Hold On'. Wendy is the daughter of Beach Boy Brian Wilson.

1977 John Mayer, US singer/ songwriter who was a 2003 Grammy award winner for 'Our Body Is A Wonderland' and had the 2004 US No.2 single 'Daughters'.

ON THIS DAY

1951 Little Richard made his first recordings for RCA in Atlanta.

1962 the first night of a two month Motown Records package tour started in Washington D.C., featuring Marvin Gaye, The Supremes, Mary Wells, The Miracles and 12-year-old Stevie Wonder.

1963 The Beatles recorded a five song session at London's Playhouse Theatre for the BBC Light programme's *Easy Beat*.

1966 the newly formed Jimi Hendrix Experience appeared at The Grand Duchy in Luxembourg.

1969 the founder of the Chess record label Leonard Chess died of a heart attack, aged 52.

1969 Bobbie Gentry was at No.1 on the UK singles chart with 'I'll Never Fall In Love Again', the singer's only UK No.1.

1975 The Who appeared at The Apollo in Glasgow during their 11 date "Back To Basics" UK tour.

1976 one-hit wonders Rick Dees And His Cast Of Idiots went to No.1 on the US singles chart with 'Disco Duck, (part one)'. Dees was a US TV and radio presenter. The song was a No.6 hit in the UK.

1976 Stevie Wonder's *Songs In The Key Of Life* went to No.1 on the US album chart, his third US No.1.

Whitney Houston.

1986 Keith Richards, Eric Clapton and Robert Cray joined other artists on stage in St. Louis for Chuck Berry's 60th birthday concert. The event was featured in the film *Hail Hail! Rock & Roll*.

1987 just back from an eight day European tour, Guns N' Roses played at The Sundance, Bay Shore, New York. It was the first of 40 dates they played before the end of the year.

1987 founder of Stiff Records Dave Robinson resigned as managing director after 11 years with the company.

1988 Whitney Houston had her third UK No.1 single with 'One Moment In Time'.

1992 Bob Dylan's 30th Anniversary Tribute took place at New York's Madison Square Garden. Guests included Neil Young, Eric Clapton, Tom Petty, George Harrison and Roger McGuinn.

1993 Aretha Franklin sang the US national anthem at a World Series baseball game in Toronto.

1999 Santana started a 12 week run at No.1 on the US singles chart with 'Smooth'.

2001 two security guards were sacked after refusing to allow Bob Dylan into his own concert. Dylan, who had demanded that security on his "Love And Theft" tour should be tighter than ever, didn't have a pass when he arrived backstage.

N° 6321

M.A.M. presents
JOE JACKSON BAND
on Thursday, 16th October '80
GLASGOW TIFFANYS
Ticket value £2.50 / £2.75

BORN ON THIS DAY

1941 Alan Howard – bass player with The Tremeloes, who had a 1967 UK No.1 & US No.11 single with 'Silence Is Golden'.

1946 Jim Tucker – guitarist with The Turtles, who had a 1967 US No.1 single with 'Happy Together' and a 1967 UK No.4 single with 'She'd Rather Be With Me'.

1968 Ziggy Marley – singer/songwriter with Ziggy Marley & The Melody Makers, who had a 1988 UK No.22 single with 'Tomorrow People'. His father Bob had his last haircut the year Ziggy was born.

1972 Marshall Bruce Mathers III (a.k.a. Eminem), who had a 2000 worldwide No.1 album with *The Marshall Mathers LP*.

1972 Wyclef Jean – rapper and guitarist with the Fugees, who had a 1996 UK No.1 single with 'Killing Me Softly'.

1977 Chris Kirkpatrick – singer with *NSYNC, who had a 2000 US No.1 single with 'It's Gonna Be Me' and a 1999 UK No.5 single with 'I Want You Back'.

ON THIS DAY

1953 Frankie Laine was at No.1 on the UK singles chart with 'Hey Joe!'. Laine spent a total of 28 weeks at No.1 with three different releases during 1953.

1960 The Drifters started a three week run at No.1 on the US singles chart with 'Save The Last Dance For Me'. It was a No.2 in the UK.

1962 The Beatles made their first TV appearance on Granada TV's *People And Places*, singing 'Love Me Do'.

1964 Manfred Mann started a two week run at No.1 on the US singles chart with 'Do Wah Diddy Diddy', possibly the first No.1 with a nonsense title. Also a No.1 in the UK, the song was first released by the US group The Exciters.

1969 Paul Kantner of Jefferson Airplane was busted for marijuana possession in Honolulu and fined $350 (£205).

1969 Led Zeppelin kicked off their third US tour at New York's Carnegie Hall.

1970 The Jackson Five started a five week run at No.1 on the US singles chart with 'I'll Be There'. The group's fourth No.1 of 1970, it made No.4 in the UK. Motown Records claimed the group had sold over ten million records during the year.

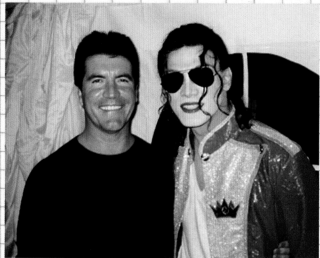

1981 Christopher Cross started a three week run at No.1 on the US singles chart with 'Arthur's Theme (Best That You Can Do)', his second US No.1 and a No.7 hit in the UK.

1981 The Rolling Stones played the first of two nights at Candlestick Park, San Francisco to 146,000 fans – the largest crowd ever for an open air show in San Francisco.

1987 Bruce Springsteen went to No.1 on the UK album chart with *Tunnel Of Love*, his second album release.

1987 The Bee Gees became the only band to have a UK No.1 in each of the three decades (60s, 70s and 80s), when 'You Win Again' went to No.1 on the UK singles chart.

1991 singer Sandie Shaw was arrested for failing to give a breath test outside her Harley Street flat in London and was fined £100 ($170).

1995 in an interview with the *Observer* magazine Noel Gallagher from Oasis said he wished Damon Albarn and Alex Cox of Blur would "die from AIDs". He later retracted his statement.

1995 Sting's former accountant Keith Moore was sentenced to six years in jail after being found guilty of embezzling £6 million ($10 million) from the singer's 108 bank accounts.

1999 it was reported that Michael Jackson had played a secret gig at a martial arts exhibition in Barnstaple, England. The man who had arrived in the white stretch limo was in fact Navi, a Londoner who claims to be the world's No.1 Jacko impersonator *(left with Simon Cowell)*.

2000 a flat in Montagu Square, London, which was owned during the 60s by Ringo Starr, went on the market for £575,000 ($977,500). The two bedrooms, two storey property was also home for Jimi Hendrix, John and Yoko and Paul McCartney during the 60s.

2004 Michael Jackson's long-time lawyer, Steve Cochran, left the star's defence team. Jackson, who was fighting child abuse charges, said in a statement that the lawyer had taken a "temporary leave of absence" but would still "collaborate".

BORN ON THIS DAY

1926 Chuck Berry – guitarist and singer/songwriter who had a 1963 UK No.6 single with 'Let It Rock' and a 1972 UK & US No.1 single with 'My Ding-a-Ling'. He was a major influence on The Beatles and The Rolling Stones. 'Johnny B. Goode' was one of the examples of Earth music sent out to space on Voyager 1 in 1977.

1938 Ronnie Bright – singer with The Coasters, who had a 1958 US No.1 single with 'Yakety Yak' and a 1959 US No.2 & UK No.6 single with 'Charlie Brown'.

1943 Russ Giguere – guitarist and vocalist with The Association, who had a 1967 US No.1 single with 'Windy'.

1947 Gary Puckett, US singer who had a 1968 UK No.1 & UK No.2 single with Union Gap, 'Young Girl'.

1949 Gary Richrath – guitarist with REO Speedwagon, who had a 1981 US No.1 & UK No.7 single with 'Keep On Loving You'.

1949 Joe Egan – guitarist, keyboardist and vocalist with Stealers Wheel, who had a 1973 UK No.8 single with 'Stuck In The Middle With You'.

1952 Keith Knudson – drummer with The Doobie Brothers, who had a 1979 US No.1 single with 'What A Fool Believes' and a 1993 UK No.7 single with 'Long Train Runnin'. Knudson died of pneumonia on February 8th 2005.

ON THIS DAY

1957 Paul McCartney made his live debut with the Quarry Men at New Clubmoor Hall Conservative Club, Liverpool.

1964 The Animals kicked off their first headlining UK tour at the ABC in Manchester with Carl Perkins, Gene Vincent and The Nashville Teens supporting.

1966 the Jimi Hendrix Experience played at the Paris Olympia, supporting French pop star Johnny Hallyday.

1968 John and Yoko were taken to Paddington Green police station charged with obstruction when cannabis was discovered at the apartment they were staying in. Lennon pleaded guilty the following month and was fined £150 ($255).

1968 The Jackson Five made their national TV debut on ABC-TV's *Hollywood Palace*.

1969 The Temptations scored their second US No.1 single with 'Can't Get Next To You'. It made No.13 in the UK.

1976 the Buzzcocks made their first recordings at Revolution Studios, Cheadle, Manchester.

1977 appearing on the UK music show *The Old Grey Whistle Test* were John Otway and Wild Willy Barrett. They performed their only hit 'Cor Babe That's Really Free'. During a flying leap Otway fell over Barrett's amp, pulling out the guitar lead. Five minutes of chaos followed on live TV.

1979 Buggles were at No.1 on the UK singles chart with 'Video Killed The Radio Star'.

1981 Dave Stewart and Barbara Gaskin were at No.1 on the UK singles chart with their version of the 1963 Lesley Gore hit 'It's My Party'.

1986 former *Eastenders* TV actor Nick Berry was at No.1 in the UK singles chart with 'Every Loser Wins'. Berry had played barman Simon Wickes in the TV show. The song also gave BBC Records its first UK No.1 single.

1987 ITV's *The South Bank Show* showed a documentary on The Smiths, filmed during the recording of the *Strangeways* album.

1989 during the first of a four night run at The Los Angeles Coliseum, Guns N' Roses frontman Axl Rose announced to the crowd that he was quitting the band. He didn't in fact and, in 2005, is the only surviving member.

1998 Jay-Z was at No.1 on the US album chart with *Vol 2...Hard Knock Life*.

2000 Internet firm DNA Visual Business Solutions filed a lawsuit against Britney Spears and her marketing company for failing to pay for the redesign of her website britneyspears.com.

2000 singer Julie London died after suffering a stroke. She had had a 1956 US No.9 & UK No.22 single with 'Cry Me A River'.

19th October

BORN ON THIS DAY

1944 George McCrae, singer who had a 1974 UK & US No.1 single with 'Rock Your Baby'.

1944 Peter Tosh – guitarist and vocalist with The Wailers, who had a 1978 UK No.43 single with 'You Gotta Walk, Don't Look Back'. He left the band in 1974. Tosh was murdered by burglars at his home on September 11th 1987.

1945 Jeannie C. Riley, singer who had a 1968 US No.1 & UK No.12 with 'Harper Valley PTA'. Jeannie won a Grammy for the Best female country singer of 68.

1946 Keith Reid – lyricist for Procol Harum, who had a 1967 UK No.1 & US No.5 single with 'A Whiter Shade Of Pale'.

1947 Wilbert Hart – vocalist with The Delfonics, who had a 1968 US No.4 & 1971 UK No.19 single with 'La-La Means I Love You'.

1957 Karl Wallinger – keyboardist with The Waterboys, who had a 1985 album *This Is The Sea*. Wallinger quit the band in 1986. He went on to be singer and guitarist with World Party, who had a 1993 UK No.19 single with 'Is It Like Today?' The Wallinger-penned song 'She's The One' gave Robbie Williams a UK No.1 hit in 1999.

1960 Jennifer Hollidy, US singer who had a 1982 US No.22 & UK No.32 single with 'And I Am Telling You I'm Not Going'.

1972 Samuel Michel (a.k.a. Pras) – rapper with the Fugees, who had a 1996 UK No.1 single with 'Killing Me Softly'.

ON THIS DAY

1961 Helen Shapiro was at No.1 on the UK singles chart with 'Walking Back To Happiness'. It was the singer's second and final UK No.1.

1963 The Beatles appeared at The Pavilion Gardens, Buxton, England.

Charles is delighted to meet members of Madness, last-minute replacements for The Three Degrees!

1968 Cream played the second of two nights at The Los Angeles Forum.

1974 Bachman Turner Overdrive went to No.1 on the US album chart with *Not Fragile*.

1974 Billy Preston went to No.1 on the US singles chart with 'Nothing From Nothing', the singer's second and last chart topper.

1974 Rod Stewart went to No.1 on the UK album chart with *Smiler*, his fourth UK No.1 album.

1979 a 2-Tone Records 40 date tour started in Brighton with ska bands The Selecter, The Specials and Madness.

1980 AC/DC kicked off a 20 date UK tour at Bristol Colston Hall. It was the band's first gigs since the death of singer Bon Scott.

1981 The Clash appeared at The Lyceum Ballroom, London.

1985 A-Ha went to No.1 on the US singles chart with 'Take On Me', making them the first Norwegian group to score a US No.1.

1989 Alan Murphy, guitarist with Level 42, died of pneumonia related to AIDs. He had also worked with Kate Bush, Go West and Mike And The Mechanics.

1991 Oasis played The Boardwalk, Manchester. It was the band's first gig with guitarist Noel Gallagher in the band.

1994 during a Pink Floyd show at London's Earl's Court a section of seating collapsed. Over 1,000 fans escaped serious injuries.

1995 Oasis played live on the *David Letterman Show* in the US.

2000 a judge ruled that Robbie Williams had substantially copied lyrics on his song 'Jesus Was A Camper Van' from the 1961 Woody Guthrie song 'I Am The Way' and also used parts of a parody by Loudon Wainwright III. EMI Records had offered 25% royalties but the publishers Ludlow Music were demanding 50%.

BORN ON THIS DAY

1890 Jelly Roll Morton, US pianist, arranger, bandleader and the first great jazz composer. He died on July 10th 1941.

1939 Jay Siegel – singer with The Tokens, who had a 1961 US No.1 & UK No.11 single with 'The Lion Sleeps Tonight'.

1951 Alan Greenwood – keyboardist for Foreigner, who had a 1985 UK & US No.1 single with 'I Want To Know What Love Is'.

1953 Tom Petty – guitarist and vocalist with Tom Petty & The Heartbreakers, who had a 1989 UK No.28 single with 'I Won't Back Down', and the Traveling Wilburys, who had a 1988 UK No.21 single with 'Handle With Care'.

1958 Mark King – bass player and vocalist with Level 42, who had a 1986 UK No.3 & US No.12 single with 'Lessons In Love' plus 19 other UK Top 40 singles.

1971 Snoop Doggy Dogg (a.k.a. Calvin Broadus), rapper who had a 1993 US No.1 album *Doggy Style* and a 1996 UK No.12 single with 'Snoop's Upside Your Head'.

ON THIS DAY

1955 appearing at Brooklyn High School auditorium, Cleveland was Elvis Presley with Bill Haley And His Comets.

1962 Bobby "Boris" Pickett And The Crypt Kickers started a two week run at No.1 on the US singles chart with 'Monster Mash'. It was a No.3 hit in the UK 11 years later. The song had been banned by the BBC as it was deemed offensive.

1967 Davy Jones of The Monkees opened his own "Zilch" boutique in Greenwich Village, New York.

1969 The Who played the first of six nights at New York's Fillmore East, performing a two hour show featuring the songs from *Tommy*.

1971 The Velvet Underground played at Birmingham University.

1973 The Rolling Stones went to No.1 on the US singles chart with 'Angie', the group's seventh US chart topper. It made No.5 in the UK.

1976 Led Zeppelin's film *The Song Remains The Same* premiered in New York, raising $25,000 (£14,706) for the Save The Children Fund.

1977 Siouxsie Sioux and Kenny Morris from The Banshees were arrested and held overnight at Holloway police station, London for causing an obstruction after a London gig. They were both fined £20 ($34).

1977 Ronnie Van Zant, Steve Gaines and Cassie Gaines of Lynyrd Skynyrd were all killed along with manager Dean Kilpatrick when their rented plane ran out of fuel and crashed into a swamp in Gillsburg, Missouri. The band was due to play at Louisiana University that evening. The other members from the band were all seriously injured.

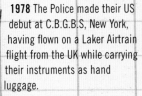

The Banshees refuse to be tainted by their brush with the law.

1978 The Police made their US debut at C.B.G.B.S, New York, having flown on a Laker Airtrain flight from the UK while carrying their instruments as hand luggage.

1979 The Eagles started a nine week run at No.1 on the US album chart with *The Long Run*, the band's fourth US No.1.

1983 US country singer/songwriter Merle Travis died, aged 65. He had invented the first solid body electric guitar. He also wrote 'Sixteen Tons', which was a 1955 US No.1 for Ernie Ford.

1990 The Charlatans went to No.1 on the UK album chart with their debut LP *Some Friendly*.

1995 Alanis Morissette appeared at The Garage, Glasgow. The date was part of her first UK tour.

2002 Nelly started a two week run at No.1 on the UK singles chart with 'Dilemma'.

2003 a jury found Girls Aloud singer Cheryl Tweedy guilty of assaulting a nightclub worker. The singer was sentenced to complete 120 hours of unpaid community service and was ordered to pay her victim £500 ($850) compensation plus £3,000 ($5,100) of prosecution costs.

BORN ON THIS DAY

1940 Manfred Mann (a.k.a. Michael Lubowitz) — keyboardist with Manfred Mann, who had a 1964 UK & US No.1 single 'Do Wah Diddy Diddy'.

1941 Steve Cropper — guitarist with Booker T & The MGs, who had a 1962 US No.3 single with 'Green Onions' and a 1969 UK No.4 single with 'Time Is Tight'.

1942 Elvin Bishop, singer/songwriter and guitarist who had a 1976 US No.3 & UK No.34 single with 'Fooled Around And Fell In Love'. He was also a member of the Paul Butterfield Blues Band (1965–68).

1953 Charlotte Caffey — guitarist with The Go-Go's, who had a 1982 US No.2 single with 'We Got The Beat' and a 1982 UK No.47 single with 'Our Lips Our Sealed'.

1954 Eric Faulkner — guitarist with the Bay City Rollers, who had a 1975 UK No.1 single with 'Bye Bye Baby', 11 other UK Top 20 singles and a 1976 US No.1 single with 'Saturday Night'.

1957 Julian Cope — guitarist and vocalist with Teardrop Explodes, who had a 1981 UK No.6 single with 'Reward'. As a solo artist he had a 1986 UK No.19 single with 'World Shut Your Mouth'.

1957 Steve Lukather — guitarist with Toto, who had a 1983 US No.1 & UK No.3 single with 'Africa'.

1971 Tony Mortimer — singer with East 17, who had a 1994 UK No.1 single with 'Stay Another Day' plus over 15 other UK Top 40 singles.

ON THIS DAY

1958 Buddy Holly's last recording session took place in New York. The songs recorded included 'It Doesn't Matter Anymore', which went on to be a worldwide No.1.

1965 Bill Black, Elvis Presley's bass player from 1954–7, died four months after receiving surgery to remove a brain tumour. He was 39.

1967 Scottish singer Lulu started a five week run at No.1 on the US singles chart with the theme from the film *To Sir With Love*.

1972 Chuck Berry started a two week run at No.1 on the US singles chart with 'My Ding-A-Ling', his first and only US and UK No.1, 17 years after his first chart hit.

1972 Curtis Mayfield started a four week run at No.1 on the US album chart with the soundtrack to *Superfly*.

1978 The Clash fired their manager Bernie Rhodes, saying that the band and record company "find him hard to deal with".

Melody Maker journalist Caroline Coon took his place.

1992 George Michael took Sony Records to court in a fight over his contract with the company. He lost the case in 1994.

1995 singer with Green Day, Billie Joe was arrested and fined $141 (£83) after mooning at the audience during a gig in Milwaukee.

1997 Elton John's 'Candle In The Wind 97' was declared by the *Guinness Book Of Records* to have become the biggest-selling single record of all time, with 31.8 million sales in less than 40 days and raising more than £20 million ($34 million) for charity.

2001 concerts at Madison Square Garden and the RFK stadium in Washington were expected to raise over $300 million (£176 million) for the victims of the September 11th attacks. Stars who appeared included Michael Jackson, Tom Petty, Aerosmith, *NSYNC, P Diddy and James Brown.

2003 US singer/songwriter Elliot Smith died from stab wounds. His song 'Miss Misery' saw him nominated for an Academy Award in 1997.

2003 Carling Live presents AC/DC at the Carling Apollo, Hammersmith, England.

2004 Jessica Simpson was being sued over her cosmetic line called "Dessert". Cosmojet, a California-based cosmetics company, filed the suit in Los Angeles County Superior Court, claiming Simpson, her cosmetic company Dessert Beauty Inc. and cosmetic retailing giant Sephora owed them nearly $200,000 ($117,647) for products they said they manufactured and sold to Dessert. Cosmojet claimed it sold nearly $1 million (£0.6 million) in products to Simpson and her company, and to date had only received close to $800,000 (£470,588) in payment.

BORN ON THIS DAY

1939 Ray Jones — bass player for Billy J. Kramer, who had a 1964 UK No.1 and US No.7 single with 'Little Children'. Jones died on January 20th 2000.

1943 Bobby Fuller — singer/songwriter with The Bobby Fuller Four, who had a 1966 US No.9 single with 'I Fought The Law' — written by Sonny Curtis of Buddy Holly's Crickets. Fuller died on July 18th 1966, mysteriously from gasoline asphyxiation while parked outside his apartment.

1945 Leslie West — guitarist with Mountain, who had a 1970 US No.21 single with 'Mississippi Queen', and West Bruce & Laing.

1946 Eddie Brigati — vocalist with The Young Rascals, who had a 1967 US No.1 & UK No.8 single with 'Groovin'.

1968 Shaggy, singer who had a 1993 UK No.1 single with 'Oh Carolina', a 2001 UK & US No.1 single with 'It Wasn't Me' and a 2001 UK & US No.1 album with *Hotshot*.

1968 Shelby Lynne, US singer/songwriter who had a 1999 album with *I Am Shelby Lynne*. Lynne was a 2001 Grammy Award winner for Best newcomer.

1985 Zachary Walker Hanson — drummer and singer with Hanson, who had a 1997 UK & US No.1 single with 'MMMbop'.

ON THIS DAY

1964 Sandie Shaw had her first UK No.1 single with '(There's) Always Some Thing There To Remind Me'.

1966 The Supremes scored their first US No.1 album with *The Supremes A Go Go*.

1969 Tommy Edwards died, aged 47. He had had the 1958 US & UK No.1 single with 'It's All In The Game'.

1973 Phonogram Records announced price increases on their albums; standard albums went up to £2.18 ($3.71) from £2 ($3.40), and Delux albums went from £2.29 ($3.89) to £2.38 ($4).

1979 The Pretenders started a run of four consecutive Monday nights at the Marquee Club in London.

1983 Culture Club went to No.1 on the UK album chart with their second release *Colour By Numbers*.

A NEMS PRESENTATION

"SUNDAYS AT THE SAVILLE"

TWO PERFORMANCES : 6.00 p.m. and 8.30 p.m.
THIS WEEK END (SUNDAY, OCTOBER 22)

THE WHO

Presenting the act which staggered fans of Herman's Hermits throughout the U.S. of A.!

VANILLA FUDGE

Performing their entire act as withdrawn from nationwide U.K. concert tour!

SUNDAY, OCTOBER 29
First appearance following fabulous U.S. tour

CREAM

... AND LOOKING AHEAD (SUNDAY, NOVEMBER 19)
RESERVE YOUR SEATS IMMEDIATELY to hear the "MASSACHUSETTS" CHART TOPPERS

THE BEE GEES

BOOK : TEM 4011

1985 R.E.M. appeared at The Octagon Centre, Sheffield during a nine date UK tour.

1986 Jane Dornacker was killed in a helicopter crash while doing a live traffic report for WNBC radio in New York.

Listeners heard the terrified voice of Dornacker screaming "Hit the water, hit the water" as the helicopter from which she and pilot Bill Pate were reporting fell from the sky and crashed into the Hudson River. Dornacker had been a member of The Tubes and Leila And The Snakes.

1988 Phil Collins started a two week run at No.1 on the US singles chart with 'Groovy Kind Of Love', his sixth US No.1.

1988 U2 scored their fourth UK No.1 album with the film soundtrack *Rattle And Hum*, which featured their first UK No.1 single 'Desire'.

1989 singer/songwriter Ewan MacColl died, aged 74. He wrote 'Dirty Old Town' and 'The First Time Ever I Saw Your Face'.

1993 Oasis signed a six album deal with Creation Records for a £40,000 ($68,000) advance.

1995 Mariah Carey was at No.1 on the US album chart with *Daydream*.

1999 it was reported that Sinead O'Connor was attempting to buy the church where she was ordained into the Catholic sisterhood. The church was on the market for £70,000 ($119,000).

2000 George Michael paid £1.45 million ($2.46 million) for the Steinway piano on which John Lennon wrote 'Imagine'. George said, "I know that when my fingers touch the keys of that Steinway, I will feel truly blessed. And parting with my money has never been much of a problem. Just ask my accountant." The singer outbid Robbie Williams and The Oasis brothers.

HASTINGS PIER
SUNDAY, 22 OCTOBER
7.30 — 11.00 p.m.
JIMI HENDRIX EXPERIENCE
TICKETS (IN ADVANCE) 12/6
(AT DOOR ON NIGHT) 15/-

BORN ON THIS DAY

1943 Greg Ridley – bass player for Spooky Tooth and Humble Pie, who had a 1969 UK No.4 single with 'Natural Born Bugie'. Ridley died of pneumonia-related complications in Javea, Spain on November 19th 2003.

1949 Michael Burston – guitarist with Motorhead, who had a 1980 UK No.15 single with 'Ace Of Spades'.

1953 Pauline Black – vocalist with Selecter, who had a 1979 UK No.8 single with 'On My Radio'.

1956 Dwight Yoakam, Grammy Award-winning US country singer/songwriter and guitarist who released the 1986 album 'Guitars and Cadilacs'. He also appeared in the 2002 film *Panic Room* with Jodie Foster.

1957 Kelly Marie, singer who had a 1980 UK No.1 single with 'Feels Like I'm In Love', which was written by Ray Dorset of Mungo Jerry.

ON THIS DAY

1961 Dion started a two week run at No.1 on the US singles chart with 'Runaround Sue', a No.11 hit in the UK.

1962 12-year-old Little Stevie Wonder recorded 'Thank You For Loving Me All The Way', which was his first single for Motown Records.

1964 all four members of US band Buddy And The Kings were killed when they hired a Cesna Skyhawk to take them to a gig in Harris County. Piloted by the band's drummer, Bill Daniles, the plane crashed nose first, killing all on board. Singer with the group Harold Box had replaced Buddy Holly in The Crickets after his death in a plane crash. He sang on 'Peggy Sue Got Married'.

1966 at De Lane Lea Studios in London the Jimi Hendrix Experience recorded their first single 'Hey Joe'.

1976 The Clash appeared at The ICA, London and The Jam played an afternoon show in Soho Market, London.

MONDAY, OCT 23rd
THE MOVE
●LIVE!

on stage at
SILVER BLADES ICE RINK
STREATHAM HIGH ROAD, LONDON, S.W.16
during the normal evening session 7.30–11.00 p.m.
ADMISSION 7/6

1976 Chicago started a two week run at No.1 on the US singles chart with 'If You Leave Me Now'. It was the group's 18th Top 40 and first US No.1, and was also a No.1 in the UK.

1980 Depeche Mode appeared at The Bridge House, Canning Town, London. Tickets cost 60p ($1.02).

1982 Culture Club was at No.1 on the UK singles chart with 'Do You Really Want To Hurt Me?', the group's first of 12 UK Top 40 hits.

1982 The Damned released an album titled *Strawberries*, packaged with a strawberry-smelling lyric sheet.

1984 Sade kicked off a 12 date UK tour at Newcastle City Hall.

1987 Madonna's film *Who's That Girl?* opened in London.

1989 Nirvana played their first-ever European show when they appeared at Newcastle's Riverside Club. It was the first night of a 36 date European tour with Tad.

1993 Meat Loaf had his first UK No.1 with 'I'd Do Anything For Love (But I Won't Do That)', which stayed at No.1 for seven weeks.

1993 Take That scored their first UK No.1 album with *Everything Changes*.

1994 the Crash Test Dummies kicked off an eight date UK tour at Rock City, Nottingham.

1995 Def Leppard put themselves in the *Guinness Book Of World Records* by playing three gigs on three continents in 24 hours. They played in Tangier, London and Vancouver.

1999 the wife of Los Lobos singer Sandra Ann-Rosas disappeared. Police charged her half brother Gabriel Gomez with the kidnapping and murder.

Crash Test Dummies

NOTTINGHAM ROCK CITY
Box Office Tel: 0602 412544
SUNDAY 23RD OCTOBER
NEWCASTLE CITY HALL
Box Office Tel: 091 261 2606
MONDAY 24TH OCTOBER
ROYAL ALBERT HALL
Box Office Tel: 071 589 8212
Tickets £15.50, £14.50, £12.50 & £11.50
WEDNESDAY 26TH OCTOBER
BRIGHTON CENTRE
Box Office Tel: 0273 202881
FRIDAY 28TH OCTOBER
CARDIFF UNIVERSITY
Box Office Tel: 0222 396421
SATURDAY 29TH OCTOBER
BRISTOL COLSTON HALL
Box Office Tel: 0272 223686
SUNDAY 30TH OCTOBER
MANCHESTER APOLLO
Box Office Tel: 061 236 9922
WEDNESDAY 2ND NOVEMBER
WOLVERHAMPTON CIVIC HALL
Box Office Tel: 0902 312030
FRIDAY 4TH NOVEMBER
Tickets £10.50 adv - except Royal Albert Hall

BORN ON THIS DAY

1936 Bill Wyman – bass player with The Rolling Stones, who had a 1969 UK & US No.1 single with 'Honky Tonk Women' and over 30 Top 40 UK & US singles and albums. Wyman left the band in 1993. He had a 1981 UK solo No.14 single with 'Je Suis Un Rock Star'.

1944 Ted Templeman – singer and guitarist with Harpers Bizarre, who had a 1967 US No.13 & UK No.34 single with 'The 59th Street Bridge Song, Feelin' Groovy'.

1946 Jerry Edmonton – drummer and vocalist with Steppenwolf, who had a 1969 US No.2 & UK No.30 single with 'Born To Be Wild'. He was killed in a car crash on November 28th 1993.

1946 Rob Van Leeuwen – singer and mandolin player with Shocking Blue, who had a 1970 US No.1 & UK No.8 single with 'Venus'.

1948 Dale Griffin – drummer with Mott The Hoople, who had a 1972 UK No.3 & US No.37 single with 'All The Young Dudes'.

1948 Paul and Barry Ryan – identical twins who had a 1965 UK No.13 single with 'Don't Bring Me Your Heartaches'. Barry also had a solo 1968 UK No.2 single with 'Eloise' written by his brother Paul. Paul died of cancer on November 29th 1992 aged 44.

1959 "Weird Al" Yankovic, composer and accordion player who had a run of minor US hits with parody songs –such as 'Eat It' (parodying Michael Jackson's 'Beat It') and 'Like A Surgeon' (Madonna's 'Like A Virgin').

1980 Monica, singer who had a 1998 US No.1 & UK No.2 single with Brandy, 'The Boy Is Mine'.

ON THIS DAY

1962 James Brown recorded his legendary *Live At The Apollo* album in New York. Released in 1963, the album spent 33 weeks on the US chart.

1964 The Rolling Stones kicked off an 11 date North American tour playing two shows at The New York Academy of Music.

1967 Pink Floyd were forced to cancel a tour of the US when Syd Barrett refused to move his lips in time to "Arnold Layne" on ABC-TV's *American Bandstand*.

1970 Santana scored their first US No.1 album with *Abraxas*, which went on to spend a total of 40 weeks on the US chart.

1973 John Lennon began litigation against the US government, accusing them of tapping his telephone.

1973 Keith Richards was fined £205 ($349) after admitting to having cannabis, tiny amounts of Chinese heroin, mandrax tablets and a revolver at his Chelsea home.

1979 Paul McCartney received a medallion cast in rhodium after being declared the most successful composer of all time. From 1962 to 1978 he had written or co-written 43 songs that had sold over a million copies each.

1986 Peter Grange, sound engineer for Dire Straits, was killed in a road accident in Gloucestershire.

1987 Sting went to No.1 on the UK album chart with his third solo release *Nothing Like The Sun*.

1998 former Stone Roses lead singer Ian Brown was jailed for four months after being found guilty of disorderly behaviour during a flight from Paris to Manchester. Brown had threatened to chop the hands off an air stewardess during a heated exchange.

1999 Westlife went to No.1 on the UK singles chart with 'Flying Without Wings'. It made the boyband only the third act to debut at No.1 with their first three singles, B*Witched and Robson & Jerome being the other two.

2001 Kim Gardner, former bassist with Ashton, Gardner & Dyke, died of cancer. The band had had a 1971 UK No.3 single with 'The Resurrection Shuffle'. Gardner had also formed The Birds with Ron Wood.

BORN ON THIS DAY

1944 Jon Anderson – vocalist with Yes, who had a 1983 UK No.28 & US No.1 single with 'Owner Of A Lonely Heart'.

1947 John Hall – drummer with The Equals, who had a 1968 UK No.1 & US No.32 single with 'Baby Come Back'.

1951 Richard Lloyd – guitarist and vocalist with Television, who had the 1977 album *Marquee Moon*.

1960 Christina Amphlett – vocalist with The Divinyls, who had a 1991 US No.4 & UK No.10 single with 'I Touch Myself'.

1962 Chad Smith – drummer with the Red Hot Chili Peppers, who had a 1992 UK No.26 single with 'Under The Bridge' and a 2002 UK No.1 album with *By The Way*.

1968 Todd Thomas (a.k.a. Speech) – singer with Arrested Development, who had a 1992 UK No.2 single with 'People Everyday'.

1970 Ed Robertson – guitarist with Barenaked Ladies, who had a 1998 US No.1 & UK No.5 single with 'One Week'.

ON THIS DAY

1958 Cliff Richard made his British radio debut on the BBC's *Saturday Club*.

1963 The Beatles played the first of a five date Swedish tour in a school hall in Karlstad.

1964 The Rolling Stones appeared on *The Ed Sullivan Show*, New York. A riot broke out in the studio and Sullivan was quoted as saying, "I promise you they'll never be back on our show again".

1968 the double album *Electric Ladyland* by the Jimi Hendrix Experience was released. It was also made available as two albums with changed artwork after complaints about the naked women who were pictured on the sleeve.

1969 'Sugar Sugar' by The Archies was at No.1 on the UK singles chart. It stayed at the top for eight weeks, and was also No.1 in the US, selling over six million copies worldwide. The Archies were a rock group based on comic book characters.

1974 Al Green was taking a shower at his Memphis home when his ex-girlfriend Mary Woodson burst in and poured boiling hot grit over him. She then shot herself dead. Green suffered second degree burns.

1980 Barbra Streisand scored her fourth US No.1 album with *Guilty*. Also on this day Streisand started a three week run at No.1 on the UK singles chart with 'Woman In Love', the singer's only UK No.1.

1980 New Order played their debut gig at The Squat in Manchester, England.

1985 actor and singer Gary Holton died of a drug overdose. He had been a member of The Heavy Metal Kids and one half of Casino Steel. He also appeared in the film *Quadrophenia* and TV's *Auf Wiedersehen Pet*.

1986 Bon Jovi went to No.1 on the US album chart with *Slippery When Wet*. It featured two US No.1 singles, 'You Give Love A Bad Name' and 'Livin' On A Prayer'. The album went on to sell over eight million copies.

1986 Cyndi Lauper started a two week run at No.1 on the US singles chart with 'True Colours'.

1986 Dire Straits guitarist Mark Knopfler crashed in a celebrity car race before the Australian Grand Prix and broke his collarbone.

1989 appearing at the Duchess Of York, Leeds were Nirvana and Tad. It was the third night of Nirvana's debut European tour.

1993 Tears For Fears appeared at The Aladdin Theater, Las Vegas with support band Radiohead.

1997 Johnny Cash announced during a gig in Michigan that he was suffering from Parkinson's disease after he fell over on stage when reaching for a guitar pick.

2001 13 law firms were involved in claims to Grateful Dead's guitarist Jerry Garcia's $10 million (£5.88 million) estate six years after his death. Former wives and girlfriends continued to fight on how to distribute his estate and annual royalties of $4.6 million (£2.7 million).

2003 Johnny Cash's stepdaughter, Rosey Nix Adams, and her fiddle player Jimmy Campbell were found dead on their tour bus in Clarksville, Tennessee from carbon monoxide poisoning.

2004 John Peel (a.k.a. John Robert Parker Ravenscoft) died in Cuzco, Peru of a heart attack, aged 65. He was BBC's longest-serving radio DJ and the first DJ to introduce The Ramones, Roxy Music, The Smiths, The Fall, Rod Stewart, Blur, the Sex Pistols, T. Rex and others to the masses. He founded Dandelion Records in 1969, which released records by Kevin Coyne, Bridget St John and Medicine Head. He as also known for his 'Peel Sessions', releases of live radio sessions. Peel was appointed OBE in 1998.

EAST ANGLIAN
DAILY TIMES

SUFFOLK TRIBUTE TO JOHN PEEL

Get more from your East Anglian Daily Times
- six days a week

BORN ON THIS DAY

1946 Keith Hopwood – guitarist with Herman's Hermits, who had a 1964 UK No.1 single with 'I'm Into Something Good' and a 1965 US No.1 single with 'Mrs Brown You've Got A Lovely Daughter'.

1951 Bootsy Collins, bass player for James Brown, Parliament–Funkadelic and Bootsy's Rubber Band.

1952 David Was – vocals, sax and flute with Was (Not Was), who had a 1992 UK No.4 single with 'Shake Your Head'.

> **SJM Concerts present**
> ## Stereophonics
> **+ Special Guests**
> **PARR HALL**
> Palmyra Square South, Warrington
> Monday 26th October 1998
> Doors 7:30pm
> Tickets £9.00 in advance
> (Subject to Booking Fee)
> **STANDING DOWNSTAIRS**   00493

1953 Keith Strickland – guitarist and keyboardist with The B-52s, who had a 1990 UK No.2 & US No.3 single with 'Love Shack'.

1963 Natalie Merchant – singer with 10,000 Maniacs, who had a 1993 UK No.47 single with 'Candy Everybody Wants'.

1978 Mark Barry – singer with BBMak, who had a 2001 UK No.5 single 'Back Here' – it went to No.1 in Japan.

ON THIS DAY

1958 Bill Haley And His Comets played the first rock 'n' roll concert in Germany. During the show 7,000 fans rioted.

1963 Bob Dylan played a sell-out concert at New York's Carnegie Hall.

1965 the Queen presented The Beatles with their MBEs at Buckingham Palace.

1966 Alma Cogan died of stomach cancer. She had had a 1955 UK No.1 single with 'Dreamboat' plus 20 other UK Top 40 hits.

She was also the youngest UK female act to top the charts during the 50s.

1974 Barry White scored his only US No.1 album with *Can't Get Enough*.

1974 Dionne Warwick And The Spinners went to No.1 on the US singles chart with 'Then Came You', the singer's 22nd US Top 40 hit.

1984 19-year-old John D. McCollum killed himself with a .22 calibre handgun after spending the day listening to Ozzy Osbourne records. One year later, McCollum's parents took court action against Ozzy and CBS Records, alleging that the song 'Suicide Solution' from the album *Blizzard of Ozz* contributed to their son's death. The case was eventually thrown out of court.

1985 Whitney Houston went to No.1 on the US singles chart with 'Saving All My Love For You', which was also a No.1 in the UK.

1991 Erasure scored their third UK No.1 album with *Chorus*, which featured the singles 'Love To Hate You' and the title track 'Chorus'.

1991 Ozzy Osbourne broke his foot after an accident on stage at a gig in Chicago, causing him to cancel the remaining dates of a US tour.

1991 legendary American promoter Bill Graham was killed when the helicopter he was flying in hit a 61m (200ft) utility tower in Sonoma County, California.

1993 Catholic churches in San Juan, Puerto Rico asked residents to tie black ribbons on trees in protest against Madonna's first live appearance there.

1996 The Spice Girls had their second UK No.1 single when 'Say You'll Be There' started a two week run at the top of the charts.

2000 Robbie Williams played a sold-out gig at the *Manchester Evening News* Arena. England.

2002 Jessica Simpson *(left)* married former 98° member Nick Lachey. The couple were featured on MTV's *Newlyweds* TV show.

2003 Sugababes went to No.1 on the UK singles chart with 'Hole In The Head', the girl group's third No.1.

2003 US TV's *American Idol* runner-up Clay Aiken was at No.1 on the US album chart with Measure Of A Man.

2004 Elvis Presley came top of a list of the highest-earning dead celebrities. Forbes.com listed the Top 5 dead music earners: No.1. Elvis Presley with $40 million (£23.5 million); No.2. John Lennon with $21 million (£12.35 million); joint 3rd, George Harrison and Bob Marley with $7 million (£4 million) and No.5. George and Ira Gershwin with $6 million (£3.5 million).

BORN ON THIS DAY

1949 Byron Allred – keyboard player with the Steve Miller Band, who had a 1974 US No.1 & 1990 UK No.1 single with 'The Joker'.

1951 Ken Downing – guitarist with Judas Priest, who had a 1980 UK No.12 single with 'Living After Midnight'.

1953 Peter Dodd – guitarist with The Thompson Twins, who had a 1984 UK No.2 single with 'You Take Me Up' and a 1984 US No.3 single with 'Hold Me Now'.

1958 Hazell Dean, singer who had a 1988 UK No.4 single with 'Who's Leaving Who'.

1958 Simon Le Bon – vocalist with Duran Duran, who had a 1983 UK No.1 single with 'Is There Something I Should Know?' plus 25 other UK Top 40 singles and a 1984 US No.1 single with 'The Reflex', and Arcadia, who had a 1985 UK No.7 single with 'Election Day'.

1984 Kelly Osbourne, singer, who had a 2002 UK No.3 single with 'Papa Don't Preach'.

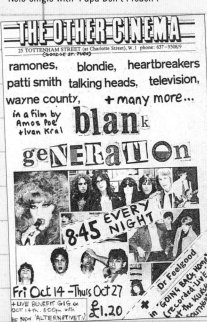

THE OTHER CINEMA
25 TOTTENHAM STREET (at Charlotte Street), W.1 phone: 637–9308/9
(GOODGE ST. TUBE)

ramones, blondie, heartbreakers patti smith talking heads, television, wayne county, + many more...

in a film by Amos Poe + Ivan Kral **blank geNERatIOn**

8.45 EVERY NIGHT

Fri Oct 14 – Thurs Oct 27

+ LIVE BENEFIT GIG on OCT 14th. 8:00pm with THE NEW 'ALTERNATIVE TV'

£1.20

Dr Feelgood in 'GOING BACK HOME' (recorded LIVE at the KURSAAL SOUTHEND)

ON THIS DAY

1957 The Crickets started a three week run at No.1 on the UK singles chart with 'That'll Be The Day'. It made No.3 in the US and sold over a million copies.

1962 The Rolling Stones made their first studio recordings at Curly Clayton Studios in Highbury, London.

1966 The Four Tops were at No.1 on the UK singles chart with 'Reach Out I'll Be There', the group's only UK No.1.

1970 Black Sabbath played their first-ever live show in the US when they kicked of a 16 date tour at Glassboro State College.

1973 Gladys Knight And The Pips started a two week run at No.1 on the US singles chart with 'Midnight Train To Georgia'. It was the group's 18th Top 40 hit and first No.1.

1975 Bruce Springsteen appeared on the covers of both *News Week* and *Time*, a move that embarrassed both magazines.

1977 Baccara were at No.1 in the UK singles chart with 'Yes Sir, I Can Boogie'.

1979 Elton John collapsed on stage at Hollywood's Universal Amphitheater suffering from exhaustion.

1980 Marc Bolan's first performing partner, Steve Took, choked to death on a cherry stone after some magic mushrooms he had eaten numbed all sensation in his throat.

1984 at a Grateful Dead concert in Berkeley the band allocated a specific recording area for fans to bootleg the show.

1984 Big Country went to No.1 on the UK album chart with *Steel Town*, the band's only No.1 album.

1989 bass player with U2 Adam Clayton was convicted of a drink driving offence by a Dublin

Skiffle king at palace

MUSIC legend Lonnie Donegan, 61, was at Buckingham Palace today to receive an MBE for services to pop. Lonnie pioneered skiffle in the 1950s and inspired a generation of teenagers to start bands, including Paul McCartney.

court after being found driving twice over the legal limit. He was fined £500 ($850) and banned from driving for one year.

1990 Michael Waite from Musical Youth was jailed for four years after being found guilty of taking part in a robbery.

1990 Paul Simon started a two week run at No.1 on the UK album chart with *The Rhythm Of The Saints*, his third UK No.1 solo album.

1991 EMF were named Best British group at the *Smash Hits* Poll Winners' Awards. Kylie Minogue won the Worst female singer award.

1992 Bo Diddley took his ex-manager to court claiming he had taken $75,000 (£44,118) through unauthorized personal expenses.

1997 34-year-old John Hector was arrested in Toronto and charged with criminal harassment after stalking U2 bass player Adam Clayton.

1999 Coldplay kicked off an 11 date UK tour at the Liverpool Royal Court Theatre.

2000 Lonnie Donegan went to Buckingham Palace *(above)* to receive his MBE for his services to pop music. Lonnie pioneered skiffle in the 1950s and inspired a generation of teenagers to start bands.

BORN ON THIS DAY

1936 Charlie Daniels — singer, songwriter, guitarist who had a 1979 US No.3 & UK No.14 single 'The Devil Went Down To Georgia'.

1937 Graham Bond, UK R&B keyboard and sax player who worked with Alexis Korner, Jack Bruce and Ginger Baker. He committed suicide on May 8th 1974 by jumping in front of a London Underground train

1940 Wayne Fontana, singer who had a 1966 UK No.2 single with Mindbenders, 'Groovy Kind Of Love' and a 1965 US No.1 single with 'Game Of Love'.

1941 Hank Marvin — guitarist with The Shadows, who had a 1963 UK No.1 single with 'Foot Tapper' plus 28 other UK Top 40 singles. They also had hits with Cliff Richard.

1948 Telma Hopkins — singer with Dawn, who had a 1971 UK & US No.1 single with 'Knock Three Times' and a 1973 US & UK No.1 single with 'Tie A Yellow Ribbon Round The Old Oak Tree'.

1957 Stephen Morris — drummer with Joy Division, who had a 1980 UK No.13 single with 'Love Will Tear Us Apart, New Order, who had a 1983 UK No.9 single with 'Blue Monday', and The Other Two, who had a 1991 UK No.41 single with 'Tasty Fish'.

WEMBLEY FESTIVAL OF MUSIC
WEMBLEY POOL
Sat. & Sun. 28-29 October 1972
Organised by the
STARS ORGANISATION FOR SPASTICS
in association with the DAILY EXPRESS

Nº 1062

ON THIS DAY

1958 Buddy Holly made his last major TV appearance on *American Bandstand*.

1961 Raymond Jones went into Liverpool's NEMS Record store trying to buy Beatles records that have been released in Germany. Shop manager Brian Epstein promised to investigate further.

1964 the first of two nights billed as the "Tami Show" at the Civic Auditorium, Santa Monica featured Smokey Robinson & The Miracles, The Beach Boys, Chuck Berry, Marvin Gaye, The Supremes and The Rolling Stones.

1972 The United States Council For World Affairs announced it was adopting The Who's 'Join Together' as its official theme song.

1973 David Cassidy was at No.1 on the UK singles chart with 'Daydreamer/The Puppy Song', the singer's second No.1.

Graham Bond (right) and that tree again.

1974 Ken Boothe was at No.1 on the UK singles chart with 'Everything I Own'.

Baby you can buy my car — 1965 McCartney Mini up for auction

By Lewis Smith

AT FIRST glance Sir Paul McCartney's old Mini, the car he used as a runabout at the height of Beatlemania, looks much like any other. The luxurious interior, however, betrays the pedigree of a 1965 vehicle customised to his personal specifications.

Designer seats, a dashboard fit for a Bentley, soundproofing, electric windows and a record player turned the Mini Cooper S, as much an icon of the 1960s as the Beatles, into the Rolls-Royce of small cars.

The Mini, registration number GGJ382C and with just 40,000 miles on the clock, is now classified in Britain as an historic vehicle. It will be auctioned next month in California by Bonhams, who estimate that it will fetch £40,000.

The vehicle is testimony to the success of the Fab Four, who were each presented with a customised Mini by their manager, Brian Epstein, as a token of thanks for their unprecedented record sales.

Ringo Starr's boasted a hatchback boot to enable him to transport his drums, John Lennon's was black like all his other vehicles at the time, George Harrison's was painted in psychedelic colours and

was used in the 1967 Beatles film Magical Mystery Tour.

Sir Paul used his to nip about the streets of London and was often seen driving from his home in St John's Wood to Primrose Hill where he liked to take his sheepdog, Martha, for walks. It is reputed to be the vehicle in which he first drove Linda Eastman, who married him in 1969, home with him, albeit with the singer Lulu.

Sir Paul's sage-green Mini, which he sold in 1970, the year the Beatles broke up, was believed lost but a motoring enthusiast found it in Canada, repainted burgundy.

1978 Nick Gilder went to No.1 on the US singles chart with 'Hot Child In The City'. It was not a hit in the UK.

1982 The Jam announced they were splitting up at the end of their current UK tour.

1989 Janet Jackson started a four week run at No.1 on the US album chart with *Janet Jackson's Rhythm Nation 1814*.

1995 Coolio scored his first UK No.1 single when his version of the Stevie Wonder song 'Gangsta's Paradise' started a two week run at the top of the charts.

1997 drummer Bill Berry announced that he was leaving R.E.M. after being a member of the group for 17 years.

2001 Mary J. Blige started a six week run at No.1 on the US singles chart with 'Family Affair'.

2001 the various artist album *God Bless America* went to No.1 on the US chart.

2004 Courtney Love was ordered to stand trial on a charge of assault with a deadly weapon after Kristin King told a Los Angeles court Ms Love threw a bottle and a lit candle at her after turning up at the home of a former boyfriend in the early hours. Ms King told the court Ms Love was "vicious" and 'erratic' when she allegedly attacked her while she slept on a sofa on April 25. She said Ms Love then sat on her, pulled her hair and pinched her left breast — the "worst pinch I ever had" — before she managed to flee.

BORN ON THIS DAY

1944 Denny Laine – guitarist and vocalist with The Moody Blues, who had a 1965 UK No.1 & US No.10 single with 'Go Now' and Wings, who had a 1974 UK No.3 single with 'Band on The Run' and a 1977 UK No.1 single with 'Mull Of Kintyre'.

1946 Peter Green – guitarist and vocalist with John Mayall's Bluesbreakers (he replaced Eric Clapton) and Fleetwood Mac, who had a 1969 UK No.1 single with 'Albatross'

1954 Steve Luscombe – synth player with Blancmange, who had a 1982 UK No.7 single with 'Living On The Ceiling'.

1955 Kevin DuBrow – singer for Quiet Riot, who had a 1983 US No.1 album with *Metal Health*.

ON THIS DAY

1965 with 'My Generation' released as a single the day before, The Who played at The Starlite Ballroom, Greenford, London.

1966 ? And The Mysterians went to No.1 on the US singles chart with '96 Tears'. It made No.37 in the UK and the song also gave The Stranglers a UK No.17 hit in 1990.

1973 Duane Allman of The Allman Brothers Band was killed in a motorbike accident.

1977 the Belgian travel service issued a summons against the Sex Pistols, claiming the sleeve to *Holidays In The Sun* infringed copyright of one of its brochures.

1983 'Islands In The Stream' gave Dolly Parton and Kenny Rogers a No.1 on the US singles chart. It was written by The Bee Gees and co-produced by Barry Gibb.

MCP, SJM, METROPOLIS MUSIC AND DF CONCERTS PRESENTS

DEL AMITRI

PLUS SPECIAL GUESTS

DON

OCTOBER
Wed 29th — BRIGHTON DOME
B/O TEL: 01273 709709
Thur 30th — TORQUAY RIVIERA CENTRE
B/O TEL: 01803 296676
Fri 31st — GLOUCESTER LEISURE CENTRE
B/O TEL: 01452 306788
NOVEMBER
Sat 1st — EDINBURGH USHER HALL
B/O TEL: 0131 228 1155/014
Sun 2nd/Mon 3rd — GLASGOW BARROWLAND
B/O TEL: 0141 339 8383
Wed 5th — PRESTON GUILDHALL
B/O TEL: 01772 258858
Thur 6th — SHEFFIELD CITY HALL
B/O TEL: 0114 278 9789
Fri 7th — YORK BARBICAN CENTRE
B/O TEL: 01904 656888
Sun 9th — CARLISLE SANDS CENTRE
B/O TEL: 01228 25222
Mon 10th — HULL CITY HALL
B/O TEL: 01482 226655
Tue 11th — NEWCASTLE MAYFAIR
B/O TEL: 0191 261 2606
Thur 13th — WARWICK ARTS CENTRE, COVENTRY
B/O TEL: 01203 524524
Fri 14th — NORWICH UEA
B/O TEL: 01603 505401
Sun 16th — CARDIFF ST. DAVIDS HALL
B/O TEL: 01222 878444

1983 Pink Floyd's *Dark Side Of The Moon* became the longest listed album in the history of the US chart when its total reached 491 weeks.

1984 Wells Kelly (45), drummer with Orleans and Meat Loaf, died after choking on his vomit.

1987 "Decades", Ron Wood's first-ever British art exhibition, opened in London, featuring portraits of friends and rock stars from the past 20 years.

1988 Dire Straits scored their fourth UK No.1 album with *Money For Nothing*.

1988 Enya started a three week run at No.1 on the UK singles chart with 'Orinoco Flow'.

1991 Memphis City Council named Interstate 55 through Jackson "The BB King Freeway".

Spice heaven

1994 Pato Banton started a four week run at No.1 on the UK singles chart with his version of the 1968 Equals hit 'Baby Come Back'.

1996 The Stone Roses split up. Singer Ian Brown said, "Having spent the last ten years in the filthiest business in the universe it's a pleasure to announce the end of The Stone Roses."

2000 Limp Bizkit started a two week run at No.1 on the US album chart with *Chocolate Starfish*.

2000 The Spice Girls went to No.1 on the UK singles chart with 'Holler/Let Love Lead The Way'. The group made musical history by scoring their ninth No.1, making them joint fourth in the list of acts that have had nine UK No.1 singles.

2001 winners at this years *Q* awards included: Ash, Best single for 'Burn Baby Burn'; Starsailor won Best new act; Travis won Best album for *The Invisible Band*; Manic Street Preachers won Best live act and John Lydon won the Inspiration award.

2003 research in the US found that songs get stuck in our heads because they create a "brain itch" that can only be scratched by repeating a tune over and over. Songs such as the Village People's 'Y.M.C.A.' and the Baha Men's 'Who Let The Dogs Out' owe their success to their ability to create a "cognitive itch", according to Professor James Kellaris of the University of Cincinnati College of Business Administration.

BORN ON THIS DAY

1939 Eddie Holland producer and songwriter (part of the Holland/Dozier/Holland team). He wrote Motown hits for The Supremes, Four Tops, Marvin Gaye, Martha & The Vandellas, Freda Payne and Chairmen Of The Board.

1939 Grace Slick – vocalist for Jefferson Airplane and Starship, who had a 1967 US No.18 single with 'White Rabbit' and a 1987 US & UK No.1 single with 'Nothing's Gonna Stop Us Now'.

1939 Otis Williams – singer with The Temptations, who had a 1971 US No.1 & UK No.8 single with 'Just My Imagination' and the reissued 'My Girl' went to No.2 in the UK in 1992.

1947 Timothy B. Schmit – bass player and vocalist with Poco, he joined The Eagles in 1977, who had a 1977 US No.1 & UK No.8 single with 'Hotel California' plus five US No.1 albums. *Greatest Hits 1971–1975* is the second biggest-selling album in the world with sales of over 30 million.

1949 David Green – bass player with Air Supply, who had a 1980 UK No.11 single with 'All Out Of Love' and a 1981 US No.1 single with 'The One That You Love'.

1967 Gavin Rossdale – singer/songwriter and guitarist with Bush, who had a 1997 UK No.7 single with 'Swallowed'. The band's first album sold over seven million copies in the US.

1969 Snow (a.k.a. Darrin O'Brien), Canadian rapper who had a 1993 US No.1 & UK No.2 single with 'Informer'.

ON THIS DAY

1967 T. Rex recorded a session for Radio 1's "Top Gear", the first group to do so without a recording contract.

1970 Hotlegs made their live debut supporting The Moody Blues at the Festival Hall, London. Their only hit, 'Neanderthal Man', made No.2 in July 1970, while the band went on to become 10CC.

1970 Jim Morrison of The Doors was fined $500 (£294) and sentenced to six months in jail for exposing himself during a gig in Miami.

1971 John Lennon And The Plastic Ono Band went to No.1 on the UK album chart with *Imagine*. It also made No.1 in the US. The album contained two attacks on Paul McCartney, 'How Do You Sleep?' and 'Crippled Inside'.

1975 Bob Dylan played the first night on his 31 date Rolling Thunder Revue tour at the War Memorial Auditorium, Plymouth, Massachusetts.

1982 Australian band Men At Work went to No.1 on the US singles chart with 'Who Can It Be Now?', the group's first US No.1. It was a No.45 hit in the UK.

1990 Axl Rose was released on $5,000 (£2,940) bail after being arrested for allegedly hitting a neighbour over the head with a bottle after a complaint to the police about loud music coming from his house.

1993 Meat Loaf went to No.1 on the US album chart with *Bat Out Of Hell II. Back To Hell*.

1998 All four original members of Black Sabbath reunited momentarily to play 'Paranoid' on US TV's *David Letterman Show*.

2000 a new website was launched to help teach children basic Physics. www.britneyspears.ac featured the singer to illustrate mathematical equations. Visitors could access physics theories generously interspersed with photos of Britney.

2002 Jam Master Jay from Run-DMC was murdered by an assassin's single bullet at his recording studio in Queens, New York.

2003 Steve O'Rourke, Pink Floyd's manager since 1968 died in Miami, Florida.

2004 Rod Stewart was at No.1 on the US album chart with *Stardust*, his third US No.1 album since 1971.

2004 An arrest warrant was issued for Motley Crue singer Vince Neil. Neil was said to have punched soundman Michael Talbert in the face at Gilley's nightclub in Dallas after he asked for more volume on his guitar.

BORN ON THIS DAY

1952 Bernard Edwards – bassist, producer and member of Chic who had a 1978 UK No.7 single with 'Le Freak'. Edwards produced ABC, Power Station and Rod Stewart. He died on April 18th 1996.

1961 Larry Mullen Jr – drummer for U2, who had a 1984 UK No.3 single with 'Pride, In The Name Of Love' plus over 25 other UK Top 40 singles and a 1987 UK and worldwide No.1 album with *The Joshua Tree*.

1963 Johnny Marr – guitarist and songwriter with The Smiths, who had a 1984 UK No.10 single with 'Heaven Knows I'm Miserable Now' plus 15 other UK Top 40 singles, Electronic, who had a 1991 UK No.8 single with 'Get The Message', and The The.

1966 King Ad-Rock (a.k.a. Adam Horovitz), rapper with The Beastie Boys, who had a 1987 UK No.11 single with 'You Gotta Fight For Your Right, To Party'.

1970 Malin Berggren – singer with Ace Of Base, who had a 1993 UK No.1 single with 'All That She Wants' and a 1994 US No.1 single with 'The Sign'.

1982 Monica and Gabriela Irimia – singers with the Cheeky Girls, who had a 2002 UK No.2 single with 'Cheeky Song'.

ON THIS DAY

1963 Gerry And The Pacemakers were at No.1 on the UK singles chart with 'You'll Never Walk Alone', the group's third No.1.

1963 The Beatles arrived at Heathrow Airport from Sweden and were greeted by hundreds of screaming girls. US talk show host Ed Sullivan was passing through the airport and witnessed the scene, which led to him booking the group on his show.

1967 Iggy And The Stooges made their live debut at a Ann Arbor, Michigan Halloween party.

1970 Michelle Gilliam from The Mamas And The Papas married actor Dennis Hopper. The marriage lasted for eight days.

1974 Led Zeppelin launched their own record label, Swan Song.

1978 Joe Jackson appeared at The Hope And Anchor, London.

1986 Roger Waters went to the high court to try and stop Dave Gilmour and Nick Mason from using the name "Pink Floyd" for future touring and recording.

1989 the very first MTV unplugged show was recorded in New York, featuring Squeeze. The programme was aired on November 26th 1989.

1992 Boyz II Men were at No.1 in the UK with the single 'End Of The Road', which was taken from the film *Boomerang*.

1996 Slash announced he was no longer in Guns N' Roses. He was quoted as saying that Axl Rose and he had only spoken to each other on only two occasions since 1994.

1998 chart history was made when the UK Top 5 was made up entirely of new entries. Alanis Morissette went in at No.5, Culture Club at No.4, U2 at No.3, George Michael at No.2 and Cher with 'Believe' at No.1. This made Cher the first female artist to have a No.1 single over the age of 50.

1999 EMI records announced that it was planning to stop paying for some of its artists to release singles. The label said that anyone who sold less than 80,000 copies would be discouraged from releasing a single.

1999 a list of "New Pop Fortunes", published in *The Sunday Times (above)*, reported that The Corrs were worth £1.5 million ($2.55 million) each, Boyzone £3 million ($5 million) each, Jamiroquai £4 million ($6.8 million), The Chemical Brothers £4 million ($6.8 million) each and Norman Cook £10 million ($17 million).

2002 the mother of pop star Bjork ended a hunger strike she had staged to protest against plans by a US company to build an aluminium smelter and hydroelectric plant power plant in the Icelandic wilderness.

SPINAL TRAP

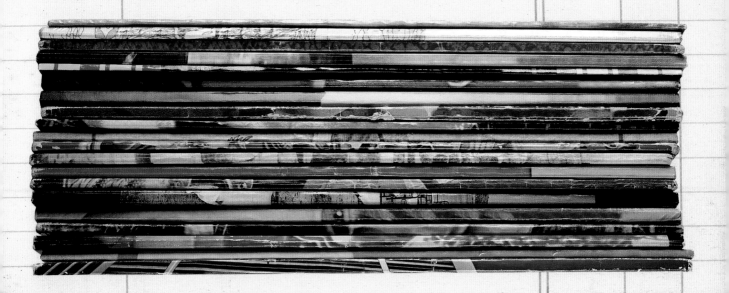

We show, here, 20 albums by their spine, and invite you to spot and name as many as you can.
This can be done by clicking on to the Competitions page at www.thisdayinmusic.com, and then the words 'Spinal Trap'.
Fill in your suggestions as to the 20, get as many as you can, and you will be contacted with your results and prizes.

The competition closes on December 25th 2006, at which point all entrants will be e-mailed the results.

The Editorial Board,
This Day In Music

BORN ON THIS DAY

1940 Sgt Barry Sadler, singer/songwriter who had a 1966 US No.1 single with 'The Ballad Of The Green Berets'. He died on November 5th 1989.

1946 Ric Grech – bass player for Family, Traffic, who had a 1970 US No.15 & UK No.11 album with *John Barleycorn Must Die*, Blind Faith, who had a 1969 UK & US No.1 album with *Blind Faith*, and Airforce. He died on March 17th 1990.

1950 Dan Peek – guitarist and vocalist with America, who had a 1972 US No.1 & UK No.3 single with 'Horse With No Name'.

1951 Jaco Pastorious – jazz bass player, had the 1976 single 'Birdland' with Weather Report, also worked with Joni Mitchell and Pat Metheny. He died on September 21st 1987, aged 35, from injuries sustained in a fight.

1951 Ronald Bell – songwriter and keyboard player with Kool & The Gang, who had a 1981 US No.1 & UK No.7 single with 'Celebration', a 1984 UK No.2 single with 'Joanna' and over 15 other Top 40 hits.

1962 Anthony Kiedis – singer with Red Hot Chili Peppers, who had a 1992 UK No.26 single with 'Under The Bridge' and a 2002 UK No.1 album with *By The Way*.

1962 Magne "Mags" Furuholmen – keyboardist for A-Ha, who had a 1985 US No.1 single with 'Take On Me' and a 1986 UK No.1 single with 'The Sun Always Shines On TV'.

1963 Rick Allen – drummer with Def Leppard, who had a 1987 UK No.6 single with 'Animal', a 1987 worldwide No.1 album with *Hysteria* and a 1988 US No.1 single with 'Love Bites'.

1981 La Tavia – singer with Destiny's Child, who had a 2000 US No.1 single with 'Say My Name'.

ON THIS DAY

1963 The Beatles' first official headline tour kicked off at The Odeon Cinema, Cheltenham. Also on the twice nightly package were The Brook Brothers, Vernon Girls and Peter Jay & The Jayhawks.

1965 The Rolling Stones played at the War Memorial Auditorium, New York during their fourth North American tour.

1969 Elvis Presley went to No.1 on the US singles chart with 'Suspicious Minds', his 18th US No.1 single. The song was a No.2 hit in the UK.

1970 Matthews Southern Comfort were at No.1 on the UK singles chart with their version of the Joni Mitchell song 'Woodstock'.

1970 Led Zeppelin started a four week run at No.1 on the US album chart with *Led Zeppelin III*, the band's second US chart topper.

1975 Elton John started a three week run at No.1 on the US singles chart with 'Island Girl', his fifth US No.1. It made No.14 in the UK.

1987 the first of three shows at the Hammersmith Odeon, London featuring LL Cool J, Eric B & Rankin and Public Enemy. Each night was marred by violence and crime.

1993 Flavor Flav from Public Enemy was arrested and charged with attempted murder of his neighbour. Flav claimed his neighbour had had sex with his girlfriend.

1996 U2 set up a video link to an Internet site from their recording studio in Dublin so fans could watch them record their new album.

2000 winners at this years *Q* Awards included: David Gray, Best single for 'Babylon'; Oasis, Best live act; Coldplay, Best album for *Parachutes*; Best act in the world went to Travis; Badly Drawn Boy won Best new act and former Clash member Joe Strummer won the Inspiration award.

2000 Robbie Williams offered to donate his bone marrow to save a fan's life after meeting leukaemia sufferer Johanna MacVicar *(above)*. Williams asked his fans to sign up as potential donors after being told of the desperate shortage of male donors.

2002 P Diddy charted two jets to fly 300 guests from New York to Marrakech to celebrate his 33rd birthday party in Morocco.

2003 organizers of the MTV Europe Awards 2003 recruited 500 "screamers" to attend this year's event. The music lovers were selected at an audition held in Edinburgh's Princes Street Gardens. About 1,500 pop-mad teenagers and adults screamed themselves hoarse in a bid to get their hands on a ticket to the exclusive event.

2004 US singer, guitarist and manager Terry Knight was stabbed to death. He had led Terry Knight And The Pack and managed and produced Grand Funk Railroad.

News 13

Robbie Williams offers bone marrow for fan

BORN ON THIS DAY

1941 Brian Poole – vocalist with The Tremeloes, who had a 1967 UK No.1 & US No.11 single with 'Silence Is Golden'. His daughters Karen and Shellie formed Alisha's Attic in the 90s.

1941 Bruce Welch – guitarist with The Shadows, who had a 1960 UK No.1 single 'Apache' plus 28 other UK Top 40 singles. Also a member of Marvin, Welch & Farrar.

1944 Keith Emerson – keyboardist with The Nice, who had a 1968 UK No.21 single with 'America', and ELP, who had a 1977 UK No.2 single with 'Fanfare For The Common Man'.

1947 Carter Beauford – drummer for the Dave Matthews Band, who had a 1998 US No.1 album with *Before These Crowded Streets*, a 2001 US No.1 album with *Everyday* and a 2001 UK No.35 single with 'The Space Between'.

1956 Chris Fairbrass – guitarist with Right Said Fred, who had a 1991 US No.1 & UK No.2 single with 'I'm Too Sexy' and a 1993 UK No.1 album with *Up*.

1961 kd lang, singer/songwriter who had a 1993 UK No.15 single with 'Constant Craving'.

1969 Reginald Arvizu – bass player for Korn, who had a 1998 UK No.23 single with 'Got The Life' and a 1998 US No.1 album with *Follow The Leader*.

1979 Nelly (a.k.a. Cornell Haynes Jr), rapper who had a 2000 US No.1 album with *Country Grammar* and a 2000 US and UK Top 10 single with 'Country Grammar'.

ON THIS DAY

1958 Tommy Edwards was at No.1 on the UK singles chart with 'It's All In The Game'.

1963 Peter, Paul & Mary started a five week run at No.1 on the US album chart with *In The Wind*, the group's second No.1.

1964 during a live *Ready Steady Go!* TV show, singing 'Donna The Prima Donna', Dion became irritated by the audience dancing around him during his performance and walked off the show.

1967 Tom Jones kicked off a 22 date UK tour at Finsbury Park, Astoria with Kathy Kirby and The Ted Heath Orchestra.

1969 'Sugar Sugar' by The Archies was at No.1 on the UK singles chart.

1974 Crosby, Stills, Nash & Young went to No.1 on the US album chart with *So Far*, the group's third US No.1.

1974 George Harrison became the first Beatle to undertake a solo world tour when he played the first of 30 dates, kicking off in Vancouver, Canada.

1984 the Rev. Marvin Gaye Sr. was sentenced to five years in prison for the manslaughter of his son Marvin Gaye.

1984 U2 kicked off a ten date UK tour at the Brixton Academy, London *(above)*.

1985 Stevie Wonder went to No.1 on the US singles chart with 'Part-time Lover', his ninth US No.1 and a No.3 hit in the UK.

1985 the TV soundtrack from *Miami Vice* went to No.1 on the US album chart. It spent a total of 11 weeks at No.1.

1987 Eric Clapton played the first of three nights at The Budokan, Tokyo.

1991 U2 had their second UK No.1 single with 'The Fly'.

1996 Counting Crows went to No.1 on the US album chart with *Recovering From Satellites*.

1999 David Gray kicked off an eight date UK tour at Leeds City Varieties.

2000 All Saints came top of a poll to find the sexiest female act. 12,000 television viewers voted for the group, The Spice Girls came second and Atomic Kitten third. The 50s group The Beverley Sisters were voted into eleventh place, beating TLC.

2001 Slipknot kicked off a six date UK tour at Cardiff Arena *(left)*.

2002 armed police arrested an international terrorist gang who were planning to kidnap former Spice Girl Victoria Beckham and her two young children. The gang had planned to ransom Victoria for £5 million ($8.5 million).

BORN ON THIS DAY

1933 John Barry – composer and leader of the John Barry Orchestra. He has written film themes such as the 'James Bond Theme', 'Zulu', and 'The Magnificent Seven'.

1946 Nick Simper – bass player with Johnny Kidd & The Pirates who had the 1960 UK No.1 single 'Shakin' All Over'. He was in the car crash that killed Johnny Kid in 1966. Simper was also a founder member of Deep Purple – he left the band in 1969.

1948 Lulu (a.k.a. Marie Lawrie), UK singer who had a 1964 UK No.7 single with 'Shout', a 1967 US No.1 single with 'To Sir With Love' plus over ten other UK Top 40 singles, including the 1993 UK No.1 'Relight My Fire' with Take That.

1954 Stuart Goddard (a.k.a. Adam Ant) – singer with Adam And The Ants, who had a 1981 UK No.1 single with 'Stand And Deliver' plus 15 other UK Top 40 hit singles.

1962 Marilyn (a.k.a. Peter Robinson), UK singer who had a 1983 UK No.4 single with 'Calling Your Name'.

1969 Mark Roberts – guitarist with Catatonia, who had a 1998 UK No.3 single with 'Mulder And Scully' and a 1998 UK No.1 album with *International Velvet*, which spent 93 weeks on the UK chart.

1969 Robert Miles, Italian instrumentalist who had a 1996 UK No.2 single with 'Children' and his 1996 album *Dreamland* spent 48 weeks on the UK chart.

ON THIS DAY

1957 Sun Records released 'Great Balls Of Fire' by Jerry Lee Lewis. It went on to sell over five million copies and became a worldwide hit.

1960 Elvis Presley had his fifth UK No.1 single with 'It's Now Or Never', which stayed at No.1 for eight weeks.

1964 a 17-year-old fan fell from the balcony during a Rolling Stones concert in Cleveland, Ohio.

1973 David Bowie scored his second UK No.1 album with *Pinups*. The set contained Bowie covering his favourite 60s songs. His version of the Mersey's 'Sorrow' made No.3 on the UK singles chart.

1977 during a concert at Wembley's Empire Pool, Elton John announced his retirement from live performances.

1979 one hit wonder M went to No.1 on the US singles chart with 'Pop Musik'. M was Robin Scott who scored one other UK Top 40 hit, while 'Pop Musik' made No.2 in the UK.

1979 The Eagles started a nine week run at No.1 on the US album chart with *The Long Run*, the group's fourth US No.1 album.

1983 Latin teen sensations Menudo were signed by RCA Records for $30 million (£17.6 million). The line up of five young boys all had to sign a contract agreeing to leave the group when they reached 16 (when they would be too old for the group). Ricky Martin was once a member.

1984 Billy Ocean started a two week run at No.1 on the US singles chart with 'Caribbean Queen', which was originally called 'European Queen'.

1987 David Bowie played the first of eight sold-out nights at The Entertainment Centre, Sydney, Australia. The shows were part of the 87 date *Glass Spider* world tour.

1990 25 years after their version was recorded The Righteous Brothers enjoyed a UK No.1 with 'Unchained Melody' after the song was featured in the film *Ghost*.

1990 'Ice Ice Baby' by Vanilla Ice became the first rap record to top the US singles chart. It was also a No.1 hit in the UK.

1997 rock group Metallica arrived at an out-of-court agreement with a fan who claimed he lost his sense of smell after being dropped on his head by fans at one of their shows four years earlier.

2002 Lonnie Donegan, the singer who launched the skiffle craze in the UK, died aged 71. He had had a 1960 UK No.1 single with 'My Old Man's A Dustman' plus over 30 other UK Top 40 singles.

BORN ON THIS DAY

1907 Bennie Benjamin, session drummer and one of 'The Funk Brothers'. He played for many Tamla Motown artists including, The Four Tops, Temptations, Marvin Gaye, The Supremes and Stevie Wonder. He died on May 2nd 1989.

1940 Delbert McClinton, US singer/songwriter who had a 1980 US No.8 single with 'Giving It Up For Your Love'. He worked with Bruce Channel and wrote 'Two More Bottles Of Wine' – a country No.1 for Emmylou Harris.

1947 Mike Smith – saxophonist with Amen Corner, who had a 1969 UK No.1 single with 'If Paradise Is Half As Nice'.

1951 Dan Hartman, multi-instrumentalist and producer who worked with Edgar Winter. He also had a 1978 UK No.8 & US No.29 solo single with 'Instant Replay'. He died on March 22nd 1994.

1954 Chris Difford – guitarist and vocalist with Squeeze, who had a 1979 UK No.2 single with 'Up The Junction'.

1957 James Honeyman-Scott – guitarist with the Pretenders, who had a 1980 UK No.1 single with 'Brass In Pocket'. He died on June 16th 1982.

1966 Damon "Kool Rock-Ski" Wimbley – rapper with The Fat Boys, who had a 1988 UK No.2 single with 'Wipe-out'.

1970 Sean Coombs (a.k.a. Puff Daddy and P Diddy), who had a 1997 US & UK No.1 single with Faith Evans, 'I'll Be Missing You'.

ON THIS DAY

1957 Jackie Wilson made his US chart debut with 'Reet Petite'. The song became a No.1 in the UK in 1986, 29 years after its first release.

1961 Bob Dylan appeared at The Carnegie Chapter Hall, New York.

1961 Cliff Richard scored his first UK No.1 album with *21 Today*.

1963 The Beatles topped the bill at The Royal Variety Show at The Prince Of Wales Theatre, London. With the Queen Mother and Princess Margaret in the audience, this was the night when John Lennon made his famous remark "In the cheaper seats you clap your hands. The rest of you, just rattle your jewellery".

1970 The Beach Boys played the first of four nights at the Whiskey A Go Go club in LA.

1972 Johnny Nash started a three week run at No.1 on the US singles chart with 'I Can See Clearly Now', his only US chart topper. It made No.5 in the UK.

1977 *The Last Waltz*, the movie of The Band's final concert, premiered in New York.

1978 Canadian singer Anne Murray went to No.1 on the US singles chart with 'You Needed Me', her only US No.1 hit. The song made No.22 in the UK.

1978 Crosby, Stills, Nash & Young were sued by former bass player Greg Reeves for $1 million (£0.6 million), the amount he claimed he was owed from sales of their album *Déjà Vu*.

1980 Bob Marley was baptised at the Ethiopian Orthodox Church, Kingston, converting to Christian Rastafarianism and taking on the new name Berhane Selassie.

The Beach Boys: neither on a beach nor at The Whiskey A Go Go.

1987 U2 appeared on the front cover of UK pop magazine *Smash Hits*. There were also features on the Pet Shop Boys, Wet Wet Wet, T'Pau, Sting and Black. The Smiths' 'I Started Something I Couldn't Finish' was reviewed in the new singles page.

1989 Elton John scored his 50th UK chart hit when 'Sacrifice' entered the charts (only Cliff Richard and Elvis Presley had also achieved this).

1989 Roxette scored their second US No.1 single with 'Listen To Your Heart', which was a No.6 hit in the UK the following year.

1993 Depeche Mode's Martin Gore was arrested at the Denver Westin Hotel after refusing to turn down the volume of his music in his room.

1998 Fall singer Mark E. Smith appeared at Manhattan Criminal Court on assault charges. He was accused of kicking, punching and choking his girlfriend and band keyboard player Julia Nagle at a New York Hotel.

2001 DMX went to No.1 on the US album chart with *The Great Depression*.

Straight Music presents

BUZZCOCKS
with guests
SUBWAY SECT
HAMMERSMITH ODEON
Queen Caroline St. W.6
SATURDAY 4th NOVEMBER at 7.30
Tickets £2.50, £2.00, £1.50 (inc. VAT) Available Box Office now. Tel. 748 4081

BORN ON THIS DAY

1931 Ike Turner, singer and producer who had a 1966 UK No.3 single with Tina Turner, 'River Deep Mountain High' and a 1971 US No.4 single with 'Proud Mary'.

1941 Art Garfunkel – actor and singer with Simon & Garfunkel, who had a 1970 UK & US No.1 single with 'Bridge Over Troubled Water'. Their 1970 album *Bridge Over Troubled Water* spent 307 weeks on the UK chart. As a solo artist he had a 1979 UK No.1 single with 'Bright Eyes'.

1946 Gram Parsons, US singer/songwriter who was part of The International Submarine Band, The Byrds and the Flying Burrito Brothers. He also released the 1973 solo album *Grievous Angel*. Parsons died on September 19th 1973 from a heroin overdose, aged 26.

1947 Peter Noone – vocalist with Herman's Hermits, who had a 1964 UK No.1 single with 'I'm Into Something Good' and a 1965 US No.1 single with 'Mrs Brown You've Got A Lovely Daughter'.

1959 Bryan Adams, guitarist and vocalist who had a 1985 UK No.11 with 'Run To You', a 1991 UK & US No.1 single with 'Everything I Do (I Do It For You)', which spent 16 weeks at No.1 in the UK, plus over 15 other UK Top 40 singles.

1959 Robert Fisher – one half of pop duo Climie Fisher, who had a 1988 UK No.2 single with 'Love Changes Everything'. They wrote songs for Rod Stewart, Milli Vanilli, Fleetwood Mac and Jermaine Jackson. Fisher died of cancer on August 25th 1999.

1971 Jonathan Greenwood – guitarist and keyboardist with Radiohead, who had a 1997 UK No.1 & US No.21 album with *OK Computer*.

ON THIS DAY

1966 The Monkees went to No.1 on the US singles chart with 'Last Train To Clarksville', the group's first No.1. They revealed during a press conference that no members of the group had played on the record.

1967 Bee Gee Robin Gibb was a passenger on a train that crashed in south east London, killing 49 people and injuring 78. Robin was treated for shock.

1973 Ronnie Lane's Slim Chance played their first-ever gig, appearing in a circus tent on Clapham Common, London.

1977 the manager of the Virgin record store in Nottingham was arrested for displaying a large poster advertising the new Sex Pistols' album *Never Mind The Bollocks, Here's The Sex Pistols*. High street stores banned the album after police warned they could be fined under the 1898 indecent advertising act.

1979 Blue Oyster Cult played the first of four sold-out nights at London's Hammersmith Odeon.

1982 Channel 4 TV's *The Tube* had its first showing. With hosts Paula Yates and Jools Holland, the show featured The Jam and an interview with Mick Jagger. The first live act on the show was local band Toy Dolls. The show helped acts such as Frankie Goes To Hollywood, Paul Young and U2 reach a larger audience.

1983 Billy Joel was at No.1 on the UK singles chart with 'Uptown Girl', his only UK No.1.

1983 Topper Headon of The Clash was arrested for walking his dog while drunk on London's Fulham Road.

1986 Billy Nunn of The Coasters died. The band had had a 1958 US No.1 single with 'Yakety Yak' and a 1959 US No.2 and UK No.6 single with 'Charlie Brown'.

1988 The Beach Boys went to No.1 on the US singles chart with 'Kokomo', a No.25 hit in the UK.

1988 the song 'The Locomotion' became the first to reach the US Top 5 in three different versions when Kylie Minogue's version made No.4. The song had also been a hit for Little Eva and Grand Funk.

1998 ex-Smiths singer Morrissey lost an appeal ruling that all band profits should have been split equally. He faced a backdated pay out to former Smiths member Mike Joyce that was estimated at £1 million ($1.7 million).

2001 *The Times* published the "Rich List" with Madonna being the highest-earning woman in Britain grossing £30 million ($51 million), while all the Spice Girls had dropped out of the listings except for Victoria Beckham. Paul McCartney had earned £20.5 million ($35 million) during the year.

2003 Bobby Hatfield of The Righteous Brothers was found dead in a hotel room in Michigan 30 minutes before he was due on stage. The Brothers had had a 1965 UK & US No.1 single with 'You've Lost That Lovin' Feelin' and a 1990 UK No.1 single with 'Unchained Melody' – the latter had first been released in 1965.

"When I was 14 I looked like a freckled baked bean."
Bono, U2

BORN ON THIS DAY

1894 Adolph Sax, inventor of the saxophone.

1938 P.J. Proby, singer who had a 1964 UK No.3 single with 'Hold Me' and a 1967 US No.23 single with 'Niki Hoeky'.

1941 Guy Clark, singer/songwriter who wrote songs for Johnny Cash and Ricky Skaggs and who released the 1997 album *Essential Guy Clark*.

1947 George Young – guitarist with The Easybeats, who had a 1966 UK No.6 & 1967 US No.16 single with 'Friday On My Mind'.

1948 Glenn Frey – guitarist and vocalist with The Eagles, who had a 1977 US No.1 & UK No.8 single with 'Hotel California' plus five US No.1 albums. *Greatest Hits 1971–1975* is the second biggest-selling album in the world, with sales over 30 million. As a solo artist he had a 1985 UK No.12 single with 'The Heat Is On'.

1964 Corey Glover – vocalist with Living Colour, who had a 1991 UK No.12 single with 'Love Rears Its Ugly Head'.

1979 Trevor Penick – vocalist with O-Town, winners of US TV show *Making The Band*, who had a 2001 US No.3 single with 'All Or Nothing' and a 2001 UK No.3 single with 'Liquid Dreams'.

ON THIS DAY

1961 Jimmy Dean started a five week run at No.1 on the US singles chart with 'Big Bad John', which was a No.2 on the UK chart. Jimmy went on to present a prime-time variety show on US TV.

1964 on their first promotional visit to the UK, The Beach Boys appeared live on ITV's *Ready Steady Go!*

1965 the Grateful Dead and Jefferson Airplane played at the opening night of San Francisco's Fillmore West.

1968 Joe Cocker was at No.1 in the UK singles chart with his version of The Beatles' song 'With A Little Help From My Friends'. The song was also a UK No.1 for Wet Wet Wet in 1988 and Pop Idol duo Sam and Mark in 2004.

1972 Bill Wyman lost his driving licence and was fined £20 ($34) by Chelmsford magistrates court after being caught speeding in his Mercedes on the A12.

1972 during a UK tour, Billy Murcia of The New York Dolls died after choking on his coffee following an overdose of Mandrax.

1973 Michael Martin and Phil Kaufman were charged and fined $300 (£176) each for the theft of a coffin containing Gram Parsons' body (after his body, awaiting shipment to New Orleans for burial, was stolen from Los Angeles Airport and partially cremated in the Californian desert). The court heard that the two men were merely carrying out singer/songwriter Parson's wishes to be cremated in the desert.

1975 the Sex Pistols made their live debut at St Martin's School Of Art in London (the performance lasted ten minutes).

1977 Abba was at No.1 in the UK with the single 'The Name Of The Game', the group's sixth No.1.

1982 Soft Cell's 'Tainted Love' achieved the longest unbroken run on the UK charts when it logged its 43rd week in the Top 100.

1993 Meat Loaf started a five week run at No.1 on the US singles chart with 'I'd Do Anything For Love (But I Won't Do That)'. The song was also a No.1 in the UK.

1993 Pearl Jam went to No.1 on the US album chart with *Vs*, selling 950,378 copies which made it the highest sales in US album history in one week.

2000 Madonna played her first show in eight years when she performed a short 20 minute set at New York's Roseland Ballroom. Madonna wore a tight black vest bearing the sequinned name of 18-year-old Britney Spears.

2001 a number of streets in the German city Frankfurt were temporarily renamed after pop stars to mark the MTV Europe Music Awards. Madonna, Robbie Williams and Janet Jackson all had avenues named after them.

2003 winners at this year's MTV Awards included: Christina Aguilera for Best female; Coldplay won Best group; Justin Timberlake (*below*) won Best album for *Justified*; The Panjabi MC won Best dance act while Best R&B act went to Beyonce. Eminem won the Best hip-hop act award for the fifth year running. Reggae artist Sean Paul took the Best new act award and Best video was won by Sigur Ros. An estimated one billion people in 28 countries watched the show, which was held in Edinburgh, Scotland for the first time.

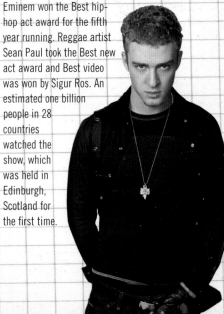

COUNTING CROWS
AND **CRACKER**

GLASGOW BARROWLANDS
Sunday 6th November
Credit Cards Tel: 031 557 6969
NEWCASTLE CITY HALL
Monday 7th November
B/O Tel: 091 261 2606
LEEDS TOWN & COUNTRY CLUB
Tuesday 8th November
B/O Tel: 0532 442999/444600
MANCHESTER ACADEMY
Thursday 10th November
Credit Cards Tel: 061 839 0858

NEWPORT CENTRE
Friday 11th November
Credit Cards Tel: 0633 259676
CAMBRIDGE CORN EXCHANGE
Saturday 12th November
B/O Tel: 0223 357851
WOLVERHAMPTON CIVIC HALL
Monday 14th November
Credit Cards Tel: 0902 312030
SHEPHERDS BUSH EMPIRE
Tues/Wed 15th/16th November
B/O Tel: 081 740 7474 or 071 344 4444

TICKETS ALL £9.00 EXCEPT SHEPHERDS BUSH EMPIRE £10.00
TICKETS AVAILABLE FROM ALL USUAL AGENTS. ALL TICKETS SUBJECT TO BOOKING FEE

BORN ON THIS DAY

1937 Mary Travers – singer with Peter, Paul & Mary, who had a 1969 US No.1 & 1970 UK No.2 single with 'Leaving On A Jet Plane', which was written by John Denver.

1942 Johnny Rivers, US singer/songwriter who had a 1966 US No.1 single with 'Poor Side Of Town' plus over 15 other US Top 40 hits.

1943 Joni Mitchell (a.k.a. Roberta Anderson) *(right)*, singer/songwriter who had a 1970 UK No.11 single with 'Big Yellow Taxi' and a 1974 US No.7 single with 'Help Me'. She wrote 'Both Sides Now', which was a hit for Judy Collins and 'Woodstock' covered by both Crosby, Stills, Nash & Young and Matthews Southern Comfort.

1951 Kevin Scott MacDonald – singer with Cutting Crew, who had a 1987 US No.1 & 1986 UK No.4 single with 'I Just Died In Your Arms'.

1951 Nick Gilder – singer with Sweeney Todd. As a solo artist he had a 1978 US No.1 single with 'Hot Child In The City'.

1967 Sharleen Spiteri – singer with Texas, who had a 1997 UK No.3 single with 'Say What You Want' and a 1997 UK No.1 album with *Blonde On Blonde*.

ON THIS DAY

1958 Eddie Cochran made his UK chart debut with 'Summertime Blues'. It reached No.18 in the UK & No.8 in the US.

1967 Reg Dwight (Elton John) and his songwriting partner Bernie Taupin signed to DJM publishing. Their signatures had to be witnessed by their parents – both were under 21.

1969 The Rolling Stones kicked off their sixth 17- date North American tour at Fort Collins state University, Colorado. Also on the bill were Ike And Tina Turner, Chuck Berry and BB King.

1970 Led Zeppelin released their third album, which entered the UK chart at No.1 and spent a total of 40 weeks on the Top 75.

1974 Ted Nugent won a national squirrel-shooting contest after picking off a squirrel at 137m (150 yards). The heavy metal guitarist also shot dead 27 other mammals during the three day event.

1975 a new world record was set for continuous guitar string plucking by Steve Anderson, who played for 114 hours 17 minutes.

1975 Elton John started a three week run at No.1 on the US album chart with *Rock Of The Westies*, the singer's seventh US No.1.

1981 Hall And Oates started a two week run at No.1 on the US singles chart with 'Private Eyes', the duo's third US No.1 and a No.32 hit in the UK.

1987 Bruce Springsteen

JONI MITCHELL
Travelogue

went to No.1 on the US album chart with *Tunnel Of Love*.

1987 at 16 years old, Tiffany became the youngest act to score a US No.1 since Michael Jackson with 'I Think We're Alone Now'.

1997 The Spice Girls sacked their manager Simon Fuller and his 19 management team.

1999 Geri Halliwell went to No.1 on the UK singles chart with 'Lift Me Up' beating former colleague Emma Bunton's single, which entered the chart at No.2. Sales of Geri's single were helped by front-page press reports about her dating TV and radio presenter Chris Evans.

2002 12 Guns N' Roses fans were arrested during a riot after a gig in Vancouver was cancelled. Promoters pulled the gig after Axl Rose's flight from Los Angeles was delayed.

2002 Whitney Houston's husband, Bobby Brown, was arrested and charged with possession of marijuana, speeding, driving without a licence and having no proof of insurance after he was stopped in Atlanta City.

A young Reg Dwight signs up to a career in music.

BORN ON THIS DAY

1927 Ken Dodd, UK singer and comedian, who had a 1965 UK No.1 single with 'Tears' plus 17 other UK Top 40 hit singles.

1942 Gerald Alston – vocalist with The Manhattans, who had a 1976 US No.1 & UK No.4 single with 'Kiss And Say Goodbye'.

1944 Bonnie Bramlett – vocalist with Delaney & Bonnie, who had a 1971 US No.13 single with 'Never Ending Song Of Love'. They also worked with Eric Clapton during the early 70s. Bramley also had acting roles in *Fame*, *Roseanne* and *The Doors*.

1946 Roy Wood – guitarist and vocalist with The Move, who had a 1969 UK No.1 single with 'Blackberry way", and Wizzard, who had a 1973 UK No.1 single with 'See My Baby Jive'.

1947 Minnie Riperton, US singer who had a 1975 US No.1 & UK No.2 Stevie Wonder produced single with 'Loving You'. Riperton died of cancer on July 12th 1979.

1949 Bonnie Raitt, blues singer/songwriter and slide guitarist who had a 1994 UK No.31 single with 'You' and a 1990 US No.1 album with *Nick Of Time*.

1954 Rickie Lee Jones, singer/songwriter who had a 1979 US No.4 & UK No.18 single with 'Chuck E.'s In Love'.

1957 Porl Thompson – guitarist with The Cure, who had a 1989 US No.2 single with 'Love Song', a 1992 UK No.6 single with 'Friday I'm In Love' plus over 20 other UK Top 40 singles.

1985 Jack Osbourne, son of Ozzy and star of MTV *The Osbournes* TV show. Also presented the UK TV show *Union Jack* and co-hosted the ITV2 show, *Celebrity Wrestling:Bring It On!*

ON THIS DAY

1952 the *New Musical Express* published the first-ever UK pop chart after staff asked 53 record shops to divulge their sales returns. 'Here In My Heart' by Al Martino was the first No.1. The song stayed at No.1 for nine weeks.

1958 the soundtrack to *South Pacific* went to No.1 on the UK album chart. It became the longest-running No.1 album of all time, spending a total of 115 weeks at the No.1 position. It also spent 31 weeks on the US album chart at No.1.

1963 Dusty Springfield set out on her first UK solo tour kicking off in Halifax. She shared the bill with The Searchers, Freddie & The Dreamers and Brian Poole & The Tremeloes.

1967 The Foundations were at No.1 on the UK singles chart with 'Baby, Now That I've Found You', the group's only UK No.1.

1968 appearing at The Walthamstow Granada Theatre were The Who, Joe Cocker And The Grease Band, The Mindbenders and The Crazy World Of Arthur Brown.

1969 'Something', the first Beatles A-side

Spice Girl Melanie C gives it both barrels.

composed by George Harrison, entered the UK singles chart. It peaked at No.4 in the UK & No.1 in the US.

1971 the UK Top 5 singles chart was: No.5, Tom Jones, 'Till'; No.4, Al Green, 'Tired Of Being Alone'; No.3, Rod Stewart, 'Maggie May'; No.2, Redbone, 'The Which Queen of New Orleans' and No.1, Slade, 'Coz I Love You'.

1975 David Bowie made his US TV debut performing 'Fame' on the *Cher* CBS-TV show.

1975 Elton John was named godfather to John and Yoko Lennon's son Sean.

1980 Bruce Springsteen *(left)* started a four week run at No.1 on the US album chart with *The River*, his first US No.1 album.

1986 taken from the film *Top Gun* Berlin started a four week run at No.1 on the UK singles chart with 'Take Your Breath Away'.

1993 Take That kicked off their 21 date, sold-out UK *Everything Changes* tour in Bournemouth.

1998 Robbie Williams scored his second UK No.1 album with *I've Been Expecting You*.

1999 Eminem played the first of two sold-out nights at the London Astoria. Tickets cost £12 ($20).

2000 Spice Girl Mel C made a foul-mouthed attack on Westlife, calling them "a useless bunch of talentless tossers" and "hyped-up shit". Mel made the attack during The Spice Girls party to launch their new album *Forever*.

BORN ON THIS DAY

1941 Tom Fogerty – guitarist with Creedence Clearwater Revival, who had a 1969 US No.2 & UK No.1 single with 'Bad Moon Rising' and a 1970 US & UK No.1 album with *Cosmo's Factory*. Fogerty died on September 6th 1990.

1948 Alan Gratzer – drummer with REO Speedwagon, who had a 1981 US No.1 & UK No.7 single with 'Keep On Loving You'.

1948 Joe Bouchard – bass guitarist with Blue Oyster Cult, who had a 1976 US No.12 & 1978 UK No.16 single with 'Don't Fear The Reaper'.

1954 Dennis Stratton – guitarist with Iron Maiden, who had a 1991 UK No.1 single with 'Bring Your Daughter To The Slaughter'.

1969 Sandra Denton (a.k.a. Pepa) – rapper with Salt-N-Pepa, who had a 1991 UK No.2 single with 'Let's Talk About Sex'.

1977 Sisqo, (a.k.a. Mark Andrews), singer who had a 2000 US & UK No.3 single with 'Thong Song'.

1984 Delta Goodrem, Australian singer and actress (she was Nina Tucker in TV's *Neighbours*) who had a 2003 UK No.3 single with 'Born To Try' and a 2003 UK No.2 album with *Innocent Eyes*.

ON THIS DAY

1955 The Everly Brothers made their first studio recordings at Nashville's Old Tulane Hotel Studios, cutting four tracks in just over 20 minutes.

1958 Elvis Presley's 'Hound Dog' exceeded three million copies in the USA, becoming only the third single to do so (Bing Crosby's 'White Christmas' and 'Rudolph The Red Nose Reindeer' by Gene Autry were the other two).

1961 Brain Epstein saw The Beatles for the first time during a lunchtime session at The Cavern, Liverpool.

1965 Wilson Pickett made his UK live debut at the Scotch Of St James Club in London.

1966 John Lennon met Yoko Ono for the first time at her art exhibition at the Indica Gallery, London.

1967 the first issue of *Rolling Stone* magazine was published in San Francisco. It came with a free "roach clip" to hold a marijuana joint.

1968 Led Zeppelin played their first-ever London show when they appeared at The Roundhouse, Chalk Farm.

1974 Bachman Turner Overdrive went to No.1 on the US singles chart with 'You Ain't Seen Nothin' Yet', the group's only No.1. It made No.2 in the UK.

1985 Jan Hammer went to No.1 on the US singles chart with the '*Miami Vice* Theme', a No.5 hit in the UK.

1990 the internal revenue seized all of country singer Willie Nelson's bank accounts and real estate holdings in connection with a $16 million (£9.4 million) tax debt.

1991 Tin Machine (David Bowie's new group) appeared at The Cambridge Corn Exchange.

1991 Prince started a two week run at No.1 on the US singles chart with 'Cream', which was a No.15 hit in the UK.

1996 actors Robson and Jerome scored their third UK No.1 single when their versions of 'What Becomes Of The Broken Hearted?/Up On The Roof/You'll Never Walk Alone' started a two week stay at the top of the charts.

1996 Oasis singer Liam Gallagher was arrested after being stopped by police in London's Oxford Street and charged with possession of a class A controlled substance.

1997 Paul Weller was arrested and spent the night in a French jail after smashing up his hotel room. His record company paid £4,000 ($6,800) to cover the damage and Weller was released the following day.

2002 it was announced that Madonna's latest movie *Swept Away* would not be released in the UK because it had been such a flop in the US. The *Washington Post* said the film was "as awful as

Madonna is swept away from UK cinemas

By A Correspondent

MADONNA'S disastrous new film Swept Away will not be released in the UK because it has been such a box-office flop in the US, it was announced yesterday.

The film, directed by her husband Guy Ritchie, was savaged by the critics and has taken barely £377,000 since its release last month. It had been due in British cinemas in March but will now go straight to video.

What a handsome pair. Everly Brothers Phil and Don.

BORN ON THIS DAY

1941 Kyu Sakamoto, singer who had a 1963 US No.1 & UK No.6 single with 'Sukiyaki', the first-ever Japanese US No.1. He was killed in a plane crash on August 12th 1985.

1948 Greg Lake – singer/songwriter and bass player with King Crimson and ELP, who had a 1977 UK No.2 single with 'Fanfare For The Common Man'. As a solo artist he had a 1975 UK No.2 single with 'I Believe In Father Christmas'.

1954 Mario Cipollina – bass player with Huey Lewis & The News, who had a 1985 US No.1 & UK No.11 single with 'The Power Of Love'.

1957 Chris Joyce – drummer with Simply Red, who had a 1986 US No.1 & UK No.2 single with 'Holding Back The Years'.

1958 Frank Maudsley – bass player with A Flock Of Seagulls, who had a 1982 UK No.10 & US No.26 single with 'Wishing, If I Had A Photograph Of You'.

1970 Derry Brownson – keyboardist with EMF, who had a 1990 UK No.3 & 1991 US No.1 single with 'Unbelievable'.

1970 Warren G, US rapper who had a 1994 UK No.5 single with 'Regulate' and a 1996 UK No.2 single with Adina Howard, 'What's Love Got To Do With It?'

1978 Eve, US female rapper who had a 2001 UK No.4 single, featuring Gwen Stefani, 'Let Me Blow Ya Mind'.

ON THIS DAY

1958 soul singer Sam Cooke was injured in a car crash in Marion, Arkansas. The driver was killed in the accident.

1961 Elvis Presley was at No.1 on the UK singles chart with 'His Latest Flame/Little Sister'. It was the singer's ninth UK No.1.

1963 The Yardbirds (with Eric Clapton) appeared at The Crawdaddy Club, Richmond, Surrey.

1967 The Beatles made the promotional film for 'Hello, Goodbye' at London's Saville Theatre.

1972 Alice Cooper appeared live at Glasgow's Playhouse, Scotland.

1973 Elton John started an eight week run at No.1 on the US album chart with *Goodbye Yellow Brick Road*, the singer's third US No.1.

1975 David Bowie was at No.1 on the UK singles chart with 'Space Oddity', (it was first released in 1969 to tie in with the Apollo Moon landing).

1979 Fleetwood Mac scored their second UK No.1 album with *Tusk*.

1979 The Eagles went to No.1 on the US singles chart with 'Heartache Tonight', the group's fifth and final US No.1.

1984 after setting a new record for advanced orders, 1,099,500 copies, Frankie Goes To Hollywood went to No.1 on the UK album chart with their debut LP *Welcome To The Pleasure Dome*. Also on this day the band made their debut US TV appearance on *Saturday Night Live* performing 'Two Tribes' and 'Born To Run'.

1984 former Rufus singer Chaka Khan was at No.1 on the UK singles chart with 'I Feel For You'. The song was written by Prince, featured Stevie Wonder on harmonica and Grandmaster Melle Mel rapped on the track.

1990 Vanilla Ice started a 16 week run at No.1 on the US album chart with *To The Extreme*.

1999 eighties hit-making team Stock, Aitken and Waterman went to court fighting over song rights. Stock and Aitken claimed they were owed hundreds of thousands of pounds, as musicians and songwriters, by Waterman.

2002 viewers of the UK music channel VH1 voted 'I Will Always Love You' as the No.1 most romantic song ever. In second place was Elvis Presley's 'You Were Always On My Mind' and third place went to 'My Heart Will Go On' by Celine Dion.

2002 Eminem was at No.1 on the US album chart with the *8 Mile Soundtrack*.

2004 Liza Minnelli's former bodyguard accused the singer of forcing him to have sex with her in order to keep his job, court documents revealed. M'hammed Soumayah was suing Minnelli for $100 million (£58.8 million) damages, saying she made "many repeated attempts" to compel him into sex and he "eventually succumbed".

ROYAL FESTIVAL HALL
DIRECTOR: JOHN DENISON. C.B.E

NEIL YOUNG AND CRAZY HORSE
WITH THE EAGLES
SAT., 10 NOVEMBER, 1973
8 p.m.
Management : M.A.M. Promotions Ltd.

TERRACE
£2.00

GANGWAY 9
ROW   SEAT
F   31

RED SIDE
Please enter the
auditorium by
DOOR
4
LEVEL
4

BORN ON THIS DAY

1927 Mose Allison, singer/songwriter, pianist and blues artist. His songs have been covered by artists including The Who, John Mayall, Elvis Costello and Georgie Fame.

1946 Chip Hawkins – singer with The Tremeloes, who had a 1963 UK No.1 single with 'Do You Love Me?' and a 1967 US No.11 single with 'Silence Is Golden'. He is the father of singer/actor Chesney Hawkes.

1946 Chris Dreja – guitarist with The Yardbirds, who had a 1965 UK No.3 & US No.6 single with 'For Your Love'.

1950 Jim Peterik – guitarist, keyboardist and vocalist with Ides Of March, who had a 1970 US No.2 single with 'Vehicle', and Survivor, who had a 1982 US & UK No.1 single with 'Eye Of The Tiger'.

1953 Andy Partridge – vocalist and guitarist with XTC, who had a 1982 UK No.10 single with 'Senses Working Overtime'.

ON THIS DAY

1955 Elvis Presley was voted the most promising new country & western artist by *Billboard* magazine.

1957 Jerry Lee Lewis secretly married his third wife and cousin, Myra Gale Brown, in Tennessee.

1969 Jim Morrison was arrested by the FBI in Phoenix, Arizona for drunk and disorderly conduct aboard a plane on the way to a Rolling Stones concert.

1971 BBC TV's *Top Of The Pops* celebrated its 400th show. It was presented by Tony Blackburn with guests Tom Jones, Dana, John Kongos, Cher, Slade, Cilla Black, The Piglets, Clodagh Rodgers and The Newbeats.

1972 bass player Berry Oakley of The Allman Brothers was killed in a motorcycle accident at the same intersection as former band member Duane Allman, who had died a year earlier. Oakley was 24 years old.

1972 Gilbert O'Sullivan was at No.1 on the UK singles chart with 'Clair', the singer's first of two UK No.1s.

1973 thirty US radio stations broadcasted a "live" Mott The Hoople concert. In reality it was the band recorded in the studio with the applause dubbed in.

1978 Donna Summer started a three week run at No.1 on the US singles chart with her version of Jimmy Webb's 'MacArthur Park', which was also a hit for actor Richard Harris in 1968. Also on this day Summer went to No.1 on the US album chart with *Live And More*.

1978 The Cars released the first-ever commercially available picture disc single, 'My Best Friend's Girl', which made No.3 in the UK charts.

1986 Big Audio Dynamite appeared at Birmingham's Powerhouse, England. Tickets cost £5 ($8.50).

1989 Chris Rea started an three week run at No.1 on the UK album chart with *The Road To Hell*.

Paddy Clancy (right).

Chris Dreja's passport.

1989 Lisa Stansfield was at No.1 in the UK with the single 'All Around The World'.

1990 a 21-year-old AC/DC fan was attacked and died outside the Brendan Byrne Arena in New Jersey, where the band was playing a gig.

1995 the Smashing Pumpkins' double album *Mellon Collie And The Infinite Sadness* went to No.1 on the US chart.

1998 Irish singer Paddy Clancy of the Clancy Brothers died, aged 76. He wrote the classic Irish songs 'Wild Mountain Thyme' and 'Carrickfergus'.

1999 Britney Spears won four MTV Awards with: Best female singer, Best pop act, Best song for 'Baby One More Time' and Best breakthrough artist. Best rock act was The Offspring, Best male act was Will Smith and Bono won the Free your mind award.

2003 The Darknesss played the Carling Homecoming gig at The Astoria, London.

2004 Robbie Williams, The Rolling Stones and Queen were inducted into the UK's first music Hall of Fame at a ceremony in London. One act had been chosen by TV viewers of a Channel 4 programme to represent each decade since the 1950s. Williams represented the 1990s, Michael Jackson the 1980s, Queen the 1970s, The Rolling Stones the 1960s and Cliff Richard the 1950s.

BORN ON THIS DAY

1943 Brian Hyland, US singer who had a 1960 US No.1 & UK No.8 single with 'Itsy Bitsy Teenie Weenie Yellow Polka Dot Bikini'.

1944 Booker T. Jones – multi-instrumentalist with Booker T And The MGs, who had a 1962 US No. 3 single with 'Green Onions' and a 1969 UK No.4 single with 'Time Is Tight'.

1945 Neil Young – singer/songwriter for Buffalo Springfield, who had a 1967 US No.17 single with 'For What It's Worth', and Crosby, Stills, Nash & Young, who had a 1970 US No.1 & UK No.5 album with *Déjà Vu*. As a solo artist he had a 1972 US No.1 & UK No.10 single with 'Heart Of Gold'.

1948 Errol Brown – vocalist with Hot Chocolate, who had a 1975 US No.3 single with 'You Sexy Thing', a 1977 UK No.1 single with 'So You Win Again' plus over 25 other Top 40 hits.

1955 Les McKeown – vocalist with the Bay City Rollers, who had a 1975 UK No.1 single with 'Bye Bye Baby' plus 11 other UK Top 20 singles.

ON THIS DAY

1956 Johnnie Ray was at No.1 on the UK singles chart with 'Just Walking In The Rain'. It stayed at No.1 for seven weeks, making it this year's Christmas No.1.

1965 having changed his name from Toby Tyler, Marc Bolan performed his first single 'The Wizzard' on the UK TV show *Ready Steady Go!*

1965 Velvet Underground made their live debut when they played at Summit High School, New Jersey. The band was paid $75 (£44) for the gig.

1966 The Monkees' debut album started a 13 week run at No.1 in the US album chart, selling over three million copies in three months.

1968 UK book and record chain WHSmith refused to display the Jimi Hendrix Experience album

THE JIMI HENDRIX EXPERIENCE ELECTRIC LADYLAND

These fine ladies get the Jimi Hendrix Experience.

Electric Ladyland due to the naked girls featured on the sleeve.

1983 Lionel Richie started a four week run at No.1 on the US singles chart with 'All Night Long', becoming Motown's biggest seller to date. The song made No.2 in the UK..

1990 Rolling Stone Ron Wood broke both his legs after his car had broken down on the M4 motorway near Marlborough, Wiltshire as he was trying to wave other cars past his.

1993 John Otway played at London's Astoria. It was Otway's 2,000th gig.

1997 singer and keyboard player Billy Preston was jailed for three years for possessing cocaine.

1997 George Michael launched his fanclub Members Online on the internet.

1998 winners at the MTV Europe Awards included: Madonna, who won Best female artist and album for *Ray Of Light*; The Spice Girls won Best group; All Saints won Breakthrough

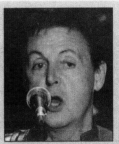

ALL CHANGE. . . Sir Paul

So now it's McCartney & Lennon

artist; Robbie Williams won Best male artist and Natalie Imbruglia won Best song for 'Torn'.

2000 Destiny's Child started an 11 week run at No.1 on the US singles chart with 'Independent Woman Part 1'.

2002 die hard Beatles fans were enraged after Paul McCartney altered the songwriting credits on original Beatles songs featured on his *Back In The US 2002* album. He changed them to McCartney and Lennon from Lennon and McCartney.

2002 the city of Atlanta declared this day as TLC Day, in order to remember Lisa "Left Eye" Lopes who was killed in a car crash on April 26th 2002, aged 30.

2004 the funeral of DJ John Peel took place at St. Edmundsbury Cathedral, Bury St. Edmunds, Suffolk. Pulp's Jarvis Cocker, Undertones singer Feargal Sharkey and The White Stripes were among mourners, while Sir Elton John left a wreath of yellow roses.

BORN ON THIS DAY

1934 Timmy Thomas, US singer who had a 1972 US No.3 & 1973 UK No.12 single with 'Why Can' We Live Together'.

1951 Bill Gibson – drummer for Huey Lewis & The News, who had a 1985 US No.1 & UK No.11 single with 'The Power Of Love'.

1953 Andrew Ranken – drummer for The Pogues, who had a 1987 UK No.8 single with 'The Irish Rover'.

1979 Nikolai Fraiture – bass player with The Strokes, who had a 2001 UK No.14 single with 'Last Nite'.

ON THIS DAY

1966 appearing live at the Birmingham Theatre were The Beach Boys, Lulu and David And Jonathan.

1968 Rolling Stone Brian Jones bought Cotchford Farm in Sussex, which was once owned by A.A. Milne the author of *Winnie The Pooh*.

1968 Hugo Montenegro was at No.1 in the UK singles chart with 'The Good The Bad And The Ugly', the soundtrack from a Clint Eastwood spaghetti western film.

1971 Santana scored their second US No.1 album with *Santana III*.

1971 The Faces appeared at The Pavilion, Bath, England. Tickets cost 75p ($1.30).

1973 Jerry Lee Lewis Jr. was killed in a car accident near Hernando, Mississippi. Lewis had been working as the drummer in his father's band.

1975 Joan Armatrading appeared at The Colston Hall, Bristol, supported by Supertramp.

1976 Led Zeppelin scored their seventh UK No.1 album with the film soundtrack to *The Song Remains The Same*. It made No.2 in the US.

1976 Rod Stewart started an eight week run at No.1 on the US singles chart with 'Tonight's The Night'. It was Rod's second US No.1. The song made No.5 in the UK after being banned by many radio stations due to it being about the seduction of a virgin.

1981 U2 kicked off a 15 date US tour in Albany, New York.

1982 Men At Work started a 15 week run at No.1 on the US album chart with their debut album *Business As Usual*. It went on to sell over five million copies in the US.

Above: Brian Jones becomes a farmer.

1982 former Equals singer Eddie Grant was at No.1 on the UK singles chart with 'I Don't Wanna Dance'.

1990 Patricia Boughton filed a lawsuit against Rod Stewart claiming that a football he kicked into the crowd at a concert at Pine Knob Music Theatre had ruptured a tendon in her middle finger and as a result made sex between her and her husband difficult.

1992 Ronnie Bond of The Troggs died. The band had had a 1966 US No.1 & UK No.2 single with 'Wild Thing'.

1999 it was announced that Cliff Richard had signed up with Internet company Remotemusic.com, making him the first major artist to sign a deal with an online company.

2000 The Beatles launched their first official website www.thebeatles.com on the same day as the release of their retrospective *Compilation 1*.

2002 the three surviving members of Led Zeppelin announced they were re-forming after 22 years for a US stadium tour.

2004 rap artist Ol' Dirty Bastard, (real name Russell Jones), collapsed and died at a Manhattan recording studio in New York, aged 35. A spokesman for his record company said the rapper had complained of chest pains, but was dead by the time paramedics reached him. He had been a founding member of the Wu-Tang Clan in the early 1990s.

Right: John Bonham and large friend in *The Song Remains The Same*.

BORN ON THIS DAY

1936 Freddie Garrity – vocalist with Freddie & The Dreamers, who had a 1963 UK No.3 single with 'You Were Made For Me' and a 1965 US No.1 single with 'I'm Telling You Now'.

1938 Cornell Gunter – vocalist with The Coasters, who had a 1958 US No.1 single with 'Yakety Yak' and a 1959 UK No.6 single with 'Charlie Brown'. He was shot dead on February 26th 1990 by an unknown person.

1949 James Young – guitarist for Styx, who had a 1979 US No.1 & 1980 UK No.6 single with 'Babe'.

1951 Steven Bishop, US singer/songwriter who wrote the 1976 album *Careless*, sang the theme for the film *Tootsie* and had a 1977 US No.11 single with 'On And On'.

1956 Alec John Such – bass player for Bon Jovi, who had a 1987 US No.1 & UK No.4 single with 'Livin' On A Prayer'.

1966 Joseph "Run" Simmons – rapper with Run-DMC, who had a 1986 UK No.8 single with Aerosmith, 'Walk This Way', and a 1998 UK No.1 single with 'It's Like That'.

1968 Brian Yale – bass player for Matchbox 20, who had a 1998 UK No.38 single with 'Push' and a 2000 US No.1 single with 'Bent'.

1970 Adina Howard, US singer who had a 1996 UK No.2 single with Warren G, 'What's Love Got To Do With It?'

1972 Douglas Payne – bass player for Travis, who had a 1999 UK No.1 album with *The Man Who* and a 1999 UK No.10 single with 'Why Does It Always Rain On Me?'

1975 Faye Tozer – singer with Steps, who had a 1998 UK No.1 single with 'Heartbeat/Tragedy'.

1975 Travis Barker – drummer with Blink 182, who had a 2000 UK No.2 single with 'All The Small Things' and a 2001 US No.1 album with *Take Off Your...*

ON THIS DAY

1954 Bill Haley scored his first US Top 10 hit with 'Shake, Rattle And Roll'.

1960 Ray Charles went to No.1 on the US singles chart with 'Georgia On My Mind'. It made No.24 in the UK.

1967 a package tour with Jimi Hendrix, Pink Floyd, The Move, Nice and Amen Corner kicked off at the Royal Albert Hall, London. The acts played two shows per night.

FLOYD JOIN HENDRIX ; FUDGE CANCELS DATES

THE Pink Floyd have been booked as an additional attraction on the Jimi Hendrix-Move-Amen Corner package tour, for which two additional dates have been set by promoter Tito Burns of the Harold Davison Organisation. Vanilla Fudge have dropped out of their current tour due to the illness of the lead singer—but they expect to undertake London dates later this month. The Mamas and Papas' London concert with Scott McKenzie has been brought forward by two days.

As it is now quite definite that the Turtles will be unable to join the Hendrix-Move-Amen tour, promoter Burns has added the Pink Floyd to the line-up. The package opens at London's Royal Albert Hall on November 14 and—in addition to the dates already exclusively reported in the NME—two new venues set for next week are NEWCASTLE City Hall (December 4) and SHEFFIELD City Hall (5th).

Mark Stein, lead singer and organist of Vanilla Fudge, collapsed last weekend as a result of nervous strain and exhaustion. By agreement with the promoter, the group withdrew from its tour with Traffic, the Flowerpot

Men and Tomorrow, and has been replaced throughout this month by the Mindbenders. It is possible the Fudge will be able to play some of the later dates on the itinerary.

Meanwhile, Vanilla Fudge plays a Sunday concert at London's Saville Theatre on October 22. They will occupy the whole first half of the show, with Who featured throughout the second half. The group also plays London's Speakeasy on December 19, and other London club dates are being lined-up —as well as concerts in Sweden, France and Germany.

The Mamas and Papas–Scott McKenzie concert at London's Royal Albert Hall, originally planned by Burns for November 1, has been brought forward a Monday, October 30. It is still probable that they will play a second date at this venue later the same week, but the plan to visit Manchester has now been scrapped.

The American stars flew this week to Paris where McKenzie is making promotional appearances. The Mamas and Papas then travelled to North Africa for a few days, where Scott will rejoin them, before they all go to Majorca for a fortnight's vacation.

1976 appearing at The Roundhouse, London were The Flamin' Groovies, The Troggs and The Damned. Tickets cost £1.70 ($2.90).

1981 The Police had their fourth UK No.1 single with 'Every Little Thing She Does Is Magic'.

1987 George Michael went to No.1 on the UK album chart with his debut solo album *Faith*, which was also No.1 in the US.

1987 T'Pau started a five week run at No.1 on the UK singles chart with 'China In Your Hand'.

1990 producer Frank Farin fired Milli Vanilli singers Rob Pilatus and Fabrice Morvan because they were insisting on singing on their new album.

Right: Mary J Blige on tour in the UK.

Below: Dusty Springfield's agent makes some plans.

NYNEX ARENA
MANCHESTER
FRIDAY 14th NOVEMBER
AT 8 pm Tickets £16.50* from NYNEX ARENA Box Office
CREDIT CARD BOOKINGS
0161 930 8000 (24hrs) · 0990 232007 (24hrs 18p per min max)

WEMBLEY ARENA
SATURDAY 15th NOVEMBER
AT 8 pm Tickets £18.50* from
WEMBLEY ARENA Box Office
CREDIT CARD BOOKINGS
0181 900 1234 (24hrs)
0990 232006 (24hrs 18p per min max)

BNB ASSOCIATES LTD.
NINETY FOUR FIFTY FOUR WILSHIRE BLVD.
BEVERLY HILLS, CALIFORNIA 90212
(213) 273-7020   CABLE: SHERMACE

November 14, 1972

Mr. David Shrimpton
Phonogram Limited
Stanhope House
Stanhope Place
London W2, England

Dear David:

Thank you for the albums. They were most appreciated. As for Dusty's schedule she will be opening at the "Talk of the Town" on December 4th, which gives her little time in front of that date because of the rehearsals of the new act.

Upon my arrival we shall sit down and talk about her available time, which should come after December 4th. I would like her to settle in the new act.

Looking forward to seeing you.

Sincerely,

Howard L. Portugais
HOWARD L. PORTUGAIS

HLP/nfs

1991 over 1,000 New Kids On The Block fans were given medical treatment after a minor riot during a concert in Berlin.

1992 Bon Jovi went to No.1 on the UK album chart with *Keep The Faith*, their second UK No.1 LP.

1995 Blur brought chaos to traffic in central London when over 3,000 fans turned up for a signing at Books Etc in Charing Cross Road.

1996 Michael Jackson married Debbie Rowe, they divorced in 1999.

1999 Robbie Williams went to No.1 on the UK singles chart with 'She's The One/It's Only Us', his second UK No.1. He had scored six other chart toppers as a member of Take That.

2000 UK music shop HMV refused to stock the new single by The Offspring after the band decided to give the track away as a free download on their official website.

BORN ON THIS DAY

1905 Mantovani, orchestra leader who had a 1953 UK No.1 single with 'Moulin Rouge' and a 1957 US No. 12 single with 'Around The World In Eighty Days'. He died on March 30th 1980.

1932 Petula Clark, singer who had a 1961 UK No.1 single with 'Sailor', a 1967 UK No.1 single with 'This Is My Song' plus over 15 other UK Top 40 singles and a 1965 US No.1 with 'Downtown'. She was the first UK female singer to score a No.1 single in the US.

1933 Clyde McPhatter – singer with The Drifters, who had a 1960 US No.1 & UK No.2 single with 'Save The Last Dance For Me'. McPhatter died on June 13th 1972.

1945 Anni-Frid Andersson – vocalist with Abba, who had their first UK No.1 hit single in 1974 with 'Waterloo', which was followed by eight other UK No.1 singles and nine UK No.1 albums as well as a 1977 US No.1 single with 'Dancing Queen'.

1954 Tony Thompson – drummer with Chic, who had a 1978 US No.1 & UK No.7 single with 'Le Freak'. He also worked with David Bowie and Madonna and appeared at Live Aid drumming with Led Zeppelin. He died on November 12th 2003.

1968 Ol' Dirty Bastard (a.k.a. ODB, Dirty, Dirt McGirt, Dirt Dog, Big Baby Jesus, Osirus and Joe Bananas but was born Russell Tyrone Jones) – founding member of the Wu-Tang Clan, who had a 1997 US & UK No.1 album with *Wu-Tang Forever*. He collapsed and died at a Manhattan recording studio in New York on November 13th 2004, aged 35.

1974 Chad Kroeger – guitarist with Nickelback, who had a 2002 US No.1 & UK No.4 single with 'How To Remind You', a 2001 US No.2 & 2002 UK No.2 album with *Silver Side Up* and a 2002 UK No.4 single with Josey Scott from Saliva, 'Hero'.

ON THIS DAY

1959 Johnny & The Moondogs (The Beatles) played in the final heat of the "TV Star Search" competition at The Hippodrome Theatre, Manchester. The band didn't win the heat due to the voting being based on a "clapometer". They couldn't afford a hotel so they took the train back to Liverpool before the voting took place.

1964 Brian Jones from the Stones was admitted to Passavant Hospital in Chicago with a temperature of 41°C (105°F), which caused him to miss the last few dates on the band's current tour.

1969 Janis Joplin was arrested during a gig in Tampa, Florida after arguing with a policeman and refusing to tell the audience to sit down.

1971 this week's *Disc And Music Echo*'s progressive album chart was as follows: No.5, Cat Stevens, *Teaser And The Firecat*; No.4, Hawkwind, *In Search Of Space*; No.3, Santana, *Santana III*; No.2,

Rod Stewart, *Every Picture Tells A Story* and No.1 was John Lennon's *Imagine*.

1980 Blondie had their fifth UK No.1 single and third No.1 of this year with 'The Tide Is High', a song written by John Holt. It was also a No.1 in the US.

1980 Kenny Rogers started a six week run at No.1 on the US singles chart with 'Lady', a song written and produced by Lionel Richie. It was a No.12 hit in the UK.

1984 R.E.M. played the first date on the band's second UK tour at Tiffany's Ballroom, Newcastle.

1986 pop history was made when the Top 5 UK singles were all by female vocalists: Corinne Drewery from Swing Out Sister; Mel & Kim; Susannah Hoffs from The Bangles; Kim Wilde and Terri Nunn from Berlin.

1990 Milli Vanilli producer Frank Farian held a press conference to confirm the rumours that the two members of the group Rob and Fab had not sung on their records.

1991 Jacques Morali, producer and songwriter who had formed The Village People, died of complications from AIDs.

1992 Ozzy Osbourne announced his retirement after a gig in California, saying "Who wants to be touring at 46?"

2000 Michael Abram, the Liverpool man who stabbed George Harrison after breaking into his home, was awarded a not guilty verdict at Oxford's Crown Court. The verdict was returned in view of Abram's mental history.

2000 winners at The MTV Europe Awards included: All Saints for Best pop act; Ricky Martin won Best male artist; Madonna won Best female artist; Red Hot Chili Peppers won Best rock band; Blink 182 won Best new act and Jennifer Lopez won Best R&B act.

LOVE BLONDIE

BORN ON THIS DAY

1916 Herb Abramson, producer, songwriter and co-founder of Atlantic Records. He wrote and produced Tommy Tucker's 1964 hit 'High Heeled Sneakers'. Abramson died on November 9th 1999.

1938 Troy Seals – guitarist with James Brown's Band, who had a 1966 US No.8 and UK No.13 single with 'It's A Man's World', a 1986 UK No.5 single with 'Living In America' and a 1963 album with *Live At The Apollo*.

1943 Winfred Lovett – vocalist with The Manhattans, who had a 1976 US No.1 & UK No.4 single with 'Kiss And Say Goodbye'.

1962 Gary "Mani" Mounfield – bass player with The Stone Roses, who had a 1989 UK No.8 single with 'Fool's Gold' and a 1989 album with *The Stone Roses*, and Primal Scream, who had a 1994 UK No.7 single with 'Rocks'.

1964 Diana Krall, Canadian singer/songwriter who has become one of the bestselling jazz artists of all time. She was nominated for Album of the Year at the 2000 Grammys and won three Juno awards in 2002: Artist of the year; Album of the year and Best vocal jazz album of the year.

1969 Bryan Abrams – singer with Color Me Bad, who had a 1991 UK No.1 single with 'I Wanna Sex You Up' and a 1991 US No.1 single with 'I Adore Mi Amor'.

ON THIS DAY

1968 the Jimi Hendrix Experience was at No.1 on the US album chart with the double album *Electric Ladyland*.

1974 David Essex was at No.1 on the UK singles chart with 'Gonna Make You A Star' the singer's first UK No.1.

1974 John Lennon was at No.1 in the US singles chart with 'Whatever Gets You Through The Night'. Elton John played on the session and made a deal with Lennon that if the song reached No.1 he would appear on stage with him. He did on the 28th of this month.

1976 Beach Boy Brian Wilson gave his first formal interview for eight years on the UK BBC 2 TV show the *Old Grey Whistle Test*. Also on the programme was Be Bop Deluxe and Cajun Moon.

1983 Frankie Goes To Hollywood kicked off a seven date UK tour at Eves, Wolverhampton.

1985 former Undertones singer Feargal Sharkey had his only UK No.1 single with the Maria McKee song 'A Good Heart'.

1985 Sade scored her first UK No.1 album with *Promise*.

1985 Starship started a two week run at No.1 on the US singles chart with 'We Built This City', which made No.12 in the UK.

1985 U2 launched their own label, Mother Records.

1987 ex-Clash drummer, Topper Headon, was jailed for 15 months at Maidstone Crown Court for supplying heroin to a man who later died.

1988 former Beach Boys manager Stephen Love was sentenced to five years probation for embezzling almost $1 million (£0.6 million) from the group's accounts.

1991 Irish singer Enya scored her first UK No.1 album with *Shepherd Moons*.

1996 The Spice Girls went to No.1 on the UK album chart with their debut release *Spice Girls*.

1996 The Backstreet Boys kicked off a 14-date UK tour at the Newport Centre.

1996 The Beatles *Anthology 3* went to No.1 on the UK album chart.

2000 Russ Conway, pianist and composer, died. He had had a 1959 UK No.1 single with 'Side Saddle' plus 17 other UK Top 40 hits.

2000 Joseph Calleja, member of Kid Rock's band, died of chronic intestinal disorder.

2002 Texan multi-billionaire David Bonderman hired The Rolling Stones to play at his 60th birthday party held at the Hard Rock Hotel in Las Vegas. The band's fee was $7.5m (£4.4m).

2002 *The Robbie Williams Show* was aired on BBC TV with the singer premiering new songs in front of a studio audience.

2003 Busted scored their second UK No.1 single with 'Crashed The Wedding.'

Frankie try to work on their macho image for this 1983 tour poster.

BLOCK 104   ROW   U SEAT   18
LOWER TIERER

25-39922   SJM CONCERTS PRESENT

‡ FOO FIGHTERS ‡
PLUS SPECIAL GUESTS

18.50   M.E.N. ARENA DOORS 6.00PM
18.50   SAT 16-NOV-2002 AT 7.30PM

BORN ON THIS DAY

1937 Peter Cook, comedian (part of duo Derek & Clive) and compere of UK TV music show *Revolver*. He had a 1965 UK No.18 single with Dudley Moore, 'Goodbye-ee'. Cook died on January 9th 1995.

1937 Geoff Goddard, songwriter who wrote 'Johnny Remember Me' and played keyboards on The Tornados' 1962 No.1 hit 'Telstar'. He died on February 15th 2000.

1938 Gordon Lightfoot, Canadian singer who had a 1971 UK No.30 single with 'If You Could Read My Mind' and a 1974 US No.1 single with 'Sundown'.

1944 Gene Clark – singer/songwriter with The New Christy Minstrels and The Byrds, who had a 1965 UK & US No.1 single with 'Mr. Tambourine Man'. As a solo artist he produced the 1974 album *No Other*. Clark died of a heart attack on May 24th 1991.

1966 Jeff Buckley, singer/songwriter who created the 1995 album *Grace*. He drowned while swimming on May 29th 1997. His singer/songwriter father Tim Buckley *(right)* died on June 29th 1975 of a heroin and morphine overdose.

1967 Ronald DeVoe – singer with New Edition, who had a 1983 UK No.1 single with 'Candy Girl', and Bell Biv DeVoe, who had a 1990 US No.3 single with 'Do Me!'

1980 Clarke Isaac Hanson – guitarist and singer with Hanson, who had a 1997 UK & US No.1 single with 'MMMbop'.

1981 Sarah Harding – singer with Girls Aloud, who had a 2002 UK No.1 single with 'Sound Of The Underground'.

ON THIS DAY

1957 Harry Belafonte was at No.1 on the UK singles chart with 'Mary's Boy Child', the first single to sell over a million copies in the UK. It stayed at No.1 for seven weeks, making it this year's Christmas No.1.

1962 The Four Seasons started a five week run at No.1 on the US singles chart with 'Big Girls Don't Cry', the group's second No.1 of the year.

1963 John Weightman, Headmaster of a Surrey Grammar School, banned any of his pupils from having Beatle haircuts saying, "this ridiculous style brings out the worst in boys physically. It makes them look like morons".

1966 The Beach Boys were at No.1 on the UK singles chart with 'Good Vibrations'. The single was taken from the album *Pet Sounds*.

1967 Pink Floyd released their third single, 'Apples And Oranges', which failed to chart.

1971 Slade were at No.1 on the UK singles chart with 'Coz I Luv You', the group's first of six No.1s.

1974 John Lennon scored his second US No.1 album with *Walls And Bridges*.

1984 Wham! Started a three week run at No.1 on the US singles chart with 'Wake Me Up Before You Go Go', George Michael's first US No.1 and also a No.1 in the UK.

1990 Dave Crosby from Crosby, Stills, Nash & Young was admitted to hospital due to breaking a leg, shoulder and ankle after crashing his Harley Davidson motorbike.

1992 at the end of a long royalties battle Jimmy Merchant and Herman Santiago, ex-Frankie Lymon & The Teenagers members, received an estimated $4 million (£2.35 million) in back payments from the song 'Why Do Fools Fall In Love?'

1999 Mariah Carey was forced to abandon a performance on Rome's historic Spanish Steps after she was swamped by crowds of tourists. She took shelter in a local shop before being given a police escort to safety.

2000 it was reported that Andy White, who played drums on The Beatles' track 'Love Me Do', featured on the new Beatles' *Greatest Hits* album, would not earn enough from it to buy his own copy. White would get no more than his original session fee of £7 ($12).

2003 21-year-old Britney Spears became the youngest singer to get a star on the Hollywood Walk of Fame. The only other performer to get a Hollywood star at her age was *Little House On The Prairie* actress Melissa Gilbert.

2003 George Michael signed a new contract with the record company he took to court in 1993. The singer re-signed to Sony in a deal that included his extensive back catalogue. Michael had failed in his court wrangle with Sony after accusing it of "professional slavery". His contract was bought out by Virgin Records.

BORN ON THIS DAY

1936 Hank Ballard, US singer/songwriter who had a 1960 US No.6 single with 'Let's Go, Let's Go, Let's Go' and wrote the 1960 US No.1 hit for Chubby Checker, 'The Twist'.

1941 Con Clusky – singer with The Bachelors, who had a 1964 UK No.1 single with 'Diane' plus 16 other UK top 40 singles. He died on March 2nd 2003.

1950 Rudy Sarzo – bass player with Whitesnake, who had a 1987 US No.1 & UK No.9 single with 'Here I Go Again'.

1953 John McFee – guitarist with The Doobie Brothers, who had a 1979 US No.1 single with 'What A Fool Believes' and a 1993 UK No.7 single with 'Long Train Runnin'.

1954 John Parr, singer and guitarist who had a 1985 US No.1 & UK No.6 single with 'St Elmo's Fire'.

1960 Kim Wilde, singer who had a 1981 UK No.2 single with 'Kids In America', a 1987 US No.1 single with 'You Keep Me Hanging On' plus 20 other Top 50 UK singles.

1962 Kirk Hammett – guitarist with Metallica, who had a 1991 UK No.5 single with 'Enter Sandman' and a 1991 US & UK No.1 album with *Metallica*.

ON THIS DAY

1956 Fats Domino appeared on US TV's *Ed Sullivan Show* performing 'Blueberry Hill'.

1965 appearing live at the ABC Cinema, Stockton, Cleveland were Manfred Mann, The Yardbirds and Paul And Barry Ryan.

1971 blues harmonica player Herman "Junior" Parker died after a series of brain operations. Parker played on Ben E. King's 'Stand By Me'.

1972 Cat Stevens began three weeks at No.1 on the US album chart with *Catch Bull At Four*.

1972 singer/songwriter Danny Whitten died of a drug overdose. He was a one time member of Neil Young's Crazy Horse and writer of 'I Don't Wanna Talk About It', which was a hit for both Rod Stewart and Everything But The Girl.

1975 Bruce Springsteen made his live debut in the UK at London's Hammersmith Odeon.

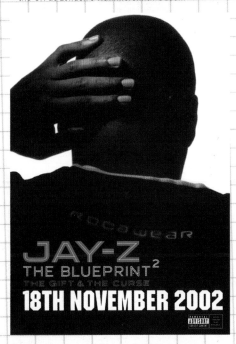

JAY-Z
THE BLUEPRINT²
THE GIFT & THE CURSE
18TH NOVEMBER 2002

1978 Billy Joel went to No.1 on the US album chart with *52nd Street*, his first US No.1 album.

1978 this week's UK Top 5 singles: No.5, The Cars, 'My Best Friend's Girl'; No.4, Rod Stewart, 'Do You Think I'm Sexy?'; No.3, Dan Hartman, 'Instant Replay'; No.2, Olivia Newton-John, 'Hopelessly Devoted To You' and No.1, The Boomtown Rats, 'Rat Trap', which gave the Irish band their first UK No.1 single.

1983 R.E.M. made their first appearance outside the US when they appeared on TV's *The Tube* on Channel 4. The following night they made their live UK debut when they played at Dingwalls, London.

1992 Black Sabbath was honoured with a star at the Rock Walk in Hollywood.

1993 Nirvana recorded their MTV unplugged special at Sony Studios, New York.

1993 Pearl Jam singer Eddie Vedder was arrested in New Orleans for disturbing the peace after a fight broke out in a bar.

1999 it was reported that Madonna had saved over £100,000 ($170,000) when buying a new South Kensington home after making a private sale and cutting out any estate agents.

2000 Craig David kicked off a 16 date UK tour of the UK at The Pavilions, Plymouth, England.

2002 Wales' Manic Street Preachers played the Carling Homecoming gig at St David's Hall, Cardiff.

2003 more than 500 Britney Spears fans camped overnight outside the Virgin Records Megastore in New York's Times Square waiting to get the star to sign copies of her new album *In The Zone*.

2003 following allegations of sexual abuse of a 12-year-old boy, police raided Michael Jackson's Neverland ranch. Jackson denied the allegations. The search came on the day that his latest greatest hits album, *Number Ones*, was released in the US.

2003 composer and arranger Michael Kamen died of a heart attack. He had worked with Pink Floyd (on *The Wall*) and Metallica, and on the film sound-tracks *Robin Hood*, *X-Men* and *Brazil*.

BORN ON THIS DAY

1937 Ray Collins – vocalist with Frank Zappa, who had a 1970 UK No.9 album with *Hot Rats*.

1938 Hank Medress – singer with The Tokens, who had a 1961 US No.1 & UK No.11 single with 'The Lion Sleeps Tonight'.

1939 Pete Moore – vocalist with The Miracles, who had a 1970 UK & US No.1 single with Smokey Robinson, 'The Tears Of A Clown'.

1943 Fred Lipsius – piano and sax player with Blood, Sweat & Tears, who had a 1969 US No.12 & UK No.35 single with 'You've Made Me So Very Happy'.

1946 Joe Correro Jr. – drummer with Paul Revere & The Raiders, who had a 1971 US No.1 single with 'Indian Reservation' plus 14 other US Top 30 hit singles.

1960 Matt Sorum – drummer with The Cult, who had a 1987 UK No.11 single 'Lil' Devil'. He joined Guns N' Roses, who had a 1989 UK No.6 single with 'Sweet Child O' Mine', in 1990.

1971 Justin Chancellor – bass player with Peach then Tool, who had a 2001 US No.1 album with *Lateralus*.

ON THIS DAY

1955 Carl Perkins recorded 'Blue Suede Shoes' at Sun Studios in Memphis. A US No.2 & UK No.10 hit for Perkins in 1956, the song became a rock 'n' roll classic and was covered by many acts including Elvis Presley and John Lennon.

1964 The Supremes became the first all girl group to have a UK No.1 single when 'Baby Love' went to the top of the charts.

1965 appearing live at the Glad Rag Ball, Empire Pool, London were The Kinks, The Who, Georgie Fame & The Blue Flames, The Hollies, Wilson Pickett and The Golden Apples Of The Sun. Tickets cost 30 shillings, ($4.20).

1967 appearing at the Saville Theatre, London were The Bee Gees, The Flowerpot Men and the Bonzo Dog Doo Dah Band.

1976 UK music weekly *Sounds* made the Sex Pistols' debut 45rpm, 'Anarchy In The UK' its single of the week.

1979 Chuck Berry was released from prison after serving a four month sentence for tax evasion.

1983 Tina Turner made her first chart appearance in over ten years with her version of the Al Green hit 'Let's Stay Together'.

1988 Bon Jovi started a two week run at No.1 on the US singles chart with 'Bad Medicine', the group's third US No.1 and a No.17 hit in the UK.

1988 Canadian singer and one hit wonder Robin Beck was at No.1 on the UK singles chart with 'First Time'. The song was from a TV advertisement for Coca-Cola.

1990 Pia King, the wife of Mark King – singer and bassist with Level 42 – was granted a "quickie" divorce after her husband ran off with their children's nanny.

1994 Nirvana entered the US album chart at No.1 with *MTV Unplugged In New York*.

1995 Alan Hull, singer/songwriter with Lindisfarne, died of a heart attack, aged 50. He had had a 1972 UK No.3 single with 'Lady Eleanor'.

2000 LeAnn Rimes started a two week run at No.1 on the UK singles chart with 'Can't Fight The Moonlight', the singer's first UK chart topper.

2000 The Beatles started an 11 week run at No.1 on the UK album chart with *The Beatles 1*.

2001 Mick Jagger released his new solo album *Goddess In The Doorway*. The first day UK sales were just 954 copies.

2002 Michael Jackson was blasted by safety experts after dangling his baby from a third floor hotel balcony *(left)*. Jacko was in Berlin for an awards ceremony and was showing his nine month old baby to his fans outside the hotel.

2003 police issued an arrest warrant for Michael Jackson following allegations of sexual abuse of a 12-year-old boy. Jackson, who was in Las Vegas filming a video, negotiated with police to arrange a time and place to hand himself in.

2003 actor and dancer Gene Anthony Ray (Leroy in *Fame*), died from a stroke, aged 41.

2004 record producer Terry Melcher, who was behind hits by The Byrds, Ry Cooder and The Beach Boys, died aged 62 after a long battle with skin cancer. The son of actress Doris Day, he co-wrote 'Kokomo' for the Beach Boys, and produced 'Mr. Tambourine Man' for The Byrds as well as hits for The Mamas And The Papas.

2004 rapper Young Buck was arrested over a stabbing at the *Vibe* hip-hop awards. Young Buck (real name David Darnell Brown) was arrested on suspicion of stabbing a man who allegedly punched rap star Dr. Dre in the face. He was released on $500,000 (£294,000) bail after surrendering to police in Los Angeles.

BORN ON THIS DAY

1942 Norman Greenbaum – singer and guitarist, who had a 1970 UK No.1 & US No.3 single with 'Spirit In The Sky'.

1946 Duane Allman – guitarist with The Allman Brothers Band, who had a 1973 US No.12 single with 'Ramblin Man'. Allman was killed in a motorcycle accident on October 29th 1971.

1947 George Grantham – drummer with Poco, who had a 1979 US No.17 single with 'Crazy Love'.

1947 Joe Walsh – guitarist and singer/songwriter with The James Gang and The Eagles, who had a 1977 US No.1 & UK No.8 single with 'Hotel California' plus five US No.1 albums. As a solo artist he had a 1978 US No.12 and UK No.14 single with 'Life's Been Good'.

1957 Jim Brown – drummer with UB40, who had a 1983 UK No.1 & 1988 US No.1 single with 'Red Red Wine' and over 30 other Top 40 singles.

1965 Mike Diamond – drummer and vocalist with The Beastie Boys, who had a 1987 US No.7 & UK No.11 single with 'You Gotta Fight For Your Right To Party'.

1966 Kevin Gilbert, multi-instrumentalist, songwriter and member of Giraffe. He worked with Sheryl Crow and co-wrote the 1994 UK No.4 hit 'All I Want To Do'. Gilbert died on May 17th 1996.

1970 Q-Tip, US male rapper who had a 1997 UK No.6 single with 'Got 'Til It's Gone'.

ON THIS DAY

1955 the song that changed popular music history, 'Rock Around The Clock' by Bill Haley And His Comets, went to No.1 in the UK singles chart for the first time.

MARQUEE
90 WARDOUR ST., W.1.
Telephone: GER 8923

Thursday, Nov. 18th   (7.30-11)
GRAHAM BOND
ORGAN-ISATION
THE GASS

Friday, Nov. 19th   (7.30-11)
DAVID BOWIE and the
LOWER 3rd
THE SUMMER SET

Saturday, Nov. 20th   (2.30-5.30)
THE MARQUEE
SATURDAY SHOW
Top of the Pops live and on disc

Monday, Nov. 22nd   (7.30-11)
JIMMY JAMES and
THE VAGABONDS
THE TRAIN

Tuesday, Nov. 23rd   (7.30-11)
THE STEAM PACKET
BO STREET RUNNERS

Wednesday, Nov. 24th   (7.30-11)
JULIE FELIX
THE SETTLERS

1965 The Walker Brothers kicked off a ten date UK tour at Buxton Pavilion.

1967 Strawberry Alarm Clock were at No.1 on the US singles chart with 'Incense And Peppermints'.

1968 The Monkees' film *Head* opened in six US cities.

1971 Isaac Hayes started a two week run at No.1 on the US singles chart with 'Theme From Shaft'. It made No.4 in the UK. Hayes also won a Grammy award for Best original film score.

1973 Allan Sherman died, aged 49. He had had a 1963 US No.2 & UK No.14 single with 'Hello Muddah, Hello Faddah'.

1974 drummer with The Who, Keith Moon, collapsed during a concert after his drink was spiked with horse tranquillizer. 19-year-old Scott Halpin from the audience took over on drums and played for the remaining three numbers.

1976 *22 Golden Guitar Greats* by Bert Weedon went to No.1 on the UK album chart.

1979 Barbra Streisand and Donna Summer were at No.1 on the US singles chart with 'No More Tears, Enough Is Enough'. The song made No.3 in the UK.

1991 Randy Jackson of The Jacksons was given a 30 day jail sentence by a Los Angeles court for violating a probation order.

1991 The Rolling Stones announced they had signed a £20 million ($34 million) deal with Virgin Records to make three albums over six years.

1994 David Crosby received a liver transplant at Dumont-UCLA Center in Los Angeles. Crosby's liver had deteriorated from extensive alcohol and drug abuse as well as hepatitis C.

1995 Whitney Houston was at No.1 on the US singles chart with 'Exhale, Shoop Shoop'. It made No.11 in the UK.

2000 Mel C announced she was quitting The Spice Girls during a TV interview on the ITV *Frank Skinner Show*.

2003 Michael Jackson flew to Santa Barbara to be arrested by police. He was seen in handcuffs being taken into the police station. The singer had his mug shot and fingerprints taken before being freed on $3 million (£1.76 million) bail.

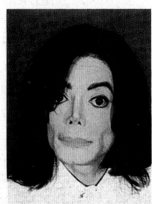

Santa Barbara County Sheriff's Dept.

11/20/2003 Photo Image of:
NAME: JACKSON, MICHAEL
RAC: B   SEX: M
DOB: 8/29/1958   AGE: 45
HGT: 511   WGT: 120
BLD: CMP:
HAI: BLK   EYE: BRO
MKS:
BOOKING #:   621785

Santa Barbara County's most high profile arrest.

BORN ON THIS DAY

1940 Dr. John (a.k.a. Malcolm John Rebennack), R&B pianist, singer and producer who wrote 'I Walk On Guilded Splinters' and 'Iko Iko.' He had the 1989 hit 'Makin Whoopie' with Ricky Lee Jones.

1948 Lonnie Jordan – singer and keyboardist with War, who had a 1973 US No.2 single with 'The Cisco Kid' and a 1976 UK No.12 single with 'Low Rider'.

1965 Bjork Gudmundsdottir – singer/songwriter with The Sugarcubes, who had a 1992 UK No.17 single with 'Hit'. As a solo artist she had a 1995 UK No.4 single with 'It's Oh So Quiet' and a 1993 UK No.3 album with *Debut*.

1968 Alex James – bass player with Blur, who had a 1994 UK No.1 album *Park Life*, which spent over two years on the UK chart, a 1995 UK No.1 single with 'Country House' plus over 12 other UK Top 40 singles. Also a member of Me Me Me, who had a 1996 UK No.19 single with 'Hanging Around'.

ON THIS DAY

1955 RCA Records purchased Elvis Presley's recording contract from Sam Phillips at Sun Records for an unprecedented sum of $35,000 (£20,588).

1960 Maurice Williams And The Zodiacs went to No.1 on the US singles chart with 'Stay', the shortest ever US No.1 single at one minute 37 seconds. It reached No.14 in the UK in 1961.

1969 T. Rex appeared live at The Free Trade Hall, Manchester, England.

1970 The Partridge Family started a three week run at No.1 on the US singles chart with 'I Think I Love You'. The song was featured in the first episode of the *Partridge Family* TV series, which was made by the same company that made *The Monkees*.

1970 two months after his death Jimi Hendrix

Phil Spector on murder charge

From James Bone
in New York

PHIL SPECTOR, the record producer whose distinctive "wall of sound" transformed Sixties pop music, was charged with murder yesterday over the death of a B-movie actress at his California mansion.

Lana Clarkson, the star of Roger Corman's cult classic *Barbara Queen*, was found dead in the entrance of Mr Spector's home in the Los Angeles suburb of Alhambra on February 3.

The actress died of a single bullet wound to the head and neck. In an interview with *Esquire* magazine in July, Mr Spector, 62, suggested that Ms Clarkson, 40, had killed herself.

"She kissed the gun. I have no idea why," he said. "I never knew her, never even saw her before that night." He said he did not witness the shooting, but went to the entrance where Ms Clarkson's body was found after he heard a shot. He said he called police himself.

Mr Spector said that Ms Clarkson was "loud and drunk" before they left the club where she worked.

was at No.1 on the UK singles chart with 'Voodoo Chile', the guitarist's only UK No.1.

1974 Wilson Pickett was arrested in New York for possession of a dangerous weapon after he pulled a gun during an argument.

1980 Don Henley was arrested after a naked 16-year-old girl was found at his home in Los Angeles suffering from a drug overdose. He received a $2,000 (£1,176) fine with two years probation.

1981 Olivia Newton-John started a ten week run at No.1 in the US singles chart with 'Physical', the singer's fourth US No.1. It went on to sell over two million copies and was a No.7 hit in the UK.

1981 Queen and David Bowie were at No.1 in the UK with 'Under Pressure' (they recorded the song together after a chance meeting in a German recording studio).

1983 Michael Jackson's 14 minute video for 'Thriller' premiered in Los Angeles.

1987 Billy Idol knocked Tiffany from the No.1 single position in the US with his version of Tommy James' 'Mony Mony'. Tiffany had

been at No.1 with another Tommy James song 'I Think We're Alone Now'.

1990 Madonna was sued by her next door neighbour for having a garden hedge that blocked his view.

1991 Aerosmith made a guest appearance in *The Simpsons* TV animated comedy.

1995 Peter Grant, legendary manager of Led Zeppelin, died from a heart attack. He had also worked with Chuck Berry and Jeff Beck.

2000 Jonathan Shalit, the former manager of singing prodigy Charlotte Church, went to court claiming he was owed £5 million ($8.5 million) of the singer's £10 million ($17 million) estate. Shalit, who originally discovered the teenage soprano, had been sacked.

2003 an acoustic guitar on which the late Beatle George Harrison learned to play fetched £276,000 ($469,200) at a London auction. The Egmond guitar was originally bought for Harrison by his father for £3.50 ($5.95). Another item auctioned was a signed invitation to the post-premiere celebrations for the Beatles' *Hard Days Night* film, which went for £17,250 ($29,325).

2003 record producer Phil Spector appeared before a California court and was formally charged with murder *(top)*. B-movie actress Lana Clarkson had been found at his mansion in February of this year with a fatal gunshot wound to her face. Spector pleaded not guilty to her murder during a brief hearing in Alhambra, near Los Angeles, and was released on $1 million (£0.6 million) bail.

2004 Carling Live presented N*E*R*D at the Carling Apollo, Manchester.

BORN ON THIS DAY

1943 Floyd Sneed – drummer with Three Dog Night, who had a 1970 UK No.3 & US No.1 single with 'Mamma Told Me Not To Come'.

1946 Aston Barrett – bass guitarist with The Upsetters and Bob Marley And The Wailers, who had a 1981 UK No.8 single with 'No Woman No Cry' plus over ten other UK Top 40 singles.

1949 Steve Van Zandt – guitarist with South Side Johnny, E Street Band, Little Steven and The Disciples of Soul.

1950 Tina Weymouth – bass player for Talking Heads, who had a 1983 US No.9 single with 'Burning Down The House' and a 1985 UK No.6 single with 'Road To Nowhere', and Tom Tom Club, who had a 1981 UK No.7 single with 'Wordy Rappinghood'.

1960 James Morrison (a.k.a. Jim Bob) – singer with Carter The Unstoppable Sex Machine, who had a 1992 UK No.7 single with 'The Only Living Boy In New Cross'.

1968 Rasa Don – percussionist with Arrested Development, who had a 1992 UK No.2 single with 'People Everyday'.

1979 Scott Robinson – vocalist with Five, who had a 1998 UK No.2 single with 'Everybody Get Up' and a 1999 UK No.1 single with 'Keep On Movin'. He is now a solo artist.

ON THIS DAY

1963 The Beatles released their second album *With The Beatles*, which went on to spend 51 weeks on the UK charts.

1965 Bob Dylan married Sara Lowndes in New York. She filed for divorce on March 1st 1977.

1965 Wilson Pickett appeared at The Flamingo Club, London.

1968 The Beatles' double *White Album* was released in the UK. It featured 'Ob-La-Di, Ob-La-Da', 'Dear Prudence', 'Helter Skelter', 'Blackbird', 'Back In The USSR' and George Harrison's 'While My Guitar Gently Weeps'. Priced at £3.13 shillings ($10.22), it spent eight weeks as the UK No.1 album.

1971 Isaac Hayes was at No.1 on the US singles chart with 'Theme From *Shaft*'. It made No.4 in the UK.

1975 Billy Connolly was at No.1 on the UK singles chart with his version of the Dolly Parton song 'D.I.V.O.R.C.E.'.

1976 Jerry Lee Lewis was arrested for drunk driving after driving his Rolls Royce into a ditch.

1983 R.E.M. appeared at the Marquee Club, London *(left)*. Tickets cost £2.50 ($4.25).

1986 The Human League went to No.1 on the US singles chart with 'Human', which made them the eighth UK act to score a US No.1 single in 1986.

1987 Jesus And Mary Chain singer Jim Reid was arrested in Canada after being accused of assaulting members of the audience with his microphone stand. He was released on $2,000 (£1,176) bail.

1990 Bill Wyman announced that his 17 month marriage to model Mandy Smith was over.

1992 appearing at The Boardwalk, Manchester were The Cherries, Molly Halfhead and Oasis.

Rock wild man Hutchence hangs himself

Michael Hutchence of INXS died on this day in 1997.

1997 INXS singer Michael Hutchence was found dead in his hotel suite in Sydney. He was 37. Hutchence's body was found at 11.50am naked behind the door to his room. He had apparently hung himself with his own belt, the buckle broke away and his body was found kneeling on the floor and facing the door. It had been suggested that his death resulted from an act of auto eroticism, but no forensic or other evidence to substantiate that suggestion was found.

2002 The surviving members of The Doors, Ray Manzarek and Robby Krieger, announced they would record and tour again with a new line up including ex-Cult singer Ian Astbury and former Police drummer Stewart Copeland. Original drummer John Densmore was not able to take part because he suffers from severe tinnitus.

2004 Ozzy Osbourne struggled with a burglar who escaped with jewellery worth about £2 million ($3.4 million) from his Buckinghamshire mansion. Osbourne told reporters that he had the masked raider in a headlock as he tried to stop him. The burglar broke free and jumped 9m (30ft) from a first floor window.

BORN ON THIS DAY

1939 Betty Everett, soul singer who had a 1964 US No 6 single with 'The Shoop Shoop Song, It's In His Kiss' and a 1965 UK No.29 single with 'Getting Mighty Crowded'. She died on August 19th 2001, aged 61.

1940 Freddie Marsden – drummer with Gerry And The Pacemakers, who had a 1963 UK No.1 single with 'How Do You Do It?' and a 1965 US No.6 single with 'Ferry Across The Mersey'.

1949 Alan Paul – singer with Manhattan Transfer, who had a 1977 UK No.1 with 'Chanson D'amour' and a 1981 US No.7 single with 'Boy From New York City'.

1954 Bruce Hornsby – keyboardist and vocalist with The Range, who had a 1986 US No.1 & UK No.15 single with 'The Way It Is'.

ON THIS DAY

1899 the world's first jukebox was installed at San Francisco's Palais Royal Hotel.

1956 sheet metal worker Louis Balint punched Elvis Presley at a hotel in Toledo claiming that his wife's love for Elvis had caused his marriage to break up. He was fined $19.60 (£11.50) but ended up being jailed because he was unable to pay the fine.

1965 Marc Bolan appeared live on the UK TV show *Five O'Clock Funfair*, performing 'The Wizard'.

The Blue Oyster Cult..

1974 one hit wonder Billy Swan started a two week run at No.1 on the US singles chart with 'I Can Help', which was a No.6 hit in the UK.

1974 The Rolling Stones scored their fifth US No.1 album with *It's Only Rock 'N' Roll* **(right)**.

1975 Blue Oyster Cult appeared live at the Hammersmith Odeon, London.

1975 Queen started a nine week run at No.1 on the UK singles chart with 'Bohemian Rhapsody'. The promotional video that accompanied the song is generally acknowledged as being the first pop video and only cost £5,000 ($8,500) to produce.

1976 The Scorpions appeared live at Accrington Town Hall, Accrington, England. They were billed as Europe's leading hard rock band.

1976 ten hours after his last arrest, Jerry Lee Lewis was nicked again after brandishing a Derringer pistol outside Elvis Presley's Gracelands home in Memphis, where he was demanding to see the "King".

1979 Anita Pallenburg, girlfriend of Keith Richards, was cleared of shooting a man who was found dead at her home.

1979 Marianne Faithfull was arrested at Oslo Airport, Norway for possession of marijuana.

1983 Tom Evans from Badfinger committed suicide. Evans co-wrote 'Without You', which was a hit for Harry Nilsson and Mariah Carey.

1985 Joe Turner, US blues songwriter, died. He wrote 'Shake, Rattle and Roll', and 'Sweet Sixteen'.

1987 Sly Stone was charged with possession of cocaine in Santa Monica.

1989 Jimmy Somerville was given a conditional discharge from Bow St. Magistrates after being found guilty of obstructing the highway during an AIDs demonstration outside the Australian commission in London.

1991 Michael Bolton scored his second US No.1 single with his version of the Percy Sledge song 'When A Man Loves A Woman', which was a No.8 hit in the UK.

1991 Michael Jackson had his fourth UK No.1 single with 'Black or White'. The song was also a No.1 hit in the US.

1994 Tommy Boyce, singer/songwriter, committed suicide. He sold over 40 million records during his career.

2004 Oasis singer Liam Gallagher was fined 50,000 (£34,000) after a fight in a German hotel in December 2002. Gallagher lost two front teeth in the fight, which led to the band abandoning their German tour.

BORN ON THIS DAY

1939 Jim Yester – guitarist and vocalist with The Association, who had a 1967 US No.1 single with 'Windy'.

1941 Donald "Duck" Dunn – bass player with Booker T And The MGs, who had a 1962 US No.3 single with 'Green Onions' and a 1969 UK No.4 single with 'Time Is Tight'.

1941 Pete Best, The Beatles' drummer 1960-62.

1942 Billy Connolly, singer, actor, comedian and part of The Humblebums with Gerry Rafferty, who had a 1975 UK No.1 single with 'D.I.V.O.R.C.E.'

1944 Bev Bevan – drummer with The Move, who had a 1969 UK No.1 single with 'Blackberry Way', and the Electric Light Orchestra, who had a 1979 UK No.3 & US No.4 single with 'Don't Bring Me Down' plus 26 other Top 40 hits. Bevan is now a DJ on UK radio station Saga FM in Birmingham.

1955 Clem Burke – drummer with Blondie, who had five UK No.1 singles including the 1979 UK & US No.1 single 'Heart Of Glass' and a 1978 worldwide No.1 album with *Parallel Lines*.

1957 Chris Hayes – guitarist with Huey Lewis & The News, who had a 1985 US No.1 & UK No.11 single with 'The Power Of Love'.

1962 John Squire – guitarist with The Stone Roses, who had a 1989 UK No.8 single with 'Fool's Gold' and a 1989 album with *The Stone Roses*, and The Seahorses, who had a 1997 UK No.3 single with 'Love Is The Law'.

ON THIS DAY

1959 Johnnie Ray was released on bail after spending the night in jail charged with accosting and soliciting.

1961 blues singer Howlin' Wolf arrived in London for his first UK tour.

1964 the first commercial radio station in the UK Radio Manx, based on The Isle of Man, started broadcasting.

1966 during an evening recording session The Beatles started work on a new John Lennon song called 'Strawberry Fields Forever'.

1973 Ringo Starr went to No.1 on the US singles chart with 'Photograph'. It was the first of two US chart toppers for him as a solo artist.

1979 Donna Summer and Barbra Streisand started a two week run at No.1 on the US singles chart with 'No More Tears (Enough Is Enough)'. The song was a No.3 hit in the UK.

1983 appearing at the Hacienda in Manchester were two local bands, The Smiths and James.

1991 Cyndi Lauper married actor David Thornton in Manhattan. The ceremony was officiated by Little Richard.

1991 Eric Carr, drummer with Kiss, died of complications from cancer in a New York hospital.

1991 Freddie Mercury died of complications from AIDs at his home in London's Holland Park, aged 45 and just one day after he publicly admitted he was HIV positive. Mercury was openly bisexual and enjoyed a colourful rock-star lifestyle. During his career with Queen he scored over 40 Top 40 UK singles including the worldwide No.1 'Bohemian Rhapsody'.

1992 Bill Wyman's divorce was finalized. The high court awarded Mandy Smith £580,000 ($986,000).

1999 at a Bonham's of London rock auction Buddy Holly's first driving licence sold for £3,795 ($6,451) and a copy of The Beatles' *White Album*, numbered 00000001, sold for £9,775 ($16,618).

2000 former husband of Spice Girl Mel B, Jimmy Gulzar, was given unconditional bail after appearing in court charged with attacking the star's sister, Danielle.

2002 Robbie Williams started a five week run at No.1 on the UK album chart with *Escapology*, his fifth UK No.1 album.

2003 'Agadoo' by Black Lace was named the worst song of all time by a panel of music writers. The song peaked at No.2 on the UK charts in 1984.

2003 after his BMW struck a Toyota Camry, country singer Glen Campbell was arrested with a blood alcohol level of .20 on charges of "extreme" drunk driving, hit and run and assaulting a police officer in Phoenix, Arizona. While in custody Campbell hummed his hit 'Rhinestone Cowboy' repeatedly.

2004 former US American Idol winner Ruben Studdard was taken to hospital, suffering from exhaustion. The 26 year old was in his Alabama hometown when he was taken ill, a spokeswoman for his record label said.

BORN ON THIS DAY

1940 Percy Sledge, soul singer who had a 1966 UK No.4 and US No.1 single with 'When A Man Loves A Woman'.

1944 Bob Lind, singer who had a 1966 US & UK No.5 single with 'Elusive Butterfly'.

1950 Jocelyn Brown, singer who had a 1997 UK No.5 single 'Something Goin' On'. She also worked with John Lennon, Bob Dylan and Bruce Springsteen.

1960 Amy Grant, singer who had a 1991 US No.1 & UK No.2 single 'Baby Baby'.

1967 Rodney Sheppard – guitarist with Sugar Ray, who had a 1999 UK No.10 single with 'Every Morning'.

1968 Tunde – singer with Lighthouse Family, who had a 1996 UK No.4 single with 'Lifted'.

ON THIS DAY

1958 Lord Rockingham's XI was at No.1 on the UK singles chart with 'Hoot's Mon'. Lord Rockingham's XI was the house band on the Jack Good TV show *Oh Boy.*

1961 the Everly Brothers started active service for the 8th Battalion, Marine Corps Reserves.

1965 London's Harrods store closed to the public so The Beatles could do their Christmas shopping.

1965 The Seekers were at No.1 on the UK singles chart with 'The Carnival Is Over', the group's second No.1.

1969 John Lennon returned his MBE to The Queen because of Britain's involvement in the Nigeria-Biafra war, America in Vietnam, and against his latest single 'Cold Turkey', slipping down the charts.

1972 Chuck Berry was at No.1 on the UK singles chart with 'My Ding-a-Ling', his only UK No.1.

1974 UK singer/songwriter Nick Drake died in his sleep of an overdose of Tryptasol, an anti-depressant. His 1972 album *Pink Moon* is regarded as a classic album.

1976 The Band made their final performance, which was called "The Last Waltz". The show also featured Joni Mitchell, Dr. John, Neil Young, Van Morrison, Neil Diamond, Eric Clapton and others. The event was filmed by Martin Scorsese.

1978 The Police appeared at The Electric Ballroom, London. Admission was £1.50 ($2.55).

1982 The Jam started their final UK tour at Glasgow's Apollo Theatre.

1984 the cream of the British pop world gathered at S.A.R.M. Studios, London to record the historic 'Do They Know It's Christmas?' The single, which was written by Bob Geldof and Midge Ure, featured Paul Young, Bono, Boy George, Sting and George Michael. It went on to sell over three million copies in the UK, becoming the bestselling record ever, and raised over £8 million ($13.6 million) worldwide.

1988 James appeared at the Irish Centre, Birmingham, supported by the Happy Mondays. Tickets cost £5 ($8.50). On the same day The Las appeared at Manchester University, and tickets cost £3 ($5).

1989 New Kids On The Block had their first UK No.1 single with 'You Got It (The Right Stuff)'.

1995 Radiohead's Thom Yorke blacked out halfway through a show in Munich, Germany, suffering from exhaustion.

1995 Whitney Houston went to No.1 on the US singles chart with 'Exhale (Shoop Shoop)', which was written by Babyface and taken from the film *Waiting To Exhale.* It gave Whitney her 11th US No.1.

2000 a burglar broke into Alice Cooper's home and made off with over $6,000 (£3,529) worth of clothes, shoes and cameras belonging to Cooper's daughter – along with four of the star's gold discs.

2001 Garth Brooks went to No.1 on the US album chart with *Scarecrow.* Robbie Williams started an eight week run at No.1 on the UK album chart with *Swing When You're Winning.*

2003 Michael Jackson launched a website to defend himself following allegations of sexual abuse of a 12-year-old boy. The singer posted a message saying the charges were based on "a big lie" and he wanted to end "this horrible time" by proving they were false in court.

2003 Meat Loaf underwent heart surgery in a London hospital after being diagnosed with a condition that causes an irregular heartbeat. The 52-year-old singer had collapsed on November 17th as he performed at London's Wembley Arena.

THE ELECTRIC BALLROOM

184 Camden High Street.

Saturday November 25th

POLICE

+ Pressure Shocks

+ Gardez Darx

Admission £1.50
8.30 pm – 2 am

Nick Drake.

BORN ON THIS DAY

1925 Michael Holliday, singer who had a 1958 UK No.1 with 'The Story Of My Life'. The song gave the writers Bacharach and David their first UK No.1 hit.

1939 Tina Turner – singer and part of duo Ike and Tina Turner, who had a 1966 UK No.3 single with 'River Deep Mountain High' and a 1971 US No.4 single with 'Proud Mary'. As a solo artist she had a 1984 UK No.3 and US No.1 single with 'What's Love Got To Do With It?' plus over 25 other UK Top 40 singles.

1944 Alan Henderson – bass player with Them, who had a 1965 UK No.2 & US No.24 single with 'Here Comes The Night'.

1944 Jean Terrell – vocalist with The Supremes (she joined in 1969), who had a 1970 US No.10 & UK No.6 single with 'Up The Ladder To The Roof'.

1945 John McVie – bass player with Fleetwood Mac, who had a 1987 UK No.5 single with 'Little Lies', and a 1977 US No.1 single with 'Dreams' taken from worldwide No.1 album *Rumours*.

1946 Burt Reiter – bass player with Focus, who had a 1973 UK No.4 single with 'Sylvia' and a 1973 US No.9 single with 'Hocus Pocus'.

1949 Martin Lee – singer with Brotherhood Of Man, who had a 1976 UK No.1 single with 'Save Your Kisses For Me'.

1964 Adam Gaynor – guitarist for Matchbox 20, who had a 1998 UK No.38 single with 'Push' and a 2000 US No.1 single with 'Bent'.

1981 Natasha Bedingfield *(below)*– singer who had the 2004 UK No.1 single 'These Words'.

ON THIS DAY

1967 the promotional film of The Beatles' 'Hello, Goodbye' was aired on *The Ed Sullivan Show* in the US. It was never shown at the time in the UK due to a Musician's Union ban on miming.

1968 Cream played a farewell concert at the Royal Albert Hall, London. The band was supported by Yes and Taste.

1969 appearing at The Civic Hall, Dunstable were Pink Floyd and Mouseproof. Tickets cost 14 shillings ($1.96).

1973 John Rostill of The Shadows died after being electrocuted at his home recording studio. The local newspaper ran the headline "Pop musician dies, guitar apparent cause".

1973 The New York Dolls made their UK live debut at Biba's Rainbow Room, London.

1975 Captain Beefheart appeared live at Brunel University, Middlesex. Tickets were £1.20 ($2).

1975 appearing live on UK TV's pop show *Supersonic* were Slade, Gary Glitter, Leo Sayer and The Troggs.

1976 Kevin Godley and Lol Creme left 10CC to concentrate on other

Good for hymn! Sir Cliff roars back to the No 1 spot

A PUNCH ON THE NOSE FOR THE MUSICAL SNOBS WHO SNEERED

projects including work on "The Gizmo", a device used to make neo-orchestral sounds on a guitar.

1976 the Sex Pistols released the single 'Anarchy In The UK'. It reached No.38 in the charts.

1982 jazz trumpeter Mile Davis married actress Cicely Tyson in New York. It was the musician's third marriage.

1991 Garth Brooks fans were asked to bring ten cans of food to a grocery store in exchange for a lottery envelope, some of which contained tickets to see Garth at a forthcoming show. Over 10,000 cans were donated to charity.

1994 Boyz II Men started their 14th and final week at No.1 on the US singles chart with 'I'll Make Love To You', giving them the longest run in chart history (along with 'I Will Always Love You' by Whitney Houston).

1994 The Eagles started a two week run at No.1 on the US album chart with *Hell Freezes Over*.

1999 Cliff Richard started a three week run at No.1 on the UK singles chart with 'Millennium Prayer' despite the record being boycotted by most radio stations *(above)*. It became Cliff's 14th UK No.1.

2000 Manchester club the Hacienda was auctioned off, raising £18,000 ($30,600) for charity. Madonna made her UK TV debut at the club when Channel 4 music show *The Tube* was broadcast live from there. Oasis, Happy Mondays, U2, The Smiths and James had also all played at the club.

BORN ON THIS DAY

1935 Al Jackson – drummer with Booker T And The MGs, who had a 1962 US No.3 single with 'Green Onions' and a 1969 UK No.4 single with 'Time Is Tight'. Jackson was shot dead by burglars inside his home on October 1st 1975.

1941 Eddie Rabbitt, singer/songwriter who had a 1981 US No.1 & UK No.53 single with 'I Love A Rainy Night'. Elvis, Dr. Hook and Tom Jones have all recorded his songs. Rabbitt died of cancer on May 7th 1998.

1942 Jimi Hendrix *(right)*, guitarist and singer who had a 1967 UK No.6 single with 'Hey Joe', a 1970 UK No.1 single with 'Voodoo Chile' and a 1968 US No.1 & UK No.6 album with *Electric Ladyland*. He died on September 18th 1970.

1944 Dave Winthrop – sax player with Supertramp, who had a 1979 US No.6 & UK No.7 single with 'The Logical Song' and a 1974 album *Crime Of The Century*.

1945 Randy Brecker – trumpeter with Blood, Sweat & Tears, who had a 1969 US No.12 & UK No.35 single with 'You've Made Me So Very Happy'.

1959 Charlie Burchill – guitarist with Simple Minds, who had a 1985 US No.1 single with 'Don't You, Forget About Me', a 1989 UK No.1 single with 'Belfast Child' plus over 20 other UK Top 40 singles.

1962 Mike Bordin – drummer for Faith No More, who had a 1993 UK No.3 and US No.4 single with 'I'm Easy'.

1978 Mike Skinner (a.k.a. The Streets), singer/songwriter and rapper who had a 2004 UK No.1 album with *A Grand Don't Come For Free*.

ON THIS DAY

1965 Herb Alpert's Tijuana Brass went to No.1 on the US album chart with *Whipped Cream & Other Delights*.

1966 The New Vaudeville Band were at No.1 on the US singles chart with 'Winchester Cathedral', which was a No.4 hit in the UK.

1973 The Carpenters were at No.1 on the US singles chart with 'Top Of The World'. The song was a No.5 hit in the UK.

1981 the British Phonographic Industry placed advertisements in the press claiming that "home taping was wiping out music". The Boomtown Rats, 10cc, Elton John and Cliff Richard all backed the campaign.

1982 Lionel Richie was No.1 in the US with 'Truly'. Richie achieved a No.1 each year from 1978–86 as a writer: 'Three Times A Lady', 'Still', 'Lady' (with Kenny Rodgers), 'Endless Love' (with Diana Ross) and the solo songs 'All Night Long', 'Hello', 'Say You Say Me' and 'We Are The World'.

1982 *The Singles – The First Ten Years* went to No.1 on the UK album chart, giving Abba their eighth UK No.1 album.

1986 Bon Jovi was at No.1 on the US singles chart with 'You Give Love A Bad Name', which made No.14 in the UK.

1995 Alice In Chains were at No.1 on the US album chart with their self-titled album.

1996 former Stones Roses' guitarist John Squires' new band The Seahorses made their live debut when they played at The Buckley Tivoli, England in front of 200 fans.

1997 a disturbed rock fan brought the funeral of Michael Hutchence to a standstill when he tried to launch himself from a 6m (20ft) high balcony with a cord around his neck. He was removed by police and taken away to a psychiatric unit.

2001 Elvis Presley was inducted into The Gospel Association Hall Of Fame.

2002 Britney Spears ended her partnership in the restaurant at the Dylan Hotel, New York after it was plagued by lousy reviews and slow business. Management had recently changed the menu to American food with an Italian flair.

2003 figures released by The Rolling Stones showed that the band had grossed £175 million ($297.5 million) from their 2002 40 Licks World Tour. The report also showed they had made over £1 billion ($1.7 billion) since 1989 from royalties, album sales and tour revenue.

BORN ON THIS DAY

1929 Berry Gordy, founder of Motown Records, former boxer and composer. He wrote with many Motown acts and co-wrote 'Reet Petite' with Jackie Wilson.

1940 Bruce Channel, US singer who had a 1962 US No.1 & UK No.2 single with 'Hey! Baby'.

1940 Glen Curtis – guitarist with The Fortunes, who had a 1965 UK No.2 & US No.7 single with 'You've Got Your Troubles'.

1943 Randy Newman, who was once hailed as the greatest songwriter alive by Paul McCartney. He was the composer of 'Mamma Told Me Not To Come', 'Simon Smith And The Amazing Dancing Bear' and the 1977 US No.2 single 'Short People'. He has also written film soundtracks, including *Ragtime*.

1958 David Van Day – vocalist with Dollar, who had a 1981 UK No.4 single with 'Mirror Mirror'.

ON THIS DAY

1960 Elvis Presley started a six week run at No.1 on the US singles chart with 'Are You Lonesome Tonight?', his third US No.1 of 1960. It reached No.1 in the UK in January the following year.

1963 'She Loves You' by The Beatles was back at No.1 for the second time on the UK singles chart.

1964 The Shangri-Las went to No.1 on the US singles chart with the "teen death song", 'Leader Of The Pack', which was a No.11 hit in the UK.

1970 Dave Edmunds was at No.1 on the UK singles chart with his version of the 1955 Smiley Lewis hit 'I Hear You Knockin'. It was also the first release on the new Mam record label.

1974 John Lennon made his last-ever concert appearance when he joined Elton John on stage at Madison Square Garden. He performed three songs, 'Whatever Gets You Thru The Night', 'I Saw Her Standing There' and 'Lucy In The Sky With Diamonds'.

1976 the Tom Robinson Band made their live debut at The Hope & Anchor, London. The band's biggest hit '2-4-6-8 Motorway' made No.5 in the UK during October 1977.

1987 Jennifer Warnes' duet with Bill Medley '(I've Had) The Time Of My Life', from the film *Dirty Dancing*, went to No.1 on the US singles chart.

1987 Rick Astley went to No.1 on the UK album chart with his debut LP *When You Need Somebody*.

1992 Whitney Houston started a record-breaking 14 week stay at No.1 in the US with a song taken from the *Bodyguard* soundtrack 'I Will Always Love You', which was written by Dolly Parton.

1993 Steppenwolf drummer Jerry Edmonton was killed in a car crash. The band had had a 1969 US No.2 & UK No.30 single with 'Born To Be Wild'.

2000 David Bowie was crowned the musician's musician. Bowie beat The Beatles and alternative rockers Radiohead in a survey by *NME*, which asked hundreds of top rock and pop stars to name their biggest musical influence.

2000 Madonna played her first British show for more than seven years at London's Brixton Academy. Tickets changed hands for more than £1,000 ($1,700) and QXL.com, the Internet auctioneers, sold one pair for £2,204 ($3,747).

2000 AC/DC kicked off the British leg of their Stiff Upper Lip Tour at the Birmingham NEC Arena.

2002 Tony McCarroll, the original drummer with Oasis, failed in a bid to sue the group's lawyers after he was sacked – because he took too long to file his claim. Judge Justice Gray at the High Court in London told McCarroll his case could not proceed because he had brought his claim outside of the six year time limit.

Bonzo Dog Doo Dah Band get the party started in 1968.

BORN ON THIS DAY

1933 John Mayall, father of the UK blues movement. His Bluesbreakers Band has featured Eric Clapton, Mick Taylor, Mick Fleetwood, John McVie, Jack Bruce, Peter Green and Jimmy McCulloch.

1941 Denny Doherty – singer and founding member of The Mamas And The Papas, who had a 1966 US No.1 & UK No.2 single with 'Monday Monday'.

1944 Felix Cavaliere – keyboardist with The Young Rascals, who had a 1967 US No.1 & UK No.8 single with 'Groovin'.

1947 Ronnie Montrose – guitarist with Montrose and the Edgar Winter Group, who had a 1973 US No.1 & UK No.18 single with 'Frankenstein'.

1951 Barry Goudreau – guitarist with Boston, who had a 1977 UK No.22 single with 'More Than A Feeling' and a 1986 US No.1 single with 'Amanda'.

1968 Martin Carr – guitarist with The Boo Radleys, who had a 1995 UK No.9 single with 'Wake Up Boo'.

1974 Apl.de.Ap – singer with Black Eyed Peas, who had a 2003 US & UK No.1 single with 'Where Is The Love?'

ON THIS DAY

1959 Frank Sinatra won Best new artist of the year at the Grammy Awards.

1965 this week's UK Top 5 albums were: No.5, *Out Of Our Heads*, The Rolling Stones; No.4, *Highway 61 Revisited*, Bob Dylan; No.3, *Help*, The Beatles; No.2, the *Mary Poppins Soundtrack* and No.1, *The Sound Of Music Soundtrack*.

1969 The Beatles went to No.1 on the US singles chart with 'Come Together/Something', the group's 18th US No.1.

1971 the UK Top 5 singles this week: No.5, The Piglets, 'Johnny Reggae'; No.4, Cher, 'Gypsies, Tramps and Thieves'; No.3, Benny Hill, 'Ernie (The Fastest Milkman In The West)'; No.2, T. Rex, 'Jeepster' and No.1, Slade, 'Coz I Love You'.

1975 Queen appeared at the Hammersmith Odeon, London.

1976 the Sex Pistols gig at Lancaster Polytechnic, England was cancelled by the local council. A spokesman said: "They didn't want that sort of filth in the town limits".

1980 Abba scored their ninth and last UK No.1 single with 'Super Trouper'. It was the group's 25th Top 40 hit in the UK.

1980 John And Yoko's *Double Fantasy* album was released 21 days after Lennon had been shot dead. The album became a worldwide No.1 and featured the No.1 single 'Just Like Starting Over'.

1986 Bon Jovi *(below)* went to No.1 on the US singles chart with 'You Give Love A Bad Name'.

1997 the Lou Reed song 'Perfect Day', performed by various artists including Elton John, Bono, Tom Jones and David Bowie, went to No.1 on the UK singles chart. The single raised over £2 million ($3.4 million) for the Children In Need charity.

2000 U2's Larry Mullen Jr. came to the rescue of a motorcyclist who had been involved in a crash. Larry was driving home when he saw the motorcyclist. He stopped and called for help on his phone and waited for the ambulance to arrive.

2001 former Beatle George Harrison died in Los Angeles of lung cancer, aged 58. Tributes to George were made worldwide by The Queen, George Bush, Paul McCartney, Ringo Starr, George Martin and Oasis guitarist Noel Gallagher.

2002 three paintings by Sir Paul McCartney were bought for just £35 ($59.50) each at the Secrets Postcard Sale at London's Royal College of Art. Members of the public gambled on whether they were buying works by celebrity artists at a fraction of their value, as each picture's creator was only made known after it has sold.

2003 a five hour charity show, to boost the fight against AIDs, was held at the Greenpoint Stadium in Cape Town. Acts who appeared included Bono, Queen, Ms Dynamite, Peter Gabriel, Eurythmics, Beyonce, Youssou N'Dour, Anastacia, The Corrs, Jimmy Cliff and Chaka Chaka. The show was also broadcast live on the Internet.

BORN ON THIS DAY

1937 Paul Stookey – vocalist with Peter, Paul & Mary, who had a 1969 US No.1 & 1970 UK No.2 single with 'Leaving On A Jet Plane'.

1945 Roger Glover – bass player with Deep Purple, who had a 1970 UK No.2 single with 'Black Night' and a 1973 US No.4 single with 'Smoke On The Water'.

1953 June Pointer – singer with the Pointer Sisters, who had a 1981 US No.2 single with 'Slow Hand' and a 1984 UK No.2 single with 'Automatic'.

1955 Billy Idol – singer with Generation X, who had a 1979 UK No.11 single with 'King Rocker'. As a solo artist he had a 1987 US No.1 & UK No.7 single with 'Mony Mony' plus nine other UK Top 40 singles.

1957 John Ashton – guitarist with Psychedelic Furs, who had a 1986 UK No.18 single with 'Pretty In Pink'.

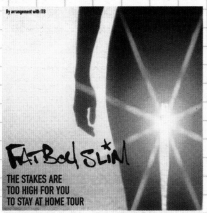

By arrangement with ITB

FATBOY SLIM

THE STAKES ARE
TOO HIGH FOR YOU
TO STAY AT HOME TOUR

NOVEMBER	DECEMBER
24 PRESSURE @THE ARCHES, GLASGOW 0141 221 4001	01 BUGGED OUT/BIG BEAT BOUTIQUE @ FABRIC, LONDON 020 7490 0444
25 CREAM, LIVERPOOL* 0151 709 1693	02 BIG BEAT BOUTIQUE @ MATRIX, READING 0118 959 0687
26 BACK 2 BASICS, LEEDS 0113 244 9474	08 BIG BEAT BOUTIQUE @ CONCORDE 2, BRIGHTON 01273 722272
30 BIG BEAT BOUTIQUE @ THE BOMB NOTTINGHAM 0115 950 6663	

WWW.GUTTERANDSTARS.COM
*check out Fatboy Slim webcast live from Cream on Saturday 25 November on www.i-gig.com
THE NEW ALBUM 'HALFWAY BETWEEN THE GUTTER AND THE STARS' OUT NOW INCLUDES THE HIT SINGLE – SUNSET (BIRD OF PREY)
WWW.SKINT.NET

1968 Des'ree, UK singer/songwriter who had a 1998 UK No.8 single with 'Life'.

1978 Clay Aiken, singer and runner-up in the 2003 US *American Idol* and who had a 2003 US No.1 single with 'This Is The Night'.

1987 Dougie Poynter – bass player with McFly, who had a 2004 UK No.1 single with 'Colours In Her Hair' and a 2004 UK No.1 album with *Room On The 3rd Floor*.

ON THIS DAY

1954 Nat King Cole played the first of six nights at Harlem's Apollo in New York.

1963 *With The Beatles* became the first million selling album in the UK.

1968 Glen Campbell started a five week run at No.1 on the US album chart with *Wichita Lineman*.

1969 The Monkees made what would be their last live appearance for 15 years when they played at The Oakland Coliseum, California.

1969 David Bowie, The Graham Bond Organization and Dusty Springfield performed at a fund raising show in London for youth magazine *Rave*.

1971 Sly And The Family Stone were at No.1 on the US singles chart with 'Family Affair', a No.15 hit in the UK.

1985 Phil Collins had his fifth US No.1 with 'Separate Lives'. The song was taken from the film *White Nights* and featured Marilyn Martin.

1985 Wham! were at No.1 on the UK singles

OH, ELTON!

Shame as star does gay dance with 'cub scouts'

EXCLUSIVE
By NICOLAS LAMBERT, Showbiz Reporter

GERMANS BLAME BRITS FOR EURO COLLAPSE – SEE PAGE TWO

chart with 'I'm Your Man', the duo's third UK No.1.

1991 Milli Vanilli singer Rob Pilatus attempted suicide at The Mondrain Hotel, Los Angeles by taking an overdose of sleeping pills and slashing his wrists.

1991 the Billboard Hot 100 chart changed by including airplay as well as sales. The US No.1 this week was PM Dawn with 'Set Adrift On Memory Bliss'.

1994 Tupac Shakur was shot five times during a robbery outside a New York Studio.

1996 Ice Cube obtained a restraining order to keep an obsessed fan away from him and his family. Cynthia Renee Collins was told to stop harassing the 26-year-old rapper, and to stay at least 30m (100ft) away from him.

1997 Chumbawamba's Danbert Nobacon was arrested by Italian police for wearing a skirt and was detained in police cells overnight.

1997 Metallica were at No.1 on the US album chart with *Reload*, the band's third US No.1 album.

1999 Elton John was blasted by the Boy Scout Association after he appeared on stage at London's Albert Hall performing 'It's A Sin' with six male dancers dressed as boy scouts *(above)*. The dancers peeled off their uniforms during the performance.

2002 high court probate records showed that George Harrison left his fortune of £99 million ($168 million) in a trust to his wife Olivia and his son Dhani, depriving the taxman of £40 million ($68 million). His English mansion near Henley-on-Thames was said to be worth £15 million ($25.5 million).

BORN ON THIS DAY

1930 Matt Monro, UK singer who had a 1964 UK No.4 & US No.23 single with 'Walk Away' plus ten other UK Top 40 hits. Monro died on February 7th 1985.

1934 Billy Paul, singer who had a 1972 US No.1 & 1973 UK No.12 single with 'Me and Mrs Jones'.

1936 Lou Rawls, singer who had a 1976 US No.2 & UK No.10 single with 'You'll Never Find Another Love Like Mine'.

1938 Sandy Nelson, US drummer who had a 1962 UK No.3 & US No.7 single with 'Let There Be Drums'. Nelson worked with The Teddy Bears and Gene Vincent. He lost his left foot in a car accident in 1963 but recovered fully to continue drumming.

1944 Bette Midler, singer and actress who had a 1989 US No.1 & UK No.5 single with 'Wind Beneath my Wings'. She worked with Barry Manilow and starred in the film *The Rose*, which was based on Janis Joplin.

1944 Eric Bloom – guitarist and vocalist with Blue Oyster Cult, who had a 1976 US No.12 & 1978 UK No.16 single with 'Don't Fear The Reaper'.

1944 John Densmore – drummer with The Doors, who had a 1967 US No.1 & UK No.49 single with 'Light My Fire' and a 1971 single with 'Riders On The Storm'.

1946 Gilbert O'Sullivan, singer/songwriter who had a 1972 UK No.1 single with 'Clair', a 1972 US No.1 single with 'Alone Again Naturally' plus 13 other UK Top 40 singles.

1977 Brad Delson – guitarist with Linkin Park, who had a 2002 US No.2 & UK No.4 single with 'In The End' and a 2002 US No.2 & 2001 UK No.4 album with *Hybrid Theory*.

1980 Michelle Williams – singer with Destiny's Child, who had a 2000 US No.1 single with 'Say My Name' and a 2001 US & UK No.1 single and album called 'Survivor'.

ON THIS DAY

1957 Buddy Holly & The Crickets appeared on *The Ed Sullivan Show*, performing 'That'll Be The Day' and 'Peggy Sue'. Sam Cooke was also on the show, and performed 'You Send Me'.

1966 Tom Jones was at No.1 on the UK singles chart with 'Green Green Grass Of Home'. It stayed at No.1 for seven weeks, giving Decca its first million-selling single by a British artist. The song was a No.11 hit in the US.

1973 The Carpenters went to No.1 on the US singles chart with 'Top Of The World', their second US No.1. It made No.5 in the UK.

1976 the Sex Pistols appeared on ITV's live early evening *Today* programme in place of Queen, who had pulled out following a trip to the dentists by Freddie Mercury. Taunted by interviewer Bill

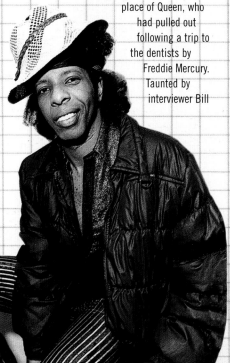

Grundy who asked the band to say something outrageous, guitarist Steve Jones said, "You dirty bastard...you dirty fucker...what a fucking rotter!"

1980 Talking Heads appeared at London's Hammersmith Palais, supported by U2.

1981 Vince Clarke announced he was quitting Depeche Mode to form Yazoo with Alison Moyet.

1982 Michael Jackson's *Thriller* album was released. It spent 190 weeks on the UK album chart and became the biggest-selling pop album of all time, with sales of over 25 million. (It was announced in 2005 that The Eagles' *Greatest Hits* had become the biggest-selling album with sales of over 28 million).

1987 a Kentucky teacher lost her appeal in the US Supreme Court over her sacking after showing Pink Floyd's film *The Wall* to her class. The court decided that the film was not suitable for minors due to its bad language and sexual content.

1989 Sly Stone *(left)* was sentenced to 55 days after pleading guilty to a charge of driving under the influence of cocaine (two weeks later he also pleaded guilty to possession of cocaine and was sentenced to spend 9-14 months in rehab).

1990 Whitney Houston went to No.1 on the US singles chart with 'I'm Your Baby Tonight', her eighth US No.1 and the first for writers and producers Reid and Babyface.

1998 this was the first night of a US tour with *NSYNC, Britney Spears and B*Witched in Columbus, Ohio.

2002 Daniel Bedingfield scored his second UK No.1 single with 'If You're Not The One'.

2002 Shania Twain started a five week run at No.1 on the US album chart with *Up!*, which was a No.4 hit in the UK.

BORN ON THIS DAY

1906 Dr Peter Carl Goldmark, who invented the long-playing microgroove record in 1945 that went on to revolutionize the way people listened to music. He was killed in a car crash on December 7th 1977.

1941 Tom McGuinness – bass player with Manfred Mann, who had a 1964 UK & US No.1 single with 'Do Wah Diddy Diddy', McGiness Flint, who had a 1970 UK No.2 single with 'When I'm Dead And Gone', and Blues Band.

1960 Rick Savage – bass player with Def Leppard, who had a 1987 UK No.6 single with 'Animal', a 1987 worldwide No.1 album with *Hysteria* and a 1988 US No.1 single with 'Love Bites'.

1968 Nate Mendel – bass player with Foo Fighters, who had a 1995 UK No.5 single with 'This Is A Call' and the 2003 US No.5 single 'All My Life'.

1978 Nelly Furtado, Canadian singer who had a 2001 UK No.5 single with 'I'm Like A Bird'.

1981 Britney Spears, singer who had a worldwide No.1 single with '…Baby One More Time'. Her 1999 album *…Baby One More Time* spent 82 weeks on the UK chart. She has been the biggest-selling teenage act in the world, with album sales of over 40 million.

ON THIS DAY

1967 The Monkees started a five week run at No.1 on the US album chart with *Pisces, Aquarius, Capricorn & Jones Ltd*, the group's third US chart topper.

1971 Led Zeppelin appeared at The Royal Ballroom, Bournemouth, England.

1978 Rod Stewart was at No.1 on the UK singles chart with 'Da Ya Think I'm Sexy?'

1982 US folk singer David Blue died of a heart attack aged 41 while jogging in New York's Washington Square Park. He had been a member of Bob Dylan's Rolling Thunder Revue during the late 70s.

1986 Jerry Lee Lewis checked into the Betty Ford Clinic to overcome his addiction to painkillers.

1987 INXS appeared at Newcastle City Hall, supported by Sinead O'Connor.

1988 The Stone Roses appeared at The London School Of Economics, supported by The Charlatans. Tickets cost £2.50 ($4.25).

1995 Mariah Carey went to No.1 on the US singles chart with her duet with Boyz II Men 'One Sweet Day'. It made Mariah the first artist in history to have two consecutive single debuts at No.1, 'Fantasy' being her first.

1997 a man died after falling from a balcony during a Rolling Stones concert at Pontiac Silverdome, Michigan.

1997 Whitney Houston pulled out of a concert sponsored by the Moonies two hours before she was due on stage. The religious group said they had no intention of suing providing the singer returned the $1 million (£0.6 million) fee she had received.

1999 it was reported that Stevie Wonder was to undergo an operation to regain his sight. The breakthrough by top eye specialists involved inserting a microchip into the retina.

2000 thieves broke into Madonna's London home. The raiders forced their way in through a basement door then took a set of car keys before loading up the singer's fiancée Guy Ritchie's car with some of the couple's possessions and driving off.

2001 Daniel Bedingfield scored his first UK No.1 single with 'Gotta Get Thru This'. The single went back to No.1 in January 2002.

2001 singer Valerie Jones, died aged 45. She had been part of The Jones Girls and worked with Lou Reed, Diana Ross, Aretha Franklin and Betty Everett.

2002 Oasis singer Liam Gallagher was arrested and charged with assault after he kung-fu-kicked a police officer. The incident happened at a nightclub in the Bayerischer Hotel in Munich. The singer lost his two front teeth in the brawl and an Oasis minder was knocked out cold. A concert in Munich had to be postponed and a show in Hamburg rescheduled as the singer underwent emergency dental work.

> ## "I'm a little fighter and I stand up for what I believe in."
> ## Avril Lavigne

The scene of Liam Gallagher's martial arts show.

3rd December

BORN ON THIS DAY

1940 John Cale – bass guitarist, keyboardist and vocalist with Velvet Underground, who released the 1967 classic album *The Velvet Underground and Nico* and solo artist.

1944 Ralph McTell, singer/songwriter and children's TV presenter who had a 1975 UK No.2 single with 'Streets of London'.

1946 Vic Malcolm – guitarist with Geordie, who had a 1973 UK No.6 single with 'All Because Of You'.

1948 Ozzy Osbourne (a.k.a. John Michael Osbourne) – singer with Black Sabbath, who had a 1970 UK No.4 single with 'Paranoid' and the 1971 *Paranoid* album which spent 34 weeks on the US chart. As a solo artist he had a 1986 UK No.20 single with 'Shot In The Dark' and a 1991 US No.7 album with *No More Tears*.

1968 Montell Jordan, singer who had a 1995 US No.1 & UK No.11 single with 'This Is How We Do It'.

1979 Daniel Bedingfield, singer/songwriter who had a 2001 UK No.1 single with 'Gotta Get Thru This'.

ON THIS DAY

1956 Guy Mitchell was at No.1 on the US singles chart with his version of the Marty Robbins song 'Singing The Blues'.

1965 Rolling Stone Keith Richards was knocked unconscious by an electric shock on stage at the Memorial Hall in Sacramento, California when his guitar made contact with his microphone.

1966 Ray Charles was given a five year suspended prison sentence and a $10,000 (£5,882) fine after being convicted of possessing heroin and marijuana.

1966 The Monkees made their live debut at the International Arena, Honolulu.

1969 The Rolling Stones recorded 'Brown Sugar' at Muscle Shoals Studios. The single made No.1 in both the US and UK.

1971 The Montreux Casino in Switzerland burned to the ground during a gig by Frank Zappa. Deep Purple, who were recording their album in the casino, immortalized the incident in their song 'Smoke On The Water'.

1976 The Stranglers signed a recording contract with United Artists.

1976 a giant 12m (40ft) inflatable pig was seen floating above London after breaking free from its moorings while being photographed for Pink Floyd's *Animals* album cover. The Civil Aviation Authority issued a warning to all pilots that a flying pig was on the run.

1976 an attempt was made on Bob Marley's life when seven gunmen burst into his Kingston home injuring Marley, his wife Rita and manager Don Taylor. The attack was believed to be politically motivated.

1976 an estimated three and a half million people applied for Abba's forthcoming Albert Hall concerts – just 11,000 tickets were available.

1977 Wings started a nine week run at No.1 in the UK with 'Mull Of Kintyre', the first single to sell over two million in the UK. It was co-written by Denny Laine, who sold his rights to the song when he became bankrupt.

1983 Duran Duran scored their first UK No.1 album with their third release *Seven And The Ragged Tiger*.

Rock solid investors

Mick Jagger and Bono: laughing all the way to the bank.

1986 Judas Priest were sued by two families who alleged that the band was responsible for their sons forming a suicide pact and shooting themselves after listening to Judas Priest records.

1994 Boyz II Men knocked themselves off the No.1 position on the US singles chart after 14 weeks with 'I'll Make Love To You' when 'On Bended Knee' went to No.1. This started a six week run at the top.

1999 prosecutors in California charged Gabriel Gomez with the kidnapping and murder of Sandra Ann Rosas, wife of Los Lobos singer and guitarist Cesar Rosas. No body had been found as yet.

2000 Hoyt Curtin, composer, died of heart failure. He wrote the theme to *The Flintstones*, *Yogi Bear*, *The Jetsons* and other cartoons.

2000 Mick Jagger and U2 formed a £100 million ($170 million) offshore investment trust to buy commercial property. Based in the Channel Islands the fund would invest in small offices and shops in London.

BORN ON THIS DAY

1940 Freddy Cannon, singer who had a 1959 US & UK No.3 single with 'Way Down Yonder In New Orleans'.

1942 Chris Hilman – bass guitarist and vocalist with The Byrds, who had a 1965 UK & US No.1 single with 'Mr. Tambourine Man', The Flying Burrito Brothers and The Souther-Hillman-Furay Band, who had a 1974 US No.27 single with 'Fallin' In Love'.

1944 Dennis Wilson – drummer for The Beach Boys, who had a 1966 UK & US No.1 single with 'Good Vibrations' plus over 25 other UK Top 40 singles. Wilson died on December 28th 1983.

1947 Terry Woods – guitarist, mandolin and banjo player with The Pogues, who had a 1987 UK No.8 single with 'The Irish Rover'.

1948 Southside Johnny – vocalist and harmonica player with Southside Johnny & The Asbury Dukes, who had a 1978 album with *Hearts Of Stone*.

1951 Gary Rossington – guitarist with Lynyrd Skynyrd, who had a 1974 US No.8 single with 'Sweet Home Alabama' and a 1982 UK No.21 single with 'Freebird'.

1969 Jay-Z, rapper who had a 1998 UK No.2 single with 'Hard Knock Life', a 1999 UK No.10 single with Mariah Carey, 'Heartbreaker' and a 2001 US No.1 album with *The Blueprint*. He is the owner of Roc-A-Fella Records.

1972 Justin Welch – drummer with Elastica, who had a 1995 UK No.13 single with 'Waking Up', and Me Me Me, who had a 1996 UK No.19 single with 'Hanging Around'.

ON THIS DAY

1956 the so-called "Million Dollar Quartet" jam session took place at Sun Studios in Memphis with Elvis Presley, Jerry Lee Lewis and Carl Perkins. Johnny Cash had been in the studio but left earlier to go shopping with his wife.

1964 The Beatles released their fourth album *Beatles For Sale*, which spent 11 weeks as the UK No.1 album.

1965 The Byrds started a three week run at No.1 on the US singles chart with 'Turn! Turn! Turn!', the group's second No.1. It made No.26 in the UK.

1971 Led Zeppelin started a two week run at No.1 on the UK chart with the *Four Symbols* album. Featuring the eight minute track 'Stairway To Heaven', the album stayed on the US chart for one week short of five years, selling over 11 million copies.

1971 Sly & The Family Stone started a five week run at No.1 on the US single chart with 'Family Affair', their third US No.1.

1976 EMI record packers went on strike, refusing to package the Sex Pistols' single 'Anarchy In The UK'.

1976 Tommy Bolin, US guitarist with Zepher, Deep Purple, The James Gang and solo artist, died from a heroin overdose, aged 25.

1979 U2 appeared at The Hope And Anchor, Islington, London.

1982 The Jam were at No.1 on the UK singles chart with 'Beat Surrender', the group's fourth UK No.1.

1982 *The John Lennon Collection* album started a six week run at No.1 on the UK chart.

1983 Tears For Fears kicked off a 13 date UK tour at Liverpool's Royal Court Theatre. Tickets cost £4 ($6.80).

1987 Madonna filed for divorce from actor Sean Penn and then changed her mind a week later.

1988 Roy Orbison played his final-ever gig when he appeared in Cleveland, Ohio. He died two days later.

1989 Lenny Kravitz made his UK live debut at London's Borderline Club.

1993 avant-garde multi-instrumentalist Frank Zappa died of prostrate cancer. Zappa recorded many albums with The Mothers Of Invention and also as a solo artist.

1999 rapper Jay-Z was released on $50,000 (£29,412) bail after being accused of attacking Lance Rivera when a fight broke out at a party for rapper Q-Tip at a Manhattan Club. Police declined to say what caused the dispute.

2000 Ronan Keating was dumped as chart-topping boyband Westlife's manager. Ronan was told his services were no longer required. Westlife had scored seven No.1 UK singles.

2002 Whitney Houston admitted in an US TV interview that drink and drugs nearly killed her. Bobby Brown's wife also admitted to being addicted to sex. She said that the music business is sex, drugs and rock 'n' roll, and that she got into the lifestyle after missing out on partying when her career kicked off aged 18.

STANDING ·149 6
FLOOR
TGN 16.00
£ 16.00
NYNE23157
Manchester

NYNEX ARENA MANCHESTER
SJM CONCERTS & KEY 103
PRESENT
BLUR
+ SPECIAL GUESTS
THU 04-DEC-1997 7.30PM

S.J.M. CONCERTS
ARTISTE The Farm
VENUE Sheffield
DATE 4th Dec
FRONT OF HOUSE

BORN ON THIS DAY

1899 Sonny Boy Williamson, US blues singer. Van Morrison, The Who, The Animals, The Yardbirds and Moody Blues all covered his songs. He died on May 25th 1965.

1932 Little Richard, singer/songwriter who had a 1956 US No.6 & 1957 UK No.3 single with 'Long Tall Sally' plus over ten other US & UK Top 40 singles.

1938 J.J. Cale, US guitarist and singer/songwriter who had a 1972 US No.22 single with 'Crazy Mama' and a 1982 UK No.36 album with *Grasshopper*.

1947 Jim Messina – bass guitarist with Buffalo Springfield, who had a 1967 US No.17 single with 'For What It's Worth'. Also a member of Loggins & Messina.

1952 Andy Kim, singer who had a 1974 US No.1 & UK No.2 single with 'Rock Me Gently'.

1960 Les Nemes – bass guitarist with Haircut 100, who had a 1982 UK No.3 & US No.37 single with 'Love Plus One'.

1965 Mike Malinin – drummer with the Goo Goo Dolls, who had a 1999 UK No.26 single with 'Iris' and a 2002 US No.3 album with *Gutterflower*.

ON THIS DAY

1960 Elvis Presley started a ten week run at No.1 on the US album chart with *G.I. Blues*, his fifth US No.1 album.

1964 Lorne Greene, star of the NBC-TV show *Bonanza*, was at No.1 on the US singles chart with 'Ringo', making him the second Canadian to have a US No.1 single. The song was a No.22 hit in the UK.

1967 the last night of a package tour arrived at Green's Playhouse, Glasgow and featured Pink Floyd, the Jimi Hendrix Experience, The Move and Amen Corner.

Amazing Grace THE BEST OF JUDY COLLINS

1970 'Amazing Grace' by Judy Collins *(above)* entered the UK singles chart for the first of eight times. It spent a total of 67 weeks on the chart but never reached the No.1 position.

1976 music weekly *NME* reviewed the Sex Pistols' debut single 'Anarchy In The UK' saying, "Johnny Rotten sings flat, the song is laughably naive and the overall feeling is of a third-rate Who imitation".

1981 Julio Iglesias was at No.1 in the UK singles chart with 'Begin The Beguine'.

1987 Belinda Carlisle went to No.1 on the US singles chart with 'Heaven Is A Place On Earth', the ex-Go-Go's first solo No.1. It was also a No.1 hit in the UK.

1987 "Fat Larry" James, drummer and leader of Fat Larry's Band, died of a heart attack, aged 38. The band had a 1982 UK No.2 single with 'Zoom'.

1987 The Jesus And Mary Chain were banned from appearing on a US music TV show after complaints of blasphemy when the group's name was flashed across the screen. The CBS show did ask them to be called Jamc but the group wouldn't agree to that.

1992 Ice Cube went to No.1 on the US album chart with *The Predator*.

1992 Whitney Houston started a ten week run at No.1 in the UK singles chart with 'I Will Always Love You', which was featured in the film *The Bodyguard*.

1993 Doug Hopkins from Gin Blossoms died of self-inflicted bullet wounds, aged 32.

1998 R. Kelly started a six week run at No.1 on the US singles chart with 'I'm Your Angel', featuring Celine Dion. The song was a No.3 hit in the UK.

2003 Courtney Love was sentenced to 18 months in drug rehabilitation after she admitted being under the influence of cocaine and opiates. She was banned from taking non-prescription drugs, drinking alcohol or being in places that serve alcohol.

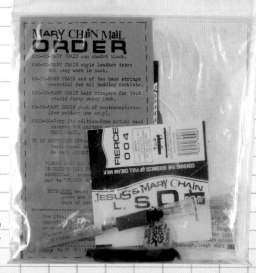

The Jesus and Mary Chain cause some more controversy.

BORN ON THIS DAY

1944 Jonathan King, singer, producer and TV presenter, who had a 1965 UK No.4 single with 'Everyone's Gone To The Moon' plus 12 other UK Top 40 singles under various names, such as Bubblerock, Shag, Weathermen, Father Abraphart and Sakkarin. He was jailed for seven years in 2001 for sex attacks against five youths aged 14 and 16 between 1983 and 1989.

1955 Edward Tudor-Pole – actor and vocalist for Tenpole Tudor, who had a 1981 UK No.6 single with 'Swords Of A Thousand Men'. He appeared in the film *Absolute Beginners* and was a presenter of UK TV's *Crystal Maze*.

1955 Rick Buckler, drums, The Jam, who had a 1980 UK No.1 single 'Going Underground' plus 14 other UK Top 40 singles.

1956 Peter Buck – guitarist with R.E.M., who had a 1991 UK No.6 & US No.10 single with 'Shiny Happy People' plus over 20 Top 40 UK singles and a 1992 UK No.1 & US No.2 album with *Automatic For The People*.

1961 David Lovering – drummer with the Pixies, who had a 1990 UK No.28 single with 'Velouria'.

1962 Ben Watt – songwriter, keyboards singer with Everything But The Girl, who had a 1995 UK No.3 & 1996 US No.2 single 'Missing'.

1970 Ulf Ekberg – keyboardist and programmer with Ace Of Base, who had a 1993 UK No.1 single with 'All That She Wants' and a 1994 US No.1 single with 'The Sign'.

ON THIS DAY

1949 US blues artist Leadbelly died. He wrote 'Goodnight Irene', 'The Rock Island Line' and 'The Midnight Special'. He was once jailed for shooting a man dead during an argument over a woman.

1959 Gene Vincent made his UK live debut at The Tooting Granada, London, when he was a guest on *The Marty Wilde Show*.

1967 Cliff Richard was confirmed into membership of The Church Of England at St. Paul's Church, Finchley, London.

1969 Led Zeppelin made their debut on the US singles chart with 'Whole Lotta Love'. It went on to make No.4 on the chart and was the first of six Top 40 singles for the group.

1969 The Rolling Stones played a free festival at Altamont in California along with Jefferson Airplane, Santana, The Flying Burrito Brothers and Crosby, Stills, Nash & Young. Stones fan Meredith Hunter was stabbed to death as the group played. It's claimed that Hunter was waving a revolver. Hell's Angels had been hired in to police the event. During it one other man drowned, two men were killed by a hit-and-run accident and two babies were born.

1971 Crosby, Stills & Nash played the first of two nights at London's Festival Hall.

1975 Rev. Charles Boykin of Tallahassee, Florida organized the burning of Elton John and Rolling Stones records, claiming that they were sinful. Boykin was reacting to the results from a survey that said 984 of the 1,000 local unmarried mothers listened to rock music while having sex.

1978 Sex Pistol Sid Vicious smashed a glass in the face of Patti Smith's brother Todd during a fight at New York club Hurrah.

1982 U2 appeared at The Hammersmith Palais, London.

1984 Frankie Goes To Hollywood were at No.1 on the UK singles chart with 'The Power Of Love'. It was the group's third No.1 of the year and final UK No.1. It also made them the first group since Gerry And The Pacemakers to have a UK No.1 with their first three singles.

1988 Roy Orbison died of a heart attack. He had had a 1964 UK & US No.1 single with 'Pretty Woman' plus over 20 US & 30 UK Top 40 singles. He had also been a member of the Traveling Wilburys, who had a 1988 UK No.21 single with 'Handle With Care'.

1990 Happy Monday's singer Shaun Ryder booked himself into the Priory Clinic Rehabilitation Detox facility in Manchester.

1997 Counting Crows kicked off an eight date UK tour at The Forum, London.

2000 the Foo Fighters kicked off a five date UK tour at the Manchester Apollo *(below)*.

2003 Elvis Costello married jazz artist Diana Krall in a ceremony at Elton John's UK mansion. About 150 guests, including Sir Paul McCartney, attended the wedding. It was Costello's third marriage.

BORN ON THIS DAY

1942 Harry Chapin, US singer/songwriter, who had a 1974 UK No.34 single with 'WOLD' and a 1974 US No.1 single with 'Cat's In The Cradle'. Chapin was killed on July 16th 1981 when a tractor trailer crashed into his car.

1949 Tom Waits, singer/songwriter who had a 1980 album with *Heart Attack And Vine*, which was used in a Levi's TV ad. He also wrote 'Ol' 55', which was a 1974 US No.17 single for The Eagles.

1954 Mike Nolan – singer with Bucks Fizz, who had a 1981 UK No.1 single with 'Making Your Mind Up' plus 12 other UK Top 40 singles.

1958 Tim Butler – bass player for Psychedelic Furs, who had a 1986 UK No.18 single with 'Pretty In Pink'.

1963 Barbara Weathers – singer with Atlantic Starr, who had a 1987 US No.1 & UK No.3 single with 'Always'.

1974 Nicole Appleton – singer with All Saints, who had a 1998 UK No.1 single 'Never Ever'. As part of duo Appleton she also enjoyed a 2003 UK No.5 single with 'Don't Worry'.

ON THIS DAY

1963 The Beatles' second album *With The Beatles* started a 21 week stay at No.1 on the UK album chart. It replaced their first album *Please Please Me*, which had been at the top since its release 30 weeks previously.

Part of a series of artworks of a Trabant car, produced by Brian Eno for U2's *Achtung Baby*.

1964 Beach Boy Brian Wilson married Marilyn Rovell in L.A. The couple divorced in 1979.

1967 Otis Redding went into the studio to record '(Sittin' On) The Dock Of The Bay'. Redding didn't live to see its release as he was killed three days later in a plane crash.

1967 The Beatles' Apple boutique opened its doors. It closed seven months later when all the goods were given away free to passers by.

1971 Genesis appeared at The Hobbits Garden, Wimbledon supported by Roxy Music.

1974 Barry White was at No.1 on the UK singles chart with 'You're The First The Last My Everything', the singer's first UK No.1.

1979 The Police had their second UK No.1 single with 'Walking on the Moon'.

1981 Duran Duran kicked off a 14 date UK tour at Canterbury University.

1985 Mr. Mister started a two week run at No.1 on the US singles chart with 'Broken Wings', which was a UK No.4 hit.

1991 George Michael and Elton John were at No.1 in the UK with a live version of 'Don't Let The Sun Go down On Me'. All proceeds went to AIDs charities.

James Brown is no stranger to Presidential honours.

1991 U2 went to No.1 on the US album charts with *Achtung Baby*. It featured the tracks 'One', 'Zoo Station', 'The Fly' and 'Even Better Than The Real Thing'.

1992 Mariah Carey's *MTV Unplugged* EP became the first Sony minidisc to be released in the US.

1996 Bush went to No.1 on the US album chart with *Razorblade Suitcase*.

1996 Toni Braxton started a 11 week run at No.1 on the US singles chart with 'Un-Break My Heart', which was written by Dianne Warren. It gave Braxton her second US solo No.1, and was also a No.2 hit in the UK.

1997 Shane MacGowan spent the night in police cells after being arrested in Liverpool following a show at the University. He was charged after he threw a mike stand into the crowd and injured a fan.

1997 the future of Black Grape was uncertain after Shaun Ryder sacked the rest of the band during a row backstage at a gig at the Doncaster Dome.

2003 James Brown and country music star Loretta Lynn were honoured for their contributions to US culture. The pair were invited to a gala attended by President George Bush at the Kennedy Arts Centre in Washington.

BORN ON THIS DAY

1925 Sammy Davis Jr., singer and actor who had a 1972 US No.1 single with 'The Candy Man'. He died of throat cancer on May 16th 1990.

1939 Jerry Butler – vocalist with The Impressions, who had a 1965 US No.7 single with 'Lilies Of The Field'. As a solo artist he had a 1969 US No.4 single with 'Only The Strong Survive'.

1942 Bobby Elliott – drummer with The Hollies, who have had over 25 Top 40 hits since 1963, including the 1972 US No.2 single 'Long Cool Woman In A Black Dress' and the 1988 UK No.1 single 'He Ain't Heavy, He's My Brother', which was first released in 1969.

1943 Jim Morrison – vocalist with The Doors, who had a 1967 US No.1 & UK No.49 single with 'Light My Fire' and a 1971 single with 'Riders On The Storm'. Morrison died on July 3rd 1971.

1944 Mike Botts – drummer with Bread, who had a 1970 US No.1 & UK No.5 single with 'Make It With You'.

1947 Gregg Allman – keyboardist, guitarist and vocalist with The Allman Brothers Band, who had a 1973 US No.12 single with 'Ramblin Man'.

1957 Phil Collen – guitarist with Def Leppard, who had a 1987 UK No.6 single with 'Animal', a 1987 worldwide No.1 album with *Hysteria* and a 1988 US No.1 single with 'Love Bites'.

1959 Paul Rutherford – vocalist with Frankie Goes To Hollywood, who had a 1984 UK No.1 & US No.10 single with 'Relax'.

1976 Corey Taylor – singer for Slipknot, who had a 2001 UK No.1 album with *Iowa*, and Stone Sour.

REGULAR MUSIC Presents

SQUEEZE
at TIFFANY'S GLASGOW
on Tuesday 8th December
Doors open 7.30 pm
Tickets £3.00 (in advance)
+ A FLOCK OF SEAGULLS.

The management reserve the right
to refuse admission
№ 1154

JOHN LENNON SHOT DEAD

THE NEW STANDARD

ON THIS DAY

1961 The Beach Boys' first single 'Surfin' was released on Candix Records, a small label based in Los Angeles.

1965 The Spencer Davis Group kicked off a nine date UK tour at The Top Rank, Southampton, England.

1968 Graham Nash left The Hollies and started work with David Crosby and Stephen Stills.

1969 on trial in a Toronto court on drug possession charges Jimi Hendrix claimed that he had only smoked pot four times in his life, snorted cocaine twice and took LSD no more than five times. After telling the jury that he has now "outgrown" drugs they find him not guilty.

1971 this week's top-selling eight track cartridges chart was: No.5, Frank Sinatra's *Greatest Hits Vol 2*; No.4, Carole King, *Tapestry*; No.3, Simon & Garfunkel, *Bridge Over Troubled Water*; No.2, *Motown Chartbusters Vol 6* and No.1, John Lennon, *Imagine*.

1973 Roxy Music had their first UK No.1 album when *Stranded* went to the top for one week. The sleeve featured *Playboy*'s Playmate of The Year, model Marilyn Cole.

1980 John Lennon was shot five times by 25-year-old Mark Chapman outside the Dakota building where John and Yoko lived. Lennon was pronounced dead from a massive loss of blood at 11.30pm. Chapman had been stalking Lennon for days outside the Dakota apartments and asked for an autograph as Lennon walked through the courtyard. As he signed a piece of paper Chapman fired.

1993 The Verve, Acetone and Oasis started a UK tour at Wulfren Hall, Wolverhampton.

1995 Courtney Love appeared on the ABC-TV show *10 Most Fascinating People*, telling the presenter that she wished she had done "eight thousand million things differently" to have prevented the death of her husband Kurt Cobain.

2000 Sting joined the ranks of tinseltown's greatest when his star was unveiled on the celebrated Walk Of Fame in Hollywood.

2003 BPI figures showed that the UK sales of seven inch singles had increased by 84 percent on the previous year. The report claimed that bands such as The Darkness, The Strokes and The White Stripes had boosted sales by releasing special limited-edition seven inch records.

2004 former Pantera guitarist Darrell Abbott was one of five people killed after a man stormed the stage during a Damageplan show at the Alrosa Villa Club in Columbus. Nathan Gale, aged 25, began firing at the band and crowd but was then shot and killed by a police officer who arrived shortly after the first shots were fired.

BORN ON THIS DAY

1932 Junior Wells, US blues singer and harmonica player who toured with The Rolling Stones in 1970. He died on January 15th 1998.

1943 Rick Danko – guitarist and vocalist with The Band, who had a 1970 UK No.16 single with 'Rag Mama Rag'. He died on December 10th 1999.

1944 Neil Innes – vocalist and guitarist with the Bonzo Dog Doo Dah Band, who had a 1968 UK No.5 single with 'I'm The Urban Spaceman'. Innes also composed music for *Monty Python's Flying Circus* and wrote and performed *The Rutles*, a TV spoof on The Beatles.

1957 Donny Osmond, singer who had a 1971 US No.1 single with 'Go Away Little Girl', a 1972 UK No.1 single with 'Puppy Love' plus seven other UK Top 40 singles. As part of The Osmonds he enjoyed a 1971 US No.1 single with 'One Bad Apple', and the 1974 UK No.1 single with 'Love Me For A Reason'.

1969 Jakob Dylan – (son of Bob), guitarist and vocalist with The Wallflowers, who had a 1997 US No.3 album with *Bringing Down The Horse*.

1970 Zak Foley – bass player with EMF, who had a 1990 UK No.3 & 1991 US No.1 single with 'Unbelievable'. He died on December 31st 2001, aged 31.

1972 Frank Wright "Tre Cool" – drummer with Green Day, who had a 1995 UK No.7 single with 'Basket Case'.

1978 Chris Wolstenholme – bass player with Muse, who had a 2003 UK No.1 album *Absolution* and a 2003 UK No.8 single with 'Time Is Running Out'.

ON THIS DAY

1964 Paul McCartney went to visit Ringo Starr at London's University hospital. Starr was recovering after having his tonsils removed.

1968 the Jimi Hendrix Experience had the US No.1 album with *Electric Ladyland*.

1971 The Who appeared at the Los Angeles Forum, California.

1972 The Moody Blues started a five week run at No.1 on the US album chart with *Seventh Sojourn*.

1978 Boney M had their second UK No.1 single with their version of the Harry Belafonte 1957 hit 'Mary's Boy Child'.

1978 Chic started a seven week run at No.1 on the US singles chart with 'Le Freak', which made No.7 in the UK.

1984 Lloyd Cole And The Commotions appeared at The Powerhouse, Birmingham and Spandau Ballet played at Wembley Arena, London.

1988 according to a poll released in the US the music of Neil Diamond was favoured as the best background music for sex. Beethoven was the second choice and Luther Vandross was voted third.

1989 Billy Joel started a two week run at No.1 on the US singles chart with 'We Didn't Start The Fire', which was a No.7 hit in the UK.

1990 Paula Abdul was taken to North Hollywood Medical Center after being involved in a car crash in Los Angeles.

1995 Michael Jackson scored his sixth solo UK No.1 single when 'Earth Song' started a six week run at the top of the charts. It also gave Jackson the UK Christmas No.1 of 1995.

1997 Oasis played the first of three sold-out nights at Wembley Arena, London, supported by Supergrass.

1998 All Saint Nicole Appleton walked out during the recording of BBC2's *Later* saying she had quit the band.

2000 Sharon Corr of The Corrs called for the legalization of cannabis, claiming that the drug has medicinal properties. Sharon said, "Certainly people with certain conditions can get a brief reprieve from their symptoms through cannabis."

2001 Channel 4 TV apologized to viewers after Madonna said "motherfucker" during live TV coverage at The Tate gallery. Madonna was presenting a prize to artist Martin Creed. A TV spokesman said that they did have a bleeper system but missed it.

2003 Ozzy Osbourne was admitted to Wexham Park Hospital in Slough, Berkshire after being injured in a quad bike accident at his UK home. The 55-year-old singer broke his collarbone, eight ribs and a vertebra in his neck. News of Osbourne's accident reached the House of Commons, where the government sent a goodwill message.

2003 a "Celebrity Thumbprints" auction took place on ebayliveauctions.com. Beyonce, Kelly Osbourne, Coldplay, Blue and Westlife were among the stars whose thumbprints went under the hammer.

Neil Diamond: music to make love to.

BORN ON THIS DAY

1910 John Hammond, producer and A&R scout. He worked with Bob Dylan, Bruce Springsteen, Leonard Cohen, George Benson and Janis Joplin. Hammond died on July 10th 1987.

1946 Ace Kefford – bass player and vocalist with The Move, who had a 1969 UK No.1 single with 'Blackberry Way'.

1947 Walter "Clyde" Orange – drummer and vocalist with The Commodores, who had a 1978 UK & US No.1 single with 'Three Times A Lady'.

1957 Paul Hardcastle, producer and keyboardist who had a 1985 UK No.1 single with 'Nineteen'.

1972 Brian Molko – guitarist and vocalist with Placebo, who had a 1997 UK No.6 single with 'Nancy Boy'.

1974 Meg White – drummer with The White Stripes, who had a 2003 UK No.1 album with *Elephant*.

ON THIS DAY

1961 the film *The Young Ones*, featuring Cliff Richard, premiered in London.

1964 The Beatles had their sixth UK No.1 single with 'I Feel Fine', which was also a US No.1.

1966 The Beach Boys went to No.1 on the US singles chart with 'Good Vibrations', the group's third US No.1. The song was also a No.1 in the UK.

1967 flying to that night's concert in Madison, the plane carrying Otis Redding and his band crashed into the icy waters of Lake Monoma near Madison. Redding died in the crash along with The Bar-Kays band members Jimmy King, Ron Caldwell, Phalin Jones and Carl Cunningham. Trumpet player Ben Cauley was the only person to survive.

1968 Led Zeppelin appeared at the Marquee Club, London. Tickets cost £7 ($12) or £6 ($10) in advance.

1971 playing the first of two nights at London's Rainbow Theatre, Frank Zappa was pushed off stage by jealous boyfriend Trevor Howell. Zappa broke one of his legs and suffered a fractured scull.

1973 the CBGB Club opened in New York's Lower East Side. It became the home for bands such as Blondie, Television, Patti Smith and The Ramones.

1976 Billy Idol's new band Generation X made their live debut at The Central College Of Art, London.

1983 Keith Richards married 27-year-old Patti Hansen on his 40th birthday.

1983 Paul McCartney and Michael Jackson started a six week run at No.1 on the US singles chart with 'Say Say Say'. It was Jackson's tenth No.1 (including his solo work and that with The Jacksons) and McCartney's 29th, (as a solo artist and part of The Beatles).

1987 New Order appeared at London's Wembley Arena, supported by Primal Scream.

1988 Cliff Richard had his 12th UK No.1 single with 'Mistletoe And Wine'.

1994 East 17 started a five week run at No.1 on the UK singles chart with 'Stay Another Day'. It also gave them the UK Christmas No.1 of 1994.

1998 Bruce Springsteen won a £2 million ($3.4 million) court battle to ban an album of his early songs. The case revolved around a dispute over copyright ownership between Bruce and a former manager.

1999 a war of words broke out between Cliff Richard and George Michael after George branded Cliff Richard's hit 'Millennium Prayer' as "vile". Cliff replied that his single was a Christian celebration.

1999 Rick Danko, guitarist and singer with The Band, died in his sleep aged 57.

2000 Eminem went to No.1 on the UK singles chart with 'Stan'.

2000 Westlife *(below)* scooped the Record of the year award at the Smash Hits Awards for 'My Love'. Other winners included: Atomic Kitten, for Best new band; Best new male was Craig David; best British band Five and Best female Britney Spears.

2003 Coldplay singer Chris Martin married actress Gwyneth Paltrow in California. Oscar winner Paltrow, 31, and 26-year-old Martin announced in a statement that they were expecting a baby the following summer.

marquee

90 Wardour Street — London W.1

Thursday, December 5th (7.30-11.00)
★ **JOE COCKER** From SWEDEN ★ **SLAM CREEPERS**

Friday, December 6th (7.30-11.00)
★ **LOVE SCULPTURE** ★ **FOOD**

Saturday, December 7th (8.00-11.30)
★ **DREAM POLICE** ★ **SLEEPY**

Sunday, December 8th (7.30-10.30)
★ **BLUE RIVERS & HIS MAROONS** ★ **TV PERSONALITY STUART HENRY**

Monday, December 9th (7.30-11.00)
★ **THE FREE** ★ **STEVE MILLER'S DELIVERY**

Tuesday, December 10th (7.30-11.30)
★ **LED ZEPPELIN** (Nee THE YARDBIRDS) ★ **BAKERLOO BLUES LINE**

Wednesday, December 10th: **CLOSED**

Tuesday, December 17th
★ **THE WHO**

marquee studios • 4 Track • Stereo • Mono • Recordings
10 Richmond Mews, W.1. 01-437 6731

BORN ON THIS DAY

1916 Perez Prado, singer and band leader who had a 1955 US & UK No.1 single with 'Cherry Pink & Apple Blossom White'. He died on September 14th 1989.

1940 David Gates — vocalist and bass guitarist for Bread, who had a 1970 US No.1 & UK No.5 single with 'Make It With You'.

1954 Jermaine Jackson — singer with The Jackson Five, who had a 1970 US No.1 & UK No.2 single with 'I Want You Back' and, as The Jacksons, a 1977 UK No.1 single with 'Show You The Way To Go'. As a solo artist he had a 1985 UK No.6 single with 'Do What You Do'.

1958 Nikki Sixx — bass player with Motley Crue, who had a 1988 UK No.23 single with 'You're All I Need' and a 1989 US No.1 album with *Dr Feelgood*.

1962 Curtis "Fitz" Williams — keyboardist and programmer with Kool & The Gang, who had a 1981 US No.1 & UK No.7 single with 'Celebration', a 1984 UK No.2 single with 'Joanna' and 15 other UK Top 40 hits.

1964 Justin Currie — vocalist and bass guitarist for Del Amitri, who had a 1990, UK No.11 single with 'Nothing Ever Happens'.

1972 Easther Bennett — vocalist with Eternal, who had a 1997 UK No.1 single with 'I Wanna Be The Only One'.

ON THIS DAY

1957 still married to his first wife, Jane Mitcham, Jerry Lee Lewis secretly married his 13-year-old second cousin Myra Gale Brown.

1961 Elvis Presley started a 20 week run at No.1 on the US album chart with *Blue Hawaii*, his seventh US No.1 album.

1964 soul singer Sam Cooke was shot dead by his manager Bertha Franklin, who claimed to have been assaulted by Cooke while staying at the Hacienda Hotel, Los Angeles. Cooke was 33 years old.

1968 The Scaffold were at No.1 on the UK singles chart with 'Lily The Pink', this year's Christmas No.1.

1971 UK comedian Benny Hill was at No.1 on the UK singles chart with 'Ernie (The Fastest Milkman In The West)', giving Hill his only No.1 and the Christmas hit single of 1971.

1972 James Brown was arrested after a show in Tennessee for trying to incite a riot. Brown threatened to sue the city for $1 million (£0.6 million) and the charges were later dropped.

1980 U2 appeared at The Mudd Club in New York, the first date of four US shows that also took the band to Boston and Washington D.C.

1982 singer, TV actress and dancer Toni Basil went to No.1 on the US singles chart with 'Mickey', making her a one hit wonder. It made No.2 in the UK.

1982 The Jam played their last-ever gig as a band when they appeared in Brighton.

1983 The Flying Pickets were at No.1 on the UK singles chart with their version of the Yazoo song 'Only You'. It was also this year's Christmas No.1.

1992 Manic Street Preacher Nicky Wire was quoted as saying, "I hope Michael Stipe goes the same way as Freddie Mercury".

1993 Snoop Doggy Dogg went to No.1 on the US album chart with *Doggy Style*.

1996 Johnny Marr and Morrissey were left with a £300,000 ($510,000) legal bill after losing a case with former Smiths members Rourke and Joyce over unpaid royalties.

1998 during a gig in Tuscon, Arizona Black Crowes singer Chris Robinson was hit by a bottle thrown from the audience. A security guard was then stabbed trying to eject a man from the crowd.

2000 former Verve frontman Richard Ashcroft was forced to cancel the remaining dates on his current UK tour after he fell on stage and broke two ribs. The accident happened during a show in Birmingham.

2001 Brian Harvey underwent surgery after suffering a serious head injury in an attack. The former East 17 singer was attacked by a group of youths as he left the Works nightclub in Nottingham, having appeared at a promotional event.

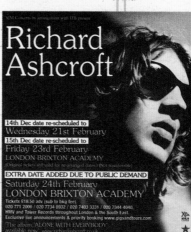

2003 Bobby Brown was charged with battery after allegedly hitting wife Whitney Houston in the face. Brown turned himself in to the police three days after a reported domestic dispute at the couple's home in Atlanta, Georgia. Houston, who accompanied her husband to court, said they were trying to work out their problems "privately".

BORN ON THIS DAY

1915 Frank Albert Sinatra, singer and actor who made his first record in 1939. He was also the first singer to encounter "pop hysteria". 'My Way' holds the UK chart longevity record of 136 weeks. He also had a 1966 UK & US No.1 single with 'Strangers In The Night'. Sinatra died on May 14th 1998.

1940 Dionne Warwick, singer who had a 1964 UK No.9 single with 'Walk On By', a 1974 US No.1 & UK No.29 single with 'Then Came You' plus over 25 US Top 40 hits.

1942 Tim Hauser – singer with Manhattan Transfer, who had a 1977 UK No.1 with 'Chanson D'amour' and a 1981 US No.7 single with 'Boy From New York City'.

1943 Dicky Betts – guitarist and vocalist with The Allman Brothers Band, who had a 1973 US No.12 single with 'Ramblin Man'.

1943 Mike Smith – singer with Dave Clark Five, who had a 1964 UK No.1 single with 'Glad All Over', a 1965 US No.1 single with 'Over And Over' plus over 15 other UK Top 40 singles.

1944 Rob Tyner – singer with MC5, who had a 1969 album with *Kick Out The Jams*. Tyner died on September 17th 1991.

1959 Sheila E., singer and percussionist discovered by Prince, she had the 1985 US & UK Top 20 single 'The Belle Of St Mark'. She also worked with Stevie Wonder, Mariah Carey, Phil Collins, Whitney Houston and Celine Dion.

1961 Daniel O'Donnell, Irish country singer who had a 1998 UK No.7 single with 'Give A Little Love'. He has had one Top 40 hit album every year since 1988.

1963 Eric Schenkman – guitarist with The Spin Doctors, who had a 1993 UK No.3 & US No.7 single with 'Two Princes'.

1966 Sinead O'Connor, Irish singer/songwriter who had a 1990 UK, US and worldwide No.1 single with 'Nothing Compares To U'.

1976 Dan Hawkins – guitarist with The Darkness, who had a 2003 UK No.2 single with 'I Believe In A Thing Called Love' and a 2003 UK No.1 album with *Permission To Land.*

ON THIS DAY

1957 Al Priddy, a DJ on US radio station KEX in Portland, was fired after playing Elvis Presley's version of 'White Christmas'. He was told by the management, "it is not in the spirit we associate with Christmas".

1963 The Beatles were at No.1 on the UK singles chart with 'I Want To Hold Your Hand', the group's third No.1 and this year's Christmas No.1.

1968 filming began for The Rolling Stones *Rock and Roll Circus.* As well as clowns and acrobats, John and Yoko, The Who, Eric Clapton and Jethro Tull all took part. The film was eventually released in 1996.

1970 Smokey Robinson And The Miracles started a two week run at No.1 on the US singles chart with 'Tears Of A Clown'. It was the group's 26th Top 40 hit and first No.1, and was also a No.1 in the UK.

1970 The Doors played what would be their last-ever live show with Jim Morrison when they played in New Orleans.

1974 guitarist Mick Taylor quit The Rolling Stones after being in the group for five years.

1980 The Human League had their only UK No.1 single with 'Don't You Want Me'. It was the Christmas hit of 1981, the biggest seller of 1981 and Virgin Records first No.1 UK single.

1985 Dionne Warwick received a star on Hollywood's Walk Of Fame.

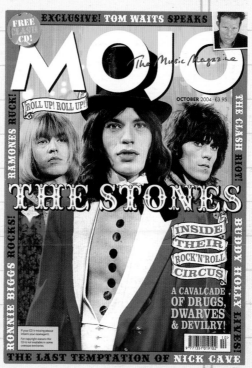

1985 The Rolling Stone's keyboard player Ian Stewart died of a heart attack in his doctor's Harley Street waiting room.

2001 Arthur Lee, guitarist and singer from Love, was released from prison after serving almost six years of an 11 year sentence. Lee had been convicted of possession of a firearm and for allegedly shooting a gun in the air during a dispute with a neighbour.

APOLLO THEATRE, GLASGOW
DEREK BLOCK PRESENTS
THE POLICE
+ WARMO NARIZ
Wednesday, 12th December, 1979
at 7.30 p.m.
UPPER CIRCLE
№ 17 G
TICKET £2.50
TO BE RETAINED
TICKETS CANNOT BE EXCHANGED

BORN ON THIS DAY

1940 Tony Gomez – keyboard player with The Foundations, who had a 1967 UK No.1 single with 'Baby Now That I've Found You' and a 1969 US No.3 single with 'Build Me Up A Buttercup'.

1945 Robert Martinez – drummer for ? & The Mysterians, who had a 1966 US No.1 & UK No.37 single with '96 Tears'. The song was also a UK No.17 hit for The Stranglers in 1990.

1948 Andy Peebles, UK radio DJ and the last person to interview John Lennon.

1948 Jeff "Skunk" Baxter – guitarist with The Doobie Brothers and Steely Dan, who had a 1973 US No.11 single with 'Reeling In The Years'.

1948 Ted Nugent – guitarist with The Amboy Dukes, who had a 1968 single with 'Journey To The Centre Of The Mind'. As a solo artist he had a 1977 single with 'Cat Scratch Fever'. He was also a member of supergroup Damn Yankees, who had a 1990 album *Damn Yankies*.

1949 Tom Verlaine – guitarist and vocalist with Television, who had a 1977 single and album called 'Marquee Moon'.

1950 Davy O'List – guitarist with The Nice, who had a 1968 UK No.21 single with 'America', and Roxy Music, who had a 1972 UK No.4 single with 'Virginia Plain' plus 15 other UK Top 40 singles.

1951 Tom Hamilton – bass guitarist with Aerosmith, who had a 1989 UK No.13 single 'Love In An Elevator' and a 1998 US No.1 single with 'I Don't Want To Miss A Thing'.

1952 Berton Averre – guitarist and vocalist with The Knack, who had a 1979 US No.1 & UK No.6 single with 'My Sharona'.

1975 Tom Delonge – guitarist and vocalist with Blink 182, who had a 2000 UK No.2 single with 'All The Small Things' and a 2001 US No.1 album with *Take Off Your...*

1981 Amy Lynn Lee – vocalist with Evanescence, who had a 2003 UK No.1 & US No.5 single with 'Bring Me To Life' and a 2003 UK No.1 & US No.3 album with *Fallen*.

ON THIS DAY

1962 Elvis Presley was at No.1 on the UK singles chart with 'Return To Sender', his 13th UK No.1.

1966 Jimi Hendrix made his TV debut on ITV's *Ready Steady Go!* Marc Bolan also appeared on the show.

1970 Dave Edmunds was at No.1 on the UK singles chart with his version of the 1955 Smiley Lewis hit 'I Hear You Knockin'.

1975 Chicago started a five week run at No.1 on the US album chart with *Chicago IX – Chicago's Greatest Hits*, the group's fifth No.1 album.

1979 Simple Minds played the first of two nights at The Marquee in London. Tickets cost £1.25 ($2).

1986 Bruce Hornsby & The Range went to No.1 on the US singles chart, with 'The Way It Is'. The song reached No.15 in the UK.

1994 The Beautiful South kicked off a five date UK tour at London's Brixton Academy.

1997 children's TV characters The Teletubbies went to No.1 on the UK singles chart with 'Teletubbies-Say Eh-Oh'.

RM CONCERTS PRESENTS

THE BEAUTIFUL SOUTH

Tuesday 13th December
BRIXTON ACADEMY
Tickets £12: Box Office 071 924 9999, Credit Cards 071 287 0932

Thursday 15th December
STOKE-ON-TRENT TRENTHAM GARDENS
Tickets £12: Box Office 0782 657777, MLN Stores Throughout
Store & Sellars

Saturday 17th December
ASTON VILLA LEISURE CENTRE
Tickets £12: Box Office 021 328 5333, Select, MLN, Ticketpro

Sunday 18th December
BLACKPOOL EMPRESS BALLROOM
Piccadilly 061 257 030 0606 & HMV 061 867 6262/34

Monday 20th December
HUMBERSIDE ICE ARENA
Tickets £12: Box Office 0482 25552, Jumbo, Generation, Sydney

1999 results in the Smash Hits readers' poll included: Back Street Boys for Best band, Best album and Best single; Britney Spears *(below)* won Best female singer; Robbie Williams Best male singer; S Club 7 won Best new band and worst group was the Spice Girls.

2000 it was announced that after 74 years the UK rock weekly *Melody Maker* was to close down. The Christmas edition would be the last one – then it would merge with the NME to create a more sizeable broadbased magazine.

2000 Sir Paul McCartney held his first-ever London book signing at Waterstone's in Piccadilly. Sir Paul was in the store to sign copies of his new book, *Paul McCartney Paintings*.

2002 David Sneddon, an unemployed busker and former children's TV presenter, won a £1 million ($1.7 million) record deal after winning the BBC TV *Fame Academy* final. The singer/songwriter from Glasgow went on to score a UK No.1 with his debut single 'Stop Living The Lie' the following month.

2002 Zal Yanovsky of The Lovin' Spoonful died of a heart attack. The band had a 1966 US No.1 & UK No.8 single with 'Summer In The City'.

2003 Lauryn Hill launched an attack on the Catholic church, urging religious figures to "repent" while speaking on a stage regularly used by the Pope. The former Fugees singer was playing at a Christmas show in Vatican City and took the opportunity to speak her mind about allegations of sexual abuse in America before an audience that included top Vatican cardinals, bishops and the cream of Italian society.

BORN ON THIS DAY

1932 Charlie Rich, country singer known as the "Silver Fox" who had a 1974 US No.1 & UK No.2 single with 'The Most Beautiful Girl'. Rich died on July 25th 1995.

1938 Gary Usher, producer and songwriter who worked with The Byrds and co-wrote The Beach Boys' 'In My Room'. He died on May 25th 1990.

1943 Frank Allen – bass player and vocalist with The Searchers, who had a 1964 UK No.1 single with 'Needles And Pins'.

1946 Jane Birkin, actress and singer who had a 1969 UK No.1 single with Serge Gainsbourg, 'Je T'aime...Moi Non', the only French language chart topper.

1946 Joyce Vincent Wilson – singer with Dawn, who had a 1971 UK & US No.1 single with 'Knock Three Times' and a 1973 US & UK No.1 single with 'Tie A Yellow Ribbon Round The Old Oak Tree'.

1949 Cliff Williams – bass player for AC/DC (he replaced Mark Evans in 1977), who had a UK No.36 single with 'Whole Lotta Rosie'. The band's 1980 UK No.1 & US No.14 album *Back in Black* sold over ten million copies.

1958 Mike Scott – singer/songwriter with The Waterboys, who had a 1991 UK No.3 single with 'Whole Of The Moon' – it was first released in 1985.

1966 Tim Skold – bass player for Marilyn Manson, who had a 1998 US No.1 album with *Mechanical Animals* and a UK No.12 single with 'The Dope Show'.

ON THIS DAY

1968 Marvin Gaye scored his first US No.1 single when 'I Heard It Through The Grapevine' started a five week run at the top of the charts. It was Marvin's 15th solo hit and also became his first UK No.1 single in March 1969.

1969 The Jackson Five made their first network television appearance in the US when they appeared on *The Ed Sullivan Show*.

1972 the *Born To Boogie* movie, directed by Ringo Starr and featuring T. Rex, premiered in London.

1977 the film *Saturday Night Fever*, starring John Travolta, premiered in New York.

1981 Adam And The Ants kicked off a 23 date UK tour at the St Austell Coliseum, Cornwall.

1984 appearing at Leeds Queens Hall, England were Wham! Tickets cost £6.50 ($11).

1985 Whitney Houston scored her first UK No.1 single with 'Saving All My Love For You'.

1991 Michael Jackson started a four week run at No.1 on the US album chart with *Dangerous*.

1997 Garth Brooks was at No.1 on the US album chart with *Sevens*, his fourth US No.1 album.

1999 Shaun Ryder **(right)** was ordered to pay £160,000, ($272,000) to his ex-management team over a dispute in his contract. Ryder said he was so high after a "joint" he didn't

Ryder: contract's small print "did his nut in"

bother to read the small print and the court was told the contract had "done his nut in".

1999 Sir Paul McCartney played a live show at The Cavern Club, Liverpool **(left)** – his last gig at the venue was in 1963. The show was filmed for TV and also went out live on the Internet.

2002 UK music channel Music Choice analyzed all the Christmas No.1 singles of the past 30 years and identified criteria for their success. These included the use of sleigh bells, children singing, church bells, harmony and references to love. They concluded that Sir Cliff Richard's 1988 hit 'Mistletoe and Wine' was the perfect Christmas hit.

2003 Ozzy And Kelly Osbourne went to No.1 on the UK singles chart with 'Changes'. It was a remake of a track first sung by Ozzy on the Black Sabbath album *Volume 4* in 1972.

2003 Dido went back to No.1 on the UK album chart for another three weeks with *Life For Rent*.

A generation later..back to where he still belongs

THEN: Young Paul at the Cavern and on his way to 60s Fab Four fame

NOW: Sir Paul back at the Cavern last night, still rockin' after all these years

MACCA'S NIGHT OF MAGIC AT BEATLES' CAVERN

By IAN DISLEY

McCartney rolled back yesterdays last night for a special night at the club where the Beatles legend was born.

The Cavern has waited more than 36 years for Macca to come back to where he once belonged.

After the show at Liverpool's most famous music venue, Sir Paul said: "I'm elated. I said I think it's a nice place to be.

"I always knew it would be a special night but this is better than I could have hoped.

"We wanted to rock out the century — we did it, we rocked Liverpool and the world loved you.

Millions more around the globe tuned into TV and radio broadcasts and 15,000 fans saw the show on a giant video screen at Liverpool's Chavasse Park.

The 75-minute gig was a live

STAR: Fans watch on a giant screen

saw the show on a live internet link. Another £½million tried to log on but found the website jammed.

Macca himself was interviewed simply enough by an anonymous voice: "Ladies and gentlemen, with his band, Paul McCartney"

"It's good here innit" and "We're

THE PLAYLIST

❶ Honey Hush
❷ Blue Jean Bop
❸ Brown-Eyed Handsome Man
❹ Fabulous
❺ What It Is
❻ Lonesome Town
❼ Twenty Flight Rock
❽ No Other Baby
❾ Try Not To Cry
❿ Shake A Hand
⓫ All Shook Up
⓬ I Saw Her Standing There
Records Party

thrash through his latest LP, Run Devil Run. Every song was greeted with rapturous applause as he lovingly tore inside the Cavern.

Macca himself was interspersed simply enough by an anonymous voice... including his fattest designer daughter Stella, his brother Mike and other relatives — went wild.

"There were loud cheers for Paul's version of Elvis's All Shook Up and Ricky Nelson's Lonesome Town.

which is dedicated to 'loved ones past, present and future'. Then the Cavern shook with delighted screams for the last song of the main set and the only Beatles number I Saw Her Standing There.

With Pink Floyd's Dave Gilmour on guitar and Deep Purple drummer Ian Paice, the music was superb.

After performing a single encore, including his fastest designer daughter ... it was time for Paul to leave.

The only complaint was that the show was too short. Jane King, 31, (Moseley, Derbyshire said: "Paul was looking great and I thought he sounded brilliant, he's never sounded so good.

"The club has been rebuilt since the Beatles' days. But no refurbishment was missing last night. A familiar scene to Paul's private room was removed in case it offended the strict expectation, whose wife Linda died of breast cancer last year.

● *Voice Of The Mirror* – Page 8

BORN ON THIS DAY

1919 Max Yasgur, owner of the Woodstock farm where the 1969 festival was held. He died of a heart attack on February 8th 1973, aged 53.

1922 Alan Freed, American DJ and the man who gave rock 'n' roll its name. Freed died on January 20th 1965.

1942 Dave Clark – drummer with the Dave Clark Five, who had a 1964 UK No.1 single with 'Glad All Over', a 1965 US No.1 single with 'Over And Over' plus over 15 other UK Top 40 singles.

1946 Harry Ray – vocalist with Moments, who had a 1970 US No.3 single with 'Love On A Two-Way Street' and a 1975 UK No.3 single with 'Girls'.

1946 Carmine Appice – drummer with Vanilla Fudge, who had a 1968 US No.6 single with 'You Keep Me Hangin' On', and Beck, Bogart & Appice.

1949 Don Johnson, Miami Vice actor and singer who had a 1986 US No.5 & UK No.46 single with 'Heartbeat'.

1955 Paul Simonon – bass player with The Clash, who had a 1979 UK No. 11 single with 'London Calling', a 1982 US No.8 single with 'Rock The Casbah, a 1991 UK No.1 single with 'Should I Stay Or Should I Go', which was first released 1982, plus 15 other UK Top 40 singles.

ON THIS DAY

1962 Bill Wyman made his live debut with The Rolling Stones at Putney Youth Club, London.

1969 John Lennon made what would be his final-ever gig in the UK when he appeared at The Lyceum Ballroom, London with the Plastic Ono Band in a UNICEF "Peace For Christmas" Benefit.

1972 Supertramp appeared at Cardiff High School, Wales.

1973 Charlie Rich started a two week run at No.1 on the US singles chart with 'The Most Beautiful Girl', the singer's only No.1 single. The song was a No.2 hit in the UK.

1973 Jermaine Jackson married the daughter of the boss of Motown Records, Hazel Gordy.

1975 Cat Stevens appeared live at London's Royal Albert Hall. Tickets cost £2.50 ($4.25).

1979 U2 appeared at the Windsor Castle Pub, Harrow Road, London. Admission was free.

1984 'Do They Know It's Christmas' by Band Aid **(below)** entered the chart at No.1 and stayed at the top for five weeks. It became the biggest-selling UK single of all time with sales of over three and a half million. Band Aid was masterminded by former Boomtown Rats singer Bob Geldof, who was moved by a TV news story of famine in Ethiopia. Geldof had the idea of raising funds with a one-off charity single featuring the cream of the current pop world.

1990 Agnetha Faltskog from Abba married Swedish surgeon Tomas Sonnenfeld.

1994 Bon Jovi guitarist Richie Sambora married actress Heather Locklear.

1998 former Backstreet Boys roadie Michael Barrett filed a $3 million (£1.76 million) lawsuit against the group claiming damages after a 23kg (50lb) cannon fell on his head during a show.

Backstreet Boys: loose cannons.

1999 Boy George was knocked unconscious when a mirror ball fell on his head during a show in Dorset, England.

2001 Rufus Thomas, singer/songwriter, died. He had had a 1963 US No.10 single with 'Walking The Dog' and a 1970 UK No.18 & US No.28 single with 'Do The Funky Chicken'.

2002 Blue featuring Elton John went to No.1 on the UK singles chart with 'Sorry Seems To Be The Hardest Word'. It had been a No.11 hit for Elton in 1976.

2004 a Detroit studio where Eminem recorded 'My Name Is' went up for auction on eBay. Studio 8, in the Detroit suburb of Ferndale, was to be listed in eBay's commercial property section for 30 days, with the minimum bid $215,000 (£126,470).

BORN ON THIS DAY

1934 Karl Denver, UK singer who had a 1962 UK No.4 single with 'Wimoweh' and a 1990 UK No.46 with 'Lazyitis – One Armed Boxer' with the Happy Mondays. Denver died on December 21st 1998.

1945 Tony Hicks – guitarist with The Hollies, who have had a over 25 Top 40 hits since 1963 including the 1972 US No.2 single 'Long Cool Woman In A Black Dress' and the 1988 UK No.1 single 'He Ain't Heavy, He's My Brother', which was first released in 1969.

1946 Benny Anderson – keyboardist and vocalist with Abba, who had their first UK No.1 hit single in 1974 with 'Waterloo', which was followed by eight other UK No.1 singles and nine UK No.1 albums. They also had a 1977 US No.1 single with 'Dancing Queen'.

1950 Bill Gibbons – guitarist and vocalist with ZZ Top, who had a 1984 US No.8 & 1985 UK No.16 single with 'Legs'.

1959 Steven Irvine – drummer with Lloyd Cole And The Commotions, who had a 1985 UK No.19 single with 'Brand New friend'.

1972 Michael McCary – vocalist with Boyz II Men, who had a 1992 US & UK No.1 single with 'End Of The Road'.

ON THIS DAY

1965 released as a double A-side The Beatles' 'Day Tripper/We Can Work It Out' became their ninth UK No.1 and their third Christmas chart topper in a row. It made US No.1 in January 1966.

1966 the first Jimi Hendrix Experience single, 'Hey Joe', was released on Polydor after being rejected by Decca Records.

1967 The Rolling Stones announced that Marianne Faithfull was the first signing to their Mother Earth label.

1971 Frank Zappa's 200 Motels film opened at London's Piccadilly Classic Cinema.

1972 Billy Paul started a three week run at No.1 on the US singles chart with 'Me and Mrs Jones', which was a No.12 hit in the UK.

1978 Alex Harvey *(below in centre)* appeared at Glasgow's Apollo. Tickets cost £1.50–3 ($2.55–5).

1983 Judas Priest played the first of two sold-out nights at London's Hammersmith Odeon.

1988 Sigue Sigue Sputnik appeared at Stourbridge Town Hall, England. Tickets cost £5 ($8.50).

1988 US singer Sylvester James died. He had had a 1978 US No.36 & UK No.8 single with 'You Make Me Feel (Mighty Real)'.

1989 Billy Joel went to No.1 on the US album chart with *Storm Front*.

1989 Jive Bunny And The Mastermixes had their final UK No.1 single with 'Let's Party'.

1991 Chubby Checker filed a lawsuit against McDonald's in Canada seeking $14,000 million (£8,235 million) for its alleged use of an imitation of his voice on 'The Twist' in a french fries commercial.

1993 Verve appeared at The Krazy House, Liverpool, supported by Oasis.

1993 MTV aired Nirvana's "Unplugged" session for the first time.

1997 American singer/songwriter Nicolette Larson died, aged 45. She had worked with Neil Young, Linda Ronstadt and David Crosby.

1999 a 28-year-old man died after falling more than 24m (80ft) at Earl's Court, London while dismantling the set at a Spice Girls concert.

2000 the estranged father and former manager of LeAnn Rimes made embarrassing allegations during a legal battle over millions of dollars. Mr Rimes told the court that LeAnn paid her mother $11,390, (£6,700) every time she styled her hair before a show.

2001 Robbie Williams and Nicole Kidman started a three week run at No.1 on the UK singles chart with their version of the Frank and Nancy Sinatra 1967 No.1 hit 'Somethin' Stupid'. The song was the Christmas No.1 for the year.

2001 Stuart Adamson, lead singer of Big Country, was found dead in Hawaii a month after disappearing from his home in the US. The 43-year-old musician had fought a long battle against alcoholism. His body was found in a hotel room.

TRIPLE A ENTERTAINMENTS
PROUDLY PRESENTS

BLONDIE & INXS
PLUS SUPPORT

SHOW 7.30PM
MONDAY 16TH DECEMBER 2002

SOUTH BALCONY

ROW C SEAT

30.00
30.00

17th December

BORN ON THIS DAY

1926 Bill Black – bass player for Elvis Presley from 1954-7 and member of the Bill Black Combo, who had a 1959 US No.17 single with 'Smokie Part 2'. He died on October 21st 1965.

1936 Tommy Steele, singer and actor who had a 1957 UK No.1 single with 'Singing The Blues' plus over 20 other UK Top 40 singles.

1937 Art Neville – vocalist and pianist with The Neville Brothers, who had a 1989 UK No.47 single with 'With God On Our Side'.

1942 Paul Butterfield, blues singer and harmonica player who had a 1965 album *Paul Butterfield Blues Band*. Appeared at The Band's Last Waltz gig. He died on May 3rd 1987.

1948 Jim Bonfanti – drummer for The Young Rascals, who had a 1967 US No.1 and UK No.8 single with 'Groovin', and The Raspberries, who had a 1972 US No.5 single with 'Go All The Way'.

1949 Paul Rodgers – singer and guitarist with Free, who had a 1970 UK No.2 & US No.4 single with 'All Right Now', Bad Company, who had a 1974 UK No.15 single 'Can't Get Enough' and The Firm.

1950 Carlton Barrett – drummer for The Wailers, who had a 1983 UK No.4 single with Bob Marley, 'Buffalo Soldier' plus ten other UK Top 40 singles. He was shot dead outside his home on April 17th 1987.

1958 Mike Mills – bass player with R.E.M. who had a 1991 UK No.6 & US No.10 single with 'Shiny Happy People' plus over 20 Top 40 UK singles and a 1992 UK No.1 & US No.2 album with *Automatic For The People*.

1962 Sarah Dallen – singer with Bananarama, who had a 1984 UK No.3 single with 'Robert De Niro's Waiting' plus over 20 other UK Top 40 singles and a 1986 US No.1 single with 'Venus'.

1969 Micky Quinn – bass player with Supergrass, who had a 1995 UK No.2 single with 'Alright'.

ON THIS DAY

1968 The Who's Christmas party gig was held at the Marquee Club, London. A new group called Yes also performed.

1973 Slade were at No.1 on the UK singles chart with 'Merry Christmas Everybody', the band's sixth chart topper. The song has re-entered the UK charts on eight other occasions.

1977 deputizing for the Sex Pistols on NBC-TV's *Saturday Night Live* Elvis Costello stopped his performance of 'Less Than Zero', saying, "there's no reason to do this", and then launched into 'Radio Radio' – a song he had been told not to perform.

1977 George Harrison played an unannounced live set for the regulars at his local pub in Henley-On-Thames.

1982 Karen Carpenter made her last live concert appearance when she performed in Sherman, California.

1984 appearing on the UK TV show *Razzmatazz Solid Gold Christmas Special* were Frankie Goes To Hollywood, Big Country, Duran Duran, Ultravox, Paul Young and Wham!

1988 Bros featured on the front page of the *NME*. The band was interviewed for the paper. Matt said, "We've got the quickest selling debut LP in the history of CBS Records. You don't do that if you're talentless."

"Anyone for a jukebox?" Lisa-Marie hawks around her late father's wares!

1995 a statue of the late Frank Zappa was unveiled in Vilnius, the capital of the Republic Of Lithuania. It had been organized by Zappa fan club president Saulius Pauksty.

1997 David Bowie launched BowieNet on the Internet.

2000 Eminem was the subject of a sick Internet hoax after MTV reported that the rapper had been killed in a car crash en route to a party.

2004 Elvis Presley's daughter Lisa Marie Presley agreed to sell 85 percent of his estate to businessman Robert Sillerman in a deal worth $100 million (£59 million). Sillerman would run Presley's Memphis home Graceland and own Elvis's name and the rights to all revenue from his music and films. In the deal Lisa Marie would retain possession of Graceland and many of her father's "personal effects".

BORN ON THIS DAY

1938 Chas Chandler – bass player with The Animals, who had a 1964 UK & US No.1 single with 'House Of The Rising Sun', and manager of Jimi Hendrix and Slade. Chandler died on July 17th 1996.

1941 Sam Andrews – guitarist with the Janis Joplin Band, who had a 1971 US No.1 single with 'Me And Bobby McGee' and a 1971 US No.1 single with 'Pearl'.

1943 Keith Richards, "The Human Riff" – guitarist and vocalist with The Rolling Stones, who had a 1969 UK & US No.1 single with 'Honky Tonk Women' and over 35 other Top 40 singles and albums. As a solo artist he released the 1988 album *Talk Is Cheap*.

1950 Martha Johnson – singer and keyboardist with Martha And The Muffins, who had a 1980 UK No.10 single with 'Echo Beach'.

1953 Elliot Easton – guitarist with The Cars, who had a 1978 UK No.3 single with 'My Best Friend's Girl' and a 1985 UK No.4 single with 'Drive'.

1964 Robson Green – actor and singer, who had a 1995 UK No.1 single with Jerome Flynn, 'Unchained Melody/The White Cliffs Of Dover'.

1980 Christina Aguilera, US singer who had a 1999 US & UK No.1 single with 'Genie In A Bottle' and a 2001 US & UK No.1 single with Mya, Lil' Kim and Pink, 'Lady Marmalade'.

ON THIS DAY

1961 The Tokens started a three week run at No.1 on the US singles chart with 'The Lion Sleeps Tonight', which was a No.11 hit in the UK. R.E.M. included a live version of the song on their 1993 'Sidewinder Sleeps Tonight' single.

1970 Pink Floyd appeared at The Town Hall, Birmingham. Tickets cost 60p ($1).

1971 Jerry Lee Lewis and his wife Myra, (who he had married when she was 13), divorced as he prepared to marry 29-year-old Jaren Elizabeth Gunn Pate. The couple separated two weeks later.

1971 Sly & The Family Stone went to No.1 on the US album chart with *There's A Riot Going On*.

1972 Bob Dylan starting filming his role in the film *Pat Garrett And Billy The Kid*.

1979 Joy Division played what would be their only ever gig in Paris when they appeared at Les Bains Club.

1982 Hall And Oates started a four week run at No.1 on the US singles chart with 'Maneater', the duo's fifth US No.1 and biggest hit in the UK – where it made No.6.

Kirsty MacColl.

1982 Renee And Renato were at No.1 on the UK singles chart with 'Save Your Love', the duo's only UK Top 40 hit and this year's Christmas No.1.

1999 The Spice Girls unveiled their waxwork lookalikes at Madame Tussaud's, London. Each of the models had cost £35,000 ($595,000) to make.

2000 singer/songwriter Kirsty MacColl was killed in a boating accident off the coast of Mexico when she was hit by a speedboat. She was 41.

2001 singer/songwriter Clifford T. Ward died, aged 57, after suffering from multiple sclerosis since 1984. He had had the 1973 UK No.8 single 'Gaye'.

2003 out on bail Michael Jackson was formally charged with seven counts of child molestation and two counts of administering intoxicating liquor to a minor with the intent of committing a crime. The abuse was claimed to have taken place between February 7th and March 10th 2003 and the alleged victim was identified only as "John Doe". Jackson's lawyer said the entertainer was "unequivocally and absolutely innocent" and would fight the charges "with every fibre of his soul".

2004 a guitar played by George Harrison and John Lennon sold for $570,000, (£294,000) at auction in New York. The Gibson SG guitar was used by Harrison from 1966 to 1969, including the recording of *Revolver*, and by Lennon during *White Album* sessions. Other items sold in the Christie's auction included a letter by Kurt Cobain, which fetched $19,400, (£10,000), and a school book report by Britney Spears, which fetched $1,860, (£1,000).

Panic grips the nation as the Spice Girls start to multiply.

BORN ON THIS DAY

1918 Professor Longhair, US rock 'n' roll piano player who influenced Fats Domino and Dr. John. He died on January 30th 1980.

1940 Phil Ochs, US folk singer/songwriter who wrote 'There But A Fortune', which was a hit for Joan Baez. He hung himself on April 9th 1976, after suffering from chronic depression.

1941 Maurice White – vocalist with Earth, Wind and Fire, who had a 1975 US No.1 single with 'Shining Star' and a 1981 UK No.3 single with 'Let's Groove'.

1944 Alvin Lee – guitarist and vocalist with Ten Years After, who had a 1970 UK No.10 single with 'Love Like A Man'.

1944 Zal Yanovsky – guitarist for The Lovin' Spoonful, who had a 1966 US No.1 & UK No.8 single with 'Summer In The City'. He died of a heart attack on December 13th 2002.

1949 John McEuen – guitarist, fiddler and mandolin player with Nitty Gritty Dirt Band, who had a 1971 US No.9 single with 'Mr. Bojangles'.

1958 Limahl – vocalist with Kajagoogoo, who had a 1983 UK No.1 single with 'Too Shy'.

ON THIS DAY

1957 Elvis Presley had his draft notice served on him for the US Army. He went on to join the 32nd Tank Battalion third Armor Corps, which was based in Germany.

1958 Conway Twitty was at No.1 on the UK singles chart with 'It's Only Make Believe'.

1964 The Beatles' fourth album *Beatles For Sale* started a seven week run at No.1 on the UK album charts.

1964 The Supremes scored their third US No.1 single of the year when 'Come See About Me' went to the top of the charts. It made No.27 on the UK chart.

1969 Mick Jagger was fined £200 ($340) at Marlborough Magistrates Court for illegal possession of cannabis.

ARENA-NEC
BIRMINGHAM **The big heart of England**
BROS
Plus Special Guests
romoted by HARVEY GOLDSMITH ENTS
:OPM MON 19 DEC 88
BLOCK 3 K 59
O   DOORS OPEN 6.00PM   CHEQUE
0.00p bkng.fee)   STRF   5-OCT-88

1969 Rolf Harris was at No.1 on the UK singles chart with 'Two Little Boys', the Christmas No.1 of 1969 and the last No.1 of the 60s. The song stayed at No.1 for six weeks.

1976 in an interview with the *Daily Mail*, Sex Pistol Paul Cook's mother said he was no longer welcome at home and she was going to turn his bedroom in a dining room.

1981 Abba scored their seventh UK No.1 album with *The Visitors*.

1987 two teenage girls died in a crush at a Public Enemy gig at the Municipal Auditorium, Nashville.

1993 Michael Clarke of The Byrds died of liver failure, aged 49.

1994 the Manic Street Preachers played the first of three nights at The Astoria, London, the last shows Richie James made with the band before disappearing.

1999 Irish boyband Westlife started a four week run at No.1 on the UK singles chart with their versions of the Abba song 'I Have A Dream' and Terry Jacks' 'Seasons In The Sun'. It gave the group the Christmas No.1 and the last No.1 of the century.

2000 10,000 Maniacs guitarist Robert Buck died. The band had had a 1993 UK No.47 single with 'Candy Everybody Wants'.

2000 Staple Singers main man Roebuck "Pop" Staples died. The group had a 1975 US No.1 single with 'Let's Do It Again'.

2000 Wu-Tang Clan rapper Ol' Dirty Bastard was returned to New York from Philadelphia in police custody in order to face outstanding drug charges for possessing crack cocaine.

2001 ex-Spice Girl Emma Bunton paid £3,000 ($5,100) for a custom built toilet. The singer ordered the hand-painted porcelain loo complete with hand-crafted toilet roll holder for her new £500,000 ($850,000) seaside apartment.

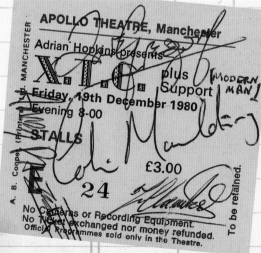

APOLLO THEATRE, Manchester
Adrian Hopkins presents
XTC
plus MODERN MAN
Support
Friday, 19th December 1980
Evening 8-00
STALLS
£3.00
24
No Cameras or Recording Equipment.
No Ticket exchanged nor money refunded.
Official Programmes sold only in the Theatre.
To be retained.
A. B. Cooper (Printers) Ltd. MANCHESTER

BORN ON THIS DAY

1944 Bobby Colomby – drummer with Blood, Sweat & Tears, who had a 1969 US No.12 & UK No.35 single with 'You've Made Me So Very Happy'.

1947 Peter Criss – drummer and vocalist for Kiss, who had a 1974 US No.5 single with 'On And On', a 1976 US No.11 album with *Rock And Roll Over*, which spent 26 weeks on the chart, and a 1987 UK No.4 single with 'Crazy Crazy Nights'.

1948 Stevie Wright – singer/songwriter with The Easybeats, who had a 1966 UK No.6 & 1967 US No.16 single with 'Friday On My Mind'.

1957 Anita Ward, singer who had a 1979 US & UK No.1 single with 'Ring My Bell'.

1957 Billy Bragg, UK singer/songwriter, who had a 1988 UK No.1 charity single with Wet Wet Wet, 'She's Leaving Home'.

1966 Christopher Robinson – vocalist with The Black Crowes, who had a 1991 UK No.39 single with 'Hard To Handle' and a 1992 US No.1 & UK No.2 album with *The Southern Harmony And Musical Companion*.

ON THIS DAY

1959 Emile Ford And The Checkmates were at No.1 on the UK singles chart with 'What Do You Want To Make Those Eyes At Me For'.

1962 The Osmonds appeared for the first time on the NBS-TV *Andy Williams Show*. They performed the song 'I'm A Ding Dong Daddy From Dumas'.

1967 folk singer Joan Baez was sentenced to 45 days in prison after being arrested during an anti-war demonstration.

1969 Peter, Paul & Mary went to No.1 on the US singles chart with 'Leavin' On A Jet Plane'.

The Pet Shop Boys: Chris Lowe (left) and Neil Tennant.

1969 The Rolling Stones went to No.1 on the UK album chart with their tenth release *Let It Bleed*, which featured 'Midnight Rambler' and 'You Can't Always Get What You Want'.

1973 Bobby Darin died of a heart attack, aged 37. He had had a No.1 with 'Dream Lover' in 1959 plus 20 other US Top 40 hits during the 60s.

1979 Dire Straits appeared at London's Rainbow and The Jam appeared at The Bath Pavilion.

1979 on the Christmas album chart at the UK high street store Our Price Records were: Michael Jackson's Off The Wall, £3.74 ($6.35); The Police, Regatta De Blanc, £3.49 ($5.93), and the No.1 album Pink Floyd's The Wall was £6.45 ($10.97).

1980 12 days after John Lennon was shot dead his 'Just Like Starting Over' was the UK No.1 single.

1980 Motorhead's Phil Taylor accidentally broke a bone in his neck when partying after a gig in Belfast.

1986 The Bangles started a four week run at No.1 on the

US singles chart with 'Walk Like An Egyptian'.

1986 The Housemartins were at No.1 on the UK singles chart with 'Caravan Of Love', a song written by Jasper Isley of The Isley Brothers.

1987 The Pet Shop Boys had their third UK No.1 single with 'Always On My Mind'. The song had been a hit for Brenda Lee in 1972 and Elvis Presley in 1973.

1992 blues singer and guitarist Albert King died.

2000 Ritchie and J from Five were remanded on bail following a court appearance in connection with a fight in a Dublin pub. They were charged with public order offences.

2001 Tommy Lee branded his ex-wife Pam Anderson an unfit mother. The drummer filed papers with the Los Angeles Superior Court alleging his sons told him "We hate Mommy" and his son Brandon had been using the F-word, which he learned from his mommy.

2003 Carling Live presents Travis and Kings of Leon at Alexandra Palace, London.

ODEON THEATRE, Birmingham

M.C.P. presents—

TOYAH

PLUS SPECIAL GUESTS
Sunday, 20th December 1981
Evenings 7-30

CENTRE STALLS
£4.00

X 29

A. B. Cooper (Printers) Ltd. MANCHESTER

No Ticket exchanged nor money refunded.
This portion to be retained   (P.T.O.)

BORN ON THIS DAY

1940 Frank Zappa *(right)*, multi-instrumentalist who had a 1970 UK No.9 album with *Hot Rats*. He died on December 4th 1993.

1940 Ray Hilderbrand – singer, songwriter with Paul & Paula, who had a 1963 US No.1 & UK No.8 single with 'Hey Paula'.

1943 Albert Lee, UK country guitarist who worked with Emmylou Harris Hot Band, Eric Clapton, Jackson Browne and Joe Cocker and was a member of Heads Hands And Feet.

1946 Carl Wilson – guitarist with The Beach Boys, who had a 1966 UK & US No.1 single with 'Good Vibrations' plus over 25 other UK Top 40 singles. He died on February 6th 1998.

1953 Betty Wright, US singer who had a 1971 US No.6 single with 'Clean Up Woman' and a 1975 UK No.27 single with 'Shoorah! Shoorah!'.

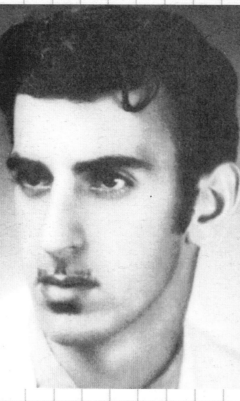

ON THIS DAY

1966 The Who played at The Uppercut, London. Tickets cost £17/6, ($2.45).

1968 Glen Campbell went to No.1 on the US album chart with *Wichita Lineman*.

1969 The Supremes made their last TV appearance together with Diana Ross on The Ed Sullivan Show, singing their last No.1 'Someday We'll Be Together'.

1974 Mud were at No.1 on the UK singles chart with 'Lonely This Christmas'.

1976 it was the first night of a two week residency by Barry Manilow at The Uris Theatre On Broadway, New York. Tickets cost $20 (£11.76).

1984 Frankie Goes To Hollywood played the first of three sold-out nights at the Liverpool Royal Court. Tickets cost £5.30 ($9).

1987 John Spence, the original singer of No Doubt in the late 1980s, committed suicide.

1988 former Cockney Rebel bass player Paul Jeffreys was one of the passengers killed by a terrorist bomb on Pan Am flight 103. The plane crashed over Lockerbie, Scotland.

1991 'Bohemian Rhapsody/These Are The Days Of Our Lives' started a five week run at No.1 in the UK, released as a tribute to Freddie Mercury.

1995 former Oasis drummer Tony McCarrol issued a writ against the band seeking damages and royalties from his work on *(What's The Story) Morning Glory*.

1996 the charity record Dunblane 'Throw These Guns Away', went to No.1 on the UK singles chart for a week.

1999 the readers of *Guitar* magazine voted Noel Gallagher the most overrated guitarist of the millennium. Jimi Hendrix was voted guitarist of the millennium and Nirvana's *Nevermind* won best album.

2000 figures from the RIA of America showed that teen pop was alive and doing very well. Pop accounted for most of the record sales in America with Jive Records, home to Britney, The Backstreet Boys and *NSYNC, selling 31 million records.

2001 police launched an investigation into why Olivia Harrison listed a non-existent Beverly Hills address as the place of George Harrison's death.

2002 Keane appeared at the 12 Bar Club, London and were spotted by Simon Williams of Fierce Panda Records, who asked them to put a single out on his label.

2003 Eminem's ex-wife Kymberley Mathers pleaded guilty to drug and driving offences. Mathers had been pulled by traffic police in June and was charged with possession of cocaine. Two other charges – driving with a suspended license and maintaining a drug house in which police discovered marijuana and Ecstasy – were dropped.

The Astoria
157 Charing Cross Road, London WC2
Phil McINTYRE PRESENTS.
ONSLAUGHT
PLUS SPECIAL GUESTS
THE CRUMBSUCKERS AND SLAMMER
Wednesday, 21st December '88
Evening 7.30
UNRESERVED
£5.00 In Advance + Agents Booking Fee
№ 0146
No Tickets Exchanged nor Money Refunded
No Cameras or Recording Equipment
Official Programme Sold Only in the Theatre
Management reserve the right to refuse admission

2003 Michael Andrews featuring Gary Jules went to No.1 on the UK singles chart with their version of the Tears For Fears song 'Mad World.' The song took just 90 minutes to record in 2001 and was featured in the film *Donnie Darko*.

BORN ON THIS DAY

1944 Barry Jenkins – drummer with The Animals, who had a 1964 UK & US No.1 single with 'House Of The Rising Sun'.

1946 Rick Nielsen – vocalist and guitarist with Cheap Trick, who had a 1979 UK No.29 & US No.17 single with 'I Want You To Want Me' and a 1988 US No.1 single with 'The Flame'.

1949 Robin and Maurice Gibb – Robin was the eldest by an hour. Singers, songwriters and producers with The Bee Gees *(right)*, who had a 1967 UK No.1 single with 'Massachusetts', a 1978 UK & US No.1 single with 'Night Fever' and over 30 UK Top 40 hits and US No.1s over four decades. Maurice Gibb died on January 12th 2003 of a heart attack.

1957 Ricky Ross – vocalist and guitarist with Deacon Blue, who had a 1988 UK No.8 single with 'Real Gone Kid' plus over 15 other UK Top 40 singles. He also works as a solo artist.

1968 Richard James Edwards – vocalist and guitarist with Manic Street Preachers, who had a 1992 UK No.17 single with 'Theme From Mash'. Ritchie disappeared on February 1st 1995, after leaving his car at a service station by The Severn Bridge.

1972 Vanessa Paradie, French singer and actress who had a 1988 UK No.3 single with 'Joe Le Taxi'.

ON THIS DAY

1962 The Tornados started a three week run at No.1 on the US singles chart with 'Telstar'. Produced and written by Joe Meek, it was the first major hit from a UK act on the American chart. It was also a No.1 in the UK.

The Gibb brothers, plus two.

1965 the Dave Clark Five scored their only US No.1 single with 'Over And Over', which made No.5 in the UK.

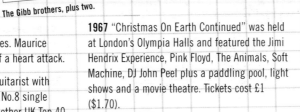

Dave Clarke, plus four.

1967 "Christmas On Earth Continued" was held at London's Olympia Halls and featured the Jimi Hendrix Experience, Pink Floyd, The Animals, Soft Machine, DJ John Peel plus a paddling pool, light shows and a movie theatre. Tickets cost £1 ($1.70).

1972 little Jimmy Osmond was at No.1 on the UK singles chart with 'Long Haired Lover From Liverpool'. At nine years of age it made him the youngest person to have a No.1 record. The song was also the biggest seller of 1972.

1973 Elton John started a two week run at No.1 on the UK chart with the album *Goodbye Yellow Brick Road*. It also had an eight week run at No.1 on the US chart, and featured the song 'Candle In The Wind'.

1979 Rupert Holmes started a two week run at No.1 on the US singles chart with 'Escape, (The Pina Colada Song)'. His only US No.1 solo hit, it made No.23 in the UK.

1979 the first of two nights at London's Marquee Club by The Pretenders. Tickets cost £1.25 ($2).

1981 at a rock 'n' roll memorabilia auction in London a stage suit worn by John Lennon sold for £2,300 ($3,910), a letter from Paul McCartney to a fan sold for £2,200 ($3,740) and a perspex sculpture of John and Yoko was bought by singer Kate Bush for £4,200 ($7,140).

1984 Madonna started a six week run at No.1 in the US charts with 'Like A Virgin', her first US No.1.

1987 Motley Crue's Nikki Sixx was pronounced D.O.A. in an ambulance, when his heart stopped beating for two minutes. He was given two shots of adrenaline in his chest to revive him. Fellow band members were prematurely informed of his death.

1988 The Smiths played their farewell gig at Wolverhampton Civic Hall (without guitarist Johnny Marr). To gain entrance fans had to wear a Smiths or Morrissey T-shirt.

2000 Madonna tied the knot with film director Guy Ritchie at Skibo Castle, Scotland. Celebrities attending the wedding included Jon Bon Jovi, Bryan Adams and Sting as well as fashion designers Donatella Versace, Jean Paul Gaultier and Stella McCartney.

2002 ex-Clash singer and guitarist Joe Strummer died of a suspected heart attack, aged 50.

2002 *Pop Stars: The Rivals* winners Girls Aloud started a four week run at No.1 on the UK singles chart with their debut release 'Sound Of The Underground'.

BORN ON THIS DAY

1935 Esther Phillips, US soul singer who had a 1975 US No.20 & UK No.6 single with 'What A Difference A Day Makes'. Phillips died on August 7th 1984.

1939 Johnny Kid – singer with Johnny Kidd & The Pirates, who had a 1960 UK No.1 single with 'Shakin' All Over'. Kidd died on October 7th 1966.

1940 Eugene Record – singer with The Chi-lites, who had a 1972 US No.1 single with 'Oh Girl' and a 1972 UK No.3 single 'Have You Seen Her'.

1940 Jorma Kaukonen – guitarist with Jefferson Airplane, who had a 1967 US No.18 single with 'White Rabbit', and Hot Tuna.

1941 Ron Bushy – drummer for Iron Butterfly, who had a 1968 US No.14 single with 'In-A-Gadda-Da-Vida'.

1941 Tim Hardin *(below)*, US singer/songwriter who had a 1967 UK No.50 single with 'Hang On To A Dream'. He also wrote 'Reason To Believe' and 'If I Were A Carpenter'. Hardin died of a heroin overdose on December 29th 1980.

1946 Duster Bennett, singer, guitarist and harmonica player who worked with Alexis Korner, John Mayall's Bluesbreakers, Fleetwood Mac and BB King. Bennett was killed in a car crash on March 26th 1976.

1949 Ariel Bender – guitarist with Mott The Hoople, who had a 1972 UK No.3 single with 'All The Young Dudes', and Spooky Tooth.

1958 Dave Murray – guitarist with Iron Maiden, who had a 1982 UK No.1 album with *The Number Of The Beast* and a 1991 UK No.1 single with 'Bring Your Daughter To The Slaughter'.

1960 Will Sinnott – bass player with The Shamen, who had a 1991 UK No.4 single with 'Move Any Mountain'. He died on May 23rd 1991.

ON THIS DAY

1959 Chuck Berry was arrested after taking 14-year-old Janice Norine (who, unbeknown to Berry, was working as a prostitute) across a state line. He was sentenced to five years jail but after racist comments by the judge Berry was freed.

1964 during a US tour Beach Boy Brian Wilson had a nervous breakdown in the middle of a flight from Los Angeles to Houston. Wilson left the band to concentrate on writing and producing. Glen Campbell replaced Wilson for the band's forthcoming live shows.

1977 Cat Stevens *(right)* formally changed his name to Yusef Islam.

1984 Howard Jones played the first of three sold-out shows at London's Hammersmith Odeon with support band Strawberry Switchblade.

1985 during a concert by LL Cool J at a roller rink in Baltimore a fight broke out – one person was trampled underfoot and three people were shot.

1985 Judas Priest fans Raymond Belknap and James Vance shot themselves after listening to the Judas Priest album *Stained Class*. The two teenagers had drunk beer, smoked marijuana and then listened to hours of the album. Afterwards they took a shotgun to a nearby school playground where Belknap shot and killed himself. Vance then blew away his jaw, mouth and nose but lived for more than three years before dying of the effects of the shooting.

1989 the second version of 'Do They Know It's Christmas' by Band Aid II made No.1 on the UK singles chart.

1996 Motley Crue bassist Nikki Sixx married TV's *Baywatch* star Donna Deruico.

1998 BBC 1 aired the programme about the life of Robbie Williams, *Some Mothers...*

2000 Simply Red singer Mick Hucknall was given a police caution for possessing cocaine and cannabis. The Class A and Class B drugs were found at his Surrey home by police after a woman falsely accused him of rape in November.

2002 Sir Paul McCartney was granted his own coat of arms by the College of Arms. The honour featured a Liver Bird, highlighting his Liverpool connections.

BORN ON THIS DAY

1924 Lee Dorsey, US singer, who had a 1966 US & UK No.8 single with 'Working In The Coalmine'.

1945 Lemmy *(right)* – bass player with Hawkwind, who had a 1972 UK No.3 single with 'Silver Machine', and Motorhead, who had a 1980 UK No.15 single with 'Ace Of Spades'.

1946 Jan Akkerman – guitarist with Focus, who had a 1973 UK No.4 single with 'Sylvia' and a 1973 US No.9 single with 'Hocus Pocus'.

1971 Ricky Martin, singer who had a 1999, US & UK No.1 single with 'Livin' La Vida Loca'. He also recorded the world's biggest-selling soccer song 'The Cup Of Life'.

1975 Joe Washbourne – singer with Toploader, who had a 2000 UK No.7 single with 'Dancing In The Moonlight'.

ON THIS DAY

1954 R&B singer Johnny Ace shot himself dead during a game of Russian roulette backstage at a concert in Houston.

1963 this was the first night of The Beatles Christmas show at The Finsbury Park Astoria, London with Billy J. Kramer, The Fourmost, Cilla Black and Rolf Harris.

1967 The Bee Gees performed their Christmas special live on national TV from Liverpool Cathedral.

1971 a Christmas Eve party was held at London's Marquee Club with Slade performing.

1972 David Bowie appeared at the Rainbow Theatre, London, giving a special Christmas Eve concert.

1977 The Bee Gees started a three week run at No.1 on the US singles chart with 'How Deep Is Your Love', the group's fourth US No.1. It stayed in the Top 10 for 17 weeks, making it the longest chart run in history. The song was a No.3 in the UK.

1977 the Sex Pistols played their last-ever UK gig (until 1996), before splitting at Ivanhoes in Huddersfield. It was a charity performance before an audience made up mainly of children.

1978 Factory Records released a double EP *A Factory Sample*, which featured Joy Division, Durutti Column and Cabaret Voltaire.

1988 Poison started a three week run at No.1 on the US singles chart with 'Every Rose Has Its Thorn'.

1988 Nirvana started recording their first album *Bleach* using a $600 (£353) loan from an old school friend.

1992 the percussion player with The Doobie Brothers, Bobby Lakind, died from cancer.

1994 Pearl Jam went to No.1 on the US album chart with *Vitalogy*.

1997 various tribute bands were appearing live all over the UK: Bi Jovi at The Wheatsheaf Stoke; T-Rextasy at Sheffield City Hall; The Silver Beatles at Portsmouth Wedgewood Rooms and Voulez Vous, The Abba tribute show, at The Venue, London.

1999 Zeke Carey of The Flamingos died. The group had had a 1959 US No.11 single with 'I Only Have Eyes For You', which was a 1975 UK No.1 hit for Art Garfunkel.

2000 Four Seasons bassist Nick Massi died. They had had a 1976 UK & US No.1 single with 'December 1963, Oh What A Night'.

2003 Jack White of the White Stripes turned himself into Detroit police to face aggravated assault charges stemming from a barroom altercation in which he allegedly attacked Jason Stollsteimer of The Von Blonds. White was also fingerprinted and formally booked on the charges before he was released on $100 (£59) bond.

BORN ON THIS DAY

1937 O'Kelly Isley – vocalist with The Isley Brothers, who had a 1968 UK No.3 single with 'This Old Heart Of Mine'. He died March 31st 1986.

1940 Phil Spector, producer known for "The Spector Wall Of Sound" and member of Teddy Bears, who had a 1958 US No.1 single with 'To Know Him Is To Love Him'. He produced many classic songs including: Ben E King's 'Spanish Harlem'; The Crystals', 'Da Doo Ron Ron'; The Ronettes', 'Baby I Love You'; The Righteous Brothers', 'You've Lost That Lovin' Feeling' and Ike And Tina Turner's, 'River Deep, Mountain High'.

1944 Kenny Everett, radio and TV presenter who had a 1983 UK No.9 single with 'Snot Rap'. He died on April 4th 1995.

1945 Noel Redding – bass player for the Jimi Hendrix Experience, who had a 1967 UK No.3 single with 'Purple Haze' and a 1970 UK No.1 single with 'Voodoo Chile'. Redding died on May 12th 2003, aged 57.

1954 Annie Lennox – singer The Tourists, who had a 1979 UK No.4 single with 'I Only Want To Be With You', and Eurythmics, who had a 1983 US No.1 single with 'Sweet Dreams' and a 1985 UK No.1 single with 'There Must Be An Angel'. As a solo artist she had a 1995 UK No.2 single with 'No More I Love Yous'.

1957 Shane MacGowan – guitarist and vocalist with The Pogues, who had a 1987 UK No.8 single with 'The Irish Rover' and a 1987 UK No.2 single with Kirsty MacColl, 'Fairytale Of New York'.

1969 Nicolas Godin – guitarist, drummer and vocalist with Air, who had a 1998 UK No.6 album with *Moon Safari*, which spent over a year on the UK chart.

Inappropriate Christmas presents: *NSYNC and Eminem.

1971 Dido, singer/songwriter who had a 2001 UK No.1 & US No.4 album with *No Angel* and a 2001 UK No.4 single with 'Here With Me'.

ON THIS DAY

1958 it was the first day of a ten day residency of Alan Freed's Christmas rock 'n' roll spectacular in New York with Chuck Berry, Frankie Avalon, Dion, Jackie Wilson, Eddie Cochran, Bo Diddley and The Everly Brothers.

1964 George Harrison's girlfriend Patti Boyd was attacked by Beatles fans as they arrived at London's Hammersmith Odeon for the evening's Beatles concert.

1965 The Beatles' sixth album *Rubber Soul* started a nine week run at No.1 on the UK chart.

1971 Melanie started a three week run at No.1 on the US singles chart with 'Brand New Key', the first release on her new label Neighbourhood Records.

1976 Johnny Mathis was at No.1 on the UK singles chart with 'When A Child Is Born', the singer's only UK No.1

1976 The Eagles started an eight week run at No.1 on the US album chart with *Hotel California*.

1978 John Lydon's new group Public Image Ltd played their first live gig at the Rainbow Theatre, London.

1981 Michael Jackson phoned Paul McCartney and suggested they write and record together, the first result being 'The Girl Is Mine'. The song was a US No.2 & UK No.8 in 1982.

1982 David Bowie had a Top 3 hit with a duet with Bing Crosby, 'Peace On Earth – Little Drummer Boy'.

1993 Mariah Carey went to No.1 on the US album chart with *Music Box*.

1995 Dean Martin, actor and singer, died. He had had a 1956 UK & US No.1 single with 'Memories Are Made Of This' plus over 15 other UK Top 40 singles.

1998 Bryan MacLean, guitarist with Love, died of a heart attack aged 62.

2003 Michael Jackson recorded his first interview since news of the allegations of sexual abuse with a 12-year-old boy broke. He told the CBS-TV network he would "slit his wrists" before he would hurt a child. He also claimed he suffered a dislocated shoulder after police "manhandled" him and treated him "very roughly" during his arrest.

BORN ON THIS DAY

1935 Abdul "Duke" Fakir – singer with The Four Tops, who had a 1965 US No.1 single with 'I Can't Help Myself' and a 1967 UK No.6 single with 'Standing In The Shadows of Love'.

1955 Lars Ulrich – drummer with Metallica, who had a 1991 UK No.5 single with 'Enter Sandman' and a 1991 US & UK No.1 album with *Metallica*.

ON THIS DAY

1963 Stevie Wonder arrived in the UK for appearances on TV shows *Ready Steady Go!* and *Thank Your Lucky Stars*.

1964 The Beatles started a three week run at No.1 on the US singles chart with 'I Feel Fine'. It was the group's sixth No.1 of the year in which they had 19 entries on the chart, giving them a total of 18 weeks at the top of the charts.

1964 The Rolling Stones placed an advertisement in the music paper *New Musical Express* wishing starving hairdressers and their families a Happy Christmas.

1966 John Lennon appeared as a men's room attendant in Peter Cook and Dudley Moore's BBC TV show *Not only... But also*.

1966 the Jimi Hendrix Experience played an afternoon show at The Uppercut Club, London. Hendrix also wrote the lyrics to 'Purple Haze' in the dressing room on the same day.

"Roll up, roll up for the mystery tour."

1967 the world TV premiere of The Beatles' film *Magical Mystery Tour* was shown on BBC TV in the UK.

1968 Led Zeppelin started their first US tour supporting Vanilla Fudge and The MC5, appearing first at Denver Auditorium, Denver, Colorado.

1970 George Harrison started a four week run at No.1 on the US singles chart with 'My Sweet Lord', making him the first Beatle to score a No.1 US hit.

1973 Paul and Linda McCartney presented the UK TV BBC's *Disney Time*.

1976 the Sex Pistols recorded 'God Save The Queen' at Wessex Studios, London.

1981 AC/DC started a three week run at No.1 on the US album chart with *For Those About To Rock We Salute You*.

1988 Shane McGowan was arrested for smashing the glass from a shop window in a drunken rage. The Pogues singer was later fined £250 ($425).

1989 U2 started a five night run at Dublin's Point Depot.

1998 The Spice Girls scored their eighth UK No.1 single with 'Goodbye', giving them the Christmas No.1 for the third year in a row. This equalled the record set by The Beatles from 1963, 64 and 65.

1999 singer/songwriter Curtis Mayfield *(left)* died, aged 57.

BORN ON THIS DAY

1931 Scotty Moore – guitarist, who's first group was Doug Poindexter & the Starlite Wranglers. He played on the first Sun Studios session with Elvis Presley and went on to a lengthy career with Presley, playing on many of his most famous recordings including 'Baby Let's Play House', 'Heartbreak Hotel' 'Mystery Train', 'That's All Right', 'Hound Dog' and 'Jailhouse Rock'.

1941 Les Maguire – pianist with Gerry And The Pacemakers, who had a 1963 UK No.1 single with 'You'll Never Walk Alone' and a 1965 US No.6 single with 'Ferry Across The Mersey'.

1941 Mike Pinder – keyboardist with The Moody Blues, who had a 1965 UK No.1 single with 'Go Now' and a 1968 UK No.19 & 1972 US No.2 single with 'Nights In White Satin'.

1944 Mike Jones – guitarist with Foreigner, who had a 1985 UK & US No.1 single with 'I Want To Know What Love Is'.

1948 Larry Byrom – guitarist with Steppenwolf, who had a 1969 UK No.30 single with 'Born To Be Wild'.

1952 David Knopfler – guitarist and vocalist with Dire Straits, who had a 1979 UK No.8 single with 'Sultans Of Swing'. He left the band in 1980.

1961 Youth – bass player with Killing Joke, who had a 1985 UK No.16 single with 'Love Like Blood'. He left to become a producer and worked with U2.

Simon Le Bon: all at sea until he married Yasmin.

1972 Matt Slocum – singer/songwriter for Sixpence None The Richer, who had a 1999 UK No.4 single with 'Kiss Me', 1999 US No.8 single 'There She Goes'.

ON THIS DAY

1969 *Led Zeppelin II* was at No.1 on the US album charts. It went on to sell over six million copies in the US.

1969 The Supremes had their 12th and last US No.1 single with 'Someday We'll Be Together'. It was also the last No.1 of the 60s.

1975 The Faces split became official. Rod Stewart went solo, Ron Wood was on permanent loan to the Stones, Ronnie Lane went on to form Slim Chance and drummer Kenny Jones joined The Who.

1975 the Staple Singers went to No.1 on the US singles chart with 'Let's Do It Again', the group's second US No.1.

1976 blues guitarist Freddie King died of heart trouble and ulcers, aged 42. Eric Clapton covered his 'Have You Ever Loved A Woman' on the *Layla* album.

1981 US singer/songwriter and bandleader Hoagy Carmichael died, aged 82. He was the composer of 'Georgia On My Mind', 'Star Dust' and 'Lazy River'.

1984 appearing on the Granada TV music show *Brighton Rock* were Frankie Goes To Hollywood, Madness, Nik Kershaw, Gloria Gaynor, Spandau Ballet, The Flying Pickets and Helen Terry.

1985 Duran Duran singer Simon Le Bon married model Yasmin Parvanah.

1989 a former chef at the Chuck Berry-owned restaurant the Southern Air started court proceedings against Berry, alleging that the singer had installed secret video cameras in the ladies toilets. A further 200 other women also took action, claiming that the recordings were used for improper sexual fetishes.

1992 Harry Connick Jr was arrested at Kennedy Airport, New York after police discovered a 9mm pistol in his hand luggage.

1997 The Spice Girls went to No.1 on the UK singles chart with 'Too Much'.

1999 Sean "Puff Daddy" Combs *(left)* and his girlfriend Jennifer Lopez were arrested after a gun was found in their car as they left a Manhattan nightclub. Police were investigating a shooting in the club.

BORN ON THIS DAY

1921 Johnny Otis, singer/songwriter and band leader who had a 1957 UK No.2 single with 'Ma, He's Making Eyes At Me' and a 1958 US No.9 single with 'Willie And The Hand Jive'.

1915 Roebuck "Pop" Staples – vocalist for the Staple Singers, who had a 1975 US No.1 single with 'Let's Do It Again'. He died on December 19th 2000.

1943 Chas Hodges – pianist with Heads Hands And Feet and Chas & Dave, who had a 1982 UK No.2 single with 'Ain't No Pleasing You'.

1946 Edgar Winter – keyboardist and vocalist with the Edgar Winter Band, who had a 1973 US No.1 & UK No.18 single with 'Frankenstein'.

1947 Dick Diamonde – bass player with The Easybeats, who had a 1966 UK No.6 & 1967 US No.16 single with 'Friday On My Mind'.

1950 Alex Chilton – guitarist and vocalist with The Box Tops, who had a 1967 US No.1 & UK No.5 single with 'The Letter'. Chilton formed Big Star in 1971.

1954 Rosie Vela, US singer/songwriter who had a 1987 UK No.27 single with 'Magic Smile'.

1971 Anita Dels – vocalist with 2 Unlimited, who had a 1993 UK No.1 single with 'No Limit'.

ON THIS DAY

1961 Danny Williams was at No.1 on the UK singles chart with 'Moon River'.

1968 The Beatles went to No.1 on the US album chart with the *White Album*, the group's 12th US No.1 album.

1968 the first major rock festival held on the East Coast of the US, the three day Miami Pop festival took place with Chuck Berry, The McCoys, Joni Mitchell, Fleetwood Mac, Marvin Gaye, The Turtles, The Box Tops, Steppenwolf, Three Dog Night, Pacific Gas And Electric, Procol Harum, Canned Heat, Iron Butterfly and the Grateful Dead. Tickets were $6 (£3.50) in advance.

1971 Mott The Hoople appeared at Plymouth Guildhall, England.

1974 Helen Reddy went to No.1 on the US singles chart with 'Angie Baby', the singer's third US No.1. The song was turned down by Cher.

1975 during a concert Ted Nugent was threatened by a member of the audience who aimed a .44 magnum gun at him. The man was removed from the audience without incident.

1978 Chris Bell, guitarist with the Big Star, was killed aged 27 after his car crashed into a telephone pole.

1980 St. Winifred's School Choir were at No.1 on the UK singles chart with 'There's No One Quite Like Grandma'.

1983 Beach Boy Dennis Wilson drowned while swimming from his boat. With the help of President Reagan he was given a burial at sea, normally reserved for navel personnel. Dennis was the only genuine surfer in The Beach Boys.

1985 Shakin' Stevens was at No.1 on the UK singles chart with 'Merry Christmas Everyone'.

1993 singer Shania Twain *(left)* married producer Mutt Lange.

1996 The Spice Girls scored their third UK No.1 single when '2 Become 1' went to the top of the charts.

1998 BBC Radio 1 aired the 100 National Anthems, songs voted by listeners. At No.5 was Radiohead, 'Creep'; No.4 Underworld, 'Born Slippy'; No.3 The Verve, 'Bitter Sweet Symphony'; No.2 Nirvana, 'Smells Like Teen Spirit' and No.1 Massive Attack's 'Unfinished Sympathy'.

2003 50 Cent's debut album *Get Rich Or Die Tryin'* was named the biggest-selling album in the US in 2003 – the album had gone Platinum six times over. Outkast came second with *Speakerboxxx/The Love Below* and Linkin Park's *Meteora* was the third biggest seller. The Top 10 albums of 2003 in the USA accounted for around 30 million sales.

A big star.

BORN ON THIS DAY

1942 Ray Thomas – flute player and vocalist with The Moody Blues, who had a 1965 UK No.1 single with 'Go Now' and a 1968 UK No.19 & 1972 US No.2 single with 'Nights In White Satin'.

1946 Marianne Faithfull, singer and one time girlfriend of Mick Jagger, who had a 1965 UK No.4 single with 'Come And Stay With Me'.

1947 Cozy Powell – drummer with Whitesnake, ELP and a solo artist. Powell also worked with Black Sabbath, Rainbow, Donovan, Roger Daltrey, Jack Bruce, Jeff Beck, Gary Moore and Brian May. Powell was killed in a car crash on April 5th 1998.

1948 Charlie Spinosa – trumpet player with John Fred, & His Playboy Band, who had a 1968 US No.1 & UK No.3 single with 'Judy In Disguise'.

1951 Yvonne Elliman, singer who had a 1978 US No.1 & UK No.4 single with 'If I Can't Have You' and also worked with Eric Clapton.

1961 Jim Reid – vocalist and guitarist with The Jesus And Mary Chain, who had a 1987 UK No.8 single with 'April Skies'.

1961 Mark Day – guitarist with the Happy Mondays, who had a 1990 UK No.5 single with 'Step On'.

1966 Bryan Holland – vocalist and guitarist with The Offspring, who had a 1999 UK No.1 & US No.59 single with 'Pretty Fly, (For A White Guy) and a 1999 US No.6 & UK No.10 album with *Americana*.

ON THIS DAY

1956 Elvis Presley made chart history by having ten songs on Billboard's Top 100 for the week ending December 29th.

1960 Cliff Richard was at No.1 on the UK singles chart with 'I Love You', the singer's fourth UK No.1.

1966 the Jimi Hendrix Experience *(below)* made their debut on *Top Of The Pops* performing 'Hey Joe'.

1967 guitarist and singer Dave Mason quit

Traffic after differences of musical opinion.

1969 The Bonzo Dog Doo-Dah Band appeared at The Lyceum, London,.

1973 Jim Croce scored his second No.1 US single of the year when 'Time In A Bottle' went to the top of the charts.

1980 US singer/songwriter Tim Hardin died of a heroin overdose. He wrote 'If I Were A Carpenter' and 'Reason To Believe'.

1982 a set of commemorative stamps in memory of Bob Marley were issued in Jamaica.

1990 Cliff Richard has his 12th UK No.1 single with 'Saviour's Day'.

1999 the Melody Maker Music of the Millennium Poll of albums placed The Smiths' *The Queen Is Dead* at No.1.

1999 three ferrets named Beckham, Posh Spice and Baby Spice were used to lay power cables for a rock concert being held in Greenwich, London. Workers were not allowed to dig the turf at the Royal Park.

2002 readers of *Sugar* magazine voted Pink as their No.1 role model. The Top 10 was: 1. Pink; 2. Britney Spears; 3. Ms Dynamite; 4. Kelly Osbourne; 5. Kylie Minogue; 6. Victoria Beckham; 7. Avril Lavigne; 8. Jennifer Lopez; 9. Sarah Michelle Geller and 10. Holly Valance.

2003 Westlife star Shane Filan married his childhood sweetheart Gillian Walsh at a ceremony in Ballintubber Abbey, Ireland.

BORN ON THIS DAY

1928 Bo Diddley, guitarist and singer who had a 1963 UK No.34 single with 'Pretty Thing'.

1934 Del Shannon, singer who had a 1961 UK and US No.1 single with 'Runaway' plus nine US and 12 other UK Top 40 singles. Shannon died on February 8th 1990.

1942 Mike Nesmith –vocalist and guitarist with The Monkees, who had a 1967 UK & US No.1 single with 'I'm A Believer' plus ten US & eight other UK Top 40 singles.

1942 Robert Quine – guitarist with Richard Hell And The Voidoids, who had a 1977 album with *Blank Generation* that featured the track 'Love Comes In Spurts'. He also worked with Lou Reed, Brian Eno, Lloyd Cole and They Might Be Giants. Quine died on June 5th 2004 of an apparent heroin overdose.

1945 Davy Jones –vocalist and guitarist with The Monkees, who had a 1967 UK & US No.1 single with 'I'm A Believer' plus ten US & eight other UK Top 40 singles. He was also an actor in the 1986 London cast of *Godspell*.

1946 Patti Smith, singer and poet who had a 1978 UK No.5 & US No.13 single with 'Because The Night', which was co-written with Bruce Springsteen.

1947 Jeff Lynne – guitarist and vocalist with Idle Race, The Move, who had a 1969 UK No.1 single with 'Blackberry Way', ELO, who had a 1979 UK No.3 & US No. 4 single with 'Don't Bring Me Down' and Traveling Wilburys, who had a 1988 UK No.28 with 'Handle With Care'.

1969 Jason Kay – vocalist with Jamiroquai, who had a 1996 UK No.3 single with 'Virtual Insanity' and a 2001 UK No.1 album with *A Funk Odyssey*.

ON THIS DAY

1962 singer Brenda Lee was slightly hurt when she attempted to rescue her poodle, Cee Cee, from her burning house. Cee Cee later died of smoke inhalation.

1962 appearing at Coconut Grove, Sacrament, California were Ike And Tina Turner, The Ike-etts, Jimmy Thomas and Mary Brown.

1965 appearing on tonight's TV pop show *Shindig!* were The Kinks, The Who, Manfred Mann *(right)*, The Hollies and Gerry And The Pacemakers.

1967 on the US singles chart The Beatles scored their 15th US No.1 with 'Hello Goodbye', Gladys Knight & The Pips were at No.2 with 'I Heard It Through The Grape Vine' and The Monkees were at No.3 with 'Daydream Believer'.

1969 Peter Tork quit The Monkees, buying himself out of his contract for $160,000 (£94,118) – which left him broke.

1978 Emerson, Lake & Palmer announced their official break up.

1978 XTC made their live debut in the US when they played a show in Philadelphia.

1989 Chris Novoselic, bass player with Nirvana, married his long-time girlfriend Shelli Dilly in Washington.

1995 Michael Jackson was at No.1 on the UK singles chart with 'Earth Song'.

1995 Clarence Satchell from The Ohio Players died. They had had a 1974 US No.1 single with 'Fire'.

1999 George Harrison and his wife Olivia were attacked when an intruder broke into their home. Olivia beat off the attacker with poker and a heavy lamp and the intruder, Michael Abram, was later arrested by police. George was stabbed in the chest and was admitted to hospital.

1999 in the Queen's Millennium Honours former Slade singer Noddy Holder was awarded an MBE and Mark Knopfler was awarded an OBE.

2001 Nickelback went to No.1 on the US singles chart with 'How To Remind Me'.

2002 Diana Ross was arrested for drink driving by the Arizona highway patrol. When asked to walk in a straight line she fell over, could not count to 30 or balance on one foot. Police said she was twice over the drink drive limit. The singer was cited with three misdemeanours, including driving under the influence, driving with a blood-alcohol level above 0.08 and "extreme DUI", driving with a blood-alcohol level above 0.15.

BORN ON THIS DAY

1942 Andy Summers – guitarist with The Police, who had a 1983 UK & US No.1 single with 'Every Breath You Take' plus four other UK No.1 singles.

1943 Henry John Deutschendorf (a.k.a. John Denver), singer/songwriter who had a 1974 UK & US No.1 single with 'Annie's Song'. He was killed in a plane crash on October 12th 1997.

1948 Donna Summer, singer who had a 1977 UK No.1 single with 'I Feel Love', a 1979 US No.1 & UK No.11 single with 'Hot Stuff' and over 25 other Top 40 hits.

1951 Fermin Goytisolo – percussionist for KC & The Sunshine Band, who had a 1975 US No.1 single with 'That's The Way, I Like It' and a 1983 UK No.1 single with 'Give It Up'.

1960 Paul Westerberg – guitarist and vocalist with The Replacements, who had a 1984 album with *Let It Be*.

1972 Joey McIntrye – singer with New Kids On The Block, who had a 1989 UK No.1 single with 'You Got It, The Right Stuff' and a 1990 US No.1 single with 'Step By Step'.

ON THIS DAY

1955 based on sales, radio and jukebox plays *Billboard* named 'Unchained Melody' the No.1 song of 1955.

1961 The Beach Boys made their live debut using their new name at the Municipal Auditorium, Long Beach, California. They were paid $300 (£176) for the gig.

1963 The Kinks made their live debut when they played at the Lotus House Restaurant, London.

1967 songwriter and producer Bert Berns died. He wrote many classic songs including 'Twist And Shout', 'Hang On Sloopy' and 'Brown Eyed Girl'.

1968 appearing at Alexandra Palace, London were Joe Cocker, Amen Corner, John Mayall's Bluesbreakers, The Small Faces, The Free and The Bonzo Dog Doo-Dah Band. Tickets cost 25 shillings, ($3.50).

1970 Paul McCartney filed a suit against the rest of The Beatles to dissolve their partnership.

1973 Journey made their live debut at San Francisco's Winterland Ballroom.

1979 Blondie's gig was broadcast live from The Apollo Theatre, Glasgow on BBC 2's Old Grey Whistle Test *(right)*.

1979 David Bowie performed an acoustic version of 'Space Oddity' on the UK TV's *Kenny Everett New Year Show*.

1981 Tom Waits married Irish playwright Kathleen Brennan.

1982 guitarist with The E Street Band, Miami Steve Van Zandt, married Maureen Santora in New Jersey. The best man was Bruce Springsteen.

1984 Def Leppard drummer Rick Allen crashed his Corvette Stingray on the A57 outside Sheffield. Allen lost his left arm in the accident.

1985 Ricky Nelson was killed along with six others when his charted light aircraft crashed in Texas. It was rumoured that an onboard explosion was caused by freebasing cocaine.

1996 Paul McCartney became a Sir after he was listed in the Queen's New Year's Honours List.

1999 The Manic Street Preachers performed to 57,000 fans at the Millennium Stadium, Cardiff. The Guinness Book of Records confirmed that the concert set a new record as the biggest indoor show ever staged in Europe. Tickets cost £30 ($51).

2003 Ringtones.co.uk announced that Beyonce's No.1 hit 'Crazy In Love' was the bestselling mobile ringtone of the year. 'Fly On The Wings Of Love' by XTM was the second-biggest and R. Kelly's 'Ignition' was third.

Acknowledgements

For Liz who makes it all possible; and Simon, Daniel, Matthew, Chloe, Lyle and Ace, and Mum and Dad.

Very special thanks to Pete Hawkins, Cally Calloman, Chris Stone, Anthony Cohen, Martin Jennings, Rob Cowley, JW Cossar, John Wadlow, Adam Walton, Andrew Sutton, Alan McBlane, Rob Partridge, Grant Cain, Martin Finn, Jason Bailey, Johnny Owen, Dave Stearn, Tony Michaelidis and Mick Brophy.

And all the music fan sites on the web. Virgin records, Polydor, Island, Universal records, RCA, Arista, Sony, Sanctuary, EMI & all the countless record labels and press departments for their continued help.

The music press *Melody Maker, Sounds, Disc, Fab 208, Record Collector, International Musician, Smash Hits, Top of the Pops, Record Mirror, NME, Select, Q, Mojo, Word, Rolling Stone, Billboard.*

The press *The Times, Telegraph, Guardian, Observer, The Sun, Daily Mirror, The Star, Daily Mail, Express, Guinness Hit Singles & Albums,* The Official UK Charts Company.

Neil Cossar has run the website www.thisdayinmusic.com on which this book is based since 1999. It's probably the largest collection of music history available on the Internet with an average of 100,000 hits from all corners of the world daily.

Neil started to collect musical facts when working as a late night DJ at a Manchester radio station. A former musician, Neil is no stranger to the musical world – his band were signed to Parlophone records in the 1980's, (they released three albums); and while working as a radio DJ he interviewed countless acts including Blur, Lenny Kravitz, Radiohead, PJ Harvey, The Cranberries, Tori Amos and The Charlatans. He also runs a music PR company with his partner Liz Sanchez – their clients have included INXS, Joan Baez, Def Leppard, LeAnn Rimes, Barenaked Ladies, Ocean Colour Scene, Holly Johnson and The Proclaimers.

Left: The author sets off to his nearest record shop, July 27th, 1961.

PICTURE CREDITS

References are supplied as day/month then position on the page; T=top, B=bottom, C=centre, L=left, R=right

All images were supplied by **The Antar Archive** apart from those listed below:

Author's Collection Page 2 TL, TR, BR, TC, Page 3 TC, C, BL. 1/1 B, 4/1 B, 5/1 T, 10/1 R,11/1 R, 16/1 B, 18/1 B, 20/1, 21/1 R, 21/1 R, 25/1 T, 26/1 R, 2/2 T, 9/2 R, 17/2 B, 18/2 B, 20/2R, 21/2 R, 22/2 T, 24/2 R, 25/2 TL&B, 23/3L, 3/4 T, 6/4 R, 8/4 T, 9/4 T, 20/4 T, 1/5 B, 4/5 T&B, 6/5 T, 11/5 L, 17/5 T, 18/5 L, 20/5 B, 21/5 T, 22/5 R, 25/5 T, 26/5 L&B, 30/5 BL, 2/6 B, 4/6 R, 11/6 T&B, 12/6 B, 13/6 L, 15/6 R, 19/6 BR, 21/6 R, 28/6 TL &B, 29/6 T, 1/7 T, 1/7 B, 3/7 R, 4/7 T, 4/7 B, 5/7 B, 6/7 T, 8/7 T, 13/7 B, 21/7 T, 26/7 B, 28/7 R, 31/7 B, 4/8 B, 7/8 B, 12/8 T, 31/8, 5/9 T&L, 7/9 T, 8/9 BR,13/9 T&L, 15/9 BL, 17/9 R, 20/9 B, 22/9 T&B, 26/9 B, 28/9 R, 29/9 T&C, 30/9 T&L, 1/10 B, 4/10 B, 9/10 T, 10/10 R, 11/10 T, 13/10T, 19/10, 21/10 B, 27/10 T, 28/10 TR, 29/10 TR, 31/10 T&B, 1/11 T&B, 2/11 T&B, 6/11 T, 8/11 B, 9/11 T, 11/11 BL, 12/11 B, 14/11 L&TR, 18/11 T&B, 19/11, 20/11 B, 21/11 T&B, 22/11 T, 24/11 T&B, 26/11 T, 28/11 R, 30/11 T&B, 2/12 B, 3/12 T, 4/12 B, 6/12 T&B, 8/12 T&B, 11/12 B, 13/12 T, 14/12 T, 16/12 B, 18/12 B, 19/12 T, 21/12 B, 22/12, 25/12 T, 27/12 B, 28/12 T, 29/12 R, Jul & Dec filler; **4AD Ltd** 6/4 L; **Clay Patrick McBride © 2003 Blue Note Records** 19/1 R; **Carling/Coors Brewers** 11/1 BR, 19/2 BR, 29/2 BR, 1/4 BR, 7/6, 26/6 TR, 9/7 CR, 15/7 B, 24/8 B, 11/11, 20/12 BR; **Chrysalis Image Library** 14/7 BR; **EMI Records Ltd** Page 2C ©Matt Jones, 27/1 T ©Xevi, 2/3 B ©Kevin Westenberg, 9/3 T ©Jason Evans, 25/7 B ©Matt Jones, 20/12 T ©Rip; ©**John Marshall/JM-Entertainment.com** 17/3 BR; ©**Judy Totton** 13/9 B; **Madame Tussauds** 31/1 C, 17/3T, 22/5 L, 23/5 B, 31/1 C; **Mercury Records Ltd.** 29/11; **Navi** 17/10; **Patrick Anderson** 27/12 T; ©**Ric Machin** 8/1 R; **Sony/BMG** page 3 R, 30/1 BR, 31/1 TR, 28/3 T, 23/6 B, 8/7 B, 8/9 B, 16/10 T, 26/10 B, 6/11 B, 26/11 B, 10/12 B, 13/12 B, 15/12 T; ©**Simon Fowler** 23/2 T; **EMI Music UK & Ireland** 8/1L, 28/9 B, 30/4 T; **Virgin Music** 5/4.